The Cousinhood

THE COUSINHOOD

CHAIM BERMANT

The Macmillan Company

New York, New York

The Genealogical Tables are not intended to be defini-
tive but are as accurate as the author could make
them from the reference books available to him when
they were prepared. The author and publisher apol-
ogise to all members of the Anglo-Jewish gentry
details of whose names, marriages and progeny have
been omitted. No inference is to be drawn from any
such omission.

The Macmillan Company
866 Third Avenue, New York, N.Y. 10022

Library of Congress Catalog Card Number: 70-103682

First American Edition 1972

Printed in the United States of America

Contents

Illustrations

22 New West End Synagogue
23 Herbert Samuel, from a drawing by Leonid Pasternak
       (*Jewish Chronicle*)
24 Sir Robert Waley Cohen, from a drawing by Sallon
       (*Jewish Chronicle*)
25 Alice Waley Cohen
26 Basil Henriques
27 Sir Henry d'Avigdor-Goldsmid
       (*Godfrey Argent*)
28 Lady d'Avigdor-Goldsmid
29 Somerhill, seat of the d'Avigdor-Goldsmids
       (*National Gallery of Scotland*)
30 Miriam Rothschild with her children
       (*Life Magazine*)
31 Mrs Edmund de Rothschild
       (*Jewish Chronicle*)
32 Rt. Revd. Hugh Montefiore

GENEALOGICAL TABLES

Foreword

I should first of all like to thank my research assistant Michael Freedman who ransacked obscure libraries in London and the shires, distilled much of the information I was seeking and prepared the genealogical tables. John Gross gave me some idea on how to put my ideas into order, Lord Cohen of Walmer my first insight into the unique character of the Cousinhood, and C. P. Snow my first insight into the unique character of the Cohens. Dr Vivian Lipman, distinguished both as a Civil servant and as a Jewish historian, read the greater part of my manuscript and saved me from errors of fact and taste. Individual chapters were read by Dr Eric Conrad, Viscount Samuel, the Hon. David Montagu, Mrs Vivian Lipman, Raphael Loewe, Alan Montefiore, Ronald Palin, Albert Polack and Mrs Edmund de Rothschild and they too lowered my quota of error. Dr Miriam Rothschild has been so helpful to me in so many ways that I came to think of her as my honorary editor. I am particularly indebted to Sir Henry d'Avigdor-Goldsmid who put the Goldsmid papers at my disposal, and also read part of my manuscript.

I am grateful to my former agent Gillon Aitken, and to my publishers for counsel and patience above and beyond the mere call of duty.

I should like to thank the National Trust for access to the Hughenden Papers and the Trustees of the British Museum for access to the Hamilton, Gladstone, Dilke and Rosebery papers, the Librarian and staff of the London Library, the Mocatta Library, the University College Library, the *Jewish Chronicle* Library and the *Sunday Times* Library.

This book arose from a chapter called 'The Cousinhood' in my book *Troubled Eden* and I am grateful to the publishers, Vallentine Mitchell for allowing me to quote liberally from myself.

I am indebted to Dr André Ungar for his recollections of Sir Basil Henriques, and to Mrs Sharon Ross who, for a period of months, forsook husband, children and dogs to type my manuscript.

And finally I am grateful to my wife and children for suffering the presence of an otherwise amiable man who becomes impossible when he is writing, and who is always writing.

1971   Chaim Bermant

Acknowledgements

Thanks are due to the following publishers for permission to quote extracts from copyright material.

George Allen & Unwin Ltd for L. Gartner, *The Jewish Immigrant in England* (1960) and I. Morris, *Madly Singing in the Mountains* (1970). Barrie & Jenkins Ltd for R. Henriques, *Marcus Samuel* (1960). G. Bell & Sons Ltd for H. B. Wheatley, *The Diary of Samuel Pepys* (1952). The Butterworth Group for H. V. Eckardstein, *Ten Years at the Court of St James'* (1921). Cassell & Co. Ltd for Lord Asquith, *Memoirs and Reflections* (1928); Lord Birkenhead, *Contemporary Personalities* (1924); M. Hardwick, *Emma, Lady Hamilton* (1969) and R. Palin, *Rothschild Relish* (1970). Cambridge University Press for J. Clapham, *The Bank of England* (1944). William Collins Sons & Co. Ltd for R. Jenkins, *Asquith* (1967) and *Sir Charles Dilke* (1968); H. Nicholson, *Diaries and Letters* (1966) and C. Sykes, *Two Studies in Virtue* (1953). Cresset Press Ltd for Lord Samuel, *Memoirs* (1945). Peter Davies Ltd for E. de Rothschild, *Window on the World* (1949). Faber & Faber Ltd for L. Cohen, *Some Reflections of C. G. Montefiore* (1940). Victor Gollancz Ltd for J. Bowle, *Viscount Samuel* (1957) and M. Lowenthal, *The Diaries of Theodore Herzl* (1958). Robert Hale & Co. for C. Roth, *The Magnificent Rothschilds* (1939). Hamish Hamilton Ltd for C. Weizmann, *Trial and Error* (1949). Rupert Hart-Davis Ltd for D. Cooper, *Old Men Forget* (1953). William Heinemann Ltd for S. Jackson, *The Sassoons* (1968). Hodder & Stoughton Ltd for W. R. Mathews, *Memoirs & Meanings* (1969). Hutchinson & Co. (Publishers) Ltd for Lord Beaverbrook, *Men and Power* (1956); B. Dugdale, *Arthur Balfour* (1936) and F. Owen, *Tempestuous Journey* (1954). Imperial Continental Gas Association for N. K. Hill, *Imperial Continental Gas Association from 1824-1900* (1950). The Jewish Historical Society for

L. Abrahams, 'Daniel O'Connell' in *Transactions*, Vol 4; H. Adler, 'Falk' in *Transactions*, Vol 5; S. Lipman, 'Judith Montefiore' in *Transactions*, Vol 21; V. Lipman, *Jews of Medieval Norwich* (1967) and *Three Centuries of Anglo-Jewish Settlement* (1961); L. Sutherland, 'Sampson Gideon' in *Transactions* Vol 17 and L. Wolf, *Essays in Jewish History* (1934). Lawrence & Wishart Ltd for I. Montagu, *The Youngest Son* (1970). Macmillan & Co. Ltd for Lady Battersea, *Reminiscences* (1922) and C. P. Snow, *The Conscience of the Rich* (1958). Martin Hopkinson for H. Cohen, *Changing Faces* (1937). Methuen & Co. Ltd for A. Hyamson, *A History of Jews in England* (1928); *David Salomons* (1939) and *The Sephardim of England* (1951). John Murray (Publishers) Ltd for L. Cohen, *Lady de Rothschild and her Daughters* (1935); Lord Crewe, *Lord Rosebery* (1931) and W. Moneypenny and Buckle, *Life of Disraeli* (1914). Nicholson & Watson for L. George, *War Memoirs* (1934) and R. Storrs, *Orientations* (1937). Oldbourne Press for K. Grunwald, *Turkenhirsch* (1966). Oxford University Press for T. E. Gregory, *The Westminster Bank* (1936) and C. Roth, *History of the Jews in England* (1964). Polak & Van Genapp for E. Conrad, *In Memory of Lily Montagu* (1967). Routledge & Kegan Paul for N. Bentwich, *My 77 Years* (1962); C. Emmanuel, *A Century and a Half of Jewish History* (1910); M. Gibbon, *Netta* (1960); R. J. D. Hart, *The Franklin Family of Liverpool and London* (1958) and V. Lipman, *A Century of Social Service* (1959). Sampson & Low for P. Emden, *Jews in Britain* (1943). Martin Secker & Warburg Ltd for R. Henriques, *From a Biography of Myself* (1969) and *Sir Robert Waley Cohen* (1966) and F. Morton, *The Rothschilds* (1962). Staples Press Ltd for D. Hopkinson, *Family Inheritance* (1954). The University of Southampton Press for C. Temple Paterson, *The University of Southampton* (1962). Vallentine Mitchell & Co. Ltd for R. Apple, *The Hampstead Synagogue* (1967); N. Bentwich and M. Kisch, *Brigadier Frederick Kisch* (1966); J. Parkes, *Antisemitism* (1963); E. Samuel, *A Lifetime in Jerusalem* (1970); L. Stein and C. C. Aronsfield, *Leonard G. Montefiore* (1964) and L. Stein, *The Balfour Declaration* (1961). George Weidenfeld & Nicholson Ltd for R. R. James, *Rosebery* (1963) and *Diaries of Sir Henry Channon* (1970); J. Watson, *The Double Helix* and Lord Davidson, *Memoirs of a Conservative* (1969).

The Cousinhood

CHAPTER I

The Cousinhood

In the beginning there was Levi Barent Cohen, merchant of Amsterdam who settled in London in 1770. And Cohen prospered and multiplied and had six sons and six daughters.

And one son married a niece of Abraham Goldsmid, a friend of Nelson and Pitt, and foremost broker of his day. A daughter married Nathan Mayer Rothschild, founder of the English branch of the banking dynasty, another married Moses Montefiore, merchant and broker. A son and daughter married a daughter and son of Moses Samuel, banker and broker. A third son married a grand-daughter of the self-same Samuel, and a fourth married a sister of Moses Montefiore whose brother, in turn, married a sister of Nathan Rothschild.

And thus there came into being the Cousinhood, a compact union of exclusive brethren with blood and money flowing in a small circle which opened up from time to time to admit a Beddington, a Montagu, a Franklin, a Sassoon, or anyone else who attained rank or fortune, and then snapped shut again.

The oldest Jewish families in England were Sephardim, that is of Spanish and Portuguese origin, while the Cousinhood was composed mainly of Ashkenazim, that is Jews of Dutch or German origin, all of them comparative newcomers and as such viewed by Sephardim with a certain amount of disdain.

Persecution in Eastern and Central Europe had occasioned a movement of Jews towards the west, but neither Cohens nor Goldsmids, neither Rothschilds nor Montefiores were victims of oppression or hunger. They had done well in Europe and hoped to do better in England, and they had chosen their country well.

England in the second half of the eighteenth century was the envy of

Europe. The pleas for enlightenment and toleration advanced by Locke almost a century before had become the guiding principle of government. There was stability and while the alien was always regarded with a certain amount of suspicion, even the Jewish alien could prosper without harassment, And England offered scope for initiative and enterprise not available elsewhere in Europe. She had triumphed in war on land and at sea. She had opened up new worlds to commerce in the Americas, the West Indies and the East. The constant movement of large armies and vast fleets offered great opportunities to merchants especially where, like the Jews, they had international connections. The valleys of Yorkshire and Lancashire were beginning to stir with the first motions of the industrial revolution. The wars were distant conflicts on distant shores. At home there was peace. England was not yet a country open to all the talents, but it was open to entrepreneurial talent and the Cousinhood grew rich and multiplied.

The first generation of the Cousinhood was content to prosper, the second wanted more. They gloried in the name of Englishmen, yet were excluded from almost every venerable English institution. They could not, as Jews, be called to the Bar or matriculate in the ancient universities and were thus virtually excluded from the professions. They were excluded from the municipalities and Parliament and were thus debarred from public service. It was doubtful whether they could own land. All this did not mean that they suffered social exclusion. They entertained courtiers and were entertained at court but this, if anything, added to their mortification at being considered second class citizens. They joined in a sustained effort to end their disabilities. By the 1830s there were Jews at the Bar. In 1855 there was a Jewish Lord Mayor of London, in 1858 a Jewish member of Parliament, in 1886 a Jewish Peer.

Nearly every country in Europe had its handful of *Hof Juden*, Court Jews, who glittered at the head of their community without being a part of them, who, indeed, often observed them with lofty contempt. The Cousinhood were not wholly free of such elements, but on the whole they took their duties to their religion and their co-religionists seriously. They organised a voluntary poor law and later the Jewish Board of Guardians and fed the hungry and clothed the poor so that no Jew was ever on the parish. They established Jewish schools and endowed them. They built synagogues and reinforced the authority of the priests. They were defenders of the faith and guardians of the faithful.

They were guided both by charity and self-interest, for to the Gentile all Jews looked alike and in the last resort their standing and fate were inseparable from that of the Jewish masses.

But basically they were responding to the confluence of two traditions, the Jewish one that a man of means must give, and the English one that the man of rank must serve, and they assumed the leadership of the community as naturally as a knight might lead in the shires. (Jewish knights, being preternaturally conscientious, tended to lead both in the shires and in the Jewish community.)

The Cousinhood were not merely a cluster of relatives. In many ways they functioned as an organic unit and even while their own rights were not yet wholly assured they threw in their wealth and influence on behalf of persecuted co-religionists in other parts of the world. Wherever Jews were oppressed emissaries hurried to England, to the Rothschilds, to Montefiore, to the Cousinhood.

Jews in other Western countries also exerted what influence they had in the same way, but English Jewry was helped by the fact that it was acting within an established liberal, humanitarian tradition. Englishmen were taking up the cause of the oppressed in Greece, Poland, Hungary, Bulgaria and Latin America, sometimes as lone idealists and romantics, but often with the active support of the Government, and the Cousinhood would have been not merely deficient as Jews but deficient as Englishmen if they had been less energetic on behalf of their co-religionists. In such a situation there was no possibility that their exertions would expose them to the charge of dual loyalties, until a movement arose which sought a solution to the Jewish problem in terms of a Jewish homeland. At which point the Cousinhood recoiled—the wane of its influence dates from the rise of Zionism.

The Cousinhood, like most of their contemporaries, were meliorists and believed that there were few problems which could not be solved through persistent efforts and good will, that the sun which shone upon them so warmly and consistently must in time spread to the bleaker parts of the globe.

And theirs, even before Jewish emancipation was complete, was a very sunny life. A few of them were too concerned for the ills of others to enjoy their own good fortune, but most, after allocating a due portion of their time and income to good work, were able to turn with an untroubled mind to good living. They had ornate homes in town and fine estates in the country and many servants to meet their many needs. Childhood was a memory of ribbons and straw hats and flouncing skirts and picnics on warm afternoons under shady trees, and ponies, and journeys in dog-carts and chaises, and then, as the year closed, boisterous gatherings in lofty halls round heavily-laden Christmas trees. The fathers hunted and shot and fished on their private lakes, and sent their sons to famous schools and famous universities and then, on a grand tour before settling down to marriage, home, a partnership and the responsibilities of their name, their rank and their faith. Victoria was on the throne, Britain was prosperous and the Empire mighty. Bliss it was that day to be middle-class, and to be English – even Anglo-Jewish – was very heaven.

CHAPTER 2

Alien Corn

The Jewish diaspora is older than Jewish exile. During the lifetime of Christ when Judea, though under the suzerainty of Rome, was still a national entity there were more Jews scattered across the Roman Empire than were to be found within Judea itself. But their wanderings began in earnest after the destruction of the second Temple in A.D. 72 and the successive abortive struggles for independence which followed. Many Jews moved eastwards to Babylon, others westwards to Egypt, or across the sea to Spain, Italy and France.

Wherever they settled they usually found themselves under the rule of Rome. Judaism in Judea was looked on as subversive, outside it was viewed with tolerance. It was with the spread of Christianity that the dark night of exile began.

The first pogroms were perpetrated in France and the Rhineland in 1096 by Crusaders *en route*[1] for the Holy Land. The Jews were gradually reduced to pariahs. Their existence became precarious and they formed melancholy, straggling bands turning now this way, now that, in the eternal hope that a change of place would bring a change of fortune. Tolerance brought an influx, oppression an exodus.

Normandy in the eleventh century offered a comparative haven, and when the Normans crossed the English Channel some Jews followed. By the middle of the twelfth century small Jewish communities were established in London, Oxford, Cambridge, Stamford and other towns, and already enjoying such prosperity as to excite the envy of their neighbours.[2]

They escaped the ravages which affected Jewish communities lying in the path of the Crusaders, but not the backwash of bigotry released by the Crusades. Some of them were comparatively rich. They were alien in habit, manner and speech and their rituals gave rise to dark conjecture. In A.D. 1144 a young boy in Norwich vanished in mysterious circumstances and the belief spread that he was slaughtered by the Jews for ritual purposes.[3]

The same accusation was to be repeated again and again, with melancholy effect, in Gloucester (1168), Bury St Edmunds (1181), Winchester (1192), London (1244) and Lincoln (1255).

The most tragic episode, however, took place in York in 1190.

By the Assize of Arms of 1181 no Jews were allowed to keep 'mail or hauberk', and it is doubtful how far they would have been able to defend themselves against an angry mob even if they had been allowed. When in danger, therefore, they generally sought the protection of the Crown. Thus, for example, when the Jews of Norwich were attacked in 1189 they found refuge in the castle. The Jews of Stamford had a similar escape in the same year. In York they also fled to the castle but there the sheriff, as well as a number of barons who were in debt to the Jews, joined the mob. The siege lasted several days and the beleaguered community, seeing no hope of escape, turned upon one another. A handful of survivors threw themselves on the mercy of the attackers, and were butchered as they emerged. Every man, woman and child of what had been a flourishing and prosperous community perished.

There were periods when the Jews were allowed to draw breath and prosper but they were nearly always exposed to arbitrary levies and imposts, and sometimes to outright confiscation. As one contemporary observer noted: "even Christians pitied and wept over their afflictions".[4] In 1275 their earning power was all but eliminated by the Statute *de Judaismo* which prevented the recovery of interest at law and thus, virtually debarred from earning a livelihood by legal means, some Jews resorted to illegal ones. In London alone 293 Jews were hanged for tampering with the currency in 1278.

In 1286 Pope Honorius IV issued a Bull denouncing the Jews as "accursed and perfidious", and requiring the archbishops of Canterbury and York to act against their "audacity in order that it may be completely suppressed and confounded and that the dignity and glory of the Catholic faith may increase". On All Saints' Day 1290, the Jews of England, whose number had by then shrunk to under 3,000 souls, were banished.

Elsewhere their situation was less doleful. The benign rule of Casimir the Great (1333-70) brought a great flood of Jews into Poland. Germany remained attractive if only because it was a patchwork of petty states and if there was trouble in one principality one could easily transfer to another. But the golden land of this time was Spain.

The Crescent, as a rule, has been more hospitable to Judaism than the Cross and in Moslem Spain Jews were able to rise to the highest offices of state. Shmuel Ha-Nagid, a prominent Jewish scholar and writer, became vizier of Granada, and under his patronage there arose a whole school of Hebrew scholarship and poetry which included Solomon Ibn Moses Ibn Ezra and Yehuda Ha-Levi.[5] This golden age was brief. Christianity spread rapidly across the country, and with it the pillory and the stake. Jews were forced into baptism at the point of the sword, and even that was not alway sufficient to save them. In 1473-4 a series of hideous massacres decimated the Jewish communities of the Peninsula. In 1478 the Inquisition was instituted, and in 1492 the Jews were expelled.

Some moved southwards into North Africa, others eastwards to Italy, Greece and the Levant. Many crossed the frontier into Portugal. Here there was a brief period of respite, but Portugal soon followed the example of her neighbour and from the beginning of the sixteenth century onwards the only Jews to be found in the Peninsula were *Marranos* who, though outwardly Christian, maintained, at the risk of martyrdom, their Jewish traditions in secret.

Numerous *Marrano* families moved northwards into the Spanish possessions in the Netherlands. When the Dutch rebelled against Spain and formed the United Provinces in 1581 a new epoch began in Jewish history. Here at last was a country where the Jew could worship in comparative freedom and prosper without molestation. The *Marranos* could be open Jews again, though many, whose families had risked martyrdom to maintain their faith, now, given freedom, chose to leave it. Jews became prominent in the trade with the West Indies, South America, North Africa and the Baltic. They established Talmudical Colleges (the young Spinoza was a student at one). They were able to enter the universities and rise in the professions. By the end of the seventeenth century Dutch Jews enjoyed all the rights and privileges which Jews elsewhere in Western Europe were not to acquire until the French Revolution.

In England the edict of expulsion still stood. In 1650 Manasseh Ben Israel a Dutch Rabbi of *Marrano* extraction published a tract *Spes Israelis* which tried to show that the millennium was nigh, for in accordance with ancient prophecy Israel was 'scattered among the nations' in all four corners of the globe, and the Jews now had only to reach England to make their dispersion complete. His ideas occasioned some excitement in England. There was in the sixteenth century a great deal of religious ferment and endless metaphysical speculation. The translation of the Bible into English had made many people familiar with Biblical prophecy and interested in the fortunes of Israel, and not a few were convinced by Ben Israel's theories. Cromwell was not among these, but he was aware of the commercial benefits which the Jews had brought to the Netherlands and could bring to England. In 1655 Manasseh Ben Israel formally approached the Lord Protector with a petition for the readmission of Jews to England and although it won some support, the balance of opinion was against it. There were churchmen to whom the Jews were still perfidious, merchants who feared Jewish competition, and others to whom the very term *Jew* evoked pictures of a dark and sinister brotherhood.

There were, however, Jews in England, *Marranos*, who now felt sufficiently encouraged to come out into the open and in 1656 they petitioned Cromwell for his 'favour and protection' and the right to meet privately for worship.

Their wish was granted. They rented rooms for a synagogue, they acquired land for a cemetery. They were established as a community, but more through squatters' rights than formal enactment. The edict of expulsion has never been rescinded and remains on the Statute Book to this day.[6]

This new settlement was in essence an offshoot of the Dutch community and was entirely composed of Sephardim, that is, families of Iberian origin. Gradually a trickle of Ashkenazim, Jews of German and Polish origin, began to come in. A succession of massacres in the mid-seventeenth century had decimated the large Jewish communities of the Ukraine and parts of Poland, and there began a great surge towards the West, from Poland into Germany, from Germany into Holland, and from there – on a pattern that was to be repeated on a larger scale two centuries later – into England. By 1690 there were enough Ashkenazim in London to establish their own synagogue.

The Sephardim differed slightly from the Ashkenazim in their ritual and significantly in their culture. The Sephardim had inherited the traditions of what had been the most illustrious Jewish community in the diaspora and which had shared in the high level of civilisation of Moorish Spain. But even after the expulsion they continued, as *Marranos*, in the main stream of European culture and were able to share in the economic opportunities created by the opening of the Cape route and the discovery of the New World.[7]

Ashkenazim, on the other hand, had been confined to their narrow ghettos in the small towns of Poland or the *Judengasse* of the German cities, and had, so to speak, been by-passed by history. They experienced all the turmoils of the post-Reformation years, but shared few of their benefits. It was mainly a matter of opportunity and environment. The Jew who moved from a benighted land to an advanced one soon made up for lost time. The first of the Anglo-Jewish magnates were Sephardim. Their successors are nearly all Ashkenazim.

The revolution of 1688 and the accession of William of Orange to the throne of England brought a number of wealthy Jews in his train, and he encouraged the arrival of more. The Suasso family financed the transfer of his Court to England. Machado, Pereira and Solomon de Medina organised the commissariat of his armies.[8] Medina, who was knighted in 1700, the first professing Jew to be so honoured, also supplied the armies of Marlborough and did for him what the Rothschilds were to do for Wellington, except that Wellington required no rake-off, whereas Marlborough demanded and received a commission of £5,000 a year.

Contracting became something of a Jewish speciality. Joseph Mendes da Costa helped to supply the army of Flanders in 1710; Abraham Prado and David Mendes da Costa were active as suppliers on the European fronts in the Seven Years War (1756-63); David Franks – here the Ashkenazim begin to appear – was commissary officer in America, and Aaron Hart was with Amherst in Canada.

As the century wore on Jews became active as brokers on the Exchange, and as bankers, and some became rich in trade with the Indies. When the daughter of Israel Levien Salomons, an East India merchant of Clapton, married Benjamin Goldsmid in 1787 she brought a dowry of £100,000.

The most prominent Jew of the age and one of the most influential bankers in the country, was Sampson Gideon born in London in 1699, the son of Rehuel Abudiente, who had amassed a fortune in the West India trade. Abudiente was an active member of the Sephardi Synagogue which had been opened in Bevis Marks in the City of London in 1702. His son at first shared his interests and was a contributor to a Hebrew literary publication produced by the synagogue. He began business life as a lottery ticket seller, and at thirty became one of the twelve Jewish brokers on the Exchange and from there his progress was rapid. In the panic during the '45 rebellion, when the Jacobites had advanced as far as Derby and were preparing to descend on London, Gideon formed a consortium of Jewish brokers who advanced over £1,000,000 to shore up public confidence in government funds, an action which in the climate of the period seemed to combine patriotism with foolhardiness.

Yet Jews still suffered from handicaps. In 1744 it was held that a bequest to a synagogue was void because, said the court, the Jewish religion was not tolerated in England but only connived at. A Jew could not normally become a Freeman of the City of London and could thus not engage in retail trade within the City boundaries. Not more than twelve Jewish brokers could operate on the Exchange at any one time. They were excluded from some of the charter trading companies. It was doubtful whether they could own land.

Some of the handicaps arose out of the fact that many Jews were aliens, and those wishing to be naturalised by Act of Parliament – in itself an expensive and ponderous operation – had to take the sacrament.

In 1753 both Jews and the Government believed that climate of opinion – partly as a result of the work of Jewish brokers during the '45 – was sufficiently favourable for a change in the naturalisation law. Both were mistaken. An Act was indeed passed, but it was rapidly rescinded, for the 'Jew Bill', as it came to be known, excited one of the wildest outbursts of anti-Jewish feeling England has known. Pamphlets denouncing the measure flooded the town. Its supporters were molested. Mobs roamed the streets shouting "No Jews, no wooden shoes". A satirist suggested that St Paul's would be converted into a synagogue, that the import of pork would be forbidden, and Christmas would be disenfranchised.[9]

The worst victim of the storm was Sampson Gideon, for he was the most prominent figure in the community, the Jew writ large. He was aware of the dangers of over-exposure and was hesitant about the wisdom of pressing for the Bill in the first place but once the *Mahamad* – the ruling body of the Bevis Marks Synagogue – had decided to go ahead he could not publicly dissociate himself from it. As a result he was mercilessly lampooned as a mock Messiah, paving a passage for the Bill with gold.

Gideon, sufficiently harassed by the mob, was outraged when he discovered that the *Mahamad* had interpreted his grudging acquiescence to their campaign as zealous support, and in September 5, 1753, he resigned from the congregation and formally sundered his links with the Jewish community.

He had already done so partially when he married out of the faith – then something almost unknown among practising Jews – his children were brought up as Christians. A lesser man would probably have been required to resign from the congregation, but Bevis Marks may have been flattered by so eminent a figure in its ranks, and even after he wrote to declare "that I am not, nor will be from henceforth, any Member of your Society or Congregation",[10] there were still some hesitancy about accepting his resignation. Did they suspect that it was not wholehearted?

In 1757 Gideon's daughter Elizabeth, with the help of £40,000 dowry, married Viscount Gage. In the following year Gideon raised a large loan in difficult circumstances for George II and as a result hoped to enter the nobility on his own account. He asked the Duke of Devonshire to press his case. He was, he pointed out, born in England, married to an English Protestant, and his sons and daughters were all baptised by the sub-Dean of St Paul's a few days after their birth.[11]

The duke returned empty-handed. The king, he reported, "seemed extremely well disposed, spoke very handsomely of you and said he should have no objection himself to oblige you, but as you were not bred in the religion of the country he was afraid that it would make a noise. . . ." As indeed it would have done[12].

The following year he tried again. He had been instrumental in helping the Government negotiate a loan of £6,600,000 which for a time threatened to overwhelm the credit structure of the country, and he felt that Jew or no Jew he was entitled to some small consideration.

And he received it, but through his son, a schoolboy at Eton. Like many a Jewish father he had to be content to secure for his children what he could not obtain for himself. A letter to his son suggests that his pride was mingled with disappointment:

Dear Sampson,

The King has been pleased to order his Letters Patents to promote you to the dignity of a baronet. It is the lowest hereditary honour, but the first step. I have hope that by your own merit you will go higher. . . .[13]

Young Sampson did go higher to become a viscount but he marked the occasion by dropping the name of his father and adopting the maiden name of his mother, Eardley. He had no heirs and the title became extinct with his death.

Gideon had a town house in Lincoln's Inn Fields and a country seat, Belvedere House, Erith, Kent, the former home of Lord Baltimore. He also bought the Manor of Spalding in Lincolnshire and as it was doubtful whether a Jew could own land, secured his estates by private Act of Parliament. In 1747 he obtained a grant of arms but a title eluded him till the end. He died of dropsy in 1762.

"Gideon is dead," wrote a contemporary, "worth more than the whole land of Canaan. He has left the reversion of all his milk and honey, after his son and daughter, and their children, to the Duke of Devonshire, without insisting on the Duke taking his name or being circumcised."[14]

In his will he left £2,000 to the Sons of the Clergy, £1,000 to the poor of Erith, £1,000 to a London hospital. And then came a clause which caused stupefaction. He left £1,000 to Bevis Marks with the request that he be buried in the Jewish cemetery, and that his name should be recalled with other benefactors of the congregation during the memorial prayers on the Day of Atonement. It was further discovered that he had maintained anonymously his annual dues to the synagogue since his resignation.

His wishes were complied with, and on the Day of Atonement those who listen carefully can hear his memory recalled by the name with which he was known to the congregation, Sampson de Rehuel Abudiente.

Gideon sought the best of both worlds and wanted to enjoy the station and life of an English country gentleman without entirely forfeiting his soul; in short, to live like a Christian and die as a Jew. To an extent he succeeded.

Gideon's successor on the Exchange was Joseph Salvador, who was one of the first Jewish directors of the East India Company, and who also owned extensive properties in Lisbon and the Carolinas. He lost one fortune in the Lisbon earthquake in 1759, another in the failure of the East India Company, and he finally emigrated to America where he died in much reduced circumstances in 1786. His nephew and son-in-law, Francis Salvador, who had preceded him to the New World some years earlier, joined the rebels in the rising against George III, rose high in their ranks, but fell into Red Indian hands in 1788 and was scalped. He was 29.[15]

An obituary notice on Joseph Salvador in an American paper recalls: "He was formerly a most eminent merchant in England, being one of those who furnished that Government with a million of money in two hours' notice, during the rebellion in the year 1745; and likewise was one of the greatest landholders in this country."[16]

Moses Mendes, a contemporary of Salvador, combined the talents of financier and dramatist, but was more successful as the first than the second. His grandfather had been physician to Catherine of Braganza, wife of Charles II. Mendes took a Gentile wife, and his children, who were brought up as Christians, discarded his name, assuming that of their mother, Head.[17] Their descendants include Sir Francis Bond Head, who was on Wellington's staff at Waterloo, and Brigadier Antony Head (now Lord Head), Minister of War from 1951-56 and later Minister of Defence.

The Sephardim, even a century after the resettlement of Jews in England, were still a small, compact, cohesive group, still inward-looking, and especially after the disturbances of 1753, somewhat apprehensive of the outside world. The *Mahamad* assumed the right to censor any publication produced by a member of the congregation, or even the sermons of the *Haham*, their Chief Rabbi, in case of controversies which might reverberate beyond the community. Disputes between members were settled internally – as they still are between Orthodox Jews – before a tribunal of Rabbis, but one dispute exploded in the open and became a *cause célèbre*.

It concerned Kitty da Costa who at the age of seventeen married an elderly member of the community, Joseph da Costa Villa Real, who died three years later leaving her a son, a daughter and an immense fortune. Within days of his death the young widow became engaged to her cousin, Philip Mendes da Costa, a young man of most objectionable character whom she had known since childhood and to whom, indeed, she had been betrothed before. Her parents objected to the match and snatched her away to their estate in Totteridge. Her fiancé tried to see her and was resolutely kept out and he thereupon took proceedings in the High Court for breach of promise. The case was dismissed. He tried again on a claim for damages and was again dismissed. Kitty eventually married William Mellish, a member of Parliament, and the children were baptised. Her daughter married the Second Viscount Galway whose descendants include the late Marquess of Crewe, whose second wife was in turn a descendant of Nathan Mayer Rothschild.[18]

There were scores of others who were loyal sons of their community for a generation or two and then vanished into Christendom to restock the thinning ranks of the English aristocracy. These included the Francos, for example, a family of Sephardi merchants, whose descendants include Lord Ludlow, and Viscount Bledisloe; the Duke of St Albans is a descendant of Jacob Israel Bernal, a treasurer of Bevis Marks Synagogue; Lord Thurlow, Lord Donington, the Countess of Loudoun, the Viscountess St Davids, Lord Grey of Ruthin, a former Duchess of Norfolk, all stem from Pellegrin Treves, an Italian Jew who settled in London in 1740 and who in turn was descended from Rashi, a medieval scholar, and one of the greatest Jewish sages of all time.[19]

There was finally the Ximenes family who first built up a considerable fortune in the City and then rose to high rank in the army. Two Ximenes brothers, Morris and David, were knighted. When in 1807 the former applied for a grant of arms he informed the College of Heralds "that he and his family have always used as arms . . . which appear to be similar to those used by Cardinal Ximenes, Archbishop of Toledo, Primate and Prince Regent of all Spain and Castile, from a branch of whose family he is traditionally descended".[20]

Not every Jew who left the fold sired a duke, but it was only the thin gilded upper crust of the community which established sufficient social contact with the outside world to marry out of the faith.

At the end of the eighteenth century there were some 20,000 Jews in England, three-quarters of them in London, and most of those huddled in the narrow streets surrounding Bevis Marks Synagogue and the three Ashkenazi Synagogues, the Great, the Hambro and the New. (The Ashkenazim were both more numerous and more fractious.) But those who prospered, while still remaining attached to the City synagogues, acquired villas on the outskirts of London.

A middle class was emerging consisting of watchmakers, opticians, physicians, teachers, traders, and below them, a substantial class of paupers.

Persecution in Eastern Europe was causing a continuous move towards the west with a consequent overflow into London. The Ashkenazim were unable to cope with them all and in 1771, in an attempt to discourage the flow, the Great Synagogue refused relief to foreign Jews "who had left their country without good cause". Some of the newcomers turned hopefully to Bevis Marks, but were given short shrift: ". . . the charitable institutions formed by the Spanish and Portuguese Jews", it was announced, "were solely directed to assist their brethren, who either fled from alluded persecution, or were reduced by other misfortunes, and not for the purpose of encouraging, German, Dutch, or Polish adventurers. . . ." [21]

It was not only at this lower level that the Sephardim wished to keep

Ashkenazim at a distance. They were prepared to meet with them on matters of concern to Jews as a whole, but socially they preferred to keep their distance. For example in 1745 Jacob Bernal gave notice that he wished to marry an Ashkenazi. The *Mahamad* grudgingly allowed the wedding to take place, but none of the Rabbis of the congregation officiated at the ceremony, and no celebrations were allowed in the synagogue. When in 1772 another member of the congregation, Asher del Banco, sought to follow Bernal's precedent, permission was refused point-blank. But even the exclusiveness was breaking. There was no religious sanction for it, and it was in the main a social prejudice. A Sephardi who married an Ashkenazi almost inevitably married out of his class. But as the century wore on there was a considerable influx of wealthy Ashkenazim, the Cohens, the Goldsmids, the Gomperts and the Waley families from Holland, and Nathan Mayer Rothschild from Germany. In 1812 Moses Montefiore, a scion of one of the leading families in Bevis Marks, married a daughter of Levi Barent Cohen of Amersfoort, Holland, and three years later his brother Abraham married a sister of Nathan Mayer Rothschild. Wealth knows few barriers, and by the end of the eighteenth century, the Cousinhood which were to rule Anglo-Jewry for the next century and a half, and contribute richly to the life of the country as a whole, were already in being.

CHAPTER 3

The Brothers Goldsmid

Goldsmith, Goldschmidt, Goldsmid, the spelling has varied with the whereabouts of the family. The English branch favoured one, the German another, the Dutch a third, but what they all had in common was a Midas touch and a concern for the welfare of their fellows. They were rich, used their riches prudently, and spread them widely.

The English branch of the family was founded by Aaron Goldsmid who came to London in 1763 and died eighteen years later leaving four sons and four daughters.

His father Benedict Goldschmidt had been a prominent member of the Amsterdam Jewish community and a merchant with numerous contacts in the various provinces of Germany. There were Goldsmids in Frankfurt, Hamlin, Cassel, Hamburg and possibly the dispatch of Aaron to London was a means of extending the network further. It proved a most fortunate move. Aaron established his own firm and built up a profitable business relationship with Abraham Mocatta and Sons, bullion merchants, and agents to the Bank of England.

Mocatta had earlier entered into partnership with another broker, A. I. Keyser, to become de Mattos and Keyser. In 1787 Asher Goldsmid, a son of Aaron, was admitted as a partner and a little later married a daughter of Keyser. In 1799 the firm became known as Goldsmid and Mocatta. Four years later its name was reversed, and it has continued as Mocatta and Goldsmid, bullion brokers, to this day, and it is still headed by a Goldsmid and a Mocatta.

George Goldsmid, Aarons' eldest son, also joined Mocatta and Goldsmid, but the younger sons, Abraham and Benjamin, branched out on their own and established themselves as brokers, first, on a humble level, in Goodman's Fields, and later, as they prospered, in

Capel Court, near the Bank. They were helped on their way with a legacy of £15,000 from a Dutch uncle and with large dowries from their brides. Abraham married a Miss Elisson of Amsterdam, described in contemporary records as 'a Lady of great fortune, and extensive family connections'.[1]

In the meantime while Abraham was consolidating his position Benjamin came near to ruining his. He had struck up a liaison with the pretty young daughter of a brewer and seriously contemplated marriage. His family got to hear of it, dispatched him on an extended tour of Europe and provided the young lady with a respectable husband and more than a respectable pension. A few years later Benjamin was introduced to Jesse Salomons, the daughter of Levien Salomons, a West India merchant. She had, it was said, a dowry of £100,000 and according to contemporaries money was not her sole asset:

> Miss Jesse, in the highest bloom of youth, was thought handsome enough to give her parents some alarm on the score of the symmetry of her person and her other accomplishments, for her education was superior to what is usually bestowed on the fair sex, and her understanding exceeded that of any of the family. In short she might be said to possess superior advantages to the ladies of her time.[2]

They were married in 1787 and both families must have greeted the occasion with relief; but the union was doomed from the beginning and it ended in tragedy.

During the French Revolutionary Wars the government had frequent recourse to the market for new funds and on occasion found itself faced with a banker's ramp which extorted rates unjustified by the state of the market. In 1792 the Goldsmid brothers broke through the ring by bidding for a government loan. The bankers looked around for the interloper and found not another bank, but a firm of brokers whose name meant little to them or anyone else. As the years wore on they were to hear more. The ring being breached, bidding for loans became more competitive and the brothers benefited from the greater activity of the market. Their combination of audacity and flair made them almost invincible. When on a black day in 1793 funds fell by nearly £4,500,000 their losses were a mere £50. "They were," wrote an historian of the Stock Exchange, "fortune's chief and most especial favourites."[3] By the end of the century they were spoken of in the same breath as Barings.

Their breach of the ramp had gained the Goldsmid brothers the friendship of the younger Pitt, but when he was out of office – as when Addington took over in 1801 – they received little government business. Also their disregard for the cliques who had rigged the market had made them many enemies, who singly, and certainly in coalition, could do them grave injury. In 1795 the Goldsmids launched an £18,000,000 loan which was to be open to the general public and was known as 'the Loyalty Loan'. It opened on December 1 and within four days was oversubscribed. In 1797 there was a run on the Bank of England and cash payments were suspended. Consols fell to $47\frac{1}{4}$ and the Loyalty Loan was discounted at 14%. The Goldsmids lost a fortune. 1801 was another disastrous year. They lost heavily on loans and also lost government patronage through the fall of Pitt. Pitt returned in 1803 and they recovered breath a little, but he died in 1806 and three years passed before B. & A. Goldsmid received another government contract. By then Abraham was on his own.

In 1792 Benjamin acquired a sixty-acre freehold site at Roehampton and built himself a mansion in keeping with what he believed was his place in society, and which was regarded in its day as 'the chief ornament in that part of Surrey'.[4] Some visitors compared it to Windsor Castle. Hills were sliced, trees moved and waters diverted to provide the right setting. Pillars and staircases were of solid Siena marble, and visitors ascended past a guard of massive bronze figures. There were numerous drawing-rooms and music rooms, a ballroom and even a private synagogue. His dining-room was sixty feet by forty, and almost everything else in the house was ancillary to it. He was a magnificent host and viewed hospitality as a vocation. Pitt, Nelson, and the Duke of Cambridge were among the distinguished guests who crowded round his table, and the fête he gave to celebrate Nelson's victory at the Battle of the Nile was recalled with awe years after the event. It was all, wrote a contemporary

> In the most splendid style possible, beyond anything that was ever attempted anywhere else . . . his Mansion was most splendidly illuminated with fireworks. Music and dancing prevailed in the house, with Masques &c. and intervals of refreshment which amused his visitants near 24 hours.[5]

His entertainments, it was suggested, were part of the price expected of the Jew anxious to keep his place in society, but he was also in need of society to offset a deeply melancholy temperament made worse, as he grew older, by gout. He was large, fat and heavy. His knees sagged under him and buckled inwards. Movement involved him in gasping exertions. On his back he was as helpless as a turtle and had to have a heavy silk cord dangling over his bed to haul himself up in the mornings. He was florid in appearance and had to be frequently bled, which did not improve his temper. He would fly into spasms of rage so dark and uncontrollable that for periods he was out of his mind.

Towards the end of his life he could not be left on his own. His wife did not share his room and a servant had to sleep near the foot of his bed. Yet he could be cheerful, affable, kind, a generous employer, an almost extravagant benefactor. He gave widely to charities, Jewish and non-Jewish alike. He was a founder of the Naval Asylum. He was a patron of the arts and scholarship and even as his body was sagging and his spirit darkening, his mind continued to be marvellously alert and his house was still a centre of lavish entertainments.

On Sunday April 10, 1808, after a happy day spent with friends and relations, he ordered his carriage to be prepared to take him to the City the next morning and retired to bed. At about eight o'clock the next morning he asked his servant to fetch him a shirt. The servant hurried out and returned a minute later to find the door locked and bolted. He raised the alarm and servants and children came rushing from all quarters. The heavy oak door was burst open with some difficulty and Benjamin was found dangling at the end of his silken cord. The coroner returned a verdict of suicide while the balance of his mind was disturbed.[6]

When Benjamin died he left a widow and seven children. His marriage had not been a happy one. He was a devout Jew and as a young man on the grand tour he took his own cook, partly because he was fastidious about food, but mainly because he wanted to be sure it was kosher. The Chief Rabbi was his occasional guest at table and sometimes conducted the family prayers. Benjamin even reserved a small plot of land in which he grew a special type of wheat for the Chief Rabbi's *matzo* (the unleavened bread eaten at Passover). But his private life, it must be added, was not all prayers and meditation, and neither his religious beliefs, nor indeed, his bloated appearance and failing health, prevented him from panting after young women, and he set up an ex-maid as a mistress. Any reservations which his wife may have had about Judaism could hardly have been lessened by his conduct, and four years after his death she and her seven children were converted to Christianity.

Abraham shared his brother's melancholy streak and for a time his family were afraid to let him out of their sight lest he should follow

Benjamin's example,[7] but he gradually recovered something of his composure.

In 1809 B. & A. Goldsmid successfully handled a £14,000,000 loan for the Government, and in the following year he joined with Barings to sponsor a further loan of £13,400,000. It was launched in a boom atmosphere. A slump followed and within a few months the stock was being quoted at a discount of 3½%. Abraham was worried – he still had £1,000,000 worth of stock in hand – but he was not desperate, for he had Sir Francis Baring behind him. On September 11 Sir Francis died, Barings bowed out, and the burden of the whole loan fell on Abraham. By the end of the month it was being discounted at 6½%. Bankers who recalled the Goldsmid audacity of the 1790s watched him stagger under his burden with grim joy. Then came the last straw. The East India Company had placed £500,000 of Treasury Bills with his company for negotiation of which only £150,000 had found a market. When the market began to sag the company recalled the balance. Loans might have been obtained to tide him over the crisis, but he was no longer fully in command of his faculties. He felt that everything and everybody was ranged against him. "I will have my revenge," he kept roaring, shaking a fist at an unseen adversary. "I will have my revenge."

His friends were alarmed at his state of mind, and one who watched him with particular concern was Emma, Lady Hamilton.

The death of Nelson at Trafalgar had left Emma with slight means and heavy debts and Abraham had organised a loan to tide her over what he hoped was a temporary difficulty. It proved to be fairly permanent and he had to come to her aid again a few years later when he joined with Sir John Perring – the Lord Mayor of London – and one or two other influential City figures to press her claims for a pension. The Crown may have felt that a pension to an admiral's mistress would set an unfortunate precedent. In any case, none was granted. Her money was running out and she felt compelled to put Merton, her country house on the market. There were no bidders. Emma's situation became desperate, and finally Abraham took it off her hands for £13,000. He was well housed at Morden Hall, and the transaction seems to have been an act of chivalry. Merton was an eerie, forbidding pile which had brought no luck to anyone. "Something gloomy hangs over the place, which time will never do away", said George Matcham, Nelson's nephew and another of Abraham's friends.[8]

The £13,000 did not last long and in 1810 Emma approached

Abraham for a further loan, and he had the matter in hand when the crisis overtook him. She heard of his difficulties. "I hope it may turn out better than he expects," she wrote on September 27. "He is a good man, it is a pity he should suffer."[9]

The next day he was found dead with a bullet through his throat.

The Goldsmid brothers had been the first Jews to penetrate the royal circle, and on Friday April 14, 1809, Abraham Goldsmid entertained three sons of George III, the Dukes of Cambridge, Cumberland and Sussex, at his town house in Finsbury Square, and took them to the evening service at the Great Synagogue, Duke's Place.

A special order of service was prepared for the occasion. Their path to the synagogue was strewn with flowers, and they were received at the door by the young Nathan Rothschild, one of the wardens. The Duke of Sussex was so impressed with the occasion as to enquire further into Jewish history. He later became a student of Hebrew and a Champion of Jewish emancipation.[10]

Abraham once entertained the king himself at Morden.

George III and Queen Charlotte had been by the Thames when they noticed a magnificent mansion standing in ornate parkland. When the king heard it was Abraham's he became quite excited. "What, what my friend Abraham! I must see it at once. Go and tell Mr Goldsmid to go and get some luncheon ready for us and we shall go to him at once."

It was, at first, an awkward meal, for while the king sat down, Abraham and family remained on their feet. After a time the king could stand it no longer. "Come Goldsmid," he growled, "if you do not sit down to luncheon I shall stand up too."

Nelson, Lady Hamilton and various members of his family were frequent guests at Morden, but not all appreciated the hospitality. "Did not like their dinner; Jewish", wrote one distinguished visitor in his diary. "The Hall, the height of the house, very gaudy; as are all the rooms; but tasteless."

Lord Nelson once found himself at table with Moses Montefiore, a distant kinsman and close business associate of his host, and as always, admiral or no admiral, the devout Montefiore closed the evening with the 'Grace after Meals' in Hebrew, verse after verse, while Nelson sat watching dumbly, wondering if it would ever end.[11]

Both the Goldsmid brothers were accused of social climbing. They may have felt flattered by royal attention and gloried in their association with famous names, but they did not thrust their way upwards so much as they were pushed upwards by the very scale of their success. Their munificence was proverbial, but they did not pave their way to eminence with gold. Abraham in particular coupled generosity with discretion, and many of his so-called loans – including those to Lady Hamilton – were really outright gifts. On his death more than £100,000 in neglected promises to pay were found among his papers.

Abraham Goldsmid, said an acquaintance, 'united in himself the rare qualities of integrity, generosity, and active benevolence'. But wealth, no matter how generously used, will always excite opprobrium, and William Cobbett (easily excited on such matters) wrote, "A man acquiring such immense wealth must see that something was necessary to keep the public from grudging, and so, tossed back to the miserable part of us in the shape of alms, the fractions of pence upon the immense sums of money that he got by his traffic in loans, bills and funds".[12]

But perhaps the last words may be left to the obituarist in *The Times*:

> There are not many men who have ever performed more kind acts in social life, or more liberal ones in what may be esteemed his public one, than Mr Abraham Goldsmid; no one indeed, of any class of description, ever became tolerably well known to him, without improving their fortunes, in some degree, by the connexion; so that the list of those whom gratitude, or the sense of kindness received in one way or other, had bound, or ought to have bound, to him was almost endless.[13]

On April 13, 1808 *The Times* had published a similarly fulsome tribute on the death of Benjamin, but on April 19, it carried an announcement which must be unique in the history of journalism, to say that the obituary was a mistake and that it was published without the editor's knowledge and disclaiming all responsibility for it.

The Goldsmid brothers rose quickly, lived magnificently, and died tragically. There was, indeed, something apocalyptic about their ending and it gave rise to the belief that they and the entire Goldsmid family lived under a curse, a belief that may have been fortified by the association between the elder Goldsmid and the dark, mysterious figure of Rabbi Samuel Jacob Falk.

Falk was a student of the Cabbalah, the great codex of Hebrew mystical thought, and he was credited by various of his followers with supernatural powers. It was said that he had been condemned to death as a sorcerer in Germany, and when he settled in London in the second half of the eighteenth century, he became the centre of an occult group of Gentiles as well as Jews, who viewed him as a new Prophet, and approached him with holy awe. He became a source of legend:

> His chamber is lighted by silver candlesticks on the walls, with a central eight-branched lamp . . . and albeit although it contained oil to burn a day and night, it remained kindled for three weeks. On one occasion he abode in seclusion in his house for six weeks without meat or drink. When, at the conclusion of this period, ten persons were summoned to enter, they found him seated on a throne, his head diademed with a gold turban, a golden chain round his neck with a pendant and silver star on which sacred names were inscribed. Verily the man stands alone in his generation, by reason of his knowledge of holy mysteries.[14]

He had a coach and four in which he made frequent excursions to Epping at the dead of night for some unnamed rite. On one occasion, it was said, a wheel came off, but the coach continued as if nothing had happened and the wheel followed all the way to the forest.

Aaron Goldsmid was perhaps too level-headed an individual to be a follower of Falk, but he was a relative and friend, acted as his financial adviser and was appointed one of his executors. When Falk died on April 14, 1782, he left a small sealed package with Aaron with strict instructions that it should never be opened. Aaron, or so the story goes, could not restrain his curiosity, broke the seal, opened the package, and was found dead – a crumpled piece of paper with Cabbalistic inscriptions in his hand.

CHAPTER 4

Arrow into the Grey
Nathan Mayer Rothschild

An American traveller, walking through the narrow streets of London in 1835, caught sight of a crowd surrounding a figure in a courtyard. He was fascinated both by the scene and the figure:

> He was a very common–looking person, with heavy features, flabby pendant lips, and projected fish eye. His figure, which was stout, awkward and ungainly, was enveloped in the loose folds of an ample surtout. Yet there was something commanding in his air and manner, and the deferential respect which seems voluntarily rendered him showed that he was no ordinary person. 'Who is that?' was the natural question. 'The King of the Jews' was the reply. The persons crowding round him were presenting bills of exchange. He would glance for a moment at a paper, return it, and with an affirmatory nod, turn to the next individual pressing for an audience. Two well-looking young men, with somewhat of an air of dandyism, stood beside him making memoranda to assist in the recollection of bargains regulating the whole Continental Exchanges of the day. Even without this assistance he is said to be able to call to mind every bargain he has made. Of these he may now be esteemed the King.[1]

The 'King' was Nathan Mayer Rothschild then near the end of his career.

Nathan stemmed from, and still bore traces of, the Frankfurt *Judengasse* in which his family had lived for generations. The very name *Rot Schild*, Red Shield, was the designation of the family abode. His father, Mayer Amschel, who was born in 1744, lost both his parents at the age of twelve and the early need to fend for himself sharpened a mind already enterprising. A Jew had to be alert to survive at all in the circumstances of the day and to prosper required genius. The young Mayer prospered.

Germany was at that time a chaos of petty states, each with its own rulers, customs barriers and currencies and one could not travel far without the services of a money-changer. While still in his teens Mayer, who may have inherited a small legacy on the death of his parents, began to provide this service, and found that occasional coins came into his hands whose worth to an antiquarian far outweighed their face value. He branched out as a coin dealer and came into contact with a zealous numismatist, Prince William of Hanau. After he had supplied the prince with a quantity of rare coins he asked to be appointed Crown Agent. To make such a request on so slight a basis required a high degree of effrontery and presumption and Mayer was deficient in neither:

> I am making so bold to beg for this with more confidence in the assurance that by so doing I am not giving any trouble; while for my part such a distinction would lift up my commercial standing and be of help to me in so many other ways that I feel certain thereby to make my way and fortune here in the city of Frankfurt.

His wish was granted and on September 21, 1769, a new sign by his door declared that M. A. Rothschild was 'Crown Agent to the Principality of Hesse-Hanau'.[2]

He was not required to pay any due for the privilege or perform any duty, but it gave him a standing which few inhabitants of the *Judengasse* possessed. He was in business with *goyim*, and royal *goyim* at that.

He had earlier courted Gutele Schnapper, the seventeen-year-old daughter of a well established Jewish trader, and he now felt sufficiently established to make a formal proposal. They married in August 1770 and the children followed at frequent intervals, a daughter in 1771, Amschel in 1773, Solomon in 1774 and Nathan in 1777. Then came a torrent of daughters and thereafter two more sons, Carl in 1788 and finally James in 1792.

In 1785 William of Hanau succeeded to the throne of Hesse-Cassel. Mayer must have extended his fortune considerably by then, especially as Gutele had brought a sizable dowry, and in 1789 he wrote to the prince to offer his services in the negotiation of money bills. The prince made inquiries which satisfied him as to Mayer's integrity if not his means, and threw occasional business in his way. The Jew proved himself energetic and efficient and the volume of transactions grew.

The French Revolutionary Wars placed a premium on the services of Hessian mercenaries – William's main export – and increased the business opportunities for the house of Rothschild. The invasion of Holland enabled Frankfurt to steal the ascendancy of Amsterdam for a time as the money market of Western Europe, and this too favoured the Rothschilds. Mayer's income in the two decades after his marriage was reckoned as between 2000 and 3000 guilden a year, a substantial sum in those days. In 1795 – the year Holland fell – it jumped to 4000 and in the following year it soared to over 15,000. By the end of the century his fortune approached the million mark.

But he still remained in the ghetto, and was still subject to all the pains and penalties of the ghetto Jew. He still had to pay a poll tax. If he travelled outside of town he paid another tax, and if he stayed overnight he was taxed again. He had twenty children, of whom ten survived, and as his family and fortune grew he moved out of the crumbling dwelling in which he had begun married life into a more substantial house in the same street. It was of stone, tall and narrow, four storeys high, with an attic on top and a small roof garden beyond and one could hardly move without going up or down stairs. The rooms were mean and the congestion was acute; every inch of space was put to use, with cupboards in alcoves under the stairs, and in every nook and cranny. There was a small bedroom for the parents, and the massive brood of children were crowded into two other rooms. The roof garden may seem something of a luxury, but no Jew in Frankfurt was allowed to own a garden and the roof garden enabled the children to come up for air. Moreover, the Orthodox Jew has to have an open space on which to build a booth for the Feast of Tabernacles and the Rothschilds were then deeply devout. Mayer had been educated in a *Yeshiva*, a Rabbinical school, and cherished every Jewish tradition. His wife Gutele, was the classical Jewish matriarch. Like other Orthodox married women she had her hair cut off and replaced with a large wig, on top of which she wore an even larger bonnet. She was a woman of simple tastes, but shrewd and outspoken, and nervous of what wealth might do to her family. Nothing could induce her to move from the old dark house in the *Judengasse*, not even after her husband was dead and her children were living in palaces. She feared that once her family was gone from the *Judengasse* its fortune would go with it.

Mayer and Gutele may not have been able to instil their personal piety into their children, but one governing principle remained, family unity. "All the brothers shall stand together in everything," declared Mayer, "all shall be responsible for the action of each one." It was almost the family motto, and it continued to hold true even after the family was scattered across Europe.

The Rothschilds dealt not only in loans and old coins but were general merchants too by this time, trading in wines, flour, textiles, and a host of other manufactured goods. The disruption of the European economies caused by the advance of French armies enabled the English manufacturer to sell almost anything he produced and made his representatives somewhat peremptory and brusque. Nathan was annoyed by their manner and he proposed to his father that he go to England to deal with the manufacturers direct. His father agreed, and in 1798 he arrived in Manchester with £20,000 in his pocket, a few letters of introduction, and not a word of English.

Manchester was enjoying a war boom. Napoleon's ambitions forced Britain to keep a large army and navy and the subsidies she was paying her friends on the Continent also kept up the demand for British goods, especially textiles. Nathan, who had been involved in textiles merely as a distributor, saw that there were also profits to be made from the various stakes in the manufacturing process. He therefore began to buy semi-finished goods, had them dyed, farmed them out for manufacture and finally sold the finished product. He also dealt in dyes and other commodities such as sugar, coffee and wine. Within five years he had doubled or trebled his original capital and turned south for London.

It was then that he met Levi Barent Cohen, who was, among other things, a linen merchant.

Levi was born in Holland in 1747 where his family had been well established for nearly a century as tobacco-growers, corn traders and general merchants with extensive contacts in Germany and the West Indies. In 1770 he crossed the Channel to establish a link with London, and opened an office in Angel Court, Throgmorton Street. He was not totally among strangers. Several Cohen sisters had married a number of Goldsmid brothers, and he could turn to Abraham and Benjamin not only as co-religionists, but as kinsmen. By the end of the century he was established in a large villa in Richmond. He retained his dwelling above his counting house in Angel Court and the young Nathan Rothschild was his guest for a while.

Levi married twice and had daughters enough for any suitor, but when in 1806 Nathan asked to marry Hannah he wanted time to think about it. Nathan's appearance was not such as to commend itself even to a father with an acute surplus of daughters. The face was astute, the eyes blue and good humoured, but goitrous and, on occasion, even a little wild. The hair was curled and reddish. The lower lip sagged. Above all, the name of Rothschild rang no bell. But the young man had winning ways and great persistence and eventually got his Hannah and a dowry of £10,000. The marriage also brought him into contact with several of the leading brokers on the Exchange and into the front rank of the small, but growing Anglo-Jewish élite.

On the advice of Mayer Rothschild, William of Hesse invested heavily in English securities. The transactions were handled in London by Nathan and as there was a gap between the dates of purchase and settlement, he used the funds for short term loans and for the purchase of bullion, the price of which was rising by the day. On one occasion he bought an entire ship-load of bullion from the East India Company which he promptly resold at a substantial profit to the Government.

The campaign against Napoleon had to be sustained by a constant outflow of bullion which was difficult to obtain and hazardous to transport and Vansittart, the Chancellor of the Exchequer, therefore turned to Rothschild who was known to have continent connections to arrange the transfers. The operation, wrote Vansittart to J. C. Herries, the Paymaster-General, was of "the utmost importance to the public service", and in view of the "dispatch and secrecy which it required and the risks which may be incurred it is not thought unreasonable to allow Mr Rothschild a commission of two per cent. . . ."[3]

Herries at once armed Nathan with an official letter dated January 11, 1814:

> In the event of your experiencing any molestation or impediment from the Civil or Military authorities . . . you will be at liberty to produce this letter as a testimony that you are employed on account of the British Government.
>
> Signed: J. C. Herries.[4]

Thus there began a relationship which was of mutual benefit to both Rothschild and the Government in the course of which he transferred no less than £11,000,000.

Nathan developed various methods of transfer and used his younger brother James, then only nineteen, and based in Paris, as his main agent. Sometimes it was an elaborate smuggling operation, with James disguised as a woman, carrying the bullion through the French lines hidden among his clothes. More often he bought bills at a discount from Wellington which he redeemed at par with the Treasury, usually in the form of guineas, and then transferred across the channel to James. James, in turn used the money to secure bills from French bankers on Spanish, Sicilian or Maltese banks, who in turn supplied Wellington with cash. The transactions enriched numerous banks along the way and Rothschild most of all.

The Government was grateful. "It is due to Mr Rothschild," wrote J. C. Herries, "that I should not omit this opportunity to be a witness to the skilfulness and zeal with which he has executed this service, while he has at the same time conducted it so quietly that no impression appears to have been made by it on the exchange."[5]

Rothschild and Herries had to work very closely on the operation and in great secrecy, and this, perhaps inevitably, gave rise to rumours that Herries had done well out of it. The rumours revived in 1827 when Prime Minister Goderich proposed to make Herries Chancellor of the Exchequer. His connections "with a certain great capitalist", wrote one paper, "made him unfit for public office."[6] The 'certain great capitalist', who was also described as 'the principal speculator on the money markets of Europe', was nowhere named, but everyone knew who he was. It is possible that Rothschild may have helped Herries with a private loan, as he had helped numerous other individuals, including the Prince Regent,[7] and that Herries may have had cause to be grateful to him, but there is no shred of evidence to suggest that he was in Rothschild's pay. Goderich assured Herries that he gave no credence to the imputations and in due course appointed him to the office.[8]

Rothschild's credit system was based on an elaborate intelligence network. There were, first of all, the brothers themselves scattered across Europe. Nathan had agents and couriers all over the south coast and the facing ports in Holland, and his servants swarmed over the the battle-fields of Europe. The captains of many of the packet boats were also in his pay, and he was often better informed about events on the Continent than the Government itself.

According to one legend, Nathan was at Waterloo presumably to be on hand in case anything important developed. Another suggests that he got first news of the victory by carrier pigeon. All relate how he then dashed to the Stock Exchange to cash in on his advance information; but instead of buying all he could, he began operations by selling and then, as prices slumped he suddenly reversed tactics and bought. Prices did slump but the cause was not Nathan's machinations but news of Wellington's setback at Quatre Bras.

Waterloo was fought on June 18. News reached Nathan via one of his agents in Dunkirk, on June 20. He at once communicated the report to the Prime Minister Lord Liverpool, who found it too good to be true until it was confirmed by a dispatch from Wellington some thirty hours later.

Nathan was less doubtful, descended joyfully on the market and bought up a huge parcel of shares. News of Waterloo broke a few hours later and prices soared.

Nathan was not averse to making a *coup* at the expense of other members of the Exchange, and indeed took a mischievous delight in leaping in one direction when the market thought he would go in another, but his *coup* after Waterloo was not due to devilish cunning but to his intelligence network. Henceforth Nathan was viewed with awe by the City as a type of miracle worker. And in finance, where so much rests on faith, the belief that a man is a miracle worker may enable him to work miracles.

After Waterloo the Rothschilds became bankers to the Holy Alliance of Christian monarchs, formed by Alexander I to maintain the stability of Europe; it consisted of Russia, Austria, Prussia and Britain.[9] The family fanned out to different capitals to direct the flow of funds. James made Paris his permanent base, Solomon moved to Vienna, Carl to Naples, Amschel remained at the home base of Frankfurt; but the main centre of operations was in New Court, London, directed by Nathan.

The end of the war did not end the flow of English money to Europe. In 1817 Prussia was in desperate need of a loan of £5,000,000. Wilhelm von Humboldt, the Prussian Ambassador to the Court of St James's, urged an appeal to New Court. "Rothschild is now easily the most enterprising businessman in the country," he wrote. "He is, moreover, a man upon whom one can rely, and with whom the Government here does considerable business. He is also, as far as I know, just, exceedingly honest, and intelligent."[10] Christian von Rother, Director of the Prussian Treasury, confirmed this opinion: "The Rothschild in this country is a most estimable person, and has an incredible influence upon all financial affairs here in London. It is widely stated, and is, indeed, almost a fact, that he entirely regulates the rate of exchange in the City. His power as a banker is enormous."[11]

Nathan undertook the loan and secured it at an average price of 72%.

It was, said Nathan, "a splendid piece of business", for the stock never fell below the issuing price in 1824 and actually rose to 100.

This was the first big state loan undertaken by the Rothschilds. Others followed in rapid succession. In 1819 he launched a £12,000,000 loan at 3% on behalf of the British Government. The lists were filled before intimation of the loan had been publicly received from the Treasury, and when bidding opened it was oversubscribed by £40,000,000. In 1821 came a loan of £2,000,000 for the Neapolitan Government; in 1823 £1,500,000 for Portugal, in 1824 £300,000 for Austria, and so on, year after year, sometimes in concert with houses like Baring Brothers, usually alone.[12] Not all of the loans were profitable, and some were disastrous, but henceforth a foreign treasury seeking money on the London market would turn to Rothschild almost as a matter of course. Nathan increased the mobility of credit and made it more international. Foreign loans before his time had been viewed with scepticism in London, for added to the normal hazards of investment were the hazards of political upheaval. Moreover dividends had generally been paid abroad, in foreign currency and subject to exchange fluctuations. Nathan made the dividends payable in London, in sterling and his name was in itself a guarantee. In 1823 for example he raised a loan of £2,500,000 for the Kingdom of Naples which had been suffering from grave internal unrest, was quartering a large Austrian army, and whose credit was at a very low point. Bidding opened at 89.8. Within a few months the price rose to 96.75 and at one point reached 108. There was little in the situation of Naples to explain this upward move, which must have been largely due to Nathan's backing.

By 1848 New Court alone had raised over £200,000,000 for foreign clients. The elaborate European system maintained by Alexander I and Metternich could hardly have functioned without Rothschild finance. Wherever armies moved, whether to quell an uprising in Naples or unrest in Spain, whether to combat nationalism in Lombardy or liberalism in France, a delegation from one Treasury or another would be found waiting hopefully at New Court.[13]

This put the family as a whole squarely on the side of reaction but, the different branches were free to act independently of one another and after the death of Castlereagh, when England tended to follow a more liberal policy, Nathan on occasion took one direction while his brothers followed another.

In 1820 Spain adopted a liberal constitution and Ferdinand VII, a virtual prisoner of the new administration, turned to his fellow monarchs for help. Sentiment in England was on the side of the liberals and rumours began to spread that the Rothschilds, presumably through Nathan, had helped them with loans. Solomon rushed to reassure Metternich that there was no truth in them:

> Your highness is far too familiar with the sentiments of myself and my brothers to give such baseless rumour more than a moment's consideration. It is so wholly inconsistent with our general reputation that I do not think it necessary for me to go into further explanation regarding the matter.[14]

The influence of the house was placed at the disposal of the powers, the liberals were suppressed, absolute monarchy was restored, and with it, the Holy Inquisition. The role of Nathan in this was uncertain but in 1829, to the dismay of his brothers, he helped Brazil, which had recently risen against Portuguese rule, to reorganise her foreign debt and secured her a loan of £800,000.

The new states of Central and South America were a hazardous field of operation, promising great rewards but often resulting in great losses, and even the Rothschilds burned their fingers. A speculative frenzy built up during 1824 akin to the South Sea Bubble of the century before. No idea was too absurd, no prospectus too vague for the mind of investors hungry to convert cash into bonds. At the end of the year the bubble burst. Large houses staggered, small ones collapsed and it looked for a time as if the Bank of England itself was in danger. Nathan, who was about to depart for the Continent, was urged by the Government to remain in London and on Christmas Eve, with the help of James he arranged an emergency transfusion of gold from France.[15]

Among the many distinguished in-laws acquired by Nathan through his marriage into the Cohen family, was Benjamin Gomperts, Fellow of the Royal Society, President of the Astronomical Society, and a renowned mathematician but who, because of his religion, was unable to get a job as an actuary with an insurance company. Jews at the time were thought of as poor insurance risks in general, and fire risks in particular, and often found it difficult to obtain policies. There was a prevailing impression, wrote an historian; "that arson had some peculiar charm for the Hebrew".[16] In 1824 Nathan, together with Moses Montefiore, another distinguished brother-in-law, launched the Alliance company which quickly grew to become one of the largest insurance companies in the country. And Gomperts, of course, became the actuary, but it is doubtful whether the company was formed to find him a job. Nathan had sufficient influence to place less gifted Jews than Gomperts in employment and was already a director of Guardian Assurance.

The place of the brothers in the European system, their role as hand-maidens of reaction, their ability to maintain and even enhance their fortunes in ventures where others lost theirs, their influence, their power, their incredible wealth, earned them the opprobrium of the left without wholly eliciting the approval of the right. They were parvenus in every sense. They had shot to the fore like comets: they were not only Jews but foreign Jews talking in foreign accents. On the Continent they were the continuing subject of anti-Semitic attacks, but Nathan was more happily placed.

In England the situation of the Jews was comparatively enviable. They could move freely and trade comparatively freely. They paid no special taxes. Above all, they were free from personal molestation. In common with Catholics and Non-conformists, they still suffered from numerous political disabilities. Nathan was active in the campaign to remove them, though less active than his brother-in-law, Moses Monte-fiore, or his distant kinsmen, Sir Isaac Lyon Goldsmid and David Salomons.

Nathan served as Warden of the Great Synagogue in 1818 in con-junction with his brother-in-law, Solomon Cohen. He may not have been as devout a Jew as his late father-in-law, but he had a greater business acumen which he applied to synagogue affairs, bringing the three Ashkenazi Synagogues in the City closer together and co-ordi-nating their work for the relief of the poor.[17] He gave his name and something of his time, but not a great deal of his money for he was not a particularly generous man. His father had died in 1812 and shortly before had disposed of his entire business to his five sons for 190,000 guilden, which was in no sense its real value, but the means of keeping the true size of his estate secret.

Nathan thus received a fifth part of a large enterprise which he quickly made larger. It is impossible to assess the size of his fortune, which was tied up in various trusts. The million or so he left in his will was certainly no indication of it, but the scale of his transactions must have made him one of the richest men in England. As he himself argued, it did not matter what one sold so long as one sold enough of it. He rarely ignored a small transaction in case it should entail a large one, and he could calculate the worth and prospects of every paper at a glance. In other respects his faculties were commonplace. This may have been one of the secrets of his success. He was the common man writ large. He had the sense of the market, but before the market sensed it and could thus make his bidding before the prices rose.

In 1822 Nathan and his brothers were made Barons of the Austrian empire, but unlike them he was not awed by the title and never used it. To be a Rothschild, and in particular Nathan Rothschild, he felt, was distinction enough. It was his saving grace. He was true to himself, and he could be brutally frank with others. He was aware that his social standing, his prestige and any esteem which he might enjoy, were not due to intellectual accomplishments or social graces, but to money. He was a boor. His awkward shape, his large belly, his goitrous eyes, his slipshod dress, his slouching posture as he stood with his coat unbuttoned and hands deep in his trouser pockets, was one of the most familiar, if not one of the most beautiful, sights on the Exchange. Yet he combined it all with a natural authority; he had the appearance of a huckster and the aura of a king. If a genius at finance, he could be backward in other respects. "Nathan Mayer Rothschild," wrote his brother Solomon, "is not particularly bright; he is exceedingly competent in his office, but, apart from that, between ourselves, he can hardly write his own name."[18] He sometimes had a dread of intellectuals. "I have seen many clever men," he said, "very clever men, who had not shoes to their feet. I never act with them. Their advice may sound very well, but fate is against them; they cannot get on themselves, and if they cannot do good to themselves, how can they do good to me?"[19]

He told the composer Spohr that he did not understand music. "That," said he, jingling the coins in his pocket, "is the music for me." And he believed it could be music for others. Of his children he said: "I wish that they may devote themselves mind, soul, heart and body to their business; that is the way to attain happiness."[20]

His own dedication to business, however, did not afford him much happiness. "Happy! – me happy!" he once protested, "What! Happy when, just as you are going to dine, you have a letter placed in your hands, saying, 'If you do not send me £500 I will blow your brains out?' Happy! – me happy!"[21] He saw threats, real and imagined, everywhere. As he grew older he slept with a loaded pistol under his pillow.

The flattery and adulation which he received made him contemptuous of mankind. In the last resort he knew on what it was all based, and was not so far removed from the Bible to have forgotten the words of Ecclesiastes: 'Vanity of vanities, all is vanity.'

He was brusque to subordinates but then he was brusque to mankind and no respecter of persons.

An illustrious prince was once ushered into his presence. Nathan, who was busy, offered him a chair and went on with his work.

"I'm afraid," said the visitor, "you did not hear who I am. I am the Prince of Puckler-Muskau."

Nathan looked up from his desk.

"Ah," he said "ah, then take two chairs."[22]

Nathan found some of the contentment he missed in business life in his family circle. His wife Hannah, a warm, amiable creature, was the centre of a large and affectionate cousinhood. Brothers, sisters, aunts and uncles, Cohens, Samuels, Montefiores, Gomperts, poured in and out. They lived first of all 'on top of the shop' at 2 New Court, but as the business and family grew they moved westwards to 107 Piccadilly. They had a country house first at Highgate, then at Stamford Hill. Finally in 1835 Nathan bought Gunnersbury, the former home of Princess Amalia, a daughter of George II, for £20,000. He never lived to use it.

He had four sons and three daughters. We shall hear more presently of Lionel, Anthony and Mayer. The fourth, Nathaniel, crippled in youth in a riding accident, married a daughter of James, and moved to Paris where he spent his limited energies and considerable fortune in amassing a large art collection. He also bought the Mouton vineyards near Bordeaux, from which were to come the famous Rothschild wines.

Of the daughters, Charlotte, the eldest, married her cousin Anselm, a son of Solomon Rothschild of Vienna. The youngest, Louisa, married another cousin, Mayer Charles of Frankfurt. A third daughter, Hannah, was the first member of the family to marry out of the faith. Others were to follow, but unlike them she embraced Christianity and married in church. Her husband was the Hon. Henry Fitzroy, a son of Lord Southampton. She never had much sympathy for or interest in Jews or Judaism which caused much consternation in the family, but she had to wait till her father was dead before she felt able to leave the fold.

Nathan took his Judaism seriously, not only as a creed but because of his position in Jewish life. "I am as good as you", he once told the Duc de Montmorenci. "You style yourself the first Christian baron, and I am the first Jew baron."[23]

In 1836 Nathan's heir Lionel became engaged to Charlotte, only daughter of his uncle Carl, of Naples. The wedding took place in June in Frankfurt so that the grandmother, who was in her eighties, could attend. A vast concourse of relatives descended on the town, Solomon from Vienna, James from Paris, cousins and second cousins, Goldsmids and Goldschmidts, Montefiores and Cohens, Oppenheimers and Sterns. Among them all, a little incongruously, was Rossini, a friend of James, who blinked and wondered at the pomp and ceremony. Gutele could not restrain her excitement at the many arrivals.

Nathan came with a large entourage, but he was less than his loud bumptious self. His health was being sapped by a large carbuncle. He staggered on till the wedding day on June 15 but when the festivities were over he took to his bed. A relay of German doctors made his condition worse and Hannah, in alarm, brought over the surgeon Benjamin Travers, a neighbour of theirs at New Court. By then it was too late. General blood poisoning had set in and on July 28 he died. He was fifty-nine.

He had rallied in his last hours and sat up to find his family weeping round him. A Rabbi gave him the confessional and he began to read: "I acknowledge unto thee, O Lord my God and God of my fathers, that both my cure and my death are in thy hands. May it be thy will. . ." He paused for a moment, and put the book aside. "It is not necessary that I should pray so much," he said, "for, believe me, according to my convictions I have not sinned."[24]

CHAPTER 5

Giant
Sir Moses Montefiore

Anyone who travelled extensively in Eastern Europe before the war would have found in many Jewish homes, sometimes among the family portraits but often in a place of honour by itself like an icon, a face that did not quite go with the setting. It was bearded and patriarchial, yet more in the manner of the *grand seigneur* than the Jewish sage, and the high collar and frilled shirt carried a hint of Regency England. The overall impression was one of power. The head was massive, the mouth firm, the chin determined, even pugnacious, the nose prominent, the eyes careworn and kindly. It was the portrait of Sir Moses Montefiore, certainly the most beloved and revered Jew to have lived in this country, and possibly the greatest.

Sir Moses bestrides the Jewish history of the nineteenth century like a colossus and for once the metaphor is entirely in place. There was something colossal about him, the span of his years, the range of his interests, the sum of his wealth, the scale of his munificence, his very size. He was six foot three in height, with massive shoulders, a grizzly beard and robust voice and he dominated any company by his presence. He was born in 1784 in the reign of George III, and died, in his one-hundred-and-first year, in the reign of Victoria. He stemmed from one wealthy family, married into another, enhanced his fortune by hard work and great enterprise, and retired at the age of forty to devote his money and the rest of his life to public welfare. There was hardly a major event in the Jewish history of his time in which he was not involved.

Much of his influence derived from the fact that the age of Montefiore in Jewish history coincided with the supremacy of Britain in the affairs of the world. It was the age of Palmerston, Russell and

39

Gladstone, when the oppressed of many lands, whether Greece, Poland, Italy or Spain, turned hopefully towards London – and there was rarely an incident of oppression which did not count Jews among the victims. Often they were the sole victims.

The Jews of Britain at this time were not numerous or powerful – in number and wealth they ranked well below those of Germany, Austria and France. But it was easier to engage British sympathy on behalf of a humanitarian cause. Britain could go beyond hints and, if necessary, beyond words. It was this which made British Jewry particularly influential and gave Montefiore the role of Prince of the Dispersion.

One first hears of the Montefiores in Moorish Spain. After the expulsion, they moved to Italy where one branch settled first in Ancona and then moved to Leghorn. In Leghorn the tolerance of the Medici gave full scope to Jewish enterprise and, in his petition for the readmission of the Jews to England in 1656, Manassah Ben Israel attributes the prosperity of Leghorn to that fact. Moses Montefiore's ancestors were among the leading merchants of the town but his grandfather, though married to the daughter of a wealthy Moorish merchant, Masshood Racah, failed to prosper and, in 1758, he emigrated to England. Having some capital at his disposal, he soon established himself as an importer of various Italian goods. He had seventeen children – eight sons and nine daughters. One son died in infancy. The eldest son, who was born in Leghorn, remained there; three sons emigrated.[1] A fourth, Joshua, began his adult life as a lawyer, but enlisted in the infantry and was the first, or claimed to be the first, Jew to hold commissioned rank in the British army. He also claimed to be the first Jewish undergraduate at Oxford, the first English Jew to be called to the Bar, and much else – claims which cannot be substantiated. He was, in fact, a sort of Baron Munchhausen and as the details of his career are based almost entirely on his own journal, it is difficult to disentangle fact from fiction, but his commission is one of the less unlikely claims.[2]

In 1792, he was, or again claimed to be, one of the leaders of an expedition to establish a new British colony in West Africa. It was ill-planned and ill-executed and collapsed almost as soon as it was established. He survived and, as he would have one believe, with his reputation enhanced – and, on his return to London was presented to George III and was offered a knighthood, which he declined. This is the unlikeliest tale of all. A report published by the head of the expedition showed that Joshua was one of the minor figures in the party, and an insubordinate one at that.[3] It is thus improbable that he was presented at Court, impossible that he was offered a knighthood. And, had it been offered, it would certainly not have been declined.

In later life he compiled a number of useful works of reference, including a *Commercial Dictionary* and a *Synopsis of Mercantile Law*. Another work, *Commercial and Notarial Precedents*, dedicated to the Lord Chief Justice, Lord Ellenborough, went into two English and three American editions.[4]

He settled in America and peddled his work among the principal commercial centres of the East Coast. At the same time, he continued to dabble in both law and journalism without much result, either by way of income or reputation. He married twice. His first wife was Esther Supino, daughter of a leading member of Bevis Marks. His second wife, Elizabeth Mahers, a Catholic, had been Esther's maid. He was seventy-three at the time of his second marriage and had moved to a farm on the outskirts of St Albans, Vermont. He lived to be eighty-one and in the last eight years of his life sired eight children. His later years were spent in near penury. Like other members of his family in similar circumstances, Joshua turned to his nephew, Moses Montefiore, for help. Sir Moses sent him an allowance of £20, how often, or for how long, is not known.

Joshua Montefiore remained a Jew, but his children, possibly to make their future less troublesome, were brought up as Protestants. During the summer of 1843, when he was dying, he told his family that he did not want to be buried in a Christian cemetery and wrote out what he could remember of the Jewish burial service which was read at his graveside. He was buried on his farm. In his family Bible there is an inscription:

> After my death, my wish and desire is that my children will add (to their prayers) the following:
> 'O my gracious God, I further humbly supplicate and pray that you will be pleased to pardon the sins of our deceased lamented Father and receive his soul with mercy and tenderness.'[5]

Horatio, one of his eight children, came to London in 1863, got into financial difficulties and finally approached the American Legation for help. Mr Benjamin M. Moran, Secretary to the Legation at the time, noted in his journal:

> A tall fine-looking Vermonter by the name of H. Montefiore came here this morning in distress to be sent home. He has an idea that he is a relative

to a Jewish Knight by that name and had come to London to beg from him. I rebuked him for his folly and gave him a few shillings to keep him from starving. It appears he has written to Sir Moses and has been at his office, but no one treated him civilly. Being a printer, he has tried to get work but failed, and I have advised him to work his way home as we can't help him. He is only twenty years of age.[6]

Horatio's first cousin, Sir Moses, was by then an almost legendary figure and must have had a considerable army of clerks about him to keep beggars and opportunists at a comfortable distance – especially where callers tried, as many did, to establish kinship. It is probable, however, that had Horatio obtained access to him he would have received a far more civil welcome and would not have gone away empty-handed. Sir Moses had fond memories of Horatio's father as a dashing and very colourful personality.[7]

The other uncles married well, settled down to safe occupations, set up homes in leafy suburbs and peopled their neighbourhoods with immense families. Samuel and Joseph Montefiore both married daughters of Abraham Mocatta. Joseph was set up by his father as an importer of Carrara marble and Italian straw bonnets. His means increased with his marriage. He was on business in Leghorn when his eldest son Moses was born. They had two other sons – Abraham and Horatio – and five daughters, Esther, Sarah, Abigail, Rebecca and Justina.

At this period no practising Jew could hope for a university education. Hence, all the boys left school early and were apprenticed to various trades. Abraham found work with a Mr Flower, an eminent silk merchant in Watling Street and gradually built up a small fortune in the silk trade. He then tried his hand on the Exchange – where he was less fortunate. He married the daughter of a Gentile stockbroker, George Hall, which virtually cut him off from his family. Since almost all the Jewish stockbrokers were in the Cousinhood, and they all depended on mutual help to carry them over the thin patches, he was ruined. Moses, perhaps the most Orthodox member of the family, was particularly distressed by the marriage but could not allow a brother to sink into penury. He helped Abraham find his feet again, and in 1812 took him in as a partner.[8]

After his wife died Abraham married Henrietta, the youngest daughter of old Mayer Rothschild of Frankfurt, and sister of Nathan. His fortune was now secure, but the lean years had sapped his health and vitality. He contracted consumption and died in 1824.

The Montefiores lived in a large terrace house in Kennington Place,

Vauxhall. The children's schooling was limited. Moses tried to supplement his with private reading of a very catholic nature with the result that he became a repository of odd bits of stray and disconnected facts. He acquired the habit of noting down passages, passing precepts, lines of poetry, epigrams, wise words – compiling a homespun guide to life and living.[9]

His first job was as a clerk with a firm of tea merchants, Messrs Johnson, McCulloch, Sons & Co. of Eastcheap. The work was hard, the hours long and the distance from home considerable. Nevertheless, he shunned transport even in the depths of winter and walked to and from work.[11] Sometimes he would not leave Eastcheap before midnight and then trudging home through slush and snow, he consoled himself with the thought of the money he was saving. Later, when he became a very rich man he still kept a careful account of every penny and, although generous with others, was by no means extravagant in his personal expenditure.

In 1803, with the help of his Mocatta uncles and the payment of £1,200, he became one of the Jewish brokers on the Exchange. "It is better to earn one pound than to toss for two" was one of his guiding maxims. Another, derived from the Talmud, was "A wise man will desire no more than what he can get justly, use soberly, distribute cheerfully, and live upon contentedly". He acted on these maxims throughout his life. His early years on the Exchange were thus not marked by any startling triumphs. He was among the first to issue a weekly price list of securities and he slowly built up a considerable clientele.

Then in 1806 he suffered a colossal setback when he was defrauded of some £30,000 by one Daniels. One does not know what form the fraud took or how a man of Montefiore's acumen allowed it to happen. He recalled it almost annually as the dark day of his career, but it does not seem to have undermined his faith in human nature.

In 1812 he married Judith, a daughter of Levi Barent Cohen, who had a sizable dowry and improved both his fortune and his standing, but more important than her dowry was the fact that her sister Hannah was married to Nathan Mayer Rothschild. A few years later, Abraham Montefiore married Nathan's sister Henrietta. With the wealthy Cohen on one side of the family and the fabulous Rothschild on the other, it was difficult for Montefiore not to prosper.

Judith and Montefiore, or Monte, as she called him were almost ideally suited. She shared his deep religious feelings, his profound sense of duty, his concern for the Jewish people, his high sense of moral purpose and his ambivalent attitude to money, open-handed and penny-pinching at one and the same time. She was a pretty young woman with a fine head framed by curls and a look of gentle determination in her large eyes. They had no children, but in every other respect, the marriage was idyllic. Moses never failed to remember their wedding anniversary without thanksgiving. In 1844 he wrote in his diary:

> On this happy day, the 10th of June, thirty-two years have passed since the Almighty God of Israel, in His Great Goodness, blessed me with my dear Judith, and forever shall I be most truly grateful for this blessing, the great cause of my happiness through life. From the first day of our happy union to this hour I have had every reason for increased love and esteem, and truly may I say, each succeeding year has brought with it greater proofs of her admirable character. A better and kinder wife never existed, one whose whole study has been to render her husband good and happy. May the God of our fathers bestow upon her his blessing with life, health, and every other felicity. Amen.[11]

According to one biographer, Judith was born in 1784, the same year as her husband. According to the figure she gave in one census return, she was born in 1796, and in another in 1794. The available evidence suggests that she was as old as her husband but would have liked to have been younger.[12]

Her upbringing was Orthodox. Admiral Sir Sidney Smith arrived unexpectedly with a party one evening to find the Cohen family seated on low chairs, attired in mourning and chanting the Book of Lamentations. "My sisters became somewhat embarrassed," she recalled, "but I quietly kept my seat, and, when Sir Sidney asked the reason for our being seated so low, I replied, 'this is the anniversary of the destruction of Jerusalem which is kept by conforming Jews as a day of mourning and humiliation . . .' Sir Sidney and the other gentlemen seemed pleased with the explanation I gave them."[13]

The wedding took place on June 10, 1812. It was a busy season for Monte. Far too busy to allow them to get away. Thus, they spent the first weeks of their married life with the bridegroom's parents in Vauxhall. "Monte has had, God be praised, a favourable day," wrote the young bride on the fifth day of her honeymoon. "He presented me with 1,000 Omnium which I have not yet disposed of. Most probably I shall have a few trifling transactions in the funds merely to amuse. I commenced yesterday by purchasing Consols, by which I have gained a few pounds."[14]

And so the days passed. Consols, family teas and prayers. On the first Friday of their married life she writes in a mood of religious exaltation:

> Nothing particular occurred throughout the day. But on lighting the candles in the evening according to my mother's wish and what is taught us, I experienced a new sensation of devotion and solicitude to act right. I trust that God Almighty will direct us how to perform that which is most pleasing to Him. I do not know any circumstances more pleasing to me than to perceive that my dear Monte is religiously inclined. It is the sort of religion which he possesses that in my opinion is most essential – a fellow feeling and benevolence.[15]

These last words are a true summary. Monte, especially in his later years, never overlooked the minutiae of religious observance, but his religious feelings more immediately took the form of concern for his fellow men. He won the esteem of his countrymen at a time when Jews were often held in opprobrium. He was, as his contemporaries might have put it, the most Christian of Jews.

At this time, the young couple were lax in only one respect. The truly Orthodox Jew will rarely eat meat or poultry outside a Jewish household, for it is not kosher unless it has been ritually prepared. This means that it must be killed by a *Sochet*, or ritual slaughterer, and then salted and soaked to be drained of blood. We know however, that in the course of their journey Monte and Judith ate beef-steak in Sittingbourne, roast duck in Margate, and duck again in Portsmouth.[16]

In later years they were to travel with a *Sochet* in their entourage so that they could eat kosher wherever they went.

During these early years the Montefiores, although much addicted to travel, did not have their own vehicle and travelled by stagecoach. They may not have had money, or they may have been keeping a careful eye on expenditure. Judith, in particular, was a careful spender and an eager saver. On June 30, at the end of her honeymoon, she hurried off to Aldgate to exchange a surplus pair of candlesticks for a set of teaspoons.[17]

They moved into New Court, next door to Nathan Rothschild and not far from her mother at Angel Court, Throgmorton Street. As individuals, Monte and Nathan were dissimilar, but they formed a happy and lucrative business association, the former acting as broker for the other. The market was kept busy with wars in Europe, and in 1819 Monte was involved in his brother-in-law's first major transaction on behalf of the Government, the £12,000,000 3% loan.

The war kept up the prices of cereals and industrial products and both landowners and industrialists had frequent recourse to loans. Consumption per head of population was rising – so also was the number of consumers. Between 1793 and 1814, the population grew from 8,500,000 to nearly 11,000,000 which was larger than the increase over the previous century.[18]

After the ending of the Napoleonic Wars, in the early 1820s, there was an immense speculative boom which burst – with disastrous results – in 1825. Naturally, such a prominent figure in the City as Montefiore was frequently approached for support. In February 1825, for example, he was asked to become director of a company set up to cut a canal through the isthmus of Panama. He did not think this a viable project. Thirty years later he was invited by de Lesseps to join the Suez Canal Company. Again, he felt better advised to say no.[19]

There were, however, three large concerns in which he did take part. One was the Provincial Bank of Ireland, an economic extension of Daniel O'Connell's Catholic Association. This Montefiore helped to establish with the support of his kinsmen, Jacob Montefiore, Ralph Ricardo (a member of an old Dutch Jewish family which had since embraced Christianity), Thomas Spring Rice and O'Connell himself.[20] Monte remained a member of the board of directors and travelled to Dublin to issue the first note over the counter. The P.B.I. was among the first joint-stock banks. It prospered rapidly and continues to prosper as one of the few surviving independent banks in the Irish Republic.

Another venture in which Montefiore was involved, but which proved less profitable – in its first years at least – was the Imperial Continental Gas Association. The idea to supply piped gas to Continental cities originated with Major-General Sir William Congreve, army engineer and inventor of the rocket, who formed a company with Mathias Attwood, M.P., Isaac Lyon Goldsmid (son of Asher Goldsmid, nephew of the late Benjamin and Abraham) and Montefiore on the board. It was launched in December 1824 with a nominal capital of £2,000,000 "at a time", to quote the prospectus, "when British capital is superabundant beyond all former precedents".[21] But the balloon was about to burst. Various I.C.G.A. projects began to show teething troubles and proved more costly than anticipated. No dividends were being paid while more money was sought and, in 1831, Montefiore had to urge his co-directors not to extend operations further until a dividend could be paid. Many years passed before that happened and, in his first seventeen years on the board, Monte did not draw one penny in fees.[22]

A letter in the *Morning Chronicle* in January 1826 accused three directors, including Montefiore, of misappropriation of £60,000 for their own use.[23] No proof was brought to support these allegations, however, and they were subsequently withdrawn with an apology.

The fortunes of the company gradually improved. By 1834, a dividend of 6% was being distributed on paid up capital – by 1840 this rose to 10.3%. Reserves grew and, by 1869, these exceeded the subscribed capital of the company. The Board proposed a bonus share issue. The chairman, Mathias Attwood, objected on the grounds that I.C.G.A. were merely leaseholders and that sizable reserves were needed against the contingency of any lease being cancelled. No compromise could be reached. Attwood resigned and Montefiore became chairman. Monte was then eighty-six years old and soon gave way to a younger man, but continued to attend board meetings until his hundreth year. In 1834, his work on the board of the I.C.G.A. led to his election as an Honorary Fellow of the Royal Society.

The largest enterprise with which Monte was concerned was Alliance Assurance. Between 1800 and 1870 over 500 new insurance companies were established, and a great many of them sprouted in the chaotic boom years of 1824-5, only to wilt as the bubble burst.[24] Some were simply fraudulent. Others, though founded under sound auspices, were under-capitalised. Still others were insufficiently aware of the character of the business.

Alliance suffered from no such defects.

The idea of the company originated with Montefiore who calculated the amount of business he and his associates gave to other insurance companies and suggested to Rothschild that it was sufficient to support a company of their own. Rothschild agreed and they invited Francis Baring of Baring Brothers, Samuel Gurney of Overend and Gurney, and John Irving (a future Chancellor of the Exchequer) to join them in the venture. Five names of greater repute could hardly have been assembled in one single enterprise. And they were needed. Montefiore wanted a concern which could win the immediate confidence of the public. The five appointed themselves presidents of the company for life. In their prospectus they did not so much invite subscriptions – rather, they laid down the conditions under which the public would be allowed to subscribe.[25] It revealed very little about the aims of the company, and declared that the presidents and directors would expect a completely free hand. In addition, every shareholder was obliged to insure a sum equal to the amount of his subscription with the Fire Department, or, £1,000 in the Life Department. No less than £5,000,000 was sought – in those days an unheard of sum for such an enterprise. Nevertheless the issue was oversubscribed[26] and the company grew in every direction.

The Alliance opened branches on the Continent, in America and throughout the Empire. It lost £40,000 in the great fire in Hamburg in 1862 and a further £690,000 in San Francisco as a result of the 1906 earthquake, but took such losses in its stride.[27] Life annuity business increased almost twentyfold. Almost until his last day, Montefiore continued to take a lively interest in the business and was on the board long after the other original presidents had died. "Among the business undertakings which Sir Moses during his long and useful life has assisted in prompting," declared the company on his hundredth birthday, "none is more prosperous or more deeply indebted to his sagacity and judgement than the Alliance Office, of which he has been President since its formation in 1824."[28]

Although active in many enterprises, Monte did not allow the business world to monopolise his time. His diary entry for a not untypical day in 1820 reads:

> With God's blessing – Rise, say prayers at 7 o'clock. Breakfast at 9. Attend the Stock Exchange, if in London, 10. Dinner 5. Read, write and learn, if possible, Hebrew and French, 6. Read Bible and say prayers, 10. Then retire.[29]

In 1824, shortly after he had launched Alliance Assurance, he retired from business, although still retaining the directorships of various concerns. He sold his place on the Exchange and devoted himself mainly to public work. He had been deeply affected by the death of his younger brother, Abraham, and appalled by the whirr of business speculation and the feverish atmosphere of the market place. In the main, also, he felt he had made enough. As with every other major decision in his life, he sought his wife's approval and support. "Thank God and be content" was her response. One does not know exactly how much he had to be content with, but he lived another sixty years after his retirement, spent lavishly (on others rather than himself) and left £310,000 – so the sum was probably more than £1m.

In 1825 the Montefiores moved from New Court, where they had begun their married life and which was now the office of Alliance

Assurance, to Green Street and from there after a short sojourn to 99 Park Lane. The house still stands.

Both Monte and his wife had a great love of the countryside and, in the early years of their marriage, bought a small retreat, Tenby Lodge Farm, near Tonbridge. In 1830, however, he bought East Cliff Lodge, a sizable villa standing on thirteen acres of ground on the eastern edge of Ramsgate, a mock Gothic structure with spires and battlements and a balcony overlooking the sea. The dining room was described by a local guide book as "the most elegant specimen of Gothic domestic architecture in England". The grounds extended to the edge of the cliff where there were subterranean passages, said to be the work of smugglers, leading from the house to the water.

The estate, although idyllic in many respects, lacked one important amenity – a synagogue. Monte promptly engaged a cousin, the architect, David Mocatta. Sacred soil was brought from Jerusalem, marble from Italy and a corps of craftsmen of all kinds was recruited to work on the carvings and upholstery. In June 1833 – on the twenty-first anniversary of their wedding – it was completed. A large part of the Cousinhood arrived for the celebrations. The Chief Rabbi of the Ashkenazi and Sephardi communities came to consecrate the building. The ceremony was followed by a banquet. A twenty-four piece orchestra entertained the guests in the dining-room. Another played in the lawn. At midnight there were the aureole splutter and shoosh of fireworks.[30]

This was only the beginning of the Ramsgate establishment. A synagogue needs an officiant. Monte brought one in and built him a house. Services require a quorum of ten men. Monte built a college for elderly scholars, who provided the quorum and received, besides accommodation, a pension. The devout Jew needs kosher meat. Monte brought in a *Sochet* and gave him a house. In time, he established a considerable colony of Jews on East Cliff, and it gave him great pleasure to walk with his wife to synagogue through the Friday twilights bent against the sea winds, to join in the familiar chants of the Sabbath service.

> O come let us sing before the Lord
> Let us shout for joy to the Rock of our salvation
> Let us come before his presence with thanksgiving
> Let us shout for joy unto Him with psalms.
> For the Lord is a great God
> And a great King above all Gods . . .[31]

All would remain for the festive *kiddush* which followed. Montefiore often stayed to listen to a discourse or to join in an hour or two of study.

He was, by the standard of knowledge common to his class, a savant. He had picked up a little from his uncles' tuition and added to this a great deal through the many hours he spent in private study. He himself, however, was aware of his limitations as a scholar. But he loved scholarship and the company of scholars and would join in the learned discussions and continue with them as he made his way homewards.

When his wife died in 1862, he built a Jewish theological college in Ramsgate as a memorial and found some consolation among the scholars, and the houses of learning and the ancient books and manuscripts he had given them. Upon a bleak Kentish promontory, he had built a small Jerusalem.

It did not survive him long, however. At the end of the century, the college was closed down after a scandal involving one or two of the students. (They were guilty of conduct unbecoming prospective Rabbis and gentlemen.) His miniature All Souls has been demolished. The houses he built are empty and in ruins. His mansion has been pulled down and the grounds are used now as a public park.

The synagogue stands; still ornate, still well preserved, and rarely used. The pews are silent, empty. At the top, by the east wall near the Ark, stands an immense chair throne, heavily upholstered in leather with leather buttons and deeply lined with use and age. There were, one feels as one looks at it, giants in those days.

CHAPTER 6

The Damascus Affair

On February 5, 1840, Father Tomaso, friar of a Capuchin monastery in Damascus, and his servant Ibrahim, disappeared without trace. A search of the Jewish quarter was begun and, on February 9, Saleun – a barber from one of the poorer streets of the quarter – was seized. He was beaten and tortured until a confession was extorted from him that he had been given 300 piastres to kill Tomaso and collect his blood for the preparation of *matzoth*, the unleavened bread eaten at Passover. He named Aaron and Joseph Arari, Joseph Legnado, Moses Abulafia and others as accomplices – nearly all of them were wealthy Jewish merchants, leading citizens of Damascus.[1] They were known to every Jew in the city and must have been the first names to enter his mind. More arrests followed. More beatings. More tortures. More confessions. And still more arrests. Before the enquiries ended over one hundred people suffered imprisonment. Among these were fifty-three children between the ages of four and eight who were kept in chains on bread and water for twenty-eight days, in the hope that they might be driven to admit some knowledge of the crime.

This was perhaps the crowning agony though the physical agonies were severe enough. Men were flogged till their flesh hung loose on their bodies. Their heads were pressed till their eyes were almost forced out of their sockets. Thorns were driven under their nails. They were made to stand without sleep for days on end, and if they sagged they were roused with bayonets. The other tortures were unmentionable. And the confessions came. They hardly corroborated one another, but they satisfied Sherrif Pasha, Governor of Damascus, that he had the culprits in hand.

But where was the body of Tomaso? Where was the blood? Passover was still six weeks away and if it had been extracted for use in *matzoth* it would still be around somewhere.

The charge of using human blood for ritual purposes was first made by the Romans against the early Christians. In turn, it was adopted by the Christians against the Jews. It was denounced by Pope Innocent IV in 1247 as a baseless calumny, but continued to be made with fearsome effect right through the centuries. As late as 1911, Mendel Beilis was tried in Russia on a charge of ritual murder. That the charge should now have been made in a Moslem country was unusual. But Syria, in 1840, although nominally under the suzerainty of the sultan was in fact under the dominion of his Pasha, Mehemet Ali, ruler of Egypt and a French protégé. Moreover, Europeans had extraterritorial rights in the Levant. Tomaso, although of Italian origin, was the father superior of a French monastery and the whole enquiry was instigated and directed by the French Consul, Ratti Menton.

Astrologers were summoned. They corroborated the evidence of the barber Saleun and for good measure named several other leading Damascus Jews as the killers of the friar's servant. Palpable evidence, however, was still lacking. But, on March 2, twenty-five days after the disappearance of Tomaso, a clue was discovered.

Mourad El-Fallat, one of the Arari servants, claimed that he had in fact killed the priest on his master's orders in the presence of the other accused and that he had disposed of the remains down a sewer. Although this contradicted Saleun's evidence, Sherrif and Ratti were unconcerned. They stopped the water supply, searched the sewers and near a butcher's stall, sunk in filth and offal, they found scraps of gristle, flesh and bones – and a piece of rag which they were assured was part of the friar's cap. There were no doctors in Damascus to establish beyond doubt whether the remains were animal or human and whether, if human, they were in fact those of Tomaso. One physician said they were mutton. Ratti, however, was satisfied that these were the remains of the priest. He had them collected and, eventually, buried with an appropriate High Requiem Mass.[2]

The case, as far as the Syrian authorities were concerned, was all but over. But where was the blood? Sherrif turned with renewed fury on the prisoners. The bastinado was brought out once again, together with the bayonets. And, again, the confessions flowed. It was in a bottle said one of the men, with Moses Abulafia. Sherrif then turned to Abulafia, who denied all knowledge of it. He was bastinadoed. One hundred blows. Two hundred. A thousand . . . but still without effect. Finally, again under torture, he gasped out that the bottle was in a drawer in his house. Where in the house? Which drawer? Abulafia, now too weak to walk, was carried by four soldiers to his home. The drawer was searched. All that was found was a large sum of money. Abulafia had hoped that the governor might accept the money in lieu of the blood. Sherrif, driven on by Ratti, was too determined to stop, even for bribes. Abulafia was hustled back to gaol. What was left of his life was almost forced out of him until he embraced Islam.[3] Two other prisoners died under torture. Ratti demanded the execution of the rest.

The Jews of Damascus were terrified. Those who could, fled. The rest huddled together, helpless, frantic. The sultan was too distant to be effective. They could expect no help from Mehemet Ali. They, themselves, were too broken, too weak and too few.

To make matters worse, the Jews of Rhodes, then still part of the Ottoman empire, were accused of abducting a Christian child and killing him for ritual purposes. There the true facts of the case were established by a judicial enquiry and the Jews were exonerated, although not before several of them had been imprisoned, beaten and tortured. The enquiry took months and during that time, anti-Jewish feeling ran high. There were riots in Beirut and Smyrna, and the Jews of Damascus lived under the threat of imminent massacre.

News of their plight appeared in sporadic reports in the British press throughout February and March. In April, a chronicle of events from the Chief Rabbi of Constantinople was received at the offices of N. M. Rothschild, together with an urgent plea for help. Baron Lionel immediately brought it before a meeting of the Board of Deputies of British Jews.

The meeting was held at Grosvenor Gate – the Park Lane home of Sir Moses Montefiore – under the presidency of Joseph Gutteres Henriques. Among those present, apart from Montefiore and Lionel de Rothschild, were Jacob Montefiore, Isaac Lyon Goldsmid and his son Francis, A. A. Goldsmid, David Salomons (a future Lord Mayor of London), Moses Mocatta, Isaac, Henry and Louis Cohen, S. J. Waley and Hiam Guedella. Some were Ashkenazi, some Sephardi. Nearly all were related to Montefiore. Also present was M. Adolphe Crémieux, a leading French lawyer and future Minister of Justice, vice-president of the *Consistoire Central des Israelites Français* (roughly the French counterpart of the Board). The president of the Consistoire was (and still is) a Rothschild.[4]

A delegation, consisting of Henriques, Rothschild, the two Monte-fiores, the three Goldsmids and David Salomons, called on Lord Palmerston at Downing Street. Palmerston showed them every sympathy and promised to use his influence with the sultan and Mehemet Ali to see that justice would be done.

The Austrian Consul in Damascus, Mr Merlato, had been helpful and sympathetic towards the Jews and had been more than sceptical about Ratti's tactics and his entire handling of the affair. The Austrian Chancellor, Metternich, sent a letter to Mehemet Ali calling for clemency.

The Pasha, worried by the build-up of pressure, promised an impartial enquiry, which was, of course, a reflection on Ratti's handling of the affair. Cochelet, the French Consul in Alexandria, protested and in Paris, the clerical party in the chamber of Deputies added its voice to the protest. The enquiry was cancelled.

London was incensed. The matter was raised in the House of Commons and Sir Robert Peel demanded that the Government put pressure on the Syrian authorities to see that justice was done. There were protests up and down the country. On July 3 a large demonstration was held at the Mansion House. The platform party included the Lord Mayor – Sir Chapman Marshall – John Abel Smith, Samuel Gurney, Daniel O'Connell and the poet Thomas Campbell. Speaker after speaker rose to condemn the Damascus atrocities and to express their sympathy with the Jews.[5] But sympathy was not enough.

Monte, who had by now succeeded Henriques as president of the Board of Deputies, determined that there was only one thing to be done – to see Mehemet Ali himself.[6] Crémieux agreed to join him.[7]

In 1833, Mehemet Ali had seized Syria from his Turkish Suzerain.[8] The province rose against his rule seven years later and the sultan, seeing an opportunity to avenge his earlier defeat, marched south – only to be crushed again. His navy surrendered. His army was chased into Anatolia. He was forced to turn to the West for help. Palmerston, worried about French connivance in the Egyptian victories, was determined to make Mehemet Ali climb down a little. On July 15, a 'Convention for the Pacification of the Levant' was signed in London between Britain, Russia, Austria and Prussia. This Convention gave Mehemet Ali an ultimatum – to withdraw from Anatolia and make his peace with the sultan, or else face action by the joint powers.[9] To show that he meant business, Palmerston ordered a naval squadron under Admiral Stopford to blockade the coast of Syria.

It was in this tense and chaotic atmosphere that Montefiore prepared for his mission. He was again received by Palmerston, who promised him any letters of introduction he might need and, shortly before embarking, he was received by the Queen. On August 4, accompanied by Lady Montefiore, and a party of orientalists and other assistants, he landed at Alexandria.

He at once rushed to see the principal Rabbis of the town for news of Damascus and visited the British Consul, Colonel Hodges; the French, Austrian and Prussian Consuls; and finally he went to the Russian consulate – to find the consul in bed and asleep. He returned to his hotel at 2 a.m. and rose again three hours later. At eight o'clock, wearing the dress of a sheriff of the City of London (an honour which had been bestowed upon him a few years previously) and accompanied by Colonel Hodges, he called on Mehemet Ali.

He came armed with a long petition but was received without any great enthusiasm either at this interview or others which he was able to arrange. Mehemet Ali seemed disposed to speak on any subject except Damascus and finally Montefiore brought together the consuls of every major European power except France and presented the petition through them. This had immediate effect, and the Pasha suggested that the Jews still in prison be released and the whole unhappy matter forgotten. "They wish this atrocious transaction to be hushed up," said Montefiore. "I will never consent to that."[10]

He had now spent two weeks in the fierce heat of Alexandria, rushing from consul to consul, from palace to palace, holding meetings, drafting petitions – all, largely, without effect. The vision of the Damascus prisoners hung heavily over him. The threat of war was imminent and the tension, heat, the general sense of frustration, all combined to sap his energies and patience.

Then Cochelet came forward with a plan. He suggested that the Pasha should declare that the Jews who had died in detention had killed Tomaso for some private motive – and that those still alive should be released as innocent, and that a public statement would be made to the effect that nothing in the Jewish creed sanctioned the use of human blood. Montefiore was aghast. He would never agree to such a scheme, he shouted. He would not allow men who had already suffered martyrdom to be charged with a crime they did not commit, could not have committed.[11]

His feelings of bitterness were intense and he proposed to go straight to the Pasha and make his feelings known there and then. Crémieux held him back. The British navy was off the coast of Beirut and a landing was imminent. It was not the best time for a *démarche*.

The summer grew more torrid and oppressive, but Montefiore still hustled around in the heat. Lady Montefiore began to have fainting fits and came down with a fever which added to his anxieties.[12]

There was a frenzy of diplomatic activity. The captain of H.M.S. *Bellerophon* called on Sir Moses and offered to take his party on board; he expected the outbreak of hostilities at any time.

Sir Moses remained. Tensions eased a little. He called once again on the Pasha and this time was received with some cordiality. Sir Moses reminded him of the petition he had presented nearly four weeks before. It had not been forgotten, said the Pasha.[13] He would order the release of the prisoners. Sir Moses wanted more than that, a fair trial of the accused and the punishment of the real culprits. But he realised that the release of the prisoners was the best he could hope for in the present confused situation. The next day the Pasha prepared a firman to that effect. Dr Loewe, Sir Moses' secretary who was an Arabic scholar, noticed that the prisoners were not being granted an honourable discharge but a pardon. Sir Moses, he said, would never agree to that – he had based his whole mission on the innocence of the victims. The Pasha did not enter into further discussion and had the document changed there and then.[14] On September 5 the prisoners were released.

When Sir Moses called on Mehemet Ali to thank him, he was taken aside and asked if he could perform a little service. Egypt, said the Pasha, often ordered armaments from Britain which tended to be slow in arriving, possibly because the manufacturers were uncertain about his means. He wondered if Montefiore could function as a sort of export guarantee bank. He would never, the Pasha assured him, have to advance money, he would merely have to act as underwriter. Montefiore was non-committal but said that he would see what could be done.[15] Presumably he was able to do a lot, for a close friendship developed between him and the Egyptian royal family and his house in Grosvenor Gate tended to be used as a hotel by any Egyptian princeling visiting London.

Crémieux returned to Paris. Montefiore went on to Constantinople determined to see the sultan. Incidents of blood seemed to be breaking out all over the Ottoman empire, with calumny feeding on calumny, and he decided to tackle the matter at source. He was received on arrival by a troop of cavalry, wafted through one marble hall after another, past bowing ranks of courtiers, and finally into the royal presence of Sultan Abdul Medjd.

His plea was heard with the warmest sympathy and the sultan issued a firman dismissing the charges against Jews and their religion as "pure calumny" and giving an undertaking that "the Jewish nation shall possess the same advantages and enjoy the same privileges as are granted to the numerous other nations who submit to our authority", and "shall be protected and defended".[16]

There was still one further matter which vexed Sir Moses. In Damascus, above the spot where, according to Ratti, the remains of Tomaso had been found, the Capuchins had placed an inscription:

Here rest the bones of Father Tomaso of Sardinia, a Capuchin missionary, murdered by the Hebrew on February 5, 1840.

Sir Moses read this as a slander on the Jewish people and, on the way home, he stopped to remonstrate with Cardinal Riverola, head of the Capuchin order in Rome, to show him the firman testifying to the innocence of the Jews and urging that the inscription be removed. The cardinal examined the document and said he would suggest that the inscription be removed, whether the firman had been obtained with Rothschild money or otherwise. Sir Moses interjected immediately and with heat. He had never attempted, nor would he ever attempt to obtain justice through bribery.[17] The prelate, who was not used to either interruptions or contradictions, most especially in a loud voice, was taken aback and would not discuss the matter further. The offending inscription was eventually removed, but most of Rome seemed to believe that the Jews had killed Tomaso and that their exoneration had been bought with cash.

Many years later when Sir Moses was again in Rome on another mission of mercy, the belief still persisted and he was asked by a cardinal, almost by the way, how much gold he had paid for the firman.

Sir Moses drew himself up to his full great height and glowered down on the little wrinkled prelate . . .

"Not so much," he retorted "as I gave your lackey for hanging up my coat in your hall."[18]

There is a postscript to the Damascus affair.

In 1859 there was a Druse rising in Syria directed mainly against the Christian inhabitants. The tribesmen swept down from the hills and devastated whole townships in their path. Hundreds of Christians perished. Thousands fled for their lives and wandered over the barren countryside without food or fuel and always in danger of attack. At the time, Sir Moses was at Ramsgate. He read the news in *The Times* and instantly sat down to draft a letter. Then he ordered his coach and drove to Printing House Square to deliver it in person. It was to launch an appeal on behalf of the refugees to which he, himself donated £200. Other donations quickly followed, and £22,500 was raised.[19]

To some who recalled the Damascus affair, it was an example of Jewish magnanimity. To others, it was a confirmation of Jewish guilt. Montefiore's appeal was spoken of as 'conscience money'.

CHAPTER 7

Emancipation

To the crowds lining the eight-mile route between Gunnersbury and Kensington, it might have been another coronation procession. Victoria had been crowned in June 1838. The concourse of noblemen which had descended on London for the occasion remained to continue the celebrations in a glorious succession of dinners and balls.

> 'London teems with foreigners,' [wrote Disraeli to his sister] 'there are fully two hundred of distinction attached to the different embassies . . . and are visible every night, with their brilliant uniforms and sparkling stars – as if their carriage at break of dawn were not changed into a pumpkin.'[1]

Lady Salisbury gave a ball on July 3, Lady Londonderry, a banquet on July 10. A few days later, it was the turn of a comparative newcomer to this London scene – the Baroness Lionel de Rothschild. The venue, Gunnersbury Park, might have evoked memories for some of the older guests. It had once been the home of Princess Amalia, daughter of George II.

Over five hundred guests assembled at Gunnersbury. The lawns were a Xanadu of tents and awnings. One band played on the terrace, another by the lake. Guests strolled through the exquisite grounds, admiring the pergolas, the climbing rose-trees, the flower-beds, the heliotropes, pausing to gaze at the strutting peacocks, or the swans on the water. The buffet was a glutton's paradise, but it was so delicately arranged in the vast marquee, that one might have hesitated to proffer one's plate for fear of disturbing the patterns.

In the evening there was a banquet. The baroness sat between two dukes of the blood royal – Prince George of Cambridge and the Duke of Sussex. Also present were the Duke and Duchess of Somerset, the Duchess of Richmond, the Duke of Devonshire, the Marquis of Londonderry. There were two ex-Prime Ministers in the gathering, Wellington and Melbourne – and a pair of future Prime Ministers, Russell and Disraeli. Every glittering name in England seemed to be present, and not a few from Europe – Prince and Princess Schwarzenberg of Austria, Prince Esterhazy from Hungary, Marshal Soult from France, a sparkle of German princelings.

Entertainments were provided by the most celebrated names of the opera – Grisi, Lablache, Tamberini, Rubini. The night closed with a ball. "It was," wrote the *Court Gazette* (with fine understatement), "one of the most delightful re-unions of the season."[2]

Yet the host, the friend of kings, the foremost banker in England, one of the most influential men in Europe (and one of the richest) was burdened with disabilities from which his humblest clerk was free.

The Rothschilds were Jewish and although the Jews in England enjoyed rights and privileges far beyond those of their fellows on the Continent, their emancipation was not yet complete. Lord Coke's doctrine that Jews were, in law, perpetual enemies 'for between them, as with the devils whose subjects they are, and the Christians there can be no peace' was upheld in an English court of law as late as 1818.[3]

Jews were excluded from office under the Crown. They could not serve in Parliament. Neither could they serve in the municipalities – and they could be debarred from voting. They could not enter the universities – and were thus virtually barred from the professions. Until 1828 Jews were limited to twelve seats on the Exchange. Until 1831 they could not become Freemen of the City of London – and could thus not engage in retail trade within the City boundaries.

Most of these disabilities were also borne by Catholics and Dissenters. The repeal of the Test and Corporation Acts in 1828, emancipating the Dissenters, might have done the same for the Jews. However, on the insistence of the Bishop of Llandaff, the words 'on the true faith of a Christian' were inserted in the oath required of anyone seeking public office.[4] These six words constituted the barrier to further progress.

Not all of these disabilities were painful and many, perhaps most, Jews were untouched by them. It mattered little to the cobbler in Hoxton or the tailor in Whitechapel that he could never become Lord Mayor of London or High Sheriff of Kent. A Whitechapel Jew, asked to subscribe to the emancipation campaign, retorted "If Rothschild wants to get emancipated, let Rothschild pay for it."

To the Cousinhood, however, the laws were an affront. They had been born in England and gloried in the title Englishmen, but they were still excluded from the most cherished institutions and from the mainstream of public life. They were tolerated rather than accepted. They were rulers in their own small communities and sought a wider outlet for their talent and zeal. They objected to being considered second-class citizens.

In 1829, while the Bill to emancipate Catholics was under debate, an attempt was made to introduce a measure for Jewish emancipation. Its prime mover was Isaac Lyon Goldsmid, nephew of Benjamin and Abraham Goldsmid, and son of Asher, senior partner in the firm of Mocatta and Goldsmid.

Isaac Lyon Goldsmid's early career was less than distinguished. He was born in 1778 and joined the family firm in 1800. Six years later he bought a seat on the Exchange. He speculated heavily in his own account and lost heavily. He was a pioneer in railway development and was concerned in the building of the Croydon and Merstham line (later sold to the Southern Railway) and in the reorganisation of the London Dock Company and was promoter and chairman of the Birkenhead Docks. He derived little joy or profit from any of these schemes. The Birkenhead Docks were a particular disappointment and they staggered from crisis to crisis until they were taken over by Liverpool Corporation.[5]

I. L. G. had been one of the original backers and life presidents of the Imperial Gas Company.[6] But he became suspicious of the integrity of the management and quarrelled with his co-directors. After five years on the board he resigned. He had remained long enough to suffer the recriminations and heartaches of the early years, without reaping the benefits of the later ones.

As a loan broker he was more successful and helped to obtain credit for Portugal, Brazil and for the Ottoman empire. The rising in Brazil against Portuguese rule in 1822 and her subsequent independence made the fiscal relationship between the two countries and their creditors extremely complicated. It was not clear who was responsible for the servicing of loans already obtained. Endless negotiations followed. Finally, I. L. G. was invited to arbitrate between all the parties concerned, which he did to the satisfaction of all and, in 1845, he was made a baron by the grateful Portuguese Crown.[7]

I. L. G. was a disciple of Jeremy Bentham, a friend of Robert Owen, James Mill, David Ricardo and William Wilberforce. He believed in the inherent nobility of the human being; that one has only to improve the circumstances to improve the man. There was hardly a progressive cause, be it the abolition of slavery, prison reform, public education or public health, which did not enjoy his support. He was a generous contributor to the London Institution for the Advancement of Literature and Useful Knowledge in Finsbury Circus and was deeply involved in the creation of London University.

The creation of a university for the capital was conceived by his friend, the poet, Thomas Campbell – a liberal Dissenter who dreamed of an institution unburdened by clergymen and free of all sectarian bias. This, of course, had immediate appeal to Jews and others excluded from the ancient seats of learning.

In 1826, I. L. G. formed a council to promote the idea of such a university with Alexander Baring (of Baring Brothers), Lord John Russell, George Birkbeck (founder of the Mechanics Institution), James Mill, Zachary Macaulay and the Duke of Norfolk. There were six Jewish members: I. L. G., his cousin Aaron, Abraham and Moses Mocatta, Nathan de Rothschild and George Magnus.[8]

Much of the groundwork for the scheme was laid down at informal gatherings in I. L. G.'s ornate home in Regent's Park – St John's Lodge. His wife, Isabel, whom he married in 1804, was a first cousin, a daughter of Abraham Goldsmid. She kept an elaborate salon in which she had at various times entertained the young Mendelssohn, Prince Alfred, son of Queen Victoria, and, on one occasion, Victoria herself.

The creation of the Mechanics Institute received general approval, but the idea of a new university was thought rather presumptious and one paper dismissed it as "a hum-bug, joint-stock subscription school for cockney boys . . . got up in the bubble season in shares sold by stockbrokers and bill-brokers and Jew brokers . . ."[9]

I. L. G. was undeterred. He bought the present site in Gower Street for £30,000 on his own responsibility and at his own risk. On April 30, 1827, the foundation stone of London University (later to be known as University College) was laid by the Duke of Sussex – a close friend of the Goldsmid family and an ardent champion of Jewish emancipation. It was ten years before the Government granted the university the right to award degrees – but it began instruction without delay.

From 1827 until the repeal of the Test Act opened Oxford and Cambridge to Jews in 1871, London University was the finishing school for the Cousinhood. Thither went Frederick David Goldsmid, son of I. L. G.; Nathaniel de Rothschild, Nathan's son; Jacob Waley, future Professor of Political Economy at the College and founder, with Lionel Cohen, of the United Synagogue; Arthur Cohen, a distinguished barrister, who served for a time as President of the Board of Deputies, and George Jessel who became Solicitor-General and Master of the Rolls. Sir Moses Montefiore, always conscious of his deficient education, attended a course of lectures in Political Economy in his seventieth year.

I. L. G. was also active in the formation of University College Hospital to which he liked to refer fondly as 'my hospital'.

Isaac Lyon Goldsmid found that working for the emancipation of his fellow Jews was a more complicated undertaking than the formation of a university. To begin with, it was uncertain whether all Jews wanted to be emancipated. Among the Sephardim, in particular, there were folk memories of the anti-Jewish feeling sparked off by the Jewish Naturalisation Bill of 1753. Even Moses Montefiore, lionhearted in other respects, thought it was best to let sleeping dogs lie. The Jews were doing well enough under toleration. Emancipation could wait for another day. The Sephardim, moreover, even at this date, did not want to be thought of as part of the same brotherhood as the Ashkenazim. Legalists pointed out that at the time of the Resettlement in 1656, Jews had given an undertaking to refrain from political activity.[10] The Ashkenazim who were not a party to the undertaking, and who did not share the memories of 1753, were less inhibited. I. L. G. was the least inhibited of all. Nathan de Rothschild, who was inclined to dither, was warned by his wife to take action or else she would.[11] Her sister, Judith Montefiore, was almost equally militant. Sir Moses himself, whatever reservations he might have had about the timing of the campaign, could not keep out of it once the machinery was in motion. He was joined by another distinguished Sephardi, Moses Mocatta. Bevis Marks Synagogue donated a considerable sum towards the expenses of the campaign. But the Sephardi community, as such, kept out of it.

I. L. G. was able to attract numerous Christian sympathisers, some of whom tended to be favourably disposed towards the Jews in general and others who found religious discrimination an ugly anachronism. These included the Irish leader, Daniel O'Connell, Lord Holland, Lord Bexley (who as Chancellor of the Exchequer at the time of Waterloo had frequent recourse to Nathan de Rothschild's advice), Foxwell Buxton and Samuel Gurney (two leading Quakers with whom I. L. G. had been associated in other reforms), and Thomas Babington Macaulay who, as a speaker and writer, proved to be the most articulate exponent of Jewish emancipation.[12]

The Duke of Sussex, brother of the King, gave every support to the cause. The King himself marshalled every impediment. "My Lord," he told a bishop while the subject was under debate, "I do not mean to interfere in any way with your vote in Parliament except on one subject, *The Jews*. and I trust I may depend on you always voting against them."[13]

And they did. A petition calling for the removal of Jewish disabilities was drafted and Nathan and Sir Moses were delegated to present it to the Government. But there was trouble in Ireland and trouble at home – much of it the result of the Catholic Bill. The pair, one tall and broad, the other short and stout, haunted the Palace of Westminster, petition in hand, for days on end and were fobbed off with apology after apology. Finally, Montefiore got hold of the Lord Chancellor for a hurried minute and was advised that the administration's plate was so full with the Catholic affairs that it would not help to pile a Jewish Bill on top of them.[14] I. L. G., however, was reluctant to hold back and carried his colleagues with him.

On February 7, 1830, Nathan had to call on the Duke of Wellington, who was then Prime Minister, about some financial matter. As if by chance, he happened to have a copy of the petition on him. "God has given your Grace the power to do good," he said, "I would entreat you to do something for the Jews." "God bestowed benefits moderately," replied the duke drily, but he agreed to read the petition.[15] A week later I. L. G., Nathan, his son Lionel, and Montefiore called on the duke and were told that he could not give government support for the measure, but he left the impression that he would not oppose it.

I. L. G. decided to go ahead and on February 22 the measure was tabled by Sir Robert Grant, a distinguished Whig parliamentarian. Its reception was mixed.

The biggest obstacle was the provision which would have allowed Jews to sit in Parliament. Had that been dropped, it seemed likely that the Bill would be passed. Montefiore thought they should take what they could get now, and perhaps ask for more later. He was something of a Fabian. I. L. G. possibly saw himself as a Jewish O'Connell. He was an admirer and friend of the Irish leader and saw what rugged determination could achieve. He insisted on everything or nothing. Again, he carried his more hesitant colleagues. The measure was debated in the House of Commons on April 16 and carried by 115 votes to 97 – a majority of 18.

On April 21, I. L. G. gave a dinner to celebrate the event, but it was a little premature. The opponents rallied and on a further reading defeated the Bill by 228 votes to 165.

When the Board of Deputies met to consider the matter, Monte again suggested that the Jews were perhaps asking for too much too soon. This view met with the evident approval of almost everyone there. I. L. G. disagreed violently and became impatient with Monte, with the Board and the cautious creaking conservatism of the official Jewish leadership.[16]

External events intervened. Wellington's administration finally collapsed. Lord Grey was sworn into office with a plan to reform the House of Commons and even I. L. G. had to recognise that, while the country was convulsed with this issue, it would be inopportune to press on with the Jewish question. After the reformed Parliament had assembled, however, Grant tabled the Bill anew. In April 1833 it passed through its various stages in the Commons by an ample majority. In the Lords, however, it met a solid wall of bishops and other opponents, and was defeated by 104 votes to 54. Grant tabled the Bill a third time. Again it passed through the Commons. Again it was killed by the Lords.

On other fronts, in the meantime, some quiet gains were being made. The chief mover there was David Salomons, a wealthy broker of Dutch extraction whose family had settled in England in the middle of the eighteenth century. His father, Salomon Levy was, to judge from a contemporary description, a fairly familiar character in and around the City:

> The Salomons are known by their connection with Dutch finance. The father . . . was remarkable for his very Jewish appearance and indeed was more to be compared with an itinerant dealer in old clothes than a merchant and money changer. To see him toddling down Bartholomew Lane, towards his offices in Shorter's Court, Throgmorton Street, with his crutch stick, his bent back and close-cut grey beard, one would have thought, giving him credit for his decency of dress, that one of the more respectable of Cutler Street or Rosemary Lane was on a visit to his dealer to invest a trifle. Although thus strange in his appearance, the older Mr Salomons was by no means parsimonious. He provided liberally for his friends, assisted many of the needy of his persuasion and is esteemed as having been a kind-hearted and benevolent man.[17]

David, who was born in 1797, inherited his father's kind heart and benevolence if not his appearance. At the age of twenty-seven he married Jeannette Cohen, grand-daughter of Levi Barent Cohen, niece of Nathan de Rothschild and Moses Montefiore, one of the most eligible heiresses in England. The ceremony was performed on the lawn of the bride's home at Canonbury by the Chief Rabbi, Solomon Hirschell. Monte toasted the bride and groom and Salomons replied.[18] Although his stately presence gained instant attention, his speeches could sometimes lose it. "There is only one mistake about Mr Salomons," wrote a contemporary, "which is, that he thinks himself an orator. . . . Although possessing commanding height and some slight intelligence of countenance, his natural defect in voice, the tone of which is more like the squeak of a penny trumpet than that of a human being, is a difficulty which we fear he will never be able to surmount."[19] However, it proved to be a difficulty which he surmounted with aplomb.

Salomons inherited one fortune, married another and enlarged both through his own enterprise. He joined the Stock Exchange in 1823, became a Lloyd's underwriter and won some renown as an authority on joint-stock banking.

Since 1709 banks, other than the Bank of England, could only function as partnerships, with the result that in the financial crash of 1825 they toppled like ninepins. In 1826 after a sustained campaign in which Salomons had joined, the Government passed an Act permitting joint-stock banks to exist beyond a radius of sixty-five miles outside London.[20] For the next seven years there was considerable antagonism between the Bank of England and these country banks anxious to obtain a foothold within the London area. Salomons suggested a division of labour which would leave the Bank of England as bankers' bank, while the others should resign the right (which they still enjoyed) to issue notes. Several of his ideas were incorporated in the Bank Charter Act of 1844.

Salomons was among the architects and was perhaps the most influential of the original directors of the London and Westminster Bank (forerunner of the Westminster). It was launched as soon as joint-stock banking in the London area was permitted in 1833 and opened its doors to the public a year later. Within a few decades it was a national institution. Salomons was chairman from 1859 to 1867.

Salomons had no academic grounding in economics, but he had an instinctive understanding of the fickle character of money and the money market. He wrote extensively on economic problems, including the operations of joint-stock banks, the Corn Laws, the fluctuations of the money market and the financing of railways. The joint-stock principle was far from universally accepted and he was frequently summoned to its defence, both as expositor and practitioner, and one is struck by his combination of plain common sense and extraordinary vision.

In 1858 he was called to give evidence before a Parliamentary Select Committee on the operations of the Bank Act. There had been a serious monetary crisis the previous year and the 1844 Act was shown to have some imperfections and the economy continued to be troubled by wild booms and calamitous crashes. Salomons rose to defend the Act.

> I think that the commercial world cannot be guarded against the effects of a long period of prosperity and success. I think that people making a great deal of money for a number of years, and carrying on extensive business without loss, become so sanguine and over-confident, that they believe no loss can possibly happen; therefore, I do not consider any human institution will make people prudent.

The best that could be done, he felt, was to give the Bank of England power to expand or contract credit to regulate the pace of the economy.[21]

The wonderful success of the Westminster, commented *The Times* on his death, "and even more the development and importance of the body of joint-stock banks in London, are greatly due to his unremitting care and attention".[22]

"By the time of his death," noted the historian of the Westminster Bank, "that system of joint-stock banking, which he had done so much to promote, had already attained pride of place in the money market, and had gained a prestige which it was never again to lose."[23]

Salomons had numerous commercial interests and among other things was a director of the South Australian Land Company, a trustee of the London Life Association and chairman of the Reading, Guildford and Reigate Railway.

His interest in emancipation was less academic and more immediate than those of I. L. G. He had pronounced political and social ambitions. The barriers which touched others merely in principle were personal impediments to him. But he shared with I. L. G. and Montefiore a concern for Jewish rights. He was an active member of the New Synagogue, a generous contributor to its charities, and its representative on the Board of Deputies. He was profoundly agitated over the Damascus affair and helped to organise the protests against it, preparing a comprehensive booklet on the subject. He took a deep interest in Jewish education and, although no Montefiore, he was active in improving the circumstances and raising the status of his fellow Jews. Ambition was thus not his sole and perhaps not even his main motive.

Whenever he climbed yet another rung of the ladder, he could feel that he was taking the Jews with him. That, indeed, was one of the reasons why he encountered so much opposition.

In his first years in the City, Salomons had witnessed some minor reforms. After 1828 the limit on the number of Jewish brokers was dropped. From 1831 Jews were no longer debarred from becoming Freemen of the City, and in that same year he joined the Coopers' Company. The City Livery Companies had at one time been guilds of artisans and traders, but by the nineteenth century they had lost all trace of these humbler origins and had become an inner club of bankers and merchants – a ruling caste from which the aldermen and mayors of the City were drawn.

In 1835 Salomons was elected a sheriff of London and Middlesex. But he was prevented from taking office by the nature of the oath. Lord John Russell, who was watching the Jewish struggle for emancipation with sympathy and interest, intervened with the sheriff's Declaration Act. Another barrier was down.

In the following year, Salomons was elected alderman for the ward of Aldgate in the City, but once again came up against an oath which he could not take. He was thus prevented from taking the seat. He believed that the situation had been changed by Russell's Act and took the case to the High Courts which ruled that his exclusion was illegal. The verdict, however, was quashed on appeal. Baulked in this direction, he turned to others.

In 1829 he bought Broomhill, a large villa in the Italian style on a hill near Tunbridge Wells. He demolished it and replaced it with a sort of Kentish Camelot, with towers, turrets and battlements. Here he held court as a country gentleman, but his wife, Jeannette, did not share his delight in the role. She was proud of him, and proud of his achievements but she preferred to keep out of the public eye.[24] The more eminent her husband became, the more she withdrew. Their failure to have children was a constant source of distress to her and she lavished abundant affection on her nephews and nieces. But they were not enough, and whether in their large town house in Great Cumberland Place, or in their mansion in Kent, she could not escape from a feeling of darkness which seemed to crowd in on her. In 1855, an *annus mirabilis* in her husband's career, her mind gave way. She died twelve years later.[25]

In 1838, Salomons was appointed a Justice of the Peace for Kent – the first Jew to hold such an office in the county. He was chairman of the

Kent agricultural society and a liberal benefactor to local schools and charities. In 1840 he was made sheriff of Kent.

The sight of a Jew holding high rank was no longer startling. Victoria had ascended the throne in 1837. She shared little of her uncle William IV's anti-Jewish feelings and, for one Jew in particular, she had the highest regard. Her mother, the Duchess of Kent, took a house occasionally at Ramsgate, where the Montefiores were their neighbours. She admired the grounds at East Cliff and Monte had a gold key cut for her so that she could come and go as she pleased.

In June 1837, Montefiore was elected sheriff of London and Middlesex. He had been nominated by T. A. Curtis, governor of the Bank of England, and seconded by his associate in many charitable undertakings, Samuel Gurney. He accepted with some misgivings, "I shall have the greatest difficulty to contend with in the execution of my duty," he wrote. "The day I enter in my office is the commencement of our New Year. I shall therefore have to walk to Westminster instead of going in my state carriage, nor, I fear, shall I be able to dine with my friends at the inaugural dinner, which, from time immemorial, is given on September 30. I shall, however, endeavour to persuade my colleagues to change the day to the 5th of October."[26]

He was also worried about the observance of the complex Jewish dietary laws – but he managed. The dinner was postponed to a more suitable date. He arrived in his state carriage, wearing his robes of office and carrying his own kosher chicken. The tenacity with which he adhered to the practices of Judaism exposed him on occasion to some ridicule and even abuse. It did not worry him: "I will not deviate from the injunctions of my religion, let them call me bigot if they like; it is immaterial to me what others do and think in this respect."

His inaugural speech had all the rotund fullness, all the predictable sentiments one would expect of such an occasion – but it contained one memorable passage.

It was, he said, looking round at the four hundred distinguished guests who had gathered to pay him tribute,

> gratifying to find that, though professing a different faith from the majority of my fellow-citizens, yet this has presented no barrier to my desire of being useful to them in a situation to which my forefathers would in vain have aspired; and I hail this as a proof that those prejudices are passing away, and will pass away, which prevent our feelings from being as widely social and just as comprehensive in their effect as the most amiable and instructed mind can desire.[27]

On the occasion of a royal visit, during the following month, Monte-fiore was knighted. "I hope my dear mother will be pleased", he thought as the queen tapped him with the sword of state.[28] In 1841 Isaac Lyon Goldsmid was made a baronet.

Salomons had not in the meantime abandoned his civic ambitions. His failure to have his election as alderman upheld in law led Sir Robert Peel, who was aware of Salomons' important contribution to the economic life of the nation, to table a Bill 'for the relief of persons of the Jewish religion elected to municipal office'. This was something like the watered-down version which the Board of Deputies had been prepared to accept nearly a decade earlier and to which I. L. G. had objected. It passed through the Commons and was killed in the Lords. In 1844 Salomons again stood for the office of alderman. Once again he was elected. Once again he refused to take the oath. Once again he was unseated. In 1845, Peel introduced the Jewish Disabilities Removal Act. Lord Chancellor Lyndhurst guided it safely through the Lords and it became law. Every municipal office was now open to Jews. Two years later Salomons finally took his seat as alderman and, in 1855 he became Lord Mayor of London.

In his chain and robes of office, with his magnificent head and stately presence, Salomons seemed born for the role. He insisted that the formalities of his installation be restricted and that the expenses be kept down to a minimum. "The new Lord Mayor," observed *The Times*, "is a graceful City King; he fills the office with a dignity unknown to many of his Christian predecessors, and Londoners can see him addressing illustrious strangers without troubling for the Queen's English."[29]

At one magnificent banquet presided over by Salomons and attended by the most eminent figures in the land, a bishop turned to the Prince Consort and said, "Thank goodness, Your Royal Highness, we've got a gentleman in the civic chair at last."

"Yes, my Lord," said the prince, "but you had to go beyond the pale of Christianity to find him."

The doors of Parliament still remained shut.[30]

CHAPTER 8

The Great Schism

"I am most firmly determined," wrote Sir Moses Montefiore while the struggle for emancipation was at its height, "not to give up the smallest part of our religious forms and privileges to obtain civil rights."[1]

But that, in essence, was what the struggle was about. No one, not even Isaac Lyon Goldsmid, the most militant of the reformers, suggested that the Jew should abandon his faith in order to claim full rights as an Englishman. To the de-Judaised Jew there were virtually no barriers, and, indeed, one such Jew, Benjamin Disraeli, the son of a former warden of Bevis Marks, was already making his way up 'the greasy pole' towards the Premiership. It was nevertheless inevitable that the mood of reform, the whole atmosphere of change, the improved status of the Jew, should give rise to pressure for changes in Jewish ritual and observance and, in fact, in the whole character of Judaism. What Montefiore feared was that the Jew could not claim a place in the outside world without losing something of his own.

He was not alone. Francis, second son of Sir Isaac Lyon Goldsmid, who was also active in the emancipation movement, noted with some regret "that there is a certain small number of Jews, who regard our application for relief not only with indifference, but even with doubt and distrust, because they imagine that our success is likely to promote among those who now adhere to Judaism, a falling off from the faith of their forefathers".[2] These fears were not unfounded. Emancipation had its price.

There were some 25,000 Jews in England in the 1830s, most of them concentrated in London, and many of them destitute. The Sephardim, who were sometimes looked on as a closed plutocracy, numbered about 2,500 families. Some were, indeed, very wealthy, but about half lived

on the charity of the other half. The situation among the Ashkenazim
was much the same, and the Great Synagogue in Duke's Place, which
was the immediate resort of any Jewish pauper who landed on these
shores, sometimes found the burden of maintaining the poor intolerable.
The main concern of the mass of the community, therefore, was with
the daily intricacies of survival. A middle class was evolving, however,
which found time for other things and which was turning with increasing
scepticism upon its most cherished institutions. The Jew was less confined to Jewish circles and the more he saw of the outside world the
more critical he became of his own. As the nineteenth century wore on,
one began to hear a growing chorus of complaint about the way the
synagogues were being run, the length of the services, the absence of
decorum.

The complaints were not without substance, but they could have
been made almost at any time in the history of the Anglo-Jewish
community. Samuel Pepys had once paid a visit to the Sephardi synagogue, in October 1663, and was dismayed by what he saw:

> . . . the disorder, laughing, sporting, and no attention, but confusion in
> all their service, more like brutes than people knowing the true God,
> would make a man forswear ever seeing them more: and indeed I never
> did see so much, or could have imagined there had been any religion
> in the whole world so absurdly performed as this.[3]

As fate would have it Pepys chose *Simchat Torah*, one of the two days
in the year, when a synagogue is given over to almost unbridled merrymaking, for his visit, but it is unlikely that he would have been particularly impressed with the proceedings at any time.

A synagogue is neither a Temple nor a Jewish church. It evolved as an
institution in Babylon, in the market place, where Jews, having assembled for trade, were encouraged to remain for prayer. In the ghettos
of Europe it was the meeting point of the community where they could
gather to pray, chant, study, talk, pass the time of day, mourn the sad
times, celebrate the glad ones. And if the services were sometimes conducted with less than perfect decorum, their very length was a cause.
On the Day of Atonement they last all day from morning till night; on
the New Year they last for five or six hours; on the Sabbath, three or
four hours.

The Jewish newcomer to Britain, whether from Poland or North
Africa, did not find this a burden, and if anything it evoked warm
memories of home. The older families did, and it is they who led the

call for change. The changes they sought, however, were largely of a technical nature. They wanted the singing to be improved and demanded a well-trained choir and more qualified cantors. They wanted a weekly sermon in English, to which they attached almost magical properties. They wanted the length of service curtailed, and they wanted something more, which was less easily defined, and which will be examined in due course.

No new theology was propounded. There was no Luther or Calvin among the party of change. Doctrine was never mentioned. Reformist ideas developed by Abraham Geiger, which were sweeping the Jewish communities of Germany, had, as yet, found no foothold in England. The Jewish middle class was no more inclined to speculate upon eternity than the English one, but as the minor changes they sought were obstructed, they came to demand major ones and in time they broke away to establish their own reformed synagogue. The Anglo-Jewish reformation happened almost in spite of itself.

The Orthodox Jew believes, or should believe, that all truth is contained in the Torah, the Law given by God to Moses, both in its written form as contained in the Pentateuch, and in its Oral form as transmitted by the Rabbis. He believes, moreover, that these laws are immutable and binding for all time even if the circumstances which gave rise to them have changed, and this applies even to laws decreed long after Sinai. At Sinai, for example, the Israelites were commanded to observe the Passover for seven days. In Babylon, because of uncertainties about the calendar, the Jews observed an extra day, and although these uncertainties have long since vanished, this extra day is still binding upon all Jews in the diaspora. And therein lies the distinguishing characteristic of Orthodoxy, the crystallisation of usage as something holy; tradition acquiring the authority of law. This principle can, of course, stultify faith, but there have always been Rabbis who were able to circumvent any impossible usage by re-interpreting the laws surrounding it. Unhappily, at the time of crisis in England, when the pressure for change became inexorable, the spiritual head of the Ashkenazi community was a sick and distraught man of eighty, and the Sephardi community was without a spiritual head. The last *Haham* had died in 1828, no successor had been appointed, and the *Beth Din*, the tribunal of Rabbis which was left to cope with the crisis, lacked authority and courage and sheltered throughout behind the book of rules.

The rumblings for reform started understandably in Bevis Marks, and in 1838 a 'Committee for promoting Order and Solemnity in the

Synagogue' was formed under Abraham Mocatta. The conservatives suspected that there was something more than a desire for 'Order and Solemnity' afoot, and countered with a 'Society for Supporting and Upholding the Jewish Religion as handed down to us by our Revered Ancestors and for preventing Innovations or Alterations in any of the recognised Forms and Customs unless sanctioned by properly constituted religious Authorities'.[4]

The society did not function for long, but two warring factions did crystallise, in the congregation, with the progressives drawing their support mainly from the older, more Anglicised families, and the conservatives from the newer families, who were at best a generation removed form Gibraltar, North Africa or the Levant. Sir Moses Montefiore kept aloof from this stage of the conflict. Finally, however, when compelled to take sides he joined with the conservatives.

All Jews were, nominally at least, bound by the *Halacha*, the Torah as interpreted by the Rabbis. Bevis Marks had a supplementary book of rules known as the *Ascamot*, which had some of the complexity of Erskine May and which had, through time, acquired something of the sanctity of holy writ. The first, and possibly most irksome of the *Ascamot*, was a rule, dating back to the reign of Charles II, against the holding of divine service in any place other than Bevis Marks within six miles of the City. The Ashkenazim, within a few years of forming their first congregation, had split up into three groups and when most Sephardim lived in or near the City, this was a reasonable device to prevent similar schisms in Bevis Marks. By 1840, however, it was impossible. The City was no longer a middle class residential area and many congregants had moved westwards to Mayfair, Kensington and beyond. Sir Moses Montefiore, who had a town house in Park Lane, walked cheerfully to the City and back – a round distance of about ten miles – every Sabbath and festival. Others, who were less robust, did so resentfully or stayed away altogether.

Thus to the old demands for modification in the order of service, was added a new one for the formation of a branch synagogue. Both demands were, however, obstructed at every turn, with procedural devices being used where it was feared a simple majority might be lacking and finally, in exasperation, the progressives formed themselves into a break-away group, nineteen in number, including nine Mocattas, three Montefiores and three Henriques. They were joined by five eminent Ashkenazim from the Great Synagogue, Albert Cohen, Montagu Levyssohn, and three members of the Goldsmid clan, Aaron Asher and two nephews,

Francis and Henry.[5] The issue had ceased to be an internal affair of Bevis Marks and was affecting the whole community.

In April 1840 the progressives resolved to establish a synagogue in West London and appointed a minister, the Rev. D. W. Marks, to draw up a revised form of service.

Their opponents were now coming round to the view that the formation of a branch synagogue was inevitable, but the progressives had moved beyond that and prepared a new prayer book which included alterations in the traditional order of service. The Rabbis were appalled. The traditional order of service, they declared, "was arranged and appointed by our sages of the Great Convocation, among whom were some of our prophets, and that those forms had been adhered to by the whole House of Israel, from generation to generation, for two thousand years".[6]

Other cautions, threats, warnings, left the reformers unmoved. They continued with their plans. They acquired their own house of prayer and organised their own style of service.

In January 1842, Sir Moses Montefiore, presiding over a meeting of all the wardens of all the London synagogues, made public an edict of excommunication pronounced by the Rabbis.

> Information having reached me, from which it appears that certain persons calling themselves British Jews publicly and in their published Book of Prayer reject the Oral Law, I deem it my duty to declare that according to the Laws and Statutes held sacred by the whole House of Israel any person or persons publicly declaring that he or they reject and do not believe in the authority of the Oral Law cannot be permitted to have any communion with us Israelites in any religious rite or sacred act.[7]

The split was complete, but Sir Moses carried it beyond the point of 'any religious rite or sacred act', and for thirty years while he was president of the Board of Deputies of British Jews, he would not allow any representative of the West London Reform Synagogue to sit on the Board.

The schism robbed the Sephardim of some of their most vital elements. It alienated Montefiore from the Goldsmids for a time and split the emancipation movement. Thus in 1845 Peel found himself faced with two Jewish delegations, the first, led by Moses Montefiore and Lionel de Rothschild representing the Board of Deputies: the other, led by the Goldsmids, did not claim to appear in any representative capacity, but in fact spoke for the West London Synagogue. The former were more cautious, gradualist in their approach; the latter were more militant, but by then the case for emancipation was so widely conceded that not even the split could affect the outcome of the campaign.

The influence of the West London Synagogue was less religious than social. It was a point of arrival and became the Temple of the assimilated, prosperous Victorian Jewish middle class. If the other synagogues had their magnates they also had their paupers, often whole floating bands of them. The West London Synagogue was prosperous almost all the way through. It contributed to the upkeep of the poor, but did not have to pray with them. Yet fashionable though it was, with many proud names, some of the proudest names held back, and it never became – what one thought it might become – the Cousinhood at prayer.

The Rothschilds and the many sons and grandsons of Levi Barent Cohen, in the main, remained loyal to the old establishment, the latter because they were mostly Orthodox, the former because they were above synagogal conflicts. The Rothschilds were the defenders of, if not necessarily believers in, the established faith. David Salomons, though infuriated by the exclusion of progressives from communal life, had his mind on other things. The role of the Goldsmids however is puzzling. How were they, scions of the Great Synagogue, drawn into the battle of Bevis Marks? Was it that they took their religion more seriously than their cousins?

Francis and Frederick Goldsmid had been brought up in a house which was a meeting place of English Utilitarianism, of Buxton and Gurney, of Brougham and Campbell, Anglicans, Quakers, Agnostics and Jews, but all with the same zeal for reform, the same readiness to probe the usefulness of any institution, no matter how ancient.

There have been Jews who combined radicalism in politics with conservatism in religion; but the Goldsmids did not keep their ideas in separate compartments, and they applied the same questioning attitudes to their faith as they did to social issues. It was perhaps natural that they should not be satisfied with the type of worship they experienced at the Great Synagogue. The defects there were much the same as in Bevis Marks. In 1822 Isaac Lyon Goldsmid had presided over a small committee of reform, but its terms of reference were nebulous and it could do nothing. The dissatisfaction felt with the service, they concluded, lay largely with the congregants themselves. The officiant "would have considerably less difficulty in exciting a proper devotion, if his audience were well acquainted with the

Hebrew language, in which prayers are delivered,"[8] But the sort of changes wanted by his sons could not in any case be achieved by an internal committee. Francis in particular wanted to rejuvenate the synagogue, and this could not be done in an institution where the slightest departure from precedent required ecclesiastical approval. Thus when the progressives at Bevis Marks were pushed to the point of secession he joined eagerly with them, and eventually took the whole movement over. "To him more than anyone else," wrote the Rev. D. W. Marks, the first minister of the Reform Synagogue, "we owe to it that our congregation was ushered into being."[9]

Francis Henry Goldsmid was born in Spitalfields in 1808. He read for the Bar at Lincoln's Inn but when called in 1833 refused to take the oath 'on the true faith of a Christian', and was instead allowed to do so on a copy of the Old Testament. He was a competent rather than brilliant lawyer, but was a skilled equity draughtsman and took silk in 1858. He was the first Jewish Q.C. and the first professing Jew to be called to the Bar. He retired from practice on succeeding to his father's title in 1859 and entered Parliament in the following year as Liberal M.P. for Reading. Jews were only admitted to Parliament in 1858 and he was among the first to take his seat.

His speeches in the House lacked lustre but rang with sincerity and they were generally concerned with humanitarian rather than political issues, rural amenities, working-class housing, popular education, religious liberty. "Descended from a race, and belonging to a religious community which were for centuries the objects of persecution", he told the electors of Reading, "I am attached alike by feeling and conviction to the great value of religious freedom."[10] In 1863 he interceded against the persecution of Protestants in Spain.

He acquired a large estate at Rendcomb Park, near Cirencester, and gave his tenants all the improvements in sanitation and housing which he sought for the working class at large. He was a model landlord and Rendcomb became a model village. His life in many ways was an example of faith in action, but he was not a happy or contented man. He had married a first cousin, Louisa Asher, in 1839, and the marriage was childless. He became prone to frequent bouts of depression which grew worse with age. On May 3, 1878, as his train was pulling in to Waterloo, he tried to alight, lost his footing and was dragged for several yards along the platform. He died of his injuries.

The Rev. D. W. Marks, who became his close friend, was not indulging in obituarese when he wrote:

What particularly distinguished him in our age of Religious indifference
. . . was his intense love of Judaism and his devotion to its principles.
Whilst he was at the head and front of the progressivists he desired that
every step should be in strict accordance with the religious consciousness,
and that the Hebrew should make it apparent, nay, clearly evident to the
world at large, that a rigid observer of Mosaism, and a loyal patriotic
citizen, capable of serving his country in every office of eminence and
every post of trust, can and does meet and combine in the same individual.[11]

Sir Francis was a deeply devout Jew. While at the Bar he arranged
his cases to avoid hearings on the Sabbath or festivals, and although
riding was his favourite relaxation, he would never mount a horse on
the Sabbath. At the same time he was the most English of English
gentlemen, an earnest, perhaps too earnest, Roger de Coverley, and his
interest in founding a new synagogue lay perhaps, not so much in the
minutiae of liturgy as the desire for an English synagogue – a national
synagogue – rather than an English branch of an international fraternity.

A clue to his feelings may be found in Marks' tribute and its references
not to the Jew, but the *Hebrew*, not to Judaism, but *Mosaism*. Jews and
Judaism were alien, rootless, in exile: Hebrews and Mosaism were established, at home, English.

This did not mean that Sir Francis disowned Jews elsewhere. On the
contrary, if Sir Moses was ambassador-at-large for the Jewish people,
Sir Francis was their parliamentary champion, and his interventions
on their behalf were forceful and frequent. As a follower of Gladstone,
one might have expected him to be pro-Russian, or at least anti-Turk,
but he was pro-Turk, probably because of the oppression of Jews in the
Russian Pale of Settlement and in Romania. His Jewish loyalties and
sense of commitment were unquestionable, but even his Jewishness was
of a very English sort. He and many of his fellow progressives wanted
a place of worship which would not remove them from the spirit of
England even for a day. The West London Synagogue is such a place.
Bevis Marks, the Great, the Hambro, the New and other Orthodox
Synagogues, were part of Judea in Exile; the West London was part of
England.

He differed from his kinsman Sir Moses Montefiore who kept his
English and Jewish worlds apart, as temporal and spiritual domains,
and believed he triumphed in the one because of his resort to the other.
To him the Sabbath, especially on his estate at Ramsgate, in his own
synagogue, among the learned tomes and the learned men, was a day

out of time, a brief restoration of the Kingdom of Heaven. Sir Francis on the other hand, sought to synthesise the two worlds, and to an extent succeeded.

In this he was perhaps a little ahead of his time. The Cohens, too, wanted a more English house of prayer but they sought it and found it within the existing ecclesiastical establishment when in 1870 they brought together the existing Ashkenazi synagogues into one union, reorganised the Rabbinate to give it a more modern character, and created an institution which, with its haughty edifices, sombre canonicals and austere services seemed, to the newcomer at least, like a Jewish branch of the established church. If the United Synagogue, as it came to be called, had come into being thirty years earlier, it is very unlikely that the Goldsmids and Mocattas would have led a breakaway movement.

As an actual *Reform* synagogue, the West London was behind its time, and that, too, was part of its Englishness. It was not very reformist – certainly not compared to the Reform synagogues springing up in Germany. If its attitude to the Oral Law was somewhat cavalier, it still held the Written Law – the Torah as contained in the Pentateuch – as sacrosanct. Theologically it was conservative, cautious, almost timid during a period when even the most advanced of churchmen were made to seem outdated by the works of Lyell and Darwin. The real, radical Anglo-Jewish reform movement did not come into being until the turn of the century, and it turned not only upon the Oral Law, but also the Pentateuch and the entire code of holy writ: it left nothing unquestioned. It was led by a nephew of Sir Francis Goldsmid, and a grand nephew of Sir Moses Montefiore – Claude Goldsmid Montefiore. What he was to offer bore little relation to the views of either.

CHAPTER 9

The Flight from Bure

Sir Isaac Lyon Goldsmid had two sons, and six daughters. Two of the daughters remained single, formidable, strong-willed, outspoken English maiden ladies. The third married a Montefiore; the fourth, a Mocatta. The fifth, Rachel, married a foreign banker, Count Solomon Henry d'Avigdor, a partner in the house of Bischoffsheim and Goldschmidt.

The d'Avigdors were to Nice what the Mocattas were to London – noble, ancient, rich. They had settled in the town in the late seventeenth century when it was under Italian rule and established themselves as the leading merchants and bankers of the region. Their wealth gave them privileges denied to their co-religionists. The gates of the Italian ghettos, thrown open by the French Revolution, were closed again in the reaction which followed, but the d'Avigdors were allowed a foothold in the outside world. They could move freely and were the intermediaries between the ghetto and authority, viewed by their fellow Jews almost as inhabitants of another planet. But there were still – until the mid-nineteenth century at least – the bonds of religion, d'Avigdors and non-d'Avigdors still prayed together. Isaac, Count Henry's father, was a pious, devout Jew.

In 1807 Napoleon summoned a Sanhedrin of Jewish notables and Rabbis to consider ways by which Jews could be assimilated and brought more fully into the life of the empire. Isaac, of course, was one of the participants and he acted as one of the secretaries of the assembly. The Sanhedrin achieved little, but the list of participants formed a sort of Jewish *Almanach de Gotha* of those chosen from the Chosen by Napoleon himself. His place on it constitutes Isaac's main claim to fame.

After the war he became Prussian Consul in Nice and Rothschild's agent. He had several tussles with authority over Jewish rights, and his own position, in spite of his wealth and influence, was far from established. In 1822 the Government ordered all Jews to return to the ghetto within a period of five years.[1] Isaac simply defied the regulation but other Jews were less well-placed to assert themselves. When Moses Montefiore visited Nice in 1838 he was appalled by the backward state of the community.[2] Jews, he found, were not allowed to enter schools or be trained for the professions. They were neither helped to improve their situation, nor were they allowed to help themselves. Even the d'Avigdors were treated with bare tolerance. When the Prince of Savoy paid a royal visit to Nice, Isaac led a delegation of notables to greet him on behalf of the Jewish community, but they were not even received. Instead they were graciously permitted to build an obelisk to commemorate the visit.

The Jews of Nice were finally emancipated in 1848, and Isaac died in the following year. He had eight children one of whom died in infancy, and his two eldest sons both married Goldsmids. Henry, as we have seen, married a daughter of Isaac Lyon and Jules – the eldest – a daughter of Aaron Asher.

Isaac d'Avigdor, in spite of his own deep religious feelings, apparently made no attempt to bring up his children in the Jewish faith. Was this due to the influence of his wife Gabrielle Raba, the daughter of a wealthy Sephardi merchant from Bordeaux? Gabrielle was extravagant, self-indulgent, a lady of fashion. Ladies of fashion rarely have patience for the minutiae of religious observance. Or was he anxious to spare his children the humiliations he had suffered himself?

Count Solomon Henry d'Avigdor (the title was derived from a tiny principality no longer extant) was a colourful character, charming, witty, hedonistic, part of the gilded Anglo-French circle which included the Count d'Orsay. In contemporary terms he might be spoken of as an international playboy. He was part Regency buck, part provençal grandee and was, at first sight, an improbable suitor for a Goldsmid daughter, brought up, as she was, on high Victorian principles of service and duty, and in the precepts of the Jewish faith.

They married in 1840 and lived for a time in London, but Henry soon tired of his role as banker. He opted for the life of a gentleman at large and moved his wife and young family from London and the reassuring proximity of St John's Lodge, to the Château de Bure in France. It was the France of Napoleon III and the Second Empire, and it formed a natural milieu for wandering courtiers like Count Henry who, in the course of time, became a duke.

It was not the sort of life to which Rachel could easily adapt herself and she would have found it trying at the best of times. And times for her were far from good. Her father had lapsed into senility and a crisis was developing in her own home. In June 1858 she came out with it all in a long and anguished letter to her brother Francis. Other letters, distraught and chaotic, followed in rapid succession:

> I grieve to be compelled, amidst your deep anxiety respecting our dear father in his present precarious condition, to intrude my private affairs on you; but alas they will soon cease to be private, and now my dear Frank, I come to seek your best advice, your most earnest consideration, feeling sure that I have on earth no truer and sincerer friend than yourself.[3]

Rachel had been brought up in a devout Jewish home and was deeply imbued with what she called "the simple and beautiful tenets of the Jewish faith".[4] Henry was not, and scorned almost everything she revered. She was aware of his feelings even at the time of their marriage, but had made him promise that he would not interfere in the religious upbringing of their children. This undertaking he kept at first, but he was somewhat more lax in others. In 1855 they began to drift apart; by 1856 they were no longer living under the same roof. She remained in the Château de Bure, where he would call occasionally to visit the children, but whatever the state of the weather or the roads, he would always leave before nine in the evening.

"I have more than once taxed him with some other connection," she wrote to her brother, "to which, of course, he always opposed the most vehement denial, and put this separation entirely to the overwhelming nature of his business transactions."[5]

She later discovered the nature of his transactions. He was living with a former actress, Mrs Fitzjames, and in 1856 had a child by her which died in infancy. In 1858 she was pregnant again. This, though painful and humiliating to Rachel was not beyond the bounds of tolerance. The real source of her anguish lay elsewhere. Her husband had turned Roman Catholic, and was planning to baptise their children, and send their daughter Isabel into a convent.

> . . . need I tell you that since he declared this to me, that I have neither slept nor had one moment's peace, that I feel as if I were surrounded by my enemies who might at any moment rob me of my children.

She was desperately afraid that in a Roman Catholic country there was no law to stop them.

> I come my dear *Frank* to *entreat*, to *implore you* to investigate all this thoroughly to try and shield our father's grandchildren from so dreadful a fate, the bare idea of which is breaking my heart and has caused me to thank God 'more than once that it has pleased Him to deprive our father of his reason, so that he is spared the knowledge of this apostasy in his last days.[6]

While all this was happening she still had to entertain guests, keep a smiling face to the world.

> You may imagine what it has cost me to rouse myself to talk to Mary Mocatta who is at present my guest, and I am writing this at 5 in the morning in order that she shall not see what sorrow overwhelms me.

The d'Avigdors had four children. Elim, the eldest, was safe. He was seventeen and being educated in England. Isabel, a year younger, was, her mother believed, "firm in the Mosaic faith", and possibly because of this had to suffer frequent harassment and bullying from her father. He had once bought her a locket containing a holy figurine and ordered her to wear it. Her mother wrenched out the figurine, her father restored it. A battle of wills ensued:

> I protested against it and said she should *not* wear such things. On which he declared in the most violent terms that unless she wore it, and never took it off, she should be carried off to a convent next Sunday . . .
> Isabel astounded me by her calm when she heard this; sat motionless and seemed determined to abstain from uttering a single word that might exasperate him still further. Of course she put the locket on because it is a matter of little importance what bit of metal it contains . . . but what a sad struggle for so young a girl. She looked death-like last evening when the excitement was over and her father had departed.[7]

The incident, if anything, drew her closer to her mother. She was moreover a Goldsmid, with a mind of her own, and could not easily have opinions thrust upon her. The two younger children, however, were in immediate danger:

> My *principal*, most *present* and most *pressing* anxiety is respecting Sergy and Boli my two youngest darlings; for I believe that if Henry could by any subterfuge see them out of my sight he would have them baptised, and then I think according to the laws here those who are not Catholics would cease to have the least power over them, and they would of course be entirely taken from me.[8]

There were numerous instances in which Catholic authorities had snatched a Jewish child from its parents, even where both were Jewish. And in that very year her brother Francis was involved in the agitation on behalf of a Jewish child in Italy who had been so abducted. This was the Mortara affair. Her fears were therefore not imaginary. Her husband, moreover, was trying to isolate her from contact with the outside world. He attempted to intercept letters to her and her children and to replace their governess, a pious Lutheran, with a Catholic. He tried to get rid of the two Protestant English girls his wife had brought over as personal maids and engage French Catholics. She countered his measures as best she could, but he was wearing her down bit by bit:

> I told him yesterday that if it were not for the children I could not stand this life; he said I might go if I liked and he wanted *none* of my money. That he had induced me to return because he wanted his children. I believe his object now is to worry me into leaving, then he thinks he shall do as he pleases with the children. But in that he is mistaken, I will endure hourly torment and nothing shall separate me from them but violence.[9]

There was only one safe course open to her – flight. Her initial plan was to set off with the governess and three children, as if going for a country drive, and then turn at full speed for Dieppe and Brighton, but she was afraid this might excite suspicion. She therefore worked out a more elaborate scheme. She would go ahead in one coach, the governess and the children in another, and their luggage would follow in a third. They would meet in St Germain, transfer to another coach and make for the Gare du Nord.[10]

It is difficult to see why a cavalcade of carriages should have excited less suspicion than a solitary vehicle, and why the rendezvous in St Germain was necessary at all. The countess was evidently taking great pleasure in the plotting, but in spite of its elaborateness, they reached London without mishap.

By the time she set out enough people were in the secret for her husband to have got wind of her scheme, but if he did, he made no attempt to foil it. Indeed the more one studies the affair the more one is left with the impression that his blusterings and threats were all part of a war of nerves to be rid of his wife and regain his freedom. He made no attempt to contact her after their flight, or reclaim his children. Possibly Mrs Fitzjames was engaging too much of his attention. He remained in Paris, a splendid courtier, continued to collect orders and titles, fought a duel with Cavour and died in 1871 shortly after the fall of the empire.[11] There was something almost symbolic about the timing of his death, as if he felt unfit to live among republicans.

The countess took a house near Hyde Park Gardens, an area of London much favoured by the Cousinhood. She became a member of the West London Reform Synagogue, but may have found it too modern for her tastes and in 1884 she, and two of her sons, Elim and Sergei, joined the Sephardi Synagogue in Bevis Marks.[12] In 1863 her daughter Isabel married Horatio Lucas, an artist and a friend of the Rosettis, and was widowed ten years later.[13] She was a keen horse-woman and rode in Rotten Row till a ripe old age. She was perhaps more at home in French culture than English, and never got out of the habit of referring to the synagogue service as "le messe".[14] Sergei and Boleslav both died in obscurity. The latter had a book dedicated to him by G. K. Chesterton, which suggests that he may have forsaken the faith of his mother for that of his father.

Elim, the oldest, had something of his father's colour, verve and extravagance, but nothing of his income. He studied at University College, London, and tried to join first the Royal Engineers and then (or so family legend avers) Garibaldi, but his weak eyesight forced him into less heroic pursuits and he finally became a civil engineer and supervised major public works projects in the Balkans and the Levant.[15]

He returned to England in the 1880s and devoted himself to the life of a country gentleman. He contributed articles on rural and sporting topics to various periodicals including *Country Gentleman, Horse and Hounds* and *Vanity Fair*. He wrote frequently on food, tried to elevate the standard of English cooking, and launched his campaign in his own house. A meal at the d'Avigdor table could be a nerve-racking affair, with his wife and six children sitting tense and upright lest a dish should occasion the master's displeasure. If it did, he would storm out in a fury, and sometimes stay out for weeks.

He wrote a number of novels under the name of Wanderer, which attracted favourable attention and a considerable readership. They were all stories of country life, of stately homes and broad acres, of baronets and squires and merry rustic folk, painfully novelettish, but revealing of certain segments of English life, and revealing also of the author. *Fair Diana* was perhaps the most successful of his books. Its hero, Sir Henry Banscombe, with his passion for hunting, his fastidious tastes, and constant debts, was virtually a self-portrait.[16]

Elim was also the author of a pamphlet on 'The New Zealand Midland Railway', which was also in its way a work of fiction. "Shareholders," he wrote, "may consider themselves exceptionally fortunate in having joined the company." The irony of the sentence may have appealed to him, for he himself held considerable blocks of shares and could do nothing with them. The pamphlet, in fact, was a shameless piece of share-pushing. The railway went bankrupt in 1895 and paid 25% on its debentures and nothing on its ordinary shares.[17]

He dabbled in other enterprises which proved hardly more fortunate. His politics matched his way of life and unlike most members of the Cousinhood, he was a Tory. He took over the *Examiner*, a lively radical paper, to further the Tory cause, but it foundered almost as soon as he laid hands on it.

Towards the end of his life he joined the *Chovevei Tzion* an association of Zionist pioneers, based mainly in Russia, who planned to establish Jewish agricultural settlements in Palestine. He became head of the English branch of the movement and drafted its constitution. It was one of the few schemes with which he was connected which came to fruition.

It is surprising that the Zionist idea, which had as yet only touched the Jewish masses, should have appealed to this choleric country squire. The Jewish communities of Russia had lately been ravaged by a series of pogroms and the Cousinhood had rushed to their aid with money and sympathy, but they thought merely in terms of ameliorative measures. Elim, from among them all, saw the need for a radical solution and advocated the need for a Jewish state in terms which anticipated Herzl's *Judenstaat*. His daughter Sylvie (who married out of the faith), translated *Judenstaat* into English and composed numerous songs which became a popular feature of Zionist gatherings.

Elim's Zionism may, paradoxically enough, have been a by-product of his Toryism. As a good Tory he was a good churchman, which is to say, a good synagogue man and was for the last decade of his life an active elder at Bevis Marks. He may have seen in Zionism a logical expression of the prayers – which have a central place in Jewish liturgy – for the restoration of Zion. As a civil engineer, he had been involved in railway construction in various parts of the Ottoman empire and was thus familiar with Palestine. He believed that Jewish settlement was an immediate way of bringing life to the moribund province. Palestine needed Jews as much as Jews needed Palestine.

Elim's tragedy was his expectations. He could never reconcile himself

to the life of a middle-class Englishman with a middle-class income. As a
d'Avigdor and a Goldsmid he felt that the world, or at least his relatives,
owed him a fortune, and it seemed for a time as if fate was working to
give him one.

When he returned to England in the 1880s he had an assured income
of £700 a year and a further £1,000 a year from his mother. He could
also look forward to inheriting her fortune, reputed to be worth about
£5,000 a year, but his main hope was fixed on the Goldsmid estates at
Somerhill, Kent, which were entailed upon the male line.

Somerhill, a Jacobean mansion standing in several thousand acres
was acquired by Sir Isaac Lyon Goldsmid in 1849. Elim's mother was
the ninth of Sir Isaac's twelve children and at the time of Elim's birth
there were some two dozen lives between him and the succession, but
one uncle died after another, then cousins began to expire in batches.

In 1866 Sir Julian Goldsmid succeeded to the estate. He married in
1868 and Elim, who was abroad at the time, must have watched with
interest and anxiety to see what fruit the union would yield. In 1869
came the first child, a daughter; in 1870, the second, another daughter;
in 1871 the third, a daughter again; in 1873 a fourth daughter; in 1874
a fifth. The family looked on incredulously. But Sir Julian, with that
aplomb which made him a favourite chairman of Committees in the
House of Commons, soldiered on. In 1877 they had a sixth daughter;
in 1879 a seventh; in 1880 an eighth. Five, six or even seven daughters
may be a sad stroke of fate, but eight was more like a conspiracy. Sir
Julian gave up.

Elim returned to England. Somerhill was as good as his, and he began
to treat it as if it were, with the money stacked up in the bank. He
borrowed widely. He borrowed heavily from his mother, uncles, cousins
and, through an intermediary, put it to Sir Julian, who had already
helped him with loans and grants, that he could do with an annual allowance on account. Sir Julian was the most understanding, the most benign,
the most generous of individuals, but this was too much even for him.
Elim had neither a legal nor moral claim on him, Sir Julian pointed out:

> The fact that Mr d'Avigdor may possibly inherit the Goldsmid estates
> would favour the argument that whilst I am in possession of them it is
> rather my duty to make the most of them for the sake of my numerous
> family and daughters, than assist Mr d'Avigdor keeping hunters or a
> yacht . . .
> Moreover the large sums (which owing to his unfortunate habit of entering
> into engagements from which his over sanguine temperament he is inclined

to think will be profitable, but which always turn out the reverse) I have paid for him to extricate him from his difficulties, are a reason why I feel disinclined to do much more. A report has reached me also, that some of the money which Sir Francis has left to the Countess, has been sold by arrangement to meet other debts of Mr d'Avigdor. This method of anticipation is, in my opinion, unsatisfactory.

But having said all that Sir Julian did not conclude, as he might well have done, with a categorical refusal. He agreed to allow Elim £600 a year:

> . . . provided he enters into a legal undertaking that if he succeeds to the Goldsmid estates, he will repay the capital to my estate.
> Provided also that he undertakes not to anticipate any further his succession to his mother's property or to the Goldsmid property. And, lastly, provided that he undertakes to enter into no engagements of any kind involving financial liability.[18]

Elim must have accepted the arrangement readily for he needed the money badly. His wife, who had given birth to a son in 1877, had lately presented him with his fifth daughter and quite apart from his own personal extravagance, the cost of his domestic establishment was becoming insupportable. A lesser man might have gone out to work. Elim waited. Sir Julian was only three years older than himself, but in frail health. He became seriously ill in the winter of 1895, staggered on into the spring, and finally died in May 1896. But Elim, alas, was by then in his grave. He had died a year earlier at the age of fifty-three and did not even live long enough to inherit his mother's estate. She died in 1916 at the age of one hundred.

CHAPTER 10

Time of Arrival

When the Catholics won their emancipation in 1829, Daniel O'Connell wrote to the Jews, who were still struggling for theirs:

> You must force your question on Parliament. You ought not to confide in English liberality. It is a plant uncongenial to British soil . . . The English were always persecutors. Before the so-styled Reformation, the English tortured the Jews, and strung up in scores the Lollards. After the Reformation, they still roasted the Jews and hung the Papists. In Mary's days, the English with their usual cruelty retaliated the tortures on the Protestants. After her short reign there were nearly two centuries of the most barbarous and unrelenting cruelty exercised towards the Catholics. . . . The Jews too suffered in the same way. I once more repeat, do not confide in any liberality, but that which you will yourself rouse into action and compel into operation.[1]

Isaac Lyon Goldsmid, O'Connell's friend and leader of the most activist wing of the Jewish emancipation movement, did not share this Irish view of history, and was content "to confide in English liberality", but he was aware that even liberals need to be nudged. By the mid-nineteenth century the nudging activities which he directed had freed Jews of most of their disabilities. There were Jewish knights and baronets, Jewish freemen, sheriffs and aldermen. Only Parliament was still closed. The emancipationists now braced themselves for the final assault and there was, of course, only one person to lead it – Baron Lionel de Rothschild.

Lionel's father, Nathan, though perhaps the most influential figure in the movement, had been compelled to take a back seat. He was too foreign, too boorish, too unattractive to be allowed to the fore. Lionel, who became head of the London bank at the age of twenty-eight, suffered from no such handicaps. He was English born and bred, with all of his father's financial genius, and none of his unfortunate mannerisms or naïvety. "It takes great wit and great caution to make a great fortune," Nathan had said, "and ten times as much wit to keep it when you've got it."[2] Lionel had such wit and was not only able to maintain his vast patrimony, but to extend it.

Nathan's particular flair had lain in gigantic speculations and in the transfer of bullion. Lionel tended to go in more for vast public works projects and in the late 1830s found much of the Fr 150,000,000 sought by the Belgian Government for a railway network round Brussels.[3] The development of Brazil rested so heavily on N. M. Rothschild & Sons that it became virtually a Rothschild fief.[4] Lionel raised the £8,000,000 sought by the British Government for the Irish Famine Relief Fund, and seven years later found the £16,000,000 necessary for the prosecution of the Crimean War. During his lifetime the London bank was involved in eighteen major government loans involving a total of £160,000,000.

The Irish Famine Relief Appeal was launched in New Court, and he opened the list with a donation of £1,000. (Generally, however, it was his wife who acted as family almoner. She left £120,000 to various charities in her will, and gave away much more than that during her lifetime.) Lionel had also served on various government committees dealing with banking and public finance, and had done much to enhance the standing and scope of N. M. Rothschild as a bank, and of the City of London as a banking centre.

The qualities which make a great merchant and a great politician are not the same. Lionel did not relish the campaigning, the speeches, the limelight, the place at the centre of controversy. It was not that commerce was the sum of his existence, but away from New Court he preferred the calm of Gunnersbury, to stroll among his exotic blooms, to relax amid his Rembrandts and Dürers. But the fight for emancipation had to be carried on, he was the best person to do it, and he did it. It took a long time. He was thirty-nine when he began knocking at the doors of Parliament. By the time he got in he was fifty, and already showing signs of the rheumatic gout which was to paralyse him in later years.

In August 1847 he stood as one of the Whig candidates for the City of London. The City had always been an outpost of independence, both as a trading community and in politics. In the eighteenth century it returned the maverick John Wilkes time after time in spite of the attempts of Parliament to unseat him, and it was now to do the same for Rothschild. He was elected with a sizable majority, but felt unable to take the oath 'on the true faith of a Christian', and was debarred from taking his seat. The trouble, said Disraeli, "arose out of this Member being not only of the Jewish race, but unfortunately, believing only in the first part of the Jewish religion".[5]

The election, the attempt to take the seat, the refusal to take the oath, were of course mere gestures, but they were made at an awkward time.

Sir Robert Peel had on the whole favoured Jewish emancipation, but in 1846 the Tory Party was torn asunder by Lord George Bentinck and Disraeli over the repeal of the Corn Laws, and the whole political scene was thrown into confusion. There was trouble on the Continent, trouble at home, acute trouble in Ireland. The Whig leader, Lord John Russell, who was returned to power in August 1847, was determined to have the Jewish question at least, out of the way.[6] In December he tabled a resolution to delete the phrase from the oath which had kept Rothschild out of the House. It received a mixed reception. Gladstone, who was then a Tory, and a member for Oxford University spoke for it. How could Jews be excluded, he asked, when Unitarians, "who refuse the whole of the most vital doctrines of the Gospel",[7] were admitted? He was answered by the other member for the university, Sir Robert Inglis. The Jews, he said, "are voluntary strangers here, and have no claim to become citizens but by conforming to our moral law, which is the Gospel".[8]

Disraeli now intervened. He was himself of old Sephardi stock. His father, Isaac d'Israeli, was a member of Bevis Marks, but did not take his Judaism seriously and after some differences with the elders he formally dissociated himself from the Jewish community without adopting any other faith. His solicitor, however, advised him that by leaving his children even nominally Jewish he was exposing them to serious handicaps and in 1817 Benjamin Disraeli, then thirteen, was baptised.

Disraeli once described himself as the blank page between the Old Testament and the New. He was a Jew of the Christian persuasion and saw no contradiction between his Jewishness and his creed. As a Jew indeed, he could claim descent from its founding fathers, but at the same time he had a strong sense of affinity with the Jewish people, to which he now gave vent in what was one of the most remarkable speeches of his career.

He had, with the fall of Peel, emerged as a major political figure, and a contender for the leadership of the Tory Party. It was not the most politic moment to intervene on behalf of the Jews, and it proved to be a most impolitic speech, which roused large sections of the House, and especially his own party, to fury.

Those in favour of Jewish emancipation had confined themselves largely to the constitutional issue or the eminent good sense of it all; those against were at pains to illustrate the differences between Judaism and Christianity. Disraeli was determined to show that, on the contrary, they were almost the same:

> If religion is a security for righteous conduct, you have that security in the instance of the Jews, who profess a true religion. It may not be in your more comprehensive form. I do not say that it is *the* true religion; but although they do not profess to all that we profess, all that they do profess is true. You must admit then that in men who are subject to the Divine Revelations that you acknowledge, whose morals are founded on the sacred oracles to which we all bow, that, as far as religion can be a security for their conduct . . . you have in the religion of the Jews the best sanction in the world except that of our own Christianity. . . . The very reason for admitting the Jews is because they can show so near an affinity to you. Where is your Christianity if you do not believe in their Judaism?

Members on all sides listened with a mixture of bewilderment and dismay. At first they were shocked into silence, but as he continued there were cries of disapproval, which stung him into some heat, and he raised his voice above the noise:

> In exact proportion to your faith ought to be your wish to do this great act of national justice. If you had not forgotten what you owe to this people, if you were grateful for that literature which for thousands of years has brought so much instruction and so much consolation to the sons of men, you as Christians would be only too ready to seize the first opportunity of meeting the claims of those who profess this religion.

The interruptions continued, grew louder; he pressed on:

> But you are influenced by the darkest superstitions of the darkest ages that ever existed in this country. It is this feeling that has been kept out of this debate; indeed, that has been kept secret in yourselves – enlightened as you are—and that is unknowingly influencing you as it is influencing others abroad . . .

And he paused to draw breath for his peroration:

I cannot sit in this House with any misconception of my opinion on this subject. Whatever may be the consequences on the seat I hold . . . I cannot, for one, give a vote which is not in deference to what I believe to be the true principles of religion. Yes, it is as a Christian that I will not take upon me the awful responsibility of excluding from the legislature those who are from the religion in the bosom of which my Lord and Saviour was born.[9]

He sat down to stony silence in the ranks behind him, and when the House divided, only he and George Bentinck out of the entire faction voted for the resolution. There were, however, enough sympathisers in the House to carry it with a majority of sixty-seven.

His speech which, according to his father was "the most important ever delivered in the House of Commons", could have ruined his career, but he was obviously fired by the subject and was responding to his favourite maxim: 'Race is all.' As an act of courage, it bordered on the reckless.

The Cousinhood were jubilant about the success of the resolution in the House of Commons, but it was promptly killed in the Lords.

Rothschild stood again for the City, was again returned, again refused to take the oath, and was again debarred. Parallel with these efforts, Russell made repeated attempts to carry an emancipation Act through Parliament. Again and again it was passed through the Commons, and on each occasion was killed in the Lords.

David Salomons now opened up a second front using different tactics. In June 1851 he was elected Whig member for Greenwich. Like Rothschild, he refused to take the oath, but unlike him, he took his seat. There was no precedent for such an action, and after the first moment of stupefaction there was uproar, with cheers from the Whigs, counter-cheers from the Tories, and members jumping up in all parts of the House to make points of order. An eye-witness described what followed:

In the middle of the House of Commons stood a peculiarly mild and gentleman-like man, looking as much like a quiet and cultivated country gentleman as the majority of Members surrounding him. Round this calm and smiling personage a war of parliamentary elements were raging loud and fierce. Amid shouts of 'Withdraw' from one side and loud cheers from the other, the hon. Member somehow gained the ear of the House. The favour of a large body of the House, the winning aspect of the

intruder, the curiosity prevailed. There was a pause and then amid
breathless silence Mr Alderman Salomons delivered his maiden speech.[10]

The gesture proved to be more memorable than the performance for
the speech, though not very long, was dreary:

> Sir . . . I trust the House will make some allowance for the novelty of my
> position, and the responsibility I feel for the unusual course which it may
> be thought I had adopted. But having been returned to this House by a
> large majority . . . I thought I should not be doing justice to my position
> as an Englishman and a gentleman did I not adopt the course which I
> thought right and proper of maintaining my right to appear on the
> floor . . . and stating before the House and the country what I believe to
> be my rights and privileges . . . I hope this House will not refuse what I
> believe no court in the country refuses the meanest subject of the realm –
> that it will not refuse to hear me before it comes to a final decision.[11]

Members could not have felt as they listened to him that they were
depriving themselves of the services of an orator, but if the rhetoric was
not impressive, his courage was, and he was cheered loudly from all
sides of the House. This did not, however, mean that they approved of
his action, and he was removed by the Serjeant-at-Arms.

The Government did not plan to take the matter further. Salomons
was indeed complimented by the Prime Minister on the calmness of his
speech, but a common informer took proceedings against him, and he
was fined £500. He appealed, but the sentence was upheld. He, however, still felt that he had acted within his rights and proposed to take
the case to the House of Lords. In the meantime a general election
intervened which robbed him of his seat, and he left the matter there.
A few years later when the old Parliament buildings were pulled down.
he bought the seat which he had so expensively occupied for a while,
and installed it in the billiard room at Broomhill.

Attention now focused once again on Lionel Rothschild. He was
returned for the City on five different occasions while Russell kept
hammering away at the House with one relief measure after another in
1849, 1851, 1853, 1856 and 1857, evidently hoping that persistence
might succeed where reasoning failed. But the Lords, with their serried
ranks of bishops could always rally a sufficient phalanx against it.

In 1853, while one such appeal to the tolerance of Parliament was in
progress, the Jews showed that they could be less than tolerant where
their own internal affairs were concerned. Some twelve years earlier,
the Board of Deputies, at a special session presided over by Sir Moses

Montefiore, had voted that no Jew who was a member of the Reform Synagogue could sit on the Board. David Salomons, though Orthodox himself, had protested against the ruling and so had other members of the Board, but without success. In 1853, however, a number of Jewish Deputies who belonged to the Reform Synagogue decided to do at the Board precisely what Salomons had done in the Commons. They took their seats, and though asked by Sir Moses to withdraw, they refused to do so. A heated debate followed in which Lionel Rothschild, his brother Sir Anthony, David Salomons and others pleaded that the Reform Deputies should be allowed to keep their seats, while Louis Cohen and Sir Moses argued that they could not. Sir Moses, indeed, had consulted two eminent lawyers and was advised that the constitution of the Board gave him no alternative. A vote followed, in which the Board was evenly divided, and Sir Moses used his casting vote against the intruders. One of them, a mine-owner from Sunderland called Jonassohn, still refused to move, till the Secretary of the Board, acting like the Parliamentary Serjeant-at-Arms tapped him on the shoulder – a gesture indicating physical ejection – and he withdrew.

All this was reported in the daily press and followed with glee by opponents of Jewish emancipation, while Rothschild and Salomons wrung their hands in despair.

Russell continued to persevere, but came to realise that, like the Catholic Emancipation Act, this was a Whig measure which only the Tories could carry. In 1858 the Tories were returned to power. Disraeli became leader of the House of Commons and immediately took steps to dispose of the issue for once and for all. A compromise was found by giving each House power to adopt its own form of oath. On July 26, 1858, Rothschild took the oath, minus the offending phrase, and finally took his seat.

"For eleven years we've had the M.P. question screaming in every corner of the house,"[12] said the baroness, but when it was finally settled it came as an anticlimax. Lionel de Rothschild remained fifteen years in the House of Commons and during that time did not open his mouth once. His struggle for entry had had nothing to do with political ambition, the desire for power or influence, for as Lord Goschen, a future Chancellor of the Exchequer, observed, he exercised more influence from New Court than most M.P.s in the House. He had sought admission to Parliament as the vindication of a right.

Once the way was open other members of the Cousinhood followed in rapid succession, Mayer Rothschild (Lionel's brother) and David

Salomons in 1859; Sir Francis Goldsmid, 1860; Nathaniel de Rothschild and Frederick Goldsmid, 1865; Julian Goldsmid, 1866 – all of
them Whigs. It was unthinkable that a Jew at this time should be anything else, for the Whigs had all along been champions of Jewish
emancipation and the Tories' opponents, and the fact that it was the
Tories who finally made it possible for the Jews to enter Parliament was
accepted as a quirk of fate. When Baron Henry de Worms, another
member of the Cousinhood, stood as a Tory candidate in 1868 he was
roundly upbraided by the *Jewish Chronicle* for doing so, and his defeat
was viewed with a certain amount of *schadenfreude*.[13]

The first Jewish Tory M.P., Saul Isaac, a wealthy colliery owner who
sat for Nottingham from 1874 to 1880, was, surprisingly, from outside
the Cousinhood. De Worms finally won a seat in 1880 and he was
joined shortly afterwards by two distant kinsmen, Lionel and Benjamin
Cohen. Lionel, indeed, became vice-president of the National Union
of Conservative Associations.

Once the Cousinhood were in the Commons it could only be a matter
of time before they were in the Lords, but the time, as it happened, was
a considerable one. The 1858 compromise on the oath admitted Jews
only to the Lower House and the position was not regularised until
1860 when one uniform oath, which could be taken by all religious
denominations, replaced the awkward oath of Allegiance, Supremacy
and Abjuration.

In 1868 the Earl of Shaftesbury approached Disraeli, who had only
just become Prime Minister, with the suggestion that Sir Moses Montefiore be raised to the peerage. Shaftesbury, a devout, indefatigable
churchman, had opposed the admission of Jews to Parliament as an
insult to Christianity, but he had since had second thoughts on the
matter. Disraeli could not have been unsympathetic to the idea, but as
he wrote to Shaftesbury, "he was less than any other Prime Minister in
a position to grant the request".[14] A few months later he fell from office
and was succeeded by Gladstone. The new Prime Minister was, of
course, more happily placed and Shaftesbury tried again:

Dear Gladstone . . .

The Jewish question has now been settled. The Jews can sit in both
Houses of Parliament. I myself resisted their admission, not because I
was adverse to the descendants of Abraham, of whom our Blessed Lord
came according to the flesh; very far from it, but because I objected to
the mode in which that admission was to be effected.

All that is passed away, and let us now avail ourselves of the opportunity to show regard to God's ancient people. There is a noble member of the House of Israel, Sir Moses Montefiore, a man dignified by patriotism, charity and self-sacrifice, on whom Her Majesty might graciously bestow the honours of the Peerage. It would be a glorious day for the House of Lords when that grand old Hebrew were enrolled on the lists of the hereditary legislatures of England.[15]

But Gladstone had another name in mind. Montefiore though, indeed, a beloved figure, was, if anything, a Tory. Lionel de Rothschild was a Liberal and in 1869 he recommended him for a peerage. The Queen was aghast at the proposal, and retorted: "To make a Jew a peer is a step she could not assent to. It would be very ill taken and would do the Government great harm." But Gladstone persevered, as he had to persevere with so much else, where the Queen was concerned:

It is extremely desirable to connect the House of Lords, in a few carefully selected cases, with the great representatives of commerce in this country. But, from the sort of parity which prevails among commercial men of the higher stamp it is extremely difficult to make the selection. Excellent candidates may easily be found but they do not stand out sufficiently from the body.

As the head of the great European House of the Rothschilds, even more than by his vast possessions, and his very prominent political position after having represented the City of London since the year 1847, Baron L. de Rothschild enjoys exactly that exceptional position, which disarms jealousy and which is so difficult to find. His amiable and popular character needs only to be named as a secondary recommendation.

He then went on to hint that the Queen was approaching dangerous constitutional grounds:

It would not be possible in this view, to find any satisfactory substitute for his name. And if his religion were to operate permanently as a barrier, it appears that this would be to revive by prerogative the disability which formerly existed by statute, and which the Crown and Parliament thought it proper to abolish. Mr Gladstone has now troubled Your Majesty to the full extent incumbent upon him, and will not think of pressing Your Majesty beyond what Your Majesty's impartial judgement may approve.[16]

The reply came almost by return of post and it was cold, curt and uncompromising:

The Queen thanks Mr Gladstone for his letter and for promising her not to press the subject of Sir (sic) L. Rothschild Peerage. The Queen really cannot make up her mind to it. It is not only the feeling of which she cannot divest herself, against making a person of the Jewish religion a Peer; but she cannot think that one who owes his great wealth to contracts with Foreign Governments for Loans, or to successful speculation on the Stock Exchange can fairly claim a British Peerage.

However high Sir L. Rothschild may stand personally in Public Estimation, this seems to her not the less a species of gambling, because it is on a gigantic scale – and far removed from the legitimate trading which she delights to honour, in which men have raised themselves by patient industry and unswerving probity to positions of wealth and influence.[17]

In 1873 Gladstone considered returning to the matter again and asked Lionel for a memorandum about his father's activities during the Napoleonic War. Lionel was either hesitant about going into his father's wartime history, or was nonchalant about the whole affair. In either case he did nothing about it and died in 1879, a commoner. Six years later Gladstone recommended his eldest son, Nathaniel the Liberal member for Aylesbury, to the peerage and he was accepted without a murmur.

Nathaniel proved himself to be a more active member of the Lords than his father had been in the Commons, but on the whole the first wave of Cousins to enter Parliament made little impact on either House. Their contributions to economic debates were followed with respect, but they were not outstanding even in the sense of being colourful. They had none of the exoticism of Disraeli. They were as English as the most English of the burghers and squires among whom they sat – as, indeed, they had to be – and blended, almost completely, into the backcloth of Westminster. Those who feared that the admission of Jews would introduce an alien strain into the mother of Parliaments were reassured.

Two of them gained some prominence. Sir Julian Goldsmid acquired an encyclopaedic knowledge of parliamentary procedure and served on occasion as Deputy Speaker. He was a widely esteemed member and had he not died at the age of fifty-eight, might possibly have been elected Speaker. Henry de Worms served as Parliamentary Secretary to the Board of Trade in Salisbury's first government, became a Privy Councillor and was in 1892 appointed Under-Secretary of State for the Colonies. In 1895 he was raised to the peerage as Lord Pirbright.

De Worms was a great-grandson of Mayer Amschel Rothschild. His father Solomon de Worms had come to England in his youth and was brought up with the Rothschild children in New Court. He had then gone out to the colonies and with his brothers established an extensive coffee plantation in Ceylon. In 1871 he was made a hereditary baron of the Austrian empire and, because of the services rendered by his family to Ceylon, he and his descendants, were allowed to use their title in the British empire.

De Worms was a good speaker – a talent in which the Cousinhood tended to be deficient – a skilled boxer, a fine shot, and showed an immense interest in an improbable variety of subjects, yet he is also recalled as an immense bore. He was the author, among other things, of books on magnetism, the Austro-Hungarian empire, and the Eastern question. He was a familiar figure on Jewish platforms and active on behalf of a variety of Jewish causes. He was president for twelve years of the Anglo-Jewish Association, and was for a time treasurer and vice-president of the United Synagogue, an office which brought him in frequent touch with Chief Rabbi Herman Adler, whose wife Henrietta was a second cousin. He was one of the defenders of the faith, and when his daughter married out of it she caused some dismay; the dismay was increased when it was learned that her father had attended the church ceremony in person, but that was nothing to the shock which was to follow. When he died in 1903 he left instructions that he was to be buried in a Christian cemetery.

No one could explain it. He had married twice and both his wives were Jewish, but in any case even those members of the Cousinhood who married out of the faith generally took pains to be buried within it. He had a reserved plot in the Jewish Cemetery at Willesden. What had made him forsake his faith in the last hour? It is suggested that he was affronted by his exclusion from the Jewish leaders, representing the Jewish community, who called on Edward VII in 1901 to congratulate him on his accession.[18] If so, he may have died as a Christian, but his sense of grievance was entirely Jewish. He lies buried at Wyke St Mark's churchyard, near Guildford, Surrey.

CHAPTER 11

Court of Last Resort

While the Jews of Britain were trying to assert their right to enter Parliament, Jews in many other parts of the world had not yet established their right to exist.

There was the threat of deportations in Russia, murder and rapine in Romania, a recurrence of the blood libel in Syria, upheaval in Morocco, and nearer home, in the papal territories of Italy, the Church still reserved the right to snatch Jewish children from their parents. In each instance the stricken communities turned westwards for help, to Britain, to the Board of Deputies, and in particular to the Cousinhood and their leading members, Lionel de Rothschild and Moses Montefiore, who functioned almost as a court of last resort.

Lionel was the premier Jew in England, in the world, but he was too eminent to travel as ambassador-at-large for the Jewish people. He did not wish to be over-exposed. Moreover, although he had two brothers in the bank, Sir Anthony and Mayer, no major decision could be taken without him and he could not be away from New Court for any great length of time. Nor did he have the necessary physical vigour for such journeys; in his last years, indeed, he was a cripple, and it was his uncle Sir Moses Montefiore who had to be Ambassador.

In the nineteenth century more than half of the Jewish population of the world lived in the Russian empire, with most of them crammed into a narrow pale of settlement in the western territories. They could not move freely or trade freely and were subject to continuous harassment. Many lived on the edge of destitution and even their meagre livelihoods were threatened by a ukase, announced in 1842, to uproot several hundred thousand of them from the western border areas and deport them into the interior. Baron Brunnow, the Russian Ambassador to

London, a frequent guest at Rothschild tables, and an acquaintance of Sir Moses, explained that it was "an act of mercy to remove Jews from the temptation of smuggling".[1] At the same time there came reports from Russia of a scheme to reform the Jewish educational structure which the Jews feared was an attempt at conversion.

In 1845 Sir Moses became a sheriff of London and for the rest of the year, though closely in touch with events in Russia, he was kept at home by his official duties. When the year was over and the Russian authorities still showed every intention of proceeding with the deportations, he decided to travel to St Petersburg and approach the czar in person. At the end of February he ordered his great coach, a veritable drawing-room on wheels, to be made ready for the roads, and on March 1 he set out.

Russia was still in the grip of winter and he had to face the hazards of swollen rivers, snow-bound roads, treacherous ice, but he pressed on relentlessly, trudging onwards on foot where the roads were impassable. Finally after a month on the move, weary and travel-stained, he reached St Petersburg, and a few days later he was received in audience by the czar. He outlined the grievances which had been brought to his attention by the Jewish community, the restrictions, the impositions, the humiliation, the harassment. Nicholas I did not listen to this in silence. He gave an account of the faults he found in his Jewish subjects which, Sir Moses later confessed, "made every hair on my head stand on end".[2]

Sir Moses did not challenge the allegations, but argued that if only the Jews could be given the same rights and privileges as other Russians they would become exemplary citizens and loyal subjects.

Nicholas did not demur. "*S'ils vous ressemblent*",[3] he said, and their meeting was at an end.

"I am satisfied," Sir Moses wrote in his diary, "that the Jews will be better off in consequence of our visit to this city. Praise be to God alone."[4]

The effects of Sir Moses' visit were not long-lasting, but in the short term he showed in his very person what a Jew living in freedom could become. He raised the standing of the Jews in the eyes of the Gentiles, and indeed he improved their own self-respect. They were cheered by his presence among them and his journey homewards through the eastern provinces was a royal progress. Cheering crowds lined his route. Flowers were thrown in his path. Poems and songs were composed in his honour. Nothing like it had been known in Europe since the days of the seventeenth-century false Messiah Sabbetai Tzvi. Sir Moses was too abundantly present in body to appear as a Messianic figure, yet his world of Victoria and England, of East Cliff and Park Lane, could not have been more remote from the wretched townships through which he passed. He had never seen such poverty. At Wilcomir, near Wilno, he learned that one Jewish family in four had perished from hunger in the previous year. He left money everywhere, a hundred roubles here, a thousand there. The experience, for all the joy his journey occasioned, was distressing. "When I see brethren suffer, I feel it painfully," he said. "When they have reason to weep my eyes shed tears."[5] He continued onwards to Kovno, Warsaw, Cracow, making detailed enquiries into the situation of the communities, taking careful notes.

As he crossed into Germany he drew nearer his own world. In Berlin he was greeted by the Bleichroder banking clan. At Frankfurt he was received by the Rothschilds. Lanterns hung from the buildings, bands played in the streets; the *Judengasse* was *en fête*.[6]

His mission had been followed with interest and sympathy by Queen Victoria and the Prince Consort and when he returned to England in June he was made a baronet.

In 1846 Sir Moses presided over a meeting of the Board of Deputies to prepare an address of appreciation to Pope Pius IX for his efforts to improve the conditions of Jews living in the Papal States of Italy. The address was forwarded first to Lord Palmerston, and then to Baron Charles de Rothschild of Naples, who in turn presented it to the Pope. A few years later came reports that the old repressive measures had been restored. Pius IX, who had begun his career as a liberal became one of the most obscurantist of all popes whose rule was described by Gladstone as "an Asian monarchy: nothing but one giddy height of despotism, and one dead level of religious observance".[7]

The pope had been forced to leave Rome during the 1848 republican uprising and take refuge in Gaeta till he was restored by French bayonets, but he was nearly ruined by the events and he turned to Charles Rothschild of the Naples house for help. His Holiness' credit at the time was not, in temporal terms, of the highest, but Charles was willing to forward the money at a low rate of interest provided the walls of the Roman Ghetto were abolished, that Jews were allowed to move freely in the Papal States, and that the special taxes paid by them were removed. He further demanded a mortgage on the ecclesiastical estates as security. The pope might have accepted the first conditions, but not the last, and he therefore turned to his protector Louis Napoleon who, in turn, introduced him to James Rothschild. James did not demand any mortgages, but still insisted on Charles' first conditions, namely the emancipation of Jews in the Papal States. He was given an assurance in the most general terms by Monsignor Fornarini, the papal nuncio in Paris, that the Holy Father had the best intentions with regard to his Jewish subjects. Pius received the loan on the most favourable terms, but the assurances given in his name remained a dead letter.[8]

In 1852 Edgar Mortara, the infant son of a Jewish merchant in Bologna (which was in the Papal States) became ill, and his nurse, a fourteen-year-old illiterate girl by the name of Mina Morisi, fearing that he was on the point of death, baptised him. Edgar recovered but his nurse kept silent about the baptism until 1858 when she mentioned it to her confessor. He, in turn, brought it to the attention of the Inquisition and on June 3, 1858 an officer of the papal police accompanied by two gendarmes seized the child and took him to a Dominican convent. He was seven years old. A few months later he was taken under armed guard and transferred from Bologna to Rome. An eye witness described how he cried continually, calling for his parents. An officer kept trying to force a rosary into his hands, which increased his tears.[9]

At first the parents were kept completely in the dark. They were not told why the gendarmes had called, why the child was seized, or what was to be done with him. It was only later that they learned of the secret baptism. Mortara appealed first to the Inquisition for the return of the child, then to Cardinal Antonelli, the Papal Secretary of State, and finally, to the pope. The Holy Father replied that there was only one way of recovering the child and that was by following him into the Church. Edgar's mother, distraught by the abduction, died of grief.

When news of the affair reached the outside world, there was an international outcry. There were protests in Turin, Paris, London, Amsterdam. There was a mass meeting in New York, one of the largest in the history of the American Jewish community. Sir Francis Goldsmid raised the issue in the House of Commons and eventually forty-nine peers and thirty-six M.P.s expressed their horror and condemnation of the affair in a letter to the Foreign Secretary. Their letter, said *The Times*, voiced the opinion of "all reasoning Europe".[10]

The Board of Deputies urged that a Jewish mission be sent to Rome, but Sir Moses still hoped that the pressure of the world opinion might yet compel the Church to return the child, but the louder the voice of protest the more obdurate the Church became.[11] "The world and all Christendom," declared a German clerical paper, "might put on sackcloth, yet the child, having received baptism, must remain Catholic."[12]

The protests began to peter out. Jewry was thrown back on its own resources. On April 5, 1859 Sir Moses arrived in Rome.

Sir Stratford de Redcliffe who, as ambassador to Constantinople had been of immense help to Sir Moses during the Damascus affair, was now living in Rome, and Sir Moses sought his guidance on this new tragedy.

"The case appears to be so clear," Sir Stratford told him, "that according to our notions, you ought to find no difficulty in obtaining justice; but judging from what reached me in conversation, I fear it will require all your ability, energy and experience to open the smallest prospect of success."[13]

Sir Moses had arrived with the blessings of the Prince Consort, letters of introduction from the British Government and Napoleon III, and Odo Russell, the British Ambassador, gave him every possible assistance, but they were all unavailing. Sir Stratford's pessimism was confirmed by events. When Russell tried to arrange an audience with the pope one Monsignor passed him on to another, who passed him on to a third, who passed him back to the first. Sir Moses was finally received by Cardinal Antonelli, but the pope refused to see him.

Mortara remained in the Church. When papal rule ended in 1870 and Italy was united under Victor Emmanuel the father appealed to the Government for the return of his son, but he refused to go back. He had entered as a novitiate of the Canons Regular of the Lateran and was ordained in 1873. He died, still a priest, in Bouhay, Belgium, shortly before the Germans entered the country in March 1940.

For the first time in his life Sir Moses returned from a mission empty-handed. He could draw no comfort from the thought that others had suffered similar frustration in dealing with Pius IX. He was seventy-five, and saw in his failures the waning of powers. "I fear increasing years may ere long impair such efficiency as I may be able to exhibit at present in the performance of my duties," he told the Board of Deputies, and warned them that he might soon have to resign from the presidency.[14]

He had many active years ahead yet, but they were lonely ones.

Sir Moses, on short journeys or long, rarely travelled without his wife. She was a poor but determined traveller, even a foolhardy one, for there were the hazards of bad roads over high mountain passes; there were brigands in Italy, pirates in the Mediterranean; there was plague in the Levant; there were sporadic uprisings throughout the near-East.

Judith's frame was unequal to her courage. She accompanied Sir Moses on three of his journeys to the East, and was ill every time. On their first journey in 1827 they stopped at Malta, and spent the Fast of Ab there. It was a heavy, torrid day, but she would not allow food or water to pass her lips. "My poor wife," lamented Montefiore, "suffered so much that I endeavoured to persuade her to break her fast about four o'clock, but she would not."[15] As a rule he knew better than to argue with her.

During his mission to Mehemet Ali in 1840 she suffered painfully from the hot weather and became gravely ill, and added to her husband's many anxieties. At Leghorn, on their return journey, she suddenly felt dizzy, with sharp pains in her head. An arm went numb and she could hardly walk or talk. She just managed to gasp out for a prayer book. She had suffered a slight stroke, and although she was able to resume the journey, she remained weak and unwell.

Her travelling days, one might have thought, were over, but when Sir Moses set out for St Petersburg in 1846 she went with him. The physical strain and the hazards of the month-long journey across the snow-bound wastes of Russia shortened her life. The emotional strain was, if anything, greater. She had seen poverty, sickness and distress on her three visits to the East, but that was almost the Englishman's picture of the Orient. Nothing prepared her for the conditions she found in the Pale of Settlement, the hungry faces, the haggard eyes, the abject misery, the sense of hopelessness. Her ladyship, noted an onlooker, "had not a dry eye for weeping over the extreme distress she here beheld".[16] She returned an invalid.

When Sir Moses set out for his abortive mission to Rome in March 1859 she could not be persuaded to remain at home, and they had to travel slowly, in easy stages, accompanied by their medical attendant, Dr Hodgkin. The Mortara tragedy affected her deeply, and she was distressed by her husband's sense of failure and frustration. On their return she was weak and in pain. In June 1861 they spent a happy wedding anniversary at Smithem Botton, a village in Surrey which they used to visit frequently during the early years of their marriage. Sir Moses was aware there could not be many such anniversaries ahead, and one can sense a melancholy tone in his diary: "At this place man appears to want but little. With peace and content and the quietness of the place . . . endeared Smithem Botton to my dear Judith and myself far beyond every other place we have ever seen, excepting Jerusalem and East Cliff."[17]

Lady Montefiore was suffering from an obstruction of the bowels which was probably cancer. In June 1862 they celebrated their golden wedding anniversary at East Cliff, but as the summer progressed she began to sink, and in September they returned to London to celebrate *Rosh Hashana*, the New Year, in Park Lane. As usual, there were numerous guests in the house for the occasion. Lady Montefiore was too weak to join them, and they assembled in an adjoining room which had been fitted up as an oratory for the evening service. The door was left open and she sat up to listen to the ancient chants and familiar melodies. Her beloved Monte then came into her room to bless her, as he had done every Sabbath throughout the fifty years of their married life, and she raised her arms weakly to reciprocate. He wanted to remain, but she urged him to join his guests below. The candles were lit, the tables were laid, the company was waiting.

He went downstairs, raised his cup of wine, and began the benediction: "Blessed art thou, O Lord, who has kept us in life, and has preserved us", when he was startled by a call from Dr Hodgkin. Judith Montefiore was dead.

Her almost grim determination to accompany Sir Moses on his missions was not the action of a worried wife anxious to keep an eye on an erring husband. They were childless. She was not greatly excited by the social life of London, and to be without him at Ramsgate was unthinkable. Sir Moses was her life. He, on his side, needed her encouragement and advice and above all her companionship to carry him through the anxieties and frustrations he often had to endure. "I am no great man," he once said. "The little good that I have accomplished, or rather that I intended to accomplish, I am indebted for it to my never-to-be-forgotten wife, whose enthusiasm for everything that is noble and whose religiousness sustained me in my career."[18] She was, he said, "a little Napoleon", and he took no major decision without her.[19]

She had a firm sense of duty which was derived partly from her religious upbringing, but also from the belief that privileges carried obligations. She was a Cohen. Her attitudes were those of her age and her class, but unlike many of her contemporaries, she lived up to them. In 1846 there was published a *Jewish Manual*, by 'A Lady', the lady in question being Lady Montefiore. In it she gives various hints on cooking, toilet, and household management. As a technical manual it did not quite enter into the Mrs Beeton class, but it does indicate some of her guiding beliefs in life.

A good skin, she advised, depended on "a strict attention to diet, regular ablutions followed by friction, frequent bathing and daily exercise, active enough to promote perspiration. . . ." She could

hardly have been more English. The next point is a little more Jewish:
". . . body and mind are, in fact, so intimately connected that it is futile,
attempting to embellish the one, while neglecting the other especially
as the highest order of beauty is the intellectual." In this instance she
may have been putting her own best points forward.

"In woman's dress," she suggested, "simplicity should be preferred
to magnificence . . ."

> All ornaments and trimmings should be adopted sparingly; trinkets and
> jewellery should seldom appear to be worn merely for display; they should
> be so selected and arranged as to seem necessary either for the proper
> adjustment of some part of the dress, or worn for the sake of pleasing
> associations.

And she concluded:

> It is, however, in bad taste to wear them [dresses] very low on the
> shoulders and bosom: in youth, it gives evidence of the absence of that
> modesty which is one of its greatest attractions; and in maturer years it
> is the indication of a depraved coquetry, which checks the admiration
> it invites.[20]

She came of age at a time when the traditional Jewish idea of modesty
was also the English one. A generation earlier or later, and she would
have been thought too proper, stuffy, too prim. It was as if she had
modelled herself on Queen Victoria. There was also something about
the manner and outlook of Montefiore, his social conscience, his sense
of duty, his rectitude, which recalled the Prince Consort; they were as
happy as the royal pair, as loyal, as affectionate, as inseparable.

Lady Montefiore kept an account of their travels and the joy she and
her husband found in each other's presence is vividly depicted in this
description of a stop at a wayside inn after a stormy day on the roads:

> Now seated by a comfortable fire with an affectionate companion, the
> table nicely prepared for tea, the kettle boiling, the rattling of the windows
> and the boisterous sound make me the more sensible of present enjoyments
> and the storm we have just escaped. Surely the German saying is true,
> 'Getheilte freud ist ganze freude; getheilter schmerz ist halber schmerz! [Joy shared
> is joy complete; sorrow shared is sorrow halved].[21]

Her writing suffered from Victorian verbosity, but it was not without
grace. She spoke French, German and Italian, and through her husband's amanuensis, the orientalist Dr Loewe, she tried to acquire a
knowledge of Hebrew and Arabic. She was an accomplished musician,
played the piano and guitar, and took great pleasure in singing the

hymns she had learned in the Great Synagogue as a child, and in Bevis Marks since her marriage. She would, where her health and the weather permitted, often accompany her husband to synagogue. "The gentlemen," she once wrote, "tell me it is not considered essential for ladies to observe that strict piety which is required of themselves; but surely at a place of devotion the mind ought to testify due respect and gratitude towards the Almighty." But her views were not widely shared and she encountered the buzz of chatter everywhere. In Alexandria she complained: "I can not say much of their devotion, conversation having been more attended to than prayers." And in Florence: "Several German females were present and they wished to be very conversant; but I, as usual, at a place of devotion was as determined to be taciturn."[22]

But even outside a synagogue she was hardly the ideal companion for a light half-hour. Scandal, she once declared, "is never my amusement".[23] She read much, but mainly stories with a moral. Yet she was no cheerless prig. In Rome in the early years of their marriage she spent a riotous couple of days at a pre-lenten carnival, joining in the masques, the balls, the parades.[24] Sir Moses was less amused by it all, but took pleasure in her pleasure. Though censorious in outlook she could be understanding to the point of indulgence. Among the many people Sir Moses supported there was one who spent everything he received on gambling and Sir Moses finally struck him off his list, whereupon Lady Montefiore pulled out her own cheque book. "My dear," she said, "I think we had better send him something. I am sure nobody else will if we do not."[25]

She was a stern believer in the stern virtues, industry, self-discipline, self-help, self-denial, but she tempered it all with charity.

Sir Moses missed her profoundly. East Cliff in the years that followed became almost a museum to her memory: she had been buried in a mausoleum there which was a replica of Rachel's tomb on the road to Bethlehem. He allowed none of her personal effects to be moved. Her room, the furniture, the furnishings remained as she had left them, and there were portraits of her, some large, some small, everywhere. Sir Moses himself was nearly eighty when she died, and he still dressed in the fashion of his younger years, with the frilled shirts and high collars of a Regency gentleman. Now he began to appear like a relic of the past, and would spend long hours among the mementoes of his married years.

He was often snatched from his reveries by events abroad.

In 1863 a Spaniard living in the Moroccan port of Safi died in mysterious circumstances, and Jacob Wizeman, a fourteen-year-old boy in his employment, was seized, tortured and 'confessed' that he had poisoned his master. The torture continued and he went on to name, one by one, eleven other Jews as implicated in the crime. The boy, once the tortures ceased, asserted his innocence but the confession was allowed to stand and he was publicly executed. The men he named were thrown into prison.

News of this reached Sir Moses in October. He at once tried to contact Lord John Russell but it was Sunday and he was out of town. He then went on to the Under-Secretary for Foreign Affairs, Sir Austin H. Layard, who promptly telegraphed Sir John Drummond Hay, the British Ambassador in Tangier, to intervene with the authorities to obtain at least a suspension of further executions. Two weeks later Sir Moses, accompanied by Dr Hodgkin, set out for Morocco. Russell telegraphed that he should be given every assistance, and the Admiralty placed a frigate H.M.S. *Magicienne* at his disposal.[26]

Sir Moses travelled overland as far as Cadiz. He stopped at Madrid where he called on the British Ambassador, the Prime Minister of Spain, and Queen Isabella.[27] He also met Mr Weisweiller, a distant kinsman and the Rothschilds' agent in Spain, who was able to give him several useful introductions. They included one to the father of the Spanish Consul in Tangier who, it appears, was the instigator of the whole affair. Thus armed, Sir Moses found no difficulty in obtaining the release of the prisoners and they were freed within hours of his arrival. He was also able to use his influence to obtain the release of a Moor who had been kept in prison for two and a half years for the alleged murder of a Jew but who had never been brought to trial.[28] Thereafter his stay in Morocco assumed the status of a royal visit. A palace was placed at his disposal. He was greeted by a band of fifes and drums; escorted to the royal palace by a squadron of cavalry, and there a body of six thousand men, who must have comprised a large part of the Moroccan army, was marshalled in his honour. The sultan received him cordially, assured him of his good will towards his Jewish subjects and issued a firman commanding that they "shall be treated in manner conformable with the evenly balanced scales of justice, and that they shall occupy a position of equality with all other people".[29]

He was fêted on his return to England. The Jewish community organised a large rally in his honour presided over by Sir David Salomons, and addressed, among others, by Gladstone, Sir Anthony Rothschild, Sir Francis Goldsmid, Lord Goschen and Jacob Waley; the Lord Mayor of London held a dinner in his honour; he was received by the

Queen at Windsor Castle. At the same time messages of appreciation poured in from all corners of the globe. He might have felt he had achieved enough in his lifetime to spend the rest of his days among his memories, but he could not rest while his co-religionists were oppressed and there was hardly a year in which some instance of serious oppression was not brought to his attention, and where there was no political oppression, there was often poverty, famine and plague. Sir Moses found more to keep him busy in his old age than in his middle years. He went on one mission in his fifties, two in his sixties, two in his seventies, four in his eighties, and four in his nineties. Most of these journeys were to the Holy Land. "In spite of old age and weakness," he said, "I would willingly undergo any fatigue and risk to benefit Jerusalem."

In 1867, Sir Moses had just returned from a mission to Palestine when he received news of a ghastly outrage in Romania.

Ten Jews from the town of Galatz who were alleged by the Romanian authorities to be Turkish vagabonds, but were in fact natives of Romania, were taken half-way across the Danube and landed on a marshy island without food or fuel. During the night one of them perished in the mud. The survivors were rescued by the Turks and returned to Galatz. But the Romanians refused them on shore and drove them into the water at the point of the bayonet, till they were drowned.[30]

Sir Moses at once set out for Bucharest, by fast train, chartering special trains where none were available, and a special steamer on the last lap of his journey to Bucharest.

Dr Hodgkin was now dead and he was accompanied by a new medical attendant, Dr James Daniel of Ramsgate, and among others his nephew Arthur Cohen, a brilliant young lawyer, whose advice he greatly valued; but before they reached their destination he received a telegram from Mrs Cohen to say that Dr Jenner, who appears to have been their family doctor, had told her it was dangerous for Arthur to go to Bucharest and that he must return at once. Sir Moses, who was nearly eighty-four, continued without him.

Mrs Cohen had presumably feared an epidemic. The dangers which faced Sir Moses were different. The *Natinuea*, an extreme right-wing paper, had been working itself into a fury at his approach:

Two weeks ago we announced to our readers the arrival of a wealthy Israelite from London, Sir Moses Montefiore, and now this personage, who is in the possession of all the keys to all the doors of the Cabinets of Europe, actually arrived yesterday in our capital. . . . Need we tell our

Rumanian brethren what these people want in our beautiful country?
Is it possible that the Rumanians should be so simple, so foolish, so led
away by the friends of the Hebrews, so betrayed by those who secretly
sell the soil of our ancestors? . . . No! No! No! Ye Rumanians; ye descendants of those who knew how to preserve this beautiful land in all storms,
who knew how to defend and rescue it from the claws of the Goths, the
Huns, Turks,. Poles, Hungarians, Germans etc; ye descendants of those
noble ancestors, you know as well as we what these Hebrews want here . . .
You will indeed still have in your veins sufficient of the blood of your
ancestors not to permit that the land should fall into the hands of the
Hebrews.[31]

When Sir Moses arrived at his hotel he found a large and menacing
mob milling in the courtyard. There was panic in the lobbies and a
terrified servant rushed into Sir Moses's room, crying "They want to
take your life!" The mob grew larger and louder and stood under the
balcony shouting threats and abuse. Sir Moses threw open his windows
and stepped out onto the balcony. The crowd was at first taken aback
by his massive presence, his wizened face, his boldness, and subsided for
a moment into silence. Somebody wielded a pistol. Sir Moses stood there
unmoved. "Fire away," he shouted, "I came here in the name of
justice and humanity to plead the cause of innocent sufferers."[32]

The mob slowly dispersed. In the evening Halfon, a banker, the
president of the Bucharest Jewish Community, came white-faced with
consternation and with tears in his eyes. "We shall all be massacred,"
he wailed. He wished Sir Moses had not come. His presence was an
affront to Prince Charles, the Government and the people of Romania.
Jews of Mr Halfon's class, as Sir Moses discovered, were doing well in
Romania, as they were doing in most places. He was concerned with the
mass of the community, and the conditions of the masses could not have
been more wretched. But he was taken aback by the sight of a banker in
tears.

"Are you afraid?" he said. "I have no fears whatever, and will at
once order an open carriage, take a drive through the principal streets
and thoroughfare, go even outside the town, and drive near some public
garden. Everyone shall see me; it is a holy cause; that of justice and
humanity. I trust in God; He will protect me."[33]

Halfon fled. Sir Moses ordered his carriage, drove about without
incident till they were outside the town, and there, on a quiet country
road they found themselves followed by a carriage moving slowly and
deliberately behind them. They took one turn, the carriage followed;

1. Moses Montefiore
as a captain of the
Surrey militia.

2. Moses Montefiore in later life. He bestrides the Jewish history
of the nineteenth century like a Colossus.

3. Judith Montefiore, devoted wife of Moses, a daughter of
Levi Barent Cohen.

4. East Cliff Lodge, home of the Montefiores at Ramsgate.

5a. Nathan Rothschild—'A View from the Royal Exchange', 1817.

5b. Nathan Rothschild
—'Fireman of the Alliance',
1824.

6. Waddesdon Manor, the Renaissance palace built by Ferdinand Rothschild in 1874-80.

7. Mentmore, acquired by Mayer de Rothschild in 1851.

8a. Nathaniel, 'Natty',
Lord Rothschild, 1888.
He was the first Jew to be
raised to the peerage.

8b. 'Potted Peers'—the first Lord
Rothschild. The legend read: 'The whole
of British Capital having been exported
to the South pole as a result of the
Budget Revolution, Lord Rothschild flees
from St. Swithin's Lane and succeeds in
escaping to the Antarctic regions
disguised as a Penguin', *National
Gazette*, 1909.

9. Lady Rosebery, *née* Hannah Rothschild, the only child of Baron Mayer.

11. David Salomons, one of
the Cousinhood's fighters for
Emancipation.

10. Walter Rothschild at Tring, riding on a giant tortoise, the gift of the ex-queen of the Sandwich Isles in 1912.

12. 'The Cohen Cab'—a contemporary caricature. Benjamin is inside on the left. Lionel on the right.

13. *Are we as welcome as ever?* A cartoon by Max Beerbohm depicting (from left to right) Ernest Cassel, Alfred Rothschild, Edward Lawson, Arthur Sassoon and Leopold Rothschild, shortly after George V's accession.

14. Aline Sassoon, from a portrait by Sargent. Aline was the beautiful daughter of Baron Gustave de Rothschild and the wife of Sir Edward Sassoon, one of the Prince of Wales' circle.

15. Samuel Montagu, a *Vanity Fair* cartoon. A successful
banker, he was described by his daughter Lilian as
'a Jew primarily—and a citizen, a politician, a business
man long afterwards'. His piety and generosity were
renowned.

16. Edwin Montagu (centre), with Lloyd George in 1916. His fight for Indian self-rule destroyed his political career.

they took another; it followed still. Sir Moses was calm, his companions were not. They stopped, and as they did so a man jumped from the carriage behind and made straight for Sir Moses. He was a businessman, and wanted Sir Moses to intervene with the prince to extend his franchise to light Bucharest with paraffin lamps.

Sir Moses was received by Prince Charles on a number of occasions and was assured that the rights and liberties of Romanian Jewry would be respected and that they would be placed on the same level in every respect as other Romanian citizens.

"Since your departure," Halfon wrote to him later, "no representation or complaint has reached me from any person. I am convinced of its being a happy prelude to the fruits of your philanthropic voyage."[34] They were both over-optimistic.

In 1872 the bicentenary of the birth of Peter the Great was celebrated in Russia and Sir Moses, despite his age, was the natural person to represent the Anglo-Jewish community. There was talk of cholera in St Petersburg, but there was always talk of one sort of plague or another every time he set out anywhere and Sir Moses ignored it. He was warmly received by Czar Alexander II and was able to see the great advances made by the Jews of Russia since his last visit in 1846.

In 1881 Alexander was assassinated and in the upheaval which followed some two hundred Jewish communities were ravaged by pogroms. Sir Moses, now nearly ninety-eight and in failing health, made urgent preparations to set out once more. "If necessary I will be carried there", he said. "Take me in my carriage to the train, put me on board ship, then again on the train, and when in St Petersburg I will be carried into the presence of the Emperor. Nothing shall prevent me from serving my unfortunate brethren if I can be of use to them."[35]

But although unwilling to recognise it, his travelling days were over. He was still mentally alert, however, and keenly in touch with all that was happening in the world. He was shocked by the attempt on the life of President Garfield of the United States in September 1881 and immediately telegraphed to Jerusalem for prayers to be offered for his speedy recovery. He also wrote a personal letter of sympathy to Mrs Garfield. But the President died and Sir Moses sent £100 to be distributed among the poor of Boston in his memory.[36]

In February 1882 there was a large meeting in the Mansion House attended by archbishops, bishops, Cardinal Manning, the heads of the Free Churches, and every eminent Jew in the country, to protest against the pogroms in Russia and to launch an appeal on behalf of the victims. Over £100,000 was raised and a special committee was formed to assist Russian Jewry. Sir Moses was too ill to attend this historic meeting, and felt too old to serve on the committee. A new generation, consisting largely of his nephews, had taken over.

Sir Moses' ninety-ninth birthday was declared a public holiday in Ramsgate and neighbouring towns. The whole Thanet coast was *en fête*. Ships in harbour were dressed over-all, the streets were decorated with triumphal arches, and hung with bunting and illuminations. Special trains deposited large crowds from London and all parts of Kent. Gifts and greetings arrived by the van-load. There was one from the Prince of Wales and another from the Duke of Edinburgh, and from Jewish communities in every country on the globe. One message, written in pure Biblical Hebrew which particularly intrigued him, was from the township of Montefiore, which had been named after him by refugees lately settled in Pratt County, Kansas. In the afternoon, a procession, organised by the chief postmaster of Ramsgate, consisting of firemen, police, lifeboat men, members of the town council, and at the end, some two thousand school children – each section preceded by a band – marched passed East Cliff villa. Sir Moses watched from his balcony. He could not stand to take the salute, but lifted his cap and waved his hand. From time to time he attempted to rise to his feet to say a few words, but was too overcome with emotion.

As his one hundreth birthday approached 'Sir Moses Montefiore Memorial Committees' were formed all over the world, and one such committee, which included many of the most distinguished names in the country, assembled in the Mansion House in January 1884 under the presidency of Sir Nathaniel Rothschild to prepare a memorial worthy of the man, but the meeting did not get far. Sir Moses wanted no such memorial. He was gratified by the intention, but aghast at the expense. He made it plain in the most emphatic terms that he would not have it.

He now rarely stirred out of East Cliff, but was not able to mark his centenary as quietly as he might have wished. There were parades again, bands, speeches, addresses, crowds, and messages and gifts by the train-load.

His memory was still sound though he often spoke of people and things past as if they were present. His beloved Judith was often in his conversation. He almost looked forward to joining her, He would recall his many missions. "Do you remember when we crossed the Dvina near Riga, and the ice broke under our feet? We had many a narrow escape; praise be God for his numerous mercies."[37] The thoughts which gave him the greatest pleasure was the work accomplished in the Holy Land.

In November 1873, when he was ninety, there had been a report in a Kent paper that he had died.[38] Sir Moses was amused by it. "Thank God," he said, "to have been able to hear of the rumour, and read an account of the same with my own eyes, without using spectacles."[39] He was now weak and his eyes began to fail him. He could still sign cheques, which he did in great number, to various charities, but his pen had to be directed.

On July 25, 1884, he began to suffer from congestion of the lungs. Physicians stood by him day and night, every medical device was tried. Prayers were said in every synagogue, but even Sir Moses could not escape the inevitable, and he died in the early hours of July 27. Another three months and he would have been a hundred and one.

During his last years he kept a piece of Jerusalem stone under his pillow and asked that it should be interred with him. He had never been sure whether he and Judith should have been buried in Jerusalem or Ramsgate. The Jerusalem stone in English soil was his compromise.[40]

Were Sir Moses's journeys really necessary? His work in Palestine was effective and lasting. The same cannot be said for his missions elsewhere. His trouble was that he put too much trust in princes. They may not have been deceitful but their writ did not always run very far. The sultans proposed, the pashas disposed, this was true of both the sultan of the Ottoman empire, and the sultan of Morocco, and Prince Charles of Romania who had received Sir Moses so warmly and with such reassurances but was not in effective control of his domains. Moreover, the promises of a monarch are not necessarily binding on his successors. Thus the sultan's firman notwithstanding, the blood libel was repeated again and again in various parts of the Ottoman empire; anti-Jewish riots continued to erupt in Morocco, and nothing Sir Moses had witnessed during his lifetime in Romania or Russia could compare to the outrages which took place after his death.

But in the short term his effect was tremendous. He not only saved lives and freed captives; he did something to alter the attitudes of many Gentiles to their Jewish neighbours. He improved for a time the material conditions of any community he visited. But above all he was a morale booster, the champion of Israel, the word 'Jerusalem' atop his family crest was in itself a form of reassurance. While he was active no Jew, whether in some dingy hamlet in Poland, or some dusty *mellah* in Morocco, no matter how wretched or oppressed, could feel completely forsaken. In the last resort, there was Britain and Sir Moses. His apotheosis was perhaps the moment he arrived in Morocco on board an Admiralty frigate.

Had he lived a little later he would have been less effective. Britain was becoming less influential (and less free with her frigates) and the age was passing when the subjects of one nation could intercede in the affairs of another, and any attempt to act the Montefiore, no matter with what diplomatic finesse, would have exacerbated a situation rather than improved it.

Anti-Semitism, moreover, was assuming a different form, and instead of being some isolated outburst of ill-feeling due to purely local circumstances, it was becoming organised, systematised, an ideology. It whispered of a Jewish conspiracy to dominate Christendom, and the descent of a Montefiore bearing official introductions would have strengthened their case. And the places affected were no longer dependent areas like the Levant, Persia, Morocco or Romania, but countries which had been in the vanguard of European civilisation, Austria, Germany, France. Sir Moses was born in time, and died in time.

CHAPTER 12

The Landed Gentry

Land has a special place in the English imagination. One speaks of the 'landed' gentry, but until comparatively recent times there was no other sort. A gentleman to be recognised as such had to own land, and lots of it. Money, no matter in what Rothschildian quantities, was merely money; land was rank. It distinguished established wealth from the upstart, secure fortunes from the ephemeral. It would pay a millionaire to sink half his fortune in 10,000 acres of land for a shilling per cent, wrote the *Economist* in 1870, for land would make him "a greater person in the eyes of more people".[1]

In the nineteenth century various members of the Cousinhood, including Moses Montefiore, David Salomons and Isaac Lyon Goldsmid, had acquired country seats, but they were hardly more than mansions surrounded by extensive parks, and could not compare to the vast estates bought by their contemporaries in the banking world, like the 15,000 acres of Hampshire acquired by Alexander Baring (the first Lord Ashburton), or the 30,000 acres spread over eleven counties bought by Lord Overstone. But in the second half of the century the Rothschilds moved into the country, and they did so on a Rothschildian scale. Between 1850 and 1880 they virtually bought up the Vale of Aylesbury, and their haughty mansions looked down from almost every ridge in the Chilterns. By the time their acquisitions were complete they owned some 30,000 acres of Buckinghamshire and a good slice of Hertfordshire.

Disraeli had settled in Buckinghamshire a little before them. In 1847, after the split in the Tory Party over the repeal of the Corn Laws, he found himself at the head of the landed wing of the party, but still landless, and in the following year he bought Hughenden, near

High Wycombe. He adored the country, his "beloved, beechy Bucks",[2] and some of his enthusiasm may have infected the Rothschilds. Another inducement was the northward thrust of the railways which brought the area within easy reach of London.

In 1851 Mayer de Rothschild acquired Mentmore, and the other members of the family followed in rapid succession with Anthony at Aston Clinton, Ferdinand at Waddesdon, his sister Alice at Eythorpe, Alfred at Halton, Leopold at Wing and Nathaniel at Tring. Nathaniel, Alfred and Leopold were Lionel's sons, and Ferdy and Alice were his nephew and niece. (Ferdy was also his son-in-law.)

This enclave in the Chilterns was merely the rural counterpart of the pattern the Rothschilds had established in London where they were within hailing distance of each other. In Bucks they were (given robust health) within walking distance. In 1865 Lionel built himself a six-storey mansion at 148 Piccadilly. Within the next few years Mayer moved into 107, Ferdinand into 143, Alice 142, Anthony, round the corner, at 19 Grosvenor Gate, Leopold at the rear of 5 Hamilton Place, and Alfred, a little down the road at 1 Seamore Place.

Buckinghamshire is thickly ringed with market towns which now reach out towards each other and threaten to form a large conurbation, but a hundred years ago the hills were wind-blown and desolate, and the villages strung out along the valleys were sunk in poverty. Agriculture, already hard-hit by the repeal of the Corn Laws, received a staggering blow from the opening of the American prairies. Corn prices fell disastrously, many farmers were unable to pay their rents, and added to these external factors was the sheer improvidence of some landlords. The Duke of Buckingham, for example, was forced to dispose of some 50,000 acres of land between 1844 and 1857 (while still retaining some 10,000 acres round his seat at Stowe).[3] Other magnates abandoned the neighbourhood and left it to decay.

> Where [asked a local historian in 1885], are the great families: Where are the Lees of Quarrendon, the Dashwoods of Halton, the Chesterfields and Stanhopes of Eythorpe, the Whartons of Upper Winchenden, the Lakes of Aston Clinton, the Dormers of Wing? All their once noble residences have been swept away by the ruthless hand of time, and their lands have become alienated. The members of the Rothschild families are now the owners of the principal of these estates.[4] [But he went on] the new owners infused new life into the neighbourhood and experience, at all events in this case, gives a denial to the saying that 'Nothing flourished under a big tree . . .

Mayer, the youngest of Nathan's sons, engaged Joseph Paxton, who had only recently completed the Crystal Palace for the Great Exhibition, to build what he called a villa at Mentmore. Paxton based his design on Wollaton, the magnificent sixteenth-century seat of the Willoughby family (and now the home of the Nottingham Natural History Museum). He used the same honey-coloured Ancaster stone and the same ornate Elizabethan detail, and added variations of his own. The result, with its massive square towers and pinnacles, was overwhelming, but it was softened by the gardens and park. The house, begun in 1852, was completed in 1854 and was among the first in the country to have hot-water heating and artificial ventilation throughout.[5]

As may be expected of the designer of the Crystal Palace, much use was made of glass. The great central hall is lit by a glass roof, and there are plate-glass windows facing out on to the Chilterns.

Baron Mayer, though a partner in the bank, spent little time at New Court. He was Liberal M.P. for Hythe, but he never spoke in the House once. His main interest was the turf. He established a stud farm at Grafton, near Mentmore, and won the Thousand Guineas in 1854 and 1864, the Goodwood Cup in 1869 and 1872, and in 1871, which became known in racing history as 'The Baron's year', the Thousand Guineas, the Oaks, the St Leger, the Cesarewitch and, as a crowning triumph, the Derby.

The baron was fond of saying that it was cheaper to buy antique French furniture than to go to Maples,[6] but the furnishing at Mentmore did not suggest any undue striving for economy. He and the baroness amassed a priceless collection of French tapestries, Limoges enamels, Sèvres porcelain. There were Renaissance furniture, and pieces bearing the cipher of Marie Antoinette, objects from the doges' palace at Venice, and a number of huge gilt lanterns from the doges' barge; and a vast chimney-piece in black and white marble which had once adorned Rubens' house in Antwerp. The rooms at Mentmore were of a proportion to accommodate such treasures. The central hall is fifty feet long, forty feet wide, and forty feet high.

The total result excited awe rather than admiration. It was, said Asquith, "a regular museum of every kind of antiquity".[7] "I don't believe," wrote another visitor, "that the Medici were ever so lodged in the height of their glory."[8]

Yet even Mentmore was not the last word in magnificence. It was outshone by Waddesdon, a Renaissance-style château built for Ferdinand de Rothschild by the French architect Hippolyte Destailleur.

Ferdinand was a grandson of Nathan's brother Solomon. His mother, Charlotte, had married Anselm, head of the Vienna house, but the marriage was not a happy one. Anselm, a devout Jew, did not carry his religious fervour to the point of marital fidelity. His wife returned to England with their son, and Ferdinand was brought up as an English gentleman, though with cosmopolitan tastes. In 1865 he married his cousin Evelina, Lionel's daughter. It was the social event of the year. Fourteen bridesmaids and a troop of pageboys followed the bride. The cream of London society and a host of glittering figures from abroad were present. The First Lord of the Admiralty proposed the health of the Rothschilds, Disraeli toasted the bride. Eighteen months later she died in childbirth. The whole family was sunk in grief.

"We were happy, merry, even joking, without the slightest thought of such a terrible event", wrote her cousin Constance in her diary. "It now seems to be impossible. . . . The house, all dark and shut up. . . . Saw the bedroom, that gay, bright room with the motionless form on the bed, with the poor tiny baby on the sofa."[9]

Ferdinand, who never married again, founded a hospital at Southwark and a girls' school in Jerusalem in Evelina's name.

He acquired the site of Waddesdon, a forbidding, chalky escarpment, from the Duke of Marlborough for £200,000. The top of the site was sliced off like the top of an egg to accommodate the building and fully grown chestnut trees were hauled up the steep gradient and planted into avenues. A specially constructed branch railway line was built half-way up the hill, and Percheron mares were imported from Normandy to haul the building materials to the top.[10] Intricate shrubberies, exotic plants, dancing fountains, elaborate statuary transformed a wilderness into a minor Versailles. The work begun in 1874, was completed in 1880.

Inside, the floors were lined with miles of Savoneries carpets. Beauvais and Gobelins tapestries stretched across the ceilings and walls. The galleries were crowded with Reynolds, Gainsboroughs, Cuyps, Watteaus, Rubens, Guardis, Van Eycks and Van Ruysdaels. And everywhere on mantlepieces, sideboards, in vitrines, were displayed the fragile masterpieces of Sèvres, Dresden and Limoges. Waddesdon, with its two hundred and twenty-two rooms, became one of the wonders of England.

It is the one Rothschild palace that remains much as the Rothschilds left it. Ferdinand died in 1898 and left Waddesdon to his sister Alice, who in 1922 passed it on to her great-nephew James de Rothschild.

James died in 1957, and bequeathed the house and all its contents to the National Trust with a large endowment to ensure its proper maintenance.

While Waddesdon was in the course of construction yet another pinnacled palace was rising on yet another ridge of the Chilterns, Halton House, near Wendover, built for Ferdinand's cousin Alfred. It was only slightly less ambitious than Waddesdon, an immense Victorian pile, looking in the main like a French eighteenth-century château but owing something to a dozen architectural styles. The interior was encrusted with ormolu. One wing was flanked by a spectacular winter garden. If Mentmore was a museum, Halton was a pleasure dome and even included a skating rink.

Halton would have seemed slightly incongruous in almost any setting, but set among the beech woods and hamlets of Bucks it was startling. Algernon West saw it as "an exaggerated nightmare of gorgeousness and senselessness and ill-applied magnificence". Eustace Balfour, a brother of Arthur Balfour, was more damning:

I have seldom seen anything more terribly vulgar. Outside it is a combination of a French château and a gambling house. Inside it is badly planned and gaudily decorated. . . . Oh, but the hideousness of everything, the showiness! The sense of lavish wealth thrust up your nose! The ugly mouldings, the heavy gilding always in the wrong place, the colours of the silk hangings! Eye hath not seen nor pen can write the ghastly coarseness of the sight.[11]

The Prince of Wales, however, appears to have found it entirely to his tastes. He was among the magnificent assembly which attended the house-warming party in 1884, and he was a frequent guest thereafter.

Alfred pushed hospitality to the point of embarrassment. Guests arriving at Tring railway station had their route illuminated by footmen with lanterns. Baskets of flowers awaited them in their rooms. Liveried coachmen with horses in harness stood by at all times of the night for anyone caring to tour the grounds by moonlight. And when guests made ready for home they would be weighed down with mementoes of their stay, flowers, hot-house fruits, chocolates and Alfred de Rothschild cigars.

At Waddesdon, Ferdinand could be equally extravagant. When he entertained Crown Prince Rudolf of Austria to dinner he offered his lady guests new dresses at Doucet. (But when Lillie Langtry tried to get a petticoat to go with her dress at Ferdinand's expense, she promptly got a bill for it, with the admonition that it was not 'authorised'.) [12]

Asquith, the Liberal leader, who was a frequent visitor at Waddesdon recalled the ritual exchange between servant and guests in the mornings:

"Which will you have, sir – tea, coffee, or chocolate?"
"Tea."
"What kind of tea, sir – China, India or Ceylon?"
"India."
"What will you take with it, sir – cream, milk or lemon?"
"Milk."
"What kind of milk, sir – Jersey, Guernsey or Alderney?"
"I confess," added Asquith, "I should have been tempted to reply 'Sark'." [13]

And he would almost certainly have got it.

Besides the establishments at Mentmore, Halton and Waddesdon, the houses kept at Tring, Wing and Aston Clinton by Lionel, Leopold and Sir Anthony respectively, were comparatively humble. Halton and Waddesdon could in no sense be thought of as country retreats. They were Mayfair *alfresco*, and whenever Alfred or Ferdy travelled down to Bucks they often brought London with them, either in special trains, or in long gilded convoys of carriages. Alfred in particular had little interest in or patience for rural pursuits. He was small, delicately formed, immaculately attired, aristocratic and urbane to the point of being unreal. He seemed to gaze a trifle disdainfully at the world through hooded, sleepy eyes, not quite knowing what to make of it, and painfully anxious not to get too deeply involved in it. He gave immense sums of money to Jewish refugees, but shuddered at the thought of any contact with them, and generous though he was he probably gave more to the rich than the poor.

If Alfred found an interest in a subject he allowed no expense to stand in his way. If he was interested in animals, he maintained his own private circus; if interested in music, he maintained a private orchestra. He kept a box at Covent Garden, but he would often engage its principal singers to perform at his own private *soirées* at Halton and Seamore Place.

One is tempted to dismiss Alfred as an incorrigible dilettante, but there was nothing dilettantish about his role at New Court. He may not have been as dedicated to the bank as other members of his family, but he had a thorough understanding of the operations of the money market and was an astute financier. He was the first Jewish director of the Bank of England, to which he was elected at the age of twenty-six but he was compelled to resign twenty-one years later after he scrutinised the account of one of the bank's clients who had sold him a painting, to see what the mark-up had been. (One is surprised that he did not look into the account *before* he bought the painting.)

Alfred never sat in the House of Commons – an election, presumably, would have exposed him to excessive contact with the masses – but he was interested in politics, and was on close terms with many of the leading statesmen of his day.

In common with his brothers, he was exceptionally well informed about the course of international events, and like them was disturbed at the growing rivalry between Britain and Germany, for he believed that the peace of Europe rested on an Anglo-German rapprochement. Possessing important contacts both in London and Berlin, he was able to use his influence to arrange informal meetings between senior British and German officials. These led in February 1898 to a round table conference at Halton attended by Arthur Balfour, the foreign secretary, Joseph Chamberlain, the Colonial Secretary, and Count Hertzfeld, the German ambassador.

"Alfred," wrote Balfour to the Prime Minister, Lord Salisbury, "abandoned his dining-room to us and provided a sumptuous 'déjeuner', between the courses of which there was an infinity of talk. . . ."[14]

Further meetings took place at Halton or at Seamore Place, though Alfred himself was rarely a party to the conversations. He was content to act as honest broker cum *maître d'hôtel*.

But the course of German policy, with its shifts and prevarications, made the whole effort futile.

"Joe [Chamberlain] who dined with me is quite disheartened," wrote Alfred in May 1901. "He will have nothing more to do with the people in Berlin. If they are so short-sighted, says he, as not to be able to see that the whole new world system depends upon it [an Anglo-German alliance], then there is nothing to be done for them."[15]

The war brought Alfred's rarefied universe to an end.

He placed Halton at the disposal of the Government, and allowed Field Marshal Lord Kitchener to use Seamore Place almost as a second home. The magnificent beechwoods surrounding his estate were cut down for use as pit-props in the trenches.

Alfred never married and when he died in January 1918, he appears to have left a little something for everyone. Halton was left to his nephew Lionel. He left Sir Ernest Cassel a pair of Louis XV lights, the Earl of Ripon, "my walking stick with bloodstone knob monogram in gold", £10,000 to Lady Curzon and each of her two sons, and £5,000 to her daughter; to Sir Philip Sassoon a Velazquez painting; £25,000 to Lord Porchester and Lady Evelyn Herbert, and sundry gifts to Lady Ripon, Lady Arlington, Lady Rocksavage, the Countess of Gosport and Mrs Asquith. Seamore Place and the bulk of his £2,500,000 estate went to Almina, Countess of Caernarvon. Almina was his natural daughter.

Alfred had two brothers, Nathaniel and Leopold. Leo was the younger, the spoilt child of an adoring mother. He was an exquisite infant and Mrs Disraeli was quite overcome by his appearance. "My dear," she exclaimed, "that beautiful baby may be the future Messiah."[16] Being a Rothschild was enough for a start.

His father left him Gunnersbury Park and a rambling farmhouse at Ascott Wing near Leighton Buzzard, which with modifications and extensions became a stately manor. He acquired a town house by the family enclave at 5 Hamilton Place, and he bought Palace House, Newmarket to be well placed for the races. He was one of the most eligible bachelors of his generation and various cousins and aunts joined in the usual conspiracies to get him married, without success. He would never marry, he said, until he found someone "as beautiful and accomplished as Mrs Arthur Sassoon" [17] They at once took him at his word and introduced him to Mrs Sassoon's sister, Marie.

The meeting was organised by Leo's cousins Constance (a daughter of Sir Anthony) and Hannah (the daughter of Baron Mayer), aided and abetted by Mrs Sassoon herself.

Marie was a member of a well-known Italian Jewish family, the Perugias, and was almost as beautiful as her sister. She was a petite, delicate-looking, sensitive woman, rather nervous of country pursuits and horses, while Leo was a bucolic squire who spoke, lived and dreamed horses. She was coaxed into taking riding lessons – a Rothschild was worth a fall – and casually introduced to Leo at a meet near Leighton Buzzard. This meeting led to others, not all of them on horseback. Leo showed her his kennels, his stables, and gave her a horse. Eventually he proposed. She was eighteen, he was twice her age, but it proved to be an enduring and happy marriage.

The wedding took place in the Central Synagogue, Great Portland Street, in January 1881 during one of the worst blizzards of the century. The Prince of Wales and Lord Rosebery were among the guests and sat with Alfred and Nathaniel in the Wardens' Box traditionally occupied by the synagogue elders. The aged Disraeli was prevented by the weather from getting to the religious ceremony, but arrived blue-nosed and breathless at the reception held in Arthur Sassoon's house in Albert Gate. He toasted the prince in champagne, who in turn toasted the health of bride and groom. Disraeli wrote to Leo to congratulate him on his choice, adding: "I have always been of the opinion that there cannot be too many Rothschilds."

Leo was the most accessible of the three brothers. Nathaniel was too eminent and preoccupied, Alfred too aloof. Leo was the people's baron, generous like most of the Rothschilds, but unlike them, involved in the lives of the people he helped. In 1912 a madman who felt the Rothschilds owed him a living tried to kill him, and thereafter Leo was somewhat more withdrawn. He was a model landlord, as were his brothers, and converted Ascott Wing into a model village. Where a Rothschild lived there was never unemployment or want.

He was the most tender-hearted of men. "I have sometimes been taken in," he confessed, "but I always felt that I had the best of the transaction, and I have never regretted my being mistaken."

But what kept him in the public eye and public imagination was his reputation as a sportsman. His uncle Baron Mayer had made the Rothschild colours famous on every major course in the land. Leo became one of the leading breeders of thoroughbreds in the country. He won the Derby in 1879 with a comparatively unknown horse called Sir Bevvys, which ambled home in one of the longest times ever taken by a Derby winner – three minutes two seconds. A few routine bets at heavy odds brought him in £50,000.

His most famous, though possible most disappointing horse, was St Frusquin, son of St Simon. In 1895, in his first appearance as a two-year-old, St Frusquin carried all before him winning the Royal Plate at Kempton Park, the Sandringham Gold Cup, the Chesterfield Stakes at Newmarket, and the Middle Park Plate and the Dewhurst Plate, both at Kempton Park. In the following year he carried off the Two Thousand Guineas and on being entered for the Derby was booked as the favourite at 13-8. But a comparatively unknown runner, Persimmon, came first. If Persimmon was a dark horse, his owner, the Prince of Wales, was not, and it was widely suggested that the other horses were loyally held back to let the royal runner win. The two horses met again shortly after at the Prince of Wales Stakes and St Frusquin won by half a length. In that year, 1896, Leo headed the list of winning owners with £46,766 in stakes.

St Frusquin could not maintain his pace and was retired to stud.

Marie had him modelled by Lutiger and cast in silver by Fabergé as a birthday present for her husband.

1898 was another triumphal year for Leo when his winnings totalled £40,000 but he did not win the Derby again till 1904. It seemed as if the very heavens intervened to compensate him for his disappointment in 1896. The thunder crashed, the lightning flashed, and the rain fell in great torrents as if the clouds had come away from their hinges. But St Amant, his eyes in blinkers, ran on, treating the elements as if they were cheering bystanders, and on past the winning post. Leo, equally mindless of the deluge, rushed out to greet him in his immaculate topper and frock-coat and was drenched to the skin.

The historian, Dr Cecil Roth, in an otherwise balanced study of the Rothschilds, wrote rhapsodically about Leo, a shortish, robust figure, with kindly, smiling eyes, and white billowy moustache:

> —the body in which there beat the most generous heart in England. All succumbed to that charm – associates and subordinates and rulers and tradesmen and children and the most casual acquaintances. It could have been said of him as truly as it was of a kinsman and contemporary:
>> Of men like you
>> Earth holds but few:
>> An angel – with
>> A revenue.[18]

CHAPTER 13

New Court

There is no official history of the Rothschilds and no historian has ever had access to the archives at New Court. The family has a passion for secrecy which, if anything, has helped to swell the Rothschild legend, but one reason for its fantastic success is fairly well known. In the course of the nineteenth century it produced at least one financial genius per generation. Thereafter it managed to make do with competence, and sometimes not even that.

First came Nathan, then Lionel, and finally Nathaniel. Between them they spanned the century from Waterloo till World War I. When the lights went out in Europe in 1914 they did not quite leave the Rothschilds in darkness, but the particular circumstances in which they flourished and prospered were no more.

Britain had her spasms of civil commotion in the nineteenth century, and there was, of course, always trouble in Ireland; but Britain was an island of tranquillity compared to Europe and the Americas, and being rich grew richer still. If a nation wanted a loan to bring order out of chaos to finance railways, to build new industries or to pay for the great volume of manufactured goods she brought in from Britain, it was to London that she inevitably turned for a loan, and usually, to the London Rothschilds. Between 1815 and 1914 N. M. Rothschild & Sons handed eighteen government loans worth £1,600,000,000.[1]

Few City bankers could as yet organise the vast amount necessary for state loans, and arrange the movement of great blocks of capital without upsetting the Exchanges. When the Government abolished slavery in the British empire in 1833, for example, £20,000,000 had to be found as compensation to slave owners, and the whole funding operation was undertaken by Rothschilds.

In 1839 Lionel floated a massive loan for America and in 1845 he mobilised British capital to finance the French Great Northern Railway. In 1846 he formed the 'British Relief Association Fund'[2] at New Court to help the victims of the Irish famine, and in the following year joined with Barings to raise £8,000,000 for the Irish Famine Loan (and waived his usual commission). In 1854 he floated a £16,000,000 loan to finance the Crimean War, and in 1871 raised £100,000,000 to help France pay her war indemnity to Prussia. He was Imperial Crown Agent for Russia in London for over twenty years and organised a constant flow of British capital to St Petersburg, but in 1861 he declined to take up a Russian loan after her brutal suppression of an uprising in Poland and his special relationship with the Romanovs ended.

In 1875 came the most memorable *coup* in the history of the bank. The sum involved was, in Rothschild terms, not great, but the consequences were tremendous.

The Suez Canal had been formally opened five years earlier, and important as it was to international trade, it was even more important to the defence of the empire, but most of the shares of the company were in French hands. In 1873 the company ran into financial difficulties and Disraeli dispatched Nathaniel de Rothschild to Paris to see if he could acquire a block of the shares. There were more than financial interests involved, however, and Nathaniel returned empty-handed.[3]

Then in 1875 came rumours that the near-bankrupt Khedive of Egypt, who owned 177,000 of the 400,000 company shares, was looking for a buyer. Disraeli first heard of it at Lionel's (where, as he once observed, "there is ever something to learn, and somebody distinguished to meet")[4] and decided to act at once. "'Tis an affair of millions," he wrote to the queen, "about four at least; but would give the possessor an immense, not to say preponderating influence in the management of the Canal".[5] He quickly got his Cabinet colleagues to agree in principle to the purchase. Parliament, which alone could have voted the necessary funds, was not sitting; there was, he felt, only one alternative ready source of money – N. M. Rothschild & Sons.

Cory, Disraeli's secretary, was sent to New Court and he left a colourful account of what followed:

How much, he was asked, was needed?

Four million pounds.

When?

Tomorrow.

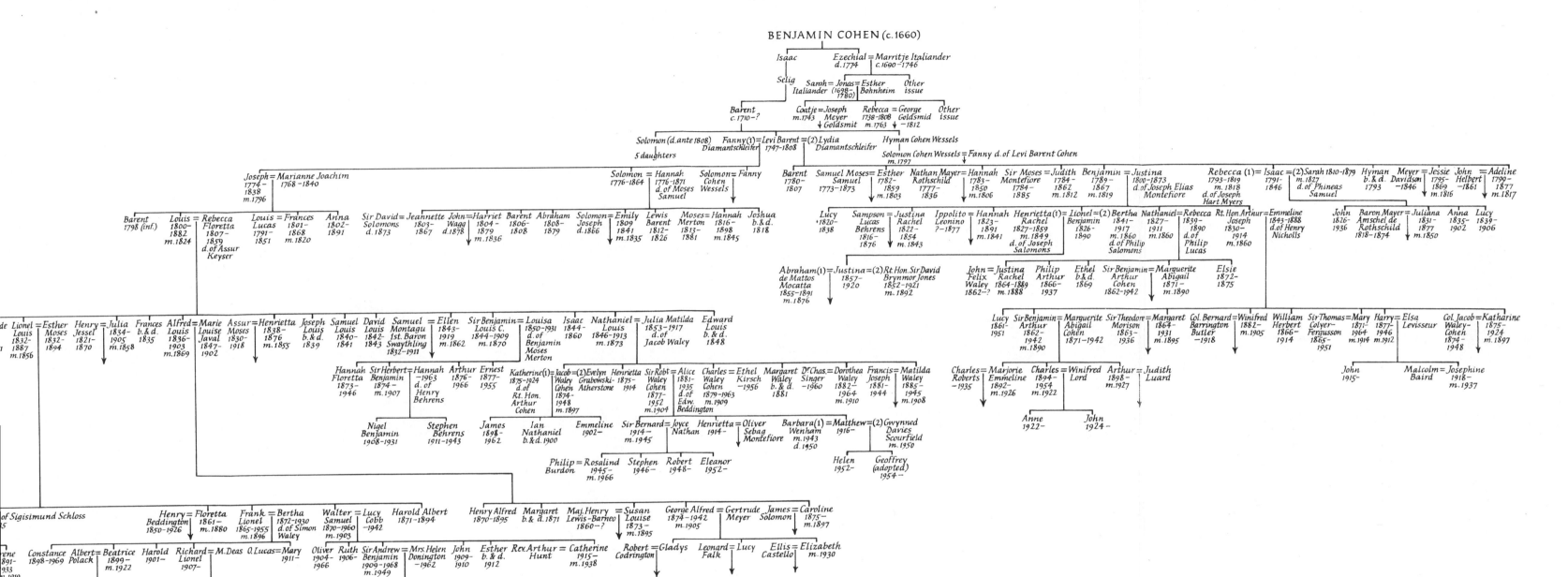

BENJAMIN COHEN (c.1660)

Lionel, fingering a muscatel grape, popped it into his mouth, and spat out the skin.

"What is your security?" he asked.

"The British Government."

"You shall have it."[6]

The meeting took place on November 18. On November 23, terms were settled with the Khedive. On December 1 he received the first instalment of £2,000,000, a third £1,000,000 on December 16 and the fourth on January 5.

The deal represented a personal triumph for Disraeli and his official report to the queen crackled with elation:

> It is just settled; you have it, Madam. . . . Four millions sterling! And almost immediately. There was only one firm that could do it – Rothschilds. They behaved admirably; advanced the money at a low rate, and the entire interest of the Khedive is now yours, Madam.[7]

Parliament was delighted with the purchase, though not every M.P. believed that the rate of interest was low. Lionel charged a commission of 2½% on the transaction, or about £100,000. Parliament voted the money on February 20 which meant that the interest worked out at about 13% per annum, this on the security of the richest state in the world. Various critics suggested that the Bank of England should have been approached for the loan, but it is doubtful whether it had the power to lend money in this way without the sanction of Parliament, and speed was essential because the French too were anxious to get hold of the shares.

Lionel in self-defence argued that the mobilisation of such a sum might have prevented his bank from satisfying the needs of regular clients, and unforeseen events could have forced up the price of money beyond the interest charged. The Rothschilds alone, moreover, had perfected ways of moving so vast a sum in so short a time without affecting the exchanges, and he therefore felt that the Government had received good value for money. Apart from the political advantages of the purchase, it proved to be, in plain commercial terms, a good buy. Disraeli paid £22. 10. 4d. per share. Within a month the price had risen to £34. 12. 6d.[8]

Lionel was the eldest of four brothers and outlived them all. Nathaniel, the third brother, was crippled in a riding accident and spent most of his time in Paris, an aesthete with a bottomless purse.

The other brothers remained rooted in England. All three were partners in the bank, but the main burden of work fell on Lionel.

In his earlier years he had shared something of the bucolic streak of Anthony and Mayer and loved a gallop on horseback across the Vale of Aylesbury. In later years, however, he was crippled with rheumatism and gout, and could not mount a horse and, indeed, could hardly move at all without grimacing with pain and gasping for breath. Towards the end of his life he was largely confined to a wheelchair, and his temperament, never particularly amiable, became explosive. His youngest daughter Evelina, who had made such a brilliant marriage and had been the source of so much hope and happiness, had died in childbirth in her twenty-first year. The large, unhappy face, with the protruding Rothschild lip and rim of white hair, seemed to shrivel and become unhappier still. His brothers died, Nathaniel in 1870, Mayer in 1874, Anthony in 1876.

Lionel continued a further three years, becoming more withdrawn, silent and morose, but his mind was still alert and his memory tenacious. He was at the bank on the morning of Friday, May 30, 1879, and in the afternoon left for his usual week-end at Gunnersbury. When he returned to Piccadilly on Sunday evening he was taken ill with a fierce spasm of gout. The next day, a Bank Holiday, he had an epileptic fit, sank into a coma and died the following morning.

He left £2,700,000 to be divided among his family, and a few words of admonition to his sons:

> . . . my last words are that they will be mindful of their duties towards God and towards all about them and that they will not forget the family union and friendship which has so much contributed towards placing us in the honourable position we now hold.

He was succeeded as head of the bank by his son Nathaniel, who figures in all the many books on the family as 'Natty'. He was generous and his benefactions were particularly numerous in the Jewish community which – with mass immigration from the pogrom-stricken areas of Russia and Poland – was in particular need. He was raised to the peerage in 1886, and when Jews consoled themselves with the expression, 'the Lord will provide', they meant Lord Rothschild. He had his principal country seat at Tring in a mansion which was once the home of Nell Gwyn (it is now a girls' school and one can still see her initials in the crevices). Here he established a private welfare state among villagers and tenants. "No one," wrote his niece, "was unemployed in the town because he took them forthwith onto his payroll and provided free medical treatment, a free reading-room, free nursing, free housing and an old age pension."[9]

He had kindly eyes set in an avuncular face, but his manner was abrupt to the point of rudeness. As he grew older he was spoken of as one of the rudest men in England.[10] He was taciturn, perhaps even shy, but in the main the brusqueness, so characteristic of his manner, grew out of a biting impatience. If he could dispose of fortunes at the wave of a hand, he grudged every wasted moment. Callers asking for a minute of his time would get a minute, that and no more. He was a miser for time and perfected a conveyor belt method of interviews by placing his callers in a succession of anterooms and disposing of them all on the trot from room to room.

He could not have got on particularly well with his brothers Alfred and Leo, who looked upon the calls of business as something which one fitted in between the more significant pleasures of life. He did not get on at all with his son Lionel Walter, whom he eventually disinherited.

The Hon. Lionel Walter Rothschild, born in 1868, was a frail, sickly child, who, it was feared, might not survive infancy. He was brought up like some exotic peach in his father's conservatory and was not allowed to be exposed to the rough-and-tumble of school friends and school play-grounds but was tutored at home. He grew up to be a burly giant, six foot three inches in height, with massive shoulders and weighing, in later life, over three hundred pounds. He had an impediment of speech which made it difficult to modulate his voice and he spoke either in a whisper or a roar. The total effect could be forbidding, even startling, but he was mild, gentle and modest. His lonely childhood had made him socially awkward and pathologically shy.

He was handsome in his youth and he exuded a virility which made him extremely attractive to women. He was a keen patron of the theatre and perhaps a keener patron of actresses.

His father felt that a Rothschild, especially of the English branch, should have his mind on higher things – like the bank.

Natty had built up N. M. Rothschild & Sons until it was the supreme merchant bank and he the supreme merchant banker in the City. He often figured in cartoons as the symbol of high finance and was quoted in the press as the voice of orthodox City opinion. He regarded his role at New Court almost as a sacred mission. To Lionel Walter it was a job, and a dull job at that and he would absent himself whenever he could.

The theatre claimed part of his time but his deepest passion was animals. He began collecting them while still only a child. As he grew older, he spent heavily on any animal that was unusual, exotic or big, especially big. He was, if one may coin a term, a gargantuaphile and put his collection to improbable uses. He went up to Cambridge with a flock of Kiwis. He once crossed Kensington Gore on a giant tortoise. At other times he harnessed an ostrich to a gig and travelled through Hyde Park in an open coach drawn by four zebras. He also kept butterflies, cranes, kangaroos, salamanders, anything which moved. In later life he applied method to his madness and brought together his collection in a natural history museum at Tring. In time this became a place of pilgrimage for naturalists from all over the world and today it attracts over 70,000 visitors a year.[11]

In 1893 he engaged Karl Jordan, a brilliant young zoologist from Germany as curator of his collection and they collaborated on several hundred scientific papers. What had begun as a hobby became his life's work and he acquired considerable standing among professional zoologists.

All this did not rehabilitate him in his father's eyes. He continued to neglect his work at the bank. In 1886 he succeeded his father as Liberal Unionist M.P. for Aylesbury (a family fief) but rarely attended sittings at the House. During his eleven years as an M.P. he spoke only once, a brief intervention on the Rickmansworth and Uxbridge Valley Water Bill.[12]

Nathaniel thought that his son's absence from the bank was due to his presence in the House, and a very diligent member he seemed to be; the true facts eventually emerged and in 1908 he was dismissed from New Court. Today he is best remembered for his work in connection with the Balfour Declaration.

The Cousinhood, and the Rothschilds in particular, were anti-Zionist almost to a man. Lionel Walter was one of the few exceptions, and as he was not merely a Rothschild, but, in 1915 he succeeded his father to the peerage and was head of the family, *the* Rothschild, his association with Zionism gave an immense boost to the Zionist movement. He was not the sort of person to be ignited by nationalist ideas, and his sudden conversion may seem strange at first sight, but his niece, Dr Miriam Rothschild, who knew him well, explains that numerous anti-Semitic incidents before and during the war made him pessimistic about the future of European Jewry. This, and a meeting with the Zionist leader, Chaim Weizmann, convinced him that the only solution to the Jewish problem lay in a Jewish State.[13] He took part in the negotiations leading up to the Balfour Declaration and when the Declaration was finally made, it was addressed not to the Chief Rabbi, nor Weizmann, but to Walter at his home in 148 Piccadilly.

Nahum Sokolow, one of Weizmann's colleagues, later observed that the Declaration had been "sent to the Lord and not to the Jewish people because they had no address, whereas the Lord had a very fine one."[14] The lord was not amused.

"In the early days," wrote Dr Rothschild, "he dutifully took the chair at the large Zionist thanksgiving meetings, but now feeling that their first and principal objective had been achieved, he turned his broad back on the world of quarrelling, intriguing politicians, and retired once again to his ivory tower at Tring, to his books and his specimens and another unbroken spell of twenty years of scientific research."[15] He died tragically, his vast frame paralysed from the waist down, and racked with cancer.

Lionel's youngest brother Charles, who was also a keen naturalist, centred his researches on entomology; but he was a diligent and conscientious young man and did not forsake the bank for his fleas. He developed the Rothschild gold refinery and on the death of Natty he became senior partner at the bank. Two years later he contacted sleepy sickness which was then incurable and in 1923, during a bout of high fever and depression, he took his own life. He was forty-six.

The loss to New Court was irreparable. The bank now devolved into the hands of Leo's two sons, Lionel and Anthony, and entered upon a period of prolonged and contented slumber.

But it was hardly a hive of activity even during the last years of Natty's reign.

In 1886 Natty, who sat as Liberal M.P. for Aylesbury, was elevated to the peerage on the recommendation of Gladstone. When the Liberals split over Gladstone's Bill to give home rule to Ireland, he joined the Liberal Unionists, the anti-home-rule faction, and gradually drifted with them into the Tory party. He shared the simple patriotism, one might even call it jingoism, of the Cousinhood, and he was too new an eminence to regard with equanimity what looked like the disintegration of the United Kingdom. He was in any case moving towards the right and the peerage accelerated the process. He opposed death duties, old age pensions, women's suffrage, almost every progressive measure of his day. In 1909, Lloyd George as Chancellor of the Exchequer imposed a series of new taxes, which were hardly punitive by today's standards; income tax was raised from 1s. to 1s. 2d in the pound and a super tax of 6d in the pound was introduced on incomes above £5,000. Natty was incensed and addressed a rally of a thousand City merchants to protest against what he called the 'Robber's Budget'.

This gave Lloyd George the perfect opening, with Natty as the perfect occasion. He recalled a meeting presided over by Natty earlier in the year at which he had demanded that eight new Dreadnoughts be laid down without delay. 'We want eight, and we can't wait' was the slogan. The Government ordered four, and now, said Lloyd George, Rothschild didn't even want to pay for them. Lord Rothschild's ancestors, he said, had had to make bricks without straw, but that was nothing compared to making Dreadnoughts without money. When the laughter subsided, he turned to his main point:

> Now we are not to have Temperance Reform in this country. Why? Because Lord Rothschild has sent a circular to the Peers to say so. We must not have Estate Duties, and a Super Tax. Why? Because Lord Rothschild signed a protest on behalf of the bankers to say that he would not stand it. We must not have Tax on Reversions. Why? Because Lord Rothschild, as chairman of an insurance company, said it would not do. We must not put a Tax on Undeveloped Land. Why? Because Lord Rothschild is chairman of an industrial dwellings company. We ought not to have old age pensions. Because Lord Rothschild is chairman of a committee which says it can't be done. Is Lord Rothschild the Dictator of this country? Are we to have all the way of reform, financial and social, blocked simply by a notice board:
>
>
>
> NO THOROUGHFARE
> by order of Nathaniel Rothschild[16]
>
>

Lloyd George was always ready to forgive his victims, and in 1914 he appointed Natty as one of his advisers on financing the war effort.[17]

Natty was just as conservative in his conduct of the bank as he was in his politics, although it could be said that external circumstances were perhaps to blame.

At the end of 1890 a rumour began to circulate in the City which informed opinion at first refused to believe. But it persisted.

"Went to the Bank," noted Lord Goschen, the Chancellor of the Exchequer, in his diary, "things queer! Some of the first houses talked about."[18] A few days later, on November 10, he was again in the Bank and found Lidderdale, the Governor, "in a dreadful state of anxiety".[19]

The anxiety spread, rumour piled on rumour. There were hurried comings and goings between the Bank and the Treasury, and long confabulations behind locked doors. On November 14 a frantic broker burst into Lidderdale's room, shouting: "Can't you do something or say something to relieve people's minds: they have made up their minds that something awful is up and they are talking of the very highest names" – his voice went hoarse and he raised his arms – "*the very highest*".[20]

They were talking of Barings, a name sufficiently famous to have passed into Gilbert and Sullivan's *Iolanthe*:

> . . . The shares were a penny
> And ever so many
> Were taken by Rothschild and Baring . . .

Rothschilds and Barings had divided up much of South America between them, with the former taking Brazil and Chile as their particular fiefs, and the latter the Argentine and Uruguay. Barings proved to be a little too anxious to do business, underwrote loans without fully examining their prospects and were left holding immence blocks of shares and this coincided with the withdrawal of funds by some large clients. There is nothing like a rumour of difficulties to create actual difficulties. Other clients rushed in to redeem their bills and there were fears for a time that Barings might close its doors.

Lidderdale acted at once, brought together an emergency committee under Natty who used his connections with the Paris Rothschilds to bring in £3,000,000 in gold from France. A further £1,500,000 was brought in from Russia, and Barings were underpinned with an emergency loan to which the Bank of England contributed £1,000,000, Rothschilds £500,000, Glyn, Mills £500,000, and various other merchant banks £1,250,000, and the next day *The Times* was able to report that 'the worst was over'.[21] The crisis passed. The City could breathe again. Within four years Barings paid off all its debts without defaulting on a penny.

Lidderdale in a letter paid generous tribute to Natty for his help in saving a firm which had always been a rival, and sometimes a hostile rival:

> When you thank the Bank of England, it is very important to bear in mind the willing and cheerful aid that we have received from others, in the first place from Lord Rothschild, whose influence with the Bank of France was of such assistance to us in obtaining those means without which we could not have rendered the aid we were enabled to give.[22]

The experience of that crisis must have added to Natty's natural wariness. Barings was reconstructed and converted into a limited liability company. Rothschild continued as a partnership. Natty felt it could take no chance and took none. N. M. Rothschild & Sons became a by-word for caution.

"The London House enjoys great prestige," wrote the German Ambassador to Britain in 1903, "but for many years no new business has come its way, and it contents itself with safe investment of its wealth."[23] It was beginning to act as if it was too grand and well-established to do business at all.

New Court at this time is charmingly recorded in Ronald Palin's *Rothschild Relish*. Mr Palin, who recently retired as secretary of the bank, entered New Court in 1925, some ten years after the death of Natty and his brothers, but their ghosts still seemed to hover about the place and memories of their day were still in circulation.

> Leopold arrived first about eleven o'clock, lunched at half past one and left about five. Alfred did not turn up until two o'clock or later, lunched between half past three and four o'clock and after his brother's departure often fell asleep on the leather-covered sofa.[24]

There is no record of the sort of hours Natty kept, but he was a public figure in great demand both at City gatherings and as the lay head of the Jewish community. He also took a considerable interest in his estates, and was a breeder of prize Jersey cattle. The routine business of the firm was carried out by about a hundred clerks and one gets the impression from Mr Palin's account that the company had reached a stage where things could not go wrong, for somewhere beyond the famous Partners' Room, with its ornate panelling, large fire places, heavy couches, huge desks and portraits of partners past, there was a Senior Partner on High watching over the affairs of N. M. Rothschild & Sons.

CHAPTER 14

Ladies in Retirement

Of all the mansions erected by the Rothschilds in the Chilterns there was only one which looked and felt like a home, Sir Anthony's two-storey house at Aston Clinton. It was a comparatively modest dwelling, of unremarkable but solid design. It was the sort of house which might have been occupied by any modestly prosperous merchant, and, if it was not entirely in keeping with what Sir Anthony might have wished, it reflected something of the retiring disposition of Lady Rothschild.

Louise Rothschild was a Montefiore, a niece of Sir Moses, and she displayed many of his characteristics, personal piety, a deep concern for the Jewish people, an affection for family life, a deep social conscience and firmness of purpose. From an early age she kept a journal in which she mapped out her guide lines in life.

At eighteen she wrote:

> I must never allow myself any preferences or antipathies which are not approved of by my conscience and reason. I must never permit myself to have any affection unfounded on esteem, and must never, either from self-interest, caprice or thoughtlessness demonstrate more affection than I really feel.[1]

Sir Anthony fitted entirely into her somewhat stringent terms of reference. He was a cousin, a Rothschild, and a good man in the simple sense of the term, kindly, generous, genial, affectionate.

At the time of their engagement Anthony was working in the Paris branch of the bank and their exchange of letters suggests that Louise was well able to contain her feelings. His letters are warm, spontaneous, hers reserved and chilly, for she may have disciplined herself to the point where she could no longer display affection even where she wished.

In 1840, on the eve of her marriage, when she was nineteen, we find her planning her days ahead:

MONDAY

Household and newspapers . . .	till ½ past 10.	
A chapter of Locke on the Human understanding .	. 11	
Drawing	. 1	
New Publications	. ½ past 1	
Geography	. 3	
Italian or German	. 4	2

And so on for the entire week, except Saturday, which she set apart as the Sabbath to be spent in religious devotions and serious study. She was not, even when in London, a frequent visitor to synagogue, for she did not travel on the Sabbath, and as her daughter adds, "she could not bear the physical fatigue of a long walk, followed by a lengthy and somewhat tiring service".

She therefore organised a form of service of her own and spent many hours in reading sermons. She appeared to prefer the works of Christian divines to Jewish ones, and took their message seriously:

> In order to regulate my conduct rightly, I must diligently study the Word of God, and pray earnestly for the knowledge of my duties and the strength to fulfil them, and be vigilant in constant self-examination. My present duties are to give an example of virtue and piety; to influence, if possible, the conduct of those around me; to make my husband as happy as lies in my power, fulfilling his desires and in all things giving way to his wishes; to employ industry, attention and judgement in directing these persons and affairs which are under my control. My first object now must no longer be simply to *know*, but to make use, and the best use, of that which I know; to advance the happiness and comfort of all those around us.[3]

Anthony left the search for a house to Louise, warning her that they "must not be too near any person. Our family is large and it will be requisite for us to live for ourselves."[4] In particular he urged her to avoid Piccadilly where his brothers lived, or Stanhope Street, the home of his mother, but in the event they settled upon Grosvenor Place, which was no distance from either. It was there that their two children were born, Constance in 1843 and Annie in 1844.

In 1847 Anthony was created a baronet and six years later he bought Aston Clinton.

"You will probably perceive, my dear Louise," Anthony warned her before their marriage, "that all the family are complete slaves to their business."[5]

This may have been true in the case of his brother Lionel; it was an exaggeration in his own case, for he found ample time for riding, hunting, shooting. He and his brothers were members of the Old Berkeley Hunt near Mentmore, and as fox hunting often meant a blank day, they resorted to stag-hunting which almost always assured a run. The kennels were at Mentmore and the Rothschilds financed the hunt. It met every Monday and Thursday and attracted a large following. As Sir Anthony rarely attended to company affairs on the Sabbath, and as New Court was closed on the Sunday, his slavery to business was far from complete.

Sir Anthony was a happy, jovial man, who made friends easily and enjoyed every sort of company. Louise was frail, delicate, shy and tended to shrink at the very thought of large gatherings. In February 1848, after a lavish dinner at Lionel's she noted sadly in her journal:

Madame Nath (her sister-in-law) looked very well, highborn, graceful, and picturesque. I was tired and felt humbled as I often do in society from comparison.[6]

She loathed such dinners but felt compelled by her position not only to participate in them, but to emulate them, and sat there, an agitated little soul among her glittering guests:

Today we have our first grand dinner party – our first grand bore. I am nervous and fidgety, principally because the rooms are so smart – much too smart for my taste. What trouble we take, what expense we incur for the so-called pleasures of society! How much more real pleasure it would give one to perform an act of generosity or to make, even, a kindly present, but I cannot follow my own inclination in this matter, and strange to say, I, who am so anti-luxurious in tastes and habits am made to appear fond of show and glitter. That is one of my vexations. . . .[7]

She was upset not merely by the extravagance of such occasions, but the vanity of them. She felt people were created for higher things. This did not mean that she abhorred all company. She spent much of her time among books and bookmen, and Aston Clinton saw a continuing succession of literary figures which included Thackeray and Matthew Arnold. She liked her gatherings to be small, informal, intimate and select. At a formal occasion she could feel ill at ease even among writers: "I sat between Mr Thackeray and Mr Charles Villiers! They were most amusing and good natured, but when I am most anxious to become least stupid I am often most so, and that was the case then."[8]

But Thackeray in fact had the highest opinion of Lady Rothschild, and in *Pendennis* one finds this almost devotional picture of her:

> I saw a Jewish lady only yesterday with a child on her knee, and from whose face towards the child there shone a sweetness so angelical that it seemed to form a sort of glory round both. I protest I could have knelt before her. . . .[9]

Both Sir Anthony and Lady Rothschild took their duties to their tenants, the village and the neighbourhood seriously, and Lady Rothschild acted as sort of almoner at large. She would call on the villagers at their homes and encouraged her daughters to do the same. On one occasion they found a young woman nursing a young baby. And how old is the infant? she was asked.

"Four months."
"And how long have you been married?"
"Half a year."[10]

Exeunt her ladyship and daughters.

She made education her particular concern, and her daughters shared her interests. When Constance was a small girl her fond father asked what she would like for a birthday present. "An infants' school," she said at once, and an infants' school she got. He also built a girls' school in the village (this was of course before education was made generally available by the 1870 Education Act). The two buildings, in what might be called pocket-Gothic, still stand on either side of the main village street.[11] The village hall, which is also still in use, was built by Lady Rothschild in 1884 as a memorial to her husband.

Constance and Annie taught at the schools from time to time. They also instituted 'penny readings' and amateur theatricals for the benefit of the villagers, and Lady Rothschild wrote a brief fantasy called 'A Dream' for the opening of the village hall. It was a sermonette, somewhat heavy with symbolism, but contrived with some delicacy and charm.[12] It is not known how the villagers took it.

Lady Rothschild's bookish disposition notwithstanding, the household was not a sedate one. The two daughters were a lively pair. There was a constant traffic of governesses and tutors, and men-servants and maid-servants. There was also a menagerie of dogs, black and tan terriers, Scotch terriers, pugs, spaniels, dachshunds, in teeming, snarling profusion. Lady Rothschild was in particular attached to a tiny Yorkshire terrier called Elfie, constant companion of her old age, and when he was killed in an accident she was overwhelmed with grief:

My darling Elfie is to be put in her last resting-place under the big yew-tree today. How I shall miss her – that constant little friend. Alas! Alas! To know I shall never see her again.[13]

The flow of guests was unending. Mrs Disraeli might drop in unannounced at almost any time of the day or night, and her ceaseless prattle, her awry wig, her flamboyant manner caused some amusement among the younger members of the family. But she was viewed with affection by Lady Rothschild: "Mrs Disraeli . . . possesses good powers of observation; strange that she should be blind to her own absurdities; however, notwithstanding them all, I like her, for she has a warm, true heart."

She could not say the same of Disraeli and believed "his own elevation has been his only aim".[14] Dizzy, on the other hand, liked and admired Lady Rothschild and had the warmest regard for her husband, "a thoroughly good fellow, the most genial being I ever knew, the most kind-hearted and most generous".[15]

Lady Rothschild's distrust of Dizzy was not shared by other members of the family, and he was virtually an honorary Rothschild. Hughenden was hardly more than twenty miles from any of the Rothschild estates, and only seventeen miles from Aston Clinton. Exchange visits were therefore frequent. Constance retained a clear memory of the statesman among the woods and fields of Hughenden:

How he loved the place! And how he tried to act up to the character he had imposed upon himself, that of the country gentleman! For dressed in his velveteen coat, his leather leggings, his soft felt hat, and carrying his little hatchet, for relieving the bark of trees from the encroaching ivy, in one of those white hands, which probably hitherto had never held anything heavier than a pen, Mr Disraeli was *the Squire*. . . .[16]

In its way it would not have been an imperfect picture of her father.

Mr and Mrs Gladstone stayed twice at Aston Clinton. On the second occasion Constance, who was by then a married woman, spent long hours walking in the garden with Mr Gladstone, discussing the Bible, the Apocrypha, and the hereafter. With the Disraelis the talk was invariably of the here and now.

The Prince of Wales came for a short visit in 1873 and spent much of his stay playing whist. In the following year his brother the Duke of Cambridge, accompanied by the Crown Prince of Russia and a large entourage, came for a day's shooting.

Lady Rothschild, a devout woman, kept open house for clergymen of all denominations and they came in a constant succession, curates, vicars, deans, bishops. Rabbis came less frequently. As a rule, they stemmed from the lower middle class, while Anglican clergy were often to be found on the periphery at least of aristocracy. Even those of humbler origin were accepted members of the gentry; Rabbis were not. Her ladyship, moreover, did not fit happily into the Jewish religious establishment of which her husband was a pillar, possibly because she took religion more seriously than he did. In 1870 the major Ashkenzai synagogues in London had been brought together to form a United Synagogue under the presidency of Sir Anthony. Lady Rothschild occasionally, when in London, attended services, usually in the Central Synagogue, but left unedified:

> What a pity that our Service is not of that impressive, solemn kind that would claim the attention of all those who assist at it and leave some good thoughts with its hearers. It might be beautiful, whereas it is not only tedious but often ridiculous and in order to keep up any devotional feeling I am often compelled not to follow the English translation but to give quite a different meaning to the Hebrew. Is it not, however, a profanation of sacred things to read prayers which one feels to be absurd? We are indeed in much need of reform . . .[17]

Her daughter Constance shared her feelings:

> We started off for Synagogue, heard a bad service, horrible singing, inferior sermon.

Lady Rothschild took pains to give her daughters a sound Jewish education:

> . . . This morning I tried to give the children a little lesson in religion, but I found it very difficult to make it interesting to them. We have no books quite fitted for that purpose, all the Jewish Manuals are bad in my opinion, being written in too concise a manner with too many long, fine words and here and there a slight colouring of superstition.[18]

She found it difficult to instruct them in Jewish customs and laws, many of which she felt were 'useless' and 'obsolete', but with the help of Dr Kalisch, a young German-born tutor, she was able to impart a considerable knowledge of the Bible and Jewish history.

The upbringing of the two sisters was almost stiflingly sheltered. They could not walk without company, ride without grooms, attend a dance without chaperones. As they grew older their mother became understandably concerned about their future. Rothschilds, wherever possible, married Rothschilds, and when none was available one looked for a Montefiore, a Cohen, a Goldsmid. Later generations of Rothschilds were less fecund than the earlier ones, and daughters tended to predominate. Carl Rothschild of Frankfurt had seven daughters, almost enough for the needs of an entire generation of male heirs. There were few cousins or second cousins available and before Lady Rothschild was the awful example of her sister-in-law Hannah.

Hannah Mayer, a daughter of Nathan Rothschild, a small, pretty, strong-willed girl, fell in love with Henry Fitzroy, a brother of Lord Southampton. There was no question of getting married while her father was alive, but in 1839 when he was safely in his grave, and against the wishes of her mother, she married in church and out of the faith. There was much head-shaking in the family, and even twenty years later when Hannah lost a young son, Annie, then fourteen years old could write:

> I cannot help thinking that all the misfortune and distress which have overwhelmed poor Aunt Hannah Mayer have been a punishment for having deserted the faith of her fathers and for having married without her mother's consent.[19]

Hannah had little patience or love for Jews or Judaism and if she had not married Fitzroy she would have found some other means of dissociating herself from both. Annie and Constance were in their own peculiar way staunch daughters of Israel, but even with them the worst could happen, and Lady Rothschild, as a cousin noted, became 'white as a ghost' with anxiety about their future.

"How extraordinary it would be if we both married Christians",[20] wrote Constance. They both did, and it would have been extraordinary if they had not. They very rarely met a Jew outside the family, and all their close friends were, with one exception, Christian. They were aware of course of the family's feeling of the matter, and in their earlier years they turned down one suitor after another, a lord, a curate, a Russian prince, and others.

As they grew older their attitude, perhaps understandably, slackened. Both of the girls were intelligent, vivacious and charming. Neither of them was unattractive, but they were not raging beauties. In 1869 when Annie was twenty-five, an Italian marquis proposed to her. Lady Rothschild had by then all but reconciled herself to the inevitable and raised no objections, but Sir Anthony, after hurried consultations with his brother, declared that the marriage could not take place. Annie who could not have been particularly excited by the proposal in any case, bowed to his wish.

Annie was approaching thirty, when the situation repeated itself, her suitor this time was an English aristocrat, the Hon. Eliot Yorke, a son of Lord Hardwicke. They had met during a house party at Wimpole Hall, the seat of the Yorke family.

Eliot was a debonair young man of striking appearance, but of less striking ability, and, as the younger son of a peer, his means were limited. In 1858 when one of H.M. Commissioners for Excise died he wrote to Disraeli to apply for the post. It would, he wrote, "make me a comfortable man for the rest of my life. . . ."[21] Annie was to do that more adequately.

Lord Hardwicke, to all appearances at least, was happy with the match:

My Dear Sir Anthony,
    I am informed that my son Eliot and your daughter Annie are deeply attached, and my consent is asked for a marriage.
    I think it is most fortunate that I and my dear wife are intimately acquainted with you and your family, I am most drawn to you personally and have great love for you, Lady de Rothschild and your two daughters and may I therefore without further preamble give my consent to the union and can add that your child will be treated in our house as a daughter.[22]

Again there were anxious family confabulations. Again Annie's father went into a huddle at New Court and came back adamant that the marriage could not take place. Annie insisted that it would, and it did, but there was no question of her marrying out of the faith. The ceremony took place in a registry office in February 1873, followed by a sort of ecumenical religious service in Wimpole Hall. "Papa looked so sad and we all felt it dreadfully, Annie included," wrote Constance in her diary.[23]

Sir Anthony bought them a house at 17 Curzon Street, but they seem to have spent much of their short married life on a rented yacht, the *Garland*. At the end of 1873 Eliot was returned as Tory M.P. for Cambridgeshire (a Yorke family fief), but he made no impression in the House of Commons. He died five years later.

Constance in the meantime remained single. "An old Russian monster proposed to me," she noted, and of course turned him down. "But good heavens, where is the right one?" In 1874 he duly appeared in the person of the tall and beautiful Cyril Flower, a Cambridge friend of her cousin Leo. He was exquisitely mannered and exotically attired. An early admirer of Burne Jones, Millais and the pre-Raphaelites, he could have walked straight out of a pre-Raphaelite painting himself. At Harrow he had been the particular protégé of the Master, Dean Farrar, who later used him as the model for the hero of his celebrated *Eric, or Little by Little.*

"The more I see Flower," wrote a contemporary, "the more interesting he becomes as a psychological study." And he went on:

> He is the only instance with which I am acquainted of a man whom the whole world had agreed, with one consent, to pet, from Whewell (the Master of Trinity) to the white-aproned men who carry the baked meats from the kitchen on their heads; nobody can resist him. . . . Artists are perpetually painting him. Bootmakers call to borrow his boots as models. . . . In short he is an irresistible man. He is the only man who has some of the qualities of a charming woman, and that without a shade of effeminacy.. . .[24]

With the precedent of Annie before her, Connie, who was already thirty-four, experienced no difficulty in getting her mother's approval. Sir Anthony, moreover, was dead. The wedding was fixed for November 1877.

In October there was another Rothschild wedding where the bride married not only within the faith, but within the family. "Today Adele and Edmond are marrying," Louise noted wistfully in her diary, "what a different wedding from the one we are looking forward to. God help dear Connie, though so many condemn her."[25].

The ceremony was performed by Dean Farrar, but like her sister, Constance did not adopt the Christian faith. The Prince of Wales, who was among their mutual acquaintances told Flower, "You are marrying a person fit to be the Queen of England."

Flower and his brothers had been left a considerable slice of Battersea by their father, and he built street after street of drab working-class tenements naming – at his mother-in-law's request, one street after Dickens, another after Thackeray and a third after her uncle Sir Moses Montefiore.

Constance, who had a strong social conscience, had visions of being to the working men of Battersea what her mother was to the villagers of Aston Clinton:

> At the beginning of my married life I was disappointed that we did not settle down in Battersea amongst the working classes. I suggested making a 'House Beautiful' in that region, allowing of closer intercourse with and better knowledge of the men and women whose paths were so different from mine. . . . But it was not to be.[26]

Cyril, who was Liberal, did not carry his sympathies to the point of going native. He was attracted by a house on the Portman Estate on the site of what is now the Marble Arch Odeon. It was Surrey House, five storeys high, with a view of Hyde Park and beyond to the Surrey Hills. There was also space at the back for extensions. Messing about with houses seemed to be Cyril's principal occupation, and as his wife confessed, it proved to be, even by their standards, 'a very expensive amusement'.

Flower had inherited a considerable fortune, and Constance had been left £300,000 by her father. This was not the full extent of her fortune, for like other members of the Cousinhood, she was the beneficiary of innumerable trusts; but her funds were not infinite and inroads were being made upon them by her husband's extravagant tastes. "It was always the very best that he cared for; he was never content with anything short of that."[27]

He collected paintings and painters, and, by way of a minor item, acquired a black African servant named Abdul. (Eliot Yorke once came back from a voyage with a pig-tailed Chinaman in his baggage.)

He would have liked to collect homes, sighed for a villa above Florence, and seriously contemplated taking a lease of Desdemona's Palace on the Grand Canal in Venice. Constance watched him apprehensively among the villas and palazzos like a wife might watch a hard-drinking husband at large in a distillery, but she knew when to put her foot down and baulked of a home in Italy, tried to introduce Italy to their homes in London and Norfolk. The result, if expensive, was not entirely felicitous. Their seaside home, the Pleasaunce at Overstrand near Cromer in Norfolk still stands and one can see the results of his work which, even after the mellowing influence of eighty years, still verges on the horrific, a sedate cottage transformed by wealth into a grotesque folly. Yet the Pleasaunce was no misnomer, for the Flowers were very happy there amidst their dogs, and their many friends. They had pleasant neighbours, and in the summer an endless succession of visitors, George Meredith, Mrs Humphry Ward, Mrs Belloc Lowndes, Lord and Lady Curzon, the Princess of Wales. Lord Morley, who was almost accepted as a member of the family wrote:

> The happiest days of my life were passed in the early times of the Pleasaunce, delightful days of friendship, gaiety, reading, and talks of serious things.[28]

He later took a house nearby.

In 1880 when Cyril Flower was returned Liberal M.P. for Brecon, they leased a house in the town and Constance even tried to learn Welsh. He was a dedicated M.P. and took a personal interest in the lives of his constituents, helping them find jobs and on occasion advancing them considerable sums of money. In 1885 came a redivision of boundaries and the Brecon seat disappeared. He found another without difficulty, in South Bedfordshire, which was the fief of the Duke of Bedford, within easy distance of Aston Clinton and was returned to this safe seat with a majority of over 2,000. In the following year he was appointed a Junior Whip by Gladstone. It was an unpaid and thankless job, which he held on to through three Parliaments. Slowly he abandoned the hope that he might get further, and in 1892 he was offered a peerage.

Constance was in two minds whether he should accept and Asquith wrote to reassure her: "I think Cyril is doing right. There is a considerable sphere for Liberal peers in these days, and not the least reason why he should regard himself or be regarded by others, as being on the shelf."[29] He took the name of Lord Battersea, a title which Connie gloried in; but she could not hide from herself the fact that his political career was over. "I had hoped for a Government appointment of interest and weight, but it was not to be," she wrote, and consoled herself with the thought that he was perhaps cut out for finer things:

> I think . . . that although Cyril was deeply interested in the House of Commons, and although he was a most popular member both there and in his constituency, his special talent did not lie in political work. His were not so much attributes of the statesman as they were those of the man of artistic taste.[30]

In 1893 he was offered the post of Governor of New South Wales. The offer, as Cyril readily confessed, was the answer to all his dreams.[31] It was a challenge which would call on all his talents, but for Constance it posed an agonising dilemma. She knew what the offer meant to Cyril, but she feared what her departure might do to her mother. It was at first suggested that Lady Rothschild might go with them, but she was seventy-two, and protested that her health would not allow it. Connie was at her wits' end and sought guidance from friends. Lord Rosebery, who was married to her cousin Hannah and was a neighbour, was quite emphatic: "It won't do if Lady de Rothschild can't go. The wrench would be terrible."[32]

Louise de Rothschild, a life-long hypochondriac, was old and frail, but not quite as frail as she or her family believed. A lady of rank at the time was expected to suffer from a certain delicacy of constitution, but though she was prone to passing ailments, her health was fundamentally sound. She, however, felt that she was not long for this world and almost every letter she received opened with an enquiry on her health, and her replies consisted in good part of medical bulletins. In 1843, for example, when she was expecting her first child she was quite convinced that she would not survive the pregnancy and went so far as to write a touching farewell to Sir Anthony:

> My dearest husband when you read this your wife will be gone to another and Oh may God grant, to a better world. . . . Forgive me dear Anthony if I have not always made you as happy as I ought, I tried to do so to the best of my powers and indeed should have been unpardonable should I have acted otherwise towards so good, so kind, so affectionate a husband. I need not tell you to take care of our dear little child if it survives me, speak to it sometimes of its dear Mamma and give it a good religious education.[33]

But she survived the birth, she survived her husband, she survived her two sons-in-law, and she would no doubt have survived the crossing to Australia. With all her indispositions she was still a Montefiore and as such prone to the longevity from which much of that family suffered. She died in 1910 in her ninetieth year.

She was a good being, but as she grew older she became entirely self-centred and had no idea of the sacrifices she was expecting Cyril and Connie to make. Constance could never forgive herself for having asked him to make it. "Were I to live again," she confessed, "I should act differently, for, to say the least, it is ill-judged, perhaps unpardonable, to stand in the way of a man's acceptance of an honourable and useful career."

Her decision, coming so soon after his disappointments at Westminster, was a staggering blow to Cyril. He was a prisoner of the family, but too concerned for the happiness of his wife and mother-in-law to make a spirited bid for freedom.

There was little now for him to do or to hope for in London. He retired with his wife to his cherished corner of Norfolk, adding a wing here, a colonnade there, and bringing in Sir Edwin Lutyens to help him with his plans. Constance watched it all indulgently, too mindful of the sacrifice he had made to curb on his extravagance.

Cyril died in 1907, leaving debts so immense that for a time it seemed that she might have to sell the Pleasaunce, but her cousin Alfred came to her aid with advice, and her mother with money, so that the house was saved. She left it on her death to her second cousin Lionel Rothschild, who in his turn left it to his daughter Mrs Denis Berry. It is today a rest home for Anglican clergy.

Annie in the meantime had remained in the home which she and Eliot had set up at Hamble Cliff on Southampton Water, easing her solitude from time to time with visits to her mother, or among the scattered homes of various uncles and cousins in France, Switzerland, Germany and Austria. She did not repine in idleness. She, like her sister, was active in the temperance movement, even to the extent of rendering the crew of her ocean-going yacht teetotal. She was a plump little rosy-cheeked woman and, like her mother, always with a dog in her lap.

Both sisters maintained their contact with Jewish institutions. They had given occasional lessons at the Jewish Free School, and finding the textbooks deficient, set about, with the encouragement of Dr Kalisch, to write one of their own. The result was the *History and Literature of the Israelites*, which was published by Longmans in 1870 and, surprisingly, went into two editions. Constance sent a copy to Disraeli, who promptly congratulated her for describing "in a style, animated and picturesque, the great story of our ancestors", and for treating "with force and feeling their immortal annals".

One must charitably assume that he had not read the book, for although it indicated a fair amount of solid knowledge and a great amount of zeal, it is anything but 'animated' or 'picturesque', and if the children at the Jewish Free School had to study it in detail then the bounties they received from the Rothschilds were well earned.

Constance was also a member of the Jewish Ladies Benevolent Loan Society, and trekked round the narrow alleys and up the rickety stairs of Whitechapel even after her weight made it cumbersome to do so, to see conditions for herself and to offer guidance and sympathy. Such guidance was sometimes less well received in Whitechapel than Aston Clinton. "We are not like the *goyim*," one mother retorted, "we do not want to be talked to or taught, we do not drink, and we know how to bring up our children religiously and soberly."[34] Constance was also active on the Jewish Society for the Protection of Women and Girls.*

This social work was undertaken during brief forays into London and most of their time was spent in the country and Constance and Annie's diaries are full of sighs over scenes past, and their isolation.

* See page 321.

"Thought much of other years, of the old synagogue days, the family meetings, the Piccadilly reunions," wrote Annie on Passover, and six months later on the Day of Atonement she lamented: "I have separated myself from the world I knew amongst my own people." And in 1904: "I have cut myself off from much of Judaism and am only at the very outer gates of Christianity. There I shall never enter, though it attracts me."[35]

She could have been speaking for her sister Constance, who found great pleasure in the visits to the local church at Overstrand or at Cromer, the old stones, the stained-glass windows, the mellowness of the surroundings, the sound of the organ, the chant of the choir, and towards Christmas, the carols, the holly, the bells, and the cheerful bustle. She loved it all, yet was alien to it all, a charmed onlooker, but never a celebrant. Annie died in 1926, Constance in November 1931. They lie buried in Willesden Jewish Cemetery.

CHAPTER 15

The Richest Woman in England

It was said of Lord Rosebery – one does not know with what truth – that he had three ambitions, to become Prime Minister, win the Derby and marry the richest woman in England. He achieved the last ambition first.

Archibald Philip Primrose, fifth Earl of Rosebery, was born in 1847. He stemmed from a Scottish lowland family of some antiquity, if no great distinction, which first made its mark during the troubled years of the seventeenth century and which, in the succeeding years, enhanced its rank and wealth till, on the death of the fourth earl in 1868, Rosebery, at twenty-one found himself heir to extensive shale mines and 230,000 acres of land, yielding between them an income of over £30,000 a year.

To wealth and rank he added a capacious mind, a sharp intelligence and almost startling good looks, so that his progress through life seemed effortless. At Eton masters recognised his ability but lamented his lack of industry. He went on to Christ Church, Oxford, which has never been known as an intellectual sweat-shop. He enjoyed gay company, good dinners, excellent wines and frequent forays to race-tracks far and near, and even bought his own race-horse. Nevertheless his tutors were confident that he was well placed for a first in 'Greats', but his ability was never put to the test. He had an aristocratic disregard for rules which the authorities would overlook, but undergraduates were not allowed to own race-horses, and a race-horse was something which even Christ Church could not overlook. He was ordered to choose the horse or Oxford, and chose the horse.[1] "I have left Oxford," he cheerfully informed his horrified mother. "I have secured a house in Berkeley Square; and I have bought a horse to win the Derby. Your affectionate Archie."[2]

His house at number two Berkeley Square, a compact residence amongst massive palatial establishments, was an ideal redoubt for a young bachelor, and in 1873, he received a discreet enquiry whether the Prince of Wales, who was no longer young nor, indeed, a bachelor, might borrow it occasionally to entertain his 'actress friends'. Rosebery replied, a trifle testily, that it was too small.[3]

Rosebery was no playboy. The race-track and fast society might occupy some of his time and a good deal of his money, but he also tried to make up for the education he had failed to receive at Oxford. He read copiously and travelled widely. In 1873 he was in America and was received by President Grant, lunched with Longfellow and witnessed a torch-light procession winding its way to the Democratic Convention in New York. He was impressed with his visit and returned again in the following year.

In 1868, while on a visit to Newmarket races, Rosebery was introduced to Hannah Rothschild by Mrs Disraeli.

Hannah, the only child of Baron Mayer, was seventeen with fine, languorous eyes and a pouting prettiness. As an infant she had laid the foundation stone of Mentmore with a small silver trowel. She had spent a lonely childhood moving from one palatial home to another, and had meagre contact with the outside world. "She was never allowed to enter a cottage," wrote her cousin Constance. "She was never brought face to face with want or sickness. 'The poor' was merely a phraseology to her."[4] She acquired an appreciation of art and literature, but her formal education was slight. Though accustomed since early childhood to move among princes and magnates, she remained indrawn, diffident and shy.

Her father, a familar and beloved figure on every major racecourse, had almost become a legend. In racing circles he was *the* Baron, and had even figured in a doggerel on Derby day written by Rosebery at Oxford.[5]

Mayer died in 1874, leaving £2,100,000 and numerous properties to his wife. The baroness died three years later, and Hannah was left alone, a small, melancholy figure among the glittering treasure and great rooms of Mentmore.

She did not remain alone for long. Her first meeting with Rosebery was followed rapidly by others and she fell deeply in love with him. It was not, at first, evident that her affections were reciprocated, for it seemed as if Rosebery might take an American wife. He was attracted by the young daughter of a Washington family. "She is a young beauty," he wrote. "I meditate over her as over a sonnet." Nothing came of that romance or others. He was in no hurry. ". . . unless his affections were irreparably involved," wrote his son-in-law and biographer the Marquess of Crewe, "there was nothing to make an early marriage urgently desirable".[6]

And it was unlikely that his affections would be "irreparably involved" in the absence of a large dowry, for as Crewe explained: "A dowerless marriage might mean then a reduced scale of living of a kind galling to his proud nature. His public career . . . would be hampered by the necessity of taking thought for the morrow."[7]

In 1876 rumours began to circulate that he was about to become engaged to Hannah Rothschild and by 1877 they came to be accepted as fact. The reports caused great distress in the Jewish community. "The Rabbinical query is on every lip", wrote the *Jewish Chronicle*:

> If the flame seized on the cedars, how will fare the hyssop on the wall? If the leviathan is brought up with a hook, how will the minnows escape? '. . . was there amongst the millions of brethren-in-faith all over Europe no one of sufficient talent, sufficiently cultured, sufficiently high-minded, to be deemed worthy to be received in the family circle, that this honour must be bestowed upon one who must necessarily estrange the partner from her people. . . . A sad example has been set which, we pray God, may not be productive of dreadful consequences. The intelligence has thrilled through the communal frame. It quivers under the impact. And shall we suppress the cry of pain heaved forth from the soul?'[8]

Hannah's mother was aware of what was happening and the prospects of the engagement cheered the last broken months of her life, but Hannah herself must have had reservations on the subject, for although very much in love with Rosebery, she was a deeply devout Jewess, more so than any other Rothschild daughter of her generation.

Annie and Constance Rothschild were, as we have seen, religious, but there was little in their beliefs which could not have been accommodated comfortably within the Unitarian Church. They believed in religion rather than Judaism and did not feel themselves to be unduly bound by its precepts, and if even after their respective marriages in church they continued to adhere, at least nominally, to the Jewish faith, it was because the God of Abraham, Isaac and Jacob was also the God of the Rothschilds, and to have formally embraced Christianity would have been an affront to the memory of their fathers. Hannah's beliefs ran deeper and it was a measure of her affection for Rosebery that she was nevertheless prepared to marry outside the faith but she was troubled by her act throughout her short life.

It cannot be said that Rosebery's family was happy about the match. His mother, the Duchess of Cleveland, disliked Jews and made no secret of her antipathy. "You can easily suppose how unhappy I must feel in finding that you have chosen as your wife, and the mother of your children, one who has not the faith and hope of Christ," she wrote. "I myself do honestly and from the bottom of my heart, disapprove of such marriages, and I could not say otherwise without acting against my conscientious convictions."[9]

Rosebery anticipated her views but did not see them as an obstacle, and they hardly impaired his own joy in the event. "My darling Connie," he wrote to his sister, Lady Leconfield, "I was engaged to Hannah yesterday. I love her so much that I can never be happy if you do not love her too." And to Gladstone:

> I want to write and explain why you have not heard from me as to my visit to Hawarden. I am engaged to be married to Miss Hannah Rothschild, and your good wishes on this the most momentous day of my life will be welcomed.[10]

The wedding was arranged for March 20, 1878. On March 18 and 19 the wedding presents were on display at the bride's Piccadilly home, and occupied three immense drawing-rooms. There was a dressing-case from the Prince of Wales, a bracelet with pink pearls of rare size and beauty from Alfred de Rothschild, ruby and diamond ear-rings and a pansy from Natty, a silver inkstand from the Duchess of Cleveland, the family diamonds from Lord Rosebery, including among various priceless gems, a diamond tiara set in primroses, and a necklace of five rows of pearls, with a diamond clasp. Lord Beaconsfield sent a framed photograph of himself.[11]

There were two wedding ceremonies, the first, a civil one, was held in the Mount Street Registrar's office, in a room swamped in blooms, in the presence of some thirty close friends of the couple. The bride wore a plain morning dress of brocaded silk trimmed with pearls, with a jewelled rose in front, and a fur cloak lined with pearls.

From there she was driven back for a quick change, and appeared an hour and a half later at Christ Church, Down Street, Piccadilly, in a white satin dress and a brocade train, with a veil of Brussels lace. She wore no jewellery except a pair of pearl ear-rings set in diamonds.

There was a large crowd inside the church and an even larger one outside. The Duke of Cambridge, a younger son of the Queen, was among the earliest guests, and he was quickly followed by a whole brigade of noblemen, the Duke of Cleveland, the Earl of Stanhope, the Marquis of Hartington, the Earl of Orkney, and others.

At 11.30 the bride arrived accompanied by her grandmother, the aged Mrs Isaac Cohen, and her cousin, Ferdinand de Rothschild. She was received by Disraeli. One important guest was missing, and he arrived, a burly figure, puffing up the aisle, just after the service began – His Royal Highness, the Prince of Wales.

The ceremony, which was in every detail that of the Church of England, was conducted by Prebendary Rogers, chaplain-in-ordinary to the Queen, and it caused some raising of eyebrows among some of the guests, for the bride, as she was frequently careful to assert, was still Jewish. Two months later, at the Convocation of Canterbury a petition was presented protesting that the blessing of a non-believer "in the name of the Father, the Son and the Holy Ghost . . . is a plain profanation of the Holy Trinity, and a great scandal in the eyes of your petitioners and many other Christians."[12]

The Rosebery-Rothschild union may seem as yet another marriage of a dwindling old fortune to a growing new one, and it may be fairly stated that the two or three millions which Hannah inherited from her parents was not amongst the least of her attractions. Some contemporary observers suspected that in the eyes of Rosebery it was the only one, but though their days together were not untroubled, they were an affectionate and devoted couple. Their marriage, though it was to be tragically short, was happy and was characterised by profound affection and respect. Hannah, however, carried her feelings to the point of awe and Rosebery was sometimes exasperated by her solicitude.

Hannah had been slender in her youth, with a fine figure, but because of ill health she was allowed little exercise and in her later years put on weight. Sir Charles Dilke, an *habitué* of several Rothschild homes, who was believed to be the lover of her cousin Alice, spoke of her as "fat Hannah".[13] Rosebery himself was inclined to make light of the matter. "I am leaving tonight," he wrote to a friend, "Hannah and the rest of the heavy baggage will follow later."

The rise of Rosebery to high office was rapid and effortless. Where others struggled, he had to be coaxed. He was a Liberal and in 1878 he turned down an offer of junior office from Gladstone. In 1880 he was offered the office of Under-Secretary of State for India and refused that, and in the following year was finally prevailed upon to become Under-Secretary at the Home Office with special responsibility for Scotland, but resigned after a few months. He believed that the Government had given Scotland too low a place in its scheme of priorities. Gladstone tried to console him with the Scottish Office itself, but he refused that. Public Works? And again the answer was no. Either office would have given him the rank of full Minister, but not a seat in the Cabinet, and it seemed that he would not settle for less. Hannah believed that anything less was beneath him. "He must not be in a hurry to mount the ladder," Mrs Gladstone told her, "he is so young."[14]

Hannah saw his exclusion from the Cabinet as a conspiracy of minnows against her beloved titan, and when friends tried to reason with her she questioned their friendship.

Her attitude gave rise to misunderstandings and worse:

> Mr and Mrs G dined with us. After dinner I seized a moment to talk about Archie, and said I wished he had some work to do, as I believed it was what his brain required and should do good to his physical health. He answered, alluding to official work, "But then there is nothing now to give him." I was horrified at seeming to hint at office, when I meant nothing of the sort, and endeavoured to explain I meant to work at a subject. Mr Gladstone may be a marvel of erudition but he will never understand a man, still less a woman.[15]

Gladstone, however, may have felt that he understood her only too well.

In 1885 Rosebery finally entered the Cabinet as Lord Privy Seal, and in the following year Hannah received a hint from Gladsone's secretary that her husband was about to rise even higher and become Foreign Secretary. Her reply did not quite hide her excitement:

> I am not sure if you yet thoroughly understand Archie. Anything right and to prevent an incompetent person to hold a particular office he will endeavour, but I doubt his even saying a syllable which would even make an idea possible of his having entertained the notion of taking a high post.[16]

Hannah's ambition for her husband was well known. It had passed into political lore and become a source of amusement, but now, when Rosebery's appointment as Foreign Secretary was in the offing, it went beyond a joke and it was rumoured that she had paved the way for his ascent by eliminating his most immediate rival, Sir Charles Dilke.

In February 1886, Dilke, a leader of the radical wing of the Liberal Party, and one of the most brilliant parliamentarians of his day, who had been widely tipped as Foreign Secretary, was sued by Mr Donald Crawford for adultery with his wife. The evidence against Dilke was dismissed but the petitioner was given a decree nisi. Dilke sought a further hearing to clear his name, and on this occasion he was subjected to merciless cross-examination and was found to be guilty both of adultery and perjury. Either count would have been harmful, together they were fatal and Dilke was ruined. Could Hannah have bribed the Crawfords to frame him? Dilke believed it was a distinct possibility and in December 1885, while the case was still pending, he wrote to Rosebery that he had heard "a statement so incredible that I hesitate to repeat to you even in a secret letter. It is that Mr Crawford states that Lady Rosebery had promised him *help* in this case."

Rosebery replied at once:

I should have thought that even in this age of lies no human being could have invented so silly a lie as that you mention. But if you wish me to contradict it I will only say that there is no vestige of truth or even possibility about it. Under no circumstances could I, much less my wife, connect myself with anything of the sort.

Dilke thanked him for his reply. "Your letter is all I could expect or wish."

But Rosebery continued to worry about the insinuation and among his papers there is found this note, dated October 27, 1909.

I think it necessary to leave on record for the information of my children, in case Sir Charles Dilke should leave any records of his life speaking ill of me, that I was compelled to cut him dead, for having declared that my wife (then dead) had inspired Mrs Crawford to make a false accusation against him in order to get him out of the way of my career.[17]

Roy Jenkins, in his biography of Dilke, suggests two factors which gave 'a certain superficial plausibility to the story'.

The first was that Dilke was a direct rival to the extremely ambitious Rosebery. . . . The second factor was Lady Rosebery's known capacity for trying to advance her husband's career by rather unfortunate methods.

But he goes on:

It is true that she [Hannah] was sometimes hysterically anxious for her husband's success and that Dilke stood directly in his way. But these truths do not begin to prove that she attempted to remove the obstacle. The theory of a conspiracy instigated by the Roseberys might be dramatically satisfying but it cannot be held to have much hard evidence in its support.[18]

Robert Rhodes James, Rosebery's latest biographer, finds no difficulty in showing that there was no hard evidence whatever, nor was there much of the soft kind. Rosebery was ambitious and Hannah could be hysterical, but neither his ambition nor her hysteria were pushed to the point of assassination.

Rosebery remained Foreign Secretary for five months. The Liberal Party split over Gladstone's plans to give home rule to Ireland, and ninety-three Liberals led by Joseph Chamberlain – and who came to be known as Liberal Unionists – voted with the Tories against the measure. Gladstone resigned, went to the country, and was roundly defeated at the polls. But even in five months Rosebery lived up to the expectations that even his wife had of him, and Gladstone singled him out as 'the man of the future'.

Gladstone was now nearly ninety, and Rosebery seemed his obvious successor. He combined charm and eloquence and tact with great administrative ability. He showed this during the brief occasion he held office and confirmed it in the last years of the decade when he became the first chairman of the London County Council. But he was a moody, temperamental man and moved among his many homes like some restless eagle; to Dalmeny Park, his family's country seat near Edinburgh, or Rosebery, his shooting lodge in the Highlands, to the Durdans, his home on the Epsom Downs, or Mentmore. His favourite retreat was perhaps Barnbougle, a lone eyrie on the grounds of Dalmeny Park, by the grey, surging waters of the Forth. In London he had his own home in Berkeley Square and Baron Mayer's mansion in Piccadilly but he found neither large enough for the scale of entertainment he had to give and hired Lord Lansdowne's vast town house for £3,000 a year.

Hannah was not happy with Lansdowne House and its many drawing rooms, each the size of a ballroom. There were times when she felt as if she were hostess to every itinerant politician and diplomat in Europe, shaking a hand there, greeting a guest here, moving from room to room, smiling bravely, striving earnestly, but doing it all unwillingly and not always well. And when an occasion arose when she had to read a paper or make a speech herself, she suffered agonies of apprehension. Would she say the right things? And say them well? Might she not let down her Archie?

Rosebery, who was almost the embodiment of calmness, found her tendency to panic trying, but even more trying was her adoration. She would fuss about him, not so much like a Jewish wife as a Jewish mother. She fussed over him when he was well, she fussed over him when he was ill. Rosebery was a bad patient and could have been made no better by her ceaseless solicitude. In June 1880 he seemed to be approaching a breakdown in health, and Mrs Gladstone urged him to take things a little more easily. Hannah was grateful for her support:

> Your letter is more than kind, and if anything could encourage Archie to three months exile, it will be your affectionate recommendation of fresh air and rest. He had promised to endeavour to carry out the doctors' injunctions, and though they assure me there is no cause for any nervousness, still I am much relieved at his decision to follow their advice.[19]

Their marriage, wrote Crewe, "was founded on admiration and warm affection on one side, admiration and adoring devotion on the other."[20] Rosebery, who had grown to manhood knowing little affection from his mother, felt, on the approach to middle age, no need for a mother substitute, and he may have found Hannah's affection, adoration and devotion, excessive and burdensome, and sometimes, in his exasperation, he exploded in her face. His tendency to poke fun at her, even in public, may be less easily explained. He could not resist a joke at anyone's expense, even his own. He cared for her dearly, was mindful of even her little idiosyncrasies. Birthdays in the Rothschild family, for example, were sacrosanct. Cyril Flower asked him out to dinner one evening. "Quite impossible," he replied, "though very tempting. Wednesday is Hannah's birthday and I am not allowed to dine out. I am never sure whether it's on the 25th, 26th, or 27th, but this year it falls on the 27th."[21]

In March 1884 Gladstone's private secretary suggested that he might care to invite the old man, who had been ill, to spend a few days at Mentmore. Rosebery, who was the most generous of hosts had to refuse. A Rothschild had died a few days previously, he explained, and the family was still in mourning. And he added:

> My feeling is all the stronger because it is not my relation who is dead, or my family who would be hurt, but my wife's, which is a matter of great delicacy to me.[22]

Later events were to show that Hannah meant far more to him than anyone could have known.

On October 5, 1890 Rosebery returned from a visit to Germany to find her gravely ill. She was suffering from typhoid. At first her doctors assured him that there was no cause for alarm, but her condition deteriorated and death seemed imminent. Lady Leconfield, Rosebery's sister, who was on the most intimate terms with Hannah, hurried north to Dalmeny Park to be at her bedside.

Hannah had remained steadfast to her faith throughout her married life and would still attend services in the Western Synagogue in London, on the anniversary of her parents' death. In 1884 when she visited Australia with her husband, she went to the Melbourne synagogue to offer a prayer of thanksgiving for their safe crossing. She fasted and prayed without fail on the Day of Atonement. She also made it her custom to open her day with a passage from the Psalms, and now on her sick bed she asked Lady Leconfield to read the Psalms to her. On Friday evening she lit her Sabbath candles and tried to say her prayer, but she became tense and agitated, and her doctor discouraged further effort.

Then, almost at the point of death, she rallied. Her improvement continued and early in November they discussed plans for a holiday in Greece. A week later she suffered a relapse, and sank into a coma. Rosebery remained at her side while the doctors battled to save her. For a moment she recovered consciousness, looked up and smiled. "Archie," she said softly, "Archie, I am going home." Some hours later she was dead. She was thirty-nine, and left four young children.

There was a large Bible at her side, a gift from Sir Moses Montefiore, open at Psalm 103:

Like as a father pitieth his children, so the Lord pitieth them that fear him.
For he knoweth our frame; he remembereth that we are dust.
As for man his days are dust; as a flower in the field so he flourisheth.
For the wind passeth over it, and it is gone;
And the place thereof shall know it no more.

The Rev M. Furst, minister of the Edinburgh Hebrew Congregation, was summoned, and he arrived with four ladies of the Edinburgh *Chevra Kadisha*, the Jewish burial society, to prepare her body for burial, according to Jewish rites.

The funeral was held at the Jewish cemetery, Willesden. The hearse was followed by Lord Rosebery and his two young sons. They were followed by carriages bearing Lord Rothschild, Leopold de Rothschild, Baron Ferdinand de Rothschild, and Baron Edmond de Rothschild of Paris. Behind them came carriages bearing representatives of the Queen, the Prince of Wales and the Duke of Connaught, and behind them, a large part of the Cousinhood.

The cortège travelled up Mount Street, along Park Lane, Edgware Road and thence along Willesden Lane to the cemetery. Crowds lined the route, and at the gates, more recent arrivals to the community hawked crude portraits of the late countess. She was buried in the

MAYER AMSCHEL ROTHSCHILD

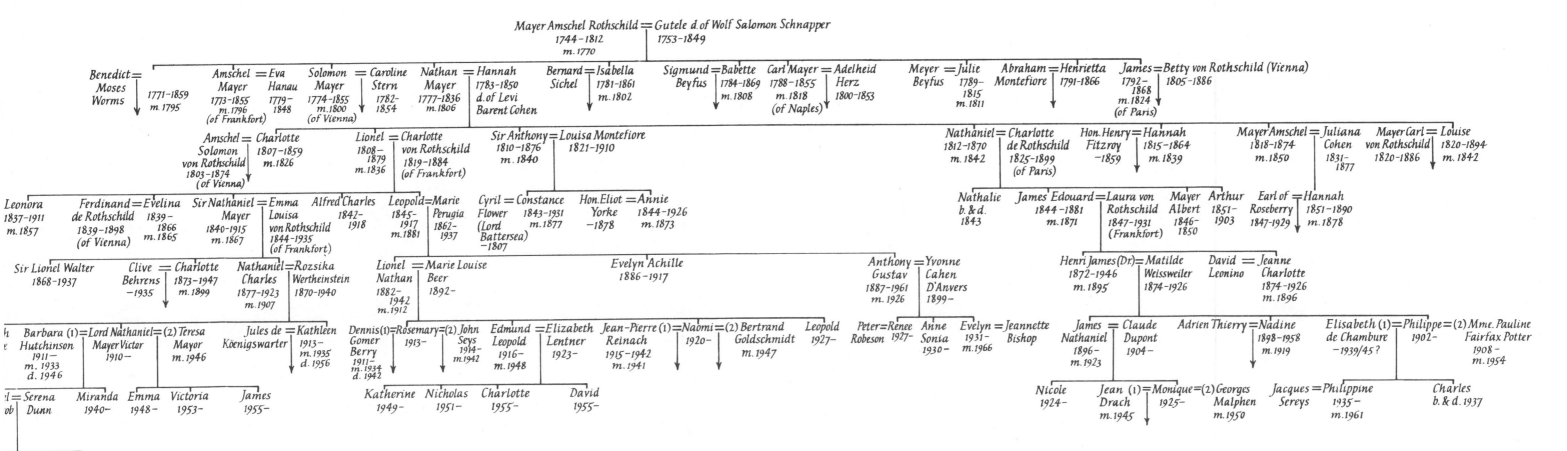

Mayer Amschel Rothschild = Gutele d. of Wolf Salomon Schnapper
1744–1812   1753–1849
m. 1770

Benedict = 1771–1859   Amschel = Eva   Solomon = Caroline   Nathan = Hannah   Bernard = Isabella   Sigmund = Babette   Carl Mayer = Adelheid   Meyer = Julie   Abraham = Henrietta   James = Betty von Rothschild (Vienna)
Moses   m. 1795   Mayer   Hanau   Mayer   Stern   Mayer   1783–1850   Sichel   1781–1861   Beyfus   1784–1869   1788–1855   Herz   Beyfus   1789–   Montefiore   1791–1866   1792–   1805–1886
Worms   1773–1855 1779– 1774–1855 1782–   1777–1836 d. of Levi   m. 1802   m. 1808   m. 1818   1800–1853   1815   m. 1839   1868
                        m. 1796   1848   m. 1800 1854   m. 1806   Barent Cohen   (of Naples)   m. 1811   m. 1824
                        (of Frankfort)   (of Vienna)   (of Paris)

Amschel = Charlotte   Lionel = Charlotte   Sir Anthony = Louisa Montefiore   Nathaniel = Charlotte   Hon. Henry = Hannah   Mayer Amschel = Juliana   Mayer Carl = Louise
Solomon   1807–1859   1808–   von Rothschild   1810–1876   1821–1910   1812–1870   de Rothschild   Fitzroy   1815–1864   1818–1874   Cohen   von Rothschild   1820–1894
von Rothschild   m. 1826   1879   1819–1884   m. 1840   m. 1842   1825–1899   –1859   m. 1839   m. 1850   1831–   1820–1886   m. 1842
1803–1874   m. 1836   (of Frankfort)   (of Paris)   1877
(of Vienna)

Leonora   Ferdinand = Evelina   Sir Nathaniel = Emma   Alfred Charles   Leopold = Marie   Cyril = Constance   Hon. Eliot = Annie   Nathalie   James Edouard = Laura von   Mayer   Arthur   Earl of = Hannah
1837–1911 de Rothschild 1839– Mayer   Louisa   1842–   1845–   Perugia   Flower   1843–1931   Yorke   1844–1926   b. & d.   1844–1881   Rothschild   Albert   1851–   Roseberry   1851–1890
m. 1857   1839–1898   1866   1840–1915   von Rothschild   1918   1917   1862–   (Lord   m. 1877   –1878   m. 1873   1843   m. 1871   1847–1931   1846–   1903   1847–1929   m. 1878
          (of Vienna)   m. 1865   m. 1867   1844–1935   1937   Battersea)   (Frankfort)   1850
                                  (of Frankfort)   –1807

Sir Lionel Walter   Clive = Charlotte   Nathaniel = Rozsika   Lionel = Marie Louise   Evelyn   Achille   Anthony = Yvonne   Henri James (Dr) = Matilde   David = Jeanne
1868–1937   Behrens   1873–1947   Charles   Wertheinstein   Nathan   Beer   1886–1917   Gustav   Cahen   1872–1946   Weissweiler   Leonino   Charlotte
            –1935   m. 1899   1877–1923   1870–1940   1882–   1892–   1887–1961   D'Anvers   m. 1895   1874–1926   1874–1926
                                          1942   m. 1926   1899–   m. 1896
                                          m. 1912

h   Barbara (1) = Lord Nathaniel (2) = Teresa   Jules de = Kathleen   Dennis (1) = Rosemary = (2) John   Edmund = Elizabeth   Jean-Pierre (1) = Naomi = (2) Bertrand   Leopold   Peter = Renee   Anne   Evelyn = Jeannette   James = Claude   Adrien Thierry = Nadine   Elisabeth (1) = Philippe = (2) Mme. Pauline
e   Hutchinson   Mayer Victor   Mayor   Köenigswarter   Gomer   1913–   Seys   Leopold   Lentner   Reinach   1920–   Goldschmidt   1927–   Robeson   1927–   Sonia   1931–   Bishop   Nathaniel   Dupont   1898–1958   de Chambure   1902–   Fairfax Potter
    1911–   1910–   m. 1946   1913–   Berry   1914–   1916–   1923–   1915–1942   m. 1947   1930–   m. 1966   1896–   1904–   m. 1919   –1939/45 ?   1908–
    m. 1933   m. 1935   1911–   1942   m. 1948   m. 1941   m. 1923   m. 1954
    d. 1946   d. 1956   m. 1934
                              d. 1942

l = Serena   Miranda   Emma   Victoria   James   Katherine   Nicholas   Charlotte   David   Nicole   Jean (1) = Monique = (2) Georges   Jacques = Philippine   Charles
b   Dunn   1940–   1948–   1953–   1955–   1949–   1951–   1955–   1955–   1924–   Drach   1925–   Malphen   Sereys   1935–   b. & d. 1937
                                                                                               m. 1945   m. 1950   m. 1961

Beth   Emily
1964– 1967–

family vault by the graves of her father and mother, and Lord Roths-child and his brother Leo said the *Kadish*. Hannah Rothschild had returned to her people.

Sir Henry Ponsonby attended the funeral on behalf of the Queen and watched Rosebery closely. His face was a mask. "He wishes to show in public that he is able to put aside his sorrow," he wrote, "but in private he breaks down." The old Queen had been fond of Hannah and wrote to express her sympathy. Rosebery took some time to reply:

> I have I confess found the greatest difficulty in addressing myself to the duty of acknowledging Your Majesty's most gracious letter. Five or six times have I began and laid down the pen. . . . I find however that delay is fatal in this case, and that the lapse of time only makes it more difficult to write. I dearly loved my wife, and our home was happiness itself: but I only now know what I have lost, and each new day represents a new desola-tion.

His bereavement, he wrote, had a particularly bitter edge.

> There is, however, one incident to this tragedy only less painful than the actual loss; which is that at the moment of death the difference of creed makes itself felt, and another religion steps in to claim the corpse. It was inevitable and I do not complain: and my wife's family have been more than kind. But none the less it is exquisitely painful.[23]

Rosebery became Prime Minister in 1894 but success now had the taste of ashes. He had come to rely on his wife to a greater extent than he thought possible. He missed her warm, cheerful presence, the affec-tion which he once thought excessive, the adoration which he once found embarrassing. The insomnia which had plagued him at times of stress before became chronic. His cheeks began to sag, his figure became heavy and a little bent. He could still attract and hold large audiences, but to those who knew him at an earlier happier age, he was a pathetic sight. ". . . he looks so sad and ill", noted a friend in her diary. "I can hardly believe, unless he gets a great deal better, that he is anything like well enough for public life."[24]

His many homes seemed larger and infinitely more empty, and he spent much time in isolation at Barnbougle.

He became Prime Minister at a difficult time and added to the nor-mal cares of office was constant harassment from the built-in Tory majority in the House of Lords, and intrigues within his own party. A more determined politician would have persevered, but he was too dispirited and broken.

"It was at this time," wrote Churchill, "that he felt the need of his wife. . . . With all her almost excessive adoration of Rosebery, she was ever a pacifying and composing element in his life, which he was never able to find again, because he could never give full confidence to anyone else. She was a remarkable woman on whom he had leaned, and without her he was maimed."[25]

In June 1895 the Government was defeated in the Commons in a small vote on a minor issue – that the War Office had failed to secure enough cordite for the army – and he resigned. He was under fifty, but his public career was behind him. His ambition had died with his wife. He lingered on a lone figure into old age, obscurity, sickness and finally, in 1929, death.

CHAPTER 16

The Distaff Line

A London Sephardi was once asked how long his family had lived in England. "Oh," he said, "from the beginning." He didn't say which beginning but left the impression it could have been the creation.

He was a kinsman of the Mocattas and his pride in his antiquity was understandable. The Mocattas were amongst the first Jews in England, amongst the founders of the Bevis Marks congregation and the West London Synagogue, amongst the leading members of the Board of Deputies. They were indeed to be found in leading positions in every institution in the community. They were bullion brokers to the Bank of England. They included philanthropists, scholars, social reformers, public servants, distinguished professional figures. They include eminent lawyers, bankers, entrepreneurs.

Lucien Wolf, the Jewish historian, traces the Mocattas back to fifteenth-century Seville,[1] but the name is Arabic and it suggests that they had lived for a time on the southern shore of the Mediterranean and had crossed over in the wake of the Moors. After the Expulsion from Spain in 1492 some members of the family moved to Italy, some to Holland and the West Indies. One branch adopted Christianity and remained in Spain, only to be expelled a century later as crypto-Jews. They too fled to Holland and branched out from there to England where one, Moses Mocatta, traded between London and Amsterdam and prospered sufficiently to leave 35,000 guilders to various charities in his will. His son Abraham joined the Royal Exchange and must have been a man of considerable means, for we find him entertaining appeals from the Sephardi community of New York which wanted help to acquire land for a synagogue and cemetery. He offered to donate the necessary cash – £150 – on condition the plots were registered in his

165

name. The offer was refused, but he was given the option of laying the foundation-stone of the synagogue instead. Abraham may have felt that this would not have given him his money's worth of eternity, but anyhow he never replied.

He died in 1751 and with him the male line of Mocattas became extinct.

Abraham had one daughter, who married a member of another prosperous clan, Moses Lombrozo de Mattos. Her eldest son Abraham succeeded her father on the Exchange and also assumed his name – Abraham Lombrozo de Mattos Mocatta. But de Mattos was dropped and Mocatta remained.[2]

In 1759 Abraham married Esther Lamego, a wealthy Sephardi heiress, and eight years later he was able to enter into partnership with another broker to establish the firm of Mocatta and Keyser. They were joined in 1787 by Asher Goldsmid, a son-in-law of Keyser and out of this partnership there evolved the firm still known as Mocatta and Goldsmid.

Abraham Mocatta had eleven children, and their progeny married into almost every family we meet in the Cousinhood, and beyond, including the Basevi family and through them, Benjamin Disraeli.

Abraham Mocatta had been among the principal upholders of tradition at Bevis Marks but several of his sons were wearied by the length of the service and the anachronisms which governed its affairs. Jacob was able to persuade the congregation that as Portuguese was no longer in use the service should be conducted in English. Other proposals were more strenuously opposed, and, as we have seen,[3] when the inevitable split finally came in 1842, no less than nine Mocattas left Bevis Marks to join the West London Synagogue and establish Britain's first Reform congregation. Among them, surprisingly, was one of Abraham's elder sons, Moses.

Moses Mocatta was a broker by profession and a scholar by disposition: he spent more time in his study than in the counting house. He was a contributor to numerous learned periodicals, including the *Hebrew Review*. He was a generous patron of Grace Aguilar, a novelist and poetess who died in 1847. Her novels, which were mainly historical romances built round the ordeals of Spanish Jewry under the Inquisition, were avidly read in the Jewish community and enjoyed a wider following as well. In 1851 he translated Isaac Ben Abraham's work of Jewish apologetics, *Hizuk Emunah*, 'Faith Strengthened'. He also compiled a work based on the wisdom of Solomon. He was one of the ornaments of Bevis Marks and his departure was a serious loss. Of brokers they had many, of scholars few.

Moses had nine children of whom the best known was perhaps David, an architect. He designed many of the stations on the London to Brighton line, Sir Moses Montefiore's synagogue at Ramsgate, and supervised the construction of the West London Synagogue. Another son, Isaac Lindo, emigrated to South America, and thence to Australia, without prospering particularly in either place, and finally set up home in Brighton where he compiled a number of minor works on biblical subjects, including one as Sabbath reading for children. Like other members of his family he was high minded; unlike them, he had small means. When he died in 1879 he left the West London Synagogue £100, the blind £50, 'Jewish Penny Dinners' £10, and his six children nineteen guineas each.

They were to an extent provided for in their grandfather's will and probably also inherited sundry sums from various other kinsmen, but the Mocattas, whether in their lifetime or as a posthumous act, looked upon charity as a primary obligation.

One member of the family, indeed, was virtual honorary almoner of the Jewish community, though his sense of concern was not confined to Jews alone. He was Frederic David Mocatta. When he died in 1905 he left £110,000 to be divided equally between Jewish and non-Jewish charities.[4]

Frederic, one of four children, was born in 1828. Dr Albert Lowy, an eminent Hebraist, taught him Jewish history and lore. His father, a partner in Mocatta and Goldsmid, taught him Hebrew. He joined Mocatta and Goldsmid when he was fifteen and became a partner six years later. He is not recalled in the firm as one of its most active or dynamic partners,[5] but he seems to have prospered sufficiently to retire from business at the age of forty-seven, to give generously, travel widely and live comfortably.

In 1856 he married Mary Ada, the second daughter of Frederic David Goldsmid, M.P. She developed rheumatoid arthritis on their honeymoon and their married life consisted of weary pilgrimages from one watering place to another, sometimes with a doctor and nurse in tow, in a constant and unavailing quest for better health. Eventually they chose Aix-les-Bains as their annual winter resort and they became familiar members of the local English colony.

They were a devoted couple, but had no children. This was perhaps the major tragedy of Frederic Mocatta's life, for he was passionately fond of children, and would show an animation in their presence which was foreign to him at most other times. To some extent he adopted the poor as his family, but he was true to his times in that he was never indulgent, and his approach to charity was cool, business-like and detached. He found many charities duplicating the efforts of one another, a great deal of administrative chaos, and the distribution of aid characterised more by good will than good sense. The task of charity, he said, was not "to aid the poor, so much as to render them independent", and he warned against the distribution of small doles, "which, while they, like strong drink, quench the wants of the moment, stimulate a craving for more, and lower the moral constitution of the recipient, thus intensifying the misery of his condition."[6]

He was an active member of the Charity Organisation Society, which was a clearing-house for all the leading charities in London, and a vice-president of the Jewish Board of Guardians. He was, wrote an historian of the Board, "the *beau idéal* of Anglo-Jewish philanthropist".[7]

Between 1880 and 1915 the Jewish population of London increased four-fold and the Board of Guardians was almost overwhelmed by the crush of applicants. One member of the Board, in a moment of panic, advocated statutory restrictions against the admission of 'Helpless' paupers.

"This class," he believed "constitutes a grave danger to the community. Its members were always paupers and useless parasites in their own country. If accepted as immigrants in England, they remained paupers and parasites. . . . The life-boat is well-nigh full. If we can admit any more passengers, they must be such as to lend a hand to the oars."[8]

Mocatta was horrified by such arguments. "It is not for us as Englishmen to try and close the entrance to our country to any of our fellow creatures, especially such as are oppressed", he wrote. "It is not for us as Jews to try and bar our gates against other Jews, who are persecuted solely for their professing the same religion as ourselves."[9]

At the same time the Board was careful not to do anything which might appear to encourage immigration and a Jew had to be at least six months in England before he could apply for relief, and even then there was no certainty that he would get it. In 1885 one recent immigrant who had made a little money established a rudimentary shelter for immigrants out of his own pocket. The Board of Guardians came to hear of it and Frederick Mocatta with Lindo Alexander, an honorary secretary of the Board, descended for a tour of inspection.

They not surprisingly found the conditions 'unhealthy'. Such "a harbour of refuge", they said, "must tend to invite helpless foreigners to this country, and therefore is not suitable to exist."[10] The Board intervened with the local sanitary authorities and the shelter was closed, but it did not provide an alternative refuge. A proper shelter, which is still in use, was eventually built in the face of considerable opposition from the old families by Herman Landau, a stockbroker of Polish extraction, and two cousins Samuel Montagu and Ellis Franklin.

Mocatta was moved by the sufferings of Russian Jewry and for a time urged mass emigration as a solution to their problem. But where to? He did not suggest that England should close its doors against Jewish refugees, but one never found him insisting that they should stay wide open. He considered Palestine as too poor, barren and chaotic to absorb any sizable number of newcomers and he was nervous of the spectre of Zionism. In 1903, after news of the Kishinev pogrom had shocked the civilised world, he wrote to the *Haham* Dr Gaster, ". . . it is most imperative – as I know you will agree with me – that the name of Zionism shall not in any way be brought into the question in discussing the horrible matter of Kishinev, or the distribution of any funds that may be raised. We must take care to keep things as calm as possible."[11]

There was a time when he believed that Russian Jewry, "before the end of the nineteenth century will be put on perfect equality with their fellow citizens".[12] By the end of the century he was no longer so optimistic, and finally he urged mass emigration to North America as the best, indeed the only solution to the Jewish problem. The possibility that North America might have some reservations on the matter does not appear to have occurred to him.

His whole attitude to charity, in common with that of the Cohens, who were the community's overseers of the poor, was Victorian, and it was exemplified by the method of interviewing applicants for relief, an occasion that was more like a trial. The honorary officers of the Board, sat at a round table raised on high. At their side was the secretary with details of the case, and at a safe distance, at the other end of the room, behind a brass rail, stood the applicants. Only the aged and infirm were allowed to sit. The standing rule, said Mocatta, was necessary for the efficient dispatch of business.[13]

Frederic Mocatta was not active in national politics, but he was conservative in outlook and was startled by innovations, especially where the state sought to intervene in social problems. He looked upon state-aided old age pensions, as "a damning heresy, which all thoughtful people should be bound to oppose with all their might".[14] Similarly he had no sympathy for a movement to control shop hours: ". . . it seems to me that people working in shops are much better left free to make their own arrangements. I always think interference in such matters does more harm than good."[15] He was doubtful about the value of trade unions: ". . . probably the selfishness of a great number of employers rendered them necessary," he wrote in 1892, "but it appears to me that they are very tyrannical in refusing full liberty to those who think right not to join them."[16]

He was an assiduous student of blue books and white papers, official reports and social studies, and where no documents were available he often made his own elaborate enquiries. He was one of the best informed men on the social conditions of the country, and was pained by what he knew, but underlying it all was the feeling that there was little wrong with society which a sufficient number of Frederic David Mocattas could not cure. At the same time he was aware that such men were few.

> Wealth and ease are apt to dull the sympathies, and those who do not come into contact with poverty and suffering are not given to realize the misery they entail. There are many who possess large fortunes who hardly contribute anything of their own accord . . . and who never recognise the *duty* of entering into friendly relations with the poor.[17]

I have italicised duty, for Mocatta was impelled by duty rather than emotion. He was no bleeding-hearted philanthropist and had a certain amount of scorn for those who reached for their wallets at the merest hard-luck story, which does not mean that he would not from time to time let his generous nature get the better of his principles. "I hope I may grow more charitable as I advance," he once wrote to Dr Gaster, "but I must be less giving to some extent, as for some years past I have been exceeding my income – a bad practice and worse example which I am determined to stop."[18] (The fact that he was exceeding his income does not mean that he was becoming poor – but the Victorian middle class had a horror of touching its capital.)

The seriousness with which Mocatta approached his work, his high sense of purpose excited awe even in Claude Montefiore, one of the uncanonised saints of Anglo-Jewry. "In nobility of character," wrote Montefiore, "he stood out head and shoulders above all the men of his community." And he went on:

How far removed his charity was from mere giving! The money, spent unstintingly was, in very truth, the least of it. The labour and the thought, the wisdom and the self-denial – these predominated. . . . He was almost restless in doing good. . . . In every class in every creed, there were innumerable persons whom he sought to make happier by personal effort and kindness. Perhaps the most beautiful trait about him was the number of dull things he would do – things, I mean, that must have been dull to himself, and that prevented him doing other things which he would personally have enjoyed.[19]

Mocatta was devoid of that bonhomie that might have enabled him to find actual pleasure in the company of people outside his class. He was not, indeed, patronising, but if he was to be seen, as one of his obituarists wrote, 'among all manners and conditions of men', it was not because he was drawn to them by a raging sense of concern but to assess for himself the extent of their need.

He was, one suspects, a little vain about his reputation as a social worker, possibly to the extent of resenting competition.

When *Darkest England*, General William Booth's study of poverty, appeared in 1890, he was not much taken with it, nor did he think highly of Booth's reformist ideas. "Though I acquit General Booth of all dishonesty," he wrote, "he must naturally be intoxicated with his own success, and I believe the prime motive is the conversion of all England, if not of the world, to 'Corybantic *or* Salvationism'."[20]

What Mocatta hated above all was what he called 'Sensationalism'. It was, he said, "one of the great vices of the present day, and one which does the greatest harm to the sensible and beneficial exercise of charity."[21]

He must have sensed more than a hint of such sensationalism both in Booth's writing and the whole manner in which Booth sought to excite public sympathy for his cause. "Those people who require to be taken up and shaken till the principle of charity is made to rise to the top of their hearts, in order that it may overflow," wrote Mocatta, "are not such from whom charity can derive any real help." Booth was a shaker, and Mocatta feared, perhaps needlessly, that he would "captivate the multitude and withdraw heaps of money and intelligence from all sensible systems, and do much to undo the work of the Charity Organisation Society."[22]

Mocatta was a devout, pious Jew. He never worked or even travelled on the Sabbath, observed the dietary laws in all their strictness, and would rarely miss a Sabbath service if he could help it.[23] He was not inclined to indulge in any metaphysical speculation. He was no theologian or philosopher. The appeal of Judaism lay in the fact that it was there and had been there for a very long time. It fitted in with his view of continuity and order.

He was more Orthodox both in conduct and outlook than most members of the Orthodox synagogue yet he himself was a member of the West London Reform Synagogue, for the very good reason that his father had been one of its founders. Mocatta, said Claude Montefiore, looked on his parents as "the representatives of God on earth". He regretted the schism that had brought the synagogue into being, he regretted the tendency of West London to drop usages cherished in the older synagogues, but he could not think of a cause in which his father had been involved as anything other than noble and true; West London remained dear to him, and he remained dear to West London, for that reason. At the same time he hankered for tradition, for the old ways, the old tunes, and finally got the best of both worlds. He rejoined Bevis Marks and for a time served both as president of the Reform Synagogue and warden of Bevis Marks. He saw himself as a possible agent for healing the schism between the two, but what time had torn apart, not even Mocatta could bring together. He loved religious ceremonies and ritual and had he not been a Jew one could imagine him as a disciple of Cardinal Newman. He used his influence to check the hunger for innovations at the Reform synagogue. While he was alive it had not in fact moved all that far from the Orthodox synagogues, though its atmosphere was distinctly churchy, and with its high, vaulted ceiling, its organ, its fine choir, and co-ordinated hymn singing, it bore more than a faint resemblance to Brompton Oratory.

Mocatta, who was deeply interested in history and antiquities, defrayed the cost of translating and condensing Graetz' eleven-volume *History of the Jewish people*, and subsidised numerous other works of scholarship. He was a member of the Palestine Exploration Fund and a vice-president of the Society of Biblical Archaeology. In 1887 he headed a committee which organised a Jewish historical exhibition as part of the Queen's Golden Jubilee celebrations, and on the eve of the opening gave a *soirée* for 3,000 people in the Albert Hall. One of the results of the exhibition was the formation of the Jewish Historical Society of England. Mocatta doubted whether such a society could flourish. The Jews of England, he believed, were mainly "commercial people, brokers, merchants, a class of people to whom I essentially belong. I have no doubt they were a very respectable sort of people, but there is very little concerning them that is interesting to the general public."[24] He was correct in his observations but mistaken in his prognostications. The Jewish Historical Society in England is still in being and flourishing.

Mocatta amassed a very considerable collection of Judaica which was presented on his death to University College, London, and which now forms the basis of the Mocatta library.

It is difficult to assess the extent of Mocatta's fortune. His father left £100,000, and his wife inherited a similar sum. His own will was proved at £134,663. He was a partner in Mocatta and Goldsmid during thirty of its most expansive years and although he was ceaselessly propelled by a sense of duty, he was not a reckless man and it is unlikely that he would have retired at the early age of forty-seven unless he had had a reasonable fortune at his disposal.

The constant travel necessitated by his wife's illness was expensive, but he did not otherwise spend much on himself. His house in Connaught Place, Bayswater, was the typical, ponderous, creamy, stucco building much favoured by Victorian merchants. He did not have a country seat, and his entertainments were infrequent and un-lavish. When he urged an immediate scheme of mass Jewish immigration to America, he offered £10,000 towards the £1,000,000 he thought necessary for such a scheme, but he did not as a rule make his offerings public. He would have considered this to be in bad taste, and an example of the 'sensationalism' he abhorred. There have been suggestions that he disbursed half a million or even a million sterling in the course of his lifetime, but whatever the actual sum, it is certain that he placed the greater part of his wealth at the disposal of others.

Mocatta was proud both of his Englishness and his Jewishness and felt the fact that he was an observant Jew somehow made him a better Englishman. "We should," he declared:

> . . . show ourselves worthy of our great country, while acting in such a manner to cause our ancient race and religion to be respected by all men. To ensure this, the first essential is that we respect ourselves, and I fear it is in this that the Jews of England and of other countries are lamentably wanting. There is nothing in the Jewish religion which militates against good citizenship; entirely the reverse, it is our most serious duty to seek by all that is in us the good of the land which we inhabit. It is not necessary to profess the religion of the majority to be a patriot.

"Our poorer brethren," he observed, were still observant, "but as a rule they live grouped together – far more so than is indeed desirable."

But can one move in the wider world and still retain one's religious loyalties? He believed one could and should, and, of course, he did, but he could not fail to notice that he was the odd man out:

> I can, however, but regret to observe that what are called the upper and middle classes, do not as a rule submit to the sacrifices entailed by the observance of their religion – sacrifices the more obligatory now that in the general relations to life, the ordinary surroundings, they are necessarily far more Christian than Jewish.[25]

Mocatta by his exertions and example helped to delay the inevitable, and throughout the Victorian age most members of the Cousinhood remained, to a greater or lesser – usually lesser – degree loyal to Judaism. By the time they began to fall away, Christianity itself was on the wane, and when they lapsed it was not so much into the arms of the Church, as was so often the case in Europe and America, but into agnosticism.

CHAPTER 17

The Victorians

The Cohens, though founder members of the Cousinhood, have tended to form a clan within the Clan, and have always been among its less exotic members. They experienced neither dramatic rise to fortune, like the Rothschilds, nor catastrophic collapse, like the Goldsmids. They never sought to have royalty at their tables, nor a place at table with royalty, and have, on the whole, been content with a comparatively humble place in society. They have lived comfortably, graciously but unostentatiously in large homes with large gardens and numerous servants. Within a generation or two they became so much part of the fabric of English upper-class life, so Anglicised in fact, and so confident of their place in England, that they have never felt the need to change their name. Cohens they were when they came from Holland in the eighteenth century, and Cohens they still are, though not all of them have remained Jews.

The Cohens and their age could have been made for one another. They were nature's own Victorians, pious, God-fearing, high-minded worthies, industrious, sober, practical, a trifle desiccated perhaps, rather colourless, a little humourless, but sensible, solid and true.

We find the Cohen family comfortably settled in Holland by the middle of the seventeenth century, and one of them was among the founders of the Amsterdam Great Synagogue in 1670, and we hear of them as prosperous corn merchants and tobacco growers round Amersfoort, in the province of Utrecht and as business associates of the Goldsmid family.[1]

Levi Barent Cohen, founder of the clan, came to this country in 1770, and prospered sufficiently as a broker and merchant to become president of the Great Synagogue, an office which in itself indicates high standing and considerable wealth.

Turmoil in Europe during the last years of the eighteenth century brought a steady stream of Jewish newcomers to London, many of them penniless, who crowded the Ashkenazi synagogues and importuned the more prosperous congregants for help. There was in every synagogue a tacit classification of worshippers, the top strata of the very rich, the middle strata of the merely solvent, and the bottom strata of the poor. Charity is not an optional extra among Orthodox Jews (at this time all Jews were Orthodox) and the pauper has, or feels he has, an automatic claim on the rich. Every synagogue had a fund to help the needy, but when the newcomers had exhausted the money and patience of one synagogue, they would immediately descend upon another. Barent Cohen sought to introduce order and in 1780, together with the Goldsmid brothers, he founded the Jewish Bread, Meat and Coal Society, Anglo-Jewry's oldest charity and the forerunner of the Jewish Welfare Board.[2]

Barent Cohen married twice, first Fanny Diamantschleifer and when she died, her sister Lydia. He had three children by his first wife, and nine by his second and, as we have seen, there is hardly a family of any eminence in the Anglo-Jewish community which is not descended from one or other of them.

Barent Cohen has been outshone by his sons-in-law, but he left certain traditions which are still largely extant in the family, and in the larger Cousinhood, of cautious conservatism. It extended to commerce, religion, conduct of communal affairs and even personal deportment.

One of his sons, for example, cast troubled glances at the plunging female necklines, a French influence, and he warns his daughters that he prefers necklines to be English and high.[3] The eldest son Joseph was troubled by less mundane affairs. He succeeded his father as lay head of the Great Synagogue and had to fend off the demands of a reform party clamouring for change.

"I will have nothing to do with this Reform business," he insisted, "it is the thin end of the wedge."[4] He died in 1838, and his son Louis had to face the split which such recalcitrance made inevitable. It was Louis who brought all the Ashkenazi synagogues in the City together to appoint one joint Chief Rabbi, a measure which led eventually to the creation of the United Synagogue.

There was more to the appointment than mere unity, or even religion. The Jews of Britain were struggling for emancipation, and it was necessary at such a time to have at their head, not merely a pious man, but an attractive public figure, learned in things secular as well as sacred who could, if necessary, act as a sort of ambassador to the outside world.

David Salomons wrote to Louis to press upon him the right scheme of priorities:

> I hope the presiding depository of the conscience of all the Jews in the British Empire will be a person who shall command the respect of all persons quite as much by his appearance as by his learning. . . . Of the two I would prefer a commanding person to a great talent. Not that I mean that I do not value talent, but there are other qualities besides this essential to the position of so important a functionary.[5]

In the event they found Nathan Adler who had both a commanding presence and great talent.

Louis had eighteen children, of whom eight died in infancy and a ninth in childhood. Adelaide, the eldest surviving daughter, married Sir Joseph Sebag-Montefiore, a broker of Moroccan origin who began life as Joseph Sebag but took on the Montefiore by deed poll when he inherited the East Cliff Lodge estate in Ramsgate from his maternal uncle Sir Moses Montefiore. Sebag-Montefiore was the founder of Joseph Sebag & Sons, which is now one of the largest stockbrokers in Britain, with branches in Chicago and Los Angeles.

The family had by now grown up not only in size but in prosperity through the activities of Louis Cohen & Sons, stockbrokers and bankers dealing mainly with the financing of foreign trade. It was a solid house of good repute, but came into being when private banks were already on the decline and in 1901 it entered into voluntary liquidation. Robert Henriques – the biographer of Sir Robert Waley-Cohen, who was a son of one of the partners, Nathaniel Cohen – states in an unpublished part of his manuscript that 'an immense and reputable offer' was made for the firm, but that the brothers refused to sell in case their good name 'might be blemished'. If the offer was indeed 'reputable' then their fear was groundless. What was more probable was that the bank had out-lived its functions. A few millions, which was all that the brothers had at their disposal, was not enough for the type of financing required at the turn of the century.[6] The joint-stock banks had come into their own, and those private banks which were not merged or absorbed tended to be shouldered out of the market altogether. Moreover, the mania for foreign loans so characteristic of the 1860s[7] and 1870s, on which the banks' fortunes were based, had abated by the end of the century and if the Cohens had not retired like gentlemen, they might have been routed like bankrupts. Alfred, the most senior of the brothers who died in 1903, left £567,000, including £120,000 to each of his three surviving children. Benjamin left nearly £400,000 and Lionel, who died before the dissolution, £434,000, enough in Victorian times for a town house and country houses, carriages and servants and all the other appurtenances of upper-middle-class life.

There seemed to have been a rule among the Cohens that every parent would leave to each of his children as much as he inherited himself, which was usually a six figure sum. If he did less he felt that he was somehow not doing his duty by them.

Duty was perhaps the Cohen watchword and each of the partners seems to have spent as much time promoting one or other of their causes as in their counting house. This was particularly true of Lionel, the fourth of Louis' sons.

Like his father, grandfather and great-grandfather, Lionel was a leading member of the Great Synagogue and as such was actively involved in helping the poor. The Jewish Bread, Meat and Coal Society was now too limited in scope, and certainly insufficient to meet the needs of the Jewish poor over half a century after its foundation. There were, according to one Victorian observer of Jewish life, some 25,000 Jews in London in the early 1850s, of whom about 5,000 were put in the 'upper class', 8,000 in the 'middle class' and 12,000 in the 'lower class'.[8] Of the last many were said to be 'in daily want of the necessities of life, and a still larger number scarcely able to obtain sufficient to support existence'. The situation was made worse by a brutally harsh winter in 1858, which resulted in great suffering and many deaths, so the three major Ashkenazi synagogues came together to form a permanent body to ameliorate Jewish poverty. The prime mover of the scheme was Ephraim Alex, an elderly dentist who was overseer of the poor at the Great Synagogue, but the most agile mind behind it was that of Lionel Cohen, who was then twenty-seven.[9]

The poor, in the main, were newcomers and Alex outlined his ideas in a pamphlet called *A Scheme for a Board of Guardians to be formed for the relief of the necessitous Foreign Poor*. It caused a certain amount of apprehension among the older families. They feared that such a board could act as a magnet to every Jewish pauper in Europe, and Sir Francis Goldsmid and Simon Waley urged that no immigrant be helped until he had been in the country for say three or five years. The Rev. Marks, minister of the West London Synagogue, felt that they should be helped at once – to go back whence they came. Sir Joseph Sebag-Montefiore, however, argued that need alone should be the criterion, and not length of residence.[10]

Already there was a conflict of principle which was to cause serious divisions within the community a generation later.

The Board was formally brought into being in March 1859 with Alex as president and Lionel as secretary. Lionel worked out the constitution of the Board, and its whole scheme of operation, and brought to his task, in the words of the historian of the Board, "matchless energy, grasp of detail and power of original and constructive thought", which was to be characteristic of his work both inside and outside the community.[11] In 1869 he became president and the Cohen family adopted the Board of Guardians as its particular responsibility. There has hardly been a time in the past century when a Cohen has not been head of the Board, the most recent one being the Hon. Leonard Cohen, a great-grandson of Lionel.

Within two decades the Board became the pride of the community and was looked on as a model of its type by non-Jewish philanthropic institutions. It was efficient and, by the standards of the day, humane. It was anxious to discourage the globe-trotting *schnorrers* and therefore adopted a rule that no one resident in the country less than six months could obtain relief: but even this was often waived, and unlike some other charitable institutions of the day, it did not regard poverty as self-evident proof of idleness or depravity.

It taught young people trades, gave small loans to petty traders to tide them over difficulties, helped families in a crisis and it was gratified to find that about a third of the applicants during any one year did not apply for relief in the next. Such people were regarded as 'cured', though, of course, among the 'cured' there must have been many who had simply died, but the problem was one of measurable dimensions until 1881. Then came the deluge.

Between 1880 and 1914 about 150,000 Jews poured into this country, and one is sometimes given the impression that they all landed at the door of the Board. Many in fact found themselves immediate employment and others had sufficient capital to set up in small trades. Dr V. D. Lipman, in his lucid centenary history of the Board, shows that the number of applicants for relief before 1880 was under 2,500 cases a year. They rose to over 5,000 in 1894, remained at that level till 1900, climbed somewhat till 1908, and then gradually declined to 3,348 before the war. But the Board dealt with immigrants only after they had settled in the country for some time. Emergency relief to newcomers was dispensed by a conjoint committee of the Board and the Russian Jewish Committee, a special body formed after the 1881 pogroms. The conjoint dealt with 1,591 applicants in its first year. From then the numbers grew to reach a peak of 3,277 in 1892, but declined again to 543 in 1902. Then in 1905, after the Kishinev pogrom, they jumped to 3,847 and fell away again to 362 in 1914.[12]

The Board panicked. Its means were not always equal to its new commitments, but this was perhaps a minor point. The main pressure was political. As immigration built up there was considerable agitation – not unlike the Powellite agitation in our times, though far more outspoken – against the newcomers. There was considerable unemployment in the country, and this too was partly blamed on the immigrants who, it was suggested, were under-cutting the wages of the working class.

In 1888 a Select Committee of the House of Lords found that "undue stress has been laid on the injurious effect on wages caused by foreign immigration, inasmuch as we find that the evils complained of . . . . trades which do not appear to be affected by foreign immigration".

These conclusions were largely confirmed by the report of Royal Commission on Aliens, published in 1903.[13]

The anti-alien agitation nevertheless continued and became more widespread and venomous and the Board itself was accused of encouraging immigration. The Board, on the contrary, did everything it could to discourage it. It published announcements in the European Jewish press warning of hardship in England, and invoked the name of the aged Chief Rabbi to show that newcomers also faced spiritual dangers.[14] It sent agents eastwards to Germany, Poland and Russia to try and stem the flow, and westwards to America and the colonies to direct it there. The Americans, who had their own problems, sent them home with fleas in their ears.

In the meantime the influx continued. The persecution of Jews in Romania, many of whom were literally faced with starvation, gave rise to a new exodus, and in 1899 to 1900 several thousand young Jews, in a gesture of protest and despair, joined in a march on foot across Europe. The Jewish community of one country helped them on to the next and finally, to the dismay of the Board, they staggered ashore in England.

"It is an outrage against the dictates of common sense and humanity that such a senseless and hopeless movement should have been directed to these shores", it declared.[15] Nearly 3,000 marchers reached England. Almost half were dispatched whence they came, "mainly", said the

Board, "at their own request, and naturally, never without their consent". Repatriation was by then an established part of the Board's policy and between 1880 and 1914 the Board sent 50,000 men, women and children back to Europe.[16]

Dr Lipman charitably assumes that the Board was throughout motivated by the fear that unless it did something to keep down immigration the doors would close altogether.[17] This might have been a convincing argument if the doors had been left open, but they were in fact closed by the Aliens Act of 1905, and among those who voted for the Act was Benjamin Cohen, Lionel's brother, a Tory M.P. who was president of the Board from 1887 to 1900.

Lionel Cohen died in 1887 before the activities of the Board became the subject of controversy, but he too was a Tory M.P., and the Tories were the anti-immigration party.

It is now perfectly clear that the Board's policy on immigration and repatriation, far from silencing the anti-immigration groups, gave them their best argument, and Major Evans-Gordon, Tory M.P. for Stepney, who seems to have been the Enoch Powell of his day, used it to the full in the 1905 debate:

> In dealing with the question of the treatment of Jews it is impossible to ignore the actions of the Jewish authorities themselves. For years past they have found it necessary to repatriate large numbers of people who, to quote the words of the Chairman of the Board of Guardians, ought never to have come here. . . . In 1903, 369 cases were sent back to their homes out of a total of 466 who applied to the Jewish Board of Guardians for assistance. . . . We have the evidence of the constant endeavours made by the Jewish authorities, not only to send them back to their homes, but to emigrate them to America and South Africa, and by means of notices posted abroad prevent them from leaving their native country. How in the face of such facts can it be asserted that the influx from Eastern Europe is wholly desirable. . . . (Hansard, 4S, Vol. 133, Col. 1086.)

How indeed? The Bill passed its second reading by 241 to 147 and became law in August 1905.

One cannot blame the Cohens alone. The Board was acting in its capacity as almoner to the Cousinhood. F. D. Mocatta was vice-president during this crucial period, and Leopold de Rothschild was treasurer.

Not all members of the Cousinhood agreed with repatriation, but they did not exert themselves sufficiently to stop it, and, for all the treasures they poured out to help immigrants, they seem to have suffered a failure of nerve. Their fear of criticism outweighed their concern for the oppressed. We have here the beginnings of the argument which divided the old families from the new at the time of the Balfour Declaration.

The death of Lionel Cohen at the age of fifty-five was a serious loss to the community. His father, as we have seen, had persuaded the three City Ashkenazi synagogues to appoint one joint Chief Rabbi. A generation later Lionel, with the encouragement of the Chief Rabbi, brought the synagogues, with their branches in the West End and Bayswater, into one joint body, the United Synagogue. The scheme was embodied in a private Act of Parliament, and given the Royal Assent in July 1870.

Once the body was in being Lionel took a back seat, for he appreciated that if it was to enjoy the allegiance of all sections of the Jewish community, it would have to be headed by the most revered name in it – Rothschild. Sir Anthony was persuaded to become president and Lionel became vice-president.

The Cousinhood, through their direction of the United Synagogue, brought decorum and order into the conduct of synagogue affairs and, without departing from any essential Jewish tradition, managed somehow to anglicise the entire religious establishment. The United Synagogue has always been, as it still is, a profoundly Orthodox body, yet at the same time, during a crucial phase in the history of the Jewish community, it served as an instrument for assimilation.

Lionel was responsible for another important institution, the Jewish house at Clifton College. The old English public schools which, in the main, began their life as teaching places for the deserving poor, were by the nineteenth century taken over by the rich, and the man of substance sent his sons to Eton or Winchester or Harrow. The industrial revolution created a new monied class, and new public schools like Marlborough, Wellington and later Clifton were opened to cater for them. The Cousinhood, who were part of this new class, at first hesitated to send their sons to such schools. In the first place they were unwilling to send their children away from home and then there was the matter of religious education and the dietary laws. But as they became more anglicised they became less hesitant, and by the 1870s there was hardly a major English public school without its quota of Rothschilds, Henriques, Mocattas and Montefiores. There were few Cohens at such schools for they were, on the whole, the most Orthodox branch of the Cousinhood.

Lionel frequently spent his holidays at Clifton, which was then a fashionable spa, and became friendly with Percival, headmaster of the College. Clifton College, at this time, was without a charter and Percival asked Lionel, who was a member of Parliament, if he could use his influence to get one. Lionel thought he could. At the same time there was something which Lionel wanted, a place where Jewish boys could receive the full benefits of an English public school education without at the same time compromising their religious observance. Could one establish a Jewish house at Clifton?

Percival's own mind had been moving in that direction for some time, for he was troubled by the number of Jewish boys scattered about the school who could not join in worship with the Anglicans, but who yet could hardly observe their own faith. Clifton got its charter and in 1879 the Jewish house was established. Thereafter Clifton became the Eton of the Cousinhood.[18]

Jewish houses were later established at Harrow, Cheltenham and The Perse, Cambridge, but the Jewish house at Clifton has outlasted them all, possibly because of the remarkable Polack dynasty which has been at its head since 1890.

Lionel was a considerable authority on the organisation and financing of railways and on Turkish finance. He was a respected City figure, shortish, stocky, bearded, with an immense forehead, and he peered at the world through thick spectacles. His brother Benjamin was similar in appearance and build and together they looked like Tweedledum and Tweedledee. They were both solid, stolid, rather cheerless personages. Their father, according to Benjamin's daughter, Hannah, was "stern and very Orthodox", and they inherited much of his sternness if not his Orthodoxy.[19] They were very English in appearance and mannerisms, the picture of Victorian *haute bourgeoisie*, and certainly when facing the outside world, models of composure. Left among themselves they were usually more voluble and Hannah recalled how a man once entered the office of Louis Cohen & Sons with a large chrysanthemum in his button-hole, "and the Cohens talked so fast and furiously that all the petals blew away".[20]

These reminiscences came from a book by Hannah Cohen called *Changing Faces* which offers an affectionate and rather charming picture of the family in its Victorian heyday.

In the beginning of the nineteenth century the whole family, father, sons, in-laws, lived together in one tight enclave in the City. The next generation scattered to Canonbury, Bloomsbury, Marylebone and beyond to what was almost rural Bayswater. An ancient of the older generation, driving from one child to another, marvelled at their growth in prosperity. "Palaces," he kept saying to himself, "by my God, palaces."[21]

Jeannette, Barent Cohen's grand-daughter, married David Salomons, who became the first Jewish Lord Mayor of London.[22] His election caused great excitement in the family: "Dear Jeannette spent both Saturday and Sunday with us, her husband being engaged with all the great people in the Mansion House."[23]

All were staunch loyalists and even stauncher royalists. Hannah Merton, another of Barent's grand-daughters, kept "ormolu-mounted photographs of the Royal Family . . . side by side with the most cherished of her own kin".[24]

A third grand-daughter, Harriet, married John Wagg, a founder of the banking house of Herbert Wagg & Co., which is now part of the Schroders group. A fourth married S. Joseph, a merchant of New York.

Changing Faces is full of chatter and bustle, of sister-in-law descending upon sister-in-law in elaborate carriages with liveried footmen for sunny afternoons of gossip and tea. One reads of extensive journeys abroad, especially to further the daughters' education. Marriage was of course their final aim, but before that they were expected to master a language or two and they were also taught embroidery, painting and the pianoforte, whether they showed any aptitude or not, to sing if their voice allowed it and entertain in one of the frequent family salons. They were encouraged to visit the poor, but not too frequently, and not without some apprehension about the fevers common to poorer parts of town. There was ample time for gossip, for the exchange of confidences, for cheerful banter, for delicious flirtations. The sterner world of commerce, of politics, of public affairs was left to the sons, but sometimes it broke in upon the charmed lives of the daughters. We find Hannah Merton disturbed and bewildered by reports of anti-Semitism in Europe:

> . . . when religion was the world's test, the Jew was condemned because he condemned the Christian creed; now that talent and skill are offered by all to all, and the Jew, as in Germany, shows more than a proportion of talent and skill, Jew-baiting arises.[25]

But such things were passing clouds. The great excitements of life revolved round family and friends. In 1869 all were agog at reports that Benjamin Cohen, at twenty-five and already a partner in Louis Cohen & Sons, a young man with political ambitions, and the ability to fulfil them, good-looking, but no dandy, was about to become engaged. But to whom? The news leaks out; it is Hannah Merton's daughter Louisa, who, like Benjamin himself, was a great-grandchild of Levi Barent Cohen.

Her cousin Marian Wagg, still a maiden lady, hurries to congratulate her:

> First I must tell you, you are a nasty, deceitful, hypocritical young humbug, but never for one instant did you deceive me. I understand the meaning of a young lady's red cheeks at the sight or mention of a particular gentleman, and for some months I foresaw the melancholy fate that awaited you, or rather the gentleman . . .[26]

It did not prove to be an entirely happy relationship. Louisa was a cultivated woman, widely read and interested in ideas, even where she could not grasp them. She was an intellectual snob among money-snobs, and a determined highbrow. Benjamin was none of these things.

In 1888 he was elected to the newly constituted London County Council and four years later entered Parliament as a Tory M.P. for East Islington. They had a large house in Hyde Park Gardens with butler and servants, but Louisa did not care for the role of Tory political hostess, the formal dinners, the endless *soirées* and *levées*. Her own sympathies were liberal and one can notice between the lines of her daughter Hannah's *Changing Faces* a longing to be free from the solid world in which she was imprisoned.

She found some escape in her children, three sons and a daughter. All four went up to Cambridge and Louisa would sometimes spend weekends with them. She also established a close and lasting association with Louis de Glehn, a young undergraduate who came to the house as a friend of her eldest son Herbert and remained as tutor to her younger son Arthur. They corresponded after he left and their letters continued over the next thirty years.

"I have often thought," she wrote on one occasion, "that one of the great needs we have, one we cry for silently, persistently, because we cry in vain, is the need to disclose ourselves to say what we think, what we feel, what we want, what we are."[27] There are no such disclosures in *Changing Faces* but rather trite observations on things seen and heard:

"I went to Ibsen's play, and enjoyed it; a lady who went with me was rather shocked until I assured her it was symbolic . . ."

Yet her *cri de coeur* was honest enough. She was a sensitive, if not overarticulate, woman with cosmopolitan tastes, or at least pretensions, caught in the stubborn provincialism of middle-class Jewish life.

In 1897 Benjamin acquired Highfields, a two-hundred acre country estate at Shoreham, near Sevenoaks, and there, at last Louisa found contentment. One hears no further Chekovian sighs for idylls. Louisa and her children took to Highfields as to the manor born. Her daughter hunted with the local fox-hounds, her sons served with the West Kent Volunteers, the youngest, Ernest, was captain of the village cricket team and Louisa presented the club with a pavilion.

In the meantime Benjamin's health began to give cause for concern, and in 1901 he resigned both from the London County Council and the Board of Guardians. He retained his seat in the House of Commons, but lost it in the Liberal landslide of 1906, an event which did not help his recovery, though he had the consolation of a baronetcy in the dissolution honours and died in 1909. He believed, wrote his daughter, "that loyalty to his faith was part of the service he owed to his country". The epitaph on his stone at Willesden Jewish Cemetery perhaps sums up his career: HE DID HIS BEST FOR HIS COUNTRY AND HIS COMMUNITY.[28]

During the war Herbert and Arthur enlisted in the army, the daughter joined the V.A.D. and Louisa dug for victory. She sold her London home and rarely stirred from Kent. She was, said a neighbouring land owner, "the greatest *grande dame* he had ever met".[29]

Her eldest son Herbert married a daughter of Henry Behrens; her other children remained single.

Hannah was no beauty – few of the females in the Cousinhood were – but she had compensating attractions. She had studied at Roedean and Newnham, had a lively, intelligent mind, a warm personality, and some talent as a writer, but there was always a shortage of eligible male cousins, and during the war years there was a famine.

It was unthinkable to marry out of her class – partly because she rarely met anyone outside it – and equally unthinkable for the daughter of a vice-president of the United Synagogue, and a niece of its founder, to marry outside the faith, and much to the disappointment of her mother, she did not marry.

The family found consolation in Herbert's sons, two splendid young boys, Nigel and Stephen, who remained unspoilt for all the affection and attention lavished upon them. They were a particular joy to Louisa and as they grew older she liked to have them round to brighten up her conversations. The boys were deeply fond of their grandmother, but they could not pretend that these gatherings were the gayest of occasions.

"I occasionally feel sorry for the people who come to tea and who generally leave with a slightly bewildered expression on their faces," wrote Stephen. "Politics or even economics they can manage, but Art and Einstein in one afternoon is too much."[30] One wonders how far

Louisa managed Einstein, for she had no training in mathematics, and it is unlikely that she understood the quantum theory. She certainly believed in making the effort however, and even in old age she tried to keep abreast of the latest ideas, and she continued to give de Glehn the benefits of her erudition.

Nigel went to Harrow, Stephen to Eton, and both went to Cambridge. Nigel, perhaps the livelier of the two, was a popular young man-about-the-quad, president of the university Tories, had expensive taste in fast cars and fast company, and was regularly seen at nearby races, point-to-point meetings and hunt balls. In 1931, when he was twenty-three, a small plane which he was flying, crashed and he was killed instantly. Louisa, who was already in failing health, took to her bed and sat propped up on pillows, gazing silently out on her beloved Kent countryside with mirrors arranged round the room to extend her vision. She died two months later.

The attention which concentrated upon Stephen at this time must have been intolerable, but he emerged as a wholesome, healthy, supremely sane young man, gay, fun-loving, enjoying the pursuits of town and country:

> I played cricket for Shoreham . . . it was all very nice and patriarchal, people quite obviously like to see me there; working men seem to weave a romantic halo round the local gentry.[31]

In 1933 he was called to the Bar. As a son of Sir Herbert and grandson of Sir Benjamin Cohen he felt compelled to take a hand in Jewish affairs and was active on the Board of Guardians, an honorary officer of the United Synagogue, and on the council of Jews' College, which had been established in 1855 to train Orthodox Jewish clergy. He was himself totally removed in thinking and way of life from Orthodoxy, had little to do with Jews outside his family, and nothing to do with Judaism and his devoted Aunt Hannah felt compelled to explain his role in the Orthodox establishment:

> It is only fair to say that he was not in sympathy with the view of the very Orthodox, but he had strong convictions and was deeply interested and not without hope of exercising in time some modernising influence. In this as in other things he believed in building on tradition and not in breaking with it.[32]

On the outbreak of World War II he enlisted, like his father and uncles before him, in the West Kent Regiment and became the battalion's Intelligence Officer. In 1941 he was transferred to Eastern Command Headquarters and there found a new broom about the place:

Have been busy with the army changes; as you will have seen we have a new general round here, youngish man for a general – 51 I think – and maybe a bit of a genius, is at any rate a fire-eater and the stormy petrel of the army, Montgomery by name.[33]

He was bored at Eastern Command and in 1942 applied for transfer to the Indian Army as the quickest means of seeing active service.

In that same year there was a rising of an extreme religious sect in Sind led by their hereditary leader the Pir Pagaro. The rising was suppressed, the Pir arrested and martial law was imposed. Stephen, as a lawyer, was summoned to the Judge Advocate's Department and charged with preparing the case against Pagaro. Pagaro had been charged once before after leading an abortive revolt in 1930. He had, wrote Stephen, "the most startling eyes, 'heaven bestowed' is the local epithet for them".[34] In the 1930 hearing Pagaro so hypnotised crown witnesses that they would not give evidence against him and the case collapsed. This time the authorities took no chances and constructed a special court so that witnesses could not see him, or he them. The evidence which Stephen brought together proved conclusive and the Pir was found guilty and hanged.

A few days later Stephen was taken ill with an internal abscess which failed to respond to treatment and he died in February 1943, a few days short of his thirty-second birthday. An army friend wrote to his parents:

I think that Stephen's short life has had a very special significance in these days when your race is suffering so atrociously, and when the plague of anti-Semitism seems even to be spreading. By his background of your country home, by Eton and King's, and now by his death Stephen was in the heart and centre of the English tradition. At the same time he was a proud Jew. No better example could be found of genuine nationalism as opposed to the cheap imitation we are fighting today. Many of Stephen's friends at Cambridge, in his regiment, or elsewhere will always remember him as the answer to cheap and ignorant criticism of your people.[35]

This letter, though true in every detail, does not convey with sufficient force the governing passion of Stephen's life, his love for England, and especially Kent. One can see this in a little couplet he wrote in his early twenties, whose very clumsiness marks it as an expression of true feeling:

> I love the Kentish woods so wild, so free
>   And yet so ordered.
> Symbolic of all England, every tree
>   Sun flecked, each stream lush-bordered.[36]

Every hope in the family of parents, uncles, aunts had been vested in Stephen. Now there was despair. Hannah died in 1946, Uncle Ernest in 1955, his mother in 1963, Uncle Arthur in 1966. His father alone remained, ambling from room to room of his large empty mansion. He died in 1968 in his ninety-fifth year, and with his death the baronetcy and a branch of the Cohen dynasty fell away.

Other branches are still flourishing.

Lionel Cohen had five sons and one daughter. His eldest, Edward died unmarried at the age of fifty-one and the youngest at twenty-three. Each of the others established considerable dynasties of their own. All three entered the family firm of Louis Cohen & Sons, and all retired in 1901 with considerable fortunes. The eldest of them, Leonard Lionel Cohen, remained an active figure in the City both as a member of the Committee of the London Stock Exchange and as a director of several railway companies. He was president of the Jewish Board of Guardians for over twenty years and president for a time of the Jewish Colonisation Association; but his principal interest was the King Edward's Hospital Fund, which he served as honorary secretary and whose financial and administrative structure he helped to reorganise. He was created a Knight Companion of the Royal Victorian Order in recognition of this work. He acquired extensive property interests and when he died in 1938 his will was proved at over £300,000. He had one daughter, Irene (who married Colonel Thomas Sebag-Montefiore) and a son, the present Lord Cohen of Walmer, one of the most eminent jurists of our day.

The second brother, Frank, seven years Leonard Lionel's junior, was a less active figure. He was thirty-six when the family bank was dissolved and he spent the rest of his long life (he died in 1955 at the age of ninety) doing nothing in particular but doing it with *élan*. He was an inveterate clubman and his favourite club was perhaps the St Stephen, opposite the Houses of Parliament. He lived in Bayswater and one of his daily activities was to traverse the four royal parks – Kensington Gardens, Hyde Park, Green Park and St James's – on his way to the club. Then there was lunch and political chit-chat, and a sleep perhaps in a deep, leather armchair, then home in a cab to tea. One could not be home too late for one always had to change, be it for a charity dinner, a family celebration, or even for a meal with one's own immediate family at home. And on Friday night he and his wife would take it in turns with his other brothers and be at home to the entire clan.

Frank married, in 1896, Bertha, a daughter of Simon Waley Waley and they had two sons and three daughters. One of the sons became friendly with C. P. Snow while at Cambridge. This friendship has lasted throughout their lifetime, and inspired one of Snow's novels *The Conscience of the Rich* in which the central figure is based on Frank Cohen. Frank was a somewhat choleric individual, even peevish and his principal preoccupation was his attempt to organise the lives of his children for them. He failed disastrously – which did not, however, prevent him from trying again, and yet again.

One of his first setbacks was when his daughter Betty announced that she wanted to marry a young man called Albert Polack. Polack? Polack? The name was Jewish and it rang a bell, but was he a member of the Cousinhood? No, he was the son of the Rev. Polack, a cleric who was master of the Jewish house at Clifton.

Young Polack, a slight, fragile figure, with a large head, who had lately come down from Cambridge and was an assistant master at Taunton School, was brought before him.

Frank looked him up and down, then down and up.

"Are you" – these were his very words – "Are you in a position to maintain my daughter in the manner to which she's been accustomed?"

Polack thought probably not.

"How much do you earn?"

"Three hundred pounds."

"*A year?*"

"A year."[37]

End of interview.

But Betty persisted in her choice, the mother was sympathetic, and finally after Polack received a promise that he would succeed his father as housemaster at Clifton, he was accepted entirely into the family. The marriage took place in the Central Synagogue, Great Portland Street, in the presence of God, the Chief Rabbi and the assembled Cousinhood, and it has been an exceedingly happy one.

Polack had been an exception for it was unusual for Jews of his class to reach Cohen tables. C. P. Snow, who is of humble origins, ate frequently at Frank's, but Snow was a goy. "Had I been a Jew," he said, "I would not have been allowed to set foot in the house. One never saw Jews of my class among the Cohens."[38]

Polack met Betty through her brothers who were boarders at Clifton. Their aunt, Mrs Robert Waley-Cohen often took a houseboat at Henley for the regatta and she would invite all the young cousins and their friends. It was an annual marriage fair. They did not see much of the races but saw a great deal of each other. It was at Henley that John Sebag-Montefiore, a Lloyd's underwriter, who is now the senior member of the Montefiore family, met his wife, and it was there that Polack first met his future wife.

"Quite irresponsible, the sort of people they invite," observed Frank.

But if he could not stop his daughter from marrying a pauper, he could see that her money was securely tied up, and drew up a marriage settlement of such complexity as to baffle all but the most brilliant lawyers. There was a large sum of money involved, but it was all tied up in trusts with the capital passing from daughter to children and from children to grandchildren unto the nth generation.

The settlement, complained the daughter in *The Conscience of the Rich*, was made "on the assumption that I was an imbecile and Francis was a crook. Francis never touches a penny. The settlement never gives him a chance. When I die the money goes straight to the children. . . . All the marriage settlements in the family followed the same pattern. None but a March should handle March money."[39]

Frank Cohen had been to Harrow, which in his day had a Jewish house. By the time he married the Jewish house was defunct and he therefore sent his own boys to Polack's, the Jewish house at Clifton. The Jewish regime at Polack's was hardly oppressive. It meant in the main being in synagogue while the others were in chapel, but the boys were unhappy at being kept apart at all.

What pained them was that it gave them a particular identity, singled them out as Jews, while they yearned to be simply boys like the others. Their feelings, many years after Clifton, are voiced by Charles March, the hero, in *The Conscience of the Rich*.

I haven't enjoyed being a Jew. Since I was a child I haven't been allowed to forget that other people see me through different eyes. They label me with a difference I cannot accept. . . .

I know that I sometimes make myself feel a stranger, I know that very well. But still other people have made me feel stranger far more than I have myself. It isn't their fault. It's simply a fact. But it's a fact that interferes with your spirit and nags at you. Sometimes it torments you – particularly when you're young. I went to Cambridge desperately anxious to make friends who would be so intimate that I would forget it. I was aching for that kind of personal success – to be liked for the person I believed myself to be. I thought if I couldn't be liked in that way, there was nothing for it: I might as well go straight back to the ghetto.[40]

Religion as practised in the Cohen family consisted of nine parts ancestor worship to one part Jehovah worship. One helped in Jewish causes because one's parents did, one did not eat pork because one's parents did not, one belonged to a synagogue without setting foot in it because it was founded by one's father or grandfather. Besides, in England at this time one jolly well had to belong to something, and one could not, if one had self-respect, belong to a church. And one celebrated the Sabbath as a family jamboree. The children thus suffered the small discomfitures of being a Jew, without any of the consolations of Judaism and it was perhaps inevitable that as they grew older they should turn against it. A son and a daughter married out of the faith, and none of Frank's grandchildren except the Polacks, have remained within it.

The Cohens are no longer a monied clan, for they are no longer a banking clan, and the talents which earlier generations of the family applied to commerce are now being applied to the professions and the civil service, and with equal distinction. Richard Cohen, the original of Charles March, is a physician and Permanent Under-Secretary of the Ministry of Health. His cousin Ruth Cohen, who held high rank in the Civil service for a time as an agricultural economist, is now Mistress of Newnham College, Cambridge. Her sister Catherine is married to the Rev. Arthur Hunt, an Anglican clergyman who was a master at Rugby. Her brother was the late Sir Andrew Cohen, who was head of the Ministry of Overseas Development at the time of his death in 1968, but who is best remembered as a Colonial administrator of almost legendary ability.

Andrew was born in 1909 and entered the Colonial Office when the sun was already beginning to set on the empire and the main energies of the service were engaged in dismantling it, for the Government was concerned that the retreat should not be a shambles, and to leave a tradition of probity, discipline and the rule of law. Andrew, who had leftish views, was very much in sympathy with this policy, and he directed it first as Assistant Under-Secretary in Whitehall from 1947 to 1951, and then from 1952 to 1957 as Governor-General of Uganda.

He was a large, robust, rumbustious, purposeful man, who knew where he was going and how to get there, and was impatient of obstruction along the way. He did not suffer fools gladly and tended to regard anyone who disagreed with him as a fool. He was perhaps the most imperious anti-imperialist in the history of the empire, and where his writ ran one somehow had the feeling that Victoria, was still on the throne.

But he was no bully, and if he had his way, as he usually did, it was by reasoning and not by rage or bluster. Andrew was a massive man – a white Lobengula somebody called him – but the most massive thing about him was his intellect. But again, he was no detached, desiccated technocrat. He had the deepest love for Africa, and the deepest sympathy for African aspirations, and although his years in the Colonial service were not devoid of clashes, he was able to win the affection and respect, and even awe, of most Africans with whom he came in contact. They came to look upon him not as the representative of an alien authority, but as their very own chief.

He became a centre of controversy in 1953 after serious difficulties developed between him and the Kabaka, or 'King Freddie' as Fleet Street dubbed him, the native ruler of Buganda, a tribal area within the Uganda Protectorate.

The Government was guiding Uganda towards independence, but the Kabaka wanted his own tribal area to be separated from the rest of Uganda and given independent status. This would have jeopardised the progress of the entire protectorate and was contrary to an agreement on the matter reached shortly before between the Kabaka and the Governor.

Inevitably there followed charges of gubernatorial high-handedness and quick temper, but Sir Andrew had shown the greatest moderation and patience and when the matter was finally raised in the House of Commons, the Colonial Secretary, Mr Oliver Lyttleton was able to reassure critics:

> Sir Andrew Cohen is a man with a long record of fruitful and enlightened work for Africans, a man of wide and liberal views, of outstanding ability and intellectual force. If anyone was likely to persuade the Kabaka, it would be the Governor. Moreover, it was known to me that on some other occasions when the Kabaka was in minor disagreement with the Colonial office, Sir Andrew Cohen had conducted the negotiations on the Kabaka's behalf with some success. I wish to dispose of any idea that these matters had been quickly and brusquely dealt with. Nothing could be further from the truth. The Governor had six long interviews with the Kabaka. . .[41]

In 1957 Sir Andrew was appointed Permanent British Representative at the United Nations Trusteeship Council. He was an articulate spokesman and skilled negotiator, but he also showed unusual qualities of diplomacy and tact. When he returned to London in 1961 he was given the task of co-ordinating the help given to former colonial territories. Three years later when the Government created a Ministry for Overseas Development, Sir Andrew was the natural figure to head it. It is not easy for a former colonial power to be helpful without appearing to be patronising. There was still, even in the 1960s, a mildly Kiplingesque air about some Civil servants on overseas duties, a slight feeling that they were still carrying something of the white man's burden. Sir Andrew gathered new men about him and inculcated a new outlook, and where there had been a sense of giver and receiver, he developed a sense of partnership. When he died suddenly in 1968 the feeling of loss in the former colonial territories was profound, as the immense assembly of African leaders at his memorial service testified.

Andrew had not followed his cousins to Clifton but went to Malvern, and thence to Trinity College, Cambridge. He married a Christian but could hardly be said to have married out of the faith, for he had none, and was so far removed from Jewish life that he suffered none of the pangs experienced by his cousins from their residual Jewishness.

When he died, the memorial service was held in St Paul's Cathedral, but his widow felt that some gesture should be made to his antecedents, and the lesson was read by Chaim Raphael, a senior Treasury official and former Hebrew lecturer at Oxford, who was trained at Jews' College and who had at one time intended to be a Rabbi.

Andrew was one of six children. Two died in infancy, two never married. Andrew's own child had not been brought up as a Jew, and his sister Catherine's children were brought up in the Church of England, and thus another branch of the family has fallen away from Jewish life. Of all Lionel's progeny, only the children of Sir Leonard have remained identifiably Jewish – Irene, who married Colonel Thomas Sebag-Montefiore, and Lionel Lord Cohen of Walmer.

The Clifton tradition in the family had weakened by the time Lionel grew to boyhood and he was sent to Eton and thence to New College, Oxford. He had hoped to enter the Civil Service, but a good understanding of either classics or mathematics was required and he excelled in neither. So he turned to law.

It was a calling which had attracted several members of his family, and one in particular, Arthur Cohen, a distant cousin, born in 1830, had overcome serious handicaps to become a Queen's Counsel and Privy Councillor and one of the most eminent jurists of his day. One of the first difficulties *he* had to surmount was that the ancient universities were closed to Jews and Non-conformists until 1870. He studied at Cambridge, and was even elected president of the Union in 1852, but he could not take his degree till after 1870. A few years later he was appointed standing counsel for the university.

GOLDSMID

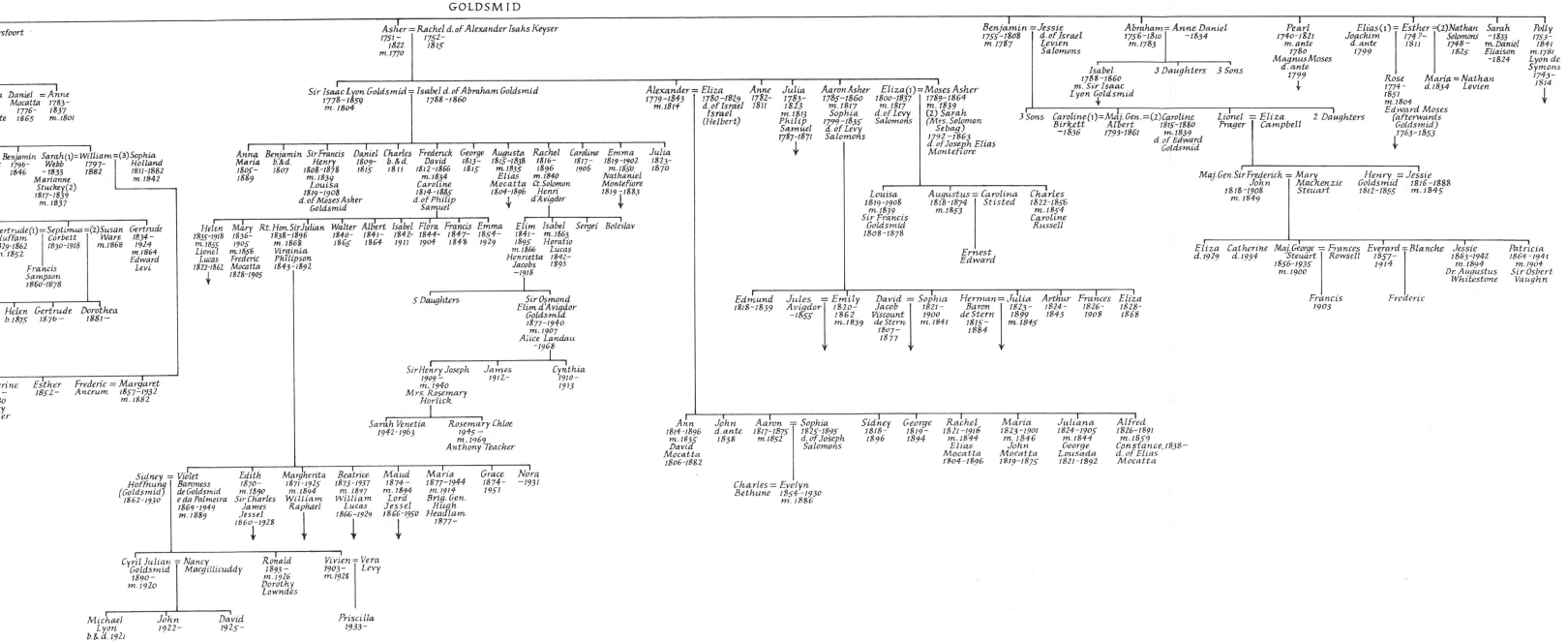

Like most members of the Cousinhood, but unlike his own immediate family, he was a Liberal in politics and sat as M.P. for Southwark from 1880-7. He was at one point in his career offered a judgeship by Lord Selborne, the Lord Chancellor, but it would have meant a by-election at an awkward moment in Liberal fortunes. Gladstone persuaded him to refuse and was given to understand that another opportunity would be forthcoming. Selborne retired and was replaced by Herschell and Herschell was less favourably disposed to him. The opportunity never came again. "What can Cohen expect of Herschel but a passover?" observed a colleague. Herschel was the son of a baptised Jew.

When Britain was involved in prolonged litigation with the United States over the depredations of the British-built and Confederate-owned warship Alabama during the American Civil War, Cohen was retained as one of Her Majesty's counsel, and he acted in a similar capacity during the litigation between the Crown and Venezuela. He was a counsel too in the Jameson Raid Inquiry.

Cohen was a believing Jew with the greatest veneration for tradition and he was attracted by Jewish ceremonies. He found the Passover ritual particularly moving, and once observed in a letter:

> It warms my Jewish blood and makes me feel that I belong to a peculiar race, of which and of whose history I am proud. There is a magnificent passage in one of Lord Chatham's speeches, and also in one of Burke's orations, in which they speak of high and noble feelings called forth by a long series of illustrious ancestors, and I sometimes think that when I retire from my profession, I may do something for Judaism, but it would be on lines very different from those of Claude Montefiore.[42]

These were passing sensations. He never acted on his intentions and far from finding time 'to do something for Judaism', he rarely found time even to be in synagogue.

In 1880 he was elected president of the Board of Deputies. As a nephew of Sir Moses Montefiore he held the office almost by hereditary succession but he felt compelled to resign fifteen years later when one of his daughters married Sir Theodore Morison, a senior member of the Indian Civil Service, who was not a Jew.

Cohen had three sons and five daughters. His oldest daughter Lucy was a gifted writer and the biographer of Claude Montefiore and Lady Louisa de Rothschild. His eldest son Benjamin was a barrister who was elected Master of the Bench of the Inner Temple in 1923 and was knighted for public services in 1929. In 1890 Benjamin married Marguerite Cohen, a first cousin. They died within a few hours of each other in 1942 and were buried under Church of England rites in Limpsfield Parish Church. It was not known when or why they converted to Christianity.

Arthur Cohen died in 1914 in his eighty-fifth year.

Cohen was a lawyer's lawyer and one found him involved mainly in cases, which though of major importance in themselves, excited little public attention. They required a keen and capacious intellect, but beyond that – and this seems to be a quality in which the Cohens excelled – an appetite for detail, the ability to assimilate endless and intricate agglomerations of fact.

Lionel Cohen has inherited this faculty to the full. In 1957 in the aftermath of the Suez campaign, there was a sharp spurt of inflation and the government appointed a special committee, with Cohen as chairman, on Prices, Productivity and Incomes. The committee was at once dubbed by the press as 'The Three Wise Men', and Cohen, with his massive head, shrewd, probing, yet pensive eyes, and his general air of sagacity, looked the part perfectly.

He was born in 1888 and called to the Bar in 1913. In 1943 he was raised to the Bench as a Justice of the High Court (Chancery Division), and three years later he was appointed a Lord Justice of Appeal and a Privy Councillor, and in 1951 he became a life peer as a Lord of Appeal in Ordinary.

Lord Cohen is a master of analysis with a homing instinct for the heart of any problem, and 'call for Cohen' has been the reaction of many a hard-pressed government committee when confronted with a particularly baffling situation. Thus he has in his time presided over the Company Law Amendments Committee, the Royal Commission on Awards to Inventors, the court of inquiry into the Comet Air Liner Disaster as well as the Council on Prices, Productivity and Incomes.

In 1918, while on leave from the army, Cohen married Adelaide Spielmann, a daughter of Sir Isidore Spielmann. Their marriage was a particularly happy one and they had two sons and a daughter.

In 1940 the daughter, Elizabeth, married Arthur Pearce-Serocold, a captain in the Welsh Guards. He was killed in action in 1942 and four years later she married Major Peter Samuel, M.C. a son of the second Lord Bearstead, and deputy chairman of Hill Samuel & Co, Ltd, merchant bankers, and a director of Shell.

The Hon. Leonard Harold Cohen, the elder son, was called to the Bar but made his career in the City and is a director of Hill Samuel. His wife, Eleanor, is a daughter of Philip Quixano Henriques, chief engineer of Shell in Australia. The youngest son, Hugh Lionel, is married to a daughter of the Rt. Hon. Sir Arthur Karminski, a High Court judge and Master of the Bench of the Inner Temple.

Lord Cohen is perhaps the most distinguished layman in the Jewish community and when, for example, the Board of Deputies wanted to send loyal greetings on behalf of Anglo-Jewry to the late George VI on the marriage of Princess Elizabeth, they called on him to lead the delegation. In 1956 when the community celebrated the tercentenary of Jewish settlement in this country, Lord Cohen was among the principal figures at the top table. He was a vice-president of the Jewish Board of Guardians before the war, the president from 1940 to 1947, but that was the discharge of a family duty: the son of Leonard and a grandson of Lionel Cohen could do no less, but after the war he found himself involved in a wide variety of causes, including some concerned with Israel.

He is a governor of the Hebrew University, an office which used to take him to Israel about once a year. He was moved by his visits, but was never tempted to stay there. He is too much a part of England, and England is too much a part of him.

Though essentially religious he is in no way Orthodox. His father had made no attempt to instil any of the family Orthodoxy into him, and he has allowed his own children to find their own way to their faith, and is rather pleasantly surprised to see that they have remained Jewish. "I wouldn't have expected them to remain in the faith if I had attempted to give them an Orthodox upbringing," he said.[43] He is a member both of the United Synagogue and the Liberal Synagogue, though he is active in the latter rather than the former, and is president of the Union of Liberal and Progressive Synagogues.

He inherited a fortune but his style of living has been almost frugal. Taxes are high, longevity runs in the family, and one has to be careful. He rode occasionally, but rides no more. He used to shoot, still does occasionally, but badly. His main love has been golf and he was for a time captain of the Royal and Ancient Golf Club, St Andrews. He used to have a fifteen–bedroom house at Walmer because it was near an excellent golf course, but the house proved to be too large and expensive and he is now largely confined to London. But he has still, at eighty-three, not entirely abandoned golf. He played four holes at the Royal St George's course last August, and a few holes on a pitch and putt course.

He is about the last survivor of the old family enclave in Bayswater and lives in a large house in Porchester Terrace. Lord Samuel used to live across the road, and the Franklins up the road, and the Montagues down the road, and the Spielmanns and the Magnuses and the Montefiores and their various collaterals all about the area. But the houses are gone, or converted into flats or private hotels – some of them very private. As people grow older they tend to surround themselves with relics of their younger days till in time their house becomes a museum with themselves as a walking exhibit. There is nothing of that about Lord Cohen's home, though there is a great deal about Lord Cohen himself which is old-worldly – the calmness, the courtesy . . . "Would you like to . . . would you care to . . . Is your chair quite comfortable? A glass of sherry?" And then the drink proffered from a crystal decanter in a crystal glass, and sipped slowly and thoughtfully. A clock in the hall ticks away with what seems to be undue excitement.

CHAPTER 18

Patriarch-Matriarch

The growth of Liverpool in the eighteenth century attracted exotic elements from all over the world, including a handful of Jews. By the end of the century the Jews were numerous enough to acquire rooms for a synagogue and bourgeois enough to require of its members certain minimal standards of deportment. No congregant, declared a synagogue by-law, "who receives a summons to the Torah dare wear jackboots outside his trousers, nor a coloured handkerchief around his neck, nor may he chew tobacco. Should he commit any of these offences he will be fined one shilling."

The spiritual head of the congregation, or the 'Jews' High Priest', as he was described in the Liverpool directory, was Rabbi Benjamin ben Elijakim Getz, who adopted the name of Benjamin Yates. His congregants could not pay him a living wage and he dabbled in various crafts, including jewellery and engraving. His brother Samuel, also an engraver, coupled his skill as a craftsman with a certain entrepreneurial flair and toured the country offering the newly rich instant antiquity by supplying them with coats of arms, either invented, or borrowed from those of another family. He himself assumed the crest of the Yates of Wiltshire.

The lay head of the community was Ralph Samuel, a clothier. Ralph Samuel had many sons, Samuel Yates had many daughters. The two families intermarried and eventually drew in another family of Samuels who had lately arrived in the north from London. They in turn were joined by the Franklin family, who claim to trace their descent from King David, and a branch of which settled in London in the eighteenth century and then moved north to Liverpool.

The Yates-Samuel, Samuel-Franklin combination was prolific and talented. The name of Samuel(s) in its various branches predominates, and some, in order to distinguish themselves from others, changed their names. One such was Montagu Samuel, who simply reversed his names to become Samuel Montagu. He was born in Liverpool in December 1832, the youngest of seven children. He was an earnest boy, passionately fond of books and study. He could vanish from view for hours on end in one of the city libraries, and could, on occasion, smuggle a novel into synagogue to read between the sober covers of a prayer book. At fourteen he was compelled to leave school to supplement the family income, and throughout his life tried to find time to make up for his lack of a formal education. He took a job with a firm of foreign exchange merchants in Liverpool one of whose principals, Adam Spielman, was married to his sister, Marian. When the arrangement did not work out happily he moved south to London to act as London agent for a small Paris bank. Then, with the help of £3,000 borrowed from his father, he opened an office in Leadenhall Street and set up in business on his own account.

The joint-stock banks were not yet very numerous nor were they as yet well known, and there was still ample scope for the small private establishments. Montagu began in business just as the British economy was gathering speed for a phenomenal leap forward, and he leapt with it. Brothers, brothers-in-law, cousins were pulled in as partners and assistants. He moved from Leadenhall Street to Cornhill and thence to Broad Street.

He was a man of great energy and perception. He also acquired an understanding of the workings of foreign exchange which at that time was rare in the City, despite the fact that London was already the commercial capital of the world. By his late twenties he had amassed a considerable fortune.

Montagu's success went with a modest bearing and earnestness of temper. He still, among all his business ventures, found time to read widely and deeply. He retained every particle of Jewish observance which he had learned at home. It was inevitable that he should marry into the Cousinhood, but he confined his choice to its most religious branch, the Cohens.

When he was thirty Montagu became a regular guest at the home of Louis Cohen, a grandson of Levi Barent Cohen. Louis' home, in Gloucester Place, Marylebone, displayed the solid opulence of an upper middle-class Victorian dwelling. Louis himself was a man of exceptional piety whom Montagu much admired. Sabbath was observed with the meticulousness ordained by tradition. Montagu would usually call on Friday evenings, when the entire family, father, mother and eight children, together with occasional visitors, were assembled for a meal which was part ritual and part banquet. Ellen, one of the younger daughters, became deeply attached to him. They married in March 1862, and had ten children.

Samuel Montagu was not a banker in the normal sense of the word. He operated on a colossal scale in the main as an exchange dealer in currency and bullion. One of his earlier transactions included a contract for the supply of £1,000,000 in silver to the German Government. His advice was frequently sought by both Liberal and Tory Chancellors of the Exchequer. He served on the gold and silver commission from 1887 to 1890 and was a tireless advocate of decimalisation. It has taken eighty years for his ideas to be adopted.

In 1885 he was elected Liberal M.P. for Whitechapel and acquired an honoured place on the Radical wing of the party though his most important contributions to debate were as a spokesman on high finance.

Although a Radical in politics, he was diehard in religion, a paradox which did not escape the obituarists. "On the surface," commented the Liberal *Daily News*, "his combination of advanced radicalism in secular affairs with conservatism in religious affairs may seem a trifle odd, but to those who penetrate below the distracting labels the essential consistency of the two attitudes will be plain."[1]

His radicalism in fact was an aspect of his religious conservatism. When one says he was a devout Jew it was not merely in the sense that, say, Lady Anthony de Rothschild was a devout Jewess. His Judaism did not consist merely of reflecting upon a page of homiletics on the Sabbath or fasting on the Day of Atonement. He was observant in the sense that Sir Moses Montefiore was, and assumed the burden of the entire *Shulchan Aruch*, the great codex of Jewish law, in all its aspects and all its minutiae, from the manifold intricacies of the dietary laws to separation from his wife during her unclean period.

He had never known a day's illness till the end of his life and attributed this to his strict adherence to Mosaic law, both in diet and personal hygiene. He was also helped by an abstemious way of life that verged on the frugal. He had a large mansion at 12 Kensington Palace Gardens and a 1,200-acre estate at Swaythling, near Southampton, but neither place saw the sumptuous banquets or the glittering assemblies that one might find at Rothschilds'. There are religious Jews who try to compensate for all the mustn'ts by over-indulging in things they may. Montagu was not among them.

His daughter Lilian painted this picture of him:

> The religion of Samuel Montagu affected his whole conception of life. He was a Jew primarily – and citizen, a politician, a business man long afterwards. It was with Jewish eyes that he judged men and things. His religion was to him a source of discipline, and he never got outside this discipline for a single instant. He believed in God with the intensity of an intense nature, and his God was a law-giver whose laws were worthy of the closest attention and most complete allegiance. Obedience and the self-sacrifice which it involved led him to holiness. He never chaffed under the discipline. He literally loved to obey the smallest enactment, and this obedience was the form of communion by which tradition told him God was to be reached.[2]

But beyond the enactment was the spirit of the faith and Montagu accepted almost literally the belief that he was his brother's keeper. He was pained by the poverty and squalor he saw around him and sought legislation which would improve the standard of industrial dwellings and a redistribution of wealth. He set aside a tithe of his income for charity as a matter of course, but gave much beyond it. C. B. Fry, the English cricketer, described one instance of his generosity. Fry, who was interested in child welfare, had established a training ship, H.M.S. *Mercury*, for boys from poor homes. Everyone he turned to gave him advice, but of money there was little, except from Montagu. "He was," wrote Fry, "the kindest of men, and with his splendid white beard accorded with one's idea of Moses. All the kinder of him in that we were nominally a Church of England training ship and he was a strict Jew."[3]

He donated twenty-six acres of land at Edmonton to the London County Council for the provision of working-class housing and followed it up with a gift of £10,000. For many years he was a director of the Four Percent Industrial Dwellings Company, a non-profit-making concern which pioneered the provision of good working-class housing. In Parliament and out he advocated the provision of evening classes and state guardianship for neglected children. He wanted legal aid for the poor and the municipalisation of public utilities like water. He was a keen supporter of death duties, and preferred a higher direct tax to purchase tax, which, he felt, weighed most heavily on the poor. He fought the 1888 Early Closing Bill which, though a progressive measure designed to help shop assistants, would have hit the small shopkeeper badly. He believed that the hereditary peerage was a serious obstacle to social reform and was treasurer of the League for the Abolition of the House of Lords. When the Liberal party split in 1886 over Gladstone's Home Rule for Ireland Bill, and the Rothschilds joined the Unionists, Montagu remained loyal to Gladstone. This was partly due to the fact that he had many Irish constituents, but he was also a great admirer, almost a worshipper of Gladstone. They had many things in common, staunch adherence to principle, high moral purpose, deep religious feelings, a close appreciation of the immaterial things which govern human conduct, sympathy for the down-trodden, the determination to do what was right at no matter what personal or political cost. Here, in short, was the man of principle as a man of action.

Montagu differed from his leader on the Eastern Question. Gladstone was anti-Turk and pro-Russian; Montagu, because of Russia's attitude to the Jews, tended to be anti-Russian and pro-Turk, but this did not impair the high regard he had for Gladstone, and the most memorable occasion in his life was the visit which Gladstone paid to Kensington Palace Gardens. He could hardly believe that he could have such a great eminence under his own roof, and, as his daughter recalled, "showed almost childlike excitement beforehand, and was supremely happy throughout the evening, particularly at the success of the party, and the evident enjoyment of the honoured guest".[4]

Montagu was heard rarely in the House of Commons and never with pleasure. His presence commanded attention. He was tall, robust, with broad shoulders, a magnificent head, long, flowing beard, and piercing eyes, but his delivery was poor, and he was apt to wander and repeat himself. He was heard with respect on financial topics, but he looked upon his function as an M.P. mainly as a servant of his constituents and in this he was unsurpassed.

He retired from Whitechapel in 1900 in favour of his nephew Sir Stuart M. Samuel and then contested Leeds Central, where he was heavily defeated. He was not unduly pained by the defeat, which was predictable. The House of Commons was for him, after the death of Gladstone, a lustreless place. In 1894, on the recommendation of Lord Rosebery, he was made a baronet, and was raised to the peerage in 1907. By then some of his radicalism had ebbed.

His political creed, wrote his daughter, was based on biblical authority:

He found in the Old Testament the expression of his faith in the separation of Church and State, in the liability of employment, in the State responsibility for human life and health, in the limitation of the hours of labour, in the laws against entail and primogeniture, and the accumulation of lands. Here, too, he found the doctrine of worth before birth revealed, and this doctrine inspired his Liberalism throughout his life.[5]

In the 1880s the small and compact Anglo-Jewish community was suddenly overwhelmed by the inrush of newcomers from Russia and Poland. The old families who had been accustomed to assimilate the newcomers as they arrived could not cope. The old institutions headed by the Cousinhood, like the Jews' Free School and the Board of Guardians which tried, and on the whole succeeded, to convert the raw sons of the ghettos into English gentlemen, were unequal to the new challenge. What was worse, the newcomers did not want to be converted. Far from wishing to shake off the dust of the ghetto, they brought the ghetto with them, and round the back alleys of Whitechapel there were formed small diasporas from Plotsk and Pinsk, Klotsk and Minsk, each with its own steamy bethel, or *Chevrot* as they were known. They were watched with frank dismay by the older families who saw them as a threat to the recently acquired respectability and standing which they enjoyed in the wider community and for which they had struggled for so long.

These *Chevrot*, declared the *Jewish Chronicle*, the mouthpiece of the older families, "originate partly in the aversion felt by the foreign poor to the religious manners and customs of English Jews. The sooner the immigrants to our shores learn to reconcile themselves to their new conditions of living, the better for themselves. Whatever tends to perpetuate the isolation of this element in the community must be dangerous to its welfare."[6]

An anonymous reader put his view in more emphatic terms:

> It is because Jews have lived within themselves in other countries on the *Chevra* principle that they have made the existence of Jews in those countries intolerable. The sooner the *Chevra* movement is crushed out of existence the sooner we will remove from our midst the only drawback to the advancement of the Jews in this country.[7]

Montagu, while not an unqualified admirer of the *Chevra*, believed that the newcomers and their institutions formed the true repositories of Judaism. He was himself a member of the United Synagogue, and recognised that its haughty edifices, their mildly episcopalian air and dog-collared, beardless Rabbis must be alien to the Jew used to the informality and the snug chumminess of the *Chevra*. At the same time he could not overlook the defects of the *Chevrot*. They were badly managed, chaotic and fractious. Some slight difference of opinion between two members could lead to the formation of yet another *chevra*, and then another, and some of the buildings were squalid, airless slums. In 1887 he therefore brought all the *Chevrot* into a Federation, supplied an architect and found them a Chief Rabbi at his own expense and established an institution which combined the warmth, comradeship and religious intensity of the old *Chevrot*, with ventilation and order. He became the first president of this Federation.

A number of observers believed that the Federation had less to do with the needs of the newcomers than with the ambitions of Montagu and they saw in it a bid to wrest control of the community from the hands of the Rothschilds. If this was his aim he never succeeded.

But he was the poor man's Rothschild. He became the champion of the new community, their spokesman in the institutions of the old, their defender in Parliament and out. His first speech in the House of Lords was to defend the interests of small Jewish shopkeepers.

In the 1880s he spent more and more time on communal work, and less and less time in the bank. He travelled to Russia and Poland to examine the situation of the Jews, and visited the various stopping points on the route to the west to facilitate the movement of refugees. In 1882 the Hebrew Immigrant Aid Society of New York protested at the influx of Jews from England and Montagu travelled to America to soothe their temper. In 1903 in order to ease the severe overcrowding in Whitechapel, Montagu established a dispersion committee which offered jobs and subsidies to newcomers prepared to move to the provinces, and a number of families were transplanted to Chatham, Reading, Leicester, Blackburn, Dover and Stroud.[8]

Many shared his acute sense of concern at the plight of Jewry, but few had his energy, his capacity for getting things done.

At the same time he kept his involvement above the personal level. He was a distant benefactor – not, indeed, so distant as the Rothschilds, whose benevolence seemed to descend from another universe – but he had no social contact with the devout Jews he admired. Some of his best friends, he once told the House of Commons, were East End Jews, but they were not to be seen at his table in Kensington Palace Gardens, nor at his house parties in Swaythling. If he reconstituted the humble bethels of the East End, he built himself a cathedral in the West End, in St Petersburgh Place. It was a lofty, pinnacled, splendid example of latter-day, mock-Gothic, adorned with marble walls, mosaic floors, stained glass, and thick gilt and elaborate carving. In its day it was the most magnificent synagogue in the community, and its splendours have still not been surpassed. He remained remote, his daughter believed "lest sentiment should affect his judgement". But as she admits, he had an almost morbid abhorrence of failure. "In spite of himself he despised the individual to whom he gave money. He himself had carved his way through very hard circumstances, he had little sympathy with the man who failed to get on."[9]

This was something which he shared with his in-laws, the Cohens, who presided over the Jewish Board of Guardians. In this, indeed, they were no more than sons of their time, but Montagu's actions were not always in keeping with his beliefs. When, as a magistrate, he actually came face to face with people whom he might otherwise have dismissed as incorrigible delinquents he was extremely lenient, and when he was called upon to intervene in the strikes of Jewish tailors and bakers his sympathies were with the strikers.

Montagu was, a little improbably, a skilled fly-fisherman, and could sometimes be seen knee-deep in the waters of the Test waiting patiently for a bite. He was also a keen horseman, and with his prophetic visage, and long white beard flowing over his shoulder he must have looked like Elijah on horseback. He was not however among the hunting, shooting members of the Cousinhood and never went to a race meeting.

He was an avid collector of works of art, and insisted that he would continue collecting in the next world even if he had to confine himself to cherubs. He did not, as an Orthodox Jew, care to harbour Italian Madonnas under his roof, but he owned several Dutch masters, including a splendid Ruysdael, and a number of paintings by Constable, Gainsborough and Turner. But these were almost obligatory adornments of a Palace Gardens mansion, and he did not claim any special understanding of painting. He was, however, a considerable authority on old silver and amassed a splendid collection in which he took particular pleasure. He liked to use the silver at his table, so that a guest might be offered salads from a Queen Anne tray and salt his food from a Lamerie celler, accompanied by a commentary on their workmanship and origins. He was a member of the Burlington Fine Arts Club and of the Society of Antiquaries, and when the Death Duties Bill was debated in Parliament, it was he who suggested the clause to exclude bequests of objects of art to galleries and museums from the provisions of the Bill.

When he was seventy-six, after a particularly bitter and foggy winter, an attack of bronchitis permanently affected his lungs and heart. He lingered on a further two years, a restless invalid. His daughter recalled his last days:

> Samuel Montagu used to join his wife and children in the Sabbath service; and the boys and girls will always remember the Friday night meal in which they took part as a privilege as well as a duty. The last night he spent with his family . . . was a Friday night, and his children and grandchildren will never forget the way in which he gave the patriarchal blessing to each in turn, in spite of the obvious weakness which grew visibly throughout the evening. With unusual docility he allowed his eldest son to read the long grace, but fought against physical weakness so strenuously that he responded to every thought expressed in the familiar words.[10]

The next morning he suffered a heart attack, but nearly a week passed before his massive strength gave out. He died on January 12, 1911, aged seventy-eight and was buried not among the other grandees of the Cousinhood at Willesden, but among the East End Jews in Edmonton. He may have been a distant figure in his lifetime, but in death he was finally gathered among his people.

He died a disappointed man. He had succeeded prodigiously in business. His will was proved at £1,150,000, but this was no indication of his real wealth which lay tied up in his banking and bullion concerns. When the firm of Montagu went public in 1964 its total assets were valued at £164,000,000. But business in a sense was the thing that mattered least to him. He found his main joy in his family, in his four sons and six daughters, and it is there that his disappointments lay. He was haunted by the fear that his children might marry out of the faith. In his will he left them all generous bequests, but all subject to the provision "that they shall respectively at my death be professing the Jewish religion and not be married to a person not professing the Jewish religion".

He was worried by two of his daughters, Marian and Lilian, devoted children in other respects, but who could not stomach his Orthodoxy and were searching for new means of religious expression. This led to deep divisions in the family which were not resolved at the time of his death. They have, he wrote in his will, "contrary to my wishes promoted and assisted a movement known as 'Liberal Judaism' the objects of which I strongly disapprove", and ordered his trustees to withhold three-fourths of their share of his estate if they should persist in their efforts. They persisted. It was not that his sons were more obedient, or ready to follow in his ways. They did not care about Judaism sufficiently one way or the other.

Marian and Lilian, and to a lesser extent Henrietta, took their religion as seriously as their father. Montagu was no theologian and for all the acuteness of his intellect – which approached genius when it came to finance – he was in essence a simple man, and his approach to his Judaism was simplistic. To him it was merely a matter of accepting and transmitting received tradition, without looking into its origins or peering too closely into its components. One arrived at its heart by living it; one did not think one's way to it, and he presumed that a creed which gave him so much satisfaction, must satisfy everyone. It did not satisfy his daughters who believed that traditional Judaism was so involved in the minutiae of observance that something of its basic spirit was being forsaken. They reserved the right to scrutinise tradition, preserve the wholesome and reject the obsolete. This meant that they no longer accepted the Rabbinical interpretation of Holy Scripture. Liberal Judaism, wrote Lily Montagu, owes its existence "to the God Within, as interpreted by the trained conscience". This was too subtle an idea for her father who tended to dismiss the whole liberal philosophy as an attempt to give moral sanctions to spiritual deficiency. When the Rev. Simeon Singer, Minister of the St Petersburgh Place Synagogue, adopted an attitude of tolerance to the heretics, Montagu quarrelled with Singer: when the Chief Rabbi, to his dismay, showed himself to be equally tolerant, he quarrelled with the Chief Rabbi. His differences with his daughters were never resolved.

When his will was published, wrote Lilian in a book intended for private circulation, people referred to "coldness and division . . . angry scenes and recrimination":

> Of course they could not tell beneath the strain occasioned by the different point of view between father and daughter there was essential sympathy and deep understanding love. The daughter felt so much reverence for her father's principles that she could never discuss them with him; the father felt such tender sympathy and yearning sorrow for the, to him, mistaken views of the daughter that he could not articulate any remonstrance, nor certainly any kind of vituperation. There was just a pained silence, beneath which hearts ached to commune.[11]

These lines were written shortly after his death, and they have more than a tinge of remorse. There was certainly deep love and respect between father and daughter, but the minds of father and children functioned in different worlds. Montagu, the son of a provincial watchmaker, had known hardship, was self-taught and self-made. His children were brought up in mansions, surrounded by servants, tutors, governesses and nannies. They went to famous public schools, studied at the ancient universities and moved freely and easily among people who still filled him with awe. He loved and cherished his children, but often could not get through to them. There were played in Kensington Palace Gardens the sort of domestic dramas that were to become commonplace in so many East End homes.

"Samuel Montagu," wrote his daughter, "never imposed his religious opinions on his children, and was satisfied so long as they conformed with the observances which he practised."[12] Affectionate children can have faulty memories, for as some of his letters which have since been published show, he made strenuous but unsuccessful efforts to impose his religious views on at least one of his children, his second son, Edwin.

There can be no doubt that Montagu's oppressive, rigorous Orthodoxy was one of the factors which turned his daughters to Liberalism, but there were others. Lilian felt that conformity to ritual was being used as a substitute for action. A photograph of her at nineteen shows her with the large dark eyes of an Italian Madonna and the determined mouth and large chin, which were the inescapable hallmark of a Montagu. Looking at the eyes and mouth one could almost see two characteristics, the spiritual and temporal, in conflict within her; but if she ever did suffer from such a conflict, it was resolved long before she reached maturity. Her life was one of piety, prayer and service. She would have fitted ideally within the Catholic Church as the Mother Superior of a Convent of a charitable order, but not, heaven forbid, within a contemplative order. Contemplation and prayer, she felt were useful as spurs to action, but she was always nervous that people might resort to them as substitutes for action. She was, deeply moved by the teachings of Jesus and looked upon him, as a great, good and wise man.[13] His ideas, however, did not draw her towards Christianity, but confirmed her belief in the eternal world of Judaism, and she worked within its context.

Her approach to her faith was instinctive. "I am not going to talk to you as a scholar because I am unlearned," she once told a gathering.[14] In this she was not being over-modest. The very scale of her activities gave her little time for study, and she derived many of her ideas from Claude Montefiore. It was she who felt the need for a more progressive

Judaism (it acquired the name Liberal later); it was Montefiore who had the scholastic stature to give it form.

Though less intellectual than Montefiore and more compassionate, they were much alike, and after his first wife died in childbirth, there was speculation that she might become the second Mrs Montefiore. She was a large, heavy-boned, rather stalwart woman, but with a warm personality and fine face, and in her youth was not unattractive. Montefiore, in any case, was unconcerned about externals, and the lady whom he eventually married, a blue-stocking from Newnham, of mature years, was no Gaiety girl. Lily's relationship with him was that of disciple and teacher. She played sister Clare to his St Francis. She also felt that there was something ungodly or, at least, not nice, about sex, and she could be deeply upset at any instance of sexual misbehaviour among the members of her youth club. She was extremely puritanical, without, however, being censorious. Before condemning anyone, she always tried to put herself in his place. Where sex was involved, she must have found it difficult, but her displeasure took the form of regret, rather than anger.

It was, of course, difficult for a young woman of her class, with her wealth, rank, intelligence and high-mindedness, to be matched. Montefiore went outside the faith for a partner. This is something she could not even have contemplated. "Intermarriage," she said, "threatens the future of our community."[15] But apart from all that her single-mindedness of purpose, her complete devotion required celibacy.

This was, of course, contrary to Jewish tradition in which "thou shalt be fruitful and multiply" is one of the earliest and most fundamental commandments. But traditional Judaism, which gives the woman a merely auxiliary role to the endeavours of her husband, would not have given sufficient scope for her dedication, and that was another reason why she found her place outside it. She was not only a founder of the Liberal Synagogue, she became one of its ministers and not even the bizarre canonicals she wore in the pulpit – the black biretta, the flapping academic gown – could lessen the impact of her message. And the impact lay not merely in her words. Her sermons, read now, seem mostly commonplace. "The deep impression they created," writes her biographer Dr Eric Conrad, "was due to the power of her personality, to her beautiful voice, to the spiritual flame within her.[16] But sermons, as she would have insisted, are a minor activity. The teachings of Lily Montagu lay in her example.

It was, of course, the custom for young ladies of her class, to do something – in the terms of the day – "for her less fortunate sisters". And the Cousinhood all did their bit. They descended on some poor quarter for an afternoon once a month – sometimes even once a week – patted a child here, gave a guinea there, scattered smiles and sympathy everywhere – and were then off back to Kensington as quickly as their carriages could take them.

When Lily launched a settlement for young Jewish people in Blooms-bury, her parents gave her every help and encouragement, until they discovered to their dismay that she was not merely intent upon a good deed, but had entered upon a vocation.

"The accepted programme for every girl in my set," she recalled, "was that she should go out as much as possible, know plenty of 'nice people' and settle down at an early age in marriage." She went on:

> My complete failure to conform with this widely supported plan brought much disappointment and anxiety to those who loved me, and the ladies of my mother's visiting circle, though generally kind and sympathetic, did not approve of my mode of life and outlook. Because I worked very hard, dressed badly, went out very little, was always shy and backward at social functions, I was held up as a warning to my mother's acquaint-ances.[17]

She was not merely held up as a warning. Mothers were nervous to expose their daughters to her company lest her example should be infectious. She was, until her fame spread and she became a beloved public figure, virtually ostracised by many of her cousins. It did not worry her. She would not have cared much for their company, and in any case she was far from friendless. There was a particularly close relationship between her and her two elder sisters, Henrietta (Netta) and Marian. Netta married her first cousin Ernest Franklin who was a partner in her father's bank. Marian remained single, and was an untiring partner in much of Netta's work. All three lived to great old age. Lilian was nearly ninety when she died, Marian was ninety-six and Netta ninety-seven. All three became beloved institutions. One could often see the trio together in Netta's chauffeur-driven Rolls pulling up for the Sabbath morning service, three large, very ancient, very English ladies with crumpled faces and large straw hats, all three hard of hearing and talking to each other at the tops of their voices. There was rapport between the sisters in their words, rapport in their silences, and singleness in their purpose. All were devoted to the Liberal Synagogue, and all were eager helpers at Lily's club.

Lily began social work at seventeen. At nineteen she founded in a few rooms the West Central Jewish Club for girls. As it grew, she moved to larger premises and it kept growing, till by the end of her life it had over a thousand members.

She was worshipped by the girls. "My approach to them was so very simple," she said, "just the kind of friendliness given by one girl to others like herself, and they gave me affection in generous measure."[18]

She began her club in Victorian times, but there was little that was Victorian in her attitudes, except, possibly her optimism and belief in progress. She believed there were few ills which education, sympathy and a hot plate of soup will not cure. Her charges came from poor homes and squalid surroundings. They had drifted from the restraints and cultural traditions of the ghetto; they were losing much that was best in Jewish life, without coming under the more wholesome influences of English life. Lily would never have been so chauvinistic as to put it in these words, but she believed that an Englishwoman of the Jewish persuasion was the highest form of moral being, and her club – which she extended into a settlement after 1919 – aimed to combine everything she worshipped in Judaism with all she adored in England. And to an extraordinary extent she succeeded.

People rarely nowadays think of any group as being by their very nature their 'betters', but the working class then did, and so did the Jew; so that it is difficult at this distance to appreciate the way in which this woman, an Honourable, the daughter of a baron, the niece of a baronet, the sister of one Cabinet minister and the cousin of another, was viewed by the working-class Jews among whom she moved. If a mere Rabbi had told them that the Kingdom of Heaven was nigh, it would have been a sermon, but if the Hon. Lily Montagu said anything like that she probably had it on good authority. It is not that she kept herself distant and aloof – quite the contrary – but her rank and connections added to her other qualities, were of immense use in her ministrations. This was true not only among the poor of London, but also among the rich of America when she made a coast-to-coast tour of the Liberal Jewish communities of America. Members of her club, as they grew to maturity, sent their daughters, and then their grand-daughters. She acted as a supernumerary mother to them all, a counsellor, a court of last resort in any family conflict. Her standing among them was that of a Chassidic Rabbi among his disciples.

She launched the evening activities at the Settlement with prayer. She went on from there to establish a synagogue and through it introduced a new stream of members into the Liberal movement. She did not do so as a missionary anxious to wean away people from Orthodox Judaism – though there were murmurings among the Orthodox that she was doing just that – but to bring religion to those who had none.

"A Jew without religion," she wrote, "is an objectionable person and a real danger to society."[19] Nor did she feel that any Jew who was not religious had a just claim to the name. It was for this reason that she opposed Zionism, which she thought of, mistakenly, as a largely political manifestation.[20]

At first glance her humble synagogue in Bloomsbury looked like a poor man's branch of the imposing Liberal temple in St John's Wood, with its massive Corinthian portico, but Lily did not approach her work with any desire to patronise. She felt more at home in Bloomsbury than in St John's Wood, and the working-class women of the former were more her type of people than the haughty dowagers of the latter. Towards the end of her life, the two streams within the Liberal movement, the rich and the non-rich, which had tended to run parallel, began to merge. The rich were less rich, the poor were infinitely less poor, and if today one were to visit a Liberal synagogue in the suburbs, it would be hard to tell the sons of St John's Wood from those of Bloomsbury.

She was among the first women in this country to be made a Justice of the Peace, and she sat first on the St Pancras Magistrates' bench and later as chairman of the Westminster magistrates. She began her day by listening to the misdemeanours of an endless succession of prostitutes. Her belief in the inherent nobility of the human being must have been severely tested, but she took the greatest interest in the personal history of the delinquents, visited some of them in their homes, or in jail, sent them books and presents. She must have been one of the few magistrates to receive a continuous flow of fan mail from H.M. Prisons and Borstal institutions.

"I am no expert on fashion," she once confessed, which was perhaps the understatement of her life. She tended to opt for styles which were fashionable when she was a girl – and they could not have been all that fashionable even then – though of good quality material, but as the material tended to last for ever, she tended to wear them for ever. She did not have a car, rarely took taxis, and generally travelled by bus or underground, or walked, with a heavy briefcase in one hand, a pile of papers under her arm, slightly bent, in flat shoes a heavy determined tread. She looked like a lady of high station come upon hard times, as had many in Bayswater, and taxi-drivers would often stop to offer a free lift, and as often as not, she would wave them on. Her nephews and nieces, who viewed her with a mixture of affection, admiration and exasperation, wanted to buy her a car, tried to buy her clothes, or persuade her to come away on a holiday, but she would refuse them all. When she lost her watch in the war, she would not allow them to buy her another and they had to enter into elaborate conspiracies to present her with even the smallest gift.

She believed that the Sabbath was Judaism's greatest gift to mankind and observed it meticulously. When she was old she would accept a lift in her sister's Rolls to synagogue, but would not travel for any lesser occasion. In later life she would be at home to friends at Red Lodge in Bayswater on Friday night, and dinner would always be preceded by a reading from scripture. The Sabbath day itself, she would spend in study, contemplation and prayer.

She kept the Jewish dietary laws, and in fact, though Liberal in belief, was far more Orthodox in observance than those members of her family who were members of, and held high office in, the United Synagogue. And when the anniversaries of her father's and mother's death came round, she would walk over to their synagogue in St Petersburgh Place to say *Kaddish*, the memorial prayer.

Her life was not all prayer and incense. She loved good music, literature, biography. She loved flowers and when she once made a confession to that effect in the course of a speech, the floral department of Harrods was emptied and deposited on her door-step. In common with Marian and Netta, she was a keen sportswoman, loved cricket and tennis, and all three would often be seen in the members' enclosures at Lord's or Wimbledon in large hats and parasols, among other ladies similarly attired, a sight so imposing, so formidable that it was difficult to watch them and believe the empire was no more.

Towards the end of her life Lily tended to look back on her career with a certain amount of disappointment. She had regarded Liberalism not as a challenge to Orthodoxy, but as another pathway to the Kingdom of Heaven for those who, like her, could not bring themselves to tread the old, and at first it seemed as if she might achieve a break-through to the Jewish masses and stem the drift from religion. But the drift, after the initial check, continued, and then accelerated, and as she grew older she seemed to be outliving not merely her friends, but her faith. A woman born in Gladstone's England could not easily reconcile herself to the "You've Never Had It So Good" universe of Mr Harold Macmillan's time. Her Jews had, indeed, become assimilated and integrated into the host society, but her Jews, she felt, were not what they were, and her England was not what it was. She suffered from passing moments of disillusionment, even in the young. "It is a curious fact," she said, "that the young people round us suffer from being tired much more than we older folk." She herself was tireless, and saw no rest even in death. "We must regard death," she said, "as an incident which provided us with a new opportunity to continue with what is worth while in eternal life."[21]

It could have been her epitaph.

CHAPTER 19

The Edwardians

There is a cartoon by Max Beerbohm showing five figures in an ante-room of Buckingham Palace shortly after the accession of George V. All are in evening dress. All are apprehensive. All are grotesque in shape and immense of nose. All are Jews – Edward Lawson, Ernest Cassel, Arthur Sassoon and Alfred and Leopold de Rothschild. "Are we," they wonder, "as welcome as ever?"[1]

All five had been friends and confidants of Edward VII. He had dined at their tables, shot on their grouse moors, stalked in their deer forests, slept in their mansions, and all had been guests at Buckingham Palace. But Edward was dead and George was now king. Would they be as welcome as ever?

It was little more than half a century since British Jews were fully emancipated, but even after the formal barriers were down, social barriers remained. The Jew – no matter how assimilated, cultivated, influential or rich – was to the Victorian mind always a Jew, still somewhat suspect and sinister, still different. There were towards the end of Victoria's reign, Jews in the House of Commons and Jews in the Lords, but there were no Jews at Court – until Edward opened his palaces to them.

His action occasioned raised eyebrows among his royal cousins in Europe, and even some muttering in England itself. Beerbohm's cartoon was one example of it; there were others. "The King, as King," noted one familiar figure in London society, "is much more useful than he was as Prince of Wales. He has a great deal of ability, but is always surrounded by a bevy of Jews and racing people."[2] The Jews and racing people were sometimes one and the same.

A bishop who called on him one afternoon found a happy ecumenical throng:

> I arrived just as they were all at tea . . . a curious mixture. Two Jews, Sir Anthony de Rothschild and his daughter; an ex-Jew, Disraeli; a Roman Catholic, Colonel Higgins, an Italian Duchess who is an English-woman, and her daughter brought up a Roman Catholic and now turning Protestant; a set of young Lords and a Bishop. . . .[3]

Edward shared something of his mother's deep affection for Disraeli, and this might have made him favourably disposed to Jews as a whole, but the simple fact was that the prince was the most broad-minded and tolerant of men. He chose people for themselves and not their ante-cedents. He was less interested in a man's convictions than his character, less in his origins than his originality.

In 1869 Victoria had refused Lionel de Rothschild a peerage because he derived his wealth from foreign loans and successful speculation. By Edward's time this was no longer a handicap. Foreign loans, indeed, had helped to give London its pre-eminence in the money-market. Capitalism and capitalists were at their apogee and the Court Jews were among their pioneers. They were extremely generous –munificence indeed, was their hallmark. They were great sportsmen; they had large estates and fine stables; they, especially the Rothschilds, had immense stores of political information; they were lavish hosts, but above all, they were all abundantly, extravagantly, spectacularly rich, and the king was fascinated by money and the men who made it. The "Court of Prince Hall", as Disraeli had called it, was open to all the talents, and money was theirs. The fact that they were Jewish was no more a disqualification than the Jewishness of Sarah Bernhardt, another of the king's friends. Their Jewishness was treated as one of the eccentricities to which the very rich and the very talented are so often prone – though assuredly, it was no advantage.

Many Jews still found it politic to drop their faith, often with their family name, as they rose in life, and where this was not a conscious choice it seemed to be a natural progression.

Edward Lawson, was born Levy. He was the son of a London printer who had acquired the *Daily Telegraph* by way of a bad debt, assumed the name of Lawson, tarried for a while as Levy-Lawson, until he was elevated to the peerage as Lord Burnham. Somewhere amid the changes of name he underwent a change of faith and died, in 1916, a member of the Church of England.

Cassel was in the words of Edward's official biographer, "the King's closest friend",[4] a fact which puzzled many of their contemporaries. It was not that he was a Jew, there were other Jews at Court: it was not that he was German, there were other Germans. He was everything the king was not and would not have wished to be. Margot Tennant, who knew Cassel well, recalled him as an austere figure. "He had no small talk," she said; the king rarely had anything else. He loathed gossip; the king loved it. He was serious, Edward was frivolous. What, then, was their relationship? It was suggested that Cassel filled the gap between the king's income and expenditure.

It was widely known that Edward was in debt. Parliament voted him £450,000 a year and £60,000 for the Queen and he derived a further £60,000 a year from the Duchy of Lancaster, but the upkeep of his palaces and estates, the large retinues which followed him on his frequent travels (except when he went *en garçon* on a furtive trip to Paris), his stables, the horses which also ran, the fortunes showered on mistresses or lost at the gaming tables, all consumed more. Cassel helped to reorganise his finances and virtually functioned as his broker. But there is no evidence whatever that he subsidised Edward or financed his peccadilloes. He did not have to buy his way into royal favour.

Cassel, the son of a small German banker, was born in Cologne in 1852. At fourteen he joined the house of Elzbacher as a clerk, at eighteen he joined Bischoffsheim and Goldsmidt in London; at twenty-two he was manager of the bank.

He made his first £1 million out of railway development in the United States, Mexico and Sweden and in 1895 formed the consortium which financed the construction of the Central London Railway (forerunner of the Central Line). He was also concerned in the formation of the Vickers combine, organised the financing of the Aswan Dam and developed vast areas of the Nile Delta for cotton growing. He became a mercantile sage at large and was involved in the formation of the National Bank of Egypt, the National Bank of Turkey and the State Bank of Morocco.

He was showered with honours by grateful governments whose finances he helped to restore and was a Commander of the Légion d'Honneur, France; Commander of the Royal Order of Vasa, Sweden; a holder of the Grand Cordon of the Imperial Ottoman Order of Osmanieh; the Red Eagle, with brilliants, of Prussia, and the Order of the Rising Sun, Japan.

He was knighted by the Queen in 1899 and appointed to the Privy

Council by Edward. Thereafter he received almost annual awards, the G.C.M.G. in 1905, the G.C.V.O. in 1906; the G.C.B. in 1909. When he appeared in full dress he almost sagged under the weight of his regalia.

Cassel, though his appearance would not have suggested it, had a bucolic streak, which broadened under Edward's influence. He was a fearless rider, came to love hunting and other rural pursuits. In 1894 he established his own stud, but here his judgement was more fallible than in banking. The nearest he came to a major prize was second place in the 1914 Derby with, having regard to the time, the unfortunately named 'Hapsburg'.

Cassel loved England, but there were qualities in his native Germany which he admired and from which he believed this country could benefit. There were many distinguished Englishmen, like Lord Haldane, who shared this view. He dreamed of a synthesis of all that was best in British and German culture and in 1911 donated £210,000 for the creation of the British-German Foundation. His dream died at Sarajevo and in the Germanophobia of the war years it was recalled against him. His loyalty was questioned. There were demands that he should be deprived of his Orders and that his name be expunged from the list of Privy Councillors. George V and his Ministers resisted the pressure. He survived with his P.C. and Orders intact, but saddened by his experience. He died in 1921 leaving £7,551,608.

Cassel had been introduced to Edward by a mutual friend, Baron Maurice de Hirsch, who had amassed a vast fortune from financing railways in Russia, the Balkans and Turkey. He entertained on a scale that made even the Rothschilds seem frugal. He had met Edward in Paris and in 1891 invited him to stay at St Johann, his hunting estate in Hungary. The Prince of Wales, as he then was, had been warned in London that Hirsch was *persona non grata* at the Austrian Court, and the fact was urgently pressed upon him when he arrived in Vienna, but he and his retinue, which included Lady Randolph Churchill, Lord Dudley, Sir Ernest and Lady Cassel and Arthur Sassoon proceeded eastwards as planned. At St Johann there was shooting on a scale unknown elsewhere. In a five-day *battue* they slaughtered over 11,000 head of game.

Apart from his estate in Hungary, Hirsch had homes in Belgium, Germany, Austria and France, and as if to complete the collection, bought another in England. He was encouraged by Edward to patronise the turf, and here, as in most of his other enterprises, his success was staggering. In one year alone (1892) his filly La Flèche won the Cambridgeshire, the One Thousand Guineas, the Oaks and the St Leger.

Baron Eckardstein, the German Ambassador to London, found Hirsch a strange mixture of generosity and greed. He once saw him squabbling with a cabman over sixpence in the pouring rain. "Why not pay him and come in out of the wet," said Eckardstein. "You'll catch cold and be laid up for weeks." "That's all very well," said Hirsch, the rain trickling down his nose, "but I have my principles."[5]

He was a product of three cultures and tended on occasion to lapse into a mixture of French, English and German. At St Johann he would bring new guests out on the terrace and explain with a wave of his hand, "And those sind die Karpaths". Edward took a fellow guest out and with the same gesture, and much the same voice, said: "And those sind die Karpaths". Everyone laughed except Hirsch.

He was in some ways a comical, pathetic figure, who more or less bludgeoned his way to social prominence with money bags, spent fortunes to see that no whim of his gilded guests went unmet, yet excited derision rather than affection. In spite of his generosity he suffered frequent and painful social rebuffs. In England, however, as a friend of the Prince of Wales, every door was open to him, and like many European Jews he became an incurable Anglophile. He could play the English country magnate on his estate or at Newmarket but was too foreign to be able to glory in the name of Englishman. He hoped his only son Lucien might do this, or at least acquire English roots by marriage, and he sought a wife for him from the English aristocracy. To this end he once invited Margot Tennant, the brilliant and beautiful daughter of Lord Glenconner, and the central figure of the English intellectual in-group known as 'the Souls' to dinner at the Café Anglais in Paris, and put the proposition to her. "I want you to marry my son Lucien," he said. "He is quite unlike me, he is very respectable and hates money; he likes books and collects manuscripts and other things and is highly educated."[6] Margot had other ambitions, and married Asquith. Lady Katie Lambton, whom he approached next, also turned him down, in favour of the Duke of Leeds.

It is unlikely that Lucien himself knew anything of the proposals; he certainly had no particular liking for Margot. He was a frail, withdrawn young man with scholarly interests, and abhorred high society, racing, shooting and all that went with it. He died in 1889 at the age of thirty-two.

Hirsch had a number of children outside his marriage and came near to attaining his ambition through one of them, Arnold de Forest, who was educated at Eton and Oxford and became Liberal M.P. for West Ham. In 1913, though sponsored by Lloyd George and Winston Churchill (or possibly because of it) he was blackballed by the Reform Club. He left England after the war and settled in Liechtenstein as Count Bendern[7] and died at his Riviera home at Cap Martin in 1968.

Hirsch died in 1896 leaving £30,000,000, one of the largest private fortunes ever recorded. He had given away over £10,000,000 in his lifetime, including over £8,000,000 to resettle Jewish refugees from Russia in America. He was richer than the Rothschilds, stemmed from nobler stock, spent more freely, entertained more lavishly, but did not quite make the social grade; where the Rothschilds moved, he pushed. Yet he did not like pushers. "All our misfortunes came from the fact that the Jews aim too high," he once said. "We have too many intellectuals, my aim is to discourage this tendency to push among Jews. They mustn't make such great progress. All the hatred of us comes from this."[8]

Hirsch himself was no intellectual, like the Prince of Wales. Like him he had a great love of the turf, the hunt, sport. There was also something colourful and breezy about him which Edward must have found attractive, but his most attractive quality – as he himself was aware – was his wealth, and even more so, his readiness to share it. He lent Edward £600,000 which according to a biographer of Hirsch, was never repaid.[9]

Cassel succeeded where Hirsch failed and obtained a secure place among the English gentry; but then he came to England at a much younger age. His wife stemmed from good, north country stock; his daughter married into the aristocracy; his grand-daughter, Edwina, married a cousin, Lord Mountbatten, a cousin of George VI and uncle of Prince Philip. Cassel married out of the faith, brought up his only child as a Christian, and died a Catholic – in accordance with the last wishes of his wife. If he had any Jewish sympathies he kept them quiet. In 1908, when the King was about to embark on a state visit to Russia, he received a plea from the Rothschild brothers to intervene with the czar on behalf of their persecuted fellow Jews. He was also approached by Cassel for an introduction to the czar in connection with a proposed loan.[10]

If Edward's close friendship with Cassel caused speculation, there was none about his friendship with the Sassoons, for they fitted perfectly into his set as nature's own Edwardians. They had the gaudiness, the grandeur, the extravagence, the vulgarity of the age. One generation they were nowhere, a wealthy tribe of oriental merchants, the next they were everywhere, at Eton, at Oxford, in Parliament, sashed, beribboned and at Court. And their rise was all the more remarkable in that they not only had to make the transition from Jewish to Gentile society, but from east to west. They were perhaps too exotic a clan to have survived into our more austere age: today they are all but extinct.

In the Orient, they were Princes of the Dispersion, and were commonly known as "the Rothschilds of the East", a description which not all members of the family found flattering. They were of greater antiquity and one could as well speak of the Rothschilds as the Sassoons of the West.

The founder of the dynasty was Sheik Sason Ben Saleh who was born in Baghdad in 1750, was chief banker to the local pasha and head of the local Jewish community, an ancient colony dating back to the days of Nebuchadnezzar. Jews and Moslems on the whole tended to live amicably together, but a succession of rapacious pashas made life intolerable for the more opulent Jews. The Sassoons being among the most opulent were particularly affected, and many of them moved eastwards to Persia, to India, among them Ben Saleh's second son, David. Most of the family's wealth was lost in the course of the flight, but they retained their commercial flair and rapidly established themselves in their new homes.

David made his home in Bombay, a wealthy, bustling port, and there he found friends, borrowed money – his very name was collateral among oriental Jews – and began trading in silks, cottons, dyes and all manner of goods. The main trade was in the hands of the East India Company and David confined himself mainly to serving the markets and bazaars dotted around the Persian Gulf. He married twice and had four children by his first wife and nine by his second, among them eight sons.

As a result of the Opium War between Britain and China, five Chinese ports were opened to British traders, and Elias, David's second son, made his base in Shanghai. In concert with his father's firm in Bombay he began dealing in metals, muslins, cottons and spices. The heavy traffic in opium to China made shipping cheaply available for the westward run. Within five years the Sassoons were established all along the China coast and reaching out to Japan. They built their own wharves and warehouses, acted as shipping brokers and financed the movement of trade. The Sassoon bill of exchange in Hebrew and English became a familiar article among oriental traders.

Abdullah, the eldest, remained at head office in Bombay, but often travelled as his father's viceroy to examine the various markets of the company in Baghdad and the Gulf ports, and eastwards in Canton, Hong Kong, Shanghai and Yokohama. The other sons were also encouraged to travel and establish contacts with local traders, or to oversee the installations of the company in the Chinese ports. A Sassoon dealing with a local representative had to explain himself in elaborate and frequent letters carried by a haphazard mail service. Sassoon dealing with Sassoon understood one another instinctively. Their trade network grew at once more extensive and tighter. Within a few years, observed a contemporary, "silver and gold, silks, gums and spices, opium and cotton, wool and wheat – whatever moves over sea or land feels the hand or bears the mark of Sassoon & Co."[11]

When the business was later incorporated as a private company its interests were spelt out in full as:

> ... dealers in any kind of good and produce, wharfingers, warehousemen, bankers, general merchants, importers, exporters and charterers of ships and vessels, ship and insurance brokers, carriers, forwarding agents, planters, growers, stockowners and breeders, etc.[12]

Each of the brothers, moreover, were encouraged to undertake investments on his own account and they did so extensively, mainly in property and acquired large areas of Bombay, Poona, Hong Kong and Shanghai.

The family, even after the sons were married and had children of their own, functioned as a tightly controlled patriarchate. David with his white beard, turban and flowing robes, could have stepped straight out of a biblical illustration, and his sons, though less exotically garbed, were careful to eschew Western dress while the father was alive; a change in dress, he believed, was but a step from a change in faith, and in their case he was proved right.

They were still at this stage a deeply pious family. Their letters, usually written in Hebrew, began with an invocation to Heaven and closed with a blessing. Business was of course closed on the Sabbath and stopped at the appropriate times of the day for prayer. Among the many servants of the household there was always a *Sochet*. A ritual bath was always available for the women of the household.

The Mosaic law as traditionally interpreted by the Rabbis, with all its impositions, was accepted without question, and Jewish tradition gave the father complete command over his sons. As he spake thus did they do, and this too hastened prosperity. "The chief cause of David Sassoon's success," said a friendly rival, "was the use he made of his sons."[13] Stanley Jackson, who has written a fascinating history of the family, has put it another way: "He trained them to be chorus masters, with himself as conductor."[14]

After Abdullah, the eldest, came Elias, who functioned mainly as his father's pro-consul in Shanghai, and then came their six half brothers, the oldest of whom was known, confusingly as Sassoon David Sassoon, and Reuben, Arthur, Aaron, Solomon and Frederick.

In 1853 David became a naturalised British subject, and although he could never learn the English language, he was an incurable Anglophile. The Union Jack fluttered above the Sassoon schools which he endowed in the Jewish quarter of Bombay; portraits of Victoria were everywhere, and pupils were taught to sing "God Save the Queen", in Hebrew, Arabic and English.[15]

The family business had now grown to the point where a European outlet was needed, and Sassoon David Sassoon, the third son, left to open an office in London. He was married, with two children, and he bought Ashley Park, a Tudor mansion standing in about two hundred acres of parkland overlooking the Thames. The fact that he, a comparatively junior figure in the family, was able to live in such style, with carriages and horses, and indoor servants and outdoor servants suggests that in the 1850s the Sassoon fortunes were already considerable, but their great extreme came during the American Civil War. The blockade of the southern states by the north resulted in a cotton famine which gave an immense boost to Indian cotton producers and everyone concerned in the Indian trade. The Sassoons, however, did not overlook the fact that the situation was temporary. They were careful not to over-expand and to build up reserves of a size able to withstand almost any contingency. When the Civil War ended and the accumulated cotton of the south was discharged upon the market, the Sassoons were among the few to survive the crash.

David died in 1864 leaving, it was said, some £4,000,000.[16] A few years later Sassoon Sassoon dropped dead in the foyer of the Langham Hotel. Abdullah, or Albert, as he preferred to call himself, succeeded his father as head of the company and was compelled to send Reuben to take Sassoon's place in London, Arthur to Hong Kong, and Solomon to Shanghai to relieve Elias who was required to act as Albert's deputy in Bombay.

It was not a role which Elias cherished. Albert had pronounced social ambitions. He sought a place on the Bombay Legislative Council, he received court emissaries from China and Persia; he mixed with Indian nobility, and he was a familiar figure at the levees of the English colony in Poona and Bombay – and breaking into English society in India was a far more formidable undertaking than penetrating English society in England, especially for someone with the sing-song accent and appearance of an Indian. Elias envisaged that he might be left to look after the shop for the rest of his life, while his brother gavotted on the public stage. In any case he was unhappy with the role of deputy, and he resigned from the company to set up on his own as E. D. Sassoon & Co. The old firm continued to act as general merchants; the new one was concerned mainly in banking and property. The Orient was big enough for them both. Of the two, the newer firm proved to be the more prosperous, possibly because its partners on the whole were more disposed to remain in the East.

The expanding interests of David Sassoon & Co., which had been given a new impetus by the opening of the Suez Canal in 1869, required a larger staff at the London office and Reuben in due course was joined by Arthur, and Arthur arrived bearing a unique asset, his wife Louise Perugia.

Albert and Reuben had made the usual carefully arranged marriages with well-endowed daughters from well-established Jewish families, who proved loyal wives and devoted mothers, but were plump and awkward, and they could not get used to their husbands' social eminence. The tradition common to Moslem and Jew, that the woman should not seek public role, was still strong in the family, and even when they moved to London they lived a more confined life in their own secluded quarters, upstairs, away from the public rooms and the public eye, like overfed, overindulged animals in some very private menageries.

"We went up to Aunt Kate's region," wrote Reuben's niece in her diary, "quite a separate establishment. She is enormous with a very pink and white face, light hair, and a mantilla – puffing away at the hookah from which she is inseparable. Her rooms are full of pretty flowers and odds and ends, and she is always carried up and down the stairs."[17]

Arthur was more fortunate. He had allowed himself the pleasures of a grand tour on his way to London, and in Vienna he met Louise Perugia, a member of one of the oldest Italian Jewish families, with looks even more exquisite than her pedigree. They set up home in a

JOSEPH ELIAS MONTEFIORE

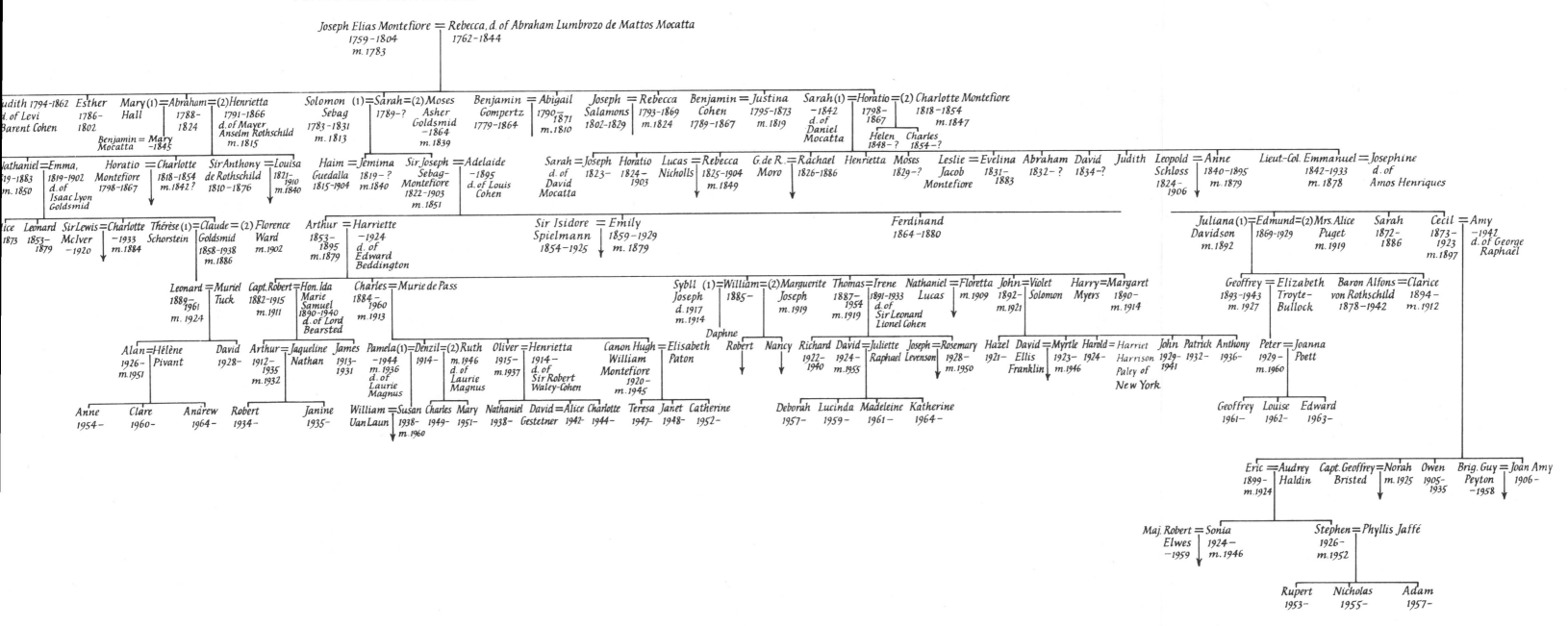

large mansion in Albert Gate which quickly became the venue of fashionable London and inevitably attracted in due course the portly presence of the Prince of Wales.

News of their glittering *soirées*, their dinners, their elaborate entertainments came back to Albert on every package, and every detail beckoned. He had risen about as far as he could hope to rise within the presidency of Bombay. Among the Jews of India, he was, of course, the Lord Bountiful. He was a leader of the commercial community. His contacts in Persia and China had proved invaluable to the British Government which was troubled by Russian ambitions both in central Asia and Persia, and in 1872 he had been knighted for his services. He was weary of the local burden of inherited responsibilities, the synagogues, the schools, the welfare institutions, the limited milieu of Poona and Bombay, and yearned to be among his peers, or at least his equals, in London.

In 1875 he felt the time was opportune to leave. He was nearly sixty. His sons and daughters had grown to maturity, and even his grand-daughter Flora, the most beautiful and exotic of the Sassoons, was now a young woman. At seventeen she married Solomon Sassoon, Albert's half-brother, her great-uncle and eighteen years her senior.

Solomon had shown pronounced ability during his years in Shanghai, and Albert brought him back to Bombay, introduced him to the responsibilities of his new office, and hurried off to London and there established himself not far from Arthur, in a baroque pile in Kensington Gore. And nearby was Reuben in a splendid mansion in Belgrave Square. They were beginning to match the Rothschild enclave just down the road in Piccadilly.

It was, of course, inevitable that the Rothschilds and Sassoons, having become neighbours, should become friends, and, having become friends, should become relatives. The two families were first drawn together through the marriage of Maria Perugia, Louise Sassoon's sister, to Leo de Rothschild, a union resulting from an inspired piece of matchmaking by Connie Battersea and Hannah de Rothschild.[18]

The second Rothschild-Sassoon union involved a younger generation, Edward, Albert's eldest son, and Aline, the second daughter of Baron Gustave of Paris. Aline, was beautiful, refined, highly educated, artistic, and barely twenty. The Prince of Wales had named his yacht after her. Edward Sassoon was thirty. He was born in Bombay and served in China and had the sallow complexion of all the family. In Rothschild terms he was not quite a catch, but he was a captain in the Middlesex

Yeomanry, a lithe, amiable dandy, with a neat, martial moustache, and the confident swagger of a Piccadilly clubman. He fell in love with Aline the moment he saw her and could not quite believe that she would have him. When it became clear that she would, he rushed off to find her some small token of his affection, a £9,000 pearl necklace.[19]

The Sassoons would have penetrated the royal circle on their own, but the Rothschild connection confirmed their place, and they became part of the standing army of royal camp followers which accompanied Edward round the watering places and shooting estates of Europe, to Homburg, to Baden, to Carlsbad, to Marienbad and, as the leaves began to fall, north to the deer forests of Scotland. Arthur and the tireless Louise seemed to be his companions everywhere, and they were in the large party which accompanied Edward on his *battue* to Hirsch's estate in Hungary.[20] Reuben, smitten with gout, was less mobile, but he too tried to keep up with the Prince and on one occasion organised an intimate picnic for some seventy guests on the lawns at Homburg.[21]

The brothers also acquired ornate villas in Brighton, which already then was London by the sea, and which the radical M.P., Henry Labouchère was to describe as "a sea-coast town, three miles long and three yards broad, with a Sassoon at each end, and one in the middle."[22] The Prince of Wales, who was fond of Brighton, found their homes convenient hostelries, and each of the brothers the most charming of *maître d'hôtel*, smiling, bowing and jumping to his every whim.

Arthur also rented a hunting lodge on Speyside, in the Highlands, a humble little place by Sassoon standards, but which Edward seemed to prefer to the much larger and more elaborate establishments nearby. He descended with a large party in knickerbockers and with guns one autumn while Arthur was celebrating the Day of Atonement, the holiest day in the Jewish Calendar, and a fast day besides.

It would never have occurred to Arthur to suggest that another day would possibly be more convenient. He placed the estate at the disposal of his guests while he went on with his fasting and prayer.[23]

The Day of Atonement apart, the brothers seemed to have kept few of the traditions of their faith. They had been warmly received by their Sephardi co-religionists at Bevis Marks, escorted to a place of honour, and elected to the *Mahamad*,[24] but such honours did not imply religious commitment. Like other members of the Cousinhood they felt that their inheritance obliged them to give their names to Jewish institutions, and something of their money. But they gave very little of their time, and hardly anything of themselves. When Victoria celebrated her Diamond Jubilee in 1897 Reuben, Arthur and Sir Edward Sassoon waited with the Rothschilds at Hyde Park Corner to present loyal greetings on behalf of the Anglo-Jewish community. They were not nearly as involved in Jewish life as the Rothschilds. They were neither leaders of the community, nor were they in any sense representative, but Anglo-Jewry felt sufficiently flattered by their place at Court to welcome them in the delegation.

The history of the Sassoons is almost a classic example of the Talmudic adage that "a name made great is a name destroyed", for though the family only sprang into prominence a century ago, it is almost completely lost to Judaism. There is but one branch which may still be thought of as Jewish in a sense that David Sassoon would recognise, and that is the branch founded by his seventh son Solomon. Solomon had been left in charge of Bombay when Sir Albert moved to London in 1875. The firm was moving through a difficult period. The opium market was vanishing; there were wild fluctuations in the value of the Indian rupee and the Chinese dollar; there was a prolonged cotton slump, and the companies numerous investments along the Chinese coast suffered heavily from the Sino-Japanese war. While the brothers in London continued on their merry way round the playgrounds of Europe, Solomon had to cope with these problems in the sweaty heat of Bombay, and the task proved overwhelming and he died in 1894, at the age of fifty-three. His widow at once announced that she would take his place.

Flora was thirty-five, without business or administrative experience and little understanding of the world of trade. Nothing in her education or training equipped her for the role she assumed, and she eventually had to be removed from the board. She was wise enough to recognise that there was nothing to be gained from any attempt at a comeback, and she gathered her court about her and moved off to London and exile.

Flora was not tall, and was somewhat top–heavy, but her bearing gave her a stateliness unrelated to her size. She had a pair of dark, luminous eyes under heavy lids, a round face, a mouth at once generous and determined. Her hands tended to be too clustered with rings, and she was sometimes overloaded with pearls, but what would have seemed ostentatious and vulgar on anyone else seemed perfectly in place on her. Her manner was innately regal and she was received like visiting royalty wherever she went. In India she had been happily at home among rajahs and rahnis, in London she was instantly received by the Rothschilds. Their enclave in Piccadilly was thrown open to her and she moved from mansion to mansion, without, however, joining them at table, for their food was not kosher.

There was always a Rabbi in her entourage, a sort of travelling family chaplain, who would lead family prayers and who could act as tutor and counsellor, with whom she could deliberate on the finer points of Jewish law. She was, said Chief Rabbi Adler, "a living well of Torah and piety".[25] But what is perhaps rarest of all within such a family, she managed to transmit her outlook to her children and grandchildren. Her grand-daughter Flora is married to an Orthodox Rabbi: her grandson Solomon is an Orthodox Rabbi.

As one studies the social engagements of the brothers Sassoon, one begins to wonder who looked after the shop? It seemed, to judge from a record which Arthur kept, to be the sort of enterprise which largely looked after itself.

> We went to the office yesterday at 11 and remained till 1, while he [Reuben] signed the Hebrew and Arabic letters. While we were there, Bishop called and offered some Persian opium and said there was a margin of more than £100 between the price here and that in Hong Kong, so we thought we might as well buy a small lot and make a little money. We went afterwards to Sandown with the Prince and Rosebery in a special and were grieved to see Ladas beaten. I had plunged on him £40 to win £70. Better luck next time.[26]

The Sassoons feature frequently in the biographies of the period, but with the exception of the occasional kindly reference to Louise, one finds little to suggest that they were cherished for themselves and not for their provender. Their gilded troughs and sweated *soirées* became the subject of derision.

"We were dragged along *both* nights," complained Arthur Balfour, "to a long, hot and pompous dinner – peopled with endless Sassoon girls – I believe the Hebrews were in an actual majority – and tho' I have no prejudice against the race (quite the contrary), I began to understand the point of view of those who object to alien immigration."[27]

But at least while Edward was on the throne there was no overlooking the fact that the Sassoons were part of the clique royal. They enjoyed a standing which died with the King.

And there arose a new king who knew not of the Sassoons, or at least was not interested. George V was no merry monarch. He was sufficiently amused by his own family, and felt comfortably accommodated in his own palaces and estates. The Sassons did not suddenly become obsolete, but they ceased to be of any particular social significance and the mockery, which had been kept in check by their place at Court, became more open. By the time Albert's baronetcy had descended to his grandson Philip, the Sassoons had become something of a joke, and Philip, a slight, exotic, precious object, with hooded eyes, who spoke with a lisp and had the mincing manner of a camp actor, was not capable of reviving their fame. He was born in 1888 one of the two children of Edward Sassoon and Aline de Rothschild.

His sister Sybil, six years his junior, made her début in 1912 and was the toast of the London Season. She was witty, well-read, an excellent athlete and superb sportswoman and combined her father's warmth of temperament with her mother's tender good looks. In 1913 she married Lord Rocksavage, an officer in the Lancers, lately A.D.C. to the Viceroy of India, and heir to the Marquess of Cholmondeley, holder of the hereditary office of Lord Great Chamberlain which gives him a leading role in such state occasions as coronations, royal funerals and the state opening of Parliament.

Philip never married and when asked why would always give the same answer: "I shall only marry when I find somebody as lovely and perfect as my sister."[28] Like nearly all the younger Sassoons, he went to Eton, but being also a Rothschild he was that much more precious. He was rather awkward at games but precocious in other things. He played bridge expertly, spoke knowledgeably of food and wine, of art and artists, and carried the languorous, world-weary air of one who had seen it all, knows it all, and for whom there is nothing new under the sun. And if as a boy he never seemed quite a child, as an adult he did not seem quite a man. Harold Nicolson, who was a frequent guest in Philip's many homes, describes him in early middle-age:

> . . . a slim, Baghdadi figure, slightly long in the tooth, dressed in a double-breasted, silk-fronted blue smoking jacket with slippers of zebra hide. He . . . is a strange, lonely, un-English little figure, flitting among these vast apartments, removed from the ordinary passions, difficulties and necessities of life. He always seems to me the most unreal creature I have known.[29]

He went to Christ Church, where he was remembered for the splendour of his wardrobe and the magnificence of his table. He also rode with the Bicester Hunt, and rode well, though, in his immaculate pink on an immaculate gelding, he looked like some sort of porcelain ornament. He was never in fact quite as fragile or as frivolous as he seemed.

Money descended upon him from all directions. He inherited part of his grandfather's estate of £400,000, part of his uncle Reuben's estate of £500,000. His mother died while he was at Oxford and left £250,000 to be divided between him and his sister, and his father who died a few years later left them over £1 million.

Edward had succeeded Albert as chairman of David Sassoon and Co., but did not involve himself too deeply in the affairs of the company. Philip joined the board and drew director's fees, but his position was nominal. He was content to derive his income from commerce but did not wish to be otherwise involved in it. His father had sat as Tory M.P. for Hythe, and at twenty-three he was adopted by the same constituency and became the youngest member in the House. It was not too formidable a feat. Hythe was a Rothschild family fief, acquired as an unstated *quid pro quo* for a £12,000 annual donation to Tory party funds.[30]

Once in the House Philip collected a rapid succession of political secretaryships, first to Sir Douglas Haig, British commander on the Western Front, then as Parliamentary Private Secretary to the Minister of Transport, and finally in 1920, as secretary to Lloyd George.

To those who wondered why so hard-headed a politician should have chosen such a frivolous-looking assistant, Lord Beaverbrook provided an answer: "Sir Philip Sassoon was a brilliant gossip and habitual flatterer. He had many houses and most capable chefs."[31] This was less than fair. Lloyd George availed himself frequently of Philip's hospitality – in fact of almost any hospitality that was going – but as Beaverbrook himself grudgingly observed in *Men and Power*, Sassoon was "a shrewd and competent adviser".[32]

He later became Under-Secretary for Air, where he was not notably successful,[33] and finally reached full ministerial office as Minister of Works. This is one of the less exacting offices in the Government but it might have been expressly created for him, for it made him virtual housekeeper of the royal palaces, including the Palace of Westminster, and other Crown properties. On state occasions, it fell to him to oversee the plate and settings at table, the accoutrements of the waiters, the liveries of the footmen and the selection of ornaments. He was hemmed in on all sides by tradition and precedent, but managed nevertheless to add his own particular touch to the public life of the nation. He died in 1939 shortly before the outbreak of war. "What a loss to the London pageant," noted "Chips" Channon in his diary:

> No one infused it with so much colour and personality. Philip was sleek, clever and amiable. Kindly, yet fickle, gay yet moody, he entertained with almost Oriental lavishness in his three rather fatiguing palaces and exerted an enormous influence on a section of London Society.[34]

Sir Henry 'Chips' Channon had arrived in Europe as a young American from Chicago in 1918, married a Guinness heiress, rose in society even more rapidly than the Sassoons, and with Philip formed part of a corps of new Edwardians who circled round Edward VIII and Mrs Simpson prior to the Abdication. In spite of the tears which Sir Henry shed over the death of Philip, he disliked him, possibly because he saw in him the parvenu he felt in himself:

> Philip and I mistrust each other; we know too much about each other, and I can peer into his Oriental mind with all its vanities.[35]

He was a frequent guest at Philip's many homes, but rarely mentions them without a sneer.

Port Lympne:

> A triumph of bad taste and Babylonian luxury, with terraces and flowery gardens, and jade green pools and swimming baths and rooms done up in silver and blue and orange. A strange hydro for this strangest of sinister men.[36]

Trent Park:

> A dream house, perfect, luxurious, distinguished with the exotic taste to be expected in any Sassoon Schloss. But the servants are casual, indeed almost rude; but this, too, often happens in a rich Jew's house.[37]

And again, back to Lympne:

> The house is large and luxurious and frankly ugly. Honor said that it was like a Spanish brothel.[38]

Philip was perhaps an obvious target. Although millionaire-baiting was never a popular sport in England, the rich are often prone to be bitchy about the rich, especially where they are very rich. He was, by English standards, an upstart, and upstarts have always been fair game among upstarts. Like his grandfather and grand-uncles, he was too eager to please and in the presence of royalty he suffered a recrudescence of his oriental blood and could almost prostrate himself with obsequiousness. When he presented the Prince of Wales with some garden plants, he not only sent the plants, but his gardener too – a detail which almost summed up the Sassoons. Finally, he could never reconcile himself to his Jewishness, possible because he moved in circles which were largely, if not always openly anti-Semitic. He tried to give the impression that he was a Parsee. He might have convinced the general public that he was not Jewish; he might have convinced Göring, who once received him at his country retreat: he did not convince his friends. "Though Jewish," wrote Channon, "he hated Jews."[39] This hatred too was perhaps part of his eagerness to please, to be like the others, part of his restless craving for acceptance.

The breakaway branch of the family, headed by Elias Sassoon, was less exotic than this branch but the firm which he founded proved to be commercially more successful. Albert, and after him Edward, had directed the fortunes of D. Sassoon & Co. from London. E. D. Sassoon & Co. was ruled by Elias's eldest son Jacob, from Bombay. He was the biggest employer in the province and the Jacob Sassoon mills which he built were one of the largest enterprises of its sort in Asia. In 1909 he was made a baronet for his public services.[40] He extended the property holdings of his company, and in 1909 launched the Eastern Bank Ltd., with head office in London and branches in Baghdad, Bombay and Singapore and, eventually throughout the East.

He was a melancholy figure, troubled by his own health, and the incessant threat of blindness, and troubled, too, by his wife's health. They had one son who died in infancy. When Jacob died in 1916 his title went to his brother Edward Elias, through whom it descended in 1924 to his nephew Victor. His estate, divided equally among his three brothers, left them very rich indeed. Albert, Reuben and Arthur, each left about £500,000. Edward left over £1 million. When Elias's son Meyer died in 1924, he left $28,000,000 (probate was granted in Hong Kong.)[41]

Victor was the new brand of Sassoon. His family stemmed from India, his fortune from China, he was born in Naples, educated at Harrow and Trinity College, Cambridge, played around much of the inhabited globe, and died in the West Indies. His father and uncle Meyer had died within days of each other. Another uncle, David Elias, an incorrigible roué, dedicated his life and fortune to a prolonged debauch round the plushier bawdy houses of Europe, and for a time, Victor himself seemed headed for the same course. He had in his early years sought to marry a Christian girl, but his parents would not hear of it[42] – their branch of the family was less assimilated than the other – and Victor consoled himself with a rapid succession of mistresses and kept on consoling himself for the rest of his life. He was handsome, gay, dashing, very rich, and would today have been spoken of as a James Bondish figure. The thing that excited him was speed – in all its applications, fast company, fast women, fast horses, fast cars, fast planes. He was one of the founders of the Royal Aero Club. Like many bachelors leading such a life, he sometimes forgot that time did not stand still and he came up against his age in 1914 when he tried to volunteer as a pilot in the Royal Naval Air Service, and discovered that at thirty-three he was too old to pass the fitness test. He was, however, taken on as an observer and even this career came to an end three months later when he crashed and smashed both his legs and one of his thighs and spent eight months in plaster. The accident left him with one leg shorter than the other, a cripple – hobbling around painfully on a pair of sticks. In his last years, he used a wheel-chair. His handicap if anything made him more attractive to women; he certainly seemed to become more voracious for them. Philip, it was said, remained a bachelor because he did not like women enough, Victor, because he liked them too much.[43]

When he succeeded his father as head of E. D. Sassoon there were doubts whether he was equal to his responsibilities.

He was. Victor had the best business head in the family. He was also a most capable administrator, but it fell to his melancholy lot to wind up the great enterprises built up by his family in the Orient. He was not sympathetic to Indian nationalism, saw no future for his firm in India and sold the Sassoon mills in 1943 for £4,000,000 and later liquidated his other Indian assets. He was less fortunate with his Chinese holdings which he had extended in the late 1920s through the purchase of the Cathay Land Company, and the construction of a new office and shopping precincts as well as the luxury Cathay Hotel. In 1945 these properties were valued at over £7,500,000 but as the Communists spread westwards from Yunnan, there were frantic efforts by Europeans all over China to dispose of their property. Victor joined a little belatedly in the race and managed to get out £1,400,000 before the curtain came down. The rest had to be written off.

During this period he regrouped his assets and invested heavily in mining and industrial and property companies in Latin America and the West Indies. He made his headquarters in the Bahamas, whose climate and tax laws he found most congenial.

Victor had always had a passion for racing which he was only able to indulge after his father's death. He began by taking over the racing interests of Mr Gocouldas, an Indian cotton magnate, who had over a hundred horses in training in India, and several in England.[44] He went on to acquire stallions and mares, including the Kingsclere stables and Lord Derby's famous stud at Thornton-le-Street. By the time he died he owned seven stables and blood stock valued at £1,500,000.

In 1925, when India was passing through an economic crisis and Sassoon mill-hands were on strike against the proposed wage cuts, he laid out £110,000 on a private race course at Poona. The Poona races, however, were a minor diversion. He had set his eyes on the English classics. "There is only one race greater than the Jews," he liked to say, "and that is the Derby."

He made his first attempt at the race in 1929 with Hot Night, which came second. When he tried again in 1953 he had built up a racing establishment of such size, and at such expense that there was almost a mathematical probability that he would win, and win he did, with Pinza ridden by Gordon Richards. From then on his horses gave the Sassoon name a prominence which it had not enjoyed since the time of Edward VII. He won the Derby in 1957 with Crepello, who also carried off the 2,000 Guineas. When he won a third time in the following year, with Hard Ridden an outsider, at 18-1, it was suggested that the Derby should be renamed the Sassoon.

Television cameras were by now becoming ubiquitous on the tracks and every time Victor was seen on the screen leading yet another victor to the paddock, he seemed, in spite of the gay, triumphant smile which was almost becoming his hall-mark, to have grown much older and more bent. The excitement was undermining his health. The 1957 victories had brought on a mild heart attack, and in the following year he was taken ill at Ascot. He was now under constant medical care and accompanied everywhere by a nurse, Evelyn Barnes, a thirty-year-old, handsome, Texan blonde. On April 1, 1959, he announced that they were to marry. "After all," he told a friend, "seventy-seven years of bachelordom are essential to acquire enough judgement to choose the right wife."[45] They were married at a simple ceremony in a registrar's office.

He was still mobile, but carried enough medical implements to equip a clinic – sticks, crutches, a wheel chair, hypodermics, drugs and oxygen cylinders.

Victor won his fourth Derby with St Paddy. The Aga Khan had five Derbys to his credit and Victor hoped to equal this record, but his 1961 entry was scratched and he died two months later after another heart attack. He was eighty.

Victor was one of the charter members of the international jet set of ageing playboys composed of Greek shipping owners, Texan oil men, large scale property developers, rootless millionaires, the familiar faces of the gossip industry on both sides of the Atlantic. They were to the post-1945 world what the Edwardians were to pre-1914 Europe, except that they were no longer under royal patronage. There might be an occasional dethroned princeling among them, an Aga Khan, a count, a baronet, but by then millions was a form of nobility in itself. They needed no royal warrant.

There have been Sassoons who were content with a humbler place in society.

When Sassoon David Sassoon of Ashley Park dropped dead in the foyer of the Langham hotel in 1867 he left a widow, two sons and a daughter.

The first son married happily, or at least suitably, and took as his wife Louise de Gunzburg, a daughter of Baron Horace de Gunzburg, a Russian nobleman of German extraction, who also happened to be a Jew.

The second son, Alfred, married out of the faith. His bride, Theresa Thornycroft, was an attractive, level-headed Englishwoman of good family, but this was no consolation to his mother, who was beside herself with grief. Such things were as yet uncommon even among the Rothschilds. Among the Sassoons they were unheard of. She ranted, she wept, and on an impulse rushed to synagogue and before the open Ark cursed her son, his bride and any offspring of their union. Alfred, she declared, was dead and she would not allow his name to be mentioned in her house.

A few years later, however, Alfred's sister, followed his example by marrying Frederick Beer. Only she carried things a step further. Alfred had married in a registrar's office; Rachel married in church.[46]

Frederick had inherited £20,000 a year from his father and a number of papers, including *The Observer*. He was always in frail health, and suffered from an undefined malady at the time of his marriage, which was later recognised as the early signs of general paralysis of the insane.[47]

Rachel took over the direction of *The Observer*, and in 1893 bought the *Sunday Times* running them in double harness until she almost ran them into the ground.[48] She was accomplished, well-educated, highly intelligent, but with a sick husband on her hands one paper would have been enough. To manage both proved impossible, and when

Frederick finally died in 1903 she went out of her mind and was committed to a lunatic asylum, where she died in 1927.

Alfred's story, if less tragic, was not altogether happy. The passionate feelings he had for Theresa did not last, It was as if his mother's maledictions weighed on them both. There was much bickering and friction and finally he eloped with Theresa's best friend and found in concubinage the bliss he had missed in marriage.

He left his wife a small country house set in unkempt fields, an allowance, which though sizable, was small by Sassoon standards. There were three children, Michael, Siegfried and Hamo. Michael, emigrated to Canada and joined the maintenance staff of a fish cannery.[49] Hamo was killed at Gallipoli. Siegfried was to become a famous poet.

Siegfried was brought up in his mother's house in the Weald of Kent far from the baroque palaces of his cousins, and here he accumulated the impressions, on which he was to draw in later years, of hopfields and orchards, of bustling hedgerows and green meadows, of hunts and huntsmen, of the clatter of hooves on springy soil:

> Memories within memories; those red and black and black and brown coated riders return to me now without any beckoning, bringing along with them the wintry smelling freshness of the woods and fields.[50]

In reading Siegfried Sassoon one can see how far his cousins were insulated from the real world and real people, and how much they missed.

CHAPTER 20

Tidings from Zion

On July 5, 1902, Lord Rothschild found among the usual flow of bankers and brokers at New Court an unusual figure, tall, erect, with black hair, dark, piercing eyes, a massive black beard, lordly personage, with the bearing of a well-kempt prophet. He was Dr Theodore Herzl, president of the World Zionist Organisation.

Herzl was a cultivated Viennese Jew, a brilliant journalist, a novelist and playwright, a charming and talented literary dilettante, who had moved far from his Jewish origins and who would in the normal course of time have vanished from Jewish reckoning altogether like so many of his Viennese friends and contemporaries.

Anti-Semitism was rife in Vienna, as it was in the whole of Central Europe, and for a time Herzl toyed with the idea of mass baptism as a solution to the Jewish problem. In the main, however, he vested his hopes in social progress. The atrocities suffered by Jews in Eastern Europe could be explained in terms of Russian barbarism, and the hostility they encountered in Central Europe to Germanic conservatism. But if one looked to the West, to France, to England, there one could see Jews living amicably among their neighbours, rising to high office and enjoying great prosperity. What the Jews of England and France enjoyed today, the Jews of Germany would have tomorrow, and those of Russia the day after. Or so he believed.

In 1891, when he was thirty-one, Herzl was appointed Paris correspondent of the Vienna liberal daily, *Neue Freie Presse*, and discovered that France, as far as the Jews at least, were concerned, was not the home of progress he imagined. He saw Jews attacked, heard anti-Jewish harangues, witnessed anti-Semitic demonstrations. Then came the arrest, trial and degradation of Captain Alfred Dreyfus on a charge of high treason. Herzl was convinced, as later events were to prove, that Dreyfus was innocent and that he was being victimised to cover up the faults of his superiors. The Jew had reverted to his traditional role of scapegoat. If this could happen in republican, modern, civilised France, a century after the publication of the Declaration of Human Rights, observed Herzl, could there be a future for Jews anywhere? There could be none, he came to believe, outside a Jewish state.

A similar conclusion had been reached by the German socialist thinker Moses Hess. Like Herzl, Hess had moved far from his Jewish origins, and like him he was compelled by the Damascus affair to think anew on the Jewish question.

The idea of a Jewish state was also put forward by Zevi Hirsch Kalischer, an East Prussian Rabbi and contemporary of Hess, and Leo Pinsker, a Russian physician. Out of their ideas there grew a movement known as the *Hovevei Zion*, the Lovers of Zion. Pinsker became head of the movement and it spread rapidly throughout Central and Eastern Europe. Its progress in France and England was less rapid.

The *Hovevei Zion* did not aim at a Jewish state, but merely the creation of Jewish colonies in Palestine. Herzl envisaged something more ambitious, an autonomous Jewish state. This, he felt, was not something which could be built up piecemeal with a farm here and a vineyard there, but through a vast chartered company floated on Jewish wealth.

"First stage," he wrote, "The Rothschilds."

"Second stage: The Midget millionaires."

"Third stage: The Little People. If it comes to the third, the first two will rue the day."[1]

In the event he first approached not the Rothschilds, but somebody equally wealthy, and even more generous, Hirsch.

In 1891 Baron Maurice de Hirsch had founded the Jewish Colonisation Association for the settlement of Jewish immigrants in agricultural colonies mainly in the Argentine. By 1895 he had already spent many millions on the scheme, but it was going far from well. Herzl regarded the whole idea "as generous as it is mistaken, and as costly as futile", and outlined his alternative.[2]

Hirsch listened at first with scepticism and then with interest, but one question troubled him. "Where," he asked, "will you get the money?"

Herzl clearly hoped to get a good part of it from Hirsch himself, but he answered in more general terms.

"I will raise a Jewish national loan of ten million marks."

Hirsch almost laughed out loud.

"Fantasy," he said. "The rich Jews will give nothing. Rich people are worthless; they care nothing for the suffering of the poor."

"You talk like a socialist, Baron de Hirsch."

"I am one. I am perfectly willing to hand over everything, provided the others do likewise."[3]

Herzl next wrote to Albert de Rothschild, of the Vienna branch of the family, and his letter was not even acknowledged,[4] but in the following year, 1896, he was received by Edmond de Rothschild of the Paris house.

The *Hovevei Zion* had established a number of colonies in Palestine in the early 1880s which showed signs of foundering and Edmond was persuaded to come to their aid. In the course of the next thirty years he helped to establish some forty agricultural settlements and numerous schools and industries and spent some £12,000,000 in an attempt to make them viable.

Herzl did not anticipate that his ideas would win much sympathy in the Rue Laffitte and his belief was confirmed by events. He did not, as he made clear, want the baron's money – though it would come in useful. He wanted at the head of his movement a man whose name meant something both in the chancelleries of Europe and to the Jewish masses. With the baron at the top everyone else would fall into place. But like Hirsch, Edmond felt the whole scheme was fantastical, if not dangerous.

"Edmond," Herzl later noted in his diary, "is a decent, good-natured, faint-hearted man who utterly fails to understand the matter and who would like to call it off as a coward tries to call off an imperative operation. I believe he is now disgusted that he ever began with Palestine, and he'll perhaps run to Alphonse [his brother] and say, 'You're right, I should have gone in for racing horses rather than wandering Jews.' And the fate of millions of persons hangs on such a man."[5]

His rebuff from Albert de Rothschild did not encourage him to pay a call at New Court as yet, but he was warmly received by other leading members of the community:

Lunched at the home of Sir Samuel Montagu, M.P. A house of English elegance, in grand style. Sir Samuel a splendid old fellow, the best Jew I have ever met so far. At table he presides over his family – which for the rest is unamiable or perhaps merely well-bred – with the air of a good natured patriarch.

Kosher food, served by three liveried footmen.

After lunch, in the smoking room, I expounded my case. I gradually roused him. He confessed to me – in confidence – that he felt himself to be more an Israelite than an Englishman. He would be willing to settle with his entire family in Palestine.[6]

Montagu was an invaluable contact, and he soon made another, the Military Commandant of Cardiff and district, Colonel Albert Edward W. Goldsmid.

Goldsmid, tall, with flushed face, billowy moustache, and staccato voice, an almost archetypal Indian colonel, seemed an unlikely figure to find at any Jewish gathering, let alone in a movement to restore the Holy Land to the Children of Israel, but he at least could not dismiss Herzl's ideas as fantastic, if only because fantasy had played so large a part in his own career.

Goldsmid, born in Poona in 1846, was the son of an Anglo-Indian Civil servant. He was destined, like so many others of his class, for a military career. He was a young man when he discovered that his parents were baptised Jews and that they both stemmed from one of the oldest and most distinguished Ashkenazi clans in Europe, the Goldsmids. His mother was a grand-daughter of the financier Benjamin Goldsmid who committed suicide in 1808 and whose widow and seven children embraced the Christian faith. His father was a grand-nephew of the same Benjamin.

Goldsmid, to the dismay of his parents, decided to return to Judaism. His fiancée, Ida Hendriks, was by chance also of Jewish origin and she enthusiastically agreed to follow his example. His parents opposed both the match and their plans, so the young couple fled to Scotland, where they married first at a civil ceremony. Ida then took instruction in Judaism, and in 1879 they were married in synagogue.

"I am a Jew," Goldsmid told Herzl proudly. "It has not prejudiced my position in England. My children Rachel and Carmel received a strict religious upbringing and learned Hebrew at an early age."[7]

From 1892-3, Goldsmid superintended Hirsch's colonies in the Argentine, and his experience there convinced him that there could not be an effective Jewish homeland outside of Palestine. In him Herzl saw another version of himself, the visionary as a man of action. "With Goldsmid," he wrote, "I stand suddenly in another world."[8]

In a long letter he urged him "to enter the services of Turkey – like Woods, Kamphovener, von der Goltz, and other foreign officers. In that capacity you could have command of Palestine under the suzerainty of the sultan. And upon the dismemberment of Turkey, Palestine would fall to us, or to our sons, as an independent country."[9]

17. Venetia Stanley, the society beauty whom Edwin Montagu eventually persuaded to marry him.

18. Lilian Montagu, a leader of the Liberal Jewish Synagogue and lifelong social worker.

19. Claude Goldsmid Montefiore, prophet of Liberal Judaism.

20. Marcus Samuel, first chairman of Shell.

21. Clifton College—the Eton of the Cousinhood.

23. Herbert Samuel, from a drawing by Leonid Pasternak. As first
High Commissioner for Palestine, he assumed the role of the
new Nehemiah.

(LEFT)
22. Interior of New West End Synagogue, St. Petersburgh Place.
Built in 1879, it became the Chapel of the Annex.

24. Sir Robert Waley Cohen—John Bull Papa.

25. Alice Waley Cohen, *née* Beddington.

26. Basil Henriques who, while still an undergraduate, was introduced to the problems of the East End and vowed to create an effective Jewish mission there.

27. Sir Henry d'Avigdor-Goldsmid.

28. Lady d'Avigdor-Goldsmid.

29. Somerhill, the country seat of the d'Avigdor-Goldsmids, a painting by J. M. W. Turner, exhibited at the Royal Academy, 1811.

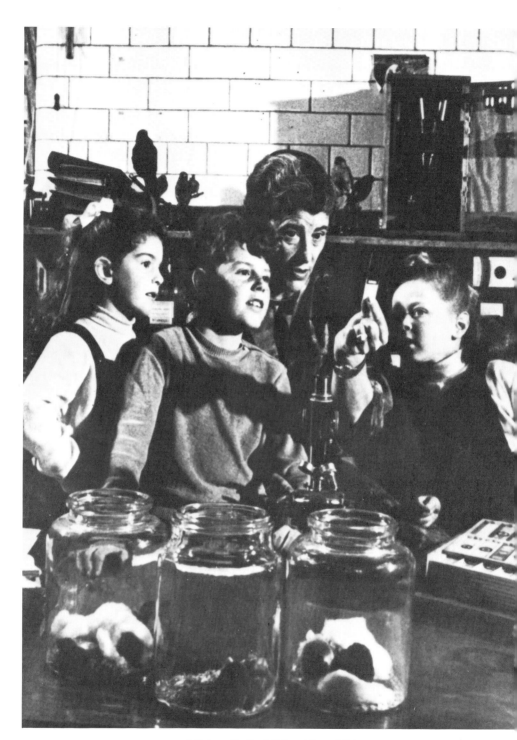

30. Miriam Rothschild and her children.

31. Mrs Edmund de Rothschild.

32. Rt. Revd. Hugh Montefiore, Bishop of Kingston.

Herzl was full of such ideas, too full for the peace of mind of his associates, but what caused the break between him and Goldsmid was his opposition to what he called the 'infiltration' policy of *Hovevei Zion*, and his determination to by-pass them and summon a Zionist Congress. Goldsmid was a leading figure in the *Hovevei Zion* as was his kinsman, Elim d'Avigdor. The *Hovevei Zion*, moreover, enjoyed the support of Edmond de Rothschild, which Herzl did not, and could not.

In April 1879 Goldsmid wrote to Herzl imploring him not to call his Congress for it would tear the *Hovevei Zion* apart, but this, if anything, was an inducement to Herzl to proceed. When the first Zionist Congress, which virtually laid the foundations of the Jewish state, opened in Basel on August 29, Goldsmid was noticeably absent. By way of compensation Herzl managed to gain the support of Sir Francis Montefiore, Bart., a grand-nephew of Sir Moses Montefiore, a barrister by profession, a staunch Conservative in politics, a high sheriff of Kent and Sussex, chairman of the Elders of the Sephardi community.

Sir Francis was an ornament of the Zionist movement in almost the literal sense of the word. A tall, elegant figure, immaculately dressed, with a flower in his buttonhole, and in white kid gloves, he stood out among the massed delegates like a sunflower in a field of turnips.[10] In 1900 he became honorary president of the Zionist Federation. He was an amiable but ineffective man, a poor speaker, but useful to Herzl, both because of his name – Sir Moses had been dead over a decade, but the name of Montefiore still struck a chord in the breast of most Jews – and his contacts in the Conservative party.

Herzl always dreamt of making a deal with the sultan by which he would obtain a charter for a Jewish settlement in Palestine in exchange for a loan. But after several visits to Constantinople he concluded that there was nothing to be gained from negotiations with Turkey. The sultan, he thought, was "the profoundly unhappy prisoner" of "a thieving, infamous, scoundrelly camarilla"[11] and there was no assurance that any agreement would ever be fulfilled. In 1902, there came the prospect of a deal with the British Government.

At the turn of the century persecution in Russia and Romania brought a new influx of Jewish refugees into Britain on top of the torrent which had arrived in the 1880s. The Conservative administration headed by Arthur Balfour felt compelled to establish a special Commission to look into the whole question of alien immigration. The Commission, headed by Lord James of Hereford, included Lord Rothschild (Natty) among its members and in June 1902 Herzl was invited to give evidence. Rothschild was apprehensive at what he might say and invited him for a preliminary meeting at New Court.

"It has taken me seven years to say to Rothschild what I will say to him tomorrow", he noted in his diary.

Herzl arrived promptly at one and was ushered into the presence of "the Lord of Banking Hosts . . . a good looking, Anglo-Jewish old gentleman. . . . He was very attractive, large Jewish eyes, and he is very hard of hearing. It would sound like a rope-dancer's patter if I were to record all the silly stuff he rattled off with great assurance."

Rothschild told him that he was not a Zionist, but an Englishman and he proposed to remain one, a subject on which Herzl had no doubt. He then tried to guide Herzl on what he should say to the Commission. Herzl, who was not an easy man to be guided by anyone, not even a Rothschild, broke in with some heat:

"I will tell the Commission what I think proper . . . I shall simply tell them what frightful misery prevails among European Jewry, and that the people must either die or get out."

Rothschild's face fell.

"I do not wish you to say that to the Commission," he said. "It will lead to restrictive legislation." But Herzl was by now in no mood to withdraw.

"Certainly I shall say it. Most certainly. You may depend on me to say it." His voice rose. "Jewish philanthropy," he cried, "has become a machine for stifling cries of distress."

Herzl later met Alfred, who spoke at length of the high decorations he had received from the Austrian and Prussian Crowns, and then turned to the question of a Jewish colony, which he thought was not a bad idea. "But why in Palestine?" he asked. "Palestine sounds so Jewish."

"How," Herzl later asked himself, "is one to negotiate with this collection of idiots?"[12]

But this was a harsh judgement certainly, as he realised himself, in the case of Natty, the first Lord Rothschild, who carried hard-headed common sense to the point of genius. Natty for his part was impressed by Herzl, both because of his firmness of purpose, and his outspokenness, which was something rare among visitors to New Court. And they discovered in the course of further meetings that their ideas were not so far apart.

Herzl had no deep sense of Jewish history. He wanted a home for Jews, in Palestine preferably, but if not there another place might do, and if it had to be another place, what could be better than a territory under British rule?

"Why not take Uganda?" asked Rothschild.

Herzl preferred something nearer Palestine, Sinai, El Arish, Cyprus. "Are you for it?" he asked.

Rothschild thought it over, chuckling: "Very much," he said.[13]

A meeting was promptly arranged with Joseph Chamberlain, the Colonial Secretary.

Cyprus, explained Chamberlain, was out of the question because the Greeks would oppose any such settlement; and as for El Arish – here there was some embarrassment for Chamberlain plainly did not know where it was, and they rummaged among atlases till Herzl pointed it out on the north-east neck of the Sinai Peninsula, abutting on Palestine.

"It was like a big second-hand store whose proprietors didn't exactly know where a particular article might be," wrote Herzl. "I need a gathering place for the Jewish people? He'll look around to see if England happens to have such a place."[14]

The area was a waterless waste, but Herzl was confident that he now had Rothschild behind him, and Rothschild's backing, he felt, was every bit as good as water. But the High Commissioner in Egypt, Lord Cromer, rejected the idea of Jewish colonies in either El Arish or Sinai. Instead Herzl was offered Uganda as the site of a Jewish colony which, under a Jewish governor, would enjoy local autonomy under the Crown. He accepted and split the Zionist movement between those who, like Weizmann, felt that there could be a Jewish home only in Palestine, and those who were desperate for any habitable corner of the globe. Herzl, already overworked and in poor health, was broken by the conflict. He died in July 1904 at the age of forty-four.

In the event Herzl could have saved himself much heartache, for it transpired that Uganda was not available after all. Even so, London, to the embarrassment of the Cousinhood, remained the focus of Zionist hope.

The death of Herzl pushed some of the younger figures in the Zionist movement to the fore. Among them was Chaim Weizmann, an industrial chemist, who settled in England in 1904 to take up a post at Manchester University. In 1906 he was introduced to Arthur Balfour and told him why Uganda was unacceptable to the true Zionist. "Supposing," he said, "I were to offer you Paris instead of London, would you take it?"

"But, Dr Weizmann, we *have* London," said Balfour.

"True," said Weizmann, "but we had Jerusalem when London was a marsh."

Their exchange continued for some time. "It is curious," said Balfour as he rose to leave, "the Jews I meet are quite different."

"Mr Balfour," said Weizmann, "you meet the wrong kind of people."[15]

Balfour was a member of the Cecil clan which had formed an inner caste within the English ruling establishment since Elizabethan times. He was a familiar figure on the Mentmore Waddesdon circuit and in the Rothschild corner of Piccadilly. He was, in particular, a personal friend of Alfred and Leo Rothschild and was a frequent visitor among the numerous Sassoons.[16]

The meeting with Weizmann though a chance informal occasion, was, in its way, epoch-making. Hitherto when a Jew wanted to approach Authority he did it through the Cousinhood. Weizmann now established direct contact. The Cousinhood were about to be by-passed. And the leading Gentiles were to prove more amenable to the Zionist idea than the leading Jews.

There was in Britain a considerable history of philo-Semitism going back to the time of Cromwell. Its character was mystical and apocalyptic, but as time progressed it grew more coherent and articulate. The Earl of Shaftesbury, the Victorian reformer and evangelist, saw the restoration of Jew to Judea as inevitable, though it would, he believed, be preceded by their conversion to Christianity.[11] In 1841 Colonel Charles Henry Churchill, a grandson of the fifth Duke of Marlborough, wrote to Sir Moses Montefiore suggesting the resettlement of the Jews in Palestine. The same course was proposed to Sir Moses a few years later by another British officer, Colonel George Gawler. The idea was taken a step further by Sir Charles Warren who proposed the formation of a Jewish charter company in Palestine which would eventually become self-supporting and autonomous.[18]

Sir Edward Cazalet, whose grandson Colonel Victor Cazalet was to become one of the staunchest proponents of Zionism in the House of Commons, proposed the mass settlement of Jews in Palestine under British protection. Sir Laurence Oliphant, the Oriental traveller and scholar, thought such a settlement was eminently practical on the East Bank of the Jordan, and even approached the sultan – without success – for consent to his idea.[19]

The Rev. William Hechler, chaplain to the British embassy in Vienna who had published a book in 1882 called *The Restoration of Jews to Palestine according to the Prophets*, saw in Herzl, whom he met a few years later, and in the Zionist movement, a fulfilment of his own prophecies. He proved to be one of Herzl's most useful and indefatigable disciples.

The Zionism of Sir Moses Montefiore falls almost into this Gentile category. It was part Messianic and part practical. He travelled to Palestine on seven different occasions, often at great hazard to himself and his companions, and out of his own pocket he established schools, dispensaries and workshops. He was appalled by the misery and destitution he found everywhere, the fatalism, the tendency to rely on almsgiving and prayers, and he concentrated on the creation of thriving, self-supporting communities. Through his friendship with the sultan and the local pashas he was able to assure the Jews the protection of the Turkish authorities, and at his request they moved cautiously beyond the old city of Jerusalem to establish a suburb outside the walls. He acquired new areas for settlement but did not envisage any mass movement of Jews to Palestine without divine intervention. "I shall await His coming daily, even though He tarry", he would say in his morning prayers, and he meant it. The tug of the Holy Land upon him was relentless.

Yet he was also an English gentleman, and a man of Kent. If these created a conflict within him, it was the conflict within a man who loved two places equally and wished to be in both at once. The advent of the Messiah would have solved his difficulty, but in His absence he resolved it, as we have seen, by being buried in Kent with holy soil beneath his head.

Montagu was in many ways like Montefiore, the mystic tycoon. He too prayed for the Messiah, but until the Messiah came along he was prepared to make do with Gladstone.

When Herzl published the plans for his Jewish state, Montagu sent a copy to the Grand Old Man, and waited breathlessly for his reply. The G.O.M. was not very forthcoming.

"The subject of the publication which you were good enough to send me," he wrote, "is highly interesting. For the outsider it is not easy to form a judgement regarding it, nor perhaps pertinent, having formed a judgement, to express it. It surprises me, however, to see how far-reaching is the distress among the Jews. I am of course strongly opposed to anti-Semitism."[20]

Had Gladstone been more enthusiastic about the scheme there can be little doubt that Montagu would have taken his wife and his younger children, his men servants and maid servants, his bag and baggage, to enter the Promised Land. But with Gladstone non-committal, and the

Rothschilds hostile or cool, he recoiled from Herzl's wild enthusiasm and confined his Zionism to his prayers.

In 1899 Herzl founded the Jewish Colonial Trust, the forerunner of the Anglo-Palestine Bank, as the financial arm of the Zionist organisation with a nominal capital of £2,000,000. He had allowed himself to hope that it would be promptly oversubscribed by the Jewish millionaires, but in the event even the 'midget millionaires', as he called them, kept away, and in the main the capital was raised in small sums from the Jewish masses.

Herzl put too much trust in princes, and this against his own better judgement. "I am an opponent of the House of Rothschild,"[21] he told the Chief Rabbi of Paris, but he wooed them relentlessly, in Vienna, in Paris, in London, wherever they occurred, with little success, and even most of the minor plutocrats proved to be cool, if not hostile.

Anti-Semitism was rife throughout Europe, and any assertion of Jewish nationalism ran counter to the claim of established Jews everywhere that they were Hungarians, Austrians, Germans, what you will. The fiercer the anti-Semitism, the louder the protests, and the greater the fear of Herzl and his visions. In England anti-Semitism was less widespread and less voluble and the Jews were less on the defensive, but here too Herzl was rebuffed by the Cousinhood and even by Chief Rabbi Adler, who dismissed his ideas as "absolutely mischievous".[22] "The Chief Rabbi has too comfortable a post to find pleasure in my project", wrote Herzl, and that, indeed, summed up the situation of the Cousinhood as a whole.[23]

It was ironical that the course of events left the Cousinhood to fight a long, inglorious struggle against Zionism, and to lose. They tried hard, but their situation was impossible. It was difficult to protest that their standing as Englishmen compelled them to oppose Zionism, when the Cecils themselves had embraced it. The truth of the matter, however, was that the Cecils could afford to espouse an alien cause while the Cousinhood felt that as yet they could not. They were not yet so established as Herzl thought, not as secure as they liked to believe. And at a crucial point in their struggle they suffered the defection of one of their most gifted sons, Herbert Louis Samuel.

CHAPTER 21

League of Loyalists

With the death of Herzl the leadership of the Zionist movement devolved upon Chaim Weizmann.

Weizmann had been one of Herzl's opponents. He had shared his basic aim, but not his trust in princes or international diplomacy. The Jewish state, he believed, could not be brought into being by a flourish of the pen and he regarded Herzl's frantic rushes between the chancelleries of Europe as futile. What counted, he felt, was the work on the soil of Palestine. The *Chalutzim* built facts, the diplomats, chimeras. But he too found himself among the diplomats, perhaps the most effective one in Jewish history. And like so much in history, it happened by chance.

The headquarters of the Zionist organisation were in Berlin. At the outbreak of war in 1914 they were shifted to neutral territory in Copenhagen, but the role of Britain was crucial in the post-war settlement and Weizmann found himself at the helm of affairs.

In 1906, while still at Manchester University, he had met Arthur Balfour. It was to have been a brief meeting; it became a long one. To Balfour it was a revelation – the facts, the ideas, above all the man.[1]

When Zionism ceased to be a vague concept and crystallised into an active force, the Cousinhood, led by a Rothschild, formed a powerful front against it, but it was on the particular stand of one man that Zionist aspirations nearly foundered. He too was a member of the Cousinhood by birth, but not wholly of them. He was the son of a peer, but not quite of the aristocracy. He rose to high office, without ever becoming an established member of the ruling class. His name was Edwin Samuel Montagu.

Montagu was born in 1879, the second son of Samuel Montagu, and

one of ten children. At the age of twelve he was sent to Clifton, and as
the son of the leading Orthodox Jew, he was naturally a member of
Polack's, the Jewish house. There he found himself among cousins,
but still lonely among them. Reverend Polack, his housemaster, recalled
him as a frail, shy, reserved boy.[2] Montagu recalled Clifton with a
shudder for added to the familiar horrors of English public-school life
was the ragging and teasing he suffered as a Jew. "Of course you take
no notice", he told his mother, but he was a sensitive child with a
strong streak of paranoia. He took a great deal of notice.

He was also racked with pains in the head. His letters home make
pathetic reading. He described how painful his headaches were and
how he could find no remedy. He could hardly 'bear the sorrow of
ending the term in such a poor way'. He asked his parents to try and
console him in the reply.

"Please *don't* worry or be miserable about me," he wrote a few
months later, "but try and come down and see me very soon."

Neither father nor mother seem to have found much time for him at
this stage. As a small child, his craving for affection was met by his
German governess, Rosie. Her name was the last word he spoke.

His parents finally took him from Clifton and sent him to the City of
London School, a day school on the Thames Embankment, where
he was much happier. In 1898 he went up to Trinity College,
Cambridge.

His father's strict orthodoxy had been the bane of his boyhood years.
His religious education was carefully supervised, and when, under the
guidance of his Hebrew tutor he went on a tour round the world, he
had to make careful arrangements to be at rest on Sabbath and Holy
Days, and for kosher food throughout.

By the time he reached Cambridge he had had enough, and wrote
home to say so. Old Montagu reminded him of his obligations to his
family and faith, but metaphysical debate was not his forte and his son
wrote back:

> Religion concerns only the individual. . . . By race I am an Englishman
> and my interests are mainly in England, but I will never forget that
> I am a Jew and the son of a Jew and I will always be a good 'Jew'
> according to my lights, my definition of a good Jew differing from yours.

He continued for the sake of his family to return home for the High
Holidays and the Day of Atonement in the autumn, and Passover in
the spring. Family feeling was his last remaining link with Judaism

and even this was becoming tenuous. His visits became fewer. His sister Lily was pained by his long absences. Although he appreciated her solicitude and her faith in him he wrote that 'her life and mine are destined always to be apart, for she works for sectarian purposes –I abominate them.' She strengthened the barriers he wanted to abolish.

Religion was not the only source of conflict. There was the matter of his career. He read Natural Sciences at Cambridge without having any clear idea what to do when he finished. "Had I been born to possess riches," he wrote, "I think my ideal would have been to possess land, to control and farm it myself and to represent the neighbourhood in Parliament."[3] But riches or no he decided on a parliamentary career.

Parliament to old Montagu was a side-employment for someone otherwise engaged. A man had to have a career and he urged his son to take up medicine, a subject in which he had no interest and for which he had no aptitude. A compromise was finally reached in which Edwin agreed to read for the Bar on completion of his science course and his father would continue to support him. When he came down from Cambridge he was given an annual allowance of £500, a substantial sum in those days, but he found it insufficient and complained bitterly:

> Oh mother darling, you have no notion of the unhappiness of my life. You and all my brothers and sisters have always been able to live at home in plenty. I am so terribly lonely seeing no friend or relation from week to week and talking nothing but politics. The work I like immensely, the life I like, but it is so terribly, maddeningly lonely, and I am driven nearly mad with money troubles.[4]

He tended to revel in self-pity. The family home in Kensington Palace Gardens was open to him, as it was to all the other members of the family, and in spite of entreaties from his mother and sisters he preferred to stay away. Nor could he have looked on his isolation from relations as a particular calamity, for he had always chosen to keep his distance. Yet it would be wrong to think of it merely as another species of begging letter which penniless sons address to rich fathers. He had a volatile temperament. One moment he would be on top of the world, happy and triumphant, the next in the dark depth of despair; and at such times he was inclined to write a tearful missive to his mother.

Then suddenly he found himself in Parliament. He had been adopted as Liberal candidate for West Cambridgeshire to cut his political teeth in what was a safe Tory seat, but in 1906 there was a Liberal landslide, and he found himself gazing around a little dazed under the arched ceiling of the Palace of Westminster, an M.P. Asquith, who became Chancellor of the Exchequer, at once invited him to become his Parliamentary Private Secretary. Edwin was only twenty-seven and already on his first rung up the ladder.

His new responsibilities involved him in new expenses, and at the same time he allowed his studies at the Bar to lapse. His father accused him of dishonesty, of broken vows, of avoiding his family, but he grudgingly increased his allowance. His mother too would hesitantly remind him of his shortcomings, which threw him into one of his frequent fits of depression. He wrote to her and said that he was too great a coward to throw up everything and leave home. He admitted their love for each other but told her how she was constitutionally incapable of writing to him without digging at him and wished that his father, whom he loves and admires and whose money he is grateful for, could 'grease the wheels with a little more kindness'.

The engagement, in 1908, of his younger brother Gerald to Florence Castello, the vivacious daughter of a wealthy stockbroker, depressed him further.

> Here is Gerald, my father's partner and trusted son, wealthy, healthy and happily settled. Here am I, un-trusted and often tolerantly condemned, poor, unhappy, unhealthy, unsettled.[5]

He would have liked to marry, and was a friend of Lady Dorothy Howard, a daughter of the Duke of Norfolk, but if he took a non-Jewish wife he would be cut off by his father, and a Jewish one was not yet in prospect. She would have had to be a member of the Cousinhood, a relative, and his relatives saw little of him.

In 1910 Edwin was appointed Parliamentary Under-Secretary of State for India. This was the lowest form of Ministerial life, but the Secretary of State for India was in the House of Lords, which left Edwin as spokesman on Indian affairs in the Commons.

He was an imposing, almost fearsome figure, with an overlarge head, a dark, saturnine, pock-marked complexion, black moustache. His mouth was large, sensual and slightly twisted. A gleaming monocle in his eye gave an impression of fierceness which bore no relation to his character.

"He was a man whose ugliness was obliterated by his charm," wrote Duff Cooper. "He had a huge, ungainly body, a deep soft voice and dark eyes that sparkled with kindliness."[6]

His speeches were characterised by good, solid sense, and if they were a little too solidly composed, they were devoid of pomposity and his opening speech as Under-Secretary of State made a pleasing impact. "The House of Commons, the most critical assembly in the world," noted a lobby correspondent, "was deeply interested in his speech. At the end of it Mr Montagu took his seat, having established himself in the course of an afternoon as a new force in English politics."[7]

In the autumn of 1910 there were rumours that Montagu, then thirty-one, was about to become engaged to a nineteen-year old cousin. His mother was delighted at the prospect and could hardly wait for the event. The son pleaded for patience. "I must be sure of myself and her before I do anything. After all, she ought to look round before joining herself to morose old me even *if* I want her and of that I'm not quite sure."[8] The fact that his father was by now a sick man with not many months to live gave some urgency to the matter, but Edwin could not be hurried, and neither for that matter could the girl. She did, as he suggested, look around, and when he finally proposed she said no.

On January 11 Samuel Montagu, who a little earlier had been raised to the peerage as Lord Swaythling, died and left over £1,000,000 to be divided among his children, "provided they shall respectively at my death be professing the Jewish religion and not be married to a person not professing the Jewish faith".

The Liberal *Nation* criticised the provisions as an example of the dead trying to direct the life of the living,[9] an observation which brought a sharp retort from G. K. Chesterton:

Many Englishmen, and I am one of them, do seriously think that the international and largely secret powers of the great Jewish houses is a problem and a peril. To this, however, you are indifferent. You allow Jews to be monopolists and wire-pullers, war-makers and strike-breakers, buyers of national honours and sellers of national honour. The one thing you won't allow Jews to be is Jews.[10]

The death of his father revolutionised Edwin's financial position He was now reputed to have an income of over £10,000 a year, but though rich, he was because of his father's will not quite independent.

His mother was proud of his political progress, but was worried by the fact that he was now over thirty and still single, and urged him to find a nice Jewish wife. "I fear it can't be done", he replied. "It is not only that I don't as a rule like Jewesses. It is also that I firmly believe that to look for a wife from one set of people is wrong as it would be to say you must look for a wife among blue-eyed women."[11]

But he was looking for a wife among blue-eyed women, or, at least, had found one, Venetia Stanley, a daughter of Lord Stanley of Alderley, a tall, elegant society beauty, and at first sight a rather frivolous creature for so earnest a figure. If she had a guiding principle, she told a friend, it was to get the maximum of fun out of life,[12] and on their first acquaintance Montagu loathed her. In time his feelings turned to adoration, feelings which were in no way reciprocated.

In 1912 he thought their relationship was sufficiently advanced to propose marriage, but she rejected him with a shudder.[13] Montagu was grieved but persisted. In time she found the idea less horrifying, and eventually agreed to marry him. Montagu was in heaven. But her feelings changed again, and she wished only to remain friends.

Venetia at this time was possibly suffering from an embarrassment of friendships and she was on particularly intimate terms with Herbert Asquith, Montagu's old chief at the Treasury, who was now Prime Minister, and thirty-two years her senior. He would write to her daily and call on her at her parents' home two or three times a week. The flow of letters became more frequent after the outbreak of war, and the visits more insistent. Neither setbacks at home nor disasters abroad affected his habit, and he would sometimes write to her three or four times a day, not resting even on Sunday, when he sent his letters by special delivery. Montagu still hovered round, ever eager, ever hopeful and they sometimes laughed together about him. Asquith did not treat him as a serious rival. On one occasion before the war all three had spent a holiday together in Sicily. All three remained close friends and Asquith thought they would remain so *sine die*. Then in May 1915 Venetia suddenly announced her engagement to Montagu.

Roy Jenkins, Asquith's latest biographer, suggests that the young woman began to find the Prime Minister's affection "a crushing and frightening emotional burden"[14] and marriage to Montagu was her best means of escape. But one can see a more likely reason. Montagu had risen to high office. In 1914 he left the India Office and served for a time as Financial Secretary to the Treasury. "My job is only that of scullery maid to the Government and the City,"[15] he told his mother, but in January 1915 he became a Privy Councillor, and in February, Chancellor of the Duchy of Lancaster, with a seat in the Cabinet. His engagement followed three months later. Lord Beaverbrook, who later became Minister of Information, was throughout this period at the very heart of affairs, spoke of Montagu as "the hope of Liberalism, the visible successor of Lord Rosebery".[16]

Venetia's father was not happy about the match, and Venetia herself could not overlook the obstacle of religion, if religion was the right word for it. Montagu had long ago abjured any belief in the Jewish faith, and Venetia herself was an agnostic, but there were the feelings of the Dowager Lady Swaythling to consider, and even more the terms of Lord Swaythling's will. If she did not become Jewish he would become a poor man. She, for her part, made her feelings perfectly clear.

> Were I to be washed a thousand times in the water of the Jordan and to go through every rite and ceremony that the strictest Jewish creed involves, I should not feel I had changed my race or nationality. I go through the formula required because you want it for your mother's sake and also (I am going to be quite honest) because I think one is happier rich than poor.

She went on to reassure him that she would marry him even if he was penniless, but wanted to know what would happen to their children:

> Is it race or religion you care about, or merely the label? If race, then you are debasing it by marrying me, whatever I do. Religion, you know I care nothing about and shan't attempt to bring up my children in. There only remains the label. And will that stick, do you think?

Such reservations were not allowed to affect their intentions. Venetia went through a form of conversion and they were married according to Jewish rites at a private ceremony in the home of his brother, the second Lord Swaythling, in Kensington Court.

The whole conversion procedure, as Montagu must have known, was a charade from beginning to end, but it satisfied his mother for whom it was better than nothing. It satisfied the terms of Lord Swaythling's will, for as far as the law was concerned Montagu had married a Jewess. It could not have entirely satisfied Montagu's biographer, the late S. D. Waley who went to some lengths to explain that the conversion was not a sordid device to hold on to Swaythling's patrimony.

Money plainly did have something to do with it. Venetia had

protested that she would have taken him without a penny, and had she done so she would still have had her own private fortune which, to use her own words, was 'vast', but Montagu who had been his father's pensioner for much of his adult life, could not have cared to be kept by his wife. Nor was it likely that with their tastes and style of life, Venetia's fortune alone would have sufficed. They kept a town house in London and a moated mansion in Norfolk, and even their combined fortunes could not keep them out of debt. Yet far more than money was involved. Montagu was also deeply concerned about his mother. She was in her seventies and in frail health. He was virtually estranged from the rest of his family, but he was particularly close to her and neither sickness, fatigue nor the worries of office could prevent him from writing his daily letter home to let her know how he was doing, what he was doing, how he was. She took a particular pride in his progress. When, for example, he toured India on official business, in the autumn of 1912 he kept a detailed diary which he sent home to his mother in regular instalments and which she read to members of the family round the Friday night table. It was almost a matter of "My son, the Secretary of State". He frequently explained the difficulty of finding a suitable Jewish wife. "I feel it would be wicked to choose a wife because of my father's will or any Jewish woman whom I did not love as I love," he wrote. "And I have never yet, though I have tried desperately, found one such."[18] Yet, having prepared her for what could happen, he could not bring himself to let it happen. He had courage, but not the sort of courage necessary to inflict pain on those he loved.

He also had certain undefined residual Jewish feelings. If his sons would marry Christians, he once told Venetia – this was before their marriage, and their discussion was hypothetical – he would look upon them as deserters.[19] He had no belief in the Jewish religion, no sense of fellowship with the Jewish people, but – it may have been the public-school element in his upbringing – he did not wish to abscond from their ranks, and he may have satisfied himself that the conversion of his wife, though made under dubious auspices, and cursory in the extreme, kept him among the Jews. It was a token act of association.

Montagu had no sooner acquired Venetia than he lost his seat in the Cabinet. He was engaged on May 12, on May 19 he was out. Asquith was deeply upset by the engagement[20] and one can almost see cause and effect, but there were, of course, far larger issues involved.

A coalition was formed in May for the more effective prosecution of the war, and a number of Liberal Ministers in the Cabinet had to make way for an influx of Tories. Herbert Samuel, was one such Minister, Montagu was another. He was asked to return to his former job at the Treasury, and a few months later was offered the Irish Office. Ireland was the graveyard of political hopes. He felt himself ill-equipped for the office, and as a Jew, he protested, he would find it difficult to cope "with religious questions in a creed which I do not believe."[21] Moreover, as he pointed out, the permanent head of the Irish Office, Sir Matthew Nathan, was a Jew, and it would not help if the political head was of the same faith.

Asquith seemed to be persuaded by his plea, though it could be added that all the arguments Montagu put forward against accepting office in Ireland applied in almost every respect against taking office in India, for when India was offered to him a year later he jumped at the opportunity.

In the meantime Asquith came forward with an offer more in keeping with Montagu's interests. In July 1916 Lloyd George became Minister of War and Montagu succeeded him as Minister of Munitions. This brought direct involvement in the war effort and he described the period as the most enjoyable and satisfying in his career. But it was brief.

A movement developed to oust Asquith from office and replace him with Lloyd George. Montagu, who was aware of what was happening at every stage in the process, was in a painful dilemma. He was drawn to Asquith by every pull of affection and friendship, and he had a high regard for the abilities, both negative and positive, of Lloyd George.

"I remain of opinion, unshakeable and based not only on affection, but on conviction, that there is no conceivable Prime Minister but you", he wrote to Asquith. "I remain of opinion that Lloyd George is an invaluable asset to any War Government. His brain is the most fertile we possess." But the value of Lloyd George inside the Cabinet was as nothing to the nuisance he would be outside. Some accommodation, he urged, must be reached.[22] None was attainable[23] and eventually Asquith resigned and Lloyd George was asked to form a Government.

Montagu took pains to "place it on record that I have not received any offer to join George's Government. . . ."[24] Lloyd George looked upon Montagu as one of the ablest members of the outgoing administration, a person of 'resource and imagination', but he was too close to Asquith to join the new Government at once.[25] At the same time he did not wish to remain out of office for ever and in March 1917, three months after the fall of Asquith, in one of his not unusual moments of whimsy, he penned a little doggerel to the Prime Minister:

> As the desert sand for rain,
> As the Londoner for sun,
> As the poor for potatoes,
> As a landlord for rent,
> As a dorsera rotundifolia for a fly,
> As Herbert Samuel for Palestine,
> As a woman in Waterloo Road for a soldier
> *I long for talk with you*[26]

In July he was offered the India Office which, he promptly accepted,[27] and wrote to Asquith for his blessing.

"In view of our past relations," came the icy reply, "it is perhaps not unnatural that I should find it difficult to understand and still more to appreciate your reasons for the course which you tell me you propose to take."[28]

The appointment caused some consternation in Tory ranks, especially among the diehards, and Lord Derby, the Secretary of State for War, was moved to utter a word of protest. "The appointment of Montagu, a Jew, to the India Office, has made, as far as I can judge, an uneasy feeling both in India and here," he said, and added quickly: "I personally have a very high opinion of his capability and I expect he will do well."[29]

This was the first mild shot against the new Secretary of State in what was eventually to become a sustained barrage.

Montagu's work at the India Office brought him into direct conflict with Balfour, Lloyd George and the Zionists. The creation of a Jewish state in Palestine would, he believed, be viewed with alarm by Indian Moslems, but he also had his own personal reservations on Zionist philosophy. In August 1916, he wrote to a friend: "It seems to me that Jews have got to consider whether they regard themselves as members of a religion or a race. For myself I have long since made the choice. I view with horror the aspiration of national unity."[30] He did not explain why what was natural, indeed commendable, in the Indian should be horrifying to the Jew. His reaction to the very idea of a national home was fierce and emotional. "All my life I have been trying to get out of the ghetto," he told Lloyd George. "You want to force me back there."[31]

It was as if the shadow of Polack's House was closing in upon him;

SAMUEL BEN AMSCHEL

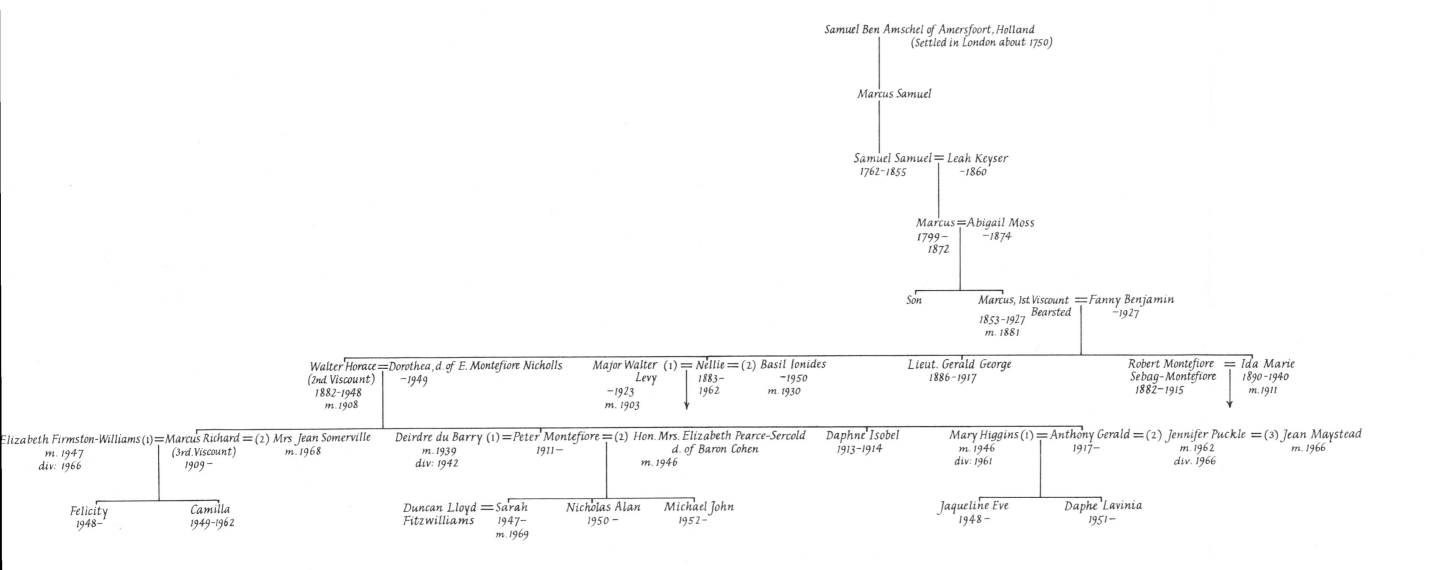

Samuel Ben Amschel of Amersfoort, Holland
(Settled in London about 1750)

Marcus Samuel

Samuel Samuel = Leah Keyser
1762-1855   -1860

Marcus = Abigail Moss
1799-   -1874
1872

Son   Marcus, 1st Viscount = Fanny Benjamin
             Bearsted   -1927
             1853-1927
             m. 1881

Walter Horace = Dorothea, d. of E. Montefiore Nicholls   Major Walter (1) = Nellie = (2) Basil Ionides   Lieut. Gerald George   Robert Montefiore = Ida Marie
(2nd Viscount)   -1949   Levy   1883-   -1950   1886-1917   Sebag-Montefiore   1890-1940
1882-1948   -1923   1962   m. 1930   1882-1915   m. 1911
m. 1908   m. 1903

Elizabeth Firmston-Williams (1) = Marcus Richard = (2) Mrs Jean Somerville   Deirdre du Barry (1) = Peter Montefiore = (2) Hon. Mrs. Elizabeth Pearce-Sercold   Daphne Isobel   Mary Higgins (1) = Anthony Gerald = (2) Jennifer Puckle = (3) Jean Maystead
m. 1947   (3rd. Viscount)   m. 1968   m. 1939   1911-   d. of Baron Cohen   1913-1914   m. 1946   1917-   m. 1962   m. 1966
div: 1966   1909-   div: 1942   m. 1946   div: 1961   div: 1966

Felicity   Camilla   Duncan Lloyd = Sarah   Nicholas Alan   Michael John   Jaqueline Eve   Daphe Lavinia
1948-   1949-1962   Fitzwilliams   1947-   1950-   1952-   1948-   1951-
                                                               m. 1969

as if his bearded father and all his fathers before him were rising to torment him. His struggle against Zionism was no mere contention with a political philosophy, it was part of a personal exorcism. He regarded Jews as a purely religious community, and himself as a Jewish Englishman.

He was certainly very English in his ways, in his style of life. He was part of the charmed circle of high-born and to an extent high-minded socialites which revolved round Duff Cooper and his beautiful wife, Lady Diana.

He had a town house in Queen Anne's Gate and the country house in Norfolk, Breccles Hall, a large Elizabethan mansion which he rebuilt at prodigious expense under the direction of Sir Edwin Lutyens, the architect of New Delhi. It had a great hall which was his particular pride, and when one saw him there, the Lord of the Manor, by the vast fire-place, under the great oak beams, amid all the solid trappings of olde-Englande, it was easy to forget that here was the grandson of a bearded Hebrew from Liverpool, three generations removed from the ghetto. He hunted and fished, shot big game and little game, stalked and walked, was a keen naturalist and ornithologist. He was no port-swilling bucolic hearty, but he loved the open air, the misty marshes of Norfolk, the wind-swept flats, the quivering reeds, the cry of the wild-fowl. There was something perhaps a trifle alien in the very depth of his affection for England, but he was the most English of English gentlemen.

He was not seen as such by his opponents, and perhaps not even by his friends. The Jew in him hit them as if he had the Star of David branded on his forehead, and it had something to do with his eventual downfall. It also had much to do with his opposition to Zionism. How, he asked, could he, a Jew, negotiate with the peoples of India on behalf of the Government, if the world had just been told that the Government regarded his national home as being in Turkish territory? Zionism, he insisted, was an alien creed, supported only by aliens and opposed by the large majority of British-born Jews.[32]

One of the leading Jewish institutions is the Board of Deputies dominated for the last part of its life by the Cousinhood. In 1917 the president was David Lindo Alexander, an eminent barrister.

There was also the Anglo-Jewish Association which had been founded in 1871 and whose president was Claude Montefiore. The Board was vaguely representative and consisted of delegates elected by the various synagogues in the country. The Anglo-Jewish Association was in effect a council of Jewish notables, manned almost entirely by the older families. Apart from a joint concern with the rights and interests of Jews in this country, both were often compelled to intervene with the government on behalf of oppressed co-religionists abroad, and for this purpose they formed a conjoint Foreign Affairs Committee. This committee became the instrument of the Cousinhood.

Zionism was making rapid headway among the Jewish masses, it was receiving support in influential sections of the British press, and in May 1917 the Conjoint Committee, fearing that its case might go by default, rushed into print with a long letter to *The Times* over the signatures of Alexander and Montefiore. Zionism, they declared:

> regards all the Jewish communities of the world as constituting one homeless nationality, incapable of complete social and political identification with the nations among which they dwell, and it is argued that for this homeless nationality a political centre and an always available homeland in Palestine are necessary. Against this theory the Conjoint Committee strongly and energetically protests. Emancipated Jews in this country regard themselves primarily as a religious community, and they have always based their claim to political equality with their fellow citizens of other creeds on this assumption, and on its corollary – that they have no separate aspirations in a political sense . . . the establishment of a Jewish nationality in Palestine founded on this theory of Jewish homelessness, must have the effect of stamping the Jews as strangers in their native lands. . . .

They also feared that Zionist plans would establish the Jews as a ruling caste in Palestine, "with certain special rights in excess of those enjoyed by the rest of the population".[33]

All these arguments had been set forth by Claude Montefiore before in various pamphlets on various occasions. What caused a storm was the presumption which lay behind the letter. Alexander had signed himself as president of the Board of Deputies of British Jews, Montefiore, as president of the Anglo-Jewish Association. They claimed to speak on behalf of British Jewry. Letters immediately poured in to show that they did nothing of the sort, from Dr Gaster, the Haham; from the Chief Rabbi, from Lord Rothschild, from others.

Dr Gaster moved a vote of censure in the council of the A.J.A., but was prevailed upon to withdraw out of respect for Montefiore, but feeling was fiercer at the Board. On June 17, by 56 votes to 51 it repudiated the Alexander-Montefiore letter and dissolved the Conjoint

Committee.[34] The community had in a passing moment of wrath asserted its independence of the Cousinhood.

But the battle was not over. The Cousinhood were regrouping for a further effort. Above all, there was still Montagu, in the Cabinet, at the very heart of affairs.

Montagu became Secretary of State for India just as a draft text of the Balfour Declaration was being prepared, and it caused understandable consternation among Zionists. "I was afraid we were done," said Lord Rothschild when he saw the announcement in *The Times*.[35] And they nearly were.

The draft text was placed before the War Cabinet, an inner committee of the Cabinet which concerned itself with the highest matters of policy and the day-to-day conduct of the war. Montagu was not a member but was brought into the discussion. He had already made his views known on several occasions and had lately circulated among his Government colleagues a memorandum headed: *The Anti-Semitism of the Present Government*.[36] Again he pointed out that such phrases as "home of the Jewish people" could prejudice the Jews elsewhere. He further felt that President Wilson should be consulted. This was a dangerous device for the President's *eminence grise*, Colonel House, was no Zionist sympathiser,[37] and Justice Brandeis, an American Zionist leader, had to make a hurried intervention with Wilson to get his support for the plan.

Montagu, who was preparing to leave for India, now played his last card. He urged that representative Jewish opinion should be sought on the draft text and again had his way. In October the draft text was circulated among what the Cabinet secretary described as "representative Jewish leaders".[38] They were ten in number and included Chaim Weizmann and his colleague in the Zionist Organisation, Nahum Sokolov, the Chief Rabbi, Lord Rothschild, Herbert and Sir Stuart Samuel, Sir Philip Magnus, Lionel Louis Cohen, Claude Montefiore and Montagu himself. The fact that Montagu could have been thought of as "a representative Jewish leader" by a senior Civil servant has both irony and significance. None of the ten was strictly speaking representative, and all but the first three were members of the Cousinhood. The Samuels and the Rothschilds favoured the draft. Cohen, Magnus, Montefiore and of course Montagu were against it.[39]

The alignment of famous Jewish names against the Declaration was impressive, and Montagu was a particularly formidable opponent, arguing both from the standpoint of the assimilated Jew and as Secretary of State for India. If it had been merely an issue between Zionist and non-Zionist factions within the community, there is little likelihood that the latter would have won, but there were the Gentile Zionists to consider and they carried the day. The most active among them was Sir Mark Sykes. He was merely an Assistant Secretary to the War Cabinet, but his particular task was to brief Ministers on the background in the Middle East and his role in the negotiations on the future of Palestine was crucial. He had been converted to Zionism by Dr Gaster, and once he espoused the cause he promoted it with all the zeal of a convert. There also was Lord Milner, the great Proconsul, who had carved a Commonwealth out of the rebel territories of South Africa, and who was now Colonial Secretary; there was Smuts, Prime Minister of South Africa, and now a member of the Imperial War Government, whose knowledge of the Old Testament had made him a keen proponent of Zionism; there were the more doubtful sympathies of Lloyd George. Above all, there was Arthur Balfour. Here too the influence of the Bible was important, but Balfour also had a deep admiration for the achievements of the Jewish people, and sympathy with their suffering. There was also something in Jewish history which answered to the broad streak of mysticism in his complex character. He could not understand how Jews could be against the idea of a Jewish state. "But why should they oppose it?" he asked Weizmann in some perplexity, "why can I afford to be a Zionist and not they?"[40]

The answer was of course that Balfour had no doubts about his own identity, while the Montagus, Montefiores and other anti-Zionists, though old-established, rich, influential, with wide contacts and of high rank, still had uncertainties; they still felt the need to assert their patriotism. They protested a little too much, and in the end they lost.

On November 2, 1917 Balfour wrote to Rothschild:

His Majesty's Government view with favour the establishment in Palestine of a National Home for the Jewish People, and will use their best endeavours to facilitate the achievement of this object, it being clearly understood that nothing shall be done which may prejudice the civil and religious rights of the existing non-Jewish communities in Palestine or the rights and political status enjoyed by Jews in any other country.

The Declaration filled Montagu with despair. He took it almost as a personal affront.

"It seems strange," he wrote in his diary, "to be a member of a Government which goes out of its way, as I think, for no conceivable purpose that I can see, to deal this blow at a colleague that is doing his best to be loyal to them, despite his opposition. The Government has dealt an irreparable blow to Jewish Britons and they have endeavoured to set up a people which does not exist. . . .[41]

He had a slight knowledge or understanding of Jewish history and in particular of Zionism, which, because its headquarters had once been in Berlin, he seemed to regard as a largely German phenomenon. He did not appreciate the religious feelings at the source of it, the extent of Jewish suffering which gave it immediate urgency or the mass following which it aroused, but once the Declaration had been made, the fight was over as far as he was concerned.[42]

The Cousinhood, however, soldiered on. They founded the League of British Jews to make known their disassociation from the Zionist creed and proclaim their patriotism. They launched a new paper *The Jewish Guardian* to counter the influence of the pro-Zionist *Jewish Chronicle*.[43] And when the Ministry of Information began to trumpet the significance of the Balfour Declaration abroad, Lionel de Rothschild pleaded with the Minister, Lord Beaverbrook, "to do nothing to encourage the idea of a Jewish National Home".[44]

Claude Montefiore went on to denounce Zionism from platform and pulpit, by letter and book, all to no avail. Whatever defects he thought he saw in Zionist philosophy, external factors settled the issue. There was chaos in Russia. Anti-Semitism was rife in Poland, the Baltic countries and Romania. It was growing apace in Germany. Anxious Jews in their thousands turned this way and that. Britain had closed its doors in 1905, and America, the great haven, did the same in 1922. Zionism was confirmed by events.

Montagu did not live to see them. He had suffered his own, private martyrdom. He was fascinated by India. "Indian problems attract me with an intensity which I can find for no other problems," he once told Asquith. "I have no other ambition save to go to India and I have had no other since I entered public life."[45] He had in particular set his heart on becoming Viceroy, and when in December 1915 he heard that Lord Hardinge, the reigning Viceroy, was about to retire, he approached the Prime Minister with a directness which was almost indelicate:

I feel I should not be doing my duty to myself or, as I conceive it, to India, if I did not once again put forward with insistence, but for the last time, my own claims. . . . I have carefully considered all the other possible names and . . . I know of no one who seems to me likely to do for India what I want done.[46]

He then turned to his Jewishness. "That," he admitted, "is the serious obstacle. It is an objection from the point of view of civil servants and perhaps of soldiers. . . . As regards the *Indians* I do not believe it to be an objection."[47]

It was a prescient observation. Asquith passed him over in spite of his entreaties, and it was Lloyd George who finally met his longing to serve India by making him Secretary of State. As such he was warmly welcomed by the Indians, and disliked and distrusted by the soldiers and the Civil Service. They viewed him as yet another 'Oriental', a fakir in morning coat, imposed upon them to bargain the empire away.

There were also strong misgivings about the appointment at home. We have seen Lord Derby's apprehensions. Bonar Law, another Government colleague, thought of him as a clever man, but with "some of the poorest qualities of his race".[48] He was viewed with particular disfavour by Tory diehards and the right wing *Morning Post* never missed an opportunity to attack him as a 'politico-financial Jew' of un-English mien and doubtful allegiance.[49] And it was this 'politico-financial Jew' who had to sell to an increasingly Conservative House what was an essentially Liberal policy.

In 1909 the Morley-Minto proposals had given India a tentative start on the road to self-rule, and in August 1917 Montagu announced a further step:

> That of increasing association of Indians in every branch of government and the gradual development of self-governing institutions with a view to the progressive realisation of responsible government in India as an integral part of the British Empire.[50]

In the following months, after an extensive tour of India, Montagu, in association with the viceroy, Lord Chelmsford, published a list of proposals on the future of India[51] which were embodied in the Government of India Act, 1919. When the Montagu-Chelmsford proposals were made there was a Liberal majority in the House. By the time they were embodied in legislation, a general election had intervened and the Tories were in the majority; and in April 1919 came the Amritsar massacre.

There was unrest in large areas of India in the post-war years and the Punjab was particularly affected. There were riots in Amritsar on April 11 and April 12 resulting in serious injury and loss of life, and a curfew was imposed. On April 13, a large crowd, estimated at between 10,000 and 20,000 people, assembled in an open space in defiance of the curfew. The local commander, Brigadier-General Dyer, without caution, without warning, without any order to disperse, commanded his troops to fire straight into the milling mass. The crowd, hemmed in by buildings on either side, turned to flee but was impeded by its own size. There were panic, screams, cries of pain. Above all came the crack of rifle fire, which continued till the ammunition gave out. When the commotion subsided 379 people lay dead, and 1,200 injured.

General Dyer later explained that he was not concerned with merely dispersing the crowd:

> there was a complete defiance of the law. They had come to fight . . . they defied me, and I was going to teach them a lesson. . . . I was going to punish them. My idea from the military point of view was to make a wide impression.[52]

Montagu was aghast. He had Dyer relieved of his command and put on half pay. There was uproar in Parliament and the press and there were complaints that a 'gallant' officer doing his duty was being made the scapegoat for the failures of politicians. Montagu in particular was singled out for attack. "Mr Montagu should never have been appointed to India," declared Sir Henry Page-Croft, a prominent Tory back-bencher. "He is in no way typical of the natives of India. He above all others is responsible for the agitation which has sprung up."[53]

In 1920 Chelmsford retired and he was succeeded as viceroy by Rufus Isaacs, the Marquess of Reading. This, of course, confirmed the suspicion of some onlookers that the Jews were conspiring to sell the Empire. India was being lost, protested a Tory diehard, "because *two* Jews, one in Whitehall and the other in India, were afraid to grapple with the extremists".[54]

Even those who were favourably disposed towards Montagu felt that a man with his antecedents must necessarily favour Indian aspirations. He was, wrote Earl Winterton, "a man of great ability, idealism and charm, who had a natural sympathy with the East, based, I think, partly on his Jewish blood".[55]

His Jewish blood had not given rise to any deep sympathies for his fellow Jews. It was not merely that he was anti-Zionist – he was totally unconcerned about the plight of his co-religionists. "I regard with complete equanimity whatever treatment the Jews receive in Russia", he wrote to a friend in 1916.[56]

One sees in such remarks an almost deliberate effort to be untouched by Jewish suffering, lest he should be overwhelmed by his feelings, for

he was a liberal, humane, compassionate man, as was evident from his
Indian policy, and given the choice between concession and oppression,
he always chose the former. This was the main complaint of the diehards. Speaker after speaker rose in the House of Commons to complain
of his pusillanimity, and that law and order in the sub-continent was
on the point of collapse.

There was at this time little law and order anywhere in the world
and Lloyd George explained events in India in a global context, but
observers were quick to notice that he did not have a word to say in
defence of his Secretary of State or in approval of his policy.

Montagu had become a political liability, and in March 1922 Lloyd
George found an opportunity to get rid of him.

The Treaty of Sèvres, which was in some ways more severe than the
Treaty of Versailles, threatened to dismember the Ottoman empire.
Both Montagu and Reading were worried about the effect of the treaty
on pan-Islamic opinion in India, and Montagu, without referring the
matter to the Government, allowed Reading to publish a statement
calling for its revision. It was not an unforgivable indiscretion, but
Lloyd George did not choose to forgive it, and on March 9, 1922 he
informed a packed House of Commons that Montagu had resigned.
At this the Tory back benches rose in a solid wall, laughing, clapping,
cheering, waving order papers, shouting. It was as if Mafeking had
been relieved all over again.

The vendetta against him did not die down. He was out of office,
but still in Parliament. In the 1922 election Tories and Lloyd George
Liberals had agreed not to oppose one another, but Montagu was
opposed with a vengeance in what was perhaps the most sordid contest
in the election. Hooligans filled his halls with noise. He was heckled
and barracked. It was a nasty and brutal campaign and he was not so
much opposed as hounded. And with the vote split three ways he lost
his seat.

During his years in office Montagu tended to leave domestic finances
to his wife. She was not an able manager and ran up enormous debts.
In 1923 he accepted a number of City appointments and joined the
Board of De Beers, and those of a couple of railway companies. He also
headed a committee of financial advisers which travelled to Rio de
Janeiro to put Brazil's economy in order. Had he lived longer he would
have risen as rapidly in the City, as he had in politics, but he knew
that his time was running out. On his return from Brazil he complained
of ill-health, as he had on frequent occasions in the past, and his

doctors tended to dismiss him as a hypochondriac. In June 1924 he wrote to his wife:

> For some time I have felt all was not right, despite the doctors. If I had more time I could have got out of debt, but it was not to be. I fear you will not have an easy time, but things are not so bad as they were and I have failed in a plan to enjoy things, both of us, while we were young because the end is coming so soon. I am miserable at going. You have made me very happy and I hope you will be happy always.[57]

He lingered on, sad and crumpled, for another five months, and died on November 15, 1924. He was forty-five.

"He was very nervous," wrote Duff Cooper later, "and absurdly pessimistic. Whenever he talked about the future he would interject 'But of course I shall be dead by then'."[58]

CHAPTER 22

The Annex

If the Cohen family provided the main framework of the Cousinhood, the Samuels have provided the annex. It was not that the one was older than the other. Both found themselves in England about the same time, but while the Cohens remained in London, the Samuels hied off north to Liverpool; and while the former were merchants and brokers the latter were watchmakers, jewellers, trinket vendors. The two were vaguely connected at the beginning of the nineteenth century through Israel Israel, a London bullion dealer, one of whose sons married a daughter of Levi Barent Cohen, and two of whose daughters married Samuel sons. They were thus, to use an untranslatable Yiddish expression, already *machatonim*. In 1862 they were brought directly together when Montagu Samuel married Ellen Cohen. They had ten children and the network thus formed spread northwards to the provinces, east into Europe westwards to America and the Indies, to include nearly every established Jewish family in the United Kingdom and to touch upon many a major Jewish clan in the diaspora.

The late Arthur Franklin[1] and Mr Ronald D'Arcy Hart,[2] both, needless to say, members of this extended Cousinhood, have traced in separate volumes the entire network with all its ramifications. Their task has been eased by some branches of the Samuel family, possibly to avoid confusing each other, altering their names. Thus, while Montagu Samuel became Samuel Montagu, Edgar Samuel became Samuel Edgar, Lawrence Samuel became – no, not Samuel Lawrence, but Lawrence Lawrence while his brother Sidney became Sidney Stevens, and one group of Samuels became Hill. (These changes were slight compared with the metamorphoses suffered by a daughter of the Samuel family and daughter-in-law of a Rabbi Hirschel Schenkolowsky, whose children's children became St Losky.)[3]

In the nineteenth century there was still much linking of wealth to wealth, and the head of each family tried to pass on at least as much as he inherited to each of his children. As time passed and taxes grew, this became increasingly difficult. The wealth began to thin out and in some cases it has grown very thin indeed. Here and there amid the crumbling terraces of West Hampstead or North Kensington, in rooms like ill-kept antique shops, one may find dusty little ladies with famous names, hugging their antecedents with a mixture of desperation and pride.

Another reason for the decline in wealth was the change in the occupational structure of the Cousinhood. By the end of the last century, as the universities and new opportunities were opened to the Jews, the sons of bankers and brokers were no longer content to be brokers and bankers. Some became scholars, statesmen, writers, social workers, spenders rather than earners, and others, while rising high and earning well in the professions did not earn nearly as well as they could have done in the banks and brokerage houses. They opted for sufficiency rather than abundance. Thus, as one turns the pages of Franklin and Hart, one finds a great variety of talents, distinctions and skills, some of them rare. One lady for example is described as "a breeder of prize-winning goats and poultry",[4]; another more simply as "a blood donor",[5] who is still happily active and alive, though of an age at which she has to keep her blood to herself.

Commerce and industry are, as one would expect, well represented. One finds a Gluckstein of the Salmon and Gluckstein dynasty, whose interests include several large West End hotels, the J. Lyons catering group, and Wimpy bars; several Van den Berghs of the Unilever combine; several members of the H. Samuel jewellery group; and members of the Liverpool Cohen family, which established the Lewis's group of department stores, came south to take over the Selfridge group, and which has since been taken over by the Clore group.

But the Annex also includes a more alien group, several artists, including the actress Rachel Gurney, the daughter of an assistant master at Eton. Her mother was the late Irene Scharrer, the concert pianist, who in turn was a distant kinswoman of the late Harriet Cohen.

Miss Cohen's mother, a grand-daughter of Walter Samuel of Liverpool, was herself a pianist of great distinction. Her father, Joseph Woolf Cohen, was an accountant by profession and a musician *manqué*. He later changed his name to Cerney, but his daughter remained Cohen.

Miss Cohen, who was born in 1895, was one of the most accomplished exponents of English piano music. The works of Vaughan Williams and Arnold Bax often had a place in her repertoire, though she was equally at home with Debussy or Bach. In 1936 she was awarded the C.B.E. for services to British music. She was a beautiful woman, elegant in dress and striking in appearance and at her concerts her many devotees would scramble for a place in the front rows to see as well as to hear. She had innumerable friends from innumerable circles and they included Elgar, Bernard Shaw, Arnold Bennett and Ramsay MacDonald.[6] In 1948 an injury to her right hand seriously affected her playing and in 1960, after undergoing two eye operations, she finally retired from the concert platform. She died seven years later.

Several members of the Annex were active feminists both during the suffragette days and after. One who rose to the front rank of the feminist movement was the late Eva Hubback, a daughter of Sir Mayer Spielmann. Her mother Gertrude was the daughter of George Raphael, a City banker of Sephardi origin, whose family had come over from Holland in the eighteenth century; the Spielmanns, from Poland, were more recent arrivals. The Raphaels had a fine Adam house in Portland Place and a country house at Castle Hill near Windsor. Eva's daughter in an affectionate memoir, describes the happy days spent at Castle Hill:

> Christmas was a fabulous occasion . . . the ceiling-high Christmas tree, the lanterns hung round the lake for skating, the sledges decorated with firs, the vast turkey and the astonishing presents. She tried to keep up this Christmas tradition in her more modest fashion in her own family all her life. A strange tradition to inherit from Jewish grandparents. . . .[7]

At the same time, her daughter recalls, "she was carefully brought up in the Jewish faith, and from it derived in part the strong moral code she retained all her life".[8]

She received Hebrew instruction and attended the New West Synagogue regularly. She was sent to a respectable but not too starchy boarding school at Southwold, and thence to a finishing school in Paris where she learned the usual subjects plus something called "Drawing Room", which is to say, the social graces, but found she couldn't learn dancing "for nuts",[9] and did not much care for the other accomplishments the young Edwardian hostess was expected to have. In 1904, when she was seventeen, she announced that she was going to Cambridge.

It was not for this that her family had sent her to a French finishing school. The idea of a young woman of good family entering upon a prolonged and serious course of study was as yet not generally accepted, and the Spielmanns did not find it quite acceptable. But her mind was made up! She went.

Eva had hitherto moved almost entirely within the Jewish community among girls from well-to-do homes with limited interests, who looked forward to happy flirtations, marriage, a home in some ornate terrace in Bayswater, and children. Cambridge opened a new world to her, new opportunities, new friends, with different interests. She was from a family with a strong social conscience. He father spent much of his time and fortune on the welfare of the young, but the Mocatta-style charity in which they were involved was already becoming outdated, and Eva, a brilliant student of economics, began to wonder whether there was not something wrong with a society where the many were so dependent on the favours of the few. She joined the Fabian Society.

While at Cambridge she met Bill Hubback, a Classics scholar from Liverpool, a large, vigorous young man, a skilled athlete and mountaineer, boisterous, good-natured and, in spite of an external air of frivolity, a brilliant scholar. Eva tended to be a little too grave, with too restless a social conscience. Bill would often make fun of her, but she took from him what she would have resented from anyone else. In June 1910 they became engaged.

The announcement caused some shock to both their families for while the Spielmanns were devout Jews, the Hubbacks were devout Christians, with clerical connections. Hubback Senior protested that no such alliance had ever to his knowledge taken place in his family. And Philip Waley, one of Eva's favourite uncles, wrote her an affectionate letter tinged with much sadness:

> . . . you won't mind my saying that I am truly sorry your choice has not fallen on one of our community; you know my views on religious as on social questions are above all liberal but it is a real regret that you are going to be lost to Judaism, and especially as I know it must and does cause such extreme pain and sorrow to your father and mother, in whose heart the cause of Judaism in its best and widest sense has only come second to their love and devotion for their children.[10]

But the truth of the fact was that even in her single state Eva was already 'lost to Judaism' much as Bill was lost to Christianity. They were both agnostics.

Theirs proved to be a happy marriage, but it was brief. Bill was killed on the Western front in 1917, leaving Eva with three young children.

She had been an active suffragette. After women won the vote in 1918, they continued to suffer from inequalities, and the various feminist organisations in the country came together to form the National Union of Societies for Equal Citizenship under the presidency of Eleanor Rathbone M.P. In 1920 Eleanor invited Eva to become Parliamentary Secretary to the Union. They were a formidable pair.

"Eva Hubback," wrote Miss Rathbone's biographer, "had a singular talent for combining pertinacious attack with friendly and reasonable co-operation. She was a trained economist with a wide circle of friends in the academic and political sphere. . . . She made easy personal contacts with male politicians whom she was called upon to pester with feminist demands – all the easier perhaps because her feminist activities were dovetailed with the upbringing of her young family rendered fatherless by the First World War."[11]

In 1927 she resigned her post to become the principal of Morley College, London, but her energies and experience continued to be at the disposal of feminists everywhere, and her large house on the Hampstead Heath extension in Golders Green tended to be a meeting point of high-powered female academics from both sides of the Atlantic and the Commonwealth. After the war she was elected to the London County Council and served until her death in 1949. She is buried near her parents in Willesden Jewish cemetery.

Eva Hubback was more of the white-haired matriarch than the detached don, but though moved by a restless compassion, her actions were always calm and considered; heart and mind worked in unison. She was a cerebral Lily Montagu, working without the benefit of religion.

Another member of the Annex on the L.C.C. was Helen Bentwich, who became a member in 1937 and rose to become chairman in 1956.

Mrs Bentwich, a daughter of Arthur Franklin, was one of the corps of well-born young ladies who helped Lily Montagu at her West Central Club, and has devoted her whole life to welfare and cultural work. During World War I, when she was forewoman in a munitions factory at Woolwich arsenal, she was horrified at the treatment of workers and tried to form them into a trade union. Her efforts were not appreciated, and she left to become an organiser in the Woman's Land Army.[12]

The office of chairman of the L.C.C. does not have any of the ceremonial or glamour attaching to the Lord Mayor of London which is regarded by some Labour members of the L.C.C. as slightly frivolous. Certainly the character of the L.C.C. (whose boundaries have since been extended and whose name is now the Greater London Council) is much more in keeping with the purposeful and business-like Bentwich temperament, and her years of office gave her great satisfaction.

Mrs Bentwich, now in her eightieth year, is still active on a large number of educational, cultural and welfare groups. One may occasionally see her, with stick in hand, walking through the White-chapel Art Gallery, of which she is treasurer, grimacing here, beaming there, as she passes from exhibit to exhibit, a white-haired, pale-faced English lady, but hardly a frail, vague little soul. The chin juts out and the almost inevitable cigarette in her mouth, gives her a mildly pugnacious appearance which is not entirely out of keeping with her character.

Her husband, the late Norman Bentwich, was Attorney-General for Palestine from 1920 to 1931 and professor of International Relations at the Hebrew University from 1932 to 1951. A lithe, slight, ageless figure, he was until his death at the age of eighty-eight chairman of the Friends of the Hebrew University, and darted from continent to continent to attend the Council of the Hebrew University in Jerusalem, the Jewish Memorial Council in New York, or the many other cultural foundations with which he was involved. He was a prolific author. Obscure works of scholarship, popular histories, memoirs, biographies, autobiographies, belles-lettres, polemics, each carefully conceived and precisely written, poured from his pen. He carried a constant sense of urgency even into old age. One tended to think of him as Quick, Quick, Bentwich.

He bore a revered name in Zionist history. His father, a wealthy barrister, was one of the few prominent English Jews to side whole-heartedly with the Zionist movement, and he did much to facilitate the efforts of both Herzl and Chaim Weizmann. In 1929 he carried his Zionist sentiments to the unusual lengths of actually settling with his family in Palestine.

As Attorney-General for Palestine Norman Bentwich thus worked on familiar territory, but it was an unhappy office for any Jew to hold. The Arabs distrusted him as a Zionist, the English – at least the subordinate officials – as a Jew, and the Jews as an Englishman. His colleague, Sir Ronald Storrs, the Governor of Jerusalem, sympathised with his predicament:

Nothing on earth would convince the Arabs of the impartial purity of his conclusions. "It is not possible," they would answer, "the better Zionist he is, the worse Attorney-General." Some of his British colleagues were inclined to agree that his position was delicate, while he was severely criticised by Zionists for excessive moderation.[13]

In February 1932 he gave his inaugural lecture as Professor of International Relations at the Hebrew University, on "Jerusalem, City of Peace". He had just gathered breath to speak and uttered his first sentence, when there was uproar. It was a year since he held Government office, but Jews have long memories, and many students felt that he had been too eager to placate Arabs at the expense of Jews. There was shouting, screaming, name-calling and the concerted chanting of slogans; papers flung through the air; stink bombs let off. The university authorities tried to restore peace, without success and finally the police were called in. The hecklers were ejected, and Bentwich, with an armed guard on each side, and fixed bayonets at the back of the hall, resumed his reflections on "Jerusalem, City of Peace".[14]

Dr Bentwich has been constantly torn between London and Jerusalem and this conflict is well symbolised in a book-plate of his design. It has one panel with his wife in an English farmhouse, and another with the Damascus Gate of the walled city of Jerusalem, and underneath the words: "If I forget Thee."[15] He was true to both. The same could be said of his wife's cousin, the late Brigadier Kisch.

Hermann Frederick Kisch, a member of a unique Anglo-Jewish-Indian clan, which included both successful merchants and distinguished civil servants, was born in Darjeeling in 1888, educated at Clifton and the Royal Military Academy, Woolwich, and was commissioned in the Royal Engineers. He was wounded in action in World War I, received the D.S.O. and *Croix de Guerre* and rose to the rank of Lieutenant-Colonel. In 1916 he was transferred to the General Staff and after the war was a member of the British delegation at the Versailles Peace Conference. In 1921 he was invited by Weizmann to supervise the work of the Zionist organisation in Palestine.

The invitation, as Kisch later recalled, "came to me out of a clear blue sky".[16] He was very English, pukka, stiff, not very approachable, somewhat clipped in utterances, a tall lean man, with a worried face and a military moustache. He was not a member of the Zionist organisation, yet the challenge and the scope of the assignment appealed to him. He accepted and at once applied himself with the zeal that was so characteristic of all his efforts. He learned Hebrew, and his fellow

Britons, who had welcomed him as an officer and gentleman, as one of them, began to suspect that he had 'gone native', which to an extent he had, but he found the in-fighting of Zionist politics tiresome, and when Weizmann resigned from the Zionist executive in 1931, he too bowed out. He had fallen in love with Palestine, however, and remained there to build himself a magnificent villa on Mount Carmel overlooking Haifa Bay.

He returned to the army on the outbreak of World War II, rose to the rank of Brigadier as Chief Engineer to General Montgomery's Eighth Army and was involved in planning the breakthrough at Alamein. He coupled great resourcefulness with rare professional skill. Montgomery said he was "the best Chief Engineer an army could hope to have".[17] In April 1943, while directing a mine-clearing operation in Tripolitania, his car hit a mine and he was killed.

Moshe Sharett, later the first Foreign Minister of Israel, broadcast a tribute from Jerusalem:

> Peace unto your dust in foreign soil, Jewish soldier! Your stout heart was beating for the redemption of Israel. Because of the contribution which you have made through your life's work for our Homeland, and because of your self-sacrifice, your name shall forever blossom in the memory of our people.[18]

At the memorial service to him arranged some days later there was present in the large congregation a heavily built man in a wheelchair, who wore a thick cluster of medals. He was Sir Brunel Cohen, a major in World War I who had lost both his legs in action.

Cohen was a member of the enterprising Liverpool Jewish family, which built up the Lewis's department stores. His father combined something of the flair of the showman with that of the businessman. He had brought Brunel's *The Great Eastern* up the Mersey for use as a floating shopping centre, and was so taken with the ship that he named his son after its designer.

Major Cohen entered Parliament in 1918 as Tory M.P. for the Fairchild division of Liverpool, and became an active member on behalf of disabled ex-servicemen. The fortitude with which he coped with his own handicap – he was a keen swimmer before he lost his legs, and somehow remained so after[19] – was in itself a source of reassurance to the disabled. He summed up his philosophy in a small volume called *Count Your Blessings*. He looked on disablement as a challenge and was on the board of a host of institutions concerned to give the disabled a useful role in life. He was a familiar and beloved figure at the annual remembrance parades of the Association of Jewish Ex-servicemen. In his bowler hat, with his long row of medals, his military moustache, his shoulders thrown back, he was still, even crippled and in a wheelchair, every inch the major. He was knighted in 1943 for his services to the disabled.

Sir Brunel was one of the few Jewish Tories in the House of Commons, but several of his kinsmen have been Tory candidates, and one of the more persistent was his brother-in-law and nephew, Gilbert Samuel Edgar, who contested Smethwick at a by-election and the General Election in 1945. He had what was then called 'a good war', in fact two good wars and had served with the Royal Horse Artillery in the first and as an R.A.F. wing commander in the second, but Smethwick was then too solidly Labour and he lost on both occasions.

His father Edgar Samuel was born in Liverpool in 1861, and finding himself one Samuel among too many, changed his name to Edgar Samuel Edgar. As a young man he had entered into partnership with his widowed mother, who had established a small jewellery and watch-making firm in 1863, and rapidly built it up into H. Samuel & Co,, the largest chain of jewellery stores in the country. Gilbert Samuel Edgar has been chairman of the group since 1935.

One of the largest clans within the Annex are the Waleys, some of whom began life as Levy and some as Schloss. The Schlosses felt compelled to change their name during the Germanophobia of World War I. Among them was David Schloss, who was educated at Rugby and Balliol – and who was a senior Treasury official when the war broke out. He enlisted in the army in 1916, was commissioned in the London Regiment and won the Military Cross for gallantry. He returned to the Treasury after the war, and was knighted in 1943. After his retirement in 1948 he joined the board of Ashanti Goldfields, International Paints and numerous other companies. He was also a director of the Palestine Economic Corporation and the Union Bank of Israel.

Sir David was a grandson of Professor Jacob Waley, who was first occupant of the Chair of Political Economy at University College, London, and first president of the Anglo-Jewish Association.[20]

The distinguished Sinologist, Arthur Waley who died in 1966, was a brother of David. He would have been horrified at any suggestion that he was a member of a clan, for he was essentially a man apart. Although he lived in Bloomsbury and had occasional contacts with some of its leading figures, such as the Sitwells, he was not part of the Bloomsbury set. He tended to treat society as one of the dispensable luxuries of life, and preferred to confine himself to essentials. A pupil recalls a meal at Waley's: "Dinner consisted of a dish of vegetables which he had himself cooked, a glass of water and, for each of us, a raw apple, which we ate unpeeled."[21]

His deep aestheticism, wrote Peter Quennell, who was to know him towards the end of his life, "was qualified by a strain of natural puritanism, which he may have perhaps inherited from his devout hardworking Jewish ancestors".[22]

Although the clan as a whole had frugal habits, the degree of puritanism displayed by Arthur Waley was as rare as his talents. Professor Ivan Morris, perhaps his leading disciple, thinks of him as a 'genius'.[23]

Waley had taught himself Chinese and Japanese while an assistant keeper in the British Museum. Although he had never received formal instruction in either subject and had never been to either Japan or China, he became the principal expositor of Chinese and Japanese literature in the Western world. "Without Waley's books," writes Professor Morris, "it is unlikely that the Classics of the Far East would have become such an important part of Western heritage."[24]

The Annex is a most catholic gathering and one tends at any turn to stumble upon unexpected people like Dr Eric Conrad, whose father Emil Conrad was editor of the Vienna *Neue Freie Presse*, and Herzl's superior at the time of the Dreyfus Affair. Eric, who was a member of the Austrian Bar, came to this country in 1933. He enlisted as a private in the Pioneer Corps at the outbreak of war, was transferred to the Intelligence Corps in 1944 and attached to the American army. He was awarded the U.S. Bronze Star for his part in the capture of Cherbourg arsenal. In 1949 he married Sheila Grenville, a daughter of the Hon. Elsie Montagu and grand-daughter of the first Lord Swaythling.

An even more unexpected figure is Alexander Poliakoff, with his long thin, almost transparent nose, a monocle in his eye, silver hair and exquisite manners. His ancestors were Rabbis in Moghilev, a celebrated dynasty of saints and sages, but they gradually spread out into this world and prospered sufficiently to become privileged Jews with the rights of residence in Moscow, St Petersburg and the other principal cities of Russia. His father, Joseph Poliakoff, organised the Russian telephone system. They lived in magnificent style with a large house in St Petersburg, a country estate, Chekovian gentry in a Chekovian setting, removed from any trace of their antecedents or from any contact with their Jewish contemporaries. Their upbringing, with Russian servants and French and German nannies, was such as to insulate them

from any Jewish awareness whatsoever. They knew that there were
Jews in the world, but not that they, the Poliakoffs, were part of the
same brotherhood. Then came the revolution. The Poliakoffs, like
almost everyone else of their class, were ruined. They arrived in England
in the 1920s, penniless, but the elder Poliakoff had specialised knowledge. More than that, he had contacts with Godfrey Isaacs of Marconi
fame and was soon re-established. In 1937 his son, Alexander, married
Ina Montagu, a grand-daughter of the first Lord Swaythling. Mr Poliakoff is a physicist by training, and is managing director of the Electronic
Instruments Company. He lives in a Regency house in Holland Park
and a country house in Sussex. At the end of December one will find
a Christmas tree in his drawing-room, and Christmas cards on the
mantelpiece and holly and ivy. The setting could not be more English,
but among it all Poliakoff still remains very much the Russian – the
accent, perhaps, or the manner, possibly the eternal air of disdain – a
living fragment of old Imperial Russia in an English drawing-room.

Although every vocation is represented in the Annex it contains only
two clergymen, one of them a Catholic priest, the late Rev Father
Ernest Hill of Newport, Monmouthshire, a grandson of Henry Israel
Samuel. The other was Sir Philip Magnus who began his career in the
1860s as minister of the West London Reform Synagogue, but found
that he could best pursue his calling as an educationalist and made
further education his particular field. He did much to interest universities and local authorities in the problem of what would now be called
'drop-outs', though it is not an expression which Magnus would have
used for he believed that children did not drop out, but were forced out
by their circumstances. He was a member of Parliament for London
University (before 1950 universities had their own M.P.s).

He was, during his days at Upper Berkeley Street, tutor to the young
Claude Montefiore and may have been in part responsible for the
latter's anti-Zionism. He was among the ten 'representative Jews'
approached by the Government in October 1917 for their opinion on
the proposed Balfour Declaration, and denounced it as dangerous. He
was, he said, in favour of a Jewish cultural centre in Palestine, but a
national home could antagonise both the local inhabitants and Turkey
and result in massacre.[25] He was among the founders of the League of
British Jews, which was formed immediately after the Declaration. He
wished, he said, to check the tendency "to fix upon the Jews the acceptance of a nationality other than, and in addition to, that of the country
of our birth and where we lived and worked".[26] The League launched

the *Jewish Guardian*, which was edited by his eldest son, Laurie. Philip was made a baronet for his services to education, and died in 1933 in his ninety-second year.

Laurie, who predeceased him, was a gifted journalist and in the *Jewish Guardian* produced a weekly paper of impressive quality. It foundered perhaps because its quality was too impressive for it to be able to attract more than a minute circulation. He was also for a time Berlin correspondent of the *Morning Post* (which, before it joined with the *Daily Telegraph* was as anti-Semitic a daily as ever appeared in Britain), and the author of several works of popular scholarship, including *Jews in the Christian Era* and a *Dictionary of European Literature*.

His son, the present baronet, who bears the resounding name of Sir Philip Montefiore Magnus-Allcroft, has not maintained the family's associations with the Jewish community. He married into an old English county family and appended his wife's surname to his own. They live in Shropshire and are active members of the Shropshire County Council, and the Ludlow Rural District Council.

Sir Philip was for a time a Civil servant, but retired in 1951 to devote himself to writing and rapidly established himself in a second career as a distinguished biographer. He has written the lives of Edmund Burke, Sir Walter Raleigh, Gladstone, Kitchener, and Edward VII and his combination of imagination and scholarship, plus a fluent prose style has gained him critical acclaim and a wide readership.

The Magnus family is linked at various points to another large and versatile clan, the Spielmans (some members of the family spelt their name with one n, some with two) whose most eminent figure was perhaps Sir Meyer Adam Spielman. Sir Meyer was on the Stock Exchange for thirty years, but retired in 1911 at the age of fifty-five to devote himself entirely to the welfare of the young, and the problems of the juvenile delinquent. He described his work in a rather maudlin little study called *Romance of Child Reclamation*. He saw juvenile delinquency largely in terms of lack of opportunity, and was one of the founders of an industrial school at Hayes, Middlesex, to provide boys from poor Jewish homes with a trade, and of Park House, a reform school for Jewish boys. He would have been happy to know that within a few decades of his death – in 1936 – there was hardly a Jewish boy at Park House. He was knighted in 1928 for his services to child welfare.

Sir Meyer had four brothers and three sisters. One of the brothers, Sir Isidore Spielman, began life as an engineer but after a few years acquired a speciality – the organisation of art collections. He was neither a student of art nor an art critic, nor yet an artist, but a sort of stage manager. He became the founder and director of the Art Exhibition branch of the Board of Trade, and as such was involved in the assembly of British works for exhibitions all over the world. He was knighted in 1905.

His younger brother Marion was an art scholar and critic and adviser to the Maharajah of Baroda on his collection of European works. He wrote a history of *Punch* in 1895, and several critical studies of artists as different as Kate Greenaway and Millais, G. F. Watts and Velasquez.

The Spielman(n) and Magnus clans have thinned out considerably, and are now hardly heard of in Jewish life, but one clan which is larger than both put together and which is still very much on the active list is the Franklins.

The Franklins, or Fraenckel as they were known on the Continent, came to this country about the same time as the Samuels, but claim descent from the House of David. A less remote but more probable ancestor was Judah Low ben Bezalel, a sixteenth-century mystic and scholar, who was Rabbi of the ancient *Altneuschul* – the building is still in use – in Prague, and is famous in Jewish legend as the creator of the *golem*, a sort of pre-Frankensteinian monster. There have been numerous tales of such mystics and monsters, but the *golem* of Prague has taken a particular grip on the Jewish imagination and the legend still circulates.

The descendants of Rabbi Low have been active in more mundane spheres, predominantly banking, but they also have interests in publishing and in tourism and own the flourishing Wayfarer's Travel Agency in Holborn.

The first of the Franklins in this country was an itinerant scholar who acted as tutor to the children of the Gomperts, Goldsmid and Waley families. Life must have been difficult in London, for his sons moved north to Manchester and then to Liverpool, from which one normally moved on to America unless one found an occupation locally. They found numerous occupations, and dabbled as money-changers, jewellers, old-clothes sellers, silversmiths. One of the sons had eleven children, the other was hardly less prolific, and Franklins spread out in all directions. One moved to London and founded the *Voice of Jacob*, the first Anglo-Jewish newspaper (which however folded after a few years).[27] Another went to Jamaica, where he became a magistrate and, for some unfathomable reason, H.M. Consul for Denmark. A third went as far west as San Francisco, where, according to the local *Hebrew Observer*, "he formed the first Minyan . . . recited the first Jewish service, married the first Jewish couple, buried the first Jew and delivered the first Jewish sermon".

The fortunes of the family were as varied as their careers, and they did not appear to have reached dry ground till the marriage of Ellis Franklin to a sister of Samuel Montagu in 1856.

Ellis had come south some years before to act as a clerk at a small private bank. He became manager and from there branched out on his own to become a bullion broker. He used to frequent the same coffee house near the exchange as Samuel Montagu. Montagu was some ten years younger than Franklin, but they became close friends, traded with each other, and when Samuel Montagu & Co. was established in 1853, Franklin was taken in as an assistant. Three years later he became Montagu's brother-in-law, and six years later, his partner.

The first offices of Samuel Montagu and Co. were in Cornhill. When it moved to larger offices in Broad Street, Cornhill was retained as a branch, and in 1868, with money supplied by Montagu, who had more relatives than he could employ in his own company, it became the independent banking house of A. Keyser & Co. Keyser was at once joined by two sons from each of the three partners of the parent bank. Since then the progeny of Samuel, Montagu and Franklin have moved now to one bank, now to the other, though in the main S.M. & Co. had been the resort of the former two, and A. Keyser of the latter. Old Samuel Montagu, however, effectively controlled both, and the Keyser bank served as a sort of second eleven. Compared to the parent bank it dabbled in small change.

In 1908 Keyser & Co. became completely independent. It concerned itself mainly with arbitrage and made a speciality out of placing U.S. railway bonds in the City. World War II virtually put an end to its arbitrage business, and since 1945 it has been involved in sponsoring new issues and in the formation and management of investment trusts. In 1956 Keyser merged with the banking partnership of Ullmann & Co. to offer a comprehensive banking service. The union proved mutually beneficial and profits rose rapidly. In 1962 Keyser Ullmann became a public company with a £3,000,000 share issue. In 1964, a little over a century after their founding fathers had come south, Keyser Ullmann Ltd joined forces with the old Liverpool house of Rathbone Bros. to open an office in the north.

Keyser Ullmann Ltd. has eight directors, including one Keyser and one Ullmann, three Franklins, Ellis and his two sons David and Ronald, and his son-in-law Ian Stoutsker, whose sister is married to Ronald Franklin. Their father, the late Rev. Aron Stoutsker, was a cantor at the Central Synagogue, London.

The Franklins have assumed the tradition of communal service maintained for so long by the Cohens. Synagogues, old peoples' homes, hospitals, their boards would not be complete without a Franklin. Jacob Franklin, the founder of the *Voice of Jacob*, was a keen student of statistical method, and applied his knowledge to the work of the Jewish Welfare Board. "His economic views," writes the historian of the Board, "led him to a view of charity administration which his colleagues sometimes resisted as due to 'the severe teachings of his economic theories'."[28] His nephew, Ellis Arthur Franklin, who was treasurer of the Board, approached his work with somewhat greater compassion. He is father of the present chairman of the Executive Committee of the Board, and grandfather of one of the present Honorary Secretaries.

The Franklins have been pillars of the Orthodox establishment, though one substantial branch of the family moved over to the Liberal Synagogue, and not a few members of the family are agnostic or militant atheists.

The shift to Liberalism was the work of Henrietta, the eldest of Samuel Montagu's many daughters who in 1885 married her cousin Ernest Franklin.

Henrietta, or Netta as she came to be known, shared the progressive religious outlook of her younger sisters Lilian and Marion and when they formed the Jewish Religious Union gave it her enthusiastic support, and swept Ernest along with her. Ernest was a partner in Montagu's, an authority on arbitrage and foreign exchange, an important figure in the City, a leader of the Jewish community, but once home at 50 Porchester Terrace, his role became subordinate. One did not have any other sort of relationship with Netta.

There is a portrait of Netta by Sargent, who painted her when she was thirty-two, a handsome young woman with the large Montagu chin, small firm mouth, and eyes looking slightly askance at the world, elegant, composed, but determined; a rare amalgam of satin and steel.

Even as a child she had a severe sense of duty; it was of course part of her upbringing, but she took it to undue lengths, as the following, composed when she was fifteen, shows:

I am goddess of duty,
And for those there is perpetual light
Who never cease to follow me,
While others dwell in endless night[29]

She was an educational reformer, served for a time as president of the National Council of Women, was a member of the Council of the Liberal Synagogue and of numerous other bodies. When she was in London there was always, or to her harassed husband there always seemed to be, a conference of one or another of her many committees in session at Porchester Terrace.

They bought a large house in a quiet corner of Donegal, with large grounds and a lake where there was fishing, and tennis, but never while Netta was about, solitude. Brothers, cousins, sisters, nephews came upon every wave, and friends, and colleagues, and occasionally some girls from her sister Lilian's West Central Club. Netta grew larger as she grew older (while Ernest seemed to shrink) and her size if anything added to her authoritarian manner, and the regimentation both in Porchester Terrace and Donegal could be severe. Some of Lilian's girls found the experience at once bewildering and overwhelming and travelled home in tears.

The Franklins had four sons and two daughters. Netta, who had strong views on education, believed in co-education and sent them to Bedales. The older boys appear to have been reasonably happy there, but Michael the third son, had to endure a considerable amount of Jew-baiting. His main tormentor, which seems to be often the case among Jew-baiters, was a boy of Jewish origin.[30]

Sidney, the eldest, became a partner in Montagu's and spent most of his free time in social work in the East End as one of Sir Basil Henriques' lieutenants in the Bernhard Baron Settlement. He never married.

The second son Geoffrey, who like other members of his family, was a keen traveller, was anxious to find a travel agency which could offer a personal service not obtainable from large organisations like Cooks or American Express, and finding none, established his own, the Wayfarer's Travel Agency[31] which is now managed by his brother Michael. There are many such agencies today, but in 1920 it was almost unique. Geoffrey died a bachelor at the age of thirty-nine.

The younger two sons married, but neither of their marriages lasted, and Netta's biographer, Monk Gibbon, suggests it was due to the dominance which the mother exercised over her sons. And it was a lasting dominance for Netta lived to be nearly a hundred.

After coming down from Oxford, where he was active in the university dramatic society, Michael decided to become a Liberal Rabbi.

The Rabbinate, as the old joke has it, is not generally considered to be 'a profession for a Yiddisher boy'. Claude Montefiore and Lilian Montagu were both lay preachers. Michael wanted to turn professional. "I believed tremendously in my vocation in the beginning," he recalls. "I felt that a Liberal Jewish Rabbi was needed from a Liberal Jewish home. And there was no one else but me to do it."[32] And he went as far as to spend two years in a Liberal seminary in New York under the guidance of perhaps the most famous of all American Rabbis, Stephen Wise.

He loved preaching. He found he could rouse his audiences to a high pitch of emotion – perhaps too high a pitch. "When I found I was bringing tears to the eyes of my congregation I couldn't go on", he told Monk Gibbon. "I realised at that moment that I was an actor, and not a preacher at all, and that I had no right to be in the pulpit."[33]

So he became a travel agent and market gardener instead.

Another branch of the Franklin family is in publishing and owned the old-established house of Routledge and Kegan Paul. The company, which was founded in 1838, was tottering towards bankruptcy when it was taken over by a new company headed by Arthur E. Franklin, of A. Keyser & Co. In 1911 it acquired the business of Kegan Paul, which included, among other things, an antiquarian bookshop opposite the British Musuem. Several Franklins have shown a distinct aversion to banking and Routledge has provided useful alternative employment, but they have shown as much flair in this more precarious type of enterprise as their cousins have shown in finance. The standard history of the British publishing trade describes the progress of Routledge as "one of the most notable revivals in modern publishing".[34] In 1967 it became a public company.

Routledge has not usually gone for the news-making, galloping bestseller. It has something of the character of a university press and tends to explore the fustier corners of scholarship. It has a good philosophy and sociology list and has also produced some notable works on folklore, literary-criticism and Judaica. It publishes the *Machzor*, the standard Jewish festival prayer book, which runs into six volumes and is found in most Jewish homes.

The chairman of Routledge is Norman Franklin, a grandson of Arthur, an intense youngish-looking man in his early forties, who cycles daily from his home in Hampstead to his office in the City. The vice-chairman until recently was his cousin Colin, a more relaxed, donnish figure, with a rosy face and prematurely grey hair. The firm continue to operate from a small side street near St Paul's which formed the heart of the publishing ghetto before the war when it was blitzed, and somehow they combine an old worldly atmosphere, and old worldly list, with this worldly profits.

There has always been a banking Franklin on the board of Routledge to act as financial adviser, but Routledge is in no sense a subsidiary of Keyser Ullman.

There are some remarkable brains in the family, and one of the most remarkable was Rosalind Franklin, a sister of Colin, a crystallographer who was part of the team which has defined the properties of DNA, deoxyribonucleic acid, which, as a chemical component of the gene, is believed to be at the very source of life. She was for a time assistant to Dr Maurice Wilkins of King's College, London, who, with Francis Crick and J. D. Watson of Cambridge, spearheaded the research. Rosalind developed new X-ray techniques which gave visual form to their theories. "The X-ray work she did at King's is increasingly regarded as superb",[35] wrote J. D. Watson, who was not otherwise one of her admirers.

A Jew often feels compelled to try that much harder than his colleagues; a woman in a man's world has a similar compulsion. Rosalind perhaps tried too hard on both scores and approached her work with a jealous determination which some of her colleagues found alarming. She seemed to carry a constant air of embattlement about her, and felt that her first-class ability and achievements were not given due recognition. This was no mere paranoia, for as Watson later confessed:

> We came to appreciate greatly her personal honesty and generosity, realising years too late the struggles that an intelligent woman faces to be accepted by a scientific world which often regards women as mere diversions from serious things. Rosalind's exemplary courage and integrity were apparent to all when, knowing she was mortally ill, she did not complain but continued working on a high level until a few weeks before her death.[36]

She died in 1958, aged thirty-seven. Four years later Crick, Watson and Wilkins won the Nobel Prize for their work on DNA.

CHAPTER 23

Midas
Marcus Samuel

In 1913 the *Sporting Times* in one of its less sporting moments launched a vicious personal attack on the chairman of the Shell Oil Company:

> Sir Marcus Samuel is a typical Jew. He is a pronounced Jew. You could never take him for anything else. He is stout, swarthy, black-haired, black-moustached, thick-nosed, thick-lipped, bulge-eyed – in short, he fulfils every expectation that one habitually forms of the prosperous Jew. . . .

The occasion was a sharp rise in petrol prices which had brought taxi-drivers out on strike. And private car owners, at that time a select, but already vociferous company, joined in the complaints. There were dark whispers of a ramp, and loud protests in Parliament and the press. Shell was not the only petrol supplier in Britain, but it was the best-known; Marcus was not the only oil-magnate, but to the public he was 'Mr Shell', and the taxi-strike became known as 'the Marcus Samuel strike'.

Such protests had been heard before and they were to be heard again, and Marcus, though not impervious to criticism, had but one answer to them all: "The price of oil is exactly what it will fetch."

He gave it so often and with such self-assurance, as if it enshrined the ultimate wisdom on the working of the market, and he was always a little surprised that it actually increased the volume of protests and left people who had been merely angry, incensed. Such *obiter dicta* seemed to give credence to the *Sporting Times* picture:

> He is cold-blooded and unmoved about it. . . . Motor-car owners may complain . . . taxi-drivers by the thousand may go on strike . . . the populace may be inconvenienced or not. . . . It is all one to Sir Marcus. He has the oil and those who want it must pay him what he asks or go without. In a transaction of this sort he is the Jew pure and simple.[1]

And again he would protest that he was but the instrument of impersonal forces and that "the price of oil is exactly. . . ."

In 1913 Shell was only fifteen years old but already it was one of the wealthiest concerns in the country with assets worth £11,500,000 and earnings in excess of £1,500,000 a year. By then he was no longer the effective controller of Shell, but he was its creator, its only true begetter. The creation of such enterprises required many qualities, but above all, vision and daring. Marcus Samuel with his podgy face, thick lips, and heavy jowls flopping over his stiff collar, did not, at first glance, strike one as either daring or a visionary, he might be taken for a curio dealer who had done well out of some fad.

And he had.

Victorians had a passion for bric-à-brac and space to indulge in it, for shell-boxes, for shell needle-cases, for shell picture-frames, for, indeed, an infinite variety of objects decorated with molluscs, or even for molluscs themselves, some gathered from British shores, but more often from more exotic places. Marcus's father (who confusingly enough was also called Marcus and who will be referred to as Samuel the elder), catered for this and similar crazes. But this was only a beginning. Through the contacts established in the shell trade he was able to branch out in other directions, and later traded in gutta percha, spices, matting, resins, tea, tin, porcelain, goatskins, wool, opium and silk. By the mid-1860s he was earning over £4,000 a year, a substantial sum in those days but he had a substantial family – eleven children, of whom nine survived, three sons and six daughters. Marcus, the tenth of the children, was born in 1853; Sam, the eleventh, in 1854.

The family lived over their warehouse opposite St Katherine's dock in the East End of London, but by 1857 they had prospered enough to move to Finsbury Square in the City, then an attractive residential area which had been favoured by the older Jewish families but was now becoming the resort of the newer ones. He became a warden of the New Synagogue, and its delegate to the Jewish Board of Guardians.[2]

When he died in 1870 he left £40,000 and the wish that his sons should remain "united, loving and considerate and keep the good name of Marcus Samuel from reproach".[3]

The eldest son, Joseph, became head of the family and of the business, but was enjoined in his father's will to "look after the interests of my said sons Marcus and Samuel and that if he finds them (as I have every reason to hope) worthy and honourable men, he will on their attaining the age of twenty-five or at an earlier age if he thinks fit, give to them respectively shares in the said business".[4]

It did not quite work out that way. They remained a united, loving and considerate family, but Marcus and Samuel were born long after the other children and they differed from them not only in years, but in outlook and temperament. Joseph was cautious, Samuel was less so, while Marcus was audacious to the point of recklessness.

In 1873, at the age of nineteen, Marcus, set out on a tour of the Far East. When he reached India he found a famine raging and promptly, with the help of his late father's contacts in Calcutta, Bangkok and Singapore, organised a small flotilla of boats to bring in rice from Siam where there was a glut. (Many years later he helped to avert famine in Japan by bringing over a sizable part of the Burmese rice harvest.) One can see already here the principle on which his fortune was to be made, marrying the nearest source of supply to the most urgent point of demand, an elementary and obvious idea but not always applied in those days.

In 1878, when Marcus was twenty-five, he inherited £2,500 apportioned under his father's will. Sam received a similar amount, and they went into partnership as M. Samuel & Co. with a branch in Yokohama, Japan, under the name of Samuel Samuel & Co.[5]

Whether by intelligent anticipation or luck their decision to acquire a firm foothold in Japan proved most fortunate, for although there was upheaval in large parts of the Orient in the years to come, Japan was stable and had embarked upon the Industrial Revolution, which within a few years was to make her a power of world rank.

By 1881 Marcus had prospered enough to marry and take a house in a terrace of substantial villas near Regents' Park. His wife was Fanny Benjamin, daughter of a merchant tailor, and the wedding ceremony was performed by Chief Rabbi Nathan Adler.[6]

They were a bulky pair, and did not look like the subjects of a true romance, but a romance it was. Marcus fell deeply in love with Fanny, never cared for or looked at another woman – this in an age when a kept mistress was almost the status symbol of the man of means. He sought her advice, deferred to her judgement, and found infinite comfort and happiness in her presence. They had two sons, Walter and Gerald, and two daughters, Nellie and Ida.

Gerald was a glum, introspective child, prone to long, brooding silences. He went to Eton and then entered M. Samuel & Co. but proved so incompetent that he had to give up business altogether: and joined Basil Henriques in social work in the East End. There he found some happiness and met with considerable success, but unlike Basil had a deep distaste for the way of life and religious outlook of the Jewish newcomers among whom he worked and saw them as sunk in darkness and superstition.[7] When war broke out in 1914 he rushed to enlist in the colours but was twice refused on account of his bad eyesight. He was more successful on his third attempt and was commissioned in the Royal Kent Regiment in 1915. He was killed on the Somme two years later.

Nellie, Gerald's sister, married Walter Levy, a major in the Royal Army Service Corps who received the D.S.O. for gallantry, but died shortly after the war as a result of his experiences in the trenches. The younger sister Ida married Robert Montefiore Sebag-Montefiore, a grandson of Sir Joseph Sebag-Montefiore. He enlisted on the outbreak of war and was killed in action less than a year later. Walter alone emerged unscathed from the war.

The growth of Marcus's many trade interests made it inevitable that he should go into oil.

Oil was then mainly refined to provide kerosene for lamps or wax for tapers. It first came into use in commercial quantities in the early 1860s. John D. Rockefeller, prompt to realise its vast potentialities quickly built up an immense refining and marketing complex which became known as the Standard Oil Company and which, through a policy of aggressive expansion, virtually cornered the American market and was thrusting out westwards into Europe and eastwards into Asia.

Marcus was aware of this. He began to ship occasional cargoes of oil to Japan in 1890, but realised that if he hoped to become a regular vendor in the product he could not survive on a small scale.

"When I started," he said, "I was convinced that only a worldwide system which would prevent my opponents from annihilating me was necessary, and so, contrary to the opinion of many of my associates, I established depots simultaneously throughout the Far East. Had I not done so, the Standard Oil Company would have made a dead set against me, and so have brought about my ruin."[8]

He was able to establish this network of depots in Singapore, Shanghai, Yokohama and throughout the Orient, through a chain of merchants with whom he dealt in other commodities. They not only acted as his local distributors, but helped to finance the whole operation and in 1893 he brought them together in a formal syndicate to share costs and profits.

LOUIS SAMUEL

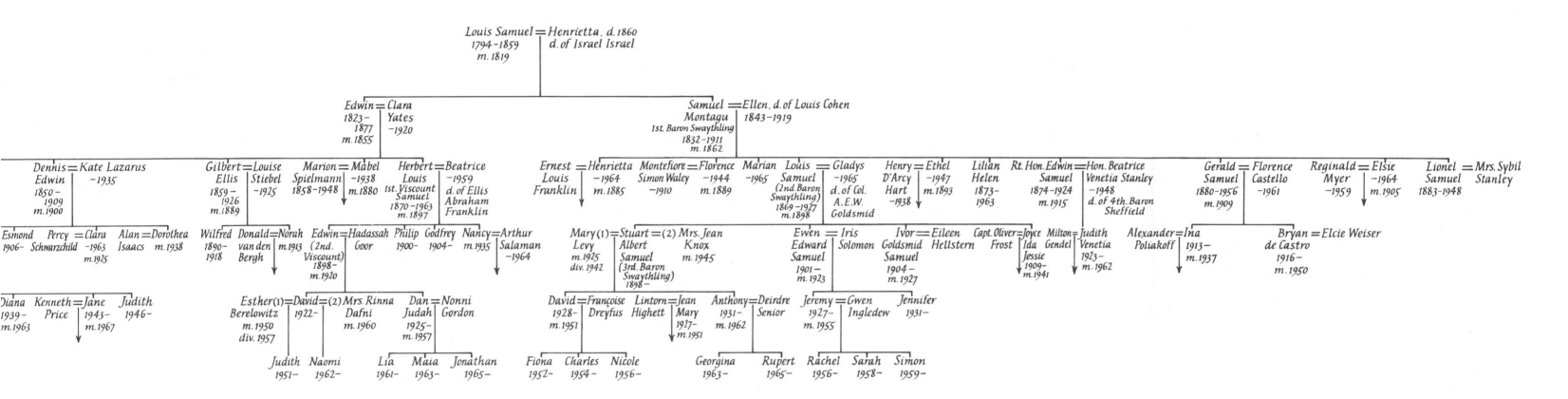

The main source of oil was America, which was of course Standard territory, but oils had also recently been discovered in considerable quantities in the Caucasus, and the Paris Rothschilds had established refineries at Batum and a marketing organisation known as Bnito, and it was to Bnito that Marcus turned for supplies. The Rothschilds were not particularly happy about entering into business relationships with Marcus. Who was he? What sort of resources did he have? They were finally reassured by Fred Lane, their agent in London, that Marcus was a man of substance and in 1891 they signed a nine-year contract for the supply of oil in bulk.

In the Far East at this time oil was distributed in five-gallon tins, which were crated together in pairs and shipped as "case-oil".[9] The canning, the crating, the handling all added to the expense of the operation, and Marcus felt he could lower costs by shipping, storing and distributing the product in bulk.

There were oil tankers in operation both in the Caspian and America, but they were merely ordinary ships with tanks built onto them and they were so hazardous to operate that no tanker was allowed through the Suez Canal.

Marcus envisaged a ship where the tank was an integral part of the structure, where the wall of the vessel in fact formed the side of the tank and which would be rendered so safe as to satisfy the stringent requirements of the Suez Canal Company. But more than that. Existing oil carriers once they had discharged their cargo, made the return journey in ballast. Marcus sought a means of cleaning the tanks which would enable them to carry general cargoes, even foodstuffs, on their homeward run, and he found a designer, Fortescue Flannery who could put all these ideas into execution. In 1892 the *Murex*, the first ship of the Shell fleet (all of whose vessels were to be named after sea-shells), was launched. It was classed A.1. at Lloyd's and, to the dismay of the Americans who had been refused passage on earlier occasions, it satisfied all the requirements of the Suez Canal Company. There were dark rumours of corruption, and one oil historian even wrote that Marcus had oiled his way through the canal "with much *baksheesh*".[10] Marcus was not that sort of merchant, and the Suez Canal Company, which was controlled by the British Government, was not that sort of enterprise, and the safety record of the Shell fleet – six other vessels followed in quick succession – showed that their performance did not fall short of their promise.

Bulk cargoes of course required bulk storage, jetties, wharves, and to this end Marcus dispatched two nephews, Mark and Joe Abrahams, the one an engineer, the other a draughtsman, at a salary of £5 a week, to lease or buy sites at the major ports throughout the Far East and erect unloading and storage installations.[11]

Standard Oil had spies everywhere, but Marcus worked with great speed and secrecy and had his network in operation before his rivals were fully aware of it. With large outlets in India, Malaya, Siam, China and Japan, he was able to withstand the war of attrition which they launched against him. Standard, with its secure home market, could afford to cut prices in some of its overseas markets all of the time and in all of them some of the time, but not in all of them all of the time. Marcus survived, grew, prospered.

In 1895, having failed to starve him out, Standard offered to buy him out[12] but Marcus had no intention of selling.

Up to this time his Syndicate only shared in the storage and distribution of oil. The tanker fleet was wholly owned by M. Samuel & Co., and in 1897 he combined his oil interests and tanker fleet into The Shell Transport and Trading Company with a capital of £1,800,000 in £100 shares.[13] All the members of the syndicate were given shares in the company and joined its board. They were all to become very, very rich.

This was a period when everything and everyone Marcus touched seemed to turn to gold. His trade connection with Japan was proving extremely profitable.

When the Sino-Japanese war broke out in 1895 Marcus and his Syndicate supplied both sides with oil, food, raw materials, manufactured goods and weapons. As a result of the war China was forced to cede Formosa to Japan and Marcus and his brother were invited to manage the island's camphor deposits as well as the Japanese state-owned opium company.[14] In 1897 Japan sought £4,500,000 from the City to go over from silver to gold. Marcus floated the loan so successfully that it was oversubscribed within a matter of hours and in the following year he was entrusted with numerous other large financial transactions on behalf of Japan.

His various trading interests left him with many bills of exchange in hand, but instead of cashing them through a discount house he held on till they matured and pocketed the premium. And thus, almost by accident, he found himself acting as a banker. He still had some forty hands employed in making knick-knacks. He was a general merchant, and large shipowner and was deriving a fortune from every activity.

And all with a minute staff, which might even have been even smaller if his relations had been less numerous.

The most important work of his organisation was carried on by Fred Lane and Fortescue Flannery, outside consultants, who called on Marcus from time to time to see correspondence and give advice. Lane had negotiated the Bnito contract with the Rothschilds and he continued to advise Marcus on shipping, insurance and brokerage and the host of problems involved in running what was by now a considerable fleet. Flannery, the marine engineer who had designed the Shell fleet, looked after the more technical problems.[15] Head office was a bleak set of rooms in a dark Houndsditch alleyway. In one room sat the partners, Marcus and Samuel, the sound of altercation rising beyond their door, Sam loud and frantic, Marcus quiet and venomous. "Idiot! Imbecile! Fool!" The deprecations echoed round the office, and then silence as one or another of the brothers gave in. They seemed to reach decisions through abuse.[16]

Sam was not a person of any particular ability and Lane, who knew something about business management, regarded him as plainly incompetent, but he was an excellent foil for Marcus; the very exasperation which he excited somehow helped Marcus to clear his mind and they were in many ways an effective partnership.[17]

There was a third partner, Henry Benjamin, Marcus's brother-in-law, who was occasionally entrusted with important decisions, but whose role was otherwise a subsidiary one and it is unlikely that he would have been taken and kept in the partnership if he had not been a relative. He was, before he joined M. Samuel, head of the family tailoring firm, and Marcus who, as we shall see, had high social ambitions, may have been embarrassed by the thought of a brother-in-law in the tailoring trade.[18]

In 1958 a biography of Marcus Samuel was written by Robert Henriques who was married to one of Marcus's grand-daughters. It traces, with meticulous skill, the various world-wide activities of M. Samuel and Co. and is also a richly human study of Marcus Samuel the man. It seems, however, to omit one vital element in the rise of Marcus – his luck, his extraordinary, inexplicable, sustained good fortune. In the first years of his career he seemed unable to put a foot wrong and even later, when nothing seemed to go right, the final course of events moved dramatically in his favour.

The Borneo project is a good example. Marcus in the early years of Shell was completely dependent on Russian oil. It was an unreliable source, first because of the erratic policies of the Russian government, second because of upheaval in the country, and third and most important there was the danger that the Rothschilds, his suppliers, might enter into partnership with Standard and leave him high and dry with a large fleet and a chain of expensive installations.

He wanted his own, assured source of oil, and to this end bought a concession over a large area of Borneo in the Dutch East Indies. The advantage of Borneo was that it was near his markets and he would be able to undercut Standard who shipped their oil from America, and compete effectively with a growing Dutch company, the Royal Dutch, which had concessions in Sumatra.

But did Borneo have oil? Was it accessible? And if accessible, was it of the right quality for the market?

None of these things were established when Marcus bought the concessions. The whole project, involving the expenditure of hundreds of thousands of pounds, was placed in the hands of the tireless Mark Abrahams, who was an engineer, but not an oil engineer, not an oil chemist, not a geologist, and in fact was devoid of any of the skills necessary for the complex operation.

For a time even Marcus wondered if he had not been too precipitate, for he seemed to be wasting fortunes on what was no more than a wild-cat scheme. From Houndsditch came angry letters demanding to know what was happening, and from Mark apologies edged with defiance, or more usually, silence.[19]

Then, at last, on April 15 1898, success. There was a loud angry rumbling, the whole earth seemed to quake, and suddenly a black column of oil shot high into the air, descended into the surrounding countryside like black lava, and flowed inexorably onwards across the white sands and into the blue waters of the bay.[20] There were no means at hand to check it.

Further oil was struck and its flow controlled, but again there was disappointment when it proved to be too heavy for kerosene. The setback was temporary, for lighter oils were found in the same concessions and even the heavy oils, which were at first feared to be useless, were found to have properties far more useful than kerosene.

Borneo oil could touch only the fringe of the vast market which Shell had built up and, given Marcus's reservations about Russian oil, the only other alternative was a marketing deal with Royal Dutch.

Royal Dutch was one of many oil concessionaires in the Dutch East Indies, but it was by far the largest and most successful. Both Royal Dutch and Shell suffered from the price-cutting activities of Standard and both were complementary to one another, for while Royal Dutch had oil it was deficient in tankers, and, while Shell had tankers, it was deficient in oil. Negotiations proceeded throughout the early 1890s without success. Output from Sumatra was too erratic to assure the large and regular supplies Marcus needed to keep his fleet occupied.

In 1897, after another period of aggressive marketing by Standard, Marcus entered into new negotiations and at one point suggested outright amalgamation, but the Dutch company was too anxious to maintain its identity and independence and talks once again broke down. Early in the following year it became clear that the Sumatra wells were running dry. Royal Dutch shares slumped catastrophically on the Amsterdam bourse. At this stage Marcus could have acquired the company for a song. He could also have pounced on its share of the eastern market. But Marcus was no Rockefeller. "The East is quite big enough for both the Royal Dutch and the Shell line," he said.[21] It would in any case not have solved his immediate problem – the assurance of an adequate oil supply to replace the Bnito contract due to expire in a few years' time. To get over the emergency the Dutch themselves had begun buying Russian oil.

Marcus was perhaps unduly nervous about the fickleness of the Rothschilds, for in 1901 they renewed the Bnito contract. He had bought immense stocks on a rising market to guard against the failure of the Bnito negotiations. Now the market had fallen and he found himself with a large and almost immovable surplus.

Early in 1901 oil was struck at Spindletop, Texas; a great black column reaching hundreds of feet into the sky rushed from the earth and was visible twelve miles away. America was full of the news, but Queen Victoria had just died, and little attention was paid to foreign news in the British press. That little, however, fired Marcus's imagination. His trading, though vast, was still confined to the Orient, whereas Standard ranged over the entire globe and was able to undercut him in the East through the high prices maintained in the West. If he could acquire an assured supply of oil in America he could fight Standard on its own ground. Under the terms of the Bnito contract he undertook not to sell Russian oil in Europe, but there was nothing to prevent him selling American oil.

The oil industry was by now becoming less dependent on kerosene. The rapid development of the motor car in the first years of the century gave rise to a growing demand for the product variously known as gasoline, benzine or petrol. Another product in growing use was solar oil, for the manufacture of gas, but Marcus had his eyes on still another possibility – the use of oil as a fuel – and it was in this particular field that he established his reputation as 'the greatest oil pioneer of our times'. He was, wrote the *Petroleum Times*, the organ of the oil industry many years later, "almost alone in his appreciation of the possibilities of oil and its uses at sea".[22]

Marcus envisaged that oil must one day displace coal as the motive power of the Navy, and it was his ambition to supply the oil, not only because of the vast contracts involved, but because he cherished the thought that he, Marcus Samuel, the son of an East End curio dealer, might keep the fleet in motion and help Britannia rule the waves.

The advantages of fuel oil, as Marcus was demonstrating in his own fleet, were overwhelming. It was smokeless, gave greater range at greater speed; two mechanics could do the work of fifty stokers; it took a tenth of the time to refuel on oil than on coal, and one could, moreover, refuel at sea.

Against this were set the facts that coal was British, abundant, and available. There was also certain technical and scientific arguments advanced against oil which Marcus had no difficulty in answering, but the main argument against it was that supplies were erratic and the sources lay, in the main, outside the empire. Spindeltop was not in the empire, but it answered one of the main arguments of the anti-oil party: supplies would be assured.

Sam urged caution. Henry Benjamin recommended further study. Marcus was too impatient. He dispatched Benjamin to Texas to examine the strike at first hand with full powers to negotiate on behalf of Shell. Benjamin shrugged his shoulders and went and eventually signed a twenty-one-year contract to take half the output of Spindeltop at 25 cents a barrel. With this in hand Marcus ordered four new 10,000-ton tankers – a prodigious size for those days – from Flannery expressly for the America run.

Standard, as if in anticipation of the new threat, launched an all out price cutting campaign both in Europe and in the East. Henri Deterding, who had revitalised Royal Dutch, adopted similar tactics, but while they battled in the market place, they smiled beatitudes in the boardrooms, for it was becoming apparent to all concerned that in a time of increasing supplies and falling prices, such campaigns were mutually murderous. The talk everywhere was of mergers.

Count de Witte, who was reconstructing the Russian oil industry, wanted Marcus as a partner, Deterding wanted him as a partner, and at the end of the year there was a personal invitation to Marcus and Fanny to visit Standard Oil.

They were received like royalty but Marcus did not allow the lavish junketings to interfere with the main purpose of his visit. Standard had made a passing overture some seven years before, but this time they were in earnest, and their terms were generous.

They proposed to form a new Anglo-American subsidiary with Marcus as chairman which would take over Shell lock, stock and barrel for the sum of £8,000,000.[23] At that time Marcus and Sam held more than half of the shares between them. The deal would have left them both very rich men.

Marcus, moreover, was now launched upon a busy civic career and had lately become a sheriff of the City of London. The Standard deal would have left him with ample time to lavish on public affairs, and in fact generally to enjoy the wealth he had accumulated and his growing acceptance as a member of the Anglo-Jewish aristocracy. He had been to an obscure school at Edmonton,[24] his sons were at Eton. He had married the daughter of a merchant tailor, his heir was about to marry a Montefiore, and there was every prospect that his daughters too would make fortunate matches. As sheriff he was in direct line of accession for the mayoralty. There was much to anticipate, much to enjoy, and he would have time in which to enjoy it. The offer was tempting, but Marcus turned it down with little hesitation.[25]

Standard did not want a mere union but sought to swallow Shell with all its assets in their entirety. It would become an American concern, and its tankers would cease to fly the British flag. He would lose control of his own creation and such things were more important to him than money.

Hell knows no fury like the Standard scorned. Marcus braced himself for the onslaught which lay ahead, and it came, with no holds barred, including intimidation and bribery, and even rumours suggesting that Shell had already been taken over by Standard. This rumour proved the most damaging of all, for Marcus still hoped for a Navy contract and such contracts were unlikely to go to a company under foreign control.

The advantages of a union with Royal Dutch, especially now that the marriage with Standard was off, were obvious. The two companies complemented each other. Without ever liking him, Marcus was dazzled by Deterding's ability and realised that he could be of immense

value to the joint organisations. And finally – and this was of crucial
importance to Marcus – as Shell was by far the larger concern, it
would be the dominant, controlling partner. Deterding for his part was
also anxious for a union, and what he could not get by direct negotiations
he obtained eventually by subterfuge.

The Paris Rothschilds now felt left out in the cold. They had had
numerous flirtations with Standard Oil which had led to various
marketing agreements, but at best they were only friends. Marcus was a
large buyer of their Russian oil, and so was Deterding. Supposing their
joint organisation should at some future time turn to a new source of
supply? A few years before, while his Bnito contract was about to
expire, Marcus was haunted by the vision of large markets and expensive
installations but no oil. The Rothschilds now had visions of abundant
oil but no markets, and found it expedient to accede to the Shell-Dutch
union.

In June 1902 they formed a triple alliance to launch the Asiatic
Petroleum Company, a £2,000,000 marketing organisation with shares
divided equally among the three principals. It was concerned mainly
with the supply of kerosene to the vast Eastern markets, and petrol
and fuel oil were outside its scope.

The Asiatic had some advantages for everyone, but to Deterding it
offered the prospect of having Shell by the throat. He was to be the
managing director of the new company, yet remain managing director
of the Royal Dutch, and he used his position on the former to further
the interests of the latter.

Deterding succeeded more rapidly than he could have hoped, for the
fates which seemed to have been conspiring to advance Marcus now
turned against him.

He had always vested great faith in fuel oil, in particular as a source
of power for the Royal Navy, so that whatever merger he contemplated,
whether with Standard or Royal Dutch, he was always careful to
exclude fuel oil from its provisions. The Hamburg-Amerika line was
now a heavy buyer of fuel oil for its ships, and it was said that the new
German navy was building up oil stores. His own ships worked
exclusively on oil and he made repeated offers to put the wealth of his
experience at the disposal of the navy, and open his fleet to navy
engineers. But for a long time the furthest that the Admiralty would
go was to fit up a shore unit for experiments.

Marcus was fortunate in that Admiral Jackie Fisher, who was to
revolutionise the Royal Navy, and who was now Second Lord of the

Admiralty, shared his enthusiasm for fuel oil, and was able to persuade his colleagues to go beyond the static stage and convert a battleship H.M.S. *Hannibal* for trials.

His day had come, or so Marcus believed. On June 26, 1902 he travelled by special train to Portsmouth in a large company of engineers and senior Admiralty officials. It was a bright day and the *Hannibal* sailed out of harbour using Welsh anthracite and emitting light smoke. At a prearranged signal it switched to oil, and almost vanished from view in smoke so thick as to be palpable. A defective vapouriser was at fault. Marcus did not know that; neither, at the time, did the navy. It was a personal calamity to Marcus, and in the opinion of his biographer it had the gravest consequences for the country as a whole: "The effect of those trials, on that day, undertaken with a type of burner that could not possibly be smokeless, was to postpone the large-scale introduction of liquid fuel to the Royal Navy for the best part of another decade. It very nearly lost us the First World War."[26]

When he returned to London news reached him of another calamity. *Spindeltop had run dry.*

And at this time when the Shell needed all his energies, initiative and resource, his mind was elsewhere. Marcus Samuel, now Sir Marcus Samuel, had become Lord Mayor of London.

Marcus had a passion for eminence, and the sort of eminence provided by great wealth did not satisfy him. He wanted to be a *public* figure, in public office – there was something, indeed, schoolboyish and pathetic about this yearning.

He was aware of himself as an upstart, and he had the presence, manner and appearance of one; if his accoutrements proclaimed a person of standing, his accent suggested humbler origins. He was slow to advance in Gentile society and was not well regarded in Jewish society. ". . . no matter how grand he might become," wrote Robert Henriques, "or in what style he might live, or how lavish his response to charitable appeals, the so-called Anglo-Jewish aristocracy were slow to receive him in their homes and accept his hospitality."[27] He was not, as they might have put it, 'one of us'. Thus he was determined to convince the world, and, above all, convince himself, that he was no mere person, but a *personage*.

In 1895, when he was still plain Mr Samuel, he bought the Mote, near Maidstone in Kent, a splendid Regency mansion, standing in five hundred acres. He bought it complete with furniture, furnishings, pictures and library; and its previous owner, Lord Romney, remained with Marcus for a month to instruct him in the ways of the place and to introduce him to his neighbours.[28]

His brother Sam, who always remained a bachelor, had similar ambitions but sought eminence through a political career. He was a member of the Tory party and generous donor to party funds, but was not particularly favoured in the constituencies. His first three attempts to enter Parliament proved abortive, but he was finally elected on his fourth in 1913. He sat first for Wandsworth and then for Putney. His magnificent flat in Hay Hill, Mayfair, became a sort of club for politicians of all parties. He had a fabulous collection of cigars, kept a splendid table, and the annual party which he gave on the eve of the Budget was one of the most popular social events of the Parliamentary year, but he did not otherwise make his mark either on his party or in the House.

He held strong anti-feminist views which were in no way diminished by his limited experience of the opposite sex, but his interventions in debate were not taken seriously. As Lady Astor, M.P., a leading feminist, observed: "We all love Sammy, and don't mind what he says."[29]

Robert Henriques recalls a dinner Sam gave for his young nephews and nieces to celebrate his seventieth birthday. At the end of the evening he asked them all to look under their plate, and there each found a cheque worth over £10,000, a fond thought from a fond uncle. He died in 1934.

Marcus, after he became a well-known and revered figure in Kent county life, was invited to contest the safe Tory seat of Canterbury. He refused because he felt happier with the less-demanding nature of civic politics. In 1891 he had sought election as alderman for the Portsoken Ward, on the eastern fringes of the City, which had a considerable Jewish population. To hold such office one had to be of high repute and wealth. The Samuel name was irreproachable, but doubts were expressed as to his means.[30] Marcus was able to reassure his critics and was elected by 485 votes to 247.

Something else intervened which fitted in so well with his ambitions that it is sometimes difficult to think of it as a mere stroke of fortune.

In February 1898, a British warship H.M.S. *Victorious* ran aground at the entrance of the Suez Canal and closed the canal to all traffic.

The Canal Company tugs tried to pull her free, but without success. Two large cruisers were diverted to Suez and rushed at full speed to her help, but they too proved ineffective. A P. & O. liner joined in; but the warship remained fast. The canal remained closed, and long queues of ships formed at both entrances. It seemed that the *Victorious* would have to be written off as a total loss and blown up.

At which point Marcus ordered the *Pectan*, the most powerful tug in the world, which had recently been commissioned by Shell, to go to the *Victorious* and it quickly pulled her free.

When the Admiralty mentioned the matter of salvage fees Marcus waved it aside. He had done nothing more than his duty, he protested.[31] Six months later he was knighted. In September 1902, he became Lord Mayor. This was not quite the 'top of the greasy pole' of which Disraeli boasted, but it was high enough. The son of a Jewish bric-à-brac dealer from the East End had become the first citizen of the City of London, would dine with kings and emperors, entertain heads of state, and would preside over ceremonies and pageantry dating back to an age when Jews were listed among royal chattels. He had arrived. The press spoke of him as 'the Modern Dick Whittington' and, indeed, his rise to eminence was no less remarkable.

November 10 was his 'Coronation Day' when he was officially installed as Lord Mayor. The whole of East End Jewry, which had lately doubled in size through mass immigration, felt elevated by his election and turned out in force to look and cheer. And there he came in his splendid robes of office, his heavy gold chain, nodding his head now to the right, now to the left, waving a hand here, a hand there, his face uncommonly jubilant.

The gold coach, drawn by six prancing white horses, was like something out of a fairy story, except that Marcus, like so many Lord Mayors before him, and many after, was more like the pumpkin than Cinderella.

The mayor, wrote one paper with brutal candour, was "short, stout and ugly, nevertheless not seeming out of place behind the State Trumpeters in black and gold, their cheeks swelling and their eyes staring under their black peaked caps".[32]

During the next twelve months he was hardly to be seen in his office for more than an hour or two at a time and sometimes not even that. His calendar was full of social functions, some arising directly out of his mayoral duties, others because of the eminence the office gave him. Henriques quotes some entries from his diary:

Wednesday November 19:
Attended Old Bailey at 10.30 . . . Received at 11.0 a.m. Alderman of Huddersfield who came to consult me as Lord Mayor having, as he said heard of my probity and ability, as to the investment of his fortune . . .

. . . At 12.30 I attended with the Lady Mayoress a Memorial Service for

Prince Edward of Saxe-Weimer. Returned at 1.30 to Mansion House and had Lord Sandhurst to lunch and arranged with him to take the Chair for a dinner in aid of the funds of the Middlesex Hospital. At 2.30 held meeting of the Port of London Committee. . . . At 4.15 gave the members tea. Dined at the Trocadero presiding for funds for the Brondesbury Synagogue. Subscription amounted to £4,200. My own donation £100. Made four speeches. . . . My health proposed by Leopold de Rothschild . . . .[33]

Amid such a whirl it was difficult for someone even with the energies of Marcus to have a mind for the affairs of Shell. Deterding waited to see him, Lane, a pair of high emissaries from the Rothschild oil interests. He had little time for any of them, and an already critical situation was allowed to slide on to disaster.

At the end of December Sam tried to draw him aside with the warning that for the first time in its history Shell was about to end the year with a loss.

Marcus was in a hurry to get to the Mote for Christmas. Family and friends were gathered for the festivities. He was busy, and would consider it later. On December 28 he received a letter which compelled him finally to sit up and take notice. It was from Lane, who had guided his first faltering steps into the oil and shipping trades, who had negotiated his major contracts, who had helped finance his first *coup*, who was one of the directors of the old Syndicate, and the most indispensable member of the board of Shell. It was to announce his resignation:

> . . . Recent events have forced me in some slight measure to become acquainted with the interior workings of the Shell Company; and it is this which has led me to the conclusion that unless some radical change be made in the policy and practice of the company, I could not afford to share the responsibility of the results. I clearly see the London management gains nothing by experience . . . but blunders along in the same feckless fashion, for want of guidance and control.

He was particularly worried about the slapdash manner in which the whole enterprise was run, without attention to detail, the tendency to leap first and look later:

> You are, and have always been, too much occupied to be at the head of such a business. Mr Sam is incompetent; and there is no one else. It is a business, I clearly see, that has no head or tail to its management. There seems to be only one idea: sink capital, create a great bluster, and trust to providence.

Companies like Shell, he went on, "cannot be conducted by an occasional glance in one's spare time, or by some brilliant *coup*." It required immense study and forethought, continued application, steady, treadmill work, in fact, for which Marcus was wholly unfitted.

And he concluded:

I see no hope for the Shell Co. conducted on such lines as I have indicated. A great splash has been made and the situation capitalised; but it cannot last, and the bubble will burst.[34]

Lane was justified on every point. Marcus's haphazard way of doing things was well exemplified by the agreement he signed on the Asiatic, and by the Spindeltop contract signed on his behalf by Benjamin. In the case of the former Marcus found that Deterding was departing so far from the spirit of their agreement as to nullify it, but when he prepared to go to arbitration he discovered that no final agreement had been concluded, but merely an agreement to make an agreement.

In the case of Spindeltop the situation was even more farcical. Spindeltop was part of the Mellon oil interests. The contract had been signed with the Mellons and Marcus was hopeful that a firm of such standing would not fall short of its undertaking. He was mistaken. Oil was obtainable elsewhere on the eastern seaboard, but at a price far higher than the 25 cents per barrel specified in their contract, and in July 1903 Mellons tore it up.

Marcus sought the opinion of the New York legal firm of Goldman & Steinhart, and was advised that he had a perfectly sound case. The question was, could he enforce it? They believed not. The whole contract, it appeared, was merely "an agreement to make an agreement, and not an agreement itself". And they added: "We are frank to confess that, in our opinion, this clause of the contract was drawn in an incredibly neglectful manner . . ."[35]

In November 1903 Marcus's mayoral year was over. ". . . thoroughly enjoyed our year of office," he wrote in his diary, "but being heartily thankful it is well over. I may truly say that I resign office without a sigh, and thank God that He has vouchsafed to myself and my dear ones good health throughout the trying and eventful year we have passed through."[36]

He could once again turn his mind to Shell, but it was too late. The bubble, as Lane had warned, had burst.

Everything seemed to happen at once. Shell, of course, was a carrier rather than a producer. The Spindeltop failure had left Marcus's four large tankers specially built for the Texas run high and dry, and he had them converted as cattle carriers. This coincided with an international recession in trade which sent freight rates tumbling. Standard launched yet another price war against him, now in Europe, now in the East, occasionally everywhere. There were angry exchanges between Marcus and Deterding and Marcus and the Rothschilds. The price of Shell shares dropped and rumours that the company was in difficulties pushed them down further. Between 1903 and 1906 they fell from £3 to 23s. Deterding, who had always cast hungry eyes on Shell, was ready to pounce.

What finally gave him control of the company was a succession of events in the European market.

At the turn of the century Marcus had formed a marketing consortium with the Deutsche Bank in the West much on the lines of the Asiatic in the East called the P.P.A.G.

This agreement had been drawn up with rather more care than his other ones. Marcus was confident that he had almost infinite supplies of oil behind him and insisted on a clause which would oblige both parties to increase their investment whenever one party chose to do so, but it was the Deutsche Bank which now invoked this clause. Having acquired a large and highly lucrative Romanian oil company, it wanted to increase the size of its oil pool and the number of installations. Marcus, who was in no position to pay his share, asked to be released from the contract. The Deutsche Bank agreed to buy him out at par on condition that it was allowed to acquire six tankers of the Shell fleet at 'book value'.

This was a harsh demand, for Marcus regarded his tankers, each flying the Union Jack, almost as his own children. In an effort to save them he had talks with Deterding about a merger with Royal Dutch. A few years earlier Shell could have bought out Deterding for a song, now Marcus wondered hopefully if he would agree to 50-50 terms. He was over-optimistic, for Deterding countered with a scheme in which Royal Dutch would have 60% of the shares and Shell 40%. Marcus wanted time to think about it but took so long that in the end he was compelled to surrender six of his ships to the Deutsche Bank at a knock-down price.

Deterding now added a number of mollifying conditions to his original offer. Marcus would be chairman of the new holding company, and retain the special 5-1 voting rights which he had enjoyed on his shares. And to assure that the Shell's interests would not be overlooked, Royal Dutch would take up 25% off its ordinary shares at 7s. above the prevailing price.

Again Marcus asked for time. "I am at present in a generous mood," said Deterding. "I have made you this offer, but if you leave this room without accepting it, the offer is off."[37] Marcus accepted.

It was a defeat, for no matter how generous the terms, ultimate control of Shell would pass into Dutch, into foreign hands. It was however a fortunate defeat both for Shell and for Marcus, because M. Samuel & Co. with its clique of brothers, brothers-in-law and nephews at the top, and its small band of clerks was, as Lane had pointed out, no longer capable of handling an organisation with the size and prospects of Shell. Marcus had a commercial flair amounting to genius, but it now also required administrative genius, the meticulous attention to detail which a Deterding could give it but a Marcus could not. Royal Dutch Shell, as the group came to be known, proved to be an invincible combination. Profits climbed inexorably, and Marcus,who was already a very wealthy man at the time of the merger, prospered to the point where he could hardly have reckoned his millions. He moved from his Georgian town house in Portland Place to a magnificent mansion in Mayfair, 3 Hamilton Place next door to Leopold de Rothschild. He bought an ocean-going yacht, the 650 ton S.S. *Lady Torfida*. He loved fishing and could relax with a rod by his own well-stocked lake on his own private grounds. He loved to watch cricket and had his own pitch, which is now the Kent County Cricket ground, and his own private pavilion. He was anxious to assure the futures of his children and grandchildren, so he bought twenty golden acres of Mayfair, in and around Berkeley Square, to establish a family trust. Money, as his biographer often repeated, meant little to him, but the things that money could buy meant a lot, and some of the things he cherished more than material things, such as social acceptance, were very expensive indeed. Only a rich man could then, as now, become an alderman of the City of London, and only the very rich could aspire to be mayor.

Money, however, meant less to him than power, and that had now passed out of his hands and into those of the Royal Dutch. The loss of power meant the end of a dream.

Marcus, said his grandson, the present Lord Bearsted, "was in some ways a very simple man, with simple instincts"[38] and he had a simple, uncomplicated, undeviating love of England. Patriotism was not as rare a quality then as it is now, but it was the dominating force in his life.

One particular incident illustrates his feelings. In March 1914, when

Ulster was on the verge of rebellion and troops were mobilised for possible action, many officers in the Cavalry Brigade resigned their commissions in protest. Marcus read of this while he was on his yacht at Biarritz, and at once cabled *The Times*:

> I am deeply moved by the patriotism of the officers who have resigned their commissions and risked the ruin of their careers rather than spill the blood of loyal subjects of His Majesty. Provided the leaders of the Unionist Party immediately announce their intention of restoring the commissions of naval or military officers resigning from conscientious objections, I will subscribe £10,000 to start a fund to relieve, in the meantime, the material needs of those officers' families who may require assistance.[39]

Once he was securely established in business he yearned to perform a service which would give him a lasting place in public esteem. His father had enjoined him to "keep the good name of Marcus Samuel from reproach".[40] He wanted to make it honoured.

He was convinced that he could render such a service to the Navy by converting it to oil and even the *Hannibal* fiasco did not halt his efforts. The German navy, it was rumoured, was going over to oil, and gradually the obvious began to impress itself even on the Admiralty; but by then Shell was no longer a British company, and this thought pained Marcus more than anything else.

He had been naïve in believing that Shell was British in the first place. It was British-*owned* but it obtained its oil from a Dutch possession through a company registered in Holland and it was a distributor of Russian, American and Romanian oil acquired through French and German companies.

But he could claim that his fleet at least was British, British built, British manned, British owned, and it too had now passed into foreign hands.

As a result of the amalgamation two new companies were established, the Baatafsche in the Hague to control production, and the Anglo-Saxon Petroleum Company, based in London, to control transport and storage. They acquired all the assets of Royal Dutch and Shell, which henceforth became holding companies, on the agreed 60-40 basis. The Asiatic was to continue as the joint marketing organisation. Marcus was to be chairman of Shell, the Asiatic and Anglo-Saxon and a director of the Baatafsche, but ultimate control remained with the Royal Dutch with its 60% holding. The Dutch, it is only fair to add, never used their majority in such a way as to harm the interests of Shell, or Britain;

and Deterding, the effective manager of the whole combine, had made his base in London, acquired a country estate, was shooting and riding to hounds, and indeed had turned native.

All that, however, did not affect the fundamental fact that Shell was now undeniably what its critics had always declared it to be, a foreign concern. When the Admiralty began to turn to oil in 1910 it obtained supplies mainly from the Burmah Oil Company.

The main driving force in favour of oil, 'the oil-maniac' as he was called, was Admiral Jackie Fisher, who had encouraged Marcus to persevere even after the Royal Dutch-Shell merger.[41] Fisher's advocacy of oil, and in particular Shell oil, was not wholly disinterested for, as he told Marcus, he had invested his 'bottom dollar' in Shell.[42] Fisher found an ally in Winston Churchill, and in 1912 a Royal Commission on Fuel and Engines was set up, with Fisher as chairman. The overwhelming advantages of oil were now self-evident and the problem was one of supply. That, Marcus believed, was not a problem. "You cannot have too much storage,"[43] was a point he made again and again.

The Royal Commission was so far impressed with his evidence that it recommended the build-up of a reserve to cover *four years'* wartime consumption. Admiral Jellicoe, the Second Sea Lord, suggested six months. The Admiralty finally decided on four-and-a-half months. The decision nearly lost Britain the war, for during the U-boat campaign of 1917, reserves were down to three-weeks supply, and the Fleet was largely confined to harbour.[44]

Early in the history of Shell, when Marcus first tried to interest the Navy in fuel oil, he had offered the Government not merely a place on the board of the company, but actual control of Shell to reassure them on the supply position.[45] This unique offer by a private company in the heyday of private enterprise was turned down. Now that the Navy was going over to oil the Admiralty adopted the procedure recommended by Marcus, but instead of buying a stake in Shell, acquired 50% of the share capital of the Anglo-Persian Oil Company.[46]

Anglo-Persian was a minnow compared with Shell, but it derived its oil from what was then a British sphere of influence, and was a subsidiary of the Burmah Oil Company, which was solidly based on the empire.

The measure, Churchill told the House of Commons, would make the Government "independent of the oil ring and oil kings". The open market, he believed, had become open mockery, and he singled out Shell for particular attention:

We have no quarrel with Shell. We have always found them courteous, considerate, ready to oblige, anxious to serve the Admiralty, and to promote the interests of the British Navy and the British Empire – *at a price*. The only difficulty had been price. On that point, of course, we have been treated to the full rigours of the game.[47]

Sam intervened with a muddled and ineffectual speech, and the best defence of Marcus was made by a Tory backbencher, Watson Rutherford. The First Lord, he suggested, had resorted to "a little bit of Jew-baiting" to rally his flagging supporters. The reason for the sharp rise in prices, he said, was simply due to a phenomenal rise in demand, "and not because some evilly-disposed gentleman of the Hebraic persuasion had put their heads together".[48]

Churchill disliked Marcus and shared the public dislike and suspicion of trusts, a very emotive word in those days, and which carried visions of hidden power, of small, rapacious cliques holding the world to ransom. Churchill was too much of a demagogue to forego the applause to be had from attacking someone who was not only the head of a vast combine but a Jew, and an unpopular Jew at that.

Marcus in his sixties came to embody the popular view of the grasping millionaire or, to use the terms of a later age, the 'bloated capitalist'. Never slender, he was now fat. His manner was pompous, aldermanic, overbearing. 'Behold, I have come', his presence would proclaim. His face, when not inscrutable, was smug. He was wholly lacking in imagination, and showed an utter insensitivity to public feeling. It is not that he was indifferent to what people thought, but it would never occur to him that he could be regarded as anything other than the admirable man he was. He meant well, he always acted in the public interest, why should anyone think ill of him? The Churchill speech must have shocked him deeply.

But if this was a dark time for Marcus, his golden moment, the opportunity to perform a unique service, lay just ahead.

In 1901 there had been complaints about the quality of the crude oil discovered at the Shell concessions in Borneo. Robert Waley Cohen, who had lately joined the company, sent a sample for analysis to a brilliant chemist at Cambridge, Dr H. O. Jones, who confirmed that the product was of little use for kerosene, but, that, by way of compensation, it was uniquely rich in toluol, an essential element in T.N.T.

Toluol in this country was normally extracted from coal, which contained about 2% of the substance; Borneo crude oil contained

10%. Marcus at once hurried to the Admiralty with the news and was rebuffed with a polite expression of disinterest.[49]

In 1914 he repeated the offer and was again rebuffed.

He thereupon took independent action. The Shell group had a toluol plant at Rotterdam. Marcus ordered that it be transferred lock, stock and barrel to a site which the company had acquired at Portishead, Somerset.

During the night of January 30, 1915 the Rotterdam factory was dismantled, each piece, numbered, loaded on a waiting fleet of lorries and driven to the docks. An army of labourers and technicians was ready for it at Portishead and, working round the clock, had it in operation within two months.

By then an explosives shortage had developed, the Government was grateful for the extra facilities provided by Shell and a further two toluol plants were erected. The three between them produced 80% of the T.N.T. used by the British armed forces. Lord Birkenhead, who was a member of the wartime Cabinet, later wrote: "I do not know how many of the victories of this last war could be counted as decisive: I think there were at least five; but if there were only three, Lord Bearstead must, in virtue of toluol, be counted as the winner of one of them."[50]

Marcus, who had become a baronet at the end of his mayoral year, was made a baron after the war "for eminent public and national services and a generous benefactor to charitable and scientific objects".[51] He took the title of Lord Bearsted after the parish in which the Mote was situated. In 1925 he became a viscount.

His vigour had been sapped by the personal tragedies he had sustained in the war and he suffered frequently from ill-health in the last years of his life. Fanny, who had been broken by the death of Gerald, also needed frequent medical attention, and during Christmas 1926 they were too unwell to leave London for the usual family celebrations at the Mote. They remained in Hamilton Place, she on one floor, he on another, with a small corps of medical attendants rushing from one to the other. Three weeks later Fanny felt an urgent desire to see Marcus, but as she stirred to get out of bed, she had a sudden seizure and died. Marcus had by then lapsed into a coma and died the following morning. They were buried on the same day at the Willesden Jewish cemetery.

Shortly before his death he asked that there should be references at his memorial service "to the action which I took on behalf of our co-religionists in Romania during my mayoralty, for I know that it bore good fruit. I had similarly, but unostentatiously and quietly intervened with the Russian authorities and had gone so far as to predict that the cruelty which they exercised to the Jews under the Czar would lead to their undoing."[52]

Marcus had a close sense of kinship with his co-religionists which seemed to grow stronger the higher he rose in life. In 1902 when Spindeltop ran dry, Lane turned up with the news that he could obtain abundant oil from Romania. Marcus, for the same reasons that he excluded the Romanian Minister from the mayoral celebrations, would not touch it.

Though conservative in politics and outlook, and with a pronounced hankering for tradition, he was perfectly content to jettison Jewish tradition. Occasionally he went to synagogue on state occasions or during the High Holiday services, but he was more meticulous in his observance of Christmas than of any Jewish festival. Certainly it gave him more pleasure, and every year there would be a great jamboree of children and grandchildren and nephews. It was not that he had any hankering for Christian ritual, for he was not a religious man; nor for endless repasts and merrymaking, for he was not a convivial man; but he loved the English countryside, its sights and sounds, and its cycle of events, of which Christmas was so important a part: the logs in the open hearth of the main hall, the great Christmas tree, and the eager excited faces of the young.

He had the parvenu's joy in titles and rank and was not ashamed to show it, or to revel in it, so that even when he was a mere alderman one had to take good care to refer to him as *Alderman* Mr Marcus.

His quest for public office was not, however, entirely due to a mania for rank and acceptance. Nowadays it may be difficult to convince a cynical public that people can be obsessively eager to serve their fellow men. With Marcus it amounted to a sense of mission. It may have been difficult to tell where this sense began and the hunger for honours finished, but the former was as strong as the latter and a host of welfare institutions benefited from his generosity, experience and wisdom. The London Hospital, not far from his birthplace in Upper East Smithfield, was perhaps his favourite cause, but he also helped the Middlesex Hospital, St Bartholemew's and St Thomas's. When an appeal was launched for the restoration of the fabric of St Paul's, he opened the subscriptions list with a donation of £1,000.[53]

The Cousinhood have always been at their most exclusive when faced with a Jewish newcomer. The Gentile with some noble association or some gift to commend him, gained quick entry, but the Jew had to kick his heels for a time while his credentials were scrutinised. Marcus was an alderman, a knight and a millionaire before he was admitted to their charmed circle, and he was a baronet and a peer before it was accepted that he had come to stay.

He was one of the richest men in England. His family-holding in Shell alone was worth £7,000,000 at the end of the World War I, and that by no means represented his complete assets. There was still the family bank of M. Samuel & Co. He could not have been worth much less than £10,000,000 and possibly more. In the first decade of this century, he could, had he wished, have bought his way into the royal circle. He was devoid of social graces, but to Edward VII millions were a grace in themselves. Marcus, however was no Hirsch or Sassoon; the Cousinhood were royal enough for him.

CHAPTER 24

Prophet
Claude Goldsmid Montefiore

In 1841, while Sir Moses Montefiore was making his way homewards from Damascus, his nephew Nathaniel, was on the grand tour. On January 9 he wrote home from Paris:

> Last Wednesday, a great day, or rather evening, I went to Court. There I was presented to His Majesty the King, afterwards to the Queen, Duc d'Orléans, and Princess. All these grand ladies and gentlemen honoured me with a few words. . . . The conversation was more novel than interesting. The Royal family are exceedingly affable, particularly the Queen who chats away, just as if she was only Mrs Snookes. . . . Next Wednesday there will be a ball given at the Palace, to which I presume I shall be invited. It is to be hoped that there will be a great many, for I want to wear my Court dress, which is too expensive an article to lay uselessly in my drawers. Last night I went to a ball given at the Embassy. . . .[1]

He had lately qualified as a doctor, but gentlemen did not dabble in medicine and this particular gentleman did not have to. His father, Abraham Montefiore, had, after a bad start, prospered on the Stock Exchange. His mother was Henrietta, the youngest daughter of Mayer Amschel Rothschild, founder of the Rothschild dynasty. Medicine was only one of his interests, and he was even elected a Fellow of the Royal College of Surgeons. He studied chemistry and literature, he was an amusing writer. He loved travel. He collected names:

> Today I give a dinner party. Bulwer, who is now on account of Lord Granville's absence, ambassador is coming. . . . I never had at my table so great a don, and therefore I am making some extra preparations, such as to have forks enough for every one, and enough clean plates.[2]

His sister Louisa married Sir Anthony de Rothschild. His niece Constance remembered him as 'dry, caustic and amusing', yet with a

313

strong romantic streak. "He had a soft heart, and was constantly falling in love with someone, but was finally anchored and proved himself to be the best, kindest of husbands."

The anchor was a formidable member of a formidable family, Emma, the fifth daughter of Sir Isaac Lyon Goldsmid.

They married in 1850 when they were both thirty-one. By then Nathaniel's more frivolous days were over, but throughout their life the more serious duties such as the education and religious upbringing of their children, were supervised by the mother. They had two sons and two daughters, who viewed their father with amused affection, their mother with affectionate respect.

Nathaniel, nominally Orthodox, took the duties of being a Montefiore seriously, served as lay head of the Spanish and Portuguese Synagogue and would even, on occasion, appear for prayers. But it was Emma a member of the Reform Synagogue who was the religious force in the household. She would conduct prayers at home, and take the children to prayer in the synagogue; she provided them with a constant succession of tutors. It was also Emma the reformist who defrayed the cost of the prayer book compiled by the Reverend Simeon Singer, the standard prayer book of the Orthodox community.

They had a large house in Portman Square and a country estate at Coldeast, near Southampton. The four children, Alice, Leonard, Charlotte and Claude, spent most of their early years at Coldeast and their friends were drawn mainly from the local gentry or some visiting member of the Cousinhood. They rarely met a Jew who was not a relation. Their mother was haunted by the fear that her children might marry out of the faith, yet she made it almost inevitable that they should.

Nearly all the children were brilliant. Alice, the eldest, born in 1851, was a first class Hebraist and a number of her translations of traditional Hebrew hymns now form part of the Liberal Jewish liturgy. Leonard, born two years later, was among the earnest élite who gathered round Dr Jowett at Balliol. After reading Modern History he rapidly established himself as an authority on German political thought; but he was interested in the main in social work, and on coming down from Oxford spent much of his time in the East End and the welfare settlement established by Canon Barnett at Toynbee Hall. Nothing in his experience had prepared him for the poverty and squalor he found in the back streets of Whitechapel, and he could not help contrasting it with the opulence he found in his own family circle.

Leonard, perhaps embarrassed by his wealth, spent much of it on others and little on himself. He avoided first-class travel, first-class restaurants, first-class shops, and bespoke tailors, and dressed like a gentleman fallen upon hard times. On his many visits to working-men's clubs he tried to identify himself with them. But he never succeeded in giving the impression that he was one of them, for if his clothes were the clothes of the people, his voice was the voice of the gentry, and prep school and of public school, of Oxford and Balliol, of privilege.

He was a gifted speaker, writer and thinker. Dr Jowett believed he had a touch of genius. It seemed inevitable that whatever course he might follow he would triumph. "You and I belong to a race which can do anything but fail," the aged Lord Beaconsfield told him. He was extremely radical in his views and toyed with the idea of a political career, but he was no young man in a hurry. In 1879 he set out on a tour of America, and there contracted rheumatic fever and died. He was twenty-six.

The family was shattered by his death, and Claude, who was five years his junior, was particularly affected. All the hope which had been vested in the older brother, now devolved upon him. Leonard was Claude's ideal against whom he measured himself. He did not fall short.

Claude Goldsmid Montefiore, born in 1858, was the youngest of the family. As a child, he had a severe attack of pneumonia which left him susceptible to bronchial ailments. He was not perhaps as delicate as his parents thought, but he was not allowed to attend school. Even when he followed his brother up to Balliol, he was considered to be too delicate for the normal spartan type of university lodging, and was housed with one of his tutors, Baron Paravicini, an Italian aristocrat.

Claude was not one of the gay bucks of Oxford. His health debarred him from sport or athletics. He neither drank nor smoked. He dismissed as frivolous all the dining clubs, the debating clubs, the literary societies, and all the fringe activities which made Oxford Oxford. Moreover he felt his pre-university schooling had been inadequate and he tried to catch up on it at Balliol, so that his student years, as indeed his later ones, were years of intense application and study. He studied Classics and of course, took a First. No other success in life, he said later, meant as much to him.

After Balliol he spent some time in Germany. Having had German governesses and German tutors, and having read German history and literature, he was almost as at home in German culture and language as in English. He grew to admire the depth and intensity of German scholarship, which was more to his taste than the frivolity to which

Oxford was sometimes prone, though he retained the deepest affection for Balliol.

When he went up to Oxford he had the vague idea of becoming a Rabbi, but exposure to the liberal ideas of T. H. Green, and the liberal Christianity of Benjamin Jowett, made it difficult for him to subscribe to the dogmas of Judaism. He still retained his sense of religious vocation, however, and even if he could no longer profess the beliefs of a Rabbi, he could still acquire the scholarship of one. He engaged as a tutor Solomon Schechter, the greatest Rabbinic scholar of his generation. Claude had met him in Germany and brought him over to England where he later became Reader in Rabbinics at Cambridge.

In 1891 Claude was invited by Dr Jowett to deliver the Hibbert Lectures at Oxford University on the 'Origin of Religion as Illustrated by the Ancient Hebrews'. The lectures were later published in book form and contained in essence a new outline of the Jewish faith. Jowett was delighted with the result.

> You seem to have done a really valuable piece of work;
> It appears to me that there is good work to be done in Judaism;
> Christianity has gone forward; ought not Judaism to make a similar progress from the letter to the spirit, from the national to the historical and ideal? The Jews need not renounce the religion of their fathers, but they ought not to fall short of the highest, whether gathered from the teaching of Jesus or from Greek philosophy.[3]

'. . . progress from the letter to the spirit . . .' This almost summed up the aims of the reforms which Montefiore envisaged.

Lily Montagu found in his ideas the answer to the many reservations she had about Judaism, and out of their common quest there grew the Jewish Religious Union, which organised 'supplementary services' on Saturday afternoons, where men and women sat together, instead of apart as in synagogues, where hymns were sung in the vernacular rather than Hebrew, and where learned discourses were heard from Jewish scholars of all shades of religious opinion, and sometimes even from Christians.

In time the Jewish Religious Union felt compelled to widen its scope. Its members, wrote Montefiore, "wanted a religion; they wanted a coherent and satisfying Judaism: they did not merely want a 'service'. They were not merely out of touch with Orthodox *services*. They were out of touch with, they doubted the truth of, Orthodox *principles*, Orthodox *beliefs*."[4]

Montagu's own views and beliefs were by then well known, but he did not wish to formulate a new theology because he wanted to keep the Jewish Religious Union catholic, an umbrella organisation for all Jews who wanted to explore the elements of their faith.

On certain basic issues he was at one with Orthodoxy. God was to him still one and alone, 'Ruler and sustainer of all, the One supreme Spirit, who is the source of all spirits and of all spiritual life'. He believed 'that the souls or spirit of men are not utterly dissolved or destroyed by death'. He believed too in 'the mission of Israel'.

The point of departure came on Revelation and authority, and the two are connected. The Orthodox Jew believes, or should believe, that in the Bible and Talmud is enshrined the will of God, that the Rabbis are the traditional interpreters of that will, and that their authority is therefore absolute.

Montefiore renounced the first part of this creed, and could therefore not accept the second:

> We recognise no binding authority between us and God, whether in a man or a book, whether in a church or in a code, whether in a tradition or in a ritual. . . .
>
> We need accept nothing which does not seem to us good. The authority of the Book, so far as it goes, is its worth, and so far as that worth reaches, so far reaches the authority. The Book is not good because it is from God; it is from God in so far as it is good.[5]

In other words, the Orthodox Jew accepted the Bible as entirely good because it was entirely from God. Montefiore, on the other hand, believed that it was something of a curate's egg – good in parts, and as such it could only be partly divine. He reserved the right to be eclectic, to select the holy from the less holy or the downright profane. Thus, for example, where he read 'And God slew Amelek', he could not reconcile it with his belief in God as a source of goodness and love. Instead of deriving guidance from Scripture and its interpreters, he accepted guidance where it fitted in with his own preconceived ideas of what was right or wrong.

"We do not deny," he wrote, "that there are many difficulties which confront us in our attitude of freedom towards the Book and the Code. But these we must accept with patience as the condition of our liberty."[6]

As Claude spread his message the more traditionalist members of the Jewish Religious Union fell away, and the society was left to its reformist core. A new sect was in being with Montefiore as the prophet in spite of himself.

A Rabbi was needed, but there was none in England whose ideas fitted within Montefiore's statement of the creed, and he travelled to find one in America. He spent over a month there, attended the Conference of American Reform Rabbis, visited Reform Temples in New York, Chicago, Pittsburg, Philadelphia and Cincinnati. His choice finally alighted on Rabbi Israel Mattuck and, under 'the Trinity of the three Ms' – Montefiore, Montagu and Mattuck – the Liberal Jewish Synagogue came into being, prospered and grew, and today, some sixty years after its foundation, it has some 12,000 members.

Solomon Schechter was disappointed with the direction which his pupil and patron had taken. "What the whole thing means," he wrote, "is not Liberal Judaism, but Liberal Christianity."[7] There was, indeed, nothing in Claude's creed to offend a Unitarian, and nothing in Unitarianism to offend any member of his creed. He did not recognise the divinity of Jesus, neither did he dismiss him as a false Messiah, but, on the contrary, looked upon him as a major, perhaps the major prophet, a universal Isaiah.

The main impact of his group lay not so much in its theology, but on the stress which it laid on the spirit of Judaism rather than its letter, and on social action as a form of ritual.

It also laid stress on the Jew as an Englishman, or a German or an American, a citizen of the Mosaic persuasion, but not a member of a wider brotherhood. Thus when Zionism began to spread in England Montefiore fought it with the vehemence of a pontiff battling with heresy.

The word Jew, he declared, "denotes not a nationality, but a religion. We want to be Englishmen or Italians by nationality; Jew by religion. We want to be Jews in the old sense – the sense of our forefathers, 'His Majesty's subjects professing the Jewish religion' – and not in the new sense of nationality."[8]

But beyond the theories, he believed that a Jewish state must adversely affect all Jews living outside it:

> Is it not natural and specious that the anti-Semites should say: The Jews now possess a country and a state of their own. Let them all go thither. Let us show them clearly where their true place is: in Asia and not in Europe, among their own people and not among ours . . . "At last," it will be said, "the Jews have shown themselves in their true colours. We anti-Semites always knew, and always declared, that their supposed desire to be Italians, Russians, or Rumanians, etcetera, was mere hypocrisy . . . they have confessed themselves to be an alien nationality,

who long to start a national life of their own. Let us be all the less disposed to listen to the few remaining hypocrites who fawn upon us, and whine about their patriotism . . . let us make things as unpleasant as we can, so that the new Jewish home in Palestine may be the more rapidly fulfilled.

It was a frightening spectre, and it certainly frightened Montefiore, for as he warmed to his argument he lost his usual composure, and concluded with what was almost a call to arms:

Are there then no dangers in Zionism? Has the time not come to expose them and fight them? It is assuredly no time for apathy and neutrality: every Jew who desires to remain an Englishman should publicly declare his standpoint. The time has come when neutrality spells betrayal.[9]

This was written after the Balfour Declaration. Montefiore had, in concert with other leading members of the Cousinhood, tried to stifle the Declaration before it was even made; but unlike the others, he continued to fight long after the battle was lost, even after the rise of Hitler. Hitler, indeed, was to him proof of his prophecies, a by-product of Zionism. "Weizmann," he wrote a year before his death, "is abler, than all the other Jews in the world put together. He is a Jewish Parnell but even abler, and alas respectably married. . . . It is appalling beyond words. But Hitlerism, is, at least partially, *Weizmann's creation*."[10]

Claude's biographer, Lucy Cohen, a gifted writer and a daughter of Arthur Cohen, looked on Liberal Judaism as "the only living and enduring form of religion possible to people brought up in English institutions and Western culture".[11] Yet the Liberal Synagogue, like the Reform, has never become the established synagogue of the Cousinhood in the sense that Temple Emanu-El in New York, became the synagogue of *Our Crowd*. The Liberal Synagogue may have been nearer to their religious thinking in so far as they thought about religion at all. It was infinitely nearer to their way of life, but most of them remained faithful to the old institutions, to the United Synagogue and to Bevis Marks.

Montefiore's father left £456,000 and his mother nearly £1 million. He was also a considerable beneficiary under the will of his uncle Sir Francis Goldsmid, and was therefore never beset with the necessity of earning a living. But he was extremely industrious. His scholarly output was prodigious. The study of the Old Testament gave him intense pleasure. He found it difficult to get its story and message across to his young son, and therefore prepared a revised version of his own, a massive work of fourteen hundred pages, with commentary, called *The Bible for Home Reading* which enjoyed wide appreciation and a ready sale. It went into three editions.

This was the nearest thing to a popular work that he wrote. He would not, however, have been ashamed to be known as a populariser, for his work, which was mainly concerned with theology and the history of religion – *Rabbinic Literature and Gospel Teachings* was a typical title – was intended to bring obscure but significant ideas to the attention of intelligent laymen. Laymen, however, were not perhaps quite as intelligent as he believed. His work was in the main taken up by scholars and his two volume *Synoptic Gospels*, in particular, which was first published in 1909, have proved invaluable to serious students of the Bible.

He gave occasional sermons at the Liberal Synagogue which were the products of much reasoning and meticulous research, but which were followed with less pleasure than respect. "Mattuck," he once said with envy, "can always feel if his audience is bored or interested, sympathetic or antagonistic. I feel nothing, one way or the other."[12] It was perhaps just as well.

It was usually better to read than to hear him (his sermons and speeches were in any case always read by him from prepared texts), except that there was a special aura about his presence. He almost literally shone. He was a tall man, well over six foot, with broad shoulders, close-cropped hair, a small beard, and a complexion the colour of ivory. But it was the eyes which immediately caught attention, large, dark, piercing, luminous, the eyes of a visionary. He was often spoken of as a saint, and his disposition was saintly, but he was devoid of all meekness, mildness or diffidence. He looked like a cross between a Victorian ironmaster and a Hebrew prophet.

He was involved with innumerable social causes. He was associated with Lily Montagu in the work of the West Central Club for Jewish girls, and with Basil Henriques in the Bernhard Baron settlement in the East End. A cause which gave him particular consternation and pain, and which consumed his time and energy over many years, was the Jewish Association for the Protection of Women and Girls.

Persecution in Russia and Romania and destitution in Galicia had caused a great movement of Jews towards the West which resulted often in the disruption of whole families. Parents too poor or broken to move themselves hoped at least for a happier future for their children by sending them off alone with a few shillings and the name of a relative on a crumpled piece of paper. Many were young girls and quite often they never reached their destination. An international network of white slavers had grown up with agents at every port, who inveigled them into prostitution. On occasion the victims were willing enough, but the girls were in the main innocent children from religious homes, friendless in a strange country, an easy prey for seducers. And once seduced they felt themselves to be unfit for anything but the streets.

Stories to this effect had been circulating in London and elsewhere for some years, but they sounded too dreadful to be true. Nothing was done until a Christian social worker brought the plight of these girls to the attention of Lady Battersea.

"Alas, I was hopelessly at sea in the matter," Lady Battersea confessed. "The subject was one I had always avoided, and I had never heard, nor, indeed, did I believe, that any so-called rescue work had been needed amongst the Jewish community."[13] She therefore wrote to Montefiore, "my dear and valued cousin . . . the most generous of individuals, with the purest and noblest of minds", and through his efforts the protection association was brought into being with Lady Rothschild as president and Lady Battersea as vice-president, and various other members of the Cousinhood active on its committees and sub-committees.

The association established hostels for young girls, and homes for the rehabilitation of former prostitutes. It had agents at the docks who worked closely with the police and kept check on the movement of known or suspected traffickers. In 1905 it came to the assistance of 1,366 girls, among them 38 who were under fourteen. Between 1906 and 1909, it found that 222 immigrant girls had vanished from the country, probably for the purposes of prostitution. In the same period it was instrumental in bringing 521 traffickers, and 151 brothel-keepers to justice.

In all this work Montefiore was no Gladstone taking nightly strolls to 'rescue' women from sin. Aware that he was dealing with a problem with the widest international ramifications, he worked with Jewish social workers in other countries to form an international committee which organised periodic conferences on the suppression of white slavery.

Not everyone viewed Montefiore's work with admiration. Some felt he exaggerated the scale of the problem, others were nervous of the prominence he gave it.

Montefiore took intense pride in his Jewishness, but even Jews, as he told a conference, could succumb to their circumstances:

If you persecute a people or community from generation to generation, you can produce, on the one hand, if it is a fine people or community – which I think ours is – much heroism, and many heroes and heroines;

but, on the other hand, alas, you can produce some human scum, and when to persecution is added social poverty and evil housing conditions, it is hardly a wonder that a certain amount of this evil should exist among us.[14]

His views was confirmed by events, for as the situation of Jews improved, the problem vanished. The association was able to close its hostels and 'rescue' homes and wind up its work.

Claude Montefiore was as active in non-Jewish as in Jewish causes, and as munificent in his help. However, he would try to appear to be less generous than he was and would offer 'loans' rather than outright grants, on which he would then waive repayment. He was, as the widowed father of a solitary child, particularly interested in infant education and was excited by the work of two disciples of Froebel who had opened a small school in London and it was largely with his help that the London Froebel Institute was able to establish a permanent home at Grove House, Roehampton.

"It is impossible to estimate the debt of the Froebel Institute to Mr Montefiore," a principal of the institute has written. "Can any educational institution ever have had as intimate friend, guide and benefactor for over forty-six years, a personality so great and humane as his? The whole life and progress of the institute have been directed and shaped by his goodness, wisdom and munificence."[15]

As a resident of Coldeast, near Southampton, he came into contact with Mrs Annie Yorke, a daughter of Sir Anthony de Rothschild who lived near Southampton Water, and who had been a generous benefactor of Hartley College, the forerunner of Southampton University. She interested him in the work of the college and in due course he joined the college council and was in 1913 elected president. This was an unpaid, but by no means nominal office, and during the next twenty-five years his exertions enabled the college to survive numerous crises and emerge finally as a university of international standing.

" . . . he threw himself heart and soul into the life of the College," the historian of Southampton University has written, "and it would be almost impossible to over-estimate the value of the services which he rendered to it."[16]

Montefiore was perhaps happier in his secular causes than his Jewish ones, for they were less fraught with ambiguities.

Of his two sisters, the elder, Alice, married Henry Lucas, a well-connected member of the faith, but the younger Charlotte, became engaged to Lewis McIver, of the Indian Civil Service, who was not. "My mother," Claude observed, was very inconsistent in allowing so many

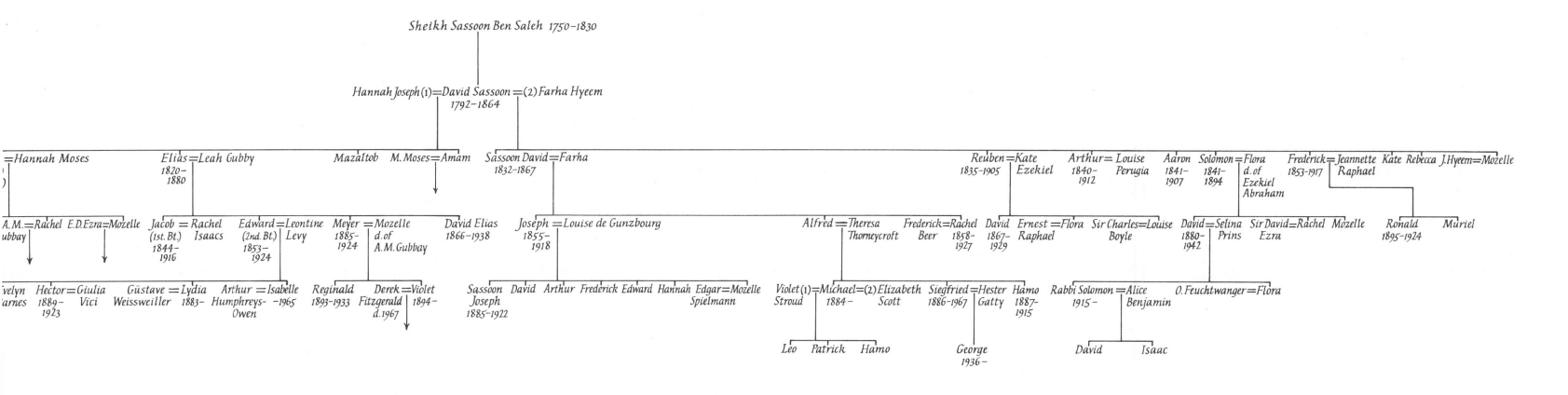

SHEIKH SASSOON BEN SALEH

Sheikh Sassoon Ben Saleh 1750–1830

Hannah Joseph (1)=David Sassoon =(2) Farha Hyeem
1792–1864

=Hannah Moses   Elias=Leah Gubby   Mazaltob   M. Moses=Amam   Sassoon David=Farha   Reuben=Kate   Arthur=Louise   Aaron   Solomon=Flora   Frederick=Jeannette   Kate Rebecca   J.Hyeem=Mozelle
1820–   1832–1867   1835–1905   Ezekiel   1840–   Perugia   1841–   1841–   d.of   1853–1917   Raphael
1880   1912   1907   1894   Ezekiel
                                                                              Abraham

A.M.=Rachel   E.D.Ezra=Mozelle   Jacob = Rachel   Edward=Leontine   Meyer = Mozelle   David Elias   Joseph=Louise de Gunzbourg   Alfred=Theresa   Frederick=Rachel   David   Ernest=Flora   Sir Charles=Louise   David=Selina   Sir David=Rachel   Mozelle   Ronald   Muriel
ubbay   (1st. Bt.)   Isaacs   (2nd.Bt.)   Levy   1885–   d.of   1866–1938   1855–   Thorneycroft   Beer   1867–   Raphael   Boyle   1880–   Prins   Ezra   1895–1924
                                1844–   1853–   1924   A.M.Gubbay   1918   1927   1929   1942
                                1916   1924

velyn   Hector=Giulia   Gustave = Lydia   Arthur =Isabelle   Reginald   Derek =Violet   Sassoon   David   Arthur   Frederick   Edward   Hannah   Edgar=Mozelle   Violet (1)=Michael=(2)Elizabeth   Siegfried=Hester   Hamo   Rabbi Solomon =Alice   O.Feuchtwanger=Flora
arnes   1889–   Vici   Weissweiler   1883–   Humphreys-   1893–1933   Fitzgerald   1894–   Joseph   Spielmann   Stroud   1884–   Scott   1886–1967   Gatty   1887–   1915–   Benjamin
     1923   Owen   d.1967   1885–1922   1915

-1965

Leo   Patrick   Hamo   George   David   Isaac
                                             1936–

Christian young men and women to stay in the house so frequently and for so long periods."[17] Jews and Christians had mixed freely in her own father's house at St John's Lodge without any untoward result, but in the early decades of the nineteenth century, Jewish and non-Jewish society, though polite, was mutually exclusive. By the end of the nineteenth century exclusiveness was breaking down. The Rothschilds had led the way, the Montefiores were following. Religious belief had slackened and the main restraint was parental. To old Mrs Montefiore intermarriage was anathema. Charlotte herself had no wish to marry in church and become a Christian and while McIver had no objections to marrying in synagogue, he had no wish to become a Jew. They reached a typically English compromise, an agreement to differ. Claude, as the surviving brother, took charge of the arrangements, but could find no Rabbi in England to solemnise the compromise, and, with the young couple in train, he scoured Europe till, in an obscure corner of Germany, he found a Rabbi willing to marry a practising Jewess to a professing Christian.

The act was completely contrary to Jewish law, and even Claude's own Liberal Synagogue would not today countenance such a marriage. He may have drawn some consolation from the thought that in Judaism it is the mother's religion which determines the faith of the child, but he must have found the whole episode unseemly and painful. Dr Jowett, the Master of Balliol, and now a family friend, on the other hand, was elated:

My dear Montefiore,

I am very glad to hear of your sister's marriage. . . .

I think it quite right that the wall of distinction between Jew and Christian should be broken down. Has it not lasted long enough? In idea it already has broken down, for all intelligent persons are agreed that in the sight of God there is no distinction of race or cast or circumcision or of uncircumcision: as a custom it will long continue. Perhaps always; there is a different tradition and it would be vain and unpopular and impossible to get rid of distinctive customs which may have their use. But it would be wrong to do violence to natural affection for the sake of always insisting upon them. It seems to me that Jewish society in England is too narrow to allow of Jews only marrying within limits of their own community, and that they would be put at a great disadvantage if such a rule was enforced. . . .[18]

The marriage, which Mrs Montefiore could not have failed to recognise as a sham was, however, sufficient to reconcile her to the *fait accompli*: but she had hardly got over this shock when another followed.

Claude was asked to interview a young graduate of Girton for a post in one of the Jewish schools, and he was so far taken with her qualifications as to ask her to become his wife. She was Thérèse Schorstein, the grand-daughter of a Polish Rabbi, a person, in Mrs Montefiore's eyes, of no rank or consequence. She was disconsolate. One son was dead. A daughter had virtually married out of the faith, and now her other son was about to marry out of his class. To his mother snobbery and religion were so intermingled that it was hard to tell where the one finished and the other began. He listened to her protestations with patience, but remained firm in his choice. He had, it was often said, the patience of a saint. He needed it. The marriage eventually took place, but three years later his young wife died in childbirth.

The child, Leonard, survived, but remained in delicate health throughout his life.

Claude married again thirteen years later. His second wife, Florence Ward, had been a vice-principal of Girton, and a tutor of his first. After the death of Thérèse she visited Coldeast a number of times and a close friendship developed between her and Claude. They had many of the same interests, and much the same outlook. She was not a Jewess, but nor was she enough of a Christian to object to becoming one. As Claude put it, "she was willing to adopt my label".[19] His mother, however, could not overlook hers and would not hear of their marriage. Claude did not press the matter. The old woman was nearly eighty and in poor health; their difference would be resolved with time. But five years passed before this happened.

The second Mrs Montefiore was formally converted to Judaism, but it took more than conversion to make her feel at ease in the wider family circle of cousins and second cousins, uncles and aunts. She was a reserved, rather dour woman at the best of times, and her dourness was by no means diminished by the chatty, clamorous bonhomie she found among the massed Goldsmids and Montefiores. She kept herself more and more to Coldeast, and Claude enjoyed a bachelor-like existence in Portman Square.

He travelled a great deal, usually without his wife. His companion on a great many of his journeys was the Reverend W. P. Jay, an Anglican clergyman. Old Mrs Montefiore had initially picked him as a travelling companion for her son, for she was always worried about his health and safety. "You will take care of him, won't you?", she charged the Reverend, "he is all I have." Claude was then over thirty.[20]

His travels were somewhat introspective affairs. Changes of scene, no matter how dramatic, meant little to him. He was not much affected by the visual or palpable, but was mainly excited by conversation and ideas, and his companion was thus more important to him than his journey.

Leonard Montefiore inherited both his father's good nature and good causes and also something of his massive intellect. He read history at Balliol, but did not prepare himself for any career. He spent his time moving from one council meeting to another, now at the Froebel Institute, now at the Board of Guardians, or some boys' club, or the West London Synagogue, or the Anglo-Jewish Association. They were numberless and their demands upon his times were relentless. He attended them all, gave money to them all, offered guidance to them all. He helped to establish on a secure footing the Wiener Library, which is now part of the Institute of Contemporary History. He was a most active figure on the emergency Central British Fund for the victims of Nazism. He helped to bring numerous children over from Germany and acted as virtual guardian to scores of them. If he accepted office it was not merely to grace a letter-heading, or to donate a few guineas; he interested himself in the organisation's day-to-day affairs to the point, almost, of being a nuisance.

He did not adopt his father's religious radicalism. An active member of the Reform Synagogue rather than the Liberal, he was something of a clergyman *manqué*, and liked when occasion permitted, to conduct services at the West London Synagogue.

Like his father he was a leading force in the Jewish Colonisation Association, like him he was an anti-Zionist, but unlike him he survived to visit the Zionist state and see its achievements with his own eyes. He was moved by his experience to confess that "events have proved false many of the fears, and, I suspect, some of the hopes entertained by Zionists and non-Zionists alike. Any Jew visiting the state of Israel, whatever his previous prejudices, feels a thrill of admiration at the labour and self-sacrifice that have gone to creating a new state."[12] He was in other ways a little removed from the realities of life, and recognised himself as such. He was, he once said, a relic of a bygone age when "the community, much smaller in numbers, was content to have its institutions managed by a group of people most of whom were related to one another. . . . I must confess that whenever I go to Woburn House (the Whitehall of Anglo-Jewry) and pass the door of the Jewish Museum, I wonder whether my appropriate place is not there rather than anywhere else in the building."[22]

In 1924 he married Muriel Tuck, a daughter of Sir Adolph Tuck, the greetings card magnate. When he died in 1961 in his seventy-third year, almost every well-known member of the Jewish community attended the funeral. Officers of every major communal institution were there and scores of unknown individuals, each of whom had some private remembrance of his kindness.

His widow, a graceful, dignified woman, who still retains the evidence of her youthful good looks, tries to keep in touch with all his interests. "But he had so many," she said, "so many, it's impossible."

They had two children. The youngest, David, born in 1929, and still a bachelor, studied at Cambridge and is now a doctor and director of a large medical establishment for the World Health Organisation in East Africa. The elder, Alan, born in 1926, took a first in P.P.E., and is a Fellow of Balliol and a philosophy don at the university. He is an agnostic and his wife is non-Jewish, a fact which caused some unhappiness in the family. His father believed that "marriage with one who comes outside the community means absorption and disappearance",[23] a view which his mother shares. "Of course, what happened was hardly Alan's fault," she explains, "we lived in the country, the children met hardly any Jewish people of their own age. It could hardly be otherwise."[24] The event did not cause any lasting rift. Mother, son and daughter-in-law are devoted to one another.

Claude Montefiore was in his seventies by the time he became a grandfather and the joy he found in his grandchildren's company was a consolation for the gathering infirmities of old age. He was almost deaf, and walked with difficulty, but could get down on all fours and frolic with them like a child among children.

He liked to think of his Jewish birth as an advantage and averred that it never interfered with his friendships. His parents and grandparents, he believed, had never been regarded as anything other than English gentlefolk. Things might be different for his descendants, he reflected sombrely, "thanks to the work of the Zionists".[25]

As he grew older his travels grew less frequent, for apart from anything else he was worried about the cost. He had, as we have seen, inherited considerable fortunes from his father, his mother and uncle; but he believed that capital should be passed on untouched and tried, as far as possible, to live on the interest. The upkeep of his two homes involved him in considerable expense, but he otherwise spent little on himself. He would wear suits till they were frayed and on the point of falling apart. He indulged in none of the pursuits of his class. He abhorred hunting, shooting, fishing and, needless to say, gambling. He did not drink and disapproved of drinkers. Even the sight of a beer advertisement on a hotel menu could annoy him. Nor was he much of an eater. He would sometimes descend on some remote farm in a large, chauffeur-driven limousine, and ask for a boiled egg, or a bowl of milk and bread. He was worried by soaring taxes, and was afraid that if they rose any further he might be unable to meet his 'commitments', by which he meant his charities. "I feel it incumbent on me as a Jew," he once said, "to do just a little more than is absolutely necessary."[26]

As squire of Coldeast, he contributed generously to parish funds, but should he, he asked the dean of St Paul's, also contribute to the diocese fund? "No," said the dean, "but don't tell the bishop I said so."[27]

Dr Gore, the Bishop of Oxford, said that the best Christian he had ever known, was a Jew. He was speaking of Montefiore.[28]

It was somehow easier for Christian clergymen than for Rabbis to regard him as one of themselves. His views were so much nearer to theirs. His house, especially in his later years, became a sort of theological club, and was on occasion as full of bishops as the Athenaeum on boat-race night. Theology was a marvellous escape from the actualities of the 1930s, and from preoccupation with his deteriorating health. To him God, Jesus, the Trinity, this world and the next, were the elements of relaxed small-talk, and the gaitered clergymen about him were not merely people who shared his interests, but intimates and friends. Among them his eyes would be alight, as they would darken in reflecting on the contemporary scene.

He at first had found it difficult to believe that Hitler was more than a passing phenomenon, and that Germany, his beloved Germany, his spiritual home, whose language he spoke, whose culture he worshipped, which was the source to him, and his son, of so many happy memories, should have gone berserk. *Crystalsnacht*, Auschwitz, the holocaust, lay ahead. He was spared knowledge of the worst and died peacefully in his sleep in July 1938.

As he lay dying he called for his friend the Reverend W. R. Matthews, dean of St Paul's to minister to him.

"This was a privilege which embarrassed me," the dean later confessed, "because he was deaf and one had to shout to make him hear, and it was difficult for me to pray in a manner which would imply no Christian belief."[29]

And so a compromise was reached. They intoned the Lord's Prayer together – to which not even the most Orthodox Jew can object – the dean at the top of his voice, the dying man in a whisper, the former addressing one Father in Heaven, the latter another.

CHAPTER 25

Carmel and Toxteth
Herbert Samuel

The House of Commons Chamber was destroyed by German bombing in World War II but the House of Lords, in another part of the Palace of Westminster, survived almost unscathed and it is still intact much as Barry built it in the 1840s, a splendid pile of Victorian Gothic, with high, vaulted ceiling, dark timbers, and stained glass. Scattered over the red, plush seats, sit the white-haired figures of lords who might have been contemporaries of the building itself.

The House as an institution has had many critics who came to love it as a place. Herbert Samuel, who as a young M.P. called for the abolition of the House of Lords, became in time one of its chief ornaments. He illuminated every subject he touched, and even in extreme old age, when he was a little bent and a little deaf, he still had power in his voice and great sagacity in his reasoning. His Semitic appearance, which had not been particularly noticeable in his earlier years, was by then very pronounced. The tone and the utterance were of England, Oxford, Balliol, but there was something about him of the Wise Man of the East, as if at the end of his days he was reverting to the archetype of his race.

Herbert Louis Samuel was born in Liverpool in November 1870. His father, Edwin, was the elder brother of Samuel Montagu, but he was the more cautious, less dynamic and less far-seeing of the pair. When the younger brother, with the help of the family, opened a small bank in Leadenhall Street, the older one was brought in as a restraining influence. Instead, he was carried headlong behind the other to the benefit of both. When Edwin died in 1877 at the age of fifty-two he left over £250,000.

The family had by then moved to London to a large house in

Kensington Gore, but the death of Edwin compelled them to move to a humbler though by no means humble dwelling in Kensington Palace Gardens. At that time several opulent members of the Cousinhood lived in the street which is still today known as 'Millionaires' Row'. There were four sons of whom Herbert was the youngest and a daughter, and Samuel Montagu became their guardian.

The eldest son Stuart succeeded his father as a partner in the family bank, and his uncle as Liberal M.P. for Tower Hamlets. An industrious but colourless member, he remained in the House for four years and resigned in 1913. He was interested in prison reform, was a Lunacy Commissioner and on the board of management of numerous hospitals and innumerable synagogues, and his very bearing tended to add to the dignity of any office he held. In 1912 he was made a baronet for his public services.

Sir Stuart was a neat, impeccable figure in suits so stiff and well-tailored as to be almost like armour. His wavy, white hair was parted carefully on one side and a pair of pince-nez was planted firmly on a rather formidable nose. He was a bachelor until his late thirties. Then, on a visit to Brighton he happened upon a crocodile of neat, trim uniformed schoolgirls, walking two by two, and guarded fore and aft by their teachers. One girl in particular caught his eye, a long-legged child with large, mischievous eyes and curly hair. He sent a clerk to enquire after her and found she was Ida Mayer. The father was French, the mother Irish, the family of slight means and no consequence. With the permission of her father, Sir Stuart had her removed from Brighton and sent to an expensive finishing school in Paris. They married in the New West End Synagogue in 1893 when she was nineteen and he twice her age.

They had two daughters, one of whom married Sir Jack Brunel Cohen, M.P., the other, Gilbert Edgar, managing director of the jewellery firm of H. Samuel, Ltd.

The Samuel boys, unlike most children of their class, did not attend boarding school, for their parents insisted on kosher food and Hebrew education. They were sent instead to University College School, an outcrop of the Gower Street College. From there Herbert went on to Balliol College, Oxford. Balliol had been the college of the philosopher T. H. Green whose *Lectures on the Principles of Political Obligation* had formed the basis of English liberal thought and action in the later years of the century, and which deeply affected the outlook of the young Samuel and perhaps inevitably tended to undermine what was left of his religious beliefs. He could not, like his uncle Montagu, view the world with one pair of eyes, and his faith with another, nor could he be a reformer in the one and remain a conservative in the other. In his third year at Oxford he wrote to his mother that he had abandoned the profession of Jewish belief. She invoked Uncle Montagu – who was having trouble with his own children on precisely the same problem – but without effect, and Herbert Samuel wrote to her:

> I shall be very pleased to discuss the question of religion with Uncle Montagu as my guardian, though there is no likelihood of such a discussion having the least effect upon me. My opinion of Uncle Montagu's theology and his philosophical qualities is not such as to lead me to bow in the matter.[1]

He did not, however, carry his views to the point of dissociation from the Jewish people, or even from Orthodox Jewish life. Above all, he did not, as his mother must have feared, marry out of the faith, or even out of the family. In 1897, at the age of twenty-six, he became engaged to Beatrice Franklin, a first cousin, whose father, Ellis Franklin, was a partner in Samuel Montagu. Their wedding, a vast reunion of the Cousinhood, took place in November at the New West End Synagogue. He noted with surprise: "I found the ceremonies, instead of being formidable and rather overwhelming, most enjoyable."[2]

They took a large house at Gloucester Terrace, Hyde Park, and in due course their three sons and one daughter were born there. As the children grew older they moved to a larger house in Porchester Terrace, a few doors away from the Franklins. Brothers and sisters, aunts and cousins were on every side.

Beatrice Samuel shared none of her husband's doubts about the basic truths of Judaism, and Samuel for his part kept his doubts to himself. In any case, whatever his doubts about Judaism, he had infinite faith in tradition. A tutor called at their home to give the children religious instruction, and every Sabbath, all four, accompanied by their mother would walk to synagogue. On high festivals, they would be joined by their father. The food at home was, of course, kosher, but when they ate out their standards were a little relaxed. Edwin, the oldest son, who was a day boy at Westminster School, recalls in his memoirs: "I was expected by my mother to follow her own peculiar version of Jewish dietary laws by picking pieces of ham out of the beef risoles served at school lunches."[3]

In later years Herbert revised some of his religious opinions. "I found," he wrote in his *Memoirs*, "I had come a long way from the negation of my earlier days; was less of an agnostic; definitely anti-materialist; convinced that the universe was charged with mind and purpose."[4]

In one respect his attitude to religion was less rational than he thought. He regarded a Jew who married out of his faith – even where he had ceased to believe in it – as a renegade. It was one thing to abandon one's God, but another to abandon one's people. When his daughter's children married Gentiles, he refused to see them or talk to them, and was reconciled with them only towards the end of his life.

If deficient in belief and indifferent to ritual and prayer, Samuel's way of life, and outlook was largely in accordance with Jewish precept. He was sober, almost ascetic. He enjoyed an occasional glass of wine but even then – to the disgust of his guests – he would dilute it with water. He did not smoke. Food was a means of keeping hunger at bay. He was a puritan even in his youth, and as he grew older he became increasingly worried by the decline of moral standards. "The moral state of the nation," he declared in the House of Lords in 1953, "is at the base of everything else, and in these days there is among careful watchers of the times, a feeling of deep anxiety."[5]

All this, of course, he had in common with most Englishmen of his class and age, but he maintained his ideas long after they were beginning to weaken elsewhere, and he carried them to greater lengths.

They had played a part in his choice of career. There was talk for a time of a place in the family bank but as it already contained two brothers, two uncles and four cousins the idea, much to his relief, was eventually ruled out. Uncle Montagu suggested the Bar, but the young man demurred:

> My father had left a large fortune; my portion would yield an assured income that was amply sufficient; and I had already determined that I would not spend my life, or any part of it, merely on labouring to increase it. Nor did the work of a barrister appeal to me for its own sake.[6]

He turned to politics.

The various social reforms undertaken by both the Tory and Liberal Parties in the latter half of the nineteenth century still left immense inequalities of wealth and opportunity and he believed that progress could be carried much further. He called himself a 'meliorist', a word he adopted from George Eliot, "meaning", as he said, "one who believes that the present is on the whole better than the past and that the future may be better still, but that effort is needed to make it so".[7] The prevailing system, with all its faults, while not forming the best of all possible worlds, was always in the process of getting better, and the role of the reformer was therefore not to upset it and start from scratch, but to jog it up a bit. He set himself to hasten the inevitable.

The Liberal Party had for a large part of the nineteenth century thrived on the belief in *laissez-faire*, and the understanding that if state intervention should be permitted at all in society, it must be kept to a minimum. As the century wore on this idea was becoming thin, and the state, through the various Factory Acts, found itself intervening more and more in the economy and in society. This new Liberalism, which might be summed up as *laissez-faire* tempered by compassion, appealed to Samuel and in 1902 he analysed the role of the party in modern times in a book he called *Liberalism*. The state, he wrote, must secure, "for all its members and all others whom it can influence, the fullest possible opportunity to lead the best life. When we speak of progress we mean . . . the enlargement of this opportunity. . . ."[8] He called for improvements in education, housing, working conditions, for more equitable taxation, and land and temperance reform. He was unapologetic about the increased role the state would have to assume. "The state is not incompetent for the work of social reform", he wrote. "Self reliance is a powerful force, but not powerful enough to cure unaided the diseases that afflict society."[9] The principles of true Liberalism, he concluded, "are nothing less than the application to public affairs of the religious spirit itself".[10]

In 1896, when he came down from Oxford, he was invited to contest on behalf of the Liberal Party the established Tory stronghold of South Oxfordshire. In those days party candidates were expected to find their own money for elections, and without it, indeed, they could hardly contemplate a candidature. "This little business," he warned his mother, "will cost me altogether £1,000, but I don't see how the money could be better spent under present conditions."[11] Then, as always, he kept careful watch on his pennies, and in the event spent £1,028. 6s. He did not attain the impossible, but did well enough both then and in the 1900 election to be given a more hopeful constituency, and in 1902 he entered Parliament for the Cleveland division of Yorkshire. In 1905 at thirty-five, he became Under-Secretary at the Home Office.

There was at this time an appalling amount of cruelty and neglect of children in the country. It was not unusual for working class mothers to dose their infants with 'drops of comfort', gin or stout, to get them to sleep. Babies were sometimes sold for adoption. Children were tried in the same courts and thrown into the same prisons as hardened criminals. These and other abuses were tackled in a Bill which Samuel called the Children's Charter and which won support from all sides of the House.

In 1908 Samuel was made a member of the Privy Council and in 1909, at the age of thirty-eight, he entered the Cabinet as Chancellor of the Duchy of Lancaster. In the following year he was made Postmaster-General, an office which, through no fault of his own, involved him in the gravest crisis of his career – the Marconi affair.

In 1911 an Imperial conference had approved a plan for the erection of a chain of wireless stations throughout the British empire, and Herbert Samuel, as Postmaster-General, was asked to take it in hand. Various systems were examined and tenders invited, and the contract was finally awarded to the Marconi Telegraph Company of Great Britain on March 7, 1912. It was placed before Parliament for ratification on July 12.

On April 17, after the tender had been accepted, but before the contract was ratified, Godfrey Isaacs, managing director of the company, offered shares in the Marconi Company of America, to his brother Harry, who in turn sold 10,000 shares to another brother Sir Rufus Isaacs, the Attorney General, at £2 per share. Rufus in turn sold 1,000 of his shares to the Chancellor of the Exchequer, David Lloyd George, and a further 1,000 tó the Master of Elibank, Chief Whip of the Liberal Party, all at £2 per share. These shares were not yet available to the general public, and when trading opened on April 19 they almost doubled in value. Samuel, one must add, was at no time involved in any of these deals.

There is conflicting evidence on the overall profits, if any, made by the various parties to the transaction, but what is not in dispute is that three members of the Government had bought shares – directly or at one remove – from the managing director of a company seeking contracts from the Government. The American company was independent of the British one, but the latter held over half the shares of the former. Isaacs was managing director of both; and independent or not, the shares of the American company could not but be affected by the massive contract about to be given to the British one. And finally the ministers had bought the shares *before* they were available to the public at especially favourable rates. They may not have been guilty of anything illegal, but as an act of political indiscretion it was monumental.

Rumours began to fly, and Cecil Chesterton (brother of G. K.), editor of the viciously anti-Semitic *New Witness*, which frequently fed its readers with hints of Jewish skulduggery, now felt he had something to go to town on. And go to town he did, with headlines screaming: MARCONI SCANDAL!

Isaacs' brother is Chairman of the Marconi Company. It had therefore been secretly arranged between Isaacs and Samuel that the British people shall give the Marconi Company a very large sum of money through the agency of the said Samuel, and for the benefit of the said Isaacs. Incidentally, the monopoly that is about to be granted to Isaacs No 1 and his colleague, the Postmaster-General, is a monopoly involving antiquated methods, the refusal of competing tenders far cheaper and far more efficient, and the saddling of this country with corruptly purchased goods, which happen to be inferior goods.[12]

Samuel had at no time touched a share of the Marconi company, American or British, nor had he in any other way profited by the contract, but his name had to be pulled in somehow to fit in to the theory, advanced by the *New Witness* that the whole affair was a Jewish ramp. They could not show that Samuel himself had derived any material benefit from it; they suggested that it was a matter of a Jew helping Jews, but in dragging in his name Chesterton and Co. weakened their case, for Samuel's role in the whole affair was entirely above suspicion. A standing sub-committee on Imperial Defence had recommended that the Marconi system was the best available, which placed Godfrey Isaacs – a shrewd negotiator – in a strong bargaining position, and the terms he exacted were high. But here again Samuel was hardly to blame for he had acted on the advice of the Permanent Secretary of his department.

In our own times a number of contractors – Ferranti and Bristol Aircraft, for example – have made such excessive profits, that they were later forced to disgorge some of them by the Public Accounts Committee, but never even in the heat of political debate, has there been any suggestion that the Ministers involved were corrupt. Political animosities were perhaps fiercer at the beginning of the century than they are now. Anti-Semitism was certainly more virulent. The scurrility of the *New Witness* was exceptional, but more than an echo of its views was to be found in Leo Maxse's *National Review*, the *Spectator*, *Morning Post* and the *Standard*. The imprudence of Rufus Isaacs, Lloyd George, and Elibank – who conveniently went off on a business trip to Colombia till the hue and cry died down – was unbelievable, but it is unlikely that Samuel's name would have been dragged into the affair at all if he had not been Jewish.

"For my part," he wrote to his mother, "I have nothing of any kind to reproach myself with in connection with this unpleasant business from first to last, and that is fully recognised by the Prime Minister (who has told me that no action of mine is fairly open to the smallest criticism) and by the Cabinet."[13]

On the other hand he was aware of his colleagues' indiscretions, which made his own disclosures less than candid. "Neither I myself nor any of my colleagues at any time held one shilling's worth of shares in this company, directly or indirectly",[14] which was perfectly true, but he surely must have known that the shareholding of Rufus Isaacs and Lloyd George in America was of more than incidental interest. His loyalty was greater than his candour.

While Samuel was defending himself on this front, he found himself attacked on another. Montagu's, as one of the leading bullion dealers in the country, were naturally large suppliers of silver to India. Edwin Montagu was at the time Under-Secretary of State for India, but not a member of the bank, and neither of course, was Samuel. But Sir Stuart Samuel, Liberal M.P. for Tower Hamlets, was, and it was suggested that between them they got the bank preferential treatment.

"What a party," declared one Tory M.P., "which has two members of the family in the Government, another brother who is a member of Parliament and another who is a member of the House of Peers and all of them are making money out of Indian finance. The Under-Secretary of State for India is a Mr Samuel; the Postmaster-General is a Mr Samuel, then there is Lord Swaythling, a pretty name for one who was a Samuel – the Infant Samuel – and also a Sir Something Samuel, all of whom were created by the Radical Party. All the silver in India is financed by the House of Samuel."[15]

One paper was inspired to poetry:

> This little Samuel went to India
> This little Samuel stayed at home.
> This little Samuel had Marconi,
> This little Samuel had none.
> This little Samuel said please, please, please
> PLEASE don't press it home.

The matter was pressed home by one Tory M.P. after another. The papers took up the chorus, but a public inquiry revealed no high crimes or misdemeanours, but only indiscretions. It showed that silver contracts which had in earlier years gone to Mocatta and Goldsmid, had been awarded to Montagu about the time that Edwin Montagu joined the India Office, but there was no proof that the one had anything to do with the other. The deal was dictated entirely by the exigencies of the market.

There was nothing to show that Samuel had the remotest connection with the entire transaction, but it was found that his brother Stuart, as a partner in Montagu's, had, contrary to the law as it then stood, voted on issues in which he had a private interest, and was forced to resign.

Samuel at this period is depicted in H. G. Wells' satirical novel *The New Machiavelli*, as the cold, pompous, desiccated Lewis, "able, industrious and invariably uninspired, with a wife in revolt against the racial traditions of feminine servitude".

At dinner one evening he is questioned about his political programme:

> Lewis laughed nervously, and thought we were "Seeking the Good of the Community".
> "How?"
> "Beneficent legislation," said Lewis.
> "Beneficent in what direction?". . .
> "Amelioration of Social Conditions", said Lewis.
> "That's only a phrase."
> "You wouldn't have me sketch bills at dinner?"
> "I'd like you to indicate directions."
> "Upward and on," said Lewis with conscious neatness, and turned to ask Mrs Bunting Harblow about her little boy's French.[16]

The picture though not too unkind is not wholly accurate. Samuel, it is true, never wore his heart on his sleeve, and even within his close family circle, he rarely registered intense feeling. ". . . he was never emotional", wrote his son. "He always seemed to be embarrassed when on our meeting again after a long absense, I kissed him lightly on his stubbly cheek."[17] His Liberalism was cerebral rather than sentimental and some of his critics felt that he was not in fact all that Liberal.

On female suffrage, for example, possibly because of what Wells had called "the racial tradition of feminine servitude",[18] Samuel was fairly conservative. The women, he felt, had a case, but their demands were premature, and one Day of Atonement, while he was at prayer in the New West End Synagogue, three Jewish suffragettes rose from their place, and in a ringing chorus cried:

May God forgive Herbert Samuel and Rufus Isaacs for denying freedom
to women. May God forgive them for consenting to the torture of women.[19]

In 1914 Samuel became president of the Local Government Board,
an office which gave him control of both health and housing. It was one
of the most arduous and least glamorous offices in the Cabinet involving
a plethora of administrative detail on local government boundaries, and
sewers and drains, but Samuel had a genius for such detail and positively relished the challenge. His farsightedness and tidiness of mind
went with a vivid imagination. He denounced the British heritage of
drabness, "the long, mean, treeless streets of our cities; our towns, ill-
planned, ill-provided with open spaces; the overcrowded houses; the
slums. . . . We have cared too much for the rights of property and too
little for the rights of life."[20]

In 1915 Samuel's career received a severe setback. Asquith felt that
the challenge facing the nation in an all-out war demanded a Government of national unity. When he brought Tories into the administration, a number of Liberal Cabinet Ministers had to resign and
Samuel was one of them.

Although Asquith had a good opinion of Samuel's clarity of mind,
he did not regard him as one of his most valued colleagues. In a list he
compiled for his amusement, Crewe, Lloyd George, Churchill and
Kitchener were among the top five or six. Samuel was among the
expendables at the bottom.[21] But there was the usual polite exchange
of notes, and Asquith protested how heavily the decision had weighed
with him. "No one knows how much I have suffered."[22]

He asked Samuel to return as Postmaster-General. Thus he remained
a member of the Government but was excluded from the Cabinet –
"only for a time", Asquith had assured him – but it felt like a long time.
He was back in his office at G.P.O. headquarters in the City, away from
Whitehall, away from the centre of power, in a comparatively minor
department, and he confessed to Asquith that after six years in the
Cabinet during which he had helped to shape national policy, the
exclusion was painful.[23]

He tried to occupy himself as fully as possible, but found insufficient
scope for his imagination and energies. For six months he moped and
fretted. On November 8, he wrote to Asquith pointing out that the
Financial Secretaryship to the War Office was vacant, could he have
that? The answer was no. Five days later Winston Churchill stormed
out of his office as Chancellor of the Duchy of Lancaster. Samuel
at once reminded Asquith of their exchange six months before:

Dear Prime Minister,

When the Coalition Government was formed and you asked me to resume the office of Postmaster-General, without a seat in the Cabinet, you were good enough to write that the suspension of Cabinet rank would be temporary; and when I saw you at the time you told me that, although the balance of number agreed with the Unionists (Tories) made it impossible for me to be included in the Cabinet, you would invite me to return to it at the first opportune vacancy among its Liberal members.

But then, having reminded Asquith of his promise, he went on to reassure him that he had nothing so ignoble in mind:

> . . . if you think it more in the public interest to leave Churchill's place unfilled than to act upon the assurances you very kindly gave me last May, I write to say, that glad as I should be to participate again in the work which I shared for six years, I ask you not to take these personal considerations into account.[24]

The message, however oblique, got through. "I remember well the assurances which I gave you," Asquith told him. "I am very anxious (apart from any assurance) to have you back again as a colleague in the Cabinet." Samuel became Chancellor of the Exchequer *and* Postmaster-General.

Samuel had a perfectly understandable hunger for office – he would have been a most unnatural politician if he had not – yet he somehow felt that there was something ignoble in such a hunger, and liked to think he was above it. He may have convinced himself that he was. He certainly convinced his son, who was not uncritical of him in other ways: "He lacked the ambition, the ruthlessness, that might have given him higher office." He was certainly not ruthless, but he was ambitious, and his attempts to keep the fact from himself involved him on more than one occasion in a degree of equivocation that could be described as both Jesuitical, or should one say, Talmudic?

In January 1916 Samuel was appointed Home Secretary, the highest office he was to reach. It involved vast responsibilities in wartime and his powers, extended by defence regulations, were almost dictatorial.

Throughout 1915 and 1916 the war went badly for the allies on almost every front and after two years of humiliation and catastrophe there was disgruntlement in the country with the Government, and disgruntlement within the Government with the leadership. The Tories who had been brought into the administration in 1915 had neither loyalty to nor confidence in Asquith and there was imperfect unity within the Liberal ranks.

In July 1916 Lloyd George succeeded Kitchener as War Secretary. Asquith's wife was convinced that he would not rest content there. "We are out," she noted in her diary, "it is only a question of time when we shall have to leave Downing Street."[25] Five months later her prediction was fulfilled.

The large Cabinet formed by Asquith in 1915 proved unwieldy, and a War Committee, a sort of inner Cabinet, was formed to deal with the day-to-day conduct of the war. Lloyd George quickly emerged as the dominant member and with the help of Bonar Law and other leading Tories he manoeuvred Asquith out of office. It was a long, intricate and sordid operation, which ended Asquith's career and led eventually to the destruction of the Liberal Party. "I felt no doubt," Samuel noted charitably, "that throughout those proceedings Lloyd George was genuinely convinced that, if he carried them through, he would be rendering an outstanding service to the country in its hour of peril."[26] At the same time Samuel felt compelled to stay out of the new coalition headed by Lloyd George. There had been reports to the contrary in *The Times* and other papers, and he assured Asquith that they were without foundation. He would "in no circumstances" serve under Lloyd George.

On the following day he was summoned by Lloyd George. There were, said Lloyd George, only two members of the old Cabinet whom he wished to include in the new one, Edwin Montagu and himself. The king, he said, had a particularly high regard for his abilities, and that at such a time he had a duty to serve.[27]

Samuel was flattered but told him frankly that he did not think the Government would last. He was also unhappy about the way the change of Government had been brought about, and to take office would be to acquiesce in it. "We parted on friendly terms", he noted.[28]

The terms were rather less friendly than he imagined, and the thought of his refusal still rankled with Lloyd George when he wrote his *War Memoirs* seventeen years later:

> In order to test the attitude of my old colleagues towards the Government, I determined to make an offer of Office to one of them, who had not displayed any antagonism to me personally. I therefore invited Sir Herbert Samuel to join the Government. He had taken no part in any of the intrigues that went on. He had always done his own snaring. He was a competent and industrious administrator, and I was persuaded that he could preside with neat efficiency over one of the Offices which owing to the War did not demand exceptional gifts of an original kind. Before the war he had won the reputation of being capable and useful in every

official sphere he had occupied. During the war he had done nothing in particular, but he had done it very well.[29]

The following morning Samuel called on Asquith and told him of his conversation with Lloyd George. "I said that my refusal of Office was definite but that if he [Asquith] would wish me to go into the Ministry, I would reconsider my position, but only at his request."

If Samuel hoped that Asquith might coax him to accept the offer, he was disappointed. "He said he could not advise me one way or the other. Each of his former colleagues must arrive at his own decision. I said that the matter would therefore, of course, remain as it stood."[30]

The Liberal Party was now in two. One section had joined Lloyd George; the other, which included most of the major party figures, remained with Asquith. From time to time one member or another from among the latter tiptoed over to the former. Samuel remained constant.

Parliament was dissolved shortly after the armistice in 1918 and in the election which followed, the Asquith Liberals were routed, and reduced to a meagre handful of twenty-six. Asquith and Samuel lost their seats.

Samuel was out of office and out of Parliament, rejected and dejected, but the most memorable phase of his career was yet ahead.

The entry of Turkey into the war on the side of the Central Powers meant the end of the Ottoman empire as it was then known, and various plans were prepared for the disposal of its various territories. The position of Palestine on the eastern flank of the Suez Canal was of crucial importance. In December 1914, in a Cabinet memorandum, Samuel had suggested the annexation of the area as a protectorate under the British Crown, and the re-creation within it of a new centre of Jewish life.

"Already there is a stirring among the twelve million scattered throughout the countries of the world", he wrote. "A feeling is spreading with great rapidity that now, at least, some advance may be made, in some way, towards the fulfilment of the hope and desire, held with unshakable tenacity for 1,800 years, for the restoration of the Jews to the land to which they are attached by ties almost as ancient as history itself."

He then went on to depict the prospects of such a centre as "the home of a brilliant civilisation. It would enable England," he wrote, "to fulfil in yet another sphere her historic part of the civiliser of the backward countries."

As he warmed to his point his terms grew more resonant and he finished with a crescendo:

The Jewish brain is a physiological product not to be despised. For fifteen centuries the race produced in Palestine a constant succession of great men – statesmen and prophets, judges and soldiers. If a body be given in which its soul can lodge, it may again enrich the world. Till full scope be granted, as Macaulay said in the House of Commons, "let us not presume to say that there is no genius among the countrymen of Isaiah, no heroism among the descendants of the Maccabees."[31]

Asquith blinked when he read it. It was unusual for Cabinet Ministers to express themselves in such language, least of all Samuel.

"It reads like a new edition of 'Tancred' brought up to date", he noted in his diary. "I confess I am not attracted by the proposed addition to our responsibilities, but it is a curious illustration of Dizzy's favourite maxim that 'race is everything' to find this almost lyrical outburst proceeding from the well-ordered and methodical brain of H. S."[32]

Samuel was not a Zionist and had until then taken no particular interest in Zionist problems. He stemmed from a sector of Jewish society which was anti-Zionist almost to a man, and he had tried to approach the issue from a purely British standpoint, but the matter, as he noted in his *Memoirs*, had "an additional and special interest" for him, as the first Jew in the Cabinet, and he therefore sought a meeting with Dr Chaim Weizmann, to learn something of the aims and achievements of the Zionist movement.

A friendship developed between them which continued, in spite of many differences, till the end of their days.[33] With the guidance of Weizmann, Samuel settled down to a serious study of Zionist literature:

The more I read the more I was impressed by the spiritual influences that evidently animated the movement; by the sacrifices that were being made, and the results already achieved, by the pioneer groups of Jewish settlers, who had succeeded in entering the country and establishing themselves there; as well as by the agricultural and industrial possibilities of the country itself. The importance of the question to the strategic interests of Great Britain stood out clearly.[34]

One almost notes in all this a determination to disclaim any emotional involvement. He may have felt that he had let his feelings run away a little in his first memorandum to Asquith, and sat down to prepare a more formal and sober document, which he circulated among his Cabinet colleagues in March 1915. It was published in full for the first time in Mr John Bowle's excellent biography in 1956, and it shows beyond doubt that if any one person may be said to have fathered the Balfour Declaration, it was Samuel.

"If war results in the break-up of the Turkish empire in Asia," he asked, "what is to be the future of Palestine?"[2]

He posed five alternatives: annexation by France; continuation under Turkey; internationalism; the creation of an autonomous Jewish state; and finally, a British protectorate.

He found no difficulty in dismissing the first three, and while he was favourably disposed towards the fourth, he felt that "the time is not ripe for it. . . . To attempt to realise the aspiration of a Jewish state one century too soon might throw its actual realisation for many centuries more." And he resorted to the last.

He was possibly naïve in his view that "a British protectorate . . . would be welcomed by a large proportion of the present population", but elsewhere he writes with extraordinary vision:

> The gradual growth of a considerable Jewish community under British suzerainty in Palestine will not, indeed, solve the Jewish question in Europe.
>
> A country the size of Wales, much of it barren mountain and part of it waterless, cannot hold 9,000,000 people. But it probably could hold in time 3,000,000 and some relief would be given to the pressure in Russia and elsewhere. Far more important would be the effect upon the character of the larger part of the Jewish race who must still remain intermingled with other peoples, to be a strength or to be a weakness to the countries in which they live. Let a Jewish centre be established in Palestine, let it achieve, as it may well achieve, some measure of spiritual and intellectual greatness, and insensibly the character of the Jew, wherever he might be, would be raised.[35]

His main concern was to show the immense benefits Britain would derive from her espousal of the Zionist cause. She would win, he argued, the gratitude of Jews throughout the world. "In the United States, where they number about two million and in all the other lands where they are scattered, they would form a body of opinion whose bias, where the interest of the country of which they were citizens was not involved, would be favourable to the British empire."

Palestine, he believed, would form a new and particularly lustrous jewel in the Imperial Crown, particularly if it was retained as "a means of aiding Jews to reoccupy the country". And he continued:

> Widespread and deep-rooted in the Protestant world is a sympathy with the idea of restoring the Hebrews to the land which was to be their inheritance, and intense interest in the fulfilment of the prophecies which have foretold it.

This last point was particularly valid, for it was the Protestant allies of Zionism who helped the Balfour Declaration to prevail against the concerted might of the Cousinhood.

But even the revised and more considered memo did not impress Asquith. It was, he said 'dithyrambic' and added:

> Curiously enough, the only other partisan of this proposal is Lloyd George, who, I need not say, does not care a damn for the Jews or their past or their future, but thinks it will be an outrage to let the Holy Places pass into the possession or under the protectorate of "agnostic, atheistic France!"[36]

Whatever Lloyd George may have felt about the past or future of the Jews the idea did genuinely excite him and at the end of the war, he invited Samuel to become first High Commissioner for Palestine. It was, said Sir Ronald Storrs, "a stroke of genius".[37]

As a result of the post-war settlement Palestine was designated a Mandated territory under the League of Nations, with Britain as the mandatory power answerable to the League. In effect it was ruled as a Crown Colony under the Colonial Office, and the High Commissioner had all the powers and privileges (and limitations) of a colonial governor. And, like a colonial governor, Samuel was knighted. In June 1920 Sir Herbert Samuel, Knight Grand Cross of the Order of the British Empire, sailed for Palestine. Britain had assumed the role of Persia in Jewish history, Balfour of Cyrus, and Samuel, prophet and courtier, Nehemiah.

In August, on the Sabbath following the Fast of Ab, which commemorates the destruction of the Second Temple and the beginning of Jewish exile, Samuel walked from Government House, on the outskirts of Jerusalem, to the Churban Synagogue in the Old City, and there, in keeping with the tradition of that day, read from the Book of Isaiah:

> Comfort ye, comfort ye my people, saith your God. Speak ye comfortably to Jerusalem, and cry unto her that her warfare is accomplished.[38]

The hour of redemption seemed to be at hand, but after the euphoria came disillusionment.

Samuel had warned Lloyd George at the outset that his appointment as High Commissioner "was open to the dangers that measures, which the non-Jewish population would accept from a British Christian governor, might be objected to if offered by a Jew".[39] In the event it was the Jews who felt that in showing his fair-mindedness he was being unfair to them, and their feelings may not have been wholly unfounded.

There had been Arab riots in the spring of 1920 in which six Jews were slaughtered. The army intervened and arrested not only the Arab ringleaders, but Vladimir Jabotinski, who headed a small group of Jewish defenders. Samuel celebrated his arrival with an amnesty in which both attackers and defenders were freed.

In 1921 the office of Mufti of Jerusalem, the religious head of the Moslem community, fell vacant and Samuel, after some hesitancy, appointed Haj Amin El Husseini, a member of a prominent Arab family. He was well qualified for the post, but he had been among the instigators of the riots of the previous year and had benefited from the amnesty. "In spite of the proverb," Weizmann observed bitterly, "poachers turned gamekeepers are not always a success."[40] Husseini, with the large funds of the chief Moslem religious foundation at his disposal, became a constant source of mischief.

Later in the year there were further Arab riots. They were quickly quelled, and quickly followed by an announcement – made by Samuel himself to Arab notables at Ramleh – that Jewish immigration was being temporarily suspended. Intimidation seemed to have its immediate reward.

The error which rankled longest in Zionist memories was the Beisan award. The administration found itself in possession of over 100,000 acres of rich, well-watered, fertile soil between the Sea of Galilee and Beisan which had once been the property of Sultan Abdul Hamid. The authorities were required by the terms of the mandate to "encourage . . . close settlement by Jews on the land, including State lands".[41] But Bedouin tribesmen who had been using the land for some time claimed squatters rights and Samuel upheld their claims. To the Jewish settlers who were trying to extort a livelihood from the barren hills of Galilee, the disposal of a vast fertile tract in this way was sacrilege.

The hopes which Samuel had roused thus gave way to bitterness. "We regarded him with reverence when he came," Ben-Gurion told the 1921 Zionist Congress. "But what did he give us? Haj Amin El Husseini as Mufti of Jerusalem."[42]

Yet taken over all, the five years of Samuel's administration, though not the golden years of the mandate, were a period of continuous progress. The Jewish population doubled from 55,000 in 1918 to 103,000 in 1925, mainly by immigration. Tel Aviv had grown from a township of 2,000 to a town of 30,000; Haifa, from 2,000 to 8,000. The waters of the upper Jordan, the Yarmuk were harnessed for electric power.[43] New industries were introduced. The standard of living was rising, the country was being transformed.

Weizmann was at times distressed by his handling of affairs, but in viewing events in perspective he could understand the difficulties which Samuel faced, the benefits he had brought, and wrote to express his gratitude:

> My dear Sir Herbert,
> I feel impelled to send you a line which will reach you only a few days before you leave Palestine. It is I think almost ten years . . . since I had the privilege of first meeting you. . . . Much has happened in this fateful decade and you were privileged – to my great joy – to play a fundamental part in the laying of the foundation of the Jewish National Home. You are leaving the country confident that the work you have done, and the wisdom with which you have guided the destinies of Palestine, have created stable conditions which will enable us to carry on further what you have begun so successfully.[44]

Sir Ronald Storrs, the Governor of Jerusalem, was particularly impressed by his resourcefulness, his fair-mindedness, his Job-like patience, his evenness of temper. "This even calm," he wrote, "was by some ascribed to his supposed incapacity for feeling either anger or joy; by those who read him better to an early acquired philosophic control. . . ."[45]

His stay in Palestine amid the shrines of Judaism, Christianity and Islam, its ancient memories and ceaseless antagonisms, had caused him to think anew on an issue which he thought he had settled during his undergraduate days at Oxford.

"What did I believe?" he asked himself. "With Judaism I kept a formal connection, and attended religious services on occasion. But the ritual did not command me; it seemed to have little relation to the known universe or to the living societies of man. The Christian ethic drew me, but the essentials were already in Judaism, and the theology could not be accepted."[46]

He planned to spend some years in reconsidering his ideas and putting his thoughts into writing. The prospect of such a life filled him with pleasure, but alas, the prospect was all he enjoyed.

He was *en route* for a holiday in Italy when a telegram arrived from Tory Prime Minister, Stanley Baldwin. The coal industry, on which much of the British economy was based, was in crisis, and a Royal Commission was being established to look into its problems. Would Samuel be chairman?

It was a small Commission consisting of Samuel, Sir William Beveridge the economist, and two industrialists. They sat for six months taking evidence, and sifting a great mass of technical information. They also visited twenty-five mines and examined reports on a further forty. Their report, which was unanimous, made far-reaching proposals on the future of the industry and was on the whole favourable to the miners.

But there was also an immediate issue at stake. The mine-owners had argued that with prevailing wage levels they could no longer market coal without loss, and the Commission agreed that wages must come down. The miners countered with their slogan: "Not a minute off the day, not a penny off the pay."

On Monday May 3, 1926, the miners went on strike. On Tuesday they were joined by railwaymen, dockers and road-transport men. Iron and steel, gas and electricity, newspapers, all followed in rapid succession. By the end of the week two-and-a-half million men were on strike. The country was paralysed.

Samuel, who was back in Italy, packed his bags and returned to London once more to enter into negotiations with trade union leaders. He acted in a purely private capacity, but his efforts enjoyed the blessing of the Government and he finally reached a formula that there would be no wage cuts until there were "sufficient assurances that the measures of reorganisation proposed by the Commission would be effectively adopted". The Government would in the meantime provide a subsidy to maintain the wage levels. The T.U.C. regarded it "as a satisfactory basis for the reopening of negotiation", but the miners did not. On May 12 the T.U.C. special negotiating committee removed its backing for the miners and called off the General Strike. Britain returned to normal.

During the hectic week of negotiations Samuel stayed with his brother Stuart in his large house in Hill Street, Mayfair. On the day the strike ended Sir Stuart complained that he felt a little unwell and went to bed early. The next morning his wife knocked on the door and there was no answer. She called Samuel who rushed to his room and found him dead. He had suffered a heart-attack in the night. He was sixty-nine.

Samuel had suffered a particularly harassing period of office as High Commissioner and had looked forward to a prolonged idyll on Lake Garda. But he had been pulled back first by the Coal Commission, then by the General Strike. He had hardly returned to Italy again when he received news that Gilbert, his sole surviving brother, was also dead. And he left for London once more.

After Gilbert's funeral he found a delegation from the Liberal Party waiting for him. The party had been split in 1918 between Asquith and Lloyd George. They had managed to come together for an uneasy truce later but had-fared disastrously at the polls. After Asquith had lost his seat in 1924 Lloyd George was elected leader, but the friction continued, and Samuel was pressed to return to politics and head the party machine as the only eminent Liberal acceptable to both wings of the party. Again Samuel could not say no.

His tact, his organisational ability, his experience, his very presence injected a new spirit into the torn and dejected party. During five by-elections in 1928 Liberals triumphed in three, a useful fillip to a party which had been reduced to forty-two seats. As 1929 and a new General Election approached, Liberal hopes rose, but the result was a disappointment. Samuel himself was returned in a three-cornered fight in the Darwen division of Lancashire, but of the five hundred Liberal candidates in the field only fifty-eight were elected. Labour under Ramsay MacDonald was returned for the first time as the largest party with 289 seats, and the Tories with 260. The Liberals held the balance.

The economic depression which had hit Central Europe and America in 1929, reached Britain the following year and rapidly grew in intensity. By the middle of 1931 there were nearly 3,000,000 unemployed. Dole payments imposed an impossible burden on the public purse. Exports were almost at a standstill. There was a flight of foreign capital from British banks. The pound was in danger. Britain had returned to the gold standard shortly after the war; it was feared that she might now topple off.

Samuel had become deputy leader of the Parliamentary Liberal Party after the election but now, at the moment of crisis, Lloyd George was struck down with a serious illness and Samuel took his place. He and Baldwin were summoned to an urgent meeting at 10 Downing Street, where they were given the full facts of the situation. The budget deficit for the current year would be £40,000,000 and £170,000,000 for the next one. The Government proposed to initiate the most rigorous economies and high taxation which alone could eliminate the deficits and save the pound. The Liberals and Tories agreed with the measures to be taken, but the Labour Party was split and MacDonald had no choice but to resign.

The most obvious alternative seemed to be a Tory-Liberal coalition, but Samuel, who was summoned to Buckingham Palace for his opinion, advised against it, and urged upon George V the necessity for a National

Government. MacDonald and Baldwin were also summoned, but in the end it was Samuel's advice which prevailed. "His Majesty found Sir Herbert Samuel the clearest mind of the three and said that he had put the case for a National Government much clearer than either of the others", wrote the King's secretary, Sir Clive Wigram. "It was after his interview with Sir Herbert . . . that His Majesty became convinced of the necessity for the National Government."[47]

At the end of August a new Government was formed, but it was not as national as was hoped, for the mass of the Parliamentary Labour Party would have nothing to do with it. MacDonald was again Prime Minister, and he brought together a Cabinet which included three of his Labour followers, four Tories and two Liberals – Reading and Samuel. The former became Foreign Secretary, and Samuel went back to the Home Office.

The life of the Government was troubled and short. Confidence in the pound was not restored. The flight of capital continued, and within four weeks the administration formed to save the pound and keep it golden, was compelled to go off the gold standard.

The Tories now felt this was the time for a new election. Labour was torn; the Liberals were again quarrelling among themselves. Mac-Donald with only twelve Labour members behind him in the House, was effectively a Tory prisoner and they were able to convince him that the national interest required an immediate election. To get the overwhelming majority they wanted they would go to the country with MacDonald at their head, and seek a vote for a *National* Government. The stumbling block were the Liberals. The Tories were determined to force through a thorough-going protectionist policy. The Liberals with their free trade traditions would oppose such a fundamental change and it was desirable therefore to edge them out of the all party line-up. Leo Amery, a former Colonial Minister and one of the principal Tory tacticians, saw that the best way to do it was to pitch "Tariff demands high enough to make sure of getting rid of Samuel and, if possible, Reading". And the demands were pitched high, but to his dismay "Samuel swallowed the formula hook, line and sinker . . . there was no way of getting rid of him".[48]

Lloyd George, who was on his sick-bed, looked upon Samuel's decision to go along with the Tories as base betrayal[49] and when he recovered sufficiently to attend the House, he sat with the opposition.

Samuel from the very moment he heard talk of an election, tried to counter it. Dissolution at a time of crisis, he warned, would undermine international confidence in Britain. Neville Chamberlain, who was now rising fast in the Tory hierarchy, agreed that his case was "very-well reasoned",[50] but the advantages to the party of an election at such a time were too obvious, and the pressure among backbenchers too relentless to be overlooked. MacDonald gave way, a majority of the Cabinet decided on an election, and Samuel's quandary became acute. Should he resign? He felt he could not:

> The Government had been in office for only a month; no one could say that the task for which it had been formed had been achieved; on the contrary, the abandonment of the gold standard made the danger of a depreciated currency all the greater. If the widest possible measure of political unity had been needed in August, the need in September was not less but greater. Nor would our resignations or the threat of them prevent an election. As to the Tariff question, our withdrawal would merely give a freer hand to our opponents. . . .[51]

The result of the election was a Tory triumph. They won 208 seats. Labour lost 312, but Liberal pickings from the Labour debacle were slight, for the party was again divided. A section under Sir John Simon which had abandoned faith in free trade, broke away to form the Liberal National party, and were barely distinguishable from the Tories. The Samuelite group had thirty-three seats, the Simonites, thirty-five.

Samuel continued as Home Secretary, but his days in office were numbered. In January 1932 the Cabinet decided to impose a general tariff on all imports. Samuel warned that if the measure went through he and his Liberal colleagues would have to resign. MacDonald, anxious to maintain at least a façade of national unity, pleaded with them to remain and finally a unique formula was evolved. The Liberal Ministers would continue in the Government, but would 'agree to differ'. When the Import Duties Bill was introduced in February, Samuel rose to assail it from the front bench.

In the summer of 1932 an Imperial Economic Conference was held in Ottawa which resulted in a system of mutual trade preferences between Britain on one side, and her Dominions and Colonies on the other but these preferences would arise not through the lowering of trade barriers between them, but by raising them against third parties. There could be no agreement to differ on that. Samuel resigned from the Government, tarried on the government benches for a while, and finally led his followers over to the opposition.

Some critics of Samuel have accused him of a determination to cling to office which was exceeded only by that of MacDonald. Samuel's actions, though well intended, gained him much unpopularity and abuse.

Lord Davidson, who was for many years chairman of the Tory Central Office, looked upon him as a Machiavelli. "The Liberals were completely untrustworthy", he wrote of this 1931 period, "especially Samuel":

> . . . great man as he was out of politics, in politics he was very unreliable. He had a very clever brain that enabled him to be really dishonest without appearing to be so. . . . It was George Younger who said that you never knew which side Samuel was supporting, for his colours were always firmly nailed to the fence.
>
> Samuel had a brain of supreme quality, he saw the essentials very quickly, but he did not impress us politically. We didn't like him, the Tories never have liked him. . . .
>
> Samuel never committed himself to anything without a getaway.[52]

Lord Davidson offers no evidence to show on what the distrust was based. Part of it, no doubt, arose out of the fact that Samuel was a rather remote figure, a philosopher fallen among politicians: he was manifestly not one of the boys. He did not play their games, he did not have their habits, and the fact that he was a Jew could not have helped. It may be added that he was admired rather than liked in the Liberal Party. He became leader of the party in the Commons after Lloyd George joined the opposition in 1931, but he was no matey chieftain clasping a hand here, slapping a back there, and resorting now and again to the smoke-room of the House for a drink or two and small talk with the rank and file. He was no genial political mine host, and Lady Samuel was no Nancy Cunard. Lady Asquith, with great diffidence and some delicacy, tried to raise the matter with him, and urged him to give "small dinners in the House of Commons for us all to meet one another":

> For instance you might ask me to bring a guest from the other side, and I would bring a young Tory, perhaps Eddy Hartington, Oliver Stanley or Bob Boothby. You must not only see, and be courteous, to our *own* lot. . . . No one need dress for dinner, and you *must* make yourself popular and personally *know* more of your own and other groups in the House. It is vital if a man is to be a *Leader* that he should be *genial* and *elastic*. . . . Forgive me saying this, but I don't like the monopoly of entertaining to be among the Simonites. Small things give great pleasure.[53]

But the trouble was that Samuel was neither genial nor elastic, and devoid of all capacity to make himself appear to be what he was not.

He had nothing of the showman, and did not much like showmanship. He did not like parties, did not like going to them, and did not like giving them. Apart from anything else, his modest, somewhat drab Victorian family house in Porchester Terrace was not equipped for it, and although never mean with money for a good cause, he resented expense on a frivolous one.

His sober demeanour was contrary to the light-hearted tradition in English politics. A Gladstone could get away with it, and even Gladstone often got on the nerves of followers as well as opponents. Samuel proceeded on the assumption that high-mindedness, dedication and ability were enough; they were not, and in part he may have been disliked for his very qualities.

The suggestion that he trimmed his sail to every passing wind may be dismissed at once, for if he was that sort of sailor he was singularly unfortunate in his choice of craft. He may have joined the Liberals during their years of triumph, but thereafter he stuck to the party through thick and thin – and after 1918 its fortune was very thin indeed. Others scattered in all directions, sometimes in groups, sometimes singly. Churchill joined the Tory party; Christopher Addison, Liberal Minister of Munitions in the wartime coalition, went to Labour (to become eventually Lord Privy Seal and Labour Leader in the Lords); W. Wedgwood Benn (Anthony's father), who began life as a Liberal, likewise joined Labour. In 1931 came the wholesale defection of twenty-five Liberal M.P.s, led by Sir John Simon, who tarried for a while as Liberal Nationals before blending completely into the Tory party. And so the loyalist group became smaller and smaller. Leo Amery believed that there was a natural tendency towards a two-party system in Britain. In 1919 he had foretold, "the gradual hiving off of Liberals to right and left, finally leaving Samuel alone to toss up which party he should join".[54]

And it nearly came to that, except that one could imagine Samuel hanging on to his Liberal label even if he was the last man to wear it. The final word on Samuel's political career may perhaps be left with Arnold Toynbee, the distinguished historian, who knew him well: "The salient feature of his character was his integrity. . . ."[55]

In 1935 Samuel lost his seat in the House of Commons. He was sixty-five, but his political days were not quite over.

He had been offered a peerage by Asquith in 1916, and again by Baldwin in 1926 and he had declined on both occasions. In 1936, on the accession of George VI the offer was made a third time and, as Samuel confessed, it placed him in a dilemma. "I was, as I always had been, an opponent of the hereditary principle in the choice of legislators. I had sons and grandsons and it would seem to be an inconsistency to inaugurate an hereditary peerage myself."[56]

It was inconsistent, but perfectly human. He had sat in Parliament for twenty-two years, mostly on the front bench, and he liked to be on the scenes of power. There was little prospect of his being returned to the Commons as a Liberal and he had no intention of defecting to any other party. A seat in the Lords was not quite like a seat in the Commons, but it would still give him a voice in the affairs of the nation. In June 1937 he took his seat in the Upper House as Viscount Samuel of Mount Carmel and of Toxteth in the City of Liverpool.

There was a fine symbolism in his title. He had toyed with the idea of calling himself Lord Paddington. It would have been somewhat nearer to his physical location in Porchester Terrace, but out of keeping with his character. Carmel and Toxteth, the incongruous union of Zion and Liverpool, were nearer to the man than the smoky terminus of the Great Western Railway.

There was a fine symbolism too in his choice of motto: "Turn Not Aside." It summed up what was for him the motivating force of Liberalism.

His role in the foreign policy debates of those years was not perhaps consistent with that motto. He supported Chamberlain's Munich policy and the harassed Prime Minister so far appreciated his gesture as to offer him the office of Lord Privy Seal. It was tempting, and Samuel was sorely tempted. "It is the case," he wrote to Crewe, the Liberal leader in the Lords, "that on the chief questions now at issue I am much more in agreement with the line taken by the Government than with that officially adopted by the Liberal opposition. . . . If I am asked to take part in carrying into effect a policy with which I agree, ought I to refuse on party grounds?"[57]

Crewe pointed out some of the dangers of accepting office, but left him to wrestle with his own conscience and he finally felt compelled to say no. He may have differed from his Liberal colleagues, but he had no wish to become another Simon.

He now spent most of his time in writing, mostly on philosophical subjects. Statesmen, wrote his son, "thought him a good philosopher, philosophers a good statesman".[58] Most of his books, however, enjoyed wide critical acclaim and one in particular, *Belief in Action*, in which he attacked the cult of abstractions, gained him a considerable following as a popular philosopher.

As one of the leading Jews of his day he was deeply involved in the harrowing refugee problem created by the Nazis. He made a number of visits to the U.S. to establish an emergency fund and in all he helped to raise some £12,000,000. He also intervened with the Home Office to ease the red-tape round the visa regulations, and as a result ten thousand German Jewish children were admitted to Britain during a period of eight months.

When Parliament was sitting it was Samuel's custom, whatever the weather, to walk across the four royal parks, Kensington Gardens, Hyde Park, Green Park and St James's Park, from his Bayswater house to the House of Commons. He also belonged at one time to a group of Liberal dons, politicians and writers, known as 'the Sunday Tramps', who would wander each weekend through the quieter parts of the home counties, marching briskly, and debating, where breath would permit them, the events of the day.

These days were now sadly over.

He was acknowledged, even in old age, as one of the best speakers in either the Commons or the Lords. He had a first class mind, but he also took infinite pains to prepare himself for even the most trivial occasion. Lord Hill of Luton, himself no mean speaker, saw him as one of the last relics "of the old school of Parliamentarians . . . serene, wise, witty".[59]

On one occasion during a long, dry speech from a Tory Peer he was observed on the front bench with eyes shut. The speaker paused. "The noble viscount opposite seems to be asleep."

Samuel opened an eye. "Unfortunately not."[60]

During the war years his fame spread beyond Parliament when, with Dr C. E. M. Joad, Julian Huxley and others he became a member of the popular B.B.C. 'Brains Trust' programme. With his calm voice, careful phrases, and deliberate tone, he seemed to be the very embodiment of sagacity.

He had enjoyed good health throughout his life. He distrusted and disapproved of medicaments and felt that there were few ills which could not be cured by a whiff of fresh air. He was greatly irritated by his wife's hyperchondrical pill-gulping. All her life she complained of ill health. Towards the end of his life, he agreed to take some vitamin tablets, but insisted that they were food and not medicine.

In 1956 the half a million Jews of Great Britain celebrated the tercentenary of Jewish settlement in this country with a great banquet in the Guildhall. It was natural that Samuel, who was a source of deep pride to his co-religionists, should be asked to preside. The Prime

Minister, Sir Anthony Eden, was present, as well as the leader of the Opposition and the Lord Mayor and Sheriffs of the City of London. The Duke of Edinburgh proposed the toast to the Anglo-Jewish community, and Samuel replied.

In 1959 Lady Samuel died. She was eighty-eight. For a time the stoicism, which had characterised Samuel for so much of his life, left him. He could not speak of her without a catch in his vioce, or tears in his eyes. They had been married for sixty-two years and, minor irritants apart, had been an extremely devoted couple.

Samuel was now in his ninetieth year, a lonely figure, made lonelier by deafness. His family was scattered. He walked with the greatest difficulty. He loved Kensington Gardens, which was only five minutes away, but could not even get as far as that. Yet even in extreme old age he had an eye for improvisation. Round the corner from his house there was a vacant strip of ground between a garage wall and the road.[61] and he persuaded the owner to turn the strip into a small garden with benches, and he would sit there, among other old men, hunched over his walking stick. Old like the others, older, but his eyes still luminous and alert.

He died in February 1963 in his ninety-third year.

CHAPTER 26

John Bull Papa
Sir Robert Waley Cohen

In 1917, Robert Waley Cohen, managing director of the Shell Transport and Trading Company, and one of the principal architects of the Shell combine, was appointed Petroleum Adviser to the War Office and asked to complete a form giving all his physical measurements. He looked down the sheet with mounting irritation, grabbed a pencil and scrawled 'huge' in block capitals right across it.

And HUGE he was, well over six foot in height, with massive, hunched shoulders, head thrust forward, long arms, fingers like bananas – and the appearance and stance of an all-in-wrestler.

Though president of the United Synagogue for many years, he was not an observant Jew, yet there was one ritual which he did take seriously and that was the Priestly Blessing, which descendants of the Temple priesthood – and as a Cohen he was one – traditionally bestowed on their fellow Jews on Passover, Pentecost and the Feast of Tabernacles. On these occasions he would be by the Ark of the Covenant in the Central Synagogue, Great Portland Street, his two sons by his side, reciting the ancient blessing of Aaron:

> The Lord bless thee, and keep thee,
> The Lord make His face shine upon thee,
> And be gracious unto thee.
> The Lord turn His face upon thee,
> And give thee peace.

But even a blessing in his mouth sounded like a threat, and with his prayer-shawl over his head, and arms outstretched he looked like some dark, avenging angel, except that angels in Jewish lore were created to receive orders, whereas Cohen believed he was born to give them. He was nature's own managing director.

When he was asked to become Petroleum Adviser he was offered the rank of colonel. He would not have it.

He wished, he said to be made "one of the higher sorts of General".

"To command what?" they asked.

"Other Generals," he said.[1]

Robert Waley Cohen, or Bob as he was known among his friends, or Uncle Bob as he was generally referred to in the Cousinhood, was a member of the remarkable Cohen dynasty. His father Nathaniel, or Natty, was the eleventh son of Louis Cohen of Gloucester Place, a brother of Lionel Cohen, a brother-in-law of Samuel Montagu and Sir Joseph Sebag-Montefiore, and a partner in Louis Cohen & Sons. Like his brothers, he retired with a fortune when the bank was dissolved in 1901.

In 1873 Natty married Julia Waley, a name which, like Mocatta and Montefiore, has been maintained through the distaff line. She was a small, wiry woman, keen on horses and horsemanship. Natty was a large, ungainly man who had never even learned to ride. This may seem a strange deficiency in a family now renowned for its love of horses, but when Natty was young the Cohens were still an urban clan with urban habits. Horses to them were merely things which pulled carriages and fouled highways.

The Cohen children knew better. They were six in number. Jacob the eldest, known as Jack, Robert and Charles, and three sisters, Hetty, Dorothea and Madge, and they were virtually brought up on horseback. Hetty was crippled by polio at the age of two and suffered from severe asthma, but neither handicap kept her from riding, although she had to use a specially designed saddle.

The family lived at Round Oak, a large country house standing in fifteen acres of ground near Windsor Great Park. There were twenty bedrooms, and the place was loud with the sound of visiting cousins and children, especially at weekends.

There was a mulberry tree in the garden which was said to have been planted by Elizabeth I, and a vast chestnut tree, in whose shade the family often had tea on hot afternoons. There were also two tennis courts, one grass and one asphalt, and a gymnasium. They had all the necessary externals for a wholesome happy life, and they enjoyed it unashamedly.

Natty and his wife were unusual for their time and class in that they did not allow servants to form a *cordon sanitaire* between them and their children. Julia in particular, though not Orthodox herself, supervised the religious upbringing of the children, and saw to it that Jewish dietary laws were strictly observed. The day would begin and end with prayer, and on Sundays the Reverend Fay came down from the Central Synagogue to give the children religious instruction. Yet the congregationalism which is so basic an element of Jewish religious life, played no part in their existence. In their Windsor redoubt they were totally removed from all contact with the Jewish community.

There was a large school-room for the children at Round Oak. In addition to their usual studies each child was expected to acquire some musical skill. Hetty learned the piano: Bob, because of his very large hands, the 'cello. Both became highly skilled performers and often entertained friends and family gatherings with duets. Bob did not have the appearance of a musician and the 'cello in his hands looked like a weapon – till he started playing. Out of the strong came forth sweetness. It was one of his many unexpected delicate qualities.

Bob and his brother went to a prep school in Wimbledon, and from there to Clifton, whose Jewish house was at that time thick with Cohens. He was not a brilliant pupil. 'Backward but working well', was the first term's report. 'Satisfactory but stupid', was the second,[2] but he worked hard and improved and, with the help of private tuition during his long holidays, he won a science scholarship to Emmanuel College, Cambridge.

Bob maintained an affection for Clifton all his life. He sent both his sons there, and later, as a member of the school council, he was instrumental in bringing it intact through two of the most serious crises in its history.[3] But he was not always happy there. Percival, the founder, had been a master at Rugby and carried over all the traditions of Rugby, not all of which were to the liking of Bob. He was not athletic, nor did he care for games. Also he was unhappy about the crushing conformity that was imposed on the boys and at times he rebelled.

He occasionally found himself charged with the obligations of wealth, but without the means, and wrote home:

> Jack has asked me to write to you for something to give to the servants before we go away. . . . Do you not think we had better give them fifteen shillings each of us, as other people do, as it seems rather hard lines that they should get half as much because we are two brothers.[4]

He does not appear to have suffered from any anti-Semitism to speak of, but when *The Merchant of Venice* was being read in class he confessed that it was "a little unpleasant for me and the other Jewish boys in my form".[5]

Whether Bob was or was not unhappy at Clifton, there can be no doubt that he came to think of the English public school as offering the best of all possible forms of education, and that for the Jewish boy there could be no better school than Clifton.

When he went on to Cambridge his father hoped that he might choose a political career and by way of encouragement bought him life membership of the Union; but Bob rarely went there and never spoke, and throughout his life had the deepest disdain for politics and politicians. He read science, but seems to have spent most of his time on music and played in a string quartet at Emmanuel.

He mixed little with Jewish undergraduates, but became friendly with Osmond d'Avigdor-Goldsmid, who while still at Cambridge inherited the Somerhill estate and a large fortune. He invited Bob to make a grand tour of the world with him. It was the chance of a lifetime and Bob took it, though it meant interrupting his studies. Various friends and relatives gave them introductions to prominent individuals in all parts of the world. They spent some time in India and the dominions and when they returned Bob read a paper on "British Character as Exemplified in India and the Colonies", which was in essence a reiteration of Kipling's idea of the white man's burden.

The Englishman in India, he declared, "far from being the John Bull Pasha, the irresponsible master of many slaves . . . acts the part of John Bull Papa. This is not only the case with the officials, who form the large majority of Englishmen in India, it is true of every Englishman who sets foot on Indian soil. . . . It is responsibility which appeals to the Englishman: it is power which appeals to the average human being. The one sobers: the other intoxicates. And of the two conditions the former is best suited to the accomplishment of great deeds. Thus it is that in India the Englishman is seen at his best. The Government is the government of English gentlemen in their capacity as such. . . ."[6]

Although this was written when Bob was twenty-two, and his biographer, Robert Henriques, quotes it with a blush,[7] it did in fact sum up Bob's philosophy on an important aspect of life and helps one to understand the role he assumed in later life as lay leader – the John Bull Papa – of the Anglo-Jewish community.

Bob came down from Cambridge with an unexceptional second class degree and took a job at the Meteorological Office. It carried vague responsibilities and no salary but it allowed him to continue on a line of research he had started at Cambridge. The arrangement displeased his father. He knew of people who enjoyed an income without work, but not of people who worked without income. He wanted Bob to have a proper job, and managed to get him one through a gentleman he met while riding in Hyde Park – Sir Marcus Samuel.

Natty would not normally have had anything to do with a Jew of such lowly origins, but Sir Marcus had risen in the world and was chairman of Shell, which was already a substantial concern. Natty asked him if he had an opening for Bob.

Sir Marcus did. Natty undertook to invest a substantial sum in Shell, and Bob would be taken on as a 'volunteer', with the prospect of higher office.

A few months later Bob noticed Sir Marcus among the High Holiday throng in the Central Synagogue, and after the service engaged him in conversation. Sir Marcus was impressed with the tall, ungainly earnest young man, and in the office next morning offered him a job directly under the partners at £500 a year. This in 1901 was a high salary. Bob respectfully declined, and said he would work for nothing until he was worth at least twice that much. In the following year Shell formed a joint marketing company with the Royal Dutch petroleum company and the French Rothschilds, to be known as 'The Asiatic'. Henry Deterding of Royal Dutch became managing director of Asiatic, with Bob as assistant manager. By 1904, when he was twenty-six, Bob was earning £2,000 a year, the equivalent of over £12,000 in our time. He could now marry a girl of his class and support her in the manner to which she was accustomed. The girl was Alice Beddington.

The Beddingtons were one of the branches of the prolific Moses family. Many of them were still in being after almost two centuries of settlement in England, but few of them were known as Moses. One famous branch of the family had assumed the name of Merton, another, a little more thoroughgoing, assumed the name of the village near which they lived – Beddington.

> They changed their name from Moses,
> but they cannot change their noses,[8]

went a jingle of the time.

The Beddingtons rapidly rose in society, bought country estates, stables, horses, distinguished themselves in the Army, became well-known sportsmen. Alice's father, Henry Beddington, was a well-known patron of the turf who led an almost itinerant life following horses round courses. His main base was at Newmarket, where he had a large country house and stables, but he would often rent houses to accommodate his family, servants and friends at Ascot, Epsom, Cheltenham, Goodwood and Doncaster – wherever there was a Classic. One could know his whereabouts by a glance at the calendar. And then, when the season was over, he would leave for an extended rest in the South of France.

His daughter Alice was brought up to share his affection for horses and racing and had a detailed knowledge of form. Bob's biographer, Robert Henriques, was the most gallant and chivalrous of men, and one can sense a touch of desperation in his efforts to bring Alice's positive qualities to the fore. She was, he said "warm and inordinately generous with very wide human sympathies, and a sincere interest in people of every class and sort". She had an "incongruous interest in mathematics extending to the calculus", but he was too honest a writer to overlook her defects.

"I do hope you are going to realise what a silly incompetent wife you are going to have," Alice wrote to Bob after their engagement and, as he discovered, she was not being modest. "She had no notion of keeping house", wrote Henriques, "and having never been without her personal maid, could scarcely look after herself. She could not, of course, sew on a button or pack a trunk and in fact had been taught very little of anything, except to behave naturally and spontaneously according to her sweet nature."[9]

She spent fortunes on clothes and, unknown to Bob, lost fortunes on gambling. This she did through her own private account and used her butler as bookie's runner. At one point, however, her losses assumed such proportions that her account could no longer carry them and she had to make a tearful confession to Bob, with the promise that she would never gamble again. She made a bonfire of her form books, credit cards and bookmakers' codes, but later relapsed, and on her death was in debt again.

Alice did not share Bob's love of music and appears to have been almost tone deaf, and although Henriques tries again to marshal all her qualities: "good complexion, blue-grey eyes, lovely hair, quite beautiful voice in conversation", he feels compelled to admit that she was "not pretty, on the contrary, she was often called plain".[10] But she was an only daughter of wealthy parents and Beddington let it be known that her prospective husband could expect a fortune.[11]

Henriques is at pains to dispel the suspicion which naturally arises that Bob married her for her money, but after their engagement there was a protracted wrangle between the families over the marriage settlement and the matter was finally taken to arbitration before a solution acceptable to both parties was reached. The wedding finally took place in June 1904.

A number of people who knew Alice well thought that Henriques' portrait was less than kind. One member of the Cousinhood who met her husband through Alice, said: "You'd think she was an imbecile from the way he describes her. She was a shrewd, sensible and sensitive woman, and kindness itself. I don't think Bob would have got as far as he did without Alice."

There was also something touching about her sense of inadequacy, her constant feelings that she was not good enough, not able enough, not wise enough. Despite her outward gaiety, she felt a sense of foreboding and nagging premonitions of death which were to be fulfilled in a dramatic way.

Her first children, Bernard and Hetty, were twins, born ten years after the marriage. A third child, Matthew, was born a few years later.

Bob and Alice began married life at a large house in Sussex Square, near Kensington Gardens, which her father gave her as a wedding present. She took her duties as a young housewife seriously, even to the extent of working out a careful annual budget:

House, rent, repairs, etc.	£400
Housekeeping £12 a week	624
Doctor etc.	30
Holidays, etc.	300
Servants' wages	100
Bob's personal money	400[12]

Alice allowed herself £220 for her own expenses, but it is unlikely that she spent as little as that, or Bob as much as £400, for in terms of personal expenditure he was the most frugal of beings and in the course of a year might spend less on clothes, food and drink than one of his junior assistants. Alice, on the other hand, was plainly extravagant.

She did not in fact have to confine herself to her budget, for quite apart from her own private income, Bob's salary increased dramatically. Within ten years of his marriage he was earning £25,000 a year, and five years later £40,000. The increase represented both the growth in the size of Shell and his rapid ascent to the top. In 1906 he became a director of Shell and Asiatic. In the following year came the merger between Shell and Royal Dutch.

As a result of the union two new companies were formed, the Baatafsche, based in Holland, which controlled production and refining, and the Anglo-Saxon Petroleum Company, based in London, which controlled transport and storage. The Asiatic continued as their joint marketing organisation. It was a complicated arrangement worked out by Bob on behalf of Shell and Deterding for Royal Dutch. Bob continued as a director both of Shell and Asiatic, and he was also the Dutch nominee to the boards of Baatafsche and Anglo-Saxon. There could have been no finer tribute to his ability.

Deterding, the effective controller of the combined group, made his headquarters in London, and Bob became his second in command.

Deterding was the great initiator and it fell to Bob to put his ideas into action, to marshal the ships, to appoint the men to discover the means.

But Bob also exercised his own initiative in many directions. During a tour of company agents and plant in India, for example, he found Standard, the Burmah Oil Company and Shell ranged against one another in murderous competition. The ideal solution, as he saw it was for Burmah and Shell to form a joint marketing board not unlike the Asiatic, but before making any such overture, he initiated an aggressive price-cutting campaign throughout India. Within a matter of months Burmah and Shell signed a marketing agreement to cover the entire sub-continent.

Such agreements, or better still, mergers, were Bob's panacea for almost all economic ills, and not only economic ones. During Deterding's many absences abroad Bob was left in command, and with the outbreak of World War I, when Shell, though foreign controlled, became an arm of the allied war effort, Deterding thought it prudent to let Bob move to the fore.

Marcus Samuel was aflame with patriotism and as soon as the fighting began ordered that the company make no profits out of the war and that the entire Shell fleet, by then the largest fleet of oil carriers in the world, be put at the disposal of the Admiralty at pre-war rates. Bob accepted that there should be no profits but was determined to see that there were no losses.

Standard Oil, Rockefeller's great American cartel and Shell's competitor in every part of the world, used American neutrality to displace Shell from some of its traditional markets. The Admiralty, moreover, bought considerable quantities of Standard oil f.o.b., which it brought over in its own vessels, and these turned out to be none other than tankers, leased to them by Shell. Shell contracts, on the other hand, were mainly c.i.f. and to meet its obligations Shell had to charter other vessels at the new inflated wartime rates – while the Admiralty used the Shell ships at the pre-war rate. The latter was

9s. 3d. a ton; the former had risen to 20s., and Standard, Shell's traditional enemy, was benefiting from the difference.[13]

There were other arrangements less obviously unjust but equally harmful to Shell, and they involved Bob in protracted exchanges in which he showed himself to be a determined, skilled, if rather short-tempered, negotiator. His explosive outbursts were genially accepted by his opposite numbers in the Admiralty as one of the hazards of war and they grew to like and respect him.

When America entered the war in 1917 the Government turned to Bob to help negotiate a transatlantic oil agreement. It was largely due to his efforts that the Inter-Allied Petroleum Council, which pooled shipping and supplies, was established, and he was knighted in 1920 for his services to the war effort.

His greatest contribution to the Shell group was, possibly, in the way he persuaded the board to pay attention to 'product research'. The oil industry until after World War I was concerned wholly and solely with providing a commodity to burn. Bob believed if one could find some use for the residues in the refining process, prices could be reduced, yet profits increased. It was not until 1927, however, that he obtained sufficient backing on the board to set aside a large sum for research. Then he invited Professor E. C. Williams, the head of the department of Chemical Engineering at University College, London, to establish a research laboratory at Emryville, California, giving him a blank cheque to gather about him the men and materials he required. This was the beginning of Shell Chemicals.[14]

In 1919 Bob bought Caen Wood Towers, a large house with twelve acres of garden, which included a tennis court and swimming pool. The land abutted on to the Kenwood estate, from whose owners he was able to rent additional ground on which to keep chickens and a few cows. There, in Highgate, some twenty minutes from the City, he and his family lived in a happy, secluded, rural setting. However, Bob's yearning for country life was not quite satisfied and in 1928 he bought Honeymead, a large farm standing on a bleak, wind-blown stretch of Exmoor. He joined the local stag hunt, became a rural district councillor and a leading figure in local society. He revelled in the new life and new setting and at the age of fifty-one decided to leave the City.

He was not to remain on his farm for long. He had hardly left Shell when he was invited to cure the ills of the African and Eastern Trading Corporation, a vast combine with head offices in Liverpool and heavy investments in Nigeria and the Gold Coast. Its one effective competitor was the Niger Company owned by Lever Brothers. Bob, who for all his belief in free enterprise had great faith in cartels, saw no reason why the two organisations should continue to contend with one another at a time when markets everywhere seemed to be shrinking. He proposed a merger. Niger was by far the smaller of the two companies, but it was more profitable, and he suggested that they should amalgamate to form the United Africa Company, with each of the parent concerns acting as holding companies and owning 50% of the shares. Once this principle was accepted Bob and d'Arcy Cooper, head of Lever Brothers, worked out the vast mass of details in a mere seven weeks. Here again the Cohen genius for detail was invaluable.

In March 1929 the United Africa Company came into being, with Bob as chairman. He remained in office for two years and it proved to be a disastrous episode in an otherwise triumphant career.

External forces were against him. The 1929 Wall Street crash caused a fall in the price of primary products everywhere, the extent of which Bob had not anticipated. He bought on a declining market which involved the company in disastrous losses.

Almost as soon as he took office he invited Edward Beddington and Frank Samuel to join him on the company executive. The one was his brother-in-law and the other a colleague from the Council of the United Synagogue, and although both were people of proven ability it is not difficult to imagine the sort of murmuring to which their appointment gave rise. He also brought in an efficiency expert, who went round the numerous establishments of the combine lopping off jobs right and left. Whatever the prospect of execution may or may not do for the mind, it manifestly unsettles the spirit and one could sense a raging neurosis through the length and breadth of the firm, which Bob's brusque hectoring manner did nothing to calm.

In August 1929 Lever Brothers itself amalgamated with *Margarine Unie* of Holland to form Unilever, and the union brought on to the board of the Lever holding company a number of Dutchmen. One of them was Anton Jurgens, an administrator of outstanding ability, but a cold, ruthless, inscrutable man who, used to the Dutch method of rule by committee, was unhappy with Bob's one man high command.

Bob had his executive below him, and the boards of the holding companies above. The former was there to receive orders, and the latter to receive results, but the day-to-day direction of policy he kept firmly in his own hands. It had worked in Shell, but it was not working in The United Africa Company and the company was totting up heavy losses. In February 1930 Bob sailed to examine the company's installations in West Africa. When he returned in April he was faced with a virtual *coup*. D'Arcy and Jurgens were insisting on the interposition of a small committee which would oversee the workings of the United Africa Company on a day-to-day basis. Edward Beddington, Bob's appointee, was to be chairman of the Committee at a salary of £10,000 and Bob who was receiving £10,000 would in future get £5,000.

Bob submitted to the humiliating terms with unusual meekness, but his old habits died hard. Instead of acting through the committee, he continued to give orders as before in a clear breach of the agreement which stated quite specifically that "no member of the Committee in the course of his interviews with the Managing Directors or the staff shall give instructions to them otherwise than through the Committee.[15] This gave Jurgens and Cooper the occasion they needed and they asked for his resignation.

It was a sad blow for Bob for he had hoped to do for the United Africa Company what he had done for Shell, and to use the resources of the combine to make a major contribution to the development of West Africa.

His children were now grown up. Bernard, his oldest son, who had yearned for a naval career, had been sent to Dartmouth Royal Naval College, but his eyesight was defective and he went on to Clifton. From there he would go to Cambridge and Bob had already envisaged the next step:

> I hope by the time he grows up the United Africa business will be worthy to receive him and, if it is, it will make a fine career with everything in his favour, and really one which is more in line with my ideal of service for this generation than the Navy itself.[16]

Bob's departure from the United Africa Company did not leave him a poor man. He still held several directorships within the Shell group, and was also a director of the Baldwin steel company. Unilevers gave him a large, parting cheque which was not wholly expected, and he was able to tell his wife: ". . . we shall now be able to pay our supertax without much borrowing."[17]

In 1935 Bob, accompanied by Alice, set out as the official representative of the Royal Dutch-Shell group at the celebrations to mark the opening of the Kirkuk-Haifa pipeline built by the Iraq Petroleum Company. On January 16, after attending the Haifa festivities, they were returning to Jerusalem by car, when they crashed head-on into a heavy lorry. Bob was severely injured. Alice seemed less injured but suffered mainly from shock. A few days later she developed pneumonia and died on January 24. She was buried on Mount Scopus overlooking the Old City.

"His loss overwhelmed him," wrote Henriques. "Unnaturally tolerant with everyone, incongruously quiet, sweet and gentle with the children, he did not smile for more than a year."

He was to find many consolations in life. His daughter Hetty made a remarkable recovery from polio and went on to lead a happy normal life. She married Oliver Sebag-Montefiore, a young Shell executive. Bob's sons were grown up, and he watched their progress with a mixture of pride and apprehension. There was not the slightest compulsion among the younger generation of the Cousinhood to confine their relationships to purely Jewish contemporaries, and many of them were marrying out of their faith. Bernard, however, found a Jewish wife, Joyce Nathan. She was a daughter of Major Nathan, a senior partner in the City law firm of Nathan, Oppenheimer and Vandyke, who was to become Minister of Civil Aviation in the Attlee administration.

"He was overjoyed," the late Rev. Ephraim Levine, minister of the New West End Synagogue, later recalled, "He came dancing into the room to tell me the news. And to see Sir Robert dance was, I can assure you, quite a spectacle."[18] His other son Matthew in fact married out of the faith, but although it occasioned some pain and embarrassment, there was no estrangement between them.

The pain and embarrassment may be easily explained, for Bob was by now lay head of the Anglo-Jewish community. It was not a role which he had sought, but once he was drawn into communal service he exerted himself with his customary energy, and it was inevitable that he should rise to the top.

Bob was by nature a religious man, with deep moments of introspection, and he found in prayer a frequent source of reassurance and comfort but he looked upon it as a very personal activity, something to be undertaken between consenting adults in private, and he did not go in for any of the externals of religious observance. He did not keep the dietary laws, worked, hunted and played on the Sabbath, and was rarely to be seen in synagogue, and he was, both in practice and belief, worlds away from the United Synagogue, the Orthodox religious establishment over which he presided.

What, as an increasing number of people were to ask, was he doing there?

He was pulled into it by his antecedents. The United Synagogue was virtually a family creation. Although a Rothschild was almost always at its head, the Cohens were its managers. It was ruled by a council of members elected by its constituent synagogues, but the actual direction of policy was in the hands of an executive consisting of a president, two vice-presidents, an honorary secretary and two honorary treasurers, who were expected to rise to office from the council, but were quite often pulled in from outside.

Bob was pulled in from outside. In 1913 Albert Jessel, an eminent lawyer who was a vice-president of the United Synagogue,wrote urging him to become treasurer, an office which had recently been held with no particular distinction by his father-in-law Henry Beddington. "I will not enlarge on the family ties which bind you to the Institution", wrote Jessel. "The important place the United Synagogue fills in the community requires that it should be guided by the best available talent."[19]

Bob demurred that he was too busy, lacked 'personal qualifications', by which he presumably meant that he was not particularly well instructed in Judaism, but the fact that he hardly subscribed to the same faith as the congregants of the United Synagogue did not enter into his reservations. He in any case had only a vague idea of the sort of Judaism the United Synagogue was meant to uphold, and even if he would have known he couldn't have felt that it mattered. Under the articles of association the Chief Rabbi headed the faith and conscience department of the United Synagogue, while the honorary officers dealt with the actual management of the synagogue, the building, the real estate. Or to put it another way, the Chief Rabbi dealt with the spiritual synagogue, and the honorary officers with the temporal. This understanding worked pretty well under the Rothschilds, but as Bob rose to high office some friction developed for he reserved the right to say what was spiritual and what was temporal.

There was another factor. Before World War I the community was monarchical in its set-up. At the very top was the royal family with Lord Rothschild as king and his brothers and nephews as dukes of the blood royal. Beneath them came the Montefiores, Mocattas, Cohens, Franklins and other courtiers, and the community was sufficiently flattered by their patronage to leave its destiny in their hands. Then in 1917 came the revolt over the Balfour Declaration, and there was some restiveness too in the United Synagogue. Indeed in the very letter in which Jessel invited Bob to assume office, there was a warning that "the Council is not so easily led (or driven) by the honorary officers as was the case when I was first elected on it twenty-four years ago" Republicanism was in the air.

There was also the matter of personalities, an inescapable problem wherever Bob was involved.

The first Chief Rabbi of the United Synagogue, who also functioned as Chief Rabbi of the British Empire, was Dr Nathan Marcus Adler, an amiable, mild, retiring scholar, who rarely cared to venture out of his study. He was succeeded by his son Hermann, who might have been custom-built as chaplain for the Cousinhood. He shared their outlook, antipathies and yearned for their milieu, and indeed he was one of them for he was a grandson of Baron de Worms, a cousin of the first Lord Pirbright, and a distant kinsman of the Rothschilds. He was a haughty, dignified, graceful figure, inclined on occasion to sport gaiters. He was also a Companion of the Royal Victorian Order, and sometimes at, say, a garden party in Lambeth Palace, or some other gathering of prelates, with his black garb, gaiters, the insignia of the Victorian Order like a pectoral cross on his chest, it was difficult to tell the Rabbi from the bishops. Edward VII spoke of him as "my Chief Rabbi", and under him the United Synagogue seemed to be the Jewish branch of the Anglican establishment.

And this, indeed, was precisely the effect which the Cousinhood wanted. If they had been anxious to detach Anglo-Jewry from ancestral traditions they would have put all the weight of their massive influence behind the Reform and Liberal Synagogues. They were sufficiently English to revere antiquity, cherish tradition, and to take a proper pride in ancestry and all that ancestors stood for. They wanted their Jews to be Jewish, but not excessively or exclusively so. They also wanted them to be English and in the United Synagogue they sought a synthesis of the two and almost found it. The doctrine of the United Synagogue was based squarely on the *Halacha*, the Mosaic law as expounded traditionally by the Rabbis, but its whole aura was Anglican, even to the mock-Gothic exterior of its buildings. The Rabbis, dressed in dog collars, were somewhat Anglican in bearing and there was even the occasional hunting parson.

By the time Bob joined the United Synagogue executive its Anglican heyday was passing, and a new Chief Rabbi had come to power, the Very Rev. Dr J. H. Hertz, Hungarian born and American trained, who had spent the first years of his ministry in South Africa and who, indeed, was appointed to the Chief Rabbinate largely on the recommendation of Lord Milner.[20]

Hertz did not resent the Anglicanism of the United Synagogue, on the contrary he revelled in it, but he did resent the encroachment of laymen on what he considered to be the Rabbinical domain. He would have taken it from the Rothschilds, but the Rothschilds were by now content merely to lend their names to the United Synagogue. The real authority had devolved, as it was bound to, into Bob's hands, and from him Hertz would not have it. The Rothschilds were gentlemen, Bob, he believed, was not. Hertz was in fact a Waley Cohen in canonicals. Both were craggy autocrats, both had violent tempers, both had fixed ideas of the role of the other in the United Synagogue, and they were involved in a demarcation dispute, which continued now quietly, now flaring into the open, until the death of Hertz.

There were also prolonged periods in which they acted happily in harness. In 1919 Bob believed that after the carnage and suffering of the war mankind was ready for a religious revival, and he felt the time was ripe to launch a great new movement for traditional Judaism, "as a monument to the Jews of the British Empire who had fallen in the war and as a thank-offering to those who had been spared".

He worked out every detail as if he was preparing the prospectus of a public company, and in a letter to Major Lionel de Rothschild, senior partner in the bank, he invited the House of Rothschild to underwrite it:

> Thus it is that we approach you and your House, to whom Jews of England and of the British Empire have always looked as their leaders, to put yourself at the head of a movement which shall establish as the undying monument of those who have sacrificed their lives for their country a religious organisation, with its college, its ministry and its religious form of Jewish religious worship – which shall carry on and interpret the Jewish and British traditions and give them their place as the permanent ennobling forces in the lives of future generations of Jewish citizens of the British Empire.[21]

It was a wildly impractical plan, but Bob's enthusiasm was such that he was able to carry with him everyone he approached including Lionel de Rothschild, the second Lord Swaythling, Lionel Cohen, the *Haham*, even the Chief Rabbi. His plan was to establish "a Great College of Jewish Learning" at Oxford or Cambridge which would provide a cadre of young rabbis to serve Britain and the empire, some on a local basis, some, like regional managers, as "District

Principal Rabbis", who would supervise religious education and stimulate Jewish religious life throughout the Empire.[22]

In 1920 Bob formally launched the appeal – for £1,000,000 – from 22 Great St Helen's, the offices of the Shell Company. It was sponsored by every distinguished name in the community, and everyone presumed that this particular issue would be promptly oversubscribed. In the event only £133,000 was raised, much of it through Bob's personal effort, and the whole ambitious scheme had to be abandoned. What went wrong?

First, the religious revival which Bob thought he could discern did not exist. On the contrary, a religious decline became evident. Bob hoped to bring every shade in the Jewish religious spectrum into one united movement. He went about it as if he was forming an oil cartel. He was resourceful, full of sound argument, energetic; but ecumenism is alien to Jewish Orthodoxy. The further one moves to the right, the greater the fractiousness, the more numerous the sects. The far right, which at that time formed a fairly sizable part of the spectrum, felt in no need of revival for they believed that they had never declined. And the left, which most favoured the scheme, was least ready with its money.

There was another occasion when Bob tried to bring together the various elements in the community and with similar lack of success, and for much the same reasons.

At the time of the Balfour Declaration Claude Montefiore and other members of the Cousinhood had established the League of British Jews which claimed to be non-Zionist rather than anti-Zionist but which opposed with great vehemence the idea of a Jewish national home. Bob was invited to join, and although he was not out of sympathy with its aims, declined to do so because he was against any divisive force in the community. He was the great amalgamator.

The Balfour Declaration was now Government policy and thus whatever reservations Bob may have had about its implications, he agreed to join the committee. He went further and tried to extend the committee as an umbrella organisation to speak with one voice on Palestine on behalf of Anglo-Jewry. He failed again because he could not understand the vast gulf which divided Chaim Weizmann and the Zionists from Claude Montefiore and the League.

Robert Henriques, who became a convert to Zionism in later life, felt that Bob and his fellows have been treated unfairly in Zionist history, and he took particular exception to a passage in Chaim

Weizmann's autobiography in which he referred to Bob and his class as "people who have cut themselves adrift from Jewry".[23]

Now, as we know, the Cousinhood had manifestly not *cut themselves adrift* from Jewry, but whether they wished it or not, they had drifted and lived, worked and drew their sensations from a different world. Henriques points to Bob's religious feelings, which were deep and sincere, while many Zionists were completely divorced from religion, and some, indeed, were militant atheists. But Zionism was a matter of involvement, of shared feelings, of common responses, and at source, a sense of unsettlement. Bob could look back on five generations of Anglo-Jewish ancestors, settled, established, accepted, and could look forward to generations ahead secure on England's soil.

This having been said one must add that Bob did much more for the development of the Jewish homeland than most active, committed Zionists. One almost suspects that he was a Zionist in spite of himself. With the help of his cousin Walter Cohen (Sir Andrew's father) he established the Palestine Corporation, which inspired a host of commercial and industrial concerns including the Nesher Cement Company, the Palestine Brewing Company, the Union Bank, the Ihud Insurance Company, the Palestine Salt Company, the Agricultural Mortgage company, the King David Hotel. It also helped to establish what is now Israel's main export, the diamond processing industry.

In 1927, in the face of considerable opposition from senior colleagues on the Shell board, Bob pushed through a scheme to build an immense oil refinery in the Middle East and on a visit to Palestine took an option on a splendid site by the River Kishon in Haifa. The refinery gave rise to a mass of ancillary industries. It gave him a particularly proud sense of achievement, for here was an occasion when he was of service to Shell, to the Empire and to Jewry at one and the same time.

Then after World War II there came a tragic moment when there was a clash of loyalties. The cause was Ernest Bevin's Palestine policy which virtually abrogated the Balfour Declaration and imposed severe restrictions on immigration. There had been such restrictions before, but now in 1945 when the full horror of the Nazi holocaust had only just become known, and while hundreds of thousands of Jews were languishing in displaced persons camps, the restrictions seemed particularly cruel. The Jews of Palestine were on the verge of rebellion, and there was a feeling of intense bitterness and betrayal among Jews everywhere.

On October 6, 1945 the Chief Rabbi sent a telegram to all synagogues under his jurisdiction calling for "a day of Jewish solidarity with the remnants of European Jewry", and declaring that the "Jews of England expect the Government to keep faith in regard to Palestine as the only haven of refuge to survivors of Nazi bestiality".

Bob had not been consulted and he at once countered with a telegram, signed by himself as president of the United Synagogue and Frank Samuel as vice-president, warning synagogues that the "last sentence of Chief Rabbi's telegram to your minister . . . may be misinterpreted as advocating introduction of politics into our religious services. . . ."

His action caused uproar in the Council of the United Synagogue and for a time it seemed that it might do what the Board of Deputies had done twenty-eight years earlier and rise in open revolt against the Cousinhood. It did not go that far, for Bob did something which he had rarely done before, he made at least a partial withdrawal. He agreed to meet the Chief Rabbi to consider the incident, and that, coming from him, was tantamount to apology. The meeting was never held for Dr Hertz died shortly after.

Some observed a sign of mellowness in Bob's readiness to withdraw, but he was not the mellowing type and in fact his temper grew worse as he grew older. A Rabbi who knew him towards the end of his life, said that his bark was worse than his bite, but in all truth his bark was bad enough. One suspected that he took a quiet pride in the terror he could instil in casual acquaintances, so that if he performed an act of kindness – as he did on countless occasions – he did so furtively lest it undermine his reputation as an ogre. He almost treated kindness as a private vice, talked loudly and carried a big stick.

While Alice was alive he would frequently be at home to young Jewish Rabbinical students. Such invitations were treated like a command performance and were viewed with apprehension, if not terror, by the young guests. But when they arrived they were taken aback by his charm, by the elegance of manner which seemed at variance with his appearance, and by the pains he took to put them at their ease. He had dignity without hauteur.

Bob had a constant urge to be of service. On the outbreak of World War II when he was living in retirement, he wrote to Churchill, whom he knew fairly well, "to say that I am free and that if you feel I can serve you or the country in any way, I hope you will send for me. I can, of course, give my whole time." The offer was not taken up, and when, in the following year, Churchill became Prime Minister, Bob tried again: "I am taking the liberty of sending you this line to tell you that

I'm available, and, of course, ready and eager to respond to any call."[24]

No call came, at least not from Churchill, but by way of consolation he was later invited by Lord Woolton, the Minister of Food, to advise him on matters relating to Jewish diet and rations, with the result that for the rest of the war he became virtual Minister of Kosher food.

Once he had retired from Shell Bob spent most of his time at Honeymead. Here in the country, in heavy tweeds, among his cattle and sheep, his horses and dogs, he was at his happiest. He joined the Exmoor Stag hunt, and he allowed nothing to interfere with the pleasures of the chase. A friend who once spent the Jewish New Year with him recalls how everybody assembled in the library in hunting pink for a brief service conducted by Bob himself, and then, the service over, tallyho, to hounds. However, if he did not observe his own Sabbath, he respected that of his neighbours and on Sundays he was always in the sombre hues of his Sunday suit and discouraged family and friends from wearing riding clothes. He was a good horseman, but with his huge bulk and awkward shape, the sight of him in full gallop frightened more than the stags.

He was as natural to the setting as the moorland crags, and one keeps asking one's self why a man with his tastes, outlook and background should have spent so much time on Jewish affairs.

There was, as we have seen, first of all the pull of his antecedents. But there was another matter. The Rothschilds were abdicating the throne and if the Jewish masses were left to their own resources, they could undo all that had been built up by earlier generations of Cohens and Rothschilds, with results that could affect the good name, the image, of the entire community. To the non-Jew all Jews looked alike.

It was for this same reason that in spite of his reservations about Zionist ideology and methods, he was of considerable help to the Zionist cause. ". . . The success or failure of the Jewish national home in Palestine", he wrote to a friend, "will now undoubtedly reflect enormously upon Jews throughout the world, and it has therefore become a matter of vital importance to all of us that we should do all that is in our power *now* to make it a success."[25]

In the same way he felt that the success or failure of the United Synagogue would undoubtedly reflect on *all* Jews – the Cousinhood perhaps most of all.

Also, though not Orthodox himself, he liked his fellow Jews to be orthodox enough to maintain the essential continuity of Jewish life.

He felt for traditional Judaism what many urban Englishmen in spacious urban flats feel for the tumbledown cottages of rural England: they would not be seen dead in them but would be sorry to see them go.

Bob was an ascetic frugal man and given his own private needs he could have lived comfortably on the salary of a suburban dentist. He did not drink or smoke, ate sparingly and had no private vices, or at least, if he did, kept them so private that no one ever caught hint of them, but he did like to be out there on high and enjoy a certain eminence. Outside the Jewish community he was just another "Bull of Bashan", to use Labouchère's phrase; inside he was King.

And finally, and this was the main cause, he cared, deeply, incessantly. He loved an argument, a fight, an occasion for a discharge of temper, but the arguments he faced in the Jewish community filled him with an exasperation which, he protested, took years off his life. In the 1930s for example, a central fund was established to help German Jewry. Bob did not like the way it was administered, but none of his colleagues shared his view. He was not used to being outvoted, and after a violent outburst, stormed out of the room like a tornado. When one of his colleagues suggested that he was perhaps overworked and should take a rest and "live the life of a country gentleman", Bob replied sadly: "I wish one could get rest, but the Hitler business is really like war, and one cannot."[26] This coming from him was an unusual confession, for he did not like to give the impression that he cared so much. And in a second letter while still protesting at the way the fund was being run, he enclosed £1,000.

After the war he learned to his horror that Jews who had miraculously survived the Nazi death camps, were being kept in the same displaced persons camps among their former persecutors. He promptly descended on the Foreign Office to protest, and, making no headway, flew out to Germany. There he spoke to the British military authorities, who made special arrangements for the Jewish displaced persons without further delay.

There have been more devout and more committed Jews at the head of the community but, with the possible exception of Moses Montefiore, none have served it with greater dedication and to better effect.

CHAPTER 27

The Gaffer

The Cousinhood took their duties to the poor seriously and gave their treasure and leisure to improve their conditions. Some like Frederic Mocatta made it their life's work, but even in his case it was always done from a distance. There was rarely a personal sense of involvement. Lily Montagu was one who was intimately involved, but even she at the end of the day returned to Kensington, to a large house and many servants, to the world of her mother, the Dowager Lady Swaythling.

For Basil Henriques, who founded the St George's and Oxford Club in the East End, the largest and most ambitious of the Jewish Settlements, there was no end of the day. He made his home in the East End, married a fellow club-worker, and remained there long after his former protégés had moved out to more attractive areas.

"Basil," I was told by one of his disciples, "turned native." This was not quite true, for no one could mistake Basil Lucas Quixano Henriques for one of the other Jewish, or even non-Jewish, inhabitants of the East End. He was tall – 6 ft 2 in height – erect, fair, with a rosy complexion and military bearing, a son of Harrow and Oxford, and every bit the toff he looked. When he first came to the East End, many people thought he was a Christian missionary.

He certainly came with a sense of mission. He wanted to transmit the values of his faith, his class, his England to the rude progeny of the Russian ghettos.

Basil was born in 1890. His father, a shipowner, was a prominent and active member of the West London Synagogue. His mother, a great-niece of Sir Moses Montefiore, was a deeply devout woman, who saw to it that prayers in synagogue were supplemented by prayers at home. Basil took to the sacred as a bear takes to honey. He loved the

377

synagogue, hymn singing, prayers and sermons. Even as a child he was obsessed with God and tended to look upon Him as a member of the family, one of his grander relations. He would on occasion compose his own sermons and, with a chair as pulpit, address his mother and aunts. By the time he went to Harrow he had learned to keep his religious feelings under control, but his letters home were somewhat in the nature of sermonettes. At Oxford, where he read history, he took virtual charge of the synagogue. He did not give any serious thought to a career, and there was certainly no pressure from his parents to acquire a livelihood.

It was common for young patricians at this time to spend a period of months or years among the London poor and various settlements had been established by undergraduates from Cambridge and Oxford in South London and the East End. Henriques was particularly attracted by the work of Alec Paterson who had founded a medical mission near the docks and warehouses of Bermondsey, and during some of his vacations he went to live in the mission. It was an illuminating experience. Paterson, he later wrote, "made me feel I had something to give and much to learn. There I saw Christianity really lived in a wonderful fellowship of dockers and undergraduates, which showed such a spirit of happiness and friendship, of service and loyalty, that I felt a challenge. Could Judaism produce such a fellowship among Jews?"[1]

Henriques was not quite certain it could and for a time he veered towards Christianity.[2] It was the teaching, example and friendship of Claude Montefiore which finally pulled him back towards the Jewish fold.

Montefiore's dry de-mythologised, de-ritualised, de-nationalised Judaism conformed very much to his own way of thinking, and especially his belief in social action as a form of prayer. It was with the encouragement of Montefiore that he went to live for a time in Toynbee Hall, the East End settlement founded by Canon Barnett; and it was again with Montefiore's encouragement that he founded the Oxford and St George's Settlement (so called because it was set among the teeming slums of the parish of St George's-in-the-East, Stepney; and Oxford because of his Alma Mater).

With the help of Montefiore, Basil brought together leading members of the West London and Liberal Synagogues to finance his scheme. He described something of the social background of St George's-in-the-East; a heavily congested area, hemmed in by docks and warehouses, criss-crossed and darkened by railway viaducts; crowded houses in mean streets, ragged children, hungry faces, poverty, ignorance, squalor, and the inhabitants mainly Jewish. The boys usually left school at fourteen, took unskilled jobs, were often unemployed or semi-employed, and spent much of their free time on the streets, 'a prey', to use the terms of the day, 'to every temptation and vice'.

Henriques hoped, through his club, to make them into "good Jews, good citizens, good sportsmen . . ."[3] The two synagogues agreed to sponsor the club and give it every support.

In 1914 Basil leased a couple of rooms in the East End, one for himself and one for his club. His mother sent her butler to look after him, but he returned a few days later. "The infestation, Madam, it was impossible." Basil however remained.

In the following year he inherited a small legacy from a brother and used it to establish a similar girls' club a few streets away, which he placed under the direction of a young social worker called Rose Loewe.

The brother, an officer in the regular army, had died at Mons in 1914. He was one of the first British casualties on the Western front, and Basil felt compelled to take his place. Before enlisting, however, he combined the boys' and girls' clubs and, as if to finalise the union, he married his co-worker, Rose Loewe. It proved to be a remarkable partnership.

He was commissioned in the Buffs and seconded to the Heavy Section Machine-Gun Corps to be trained in the use of a new and still secret weapon – the tank.[4] He had all the courage necessary for the undertaking, but at 6 ft 2 he was the wrong build. He was wounded when he drove the first tank into action in September 1916. Thereafter he served in reconnaissance. He was twice mentioned in dispatches and received the Italian Silver Medal for bravery.

The war if anything reinforced his strong religious feelings and he found time amid the mud and misery of Flanders to compose his own prayers:

I believe, O Lord, that our cause is righteousness, and that we are fighting for the suppression of Evil – for Honour, Justice and Liberty. Inspire our Leaders with wisdom and foresight, that they may so direct this war that victory may soon be ours. Give unto every man soldier, sailor and airman that courage and determination by which he may bravely and manfully fulfil his duties which are imposed upon him, and grant that I too may do my share with a stout heart and a steady hand. . . . Grant peace unto us and unto all mankind. Amen.[5]

The club grew rapidly after the war, was formed into a settlement and synagogue and Henriques became its lay preacher. His theology, derived partly from Claude Montefiore and partly from Baden-Powell, was not of a very profound order. Throughout his life he continued to address God with perfect certainty that He was up there listening. And coupled with this were the exhortations, familiar to every English public schoolboy, 'Fight the Good Fight', 'Paddle Your Own Canoe', 'Play the Game'. To the youngsters of Stepney, at all events, it was unfamiliar, and they took it seriously in the way that they would not accept the exhortations from their Rabbis. Rabbis, apart from anything else, were paid to exhort and they were also a familiar, perhaps too familiar, part of the East End Jewish scene. They tended to be white-faced, unworldly men, a little bent, still bearing the aura of the Pale, of poverty and oppression; whereas there was about Henriques everything a boy admires in a man. He had a commanding presence and a commanding voice; he was a gallant soldier, with medals and war-wounds and war-stories, an officer and gentleman – all that and pious too.

The boys idolised him and he became known among them affectionately as 'The Gaffer', or 'Long 'Un'. His wife became known as 'The Missus'.

In 1919 he established a one-man citizens' advice bureau in the Settlement.[6] He let it be known that he would be available in his office from nine to eleven every morning to offer counsel on any problem anyone in the neighbourhood might care to bring to him. And they came in a steady succession to this man who soon came to be known as the local Solomon, some with family disputes, some to correct an erring son, some to complain about their landlords, some about their tenants, some merely to ask for help. And he turned this way and that dispensing wisdom, chastisement, sympathy and old clothes.

New and larger premises were acquired after the war with the help of Marcus Samuel's son, Lord Bearsted, which were formally opened in 1919 by Clement Attlee. Within a few years they were too small and Henriques acquired an old London County Council School in Berner Street with a gift of £65,000 from Bernhard Baron, head of the Carreras tobacco empire. It was opened by the Duke of Gloucester in 1930 as the Bernhard Baron Settlement. By the time World War II broke out it had over three thousand members.

There were gymnastics, drama classes, painting, dancing, lectures, foreign language lessons; there was an annual summer camp, and an open-day concert, always followed by prayers. But there can be no doubt that the highlights of the year, as far as Henriques was concerned, were the High Holy Day Services which he conducted himself.

"A marvellous day", he noted after one Day of Atonement, "about 1,000 present. For one and a half hours at the end, decorum perfect and tension almost unbearable. . . . Preached three sermons during the day. One on sex and gambling, one on Jonah, and one on peace."[7]

When the Settlement was first launched it had the blessings of the then Chief Rabbi Dr Hertz, and even after World War I, the Rev. Israel Brodie, who was to succeed Dr Hertz as Chief Rabbi, was a resident in the Settlement. In time, and especially after it opened its synagogue, Orthodox leaders began to feel, with some justification, that Henriques was drawing young people away from traditional Judaism.

He had not set out with any such intention. He was himself brought up in the Reform Synagogue, but his wife was traditionally-minded and he was also deeply influenced by the example and beliefs of his brother-in-law Herbert Loewe, an Orthodox Jew who was Reader in Rabbinics at Cambridge. In addition he realised that the young people among whom he worked were from Orthodox homes. Thus, for example, he encouraged the older boys to don phylacteries, though it was not a rite which he observed, and although he had no belief in Jewish dietary law himself, he was always careful to keep a kosher home so that club members and their families could be at ease at his table. But there is among Orthodox Jews also such a thing as kosher theology and his de-Judaised Judaism and home-made liturgy plainly were not. He would, for example, occasionally introduce readings from the New Testament at his Sabbath services. Or to mention a lesser, though more characteristic offence, he liked to lead the singing of *Adon Olam*, which closes the Sabbath service, not to traditional Jewish melodies, but to the tune of his school song 'Forty Years On'.

The unease which he occasioned was at first muted by the awe in which he was held in the East End, and by the general admiration for the man and his work in the wider community. In time, however, it grew to a hostile clamour, which was aggravated by Henriques' anti-Zionism.

After the Balfour Declaration the Cousinhood more or less gave up the fight and some elements, though careful to disown any Zionist allegiance,were involved in the Jewish economic enterprises in Palestine. But Henriques never rested from the struggle. He found Zionism well entrenched in the East End with flourishing Zionist youth groups and he feared that they must somehow undermine the British loyalties of the Jewish youngster.

In 1943 post-war plans for Palestine came under review and Zionists reiterated their demands for a Jewish state, urging Britain to stand by the pledges made in the Balfour Declaration. Henriques chose this occasion to reopen the Anti-Zionist fight and with Sir Jack Brunel Cohen formed the Jewish Fellowship which was akin in many ways to the League of British Jews formed in 1917.[8] The League had at least attracted most of the leading members of the Cousinhood. The Fellowship was a much less significant affair. Events in Europe since the rise of Hitler had killed confidence in the idea that 'progress' must in time improve the situation of world Jewry, and though members of the Cousinhood continued to be apprehensive about the idea of a Jewish state, few saw any better solution to the Jewish problem. Henriques and Cohen, however, kept their Fellowship flag flying right up to the creation of Israel, and even afterwards continued to make hostile murmurs.

In 1948 Henriques retired from his wardenship of the Settlement. He had held the office for thirty-three years and had seen his club grow from a mere handful of youngsters into a unique social welfare institution serving the entire East End. The character of the area had been altered by the war. It had been devastated in the blitz and large council estates were rising on the ruins of the old slums. Most of the Jews and many of the Jewish institutions had moved out, and the Jews who remained were in the main non-religious. They did not feel in need of the sort of moral guidance they could receive in Berner Street. Old Boys of the Settlement still descended in their cars from the suburbs in the evenings at week-ends, to meet friends and talk over old times, but there were fewer youngsters about. The golden days of the East End Settlements were over.

Henriques was for many years chairman of the East End Juvenile Court and brought to the bench the imagination and insight which he showed in the Settlement. The court sat at Toynbee Hall and he tried as far as possible to remove the atmosphere of intimidation that normally surrounds court proceedings. He always began the day with prayers and sat behind a narrow table, face to face with the child and his or her parents and would try to address them as a friend of the family. He was by no means lenient with the youthful offender. At the same time he felt that their very presence in court was in part due to the failure of his own class. He would visit the boys in Borstal and follow their fortunes after they had been discharged. He was anxious that the sentences he imposed served as a corrective rather than a punishment.

He and his wife waged a constant war against proprietors of amusement arcades and dance-halls which he felt were glittering inducements to vice. In the 1950s he was horrified to find that contraceptive vending machines were sprouting outside tobacconists and sweetshops all over the East End. With Lady Cynthia Colville, another member of the East London bench, he launched a campaign against them, with urgent representations to the press, Parliament and the Home Office, and within a short time the machines were removed.[9]

He was worried too about the large number of young male prostitutes active in the West End of London and he spent many nights in and around Piccadilly speaking to the boys and evaluating for himself the extent of the problem.[10] Such activities, like Gladstone's salvation work among female prostitutes, are naturally liable to misinterpretation, but Henriques was unperturbed. Those who knew him, he believed, could not possibly misconstrue his efforts; others, who might, did not count. The extent to which he was able to rehabilitate youngsters who had been written off as wholly incorrigible made his court a place of pilgrimage for social workers from all over London. In 1948 Princess Margaret attended a session of the court and then lunched with him at the Settlement.[11] He retired from the bench in 1955 and was knighted for his services to youth welfare.

His health was by then in a parlous state. He suffered from diabetes which made him ill-tempered and irritable. Then in 1956 he was found to have cancer, and he calmly prepared himself for death. The surgeons decided to operate, and much to his surprise – one almost noticed an element of chagrin in his reaction – he survived. He died four years later of a heart attack.

Few Jews in this century have had such an influence on the young as Basil Henriques, but not everyone is convinced that the influence was entirely for the good. Sir Israel Brodie, the Chief Rabbi Emeritus, who served his apprenticeship as a resident minister in Berner Street, has pointed out that the boys who flocked to the Settlement were by no means young heathens.[12] Most of them, as Henriques himself was aware, came from religious homes, and he therefore did not instil religious feelings where none existed, but merely replaced one form – and in Sir Israel's opinion more lasting and relevant form – of Judaism with another.

Sir Israel was resident in St George's in the 1920s. Dr André Ungar, who is now a Rabbi in the United States, was resident in the late 1950s.

Sir Basil had by then been in retirement for nearly a decade, but although he was able to withdraw from the day-to-day direction of the Settlement he could not withdraw from its synagogue, and in particular the pulpit.

Once the two men preached on the same subject on two successive Sabbaths but reached diametrically opposite conclusions. God, declared Sir Basil – and when he spoke of the Almighty he gave the impression that they had lately had a private exchange – God, he declared, did not care a hoot if one prayed in Hebrew, English or Chinese. It was not the language, which counted, but the thought. If that was the case, added Ungar in his sermon, why not pray in Hebrew, which did something to unite and perpetuate the Hebrew people, why discard it for English?

A painful confrontation followed, not, to be sure, in synagogue itself, but the next day in Sir Basil's flat.

"Rabbi," he said, trying with difficulty to stifle his rage, "are you defying me?" Ungar explained that he was simply telling the truth as he saw it.

Sir Basil's more martial relatives might have invited Rabbi Ungar to a duel, but he was invited instead downstairs, along a draughty corridor, and into the synagogue. There Sir Basil opened the Ark and stood with Ungar before the Scrolls of the Law. "I think we need God's guidance at a time like this," he said and closing his eyes prayed fervently and at length in English. When he had finished, he opened his eyes, smiled, shook Ungar's hand, closed the Ark and they went up the stairs together talking of Pergolesi and Bach.[13]

England and things English were extremely important to Henriques. When Dr Ungar, a Hungarian, confessed that he had no strong feelings for Hungary, England or, indeed, any one particular country, he blinked with disbelief. "But patriotism," he said in a pained voice, "patriotism, it's the noblest of sentiments. I just cannot see how a man can feel complete without it. It is one of the most precious things in my life."[14]

His Englishness, indeed, was one of the reasons why he was so intent on using English rather than Hebrew in his prayers. It is not that he positively believed – though he may have done – that God was an Englishman, but he liked to think that the language of Shakespeare and Milton was the most appropriate tongue in which to address one's maker.

He was, Dr Ungar recalls, "a damn good preacher":

There was fire in his eloquence, suspense in his pauses, power in his innuendoes. That he essentially repeated the same dozen sermons over and over again, ought not to be held against him; many professionals do no better.[15]

His material was in the main admonitory. He hated falsehood, duplicity, cupidity, lust – especially lust, and he would hiss the sibilants like a burst tyre. In speaking he could draw on a very considerable knowledge of English literature and history to colour his language and illustrate his points. He would draw less frequently on Jewish literature and history, for he had a scanty knowledge of either. Jewish philosophy and law he hardly knew at all, but he believed that conviction was more important than knowledge, and it was conviction which gave force to his utterances.

But sermons have rarely moved worlds and Henriques definitely moved his world and fundamentally affected the lives and fortunes of hundreds, perhaps thousands, of young men and women. As we have seen, the Orthodox viewed his influence with some misgivings because of his Liberal views, but by the 1930s, when his influence was at its height, the religious traditions and observances which the immigrants had brought with them had atrophied. Partly as a reaction to fascism, extreme leftist views coupled with militant atheism were winning over large parts of the Jewish East End, and he was able to retain thousands of young people within the faith who would almost certainly have been lost to it.

How did he do it? There was first of all his personality. He was, as we have seen, a tall blond god of a man, a person of heroic stature, a soldier, the sort of man every schoolboy worships yet with none of the remoteness that sometimes goes with godliness, and in a sense he never grew up. One can see photos of him in summer camp in short trousers, long stockings and boots, bright-faced, eager, ready for fun, a boy among boys.[16]

He was, in fact, the eternal boy scout in his love of sportsmen and sportmanship, fair play, doing his bit (and more than his bit) for others, songs round the camp-fire, the game spirit, and plain, unsophisticated, decent, warm, boyhood chumminess. He continued to haunt the Settlement long after he retired and could not bear to be parted from the boys or the place.

His success as a magistrate can be explained in the same terms. He was a boy listening to the misdemeanours of boys, and although his own background was worlds removed from theirs, he had lived in the East End long enough to see the effects of poverty with his own eyes, and to understand what made them go wrong and what could possibly be done to make them go right.

The fact that he came from a wealthy family was no handicap in the courts and was an immense advantage in the Settlement. Most of his boys were from immigrant families, and the Jews from Poland and Russia approached the young Jewish aristocrats who came among them with almost speechless awe. There were few Jewish aristocrats in Eastern Europe, and of them very few remained Jewish. It was almost taken for granted that as one rose in life one moved out of one's faith, and if such a Jew did remain Jewish and deigned to move among them, they could hardly believe their eyes. Thus, as we have observed, Sir Moses Montefiore was regarded by the Jewish masses as a sort of acting Messiah. And even Sir Moses was only seen in passing and retained as a memory. Henriques came to live with them, work with them, be with them.

But beyond all that was his simple, transparent goodness. He could have bouts — and towards the end of his life they were frequent — of ill temper, he could be arrogant, domineering, vain, but never sufficiently to obscure the fact of his essential goodness. He was the most chaste of men and was pained by unchastity in others. Prosperity meant nothing to him and he adopted what to someone with his background was a vow of poverty. He inherited small sums and large from various relatives, but little of it was spent on himself or his wife. Their small flat at the top of the Bernhard Baron Settlement, was about the standard of the 4% dwellings provided in the locality for the poor. And if their flat itself was brightened by a cheerful clutter of personal possessions, the immediate surroundings were of unrelieved squalor and the street was narrow and mean. They lived in an eternal twilight hemmed in at every side. Mrs Leopold de Rothschild, a great admirer of Henriques and his wife, shuddered at their amenities and placed a 'cottage' — in effect a substantial country house — on her estate near Leighton Buzzard at their disposal. Sometimes they would snatch a weekend there, but even the cottage was hardly a private retreat, since they used it as a sort of convalescent and holiday home for members of the Settlement.[17]

His influence waned with the end of the 1930s. His boys were now mostly English-born and neither they nor their parents were so awestruck by the presence of this tall English milord among them, and after the rise of Hitler, his rampant anti-Zionism alienated many of his followers.

Then came the war and the blitz, and when the smoke cleared the

East End over which he had ruled was no more ; nor, indeed, was the England he cherished and into whose ways he had introduced successive generations of newcomers.

His legend is kept alive today by his widow, who had a greater part in creating it all than she would perhaps care to admit.

Rose Henriques comes from an old, scholarly Jewish family. Her brother, the late Herbert Loewe, was Reader in Rabbinics at Cambridge. Her grandfather Dr L. Loewe was Sir Moses Montefiore's amanuensis, travelling companion and, alas, rather inadequate Boswell. She was a nurse in a Maida Vale hospital when she met Henriques.

She had his high sense of public duty, his complete selflessness, his deep religious feeling, his gamesmanship, his sense of fun. She was matron and mother-at-large, not quite the heart-throbbing Yiddishe mama, but her name sprang immediately to mind when one was in difficulties. She would tend the sick, lay out the dead, and stay up with them, not only because Jewish ritual requires it, but because rats would often make for any corpse left by itself. There was no vermin, no infestation with which she did not become familiar during her years in the East End, not mere columns of fleas, but solid teeming masses on every side of her like moving wallpaper. She has shared every nightmare of poverty, and today at eighty, though half blind, if she hears of anyone in trouble she will descend with umbrella in hand as if to tackle adversity in person. There are some who would explain the success of Basil Henriques largely in terms of Rose Henriques.

"What a most able and remarkable woman she is," Claude Montefiore once observed with awe, "there is nothing she can't do."[18]

Lady Henriques does not blush at such statements. She hates false anything, even false modesty, but she would resent any suggestion that her husband's own, personal contribution to the welfare of the East End was anything less than unique.

She felt that he encompassed something divine, and that if not in actual touch with God was definitely inspired by Him. Yet at the same time 'Bunny', as he called her, exercised a certain subtle domination over him, which could on occasion drive him to exasperation. "Oh Bunny, for heaven's sake will you please leave me alone."[19] And exasperation would be followed by mortification and apologies, for he hated to lose his temper, and he lost it frequently during his last, sad, pain-stricken years.

Lady Henriques continues to live in the small, low-ceilinged flat, in which they had spent their happiest years together, and which is now a veritable museum of Henriquiana, his books, his papers (he kept a copy of every letter he wrote), his desk-furniture, his medals and decorations, his collected sermons, the clippings from his first haircut. Everywhere there are photographs, of Basil in the army, Basil with the Queen, Basil among his boys, Basil on his wedding day. Amid them all is a large painting in bright colours of his lying-in-state, his coffin on a trestle in a jungle of flowers and wreaths. He died on December 2, 1961.

Some years earlier when he was discovered to have cancer, he thought his end was near. "I was quite ready for death," he wrote, "and was not in the least afraid of it."[20] He approached his final end with the same calm resignation. His very composure, indeed, made one believe that he expected to rise again.

During his many years at the Settlement Basil roped in various members of the Cousinhood to help him including Sydney Franklin, Ben Mocatta, Philip Waley and Walter Samuel.

Franklin in particular, though a partner in Samuel Montagu & Co., seemed to spend most of his time at the Settlement, and like Henriques, actually lived there. Being a bachelor, he did not even have the benefit of a self-contained flat, but made his home in a bleak room overlooking an even bleaker back alley. Like Henriques he found the contentment one usually finds in family life in the company of boys, and like him he had a particularly close relationship with his mother.

Once, in his late seventies, he was gravely ill in hospital and a nurse came into his room with a sleeping pill and a glass of water.

"Oh I can't take that," he said, "my mother'll be here any minute."

"Your mother?"

"She'll be here any minute." The nurse nodded sadly, obviously thinking he was delirious, but she was firm and the patient took his pill and dropped off to sleep. A minute later his mother came sailing in, Henrietta Franklin, in her ninety-sixth year.

Another member of Basil's entourage was his nephew Robert Henriques, a white, undersized unhealthy-looking boy in his early teens, a pupil at Rugby.

Rugby was, of course, the school in *Tom Brown's Schooldays* (which was written about 1857) and when Robert was there shortly after World War I, conditions had hardly changed. He was to experience at first hand all the bullying, savagery and rigours he had found in the book.

He came from a wealthy upper-middle-class home, His father, a barrister by profession, never practised. In those days doing nothing was not in the least frowned upon, and Henriques Senior did nothing blissfully. He shot, fished, hunted, spent much time on horseback, galloping over his large Cotswold estate, a landed gentleman.

Robert's mother was a Beddington (Her grandfather, who was born Hyam Leopold Moses, was a stockbroker, and it was said that the day he changed his name by deed poll to Beddington, a large banner was spread across 'Change with the message: AND THE LORD SAID UNTO MOSES GOOD MORNING BEDDINGTON.) Like the Henriques, the Beddingtons prospered sufficiently in trade to become landed gentry, and Robert, a scion of two families thus established upon the soil of England, should have felt as English as the Cotswolds. But there was something about him of the eternal alien. He was uncertain in later life whether this was the result of the hell he went through at school, or whether he had to go through hell at school because he was so much of an outsider.

He was rarely allowed to forget that he was a Jew. His family had lived in England for nearly three centuries, but it can take longer than that to get accepted, especially at public school. He was, or felt, hounded at Rugby, but his particular tormentor was a boy called Connelly, of Jewish extraction, whose parents had done well out of the war and had changed their name and religion to accompany their change of fortune. He later recalled this period in an autobiographical fragment written in the third person in which he assumed the name of Laurence Lamego.[21]

Connelly was a prefect in the upper school and he found Lamego's very presence unseemly.

"You admit you are a Jew, Lamego. You are filthy, Lamego, as we can all see for ourselves. Therefore Lamego, you are a filthy Jew!"[22] These encounters generally took place in the school bathroom. "The low room would be thick with steam, the unshaded lights blurred like lamps in a city fog, the atmosphere heavy with sweat, the tiled floor slippery and awash. Laurence's naked and undersized, under-developed body which showed no signs of adolescence at that time, although he was well past his fourteenth birthday, was certainly an unpleasant sight. He stood in a kind of trance, his eyes fixed on Connelly's pubic hair and all his senses suffocated. . . ."

"Do you agree, Lamego? Do you? So he . . . he won't talk. . . . Tickle him up, somebody."

Bartlett or Fowler, Lambert, Moore, Jackson, Freeman or Barker would draw out his towel, stretch it, wet the end of it on the floor and flick it like a stock whip against Laurence's backside. . . . The others would take their turn. When it was necessary, somebody would spin Laurence round with his foot in order to present the target area in the

right direction. . . . By then Laurence would be blubbing . . . sobbing . . .
gasping for breath. . . .

"Now Lamego, why do you cheat? You do cheat, don't you, don't you?
Don't you? You must cheat because you're a Jew, mustn't you? You don't
deny that, Lamego? You can't, can you? Didn't I tell you on Thursday
to look up Jew in the Oxford Dictionary? Didn't I? . . . Didn't I tell you
that the Oxford Dictionary says in black and white that to Jew is to cheat.
So you must cheat, mustn't you? Why, why, Lamego, do you cheat?
Oh for Christ's sake tickle the bugger up; he makes me sick. . . ."[23]

And so the torments continued. 'Lamego', Jew or not, used to attend
chapel with the rest of the boys, but the anguished cry to Heaven he
would make at such times was found nowhere in the Book of Common
Prayer:

"Lord God of Israel, help Thou thy people and me in particular to
vanquish mine enemies and Connelly in particular."[24]

The humiliation and anguish did not go on for long but they affected
Henriques for the rest of his days and he became obsessed with the
belief that he was a cringing coward. It engendered within him a
nagging feeling of inadequacy amounting to self-hate. One can see it all
in the opening paragraph of his autobiography:

At various times, at various ages of my life, I have been so miserable a
failure in several different spheres of endeavour, so sunk in the glutinous
sin of self-pity and allowing myself to suffer so intolerably, that I cannot
possibly write autobiographically of the constituent events. I must write
as a novelist, who, myself, in the main dislikes my hero.[25]

And in the last paragraph:

He wasted his powers in the pursuit of courage, in flight from cowardice in
trying to expunge shame which he was never really justified in feeling. . . .[26]

And it was this flight from cowardice which finally drove him, the
least soldierly of men, into the regular army. He was commissioned in
the Royal Artillery and proved a highly competent officer. After his
retirement in 1933, he joined the Territorials, and was mobilised on the
outbreak of World War II, as an artillery officer. In the following year
he volunteered for service with the Commandos, and in due course
became chief of staff, with the rank of major, to the Special Services
Brigade which organised landings in enemy occupied Europe. In the
following year he was transferred to Combined Operations Headquarters under Admiral Lord Louis Mountbatten, and was then
seconded to General Eisenhower's headquarters in London. He was

involved in organising the North African landings, went ashore with the first American assault troops at Fedala and received the American Silver Star for his part in the operation. He accompanied the U.S. 7th Army throughout the campaign as General Patton's senior British Staff Officer, and in 1943 he took part in the Sicily landings. These were the most exhilarating years of his life. His constant introspection, who am I, what am I, how am I doing, stopped. At last, as he wrote in his autobiography, he had a sense of fulfilment:

> There was just one period when Laurence Lamego was right by those standards of his which were such a burden and torment to him. Naturally this was during the war, when a soldier was relieved of many of his moral responsibilities as a human being, when mental competence, physical courage and endurance were all that were required of him.[27]

There was one other period in his life when he had this feeling of exhilaration.

Henriques was a gifted writer, and his first novel, *No Arms No Armour* written shortly before the war, won the All Nations Prize Novel Competition. Throughout the war years he travelled with a notebook in his knapsack and made copious jottings which were later to be incorporated into one or another of his books.

The Journey Home which was published shortly after the war was sold out on the day of publication. Another, *Through the Valley*, won the prestigious James Tait Black Memorial Prize. His seventh and last novel, *The Commander*, was published posthumously. It dealt with the formation of a Commando Unit and covered the twelve-month period after Dunkirk. The commander was Captain Laurence Lamego, alias Henriques, and the account is largely autobiographical.

Although it is perhaps the least satisfactory of Henriques' novels, it shows a new, confident, dynamic, self-assured Lamego replacing the hesitant, anguished, nail-biting creature of the autobiography. But one wonders if his vision of himself was not pure fantasy.

In 1943 he was promoted to the rank of colonel and was made chief military planner at Combined Operations Headquarters. He was then thirty-eight and such a rank carrying such responsibilities at such an age is not generally accorded to spineless nincompoops, not even in the exigencies of war. After the Sicilian campaign he saw active se vice in France, Belgium and Holland. Both his courage and powers of endurance were tested to the full and he was found wanting in neither.

Similarly he thought of himself as a failed writer. He was the author of two memorable biographies, one on Sir Robert Waley Cohen, and the other, a work monumental in scale and achievement, of Marcus Samuel, the founder of Shell. He also wrote a travel book, a collection of essays on the Cotswolds, a history of the Suez War which was a best-seller.

It may be plainly said that Henriques was no Dickens, but he writes with great economy, clarity and power and is always in complete command of his material, so that even when he describes the chaos of an abortive military operation one never loses the thread of the narrative. His characters are perfectly realised, palpable, living creatures, not, perhaps, always likeable, but invariably engaging. They are the work of an accomplished creative artist and if he had cared to devote himself entirely to writing there is no doubt that his work could have yielded a considerable income.

He was, like so many colonels in their own neighbourhoods, the local Bull of Bashan, a member of the local parish council, president of the local cricket club, a familiar figure at local markets and fairs, at point to point races and hunt balls. He was no brick-faced, bull-necked blimp. That he was a refined and cultured man was quickly apparent, but otherwise, with his tweed suit, battered hat, everlasting brown waterproof shoes, thornproof jacket, he was as much part of the neighbourhood as the honey-coloured stone. Yet from time to time on the approach of the Sabbath he could remember with a start that he was a Jew. This, as his daughter recalls in a moving biographical note, did not happen often:

> My father was a very liberal Jew and although he considered it an important duty to participate himself in Anglo-Jewish life . . . he rarely went to synagogue or imposed a similar sense of obligation on his family. His sons were vaguely encouraged to learn Hebrew and there was, an amazing and somewhat hilarious emotional outburst about twice a year at his home deep in the Cotswold countryside, when candles were lit on a Friday night and dusty prayer books suddenly produced.[28]

Robert could not describe himself as a believer or disbeliever, but he did believe in continuity. That, and a deep ancestral pride, were sufficient to keep him active within the fold. He was a vice-president of the Reform Synagogue, a vice-president of the Association of Jewish Youth, on the council of the Anglo-Jewish Association, but what made him remarkable for a member and especially a Sephardi member of his caste, who at one time supported his uncles' Jewish Fellowship, was that he became a Zionist and a passionate one.

He arrived at his Zionism rather late in life, and he was brought to it not by any religious feeling, understanding of Jewish history, but out of admiration for the Israeli army, its achievements in the field, and its *blitzkrieg* in Sinai in 1956 which he described in his *One Hundred Hours to Suez*. In watching the Israel army, its courage, pugnacity, and genius for improvisation, he not only relived his own finest hour, he finally came to terms with something in himself.

With all his ancestral pride Henriques had a certain degree of ambivalence about his Jewishness. One can see it in this description of a handful of Orthodox Jews he saw at Cyprus airport:

> Those three other newcomers were not a credit to humanity . . . they were young men with an unhealthy translucent glaze to the skin of their unshaven bearded faces, with greasy ringlets and strange clothes. . . . Like three malevolent black creatures, more bird of prey than beast, nodding their fur-trimmed hats at the pivot of their assemblage, their power like a private joke.[29]

His abhorrence of 'these three ghouls', as he called them, may have stemmed from his distaste for Orthodoxy, but his Jewishness may have been at the source of the sense of inadequacy which haunted him during so much of his life, and the fear that he was deficient in courage or stamina. Jewish history, to those superficially versed in it, is one long, agonising martyrdom, and in his own lifetime he could see wave after wave of refugees, white-faced with terror, turning this way and that, helpless, hapless, hounded in *flight*. This was the picture many Jews had of themselves before the rise of Israel, and it fits in with the picture Henriques had of Lamego.

Then suddenly it changed. Israel's successes in the 1948 war were won slowly, in instalments and were not dramatic. But the 1956 Sinai campaign came as a lightning stride. Within days the Egyptians were shattered and Israel was by the canal. It must have seemed to Henriques at that moment as if his prayer in Rugby Chapel, "Lord God of Israel, help Thou thy people . . .", had finally been answered and Lamego vindicated.

CHAPTER 28

Final Generation?

The papers agreed it was a brilliant choice, but they could not agree in their assessment of the man.

In October 1970 Prime Minister Edward Heath established what he called a Central Capability Unit of special advisers to question and challenge policies put to the Cabinet by government departments, and appointed Lord Rothschild to head the unit.

The name was familiar, the man was not, for Nathaniel Mayer Victor, the third Lord Rothschild, shuns the limelight to the point almost of being a recluse. A *Sunday Times* reporter who tried to find out something about him did not find the experience illuminating:

> When asked about Victor Rothschild his friends variously describe him as a genius, an oaf, an academic recluse, a man of the world, a frustrated failure, a remnant of old Bloomsbury, a fierce perfectionist, a character out of one of Scott Fitzgerald's poorer novels, and an administrator of immense skill. They all agree, however, that the quadruple burden of his name, his race, his money and his intelligence have made him one of the most complicated personalities in contemporary life.[1]

He has inherited something of his grandfather's proverbial rudeness, but he can also be extremely courteous. He is perhaps more a respecter of persons than of personages. An editor who once tried to approach him at short notice was sent off with a flea in his ear, yet he has received young reporters with warmth and geniality. He is moody and unpredictable. Richard Crossman, an ex-Cabinet Minister who has met him on a number of occasions, observed in the *New Statesman*:

> By persuading Victor Rothschild to leave Shell and head his new central brains trust, Ted Heath has accepted a rival's advice and put 'a tiger in the tank'. Here is a new type of Whitehall warrior who combines scientific

395

eminence and managerial drive with a dialectical diabolism which whenever I meet him leaves me (nearly) speechless. He is a Lindemann and
Balogh rolled into one and stiffened with a strain of sardonic tycoonery.
The furies roused by the 'Prof' under Churchill and by Thomas Balogh
during his more recent stay at No 10 were as nothing compared with the
rows I confidently expect to erupt when Lord Rothschild really gets to
work under the protection afforded by Sir Burke Trend's cabinet secre-
tariat. I congratulate the Prime Minister on a really adventurous appointment.[2]

Lord Rothschild at sixty is a robust, vigorous but rather restless
man. His face is round and tending a little to fat, but is still handsome.
His chin is pugnacious and looks unshaven even when it is shaved. He
is impatient, does not suffer fools gladly, and is disposed to treat most
people as fools unless they can show ready proof to the contrary. The
effect is intimidating but his eyes, kindly, good-humoured and a little
care-worn, are perhaps the best clue to his character.

His father, the Hon Charles de Rothschild, a benign, gentle, unas-
suming man, had joined the family bank after coming down from
Cambridge. He was the author of a volume called *Synopsis of British
Siphonaptera*. Like his brother, the second Lord Rothschild, he was a
keen zoologist; but unlike him, he confined his studies to small creatures
and did so, moreover, in his spare time. He continued at the bank,
he said, "out of a sense of filial devotion",[3] and sighed for distant places
of exotic fleas. "Had I my way England would see little of me," he
wrote. "What I would really like is to live in a nice island or settle in
Japan or Burma and be a professional bug-hunter."[4]

Lord Rothschild is an authority on spermatozoa and he is both a
Doctor of Science and a Fellow of the Royal Society.

He was born in his father's town house in Kensington Palace
Gardens, now the home of the Romanian Embassy, was educated at
Harrow, excelled both academically and as an athlete and at seventeen
played cricket for Northampton County. He won a scholarship to
Cambridge where he took a first in English, then switched to science
and was elected a Fellow of Trinity College. He also found time to
become a skilled jazz pianist.

Like his father, he was carried by filial devotion into the bank but,
unlike him, he did not remain there. After a desultory spell in the gold
refinery he returned to Cambridge and research.

He joined the Ministry of Supply on the outbreak of war, turned his
mind to explosives and was awarded the George Medal, 'for', in the

words of the official citation, 'dangerous work in hazardous circumstances'. He was involved in dismantling the first of the German magnetic mines which were causing havoc to allied shipping and, as he half expected to be blown up in the course of the operation, described each meticulous step on a tape recorder.

In 1948 he was appointed chairman of the Agricultural Research Council and in 1965 became co-ordinating head of all the chemical research work undertaken by Royal-Dutch Shell. This is one of the most important scientific research posts in the world, and he controlled a budget of over £34,000,000 and a scientific staff of over five thousand.

Victor inherited £2,500,000 on the death of his father, and succeeded to the title in 1937 when his bachelor uncle Lionel Walter died. He is sometimes bothered by both inheritances for he does not believe in privilege. "I do not believe that people should have a lot of money unless they've earned it," he once said. He sits on the Labour benches in the House of Lords and was offered the post of Minister of Technology by Mr Harold Wilson in 1966, which he regretfully declined. He had, he said, a larger budget and a freer hand at Shell.

Although technically a scientist, his main work at Shell apart from long-term planning of research, was the allocation of funds and he could not have been more closely involved with finance if he had remained at New Court. It is as if money follows the Rothschilds even when they do not follow money.

Lord Rothschild married twice and although he is not a practising Jew, his first wife, Barbara Hutchinson, was converted with full Orthodox rites into the Jewish faith.

His second wife, Teresa Mayor, is not Jewish. There are three children by the first marriage, which ended in divorce, and three by the second.

Sarah, his eldest daughter, flitted in and out of the gossip columns in the 1950s while she was an undergraduate at Oxford. One heard of her complaining that Oxford men were unromantic and rarely gave flowers (and received a pair of cauliflowers for her pains). She modelled in Dior's boutique, organised fashion shows, and – this was part of the finishing education of any glittering young thing of the period – worked in a coffee bar. She was rusticated by her college (St Hilda's) for staying out overnight at a dance, and went down without taking her degree.

By way of compensation Emma, her half-sister, won scholarships to Oxford and Cambridge at fifteen, opted for Oxford and entered

Somerville at sixteen, probably the youngest under-graduette since the war. She was a particularly brilliant and precocious child, and her father took extraordinary pains to give her the best possible education.

A remarkable governess, Miss Lamb, was engaged for his younger children, as well as those of his sister, Miriam. Miss Lamb has no doubt that Emma's subsequent triumphs were entirely due to her efforts.[5]

He later formed a private school at his home in which Emma was joined by the sons and daughters of various Cambridge dons. She went on to take a first in P.P.E. and won a Kennedy Memorial Fund Scholarship to the Massachusetts Institute of Technology. She now commutes between London and New York, is a disciple of Tynan and Co and the glossy left and has been active on behalf of several of its causes, including the Black Panthers.

Lord Rothschild once described himself as "the most pro-Arab Jew in the country",[6] a description which could more adequately fit his daughter. He himself tries to keep an open mind on Middle Eastern questions, and has been helpful to Israel on several publicised, and numerous unpublicised occasions. They were unpublicised not because he is in any way nervous of appearing to be a supporter of Israel, but because he hates publicity in general.

The career of Lord Rothschild's heir, Jacob, has followed a rigidly orthodox pattern, the set route for every highborn, intelligent young Englishman – Eton, Christ Church, the Life Guards and then straight into the City and a partnership in N. M. Rothschild & Sons.

There is no talk of 'filial devotion' about his association with the bank. He loves it. There is nothing else he would rather do, and he does it exceedingly well. Jacob stands in direct succession to Nathan, Lionel and Nathaniel.

N. M. Rothschild and Co. is a little more than 160 years old and for the second half of its life it ticked over largely on the impetus it received from the first. It could occasionally leap into life for a major overseas project, but generally it was in the doldrums, venerable, august, but inert. Natty, Leo and Alfred, who died within a few years of each other, were succeeded by Leo's two sons, Lionel and Anthony, and they were not a particularly inspired pair. Lionel was more interested in motoring, yachting, fishing and his rhododendrons than in business. Anthony was interested in business, but not so interested as to go searching for it. "They know where we live," he would say of potential clients, "and if they want to do business with us let them come and talk to us."[7] And when they did come, and he did not like their faces or manners, he showed them to the door.

At the outbreak of World War II it occurred to the brothers that one bomb on New Court could put an end to the dynasty for good. They therefore formed Rothschild Continuations Ltd, a corporate partner, to succeed them in case they should both die in the war. Lionel died in 1942, and Anthony continued for a while alone until he was joined at the end of the war by Lionel's sons Edmund and Leo, and his own son Evelyn.

Much of the City was devastated in the blitz. Buildings on every side of New Court lay in ruins, but New Court itself remained erect, almost unscathed, as if, indeed, a Senior Partner on High had kept watch over it. It survived, moreover, as the most prestigious name in the City.

Thus when Sir Joseph Smallwood, Prime Minister of Newfoundland, came to London in 1952, for help to develop the natural resources of his province, Sir Winston Churchill put him in touch with Rothschilds and on August 19 he came to lunch at New Court.

Luncheons at New Court begin promptly at 1 p.m. and Anthony, who was then Senior Partner, made it his custom, whether the meal was over or not, to rise promptly at 2 p.m. and get back to work. That day they continued at table till 3 p.m., and the staff waiting outside concluded that something momentous was happening.[8] They were right. As a result of the meeting Rothschilds joined with the Anglo-American Corporation of South Africa, the Anglo-Newfoundland Development Company, Bowaters, English Electric, the Frobisher Mining Company, and Rio Tinto to form the British Newfoundland Corporation (Brinco) which was responsible for the Churchill Falls hydro-electric scheme, Labrador.

It was Anthony who set the machinery in motion, but it was his nephew Edmund, then Junior Partner, who carried the main burden of the work. He was the principal architect of the project which covers an area the size of England and Wales, involves an investment of $1,000,000,000 and is the biggest single private enterprise of its kind in North America.

Edmund became Senior Partner on the death of Anthony in 1961 and his attention was forcibly turned to domestic matters by the failure of Rothschilds to defend one of its major clients, Odhams Press, which owned *The People* and the *Daily Herald*, from a takeover bid by the *Daily Mirror* group (now part of Reed International). "The boom years for takeover struggles had begun", wrote a City commentator, "and Rothschilds was publicly seen to be not as much of an adept as it ought to have been in this branch of banking practice."[9]

Edmund introduced new attitudes and new people and for the first time in the history of the bank brought in a partner who was neither a member of the family, nor even a Jew, Mr David Colville, an ex-treasurer of Lloyd's Bank who had been personal assistant to Anthony.

The old New Court building, which had been reconstructed in 1860, was pulled down in 1962. A new edifice of concrete and glass was built on the site, and the new Rothschild outlook may be said to date with the building. In that year the company started a corporate finance department to handle company reconstructions and mergers. It began with a staff of one. Today it employs twenty to thirty people, including five partners. In 1968 alone it was involved in £400,000,000 worth of mergers, including those between Showerings and Allied Breweries, Associated British Foods and Allied Farm Foods, Yorkshire Copper and Imperial Metal Industries. It was also concerned in the merger between the National Provincial Bank and the Westminster, and acted for Unilever in the merger talk with Allied Breweries, until the Monopolies Commission announced that it would not allow the marriage to proceed.

Rothschilds was amongst the first to realise the possibilities opened up by the sale of Eurobonds. It is second only to Warburgs in its handling of Eurodollar loans.

To further this work it has strengthened its links with the Paris Rothschilds, and Guy, head of the Paris House, is now a partner in NMR, while Evelyn sits on the board of Banque Rothschilds.

Rothschilds was for a long time the last surviving major partnership in British banking, though the partners grew till they were sixteen in number. This was six beyond the legal maximum and Parliament was induced to insert an extra clause in the Companies Act to make this possible. Five of the partners were Rothschilds, three were corporate (like Rothschild Continuation) and eight were from outside the family.

By 1970 the structure proved to be unworkable. "A partnership where the partners have an equal say in certain respects on how the business is run", said Jacob Rothschild, "is an unwieldy structure and not a streamlined way to run a merchant bank."[10] On September 30 it was incorporated as a limited liability company with an issued and paid up capital of £10,000,000, the family holding 95% of the shares.

The bank stressed that there was no intention of seeking a stock market quotation for Rothschild shares.[11]

The division of responsibilities will continue much as it did under the partnership. Edmund is head of the bank, Leo (who is also a director of the Bank of England) looks after the banking side, Evelyn is responsible for investment and administration and Jacob is in charge of the finance department.

As such, Jacob heads the branch which gets the most publicity, something the Rothschilds have always shunned. He does so with a briskness, agility and push which would have appalled Anthony, and delighted Nathan Mayer. He has been at the centre of all the great mergers in which the Rothschilds have been involved in recent years, including the controversial Pergamon-Leasco imbroglio, and the great flotations of Eurobonds for such international giants as Philips, Rio Tinto and De Beers.

Jacob has set about his work as if there were not five generations of Rothschilds before him, to become, so to speak, a Rothschild in his own right and through his own efforts. He is an earnest, slightly-built young man with a high forehead and apart from his prominent lower lip he does not look like a Rothschild. The impression he gives after a brief encounter is of great compressed energy, and he seems driven on by some internal fury, a harnessed wrath. His boyhood was not untroubled. He grew up in the war years and his father could not give him the attention he later lavished on his daughters. He was intensely unhappy at Eton and suffered from anti-Semitism, no actual baiting of the type that Robert Henriques suffered at Rugby, but slighter harassments like name-calling – he was known as 'Hookie' throughout the school.

(One of his cousins arrived at the school to find '. . . you are a dirty little Jew-boy' scrawled on his desk. The boy at once took it up with the housemaster, who promptly traced the culprit. The cousin was half Jewish, so was the housemaster and so, it turned out, was the culprit.)

Jacob was happier at Oxford where he took a first in P.P.E. but here too his origins involved him in occasional embarrassments. He was once a guest at the table of the late Cecil Roth, Reader in Jewish studies at the university, and when the last course had been served he was invited to recite the usual Hebrew grace after meals. He turned this way and that and finally blurted out that he couldn't read a word of Hebrew.

Jacob is married to Serena, a daughter of Sir Philip Dunn, the industrialist. They have three daughters. Serena is a Roman Catholic, but their children are not being instructed in any faith.

Jacob is rather more active in Jewish affairs than his father has been and is treasurer of the Residential Centre for Jewish Deaf Children and on the council of the Weizmann Institute, but in general he finds time for little beyond his tremendous responsibilities in the bank. He was already handling multi-million pound deals in his early twenties. Now at thirty-four he is one of the most powerful men in the company and in the course of a year handles sums larger than the budget of many states.

His aunt Dr Miriam Rothschild is an entomologist of international standing with fleas as her particular speciality. She has written a book called *Fleas, Flukes and Cuckoos* which, a little improbably, proved to be something of a best-seller and has gone into four editions. She is an Honorary Fellow of St Hugh's College, Oxford, an Hon. D.Sc. and a Professor of biology at London University.

She lives in a large mansion of Cotswold stone on the outskirts of Oxford, and drives a Bentley, which she considers to be the best car in the world. Her front door is always open and anyone can wander in. Lunch is laid out on a large hot-plate and one serves oneself. The wine is not Mouton Rothschild but a plain Burgundy. There are line drawings on the wall, prints, sketches, all fitting well with the plain white décor, but nothing which could find its way into a Sotheby catalogue. What distinguishes the house from that of any number of prosperous households, is the large library with shelves stretching from floor to ceiling, and overflowing into the corridors, and strange exotic creatures fluttering behind wire cages in a specially heated room. They turn out on closer examination to be giant butterflies of an obscure Andean variety, and they are velvety, many-coloured, about the size of bats, and fix one with a nasty, unwelcoming stare. Lepidoptera seem to be a Rothschild obsession and one can find handsome specimens behind glass in several Rothschild homes.

His admiring aunt Miriam puts it all with simple candour. "His father is a genius and so is the boy, a different sort of genius, but a genius."

One has heard the expression used of Dr Rothschild herself, but she disowns it with a shrug. "Nonsense."

She farms 2,000 acres in Northamptonshire but currently lives outside Oxford to be near her children's schools. If one asks why she did not send them to public schools like all the other members of the family, her eyes widen, as if one had asked a silly question. She regards the whole public-school system as outdated.

Dr Rothschild is in some ways the archetypal English dowager, with a mind of her own and a forceful way of expressing it, but with intense Jewish feelings. The net effect is of a cross between Lady Bracknell and the Yiddishe Momma.

On the eve of the Six Day War in 1967 she had to be restrained by her family from dashing on board a plane to volunteer for service in the Israeli army. She was sixty at the time and recovering from a major operation, and was reluctantly made to see that she would be a hindrance rather than a help.

But somebody from the family had to go out, she insisted. Victor had donated £1,000,000 to Israel on behalf of the family, but she felt that that was not good enough. A Rothschild had to be there, on the spot, in person, and she was finally reassured by the news that Baron Elie of the French house had flown out in his own private plane.

Whether by conscious selection or natural evolution every generation of Rothschilds has had its own particular ambassador to the Jewish community. It was not that the rest of the family were un-Jewish, but that one of their number tended to be more Jewish than the rest. In Lionel's generation there was Anthony, in Natty's generation, Leo. After Leo came his son Lionel, and in our time it is the Senior partner, Edmund, or Eddy.

The diminutive is so widely used that one expects to meet some breezy, hand-pumping hail-fellow-well-met, but in fact the name Edmund is more fitting, for there is nothing breezy about the Senior Partner of N. M. Rothschild & Sons. He is courteous, charming, the blue eyes twinkle in a friendly face, but the voice is earnest and one is aware of a constant wariness and reserve.

Born in 1916, he was educated at Harrow and Trinity College, Cambridge and then, to complete his education, his father sent him on a world tour. The year was 1938, the shadow of Hitler was spreading over Europe and the Jewish question weighed heavily on Eddy, as may be seen from an account which he kept of his journey. On October 5, the Day of Atonement, he was in the jungles of Indo-China:

> . . . Yom Kippur. Did nothing all the day and observed the Fast. My thoughts went home again and then to a review of the year. What misdeeds one seems to do and how easily one slips into them. Perfect men are rare . . . I do not know of one . . . My thoughts turn to what the day stands for. Is the Jewish question soluble? Nicky [his companion] says it is by intermarriage. I say it is by the island solution [Madagascar] and Palestine. The day may come when I shall be able to do something. Yet I am going to encounter terrible opposition; the world today is

racially divided. Am I *Civis Britannicus*, or have I to give everything I know and have and become *Civis Judaus?*. . . .

A day of almost unceasing rain. The world seems to weep for the tormented people of Israel – or is it fancy?[12]

In Singapore he was invited to a charity film show on behalf of Jewish refugees, and found himself watching George Arliss in *The House of Rothschild*.[13]

During the war he was commissioned in the Royal Artillery and rose to the rank of major, and in 1943 was seconded to the Jewish Brigade as commander of their field battery in Italy. Many of his troops were from Palestine. In 1957 he visited the Israeli army and when he sat down to lunch he found twelve colonels and one major who had been bombardiers or gunners in his battery. By 1967 several of them had become generals.

Nathan Mayer had been warden of the Great Synagogue in Duke's Place, and there had always been a Rothschild in the warden's box. The building was destroyed in the blitz, and to keep the name alive a small synagogue in Adler Street, also in the East End, was renamed the Great, and Edmund is there at prayer every Day of Atonement.

"I immensely enjoy the meetings down at the synagogue and I have a lot of friends down there," he said. "They are very different from the people I normally meet, but they are absolutely wonderful – salt of the earth, couldn't be nicer."[14]

His sons Nicholas and Lionel had their Barmitzvahs in Adler Street in 1964. Chief Rabbi Brodie gave the sermon, and the service was followed by a sherry reception for the congregation, and then a small family luncheon. He finds the lavish type of Barmitzvah common in the community – 'ghastly'.

He is, as he will readily confess, "definitely not Orthodox", yet he is moved by deep religious impulses which he cannot quite define. When he was in Jerusalem after the Six Day War, for example, he felt compelled to make a pilgrimage to the West Wall and was deeply moved by his experience.

Edmund was greatly agitated by the war and after the ceasefire he was hopeful enough to believe that the day had come when, to use his phrase, he "might be able to do something". He wrote a letter to *The Times* suggesting a de-salination scheme which would open vast acres of desert to the plough, offer new room for the resettlement of refugees, the prospects of a much higher standard of living and peace for the entire area. The scale of the scheme, though tremendous, was not much larger than that undertaken by the British Newfoundland Corporation. His letter was based on a detailed assessment of the potential of the area, and the new possibilities opened up by atomic energy (he was for a time attached as an observer to the United Kingdom Atomic Energy Authority), and he showed his scheme to be eminently practical in the plainest accountancy terms. The missing factor was good will, but he believes that even that will in time be found.

Edmund has a deep sense of family history and his room at New Court is virtually a museum of Rothschildiana. He sits behind the great desk which, he proudly points out, his great-grandfather Baron Lionel used a century before him. At his side, in a solid gold frame is the letter sent by Disraeli to his grandfather, Leo, declaring that "there cannot be too many Rothschilds". There are numerous momentoes connected with Brinco, in whose progress he takes a justifiable pride and whose formation he regards as his finest achievement.

The present Lord Rothschild has been known to use a gold ingot as a paperweight. Edmund uses something more ornate, the number 22 fashioned in solid gold and weighing perhaps half a pound, and he wears gold cuff-links in the same design. He met his wife on the 22nd, proposed on the 22nd, got married on the 22nd, and his daughter Kate was born on the 22nd. It is his lucky number.

Edmund's father had inherited Halton House in the Chilterns from Alfred, sold it to the Air Ministry and used the money to indulge in his three main passions, rhododendron breeding, fishing and yachting, and he was able to do all three in the 3,000 acre estate he bought in the New Forest at Exbury, with the river Beaulieu on one side and the Solent on the other. He used Exbury with its exotic blooms as a pleasure garden. Edmund, living in a much taxed age, has had to make it pay, and has cut down the number of gardeners from sixty to thirty. He exports plants to all parts of the world, and has turned his gardens – which attract some 30,000 visitors during the flowering season – into a charitable foundation.

Inchmery House, on the edge of the estate, stands on broad lawns overlooking the murky sea-lanes of Southampton. It is a grey-brick villa, not particularly big and of no particular distinction, of a type which one finds in any number in the southern counties, the sort a tea planter might have built himself at the end of the last century after doing well in Assam.

A black-coated butler opens the door, and one is admitted into a large, comfortable, middle-class residence. Edmund's wife Elizabeth receives visitors in a small carpeted study, with books ranged round the walls, some of them in expensive bindings, but they are in the main the haphazard collection of people who find pleasure in books.

Elizabeth is a tall, shapely, handsome woman. She was born in Vienna and there is a slight Viennese tinge to her accent. She dresses casually, English country style, in tweeds and good solid walking shoes, with the easy assurance of the woman who knows she can look good in anything. The house displays much of her personality. There are treasures, rare furnishings, rare carpets. There are paintings by Cuyp, Romney, Reynolds and Cellini. All blend with the setting in what is essentially a home rather than a show place. They are there to be seen if one looks for them, but they do not impose themselves on the eye.

One is conscious everywhere of a distaste for extravagance.

They have four children. Kate, who is twenty, is a student of fine arts at London University; Nicholas, eighteen, is at Cambridge; and the twins, Charlotte and Lionel, are fourteen. When Kate and Nicholas were in their early teens their pocket money was 5s. a week. "It is so important for us to teach our children the value of money", said Elizabeth. "We have supplied them all with savings books and expect them to make use of them."[15]

The wealth of the English Rothschilds has not been Rothschildian for some time. During World War I Natty, Leo and Alfred died within a few years of each other and a large part of the family's wealth was swallowed in death duties. And while the old money was being soaked up, New Court was in the doldrums and little new money was being made.

The only Croesus among them after 1918 was Jimmy, and he was descended from the French Rothschilds, who were by far the wealthiest branch of the family. When he died in 1957 he left over £12,000,000, of which £7,000,000 went in death duties.

The Rothschilds enclave in Piccadilly is no more. Alfred's large pile in Seamore Place was demolished to give Curzon Street access to Park Lane. Lionel's house at 148 Piccadilly was demolished in 1937 for a Hyde Park Corner improvement scheme. The collection of Dutch and Flemish paintings, French eighteenth-century furniture, carvings, crystal, glass and porcelain, cloisonné and tapestries, which had been built up by Lionel in the 1830s, was auctioned when money generally was tight. It fetched a mere £125,000.[16]

The family has largely forsaken the Chilterns. Halton is an R.A.F.

officers' mess; Tring is a girls' school; Aston Clinton has been demolished. Waddesdon was made over by Jimmy, with a gift of £50,000, to the National Trust (though his widow Dorothy still has a house in the park). Evelyn still lives at Ascott Wing, but it too has been made over to the National Trust. Mentmore remains a Rosebery residence.

Compared with the French cousins who still own palaces and great estates and employ armies of servants, the English Rothschilds live modest lives in modest homes.

Lord Bearsted, whose grandfather, Marcus Samuel, created the Shell oil empire and the bank which is now part of the Hill Samuel group, was once described in a newspaper as one of the wealthiest men in England, but he denied it. "Wealthy," he said, "yes. Wealthiest, no."[17] He enjoys his wealth unashamedly, and bears every mark of enjoyment on his face, which is never without a tan and is wrinkled with smiles. He has a home in Chelsea, a country house in Warwick-shire, a shooting lodge in the Highlands and a villa on the Riviera.

The Samuel family is no longer in oil (though Lord Bearsted's brother Peter is on the board of Shell), and the family bank, though a substantial enterprise, was in danger of becoming too small to attract the large international corporation seeking funds on the London market or contemplating mergers. In 1964 it joined with the Philip Hill Investment Trust to form a combine with disclosed assets worth nearly £600,000,000. The First National City Bank of New York currently has a 10% holding in the bank. Charles Clore, for whom Samuels acted in his successful bid for Selfridges, has a 7% holding and the Samuel family over 24%. Hill Samuel is now one of the largest merchant banks in the City in terms of deposits and profits as disclosed after tax.

Lord Bearsted has a parched, crackling voice with the warm, easy manner of the bon-viveur and one half expects him to speak with a French accent. He is a keen farmer, "no not a gentleman farmer", he insists, "I get my hands dirty", and farms some 1,500 acres on his estate.

He has helped to endow the Bearsted Readership in Jewish History at Warwick University and is active on the Bearsted Hospital and the Tottenham Jewish hospital, both of them charities endowed by his father and grandfather. "One is pulled in, I suppose, because one feels one has to, but one is active because one enjoys it." He is not otherwise involved in the Jewish life, and keeps neither the Day of Atonement nor Passover. "My behaviour pattern as far as these things are concerned", he adds with an apologetic smile, "is not altogether correct."[18]

He has been married twice, both times out of the faith, and he expects that his daughter, who is now twenty-two, will do the same.

He finds taxes a bit mortifying. "One hears suggestions about living abroad, but I'd rather live in a cottage in England than in a mansion anywhere else." For the time being, however, he is able to continue to have a mansion in England.

Hill Samuel is an example of a family bank which through a process of growth and merger has lost its original compact family character. Samuel Montagu is another.

The founder of the bank, Samuel Montagu, had secured within his own lifetime everything necessary to establish the Montagus on English soil in perpetuity, a large family, great wealth, landed estates and an hereditary peerage. The estate was first to go. South Stoneham, the splendid Queen Anne mansion standing in a large park laid out by Capability Brown, was sold to Southampton University.[19] The ablest of the sons, Edwin, went into politics. Those who went into the bank applied themselves with greater determination than skill, and sometimes they did not even show determination. When Lionel, the youngest son, came down from Oxford he was told by his father that a job awaited him in Broad Street.

"On what terms," he asked.

"Precisely the same as for the rest of the family," said his father. "Five per cent of the profits."

"In that case," said Lionel, "might I have two-and-a-half per cent and leave at lunch time?"[20]

In effect it almost worked out that way. He began at Keyser's before World War I, and did not join Montagus till 1927 and remained till 1948. It was a quiet time in the bank, and it became quieter. He was chairman of Tattersalls Committee, a member of the Jockey Club and kept a large stable of race-horses. When there was racing within easy reach of the City he appeared at the bank two or three mornings a week. When the meetings were more distant he did not come at all.

Through his social and sporting contracts, however, he was able to introduce some important clients to the bank. He also brought in two outsiders, David Keswick, a Scot, and Louis Franck, a Belgian, who together jolted the firm into life. They extended its activities in the domestic market, opened a banking subsidiary in Zürich to strengthen the European connections, acquired extensive insurance and brokerage interests and launched several investment trusts. Within the decade 1954-63 profits increased from under £400,000 to nearly £2,000,000. In 1969 the group profits after tax were £2,245,000. It is now one of the two or three biggest merchant banks in the City, with assets, at 1969 prices, worth nearly £300,000,000.

The involvement of the Montagus and the Franklins in the bank has declined. The late Sidney Franklin was the last member of his family on the board. The Hon. David Charles Samuel, the third Lord Swaythling's heir, became a director of the bank in 1954, a few years after coming down from Cambridge. He is now, at forty-two, chairman.

Being a Montagu did not bring him to the top. By 1954, the name of Montagu carried no great weight in the City, and being an Honourable he believes, was, if anything, a disadvantage. Even the City was beginning to show a preference for self-made men, and David thinks of himself as entirely self-made. He was born to some wealth for apart from the fortune inherited by his father, his mother was a granddaughter of the first Lord Bearsted. His childhood was unhappy. During an air raid on London, his left leg was injured and developed gangrene. He spent weeks in agony and finally lost the use of his leg. Added to physical injury was the trauma of a broken home. His parents separated and his upbringing was left entirely to his mother.

"If you ask me whether I had a good start in life," he said, "I suppose you might call such handicaps a start."

He looks like the first Lord Swaythling without the beard, and with eyes so lively that they threaten at times to leave his face. His voice is slightly somnolent and solemn and he has a tendency to be portly, but in all other respects he looks younger than his years.

He does not recall that his Jewishness was ever a handicap or source of embarrassment. "My experience is that the sort of people who suffer at school from anti-Semitism would suffer in any case, but see the cause in their Jewishness rather than themselves."[21]

He believes that in the City a man's religion, or lack of it, is of no consequence whatever. This point was also made by Lord Bearsted, by Mr Edward Mocatta and by almost every Jewish banker one meets.

The late Lionel Fraser, a non-Jew who began his working life in a small Jewish bank, and eventually became one of the most powerful figures in the City, could view the situation with some detachment. He had to confess that "even in these more enlightened days, it is impossible to disguise the fact that in many minds in this country there exists a deep suspicion of, and prejudice against, Jews as a race which prevents individual cases from being judged on their merits. The undercurrent is strong and clamorous. There is no doubt about it."[22]

"That has not been my experience," said Mr Montagu emphatically, and he believes the City is now wide open to talent – whatever its source.

"We see it in the whole country," he added, and referred to the rise of Edward Heath, whom he greatly admires. "A self-made man like Heath? It couldn't have happened a generation ago."

At Cambridge he toyed with the idea of entering journalism and was interviewed by a number of Fleet Street papers after he came down. But the bank inevitably claimed him and in it he found his true calling.

"There was no pressure on me to join the bank, I suppose I gravitated towards it." After a gap of three generations there was again a Montagu with banking in his blood.

Montagus are the world's largest bullion dealers, and have particularly close relations with the Far Eastern markets. They were the first international dealers to fly gold to Hong Kong in the late forties and shipped the last cargo of gold to India before the import of gold was barred in 1947. They are also major dealers in gold coins, and in 1963, in conjunction with the Bank of Nova Scotia, they won a contract worth between sixty and eighty million dollars to replace the Central Bank of Uruguay's holding of gold coin with gold bars.[23]

The most venerable firm in the bullion market, Mocatta and Goldsmid, is still very much in business and is still headed by a Mocatta and a Goldsmid, but the sums involved are so vast that it needed the resources of a merchant bank to support it and it is now a wholly owned subsidiary of Hambros. Montagus was startled from its slumbers in time to survive on its own.

If Keswick and Franck brought it out of its slough, it was Montagu who pushed it to the fore, and while the former pair specialised mainly in foreign business, he has concentrated on domestic affairs, invented the split trusts and developed the numerous investment trusts of the company. His quiet manner and soft languorous voice go with a brisk and purposeful personality and an immaculate sense of direction. He combines resource with resourcefulness. He is quick in reaching decisions and relentless in putting them into action. City editors speak of him with some awe, as they do of the young Jacob Rothschild. After over sixty years Montagu is once again a name to conjure with in the City.

Rothschilds also had its sleepy period, but it never lost its mystique, and it has, therefore, been easier for New Court to make a comeback.

Montagus, on the other hand was a specialist concern dealing in bullion and foreign exchange. It became known because it performed a particular type of service particularly well, and when it ceased to be effective in its own particular line, it was almost forgotten. Keswick, Franck and Montagu have created what is virtually a new force in the City.

The reward for such efforts, even in pre-tax terms, is not as high as is generally believed. The total family holding in the bank yields about £100,000 a year, but that is for the whole Montagu clan, which is a very extensive one. The chairman's fees are £16,000 a year, but he has inherited considerable wealth and lives, as he says, "comfortably by any standards," if not quite on the Bearsted standard. He has a flat in Kensington and a large country-house at Newmarket, but, he is careful to point out, "no estate – only six acres of garden". He is keen on racing, and keeps a profitable stable, where the good horses pay for the bad. Anyone who can make racing stables pay for themselves could perhaps keep anything solvent.

Montagu's favourite relaxation is reading political biographies. He is a fast reader, and if he goes away for ten days will have ten books in his case. But he also takes Samuel Montagus with him, for he always leaves forwarding addresses and telephone numbers and is always on call – and is often called – at short notice.

He is, as he will confess, bad at resting, but adds, "I doubt if one can rest in this sort of game. It's an international business with international ramifications, and there is always something happening somewhere which can have serious consequences for the bank."

He was the central figure in organising the funds which served London Weekend Television its contract – "once his name is on a prospectus," said a partner in a large firm of commercial lawyers, "the money is as good as bespoke." Whenever City opinion is sought on some new fiscal measure one will generally find his well-rounded features on the television screen. He is not *the* voice of the City in the sense that, say, the first Lord Rothschild was – such dominance does not exist any more – but he is well informed, has his finger on the pulse of City opinion and is articulate.

He may on occasion find himself at a *Seder* or some other religious ceremony involving the family, but he is never quite sure what it is all about, and it holds no meaning for him. Judaism, or indeed religion of any sort, played so little a part in his upbringing that he never had to rebel against it, and his Jewishness is one of the incidental factors in his make-up, and one of the least significant at that. "One is proud of the things one's people did in the community, and one tries to do something oneself" – he is president of the Association for Jewish Youth – "but I'm afraid that that's about all there is to it."

His wife, *neé* Dreyfus, comes from an Alsatian Jewish family, and they have two daughters and a son. He would like his son to go into the bank – "if he does he will have to make his own way as I did". He would like his children to remain Jewish, but feels that they should be free, as he was, to choose their own direction in life. He is not hopeful that they will remain Jewish.

If Edmund is the representative of the Rothschilds to the Jewish community, the representative of the Montagus has been Mr Ewen Montagu, Q.C., David's uncle. He was educated at Cambridge and Harvard and then read for the Bar, and as a young man was so little bound by Jewish tradition that he could even absent himself from the ultimate Jewish occasion, the family *Seder*[24] – something which his younger brother, Ivor, a communist, would not dare to do. In the 1930s, however, he was approached by Sir Robert Waley Cohen – "Uncle Bob" as he called him – and urged to join the council of the United Synagogue. Ewen raised some objection but Bob waved them all away: "We've got to do something for these people you know, things are in a bad way."[25]

Ewen joined the council and in 1954 was elected president.

While he was in Naval Intelligence during the war years he thought up the ruse of *The Man Who Never Was* which became the subject of a best-selling book and a film.

After the war Montagu became the recorder of Southampton and chairman of the Middlesex Quarter Sessions.

He is a long, lean, choleric-looking man, with a prominent nose, determined chin. He is wont to smoke a curved pipe and, but for the absence of a deer-stalker, he could have served as the original for Sherlock Holmes. He can be impatient and brusque.

When he rose from the bench and hurried to a meeting of the United Synagogue he did not always leave the manners of the court room behind him and sometimes addressed council members as if they were petty felons. But that was perhaps a minor fault. He had become an anachronism.

A new generation of congregants had grown to maturity who felt that the United Synagogue, which is formally an Orthodox institution, should be ruled by Orthodox, or at least, practising Jews. They respected Montagu as a person. He had brought a ready intelligence to their complex affairs. His name still carried great weight, and nothing so commends a man to the Jewish world as renown in the outer world. He was a well-known public figure, a commanding personality, and they stood in awe of him, but at the same time they resented what one member called "government by goyim". Montagu made no secret of the fact that he did not conform to the usages the United Synagogue was established to uphold. Members became increasingly restive under his rule and in 1962 he resigned and Sir Isaac Wolfson took his place. The Cousinhood had retired from the Orthodox establishment.

One family who were once staunch defenders of the faith and the faithful – the Goldsmids – are now on the verge of extinction.

Sir Henry Joseph d'Avigdor-Goldsmid, the present head of the family, has only one daughter. His heir, Major General James d'Avigdor-Goldsmid, his brother, is fifty-eight and a bachelor.

Sir Henry, or Sir Harry as he is generally called, is tall, ram-rod straight, a former major and every inch the soldier. One is inclined at first encounter to jump to attention in his presence, though there is nothing imperious in his manner and he is one of the most charming and amiable of men. He had a distinguished war career, was wounded in action and received the D.S.O. and the M.C. for gallantry, but dismisses them as baubles: "The sort of thing any officer of the line who survives can expect to pick up."

He alone of the Cousinhood still lives in princely, or at least baronial style at Somerhill, the ancestral home of the Goldsmids which looks out over the Kent countryside. It is a large Jacobean mansion with typical lead-latticed windows. It has inner and outer courts, and endless galleries hung with Flemish tapestries. The great hall contains an open fireplace large enough to take an ox on a spit, and there is a Justice Room where in earlier days local magistrates dispensed justice among the local populace. There are battlements and turrets, and steep winding staircases that seem to thrust upwards into a dark eternity, and even a bedroom which is said to be haunted. In 1945 Sir Harry commissioned Sir Hugh Casson to adapt what were the servants quarters of the building into family flats. The result blends perfectly with the rest of the house and has a sort of compact grandeur. One is served at table by two butlers. The tableware is exquisite. The cruets are of ivory, the cutlery of solid silver; the plates are crested, and this at a casual Sunday lunch. Lady Goldsmid, dark-haired, attractive, with bright eyes and a fresh complexion, seems a little too young, too lively and too gay for the setting which reminds one of High Table of a Cambridge College. Sir Harry, on the other hand, seems as naturally part of it all as the oak panelling, for if his bearing is martial, his mind, as one discovers on closer acquaintance, is donnish, with hints of obscure knowledge and old port. He has travelled widely, read extensively and contributes the occasional unsigned learned review to the *Times Literary Supplement* and other journals. He is chairman of the Anglo-Israel bank and is a director of Mocatta and Goldsmid, but his City interests make no great demands upon him. He has been Tory M.P. for Walsall since 1955, and there was some speculation during Mr Macmillan's premiership that he was being considered for government office. He is well-informed on a variety of issues, particularly finance, and it was thought that he might become a junior minister at the Treasury but he was passed over. He is now sixty-one, which, in contemporary terms, makes him an old man. He was re-elected with an increased majority in the 1970 election, but like so many other wealthy Tory aristocrats does not fit easily into Heath's new model Tory Party and Heath's England. He regards himself as a mild, unobtrusive anachronism. His political career is virtually over and he hopes in the coming years to find time for writing.

His father, Osmond d'Avigdor, after an impoverished boyhood inherited the Goldsmid fortune and estate from his great-uncle Sir Julian, while he was still an undergraduate. He had looked upon himself as a young man in temporarily reduced circumstances and quickly adapted himself to his new status. He married the daughter of a Polish Jewish banker who had settled on the Riviera and she took to the role of lady of the manor with rather greater intensity than the lord himself. Osmond, like other members of the Cousinhood, conscientiously assumed the duties of his class and was active on the Board of Deputies and the Jewish Colonisation Association. In other respects, however, he was strangely ambivalent about his background and faith.

Henry entered Harrow on a scholarship in 1922 and the headmaster insisted that he be known merely as d'Avigdor in order, as he said, "to keep that dreadful German name out of the papers".

The other Jewish boys received weekly religious instruction from Sir Israel Gollancz, who was renowned both as a Rabbi and as one of the foremost Shakespearean scholars of his day; but Henry was, on his father's instruction, told to go to chapel. His housemaster told him that he understood he was being brought up as a Christian. Gollancz at once took the matter up with the highest authority, which in this case was Lionel de Rothschild. Osmond was summoned to New Court and made to see the error of his ways, and his son was withdrawn from chapel.

All this happened during Henry's first term. His younger brother, who arrived three years later, was unaffected by the incident. Osmond appears to have suffered from a great deal of Jew-baiting while he was at school and he wanted to shield his sons from a similar experience. A disbelief in Judaism or belief in Christianity did not enter into his actions. He was, Sir Henry recalls, "a moral as well as a physical coward".[26]

If the young Goldsmids never became Christian, they were hardly instructed as Jews. Sir Henry may occasionally find himself in synagogue on some state occasions, but then he may, as frequently, find himself in church. His wife, the daughter of an army officer, is not Jewish. He had two daughters. One, who was unfortunately drowned in a boating accident, is commemorated in an exquisite stained-glass window designed by Chagal in Tudeley parish church. The other has married out of the faith.

Sir Harry is active in several Jewish institutions and is regarded in the Jewish community with affection and pride, and indeed he takes some pride in his Jewishness, but religious belief hardly enters into his feelings. It is rather a matter of antecedents, but near antecedents rather than distant ones, Isaac Lyon Goldsmid rather than Abraham, Isaac and Jacob.

His brother James has had a distinguished career as professional soldier. As a commander of the 20th Armoured Brigade group he achieved a spectacular success in the Normandy landings in 1944. He was awarded a D.S.O. in the field by Field Marshal Montgomery, but this was later downgraded to the M.C. by Whitehall, for reasons which were never explained.[27] He later became director of the Royal Armoured Corps and rose to the rank of major general, the highest rank attained by a Jew in the British army. In 1970, at the age of fifty-eight, he embarked on a political career and was elected to Parliament as Tory M.P. for Lichfield and Tamworth.

The fact that his distinguished family has come to the end of the line does not bother Sir Harry at all, for he has long ago become reconciled to it. "It's sad," he said with a sigh, "but isn't it inevitable?"[28]

Sir Bernard Waley-Cohen, on the other hand, is confident about the future of his family. There will, he believes, always be a Cohen.

Sir Bernard has his father's broad shoulders, without his great height, some of his ruggedness and much of his charm.

It is always something of a handicap to be born the son of a great man, and the handicap can assume extra dimensions if the man happened to be also rather fierce and cantankerous. Sir Robert hoped that his association with firms like Unilever and Shell would offer an immediate opening for his son, but in fact one only had to breathe the name Waley-Cohen and directors ran for cover. Bernard was born to a considerable fortune but has otherwise had to make his own way in the City and has gone far. His main quality, a business colleague said, was common sense in uncommon quantities. "When he has spoken you feel there is nothing more to be said on the matter." He has very extensive business interests mainly in urban property, is an underwriter at Lloyds, is chairman of eight companies and on the board of a further nine. He occasionally applies himself with excessive energy and one can see him rushing from one appointment to another, his brows awash with perspiration.

In 1949 at the age of thirty-five he was elected an alderman of the City of London. In 1955 he became sheriff, and was later knighted for his civic services, and in 1961 he became lord mayor.

It was compensation for some of the disappointments he suffered in early life. As a boy he had hoped for a naval career, and was sent to the Royal Naval College at Dartmouth, but he had to be withdrawn because of poor eyesight. As a young man he became a member of the Honourable Artillery Company, but in 1938 lost an eye in a riding accident, and when the war came while other Cousins rose to high rank in the armed forces, he had to be content with a job at the Ministry of Fuel and Power.

Now finally, he could be of service, and be seen to be of service. The bonhomie which he brought to his office, the elegance and charm of the lady mayoress, made his year a memorable one. He introduced a Midsummer Banquet which proved to be a great success and which is now an established and popular event in the City calendar. At the end of his year he was made a baronet.

The Waley-Cohens have a compact neo-Georgian house which they built on a bombed site in St James's in 1959. It has four bedrooms and the kitchen is separated from the dining room by a wall of cupboards. "I am usually the cook so I wanted everything close at hand," said Lady Waley-Cohen.[29] Their true home however is Honeymead, which overlooks the bleak, wind-blown stretches of Exmoor. They are now a familiar and beloved part of the Somerset scene, and feature frequently in the local press, *Country Life* and *Horse and Hounds* and the other mandatory reading of county society. Sir Bernard is chairman of the Exmoor Stag Hunt, a position of great honour in the county, and there are acquaintances who even claim to have noticed a slight Somerset burr in his accent. His eyes light up and his voice softens at any mention of country life or country pursuits.

He is a keen and skilled rider. In 1950 at the age of thirty-six and forty-three pounds overweight, he won the Minehead harriers point-to-point race.

In 1953 the *City Press* reported that he had fallen off his horse and was severely concussed.[30] A hasty correction followed a week later:

Mr Alderman Waley-Cohen never falls off his horse. We are quite prepared to believe, for he is a courageous and renowned horseman. Mrs Waley-Cohen tells us that his injury referred to here last week was caused by his horse falling on the hard, frosty ground.[31]

But, whatever the cause, he cracked his skull and was out of action for weeks. Such falls have not diminished his enthusiasm for horses and riding and hounds.

"Our country sports are part of our way of life," he once told a large and distinguished gathering which included among other indefatigable country sportsmen, the then Prime Minister, Mr Harold Macmillan, and he went on:

At weekends I yield to no one in enjoying the exhilaration and good fellowship of a day's hunting, as doubtless many of you do. We are all animal lovers and are stirred and stimulated by the joys of a gallop across country and the thrill of seeing hounds work out their line, and we know that hunts up and down the country help forward the fellowship because here is a sport that all can join in and enjoy.[32]

After the 1967 Israeli-Arab war there was a prolonged correspondence in *The Times* on the future of the Middle East. There was a letter from Mr Edmund de Rothschild suggesting a de-salination programme. There were letters from Jewish M.P.s, like David Weitzmann, or M.P.s of Jewish origin, like Captain Philip Goodhart. Then one morning a letter was printed from Sir Bernard Waley-Cohen. It got star billing right at the top of the page – in defence of stag-hunting.

Sir Bernard, being the son of his father, has had to serve for a time on the United Synagogue, the Jewish Welfare Board and the Anglo-Jewish Association.

"Why," he asked, "am I going to be guest of honour at the annual dinner of the Anglo-Jewish Association while I have an invitation to dine at the Mansion House the same evening? You get pulled in."[33]

But he does not say it by way of complaint. One suspects he likes being pulled in and would be sorry if the pulling were to stop.

After leaving Dartmouth naval college Bernard went on to Clifton and never regretted the change. "It was running wild with cousins," he recalls, "but I loved the place. The fact that you were Jewish and a member of a Jewish house made no difference. The boy who stuck to his own principles, his own religion, was admired. A great place, a great school." He is a governor of Clifton, but has sent his own boys to Eton. His two girls went to Cranborne Chase.

In 1966 his older daughter Rosalind, a trainee with Lyons, the hotel and catering group, became engaged to Philip Burdon, a young New Zealander who is not Jewish. They were married first at a civil ceremony in Caxton Hall and then at a small private religious ceremony at her parents' home in St James's.

The service was ecumenical, with readings from the Old Testament and the New, though the name of Christ was never mentioned. They then recited the Lord's Prayer, and the *Shema*, "Here O Israel, the Lord Our God, the Lord is One", and they closed finally with the priestly blessing, so beloved of the girl's grandfather, Sir Robert:

> The Lord Bless thee and keep thee,
> The Lord make his face to shine upon thee,
>   and be gracious unto thee:
> The Lord turn his face unto thee,
>   and give thee peace.

The ceremony perhaps sums up the dilemma that faces all members of the Cousinhood. One who has solved it in his own way is Hugh Montefiore, the son of a president of the Spanish and Portuguese Synagogue, who is now Bishop of Kingston.

Revd Montefiore is a tall, well-built man with a massive head, athletic figure and a look of perpetual amusement in his grey eyes, as if the world was a mildy ridiculous place which, from his stance, it possibly is.

His family was prosperous and they lived in a large mansion in Palace Green, Kensington, now the home of the Israeli Embassy, with a *cordon sanitaire* of servants between parent and child. "One was brought downstairs at teatime to have one's head patted" he recalls. "I should have liked to see my parents more often."[34]

His father, Charles Edward Sebag-Montefiore, a partner in Joseph Sebag and Co., had jerked the firm from its slumbers and pushed it to the fore as one of the principal stockbrokers in the City.

Charles had been a keen athlete and was in the rugby XV at Clifton, but being a member of the Jewish house could not represent the school at Saturday matches. He was determined that his own sons should suffer from no such handicaps.

Denzil and Oliver went to Wellington, Hugh to Rugby. A man travelled up from London once a week to give him religious instruction, but it did not make a deep or lasting impression.

His family, he recalls, "was deeply religious. No bacon, of course. Candles on Friday night, family prayers now and again." He himself was a believing Jew if not always an observant one until about the age of sixteen, and then the doubts and frustrations which are so common to adolescence set in, until they were suddenly and dramatically resolved by, as he put it, "the vision of Christ". It was a sudden illumination – I quite literally 'saw the light'. I had not been 'got at' by anyone at school. Quite the contrary. They were rather embarrassed about it. They didn't want to be accused of proselytisation. They wouldn't touch me." He went to the local vicar for instruction and baptism.

He went on to Oxford but his studies were interrupted by the war and he joined an artillery unit commanded by his uncle, Colonel Thomas Henry Montefiore – "Can't avoid the family wherever you go" – and saw service in Burma. He returned to Oxford in 1945, took a first in theology and was ordained in the Church. He later became vicar of St Mary's, Cambridge, the university church and in 1970 was elevated to the bench of bishops.

He is widely regarded as one of the most original and brilliant thinkers in the Church, a point on which he himself is rather modest. "They think, he's Jewish you know, he must be bright." His sermons have always attracted large, if occasionally critical audiences. He is a sharp controversialist on the radical wing of the Church, but even fellow radicals are occasionally left gasping by some of his ideas; in particular, his speculation that the love which Christ bore for his fellow men may have been homosexual in nature caused a sensation.

He inherited a considerable fortune and agrees that there is nothing so conducive to an independent mind than independent means, but he is not as wealthy as some people believe. "Most of the money is in trusts so that the tax people shouldn't get their hands on it, but it's so securely tied that nobody gets their hands on it, except the lawyers." He is married with three daughters, and while at Cambridge lived in a large draughty Victorian house standing in a large unkempt garden. He has a cottage in the Welsh hills to which he tries to get away whenever he can, which is not often.

His conversion pained his parents, "but they did not remonstrate and were most loving. They saw that my beliefs were deeply felt and in the last resort were happy to see me happy." But it does mean that he sees much less of the rest of the family than he might otherwise have done, a thought which does not pain him unduly. "All our family are proud of our Anglo-Jewish status with not all that much to be proud about." They are, as he pointed out, no longer even rich, and he paused for second thoughts.

"No, I suppose if you've had old Sir Moses among your ancestors you've got something to be proud about. A very great man, a saint. I don't suppose he would have been particularly proud of me, poor man, but I am immensely proud of him."

He is critical of the way his family have let Sir Moses' estate at East Cliff run down. East Cliff, he explained, had descended to a great-nephew of Sir Moses, Arthur Sebag-Montefiore, "a young dare-devil", who broke his neck in a flying accident. His wife, who inherited the estate, remarried, and neither she nor her second husband found much time for it. "A terrible shame. One would have thought that a place like that would have become a place of pilgrimage."

He is not a Zionist, "but I was never, like the rest of my family, anti-Zionist." He is worried about the fate of Israel, and anxious about her chauvinism.

He thinks of himself as a Jew – "more consciously a Jew, I dare say, than some Montefiores" – and enjoys synagogue service, "though, of course, I would not intone such passages as 'I await His coming daily', for, of course, I believe that He has already come." Orthodox Jewish leaders were nervous of his presence in Cambridge, and the former Chief Rabbi, Dr Israel Brodie, warned Jewish students at the university to keep away from him.

It was possibly because of this warning that Dr Montefiore was later invited to address a seminar of Jewish students at Carmel College, the Jewish public school in Berkshire. This caused a great furore and the invitation was withdrawn after the late Charles Wolfson, a brother of Sir Isaac and a major benefactor of the school, had intervened.

"Perfectly understandable," said Montefiore. "There's the feeling, this man has gone over to the enemy. It was courageous – perhaps even foolhardy – of the students to invite me in the first place."

He has the Englishman's regard for the man who adheres to his views whatever the handicaps, but he has none for the Cousinhood as a whole.

"The trouble with them is that they try to have their cake and eat it. If they will cut their children off from Jewish life and send them to schools which are after all Christian foundations, then the occasional conversion is inevitable. I'm surprised it doesn't happen more often."

In fact outright conversions of this sort have been rare and are getting rarer.

In the early years of the Cousinhood Jews were kept together by internal cohesion and external exclusion. As the latter eased the former weakened, but the assimilation of the Cousinhood followed a unique path. They did not seek to become as the English, but *like* them, and through the later years of the nineteenth century the Jews were in the main kept Jewish by the fact that Gentiles were Christian. English gentlemen believed in believing, and so did they. They were patrons of the Church and upholders of tradition; so were they.

But few English gentlemen today are believers. They have moved so far from their faith that they no longer even feel that others should believe. And as Christians go, so do the Jews, only they go a little further and faster. The Jewish house at Clifton which was established virtually for the education of the Cousinhood has not a single Cousin among its boarders today, never a Waley-Cohen, a Mocatta, a Montefiore, a Goldsmid, a Montagu, a Samuel, a Franklin, none. The house is bursting at the seams with the sons and the grandsons of the immigrants. The older families have sought out older schools with, as one of them put it, "no damned nonsense about a Jewish house".

CHAPTER 29

The Society of Friends

The Cousinhood of Rothschilds, Montefiores, Cohens and others, still exist, but they no longer comprise the ruling élite of Anglo-Jewry and they no longer control the institutions graced by their names.

They possessed unique characteristics, but were not an entirely unique entity. Levi Barent Cohen, with his two wives and his twelve children, brings to mind the great Quaker merchant William Barclay, with his two wives and fourteen children. The union of the banking families of Cohen, Rothschild, Montefiore, Goldsmid, Samuel and Montagu is in many ways akin to the union of Barclay, Kett, Freame, Gurney, Lloyd, Bevan and Willett.

The Cousinhood had much in common with these Protestant non-conformists, except that their Jewishness added an extra dimension to their non-conformity. They suffered from all the disabilities of the non-conformists and suffered from them longer and were thus thrown even further upon themselves. Like them they were excluded from many careers, and their talents, which might have flourished in other fields, were confined to commerce.

This exclusion was not without benefit for it maintained a close sense of fraternity which proved invaluable as trade horizons widened. Communications before the coming of the railways were slow, uncertain and hazardous. Agents in distant places had to be given a virtual free hand and it helped in such a situation if they happened to be co-religionists, or better still, cousins.

"Quaker meetings", Professor Peter Mathias, a distinguished economic historian, has written, "were under the obligation of helping any member in difficulties. They boasted that no Quaker received poor relief."[1] This was equally true of the Jews. The Cousinhood in their early days functioned as a mutual friendly society.

Jews and Dissenters had their teaching as well as their handicaps in common. Both laid great stress on the ancient virtues of industry, piety and thrift, for as self-conscious, vulnerable and exposed minorities, they felt deeply obliged not only to behave well but to be seen to be well behaved. The conduct of the Cousinhood was so exemplary that one begins to ask oneself whether even after a century's sojourn in England, they ever felt at home. They were, with few exceptions, either models of virtue or marvels of discretion.

The Quakers rose to wealth in the eighteenth century and were among the pioneers of the Industrial Revolution. The Cousinhood were in the main a nineteenth-century phenomenon and at no other time could they have flourished so phenomenally. A century earlier the situation of the Jew was too cramped, his burdens too many, his resources too few for the sort of *coups* managed by the Goldsmids or Rothschilds. A century later and the outlets for individual enterprise, in Britain at least, were too restricted.

There is almost a parallel movement between the rise in the power and wealth of the Cousinhood and the tendency towards free trade in the British economy. The early fortunes of the Rothschilds and their associates were made in helping the various European powers back to stability in the aftermath of the Napoleonic wars. Once they were stable, however, they financed themselves in the main and the Cousinhood found new outlets for their capital and enterprise in the new territories overseas, in America, in Latin America and later, in South Africa. They were comparatively inactive in the East, for the Orient had been divided up between the East India Company and the Levant Company. Even after Parliament abolished the monopolies of the two concerns in 1834 and 1825 respectively, old connections usually sufficed to keep new interlopers out. Nor was there much outlet for Jewish capital in the home market. Stock Exchange trading until about 1830 was largely confined to Government securities. The expansion of the railways in the 1840s brought a great surge of new business, but the Cousinhood, rather prudently, appear to have kept well out of this. Manufacturers tended to raise their capital from among their friends and they expanded their businesses by ploughing back profits. The Industrial Revolution, until well into the nineteenth century, was largely self-financed.

The Cousinhood thus had every incentive to look overseas, but in the early part of the century their efforts were hampered by the numerous restrictions on trade, by the navigation Acts, by the monopolies enjoyed by the great charter companies and by the high tariffs. As the century wore on one impediment after another was eased or abolished, culminating in Gladstone's Act of 1860 which finally opened Britain to the world, and the world to Britain. United Kingdom exports which had averaged £44,000,000 a year in the decade 1830-9, leapt to £100,000,000 two decades later, and to £160,000,000 in the decade after that.[2] The Cousinhood were involved in many stages of the marketing process, in the financing of stock and the movement of goods, in insurance, in the discounting of bills. It was during the 1860s that Samuel Montagu established his fortune through his remarkable grasp of the intricacies of foreign exchange. This too was the heyday of Louis Cohen & Sons, a small merchant bank specialising in foreign trade, and also of the Keyser bank. The Rothschilds were in the meantime concerned with what would now be called the infrastructure of the new republics of Latin America, with the provision of docks and harbours and other transport facilities and the development of their natural resources, and although, of course, the Cousinhood were hardly involved in the British railroad boom, they helped to find British money for railways on the Continent and in the Americas.

There were great fortunes to be made by men with capital and vision and the Cousinhood were deficient in neither, nor was there any odium attached to the creation of fortunes and the accumulation of wealth. In this too the Cousinhood were fortunate in their age.

Never before and never again was individualism so highly valued. Samuel Smiles' *Self Help*, published in 1859, was read as a supplement to the Bible, and its opening line, 'God helps those who help themselves', was almost the credo of the age. No Jew needed the admonition of a Smiles to accept this idea. It is part of traditional Jewish teaching and confirmed by everything in Jewish experience. The Cousinhood were thus Smilesian before Smiles and Victorian before Victoria. They could perhaps even be called super-Smilesians, for where others needed that extra effort to get ahead the Jew required it to arrive at all. This extra effort, which began as a condition of survival, remained as a habit of mind, and it was a habit which, in Victorian England at least, was admired.

The nineteenth century, and we use the term loosely to include the years up to World War I, was a time when the traditional Jewish virtues were the accepted English ones and to be a staunch Jew was to be a sound Englishman. The old Jewish families were kept in their faith less by their convictions than by their milieu. Apart from occasional individuals like Claude Montefiore, Lily Montagu and Herbert Samuel, they were no more inclined to philosophical speculation than most Englishmen of their class; but they liked their religion, even if they did not always observe it religiously, and they liked to be or at least appear to be religious. They were high-minded and where they were not generous by instinct they were compelled to acts of generosity by a severe sense of duty. To an earlier or later age they would have seemed insufferably starchy, priggish and smug. Their complacency was a little shaken at the end of the century by the growth of anti-Semitism in Germany, which, unlike anti-Semitism in Russia, Poland and Romania, was directed against Jews of their class; but even that they could dismiss as foreign manifestations in a foreign land. England was different.

And to an extent England *was* different, though not, perhaps, as different as they liked to think; so that when between 1881-1905 there was mass Jewish immigration and English anti-Semitism assumed a scale which even they could not overlook, they panicked. They connived at a closed doors policy, and tried to stifle the Balfour Declaration at birth, but by then they were already coming to the end of their age and had, indeed, already become an anachronism.

The Cousinhood were fortunate in their century in one other respect. It was the golden age of the family as almost symbolised by Victoria and Albert and their numerous children, and the Cousinhood were the family writ large. When Constance and Annie de Rothschild contemplated marrying Gentiles, for example, it was not the tenets of their faith which worried them, but the feelings of their family. In the last resort the ties were strong enough to withstand the jolts of exogamy when they came, but they were the main defence against it. And it was this sense of family, continuing long after religious convictions lapsed, which helped to keep the Cousinhood Jewish.

The sense of family also had its commercial uses. It married fortune to fortune, offered partners for expanding enterprises and sustained and enriched the flow of capital. It also had the disadvantages of nepotism in that one felt compelled to take into partnership sons-in-law and brothers-in-laws, nephews and cousins, whom one otherwise might have strenuously avoided. But in an earlier age, before railways and telegraphs, kinship was a form of communication in its own right.

There is a direct parallel between the Cousinhood as a commercial network and the experience of the great Quaker families as described by Professor Mathias:

A bond of confidence in business was very commonly reinforced by kinship: marriage partners were chosen from the same charmed circle. Recruits for partnership were also to be found from the cadets of other families in the same clan. Ownership, capital, succession to partnerships, extension of enterprise all tended to run within the same social and religious enclave and often be sealed by a kinship link.[3]

What kept the Cousinhood somewhat tighter and more exclusive than any Quaker clan was the snobbery which they had absorbed from their English environment.

In an earlier age the Cousinhood would have been regarded as up-starts, but the upstarts were now numerous enough, influential enough and rich enough to impose their own mores on society, and wealth, even in England, was accepted as an adequate substitute for antiquity. The nineteenth century discovered money much as the twentieth century has discovered sex. Balzac may have been the Henry Miller of money, but Jane Austen, Dickens and George Eliot were also obsessed with it. They did not seek to sanctify it, but few questioned the tacit assumption that wealth was a form of grace in its own right. There was a shift of social power from the shires to the cities, from the landed gentry to the city magnates; though to be sure, the land has never lost its influence because many city magnates, like the Rothschilds, tended to become landed gentlemen.

It was of course natural that the Jews of England should regard their plutocracy as a meritocracy, for beneficence rained down from them with such regularity and abundance that they seemed like heaven's own dispensers. The Jews may not have shared the general Victorian view that poverty was a proof of degeneracy, but they did think that wealth was a proof of merit, and this belief is to an extent still extant.

The Cousinhood paid for the schools in the Jewish community, the synagogues, the hospitals and the soup kitchens. They inculcated the essential optimism of the age, not so much through their teaching as through their example. "The history of our country during the last 160 years," wrote Macaulay in 1848, "is eminently the history of physical, of moral and of intellectual improvement." Macaulay, a leading champion of Jewish emancipation, might have seen in the Cousinhood a confirmation of his case.

To the Jewish newcomer the Cousinhood were a constant reminder of how far honest exertion could get one in England and to the spur of need was added the thrust of hope. Not every Jew could aspire to become a Rothschild, but they could all hope to become solvent or even rich.

The Jewish merchant class widened and grew. New fortunes were acquired in new fields by new men, most of them of Russian origin. The main contribution of British Jews to British life has been a commercial one. Their achievements in science, literature and the arts, though by no means unimportant, have been comparatively slight.

The influence of the Cousinhood both within the Jewish community and the country at large was a conservative one. The first Jews to be active in politics were Liberals, for the champions of Jewish emancipation came mostly from the Liberal Party. Its opponents generally came from the Tory ranks. But in time, as Jews took for granted their place in Parliament, Jewish Tories appeared, and when the Liberal Party split over Irish Home Rule in 1886, the Jewish members of the party mostly sided with the Unionist wing. They had not become burgesses of the town and knights of the shire to witness the dissolution of the United Kingdom. Within the community it was suggested that they used their influence to convert the Jewish sons of the ghetto into Englishmen, which they did, but Englishmen of a markedly Jewish sort. This was in contrast to the sons of the ghetto who grew to maturity in Germany and France, and who did not have a similar penumbra of patrons. They grew to regard themselves (though they were not regarded by others) as Germans or Frenchmen pure and simple. The Cousinhood though assimilationists in one way were conservationists in another and sought for Anglo-Jewry what Disraeli sought for England, to marry continuity with change. They were a living proof that it could be done.

Again one finds a striking parallel to what happened to the Cousinhood in the experience of the Quakers:

> With great wealth, in the second and third generations, a lapse in the strict tenets of the sect commonly matched a slide towards the establishment. Very often it began with educating one's children at a famous school, the choice of a marriage partner, the accumulation of landed estates and with this the temptation to be pressed into the magistracy or a knighthood.[4]

With the Cousinhood there was the added factor of their unutterable Englishness. Victorian attitudes lingered among them long after they lapsed elsewhere, but in time they caught up with the spirit of the new England. The gaudy Edwardian splutter of the Sassoon contingent was perhaps their last effulgence, for if much about the last century – even its hypocrisy – tended to enhance the Cousinhood, almost everything about the present century has tended to undermine them.

Ours is too harsh an age even for benign anachronisms.

Notes

Notes

Chapter 2

1. J. Parkes, *Antisemitism* (Vallentine Mitchell, 1963), p. 63.
2. C. Roth, *History of the Jews in England* (Oxford, 1964), p. 17.
3. V. D. Lipman, *The Jews of Medieval Norwich* (Jewish Historical Society, 1967), p. 56.
4. A. Hyamson, *A History of the Jews in England* (Methuen, 1928), p. 46.
5. C. Roth, *A Short History of the Jewish People*, (East and West Library, 1959), p. 173.
6. C. Roth, *Three Centuries of Anglo-Jewish Settlement* (Jewish Historical Society, 1961), ed. V. D. Lipman, pp. 1-21.
7. R. D. Barnett, *Three Centuries of Anglo-Jewish Settlement* (Jewish Historical Soc., 27/4/1955), p. 58.
8. L. Simmonds, *Jewish Chronicle*.
9. Roth, *op. cit.*, p. 218.
10. C. Roth, *Anglo-Jewish Letters* (Soncino, 1938), pp. 130-2.
11. Quoted by L. S. Sutherland, *Transactions of Jewish Historical Society* (London, 1953), Vol. 17, pp. 87-8.
12. *ibid.*, p. 88.
13. *ibid.*, p. 89.
14. Quoted by J. Francis, *Chronicles of the Stock Exchange* (Longman Green, 1855).
15. A. M. Hyamson, *The Sephardim of England* (Methuen, 1951), p. 117.
16. *Charleston Morning Post and Advertiser*, 30/12/1786, quoted by Hyamson.
17. A. M. Hyamson, *op. cit.*, p. 111.
18. *ibid.*, pp. 118-19.
19. *ibid.*, p. 212.
20. *ibid.*, p. 202.
21. C. H. H. Emmanuel, *A Century and a Half of Jewish History* (Routledge, 1910), p. 11.

Chapter 3

1. L. Alexander, *Memoirs of the Life of Benjamin Goldsmid* (London 1808), p. 6.
2. *ibid.*, p. 42.
3. J. Francis, *Chronicles of the Stock Exchange*, p. 182.
4. Alexander, *op. cit.*, p. 95.
5. *ibid.*, p. 101.

6. Alexander, *op. cit.*, p. 124.
7. *Gentlemen's Magazine*, Vol. 80, 1810, pp. 382-5.
8. M. Hardwick, *Emma, Lady Hamilton* (Cassell, 1969), p. 238
9. *ibid.*, p. 251.
10. C. Roth, *History of the Great Synagogue* (Goldstone, 1950), p. 206.

11. P. Emden, *Jews in Britain* (Sampson Low, 1944), p. 96.
12. *Weekly Political Register*, 3/10/ 1810, p. 513.
13. *The Times*, 29/9/1810.
14. H. Adler, *Transactions of the Jewish Historical Society*, Vol. V, pp. 148-73.

Chapter 4

1. *An American in England* (London, 1835), quoted in *Transactions of the Jewish Historical Society*, Vol. 13.
2. Corti, *The Rise of the House of Rothschild* (Gollancz, 1928), p. 21.
3. Rothschild Archives, London.
4. *ibid.*
5. E. Herries, *Memoirs of J. C. Herries* (John Murray, 1830), Vol. I, p. 87.
6. *Morning Chronicle*, 24/8/1827.
7. A. Aspinall, ed., *The Letters of King George IV* (Cambridge University Press, 1938), Vol. III, pp. 47-8.
8. *The Times*, 27/8/1827.
9. L. Wolf, *Essays in Jewish History* (Jewish Historical Society, 1934), p. 285.
10. Corti, *op. cit.*, p. 214.
11. *ibid.*, p. 215.

12. A. Ayer, *A Century of Finance* (London, 1905), pp. 16-19.
13. Corti, *op. cit.*, p. 306.
14. *ibid.*, p. 349.
15. L. Wolf, *Moses Montefiore* (Harper Bros, New York, 1885), p. 22.
16. C. Roth, *History of the Great Synagogue*, p. 236.
17. Corti, *op. cit.*, p. 123.
18. Corti, *The Reign of the House of Rothschild* (Gollancz, 1928), p. 133.
19. C. Buxton, *Memoirs of Sir Thomas Fowell Buxton* (Murray, 1848), pp. 343-5.
20. *ibid.*
21. *ibid.*
22. Quoted in Reeves, *The Rothschilds* (London, 1885), p. 196.
23. Quoted in Morton, *The Rothschilds* (Secker & Warburg, 1962), p. 67.
24. Corti, *op. cit.*, p. 152.

Chapter 5

1. L. Wolf, *Moses Montefiore* (Harper, New York, 1885), p. 6.
2. L. M. Friedman, *Joshua Montefiore of St Albans, Vermont* (American Jewish Historical Society), Vol. XL, pt. 2, pp. 119-34.
3. *ibid.*

4. *ibid.*
5. *ibid.*
6. *The Journal of Benjamin Morgan* (Chicago, 1948), ed. Wallace and Gillespie. Quoted by Friedman.
7. Wolf, *op. cit.*, p. 9.

8. Paul Emden, *The Jews of England* (Sampson Low, 1943), p. 158.
9. *Diaries of Sir Moses and Lady Montefiore* (Griffiths Farran Okeden and Welsh, London, 1890), ed. L. Loewe, pp. 8-9, referred as *Diaries* in notes.
10. *Diaries*, Vol. 1, p. 30.
11. *ibid.*
12. S. Lipman, *Judith Montefiore, Transactions of the Jewish Historical Society* (London, 1968), Vol. XXI, p. 287.
13. *Diaries*, Vol. 11, p. 3.
14. L. Wolf, *Essays in Jewish History* (Jewish Historical Society, London, 1934), p. 244.
15. *ibid.*, p. 242.
16. *ibid.*

17. *ibid.*
18. G. Slater, *Growth of Modern England* (Constable, 1932), p. 216.
19. *Diaries*, Vol. 1, p. 31.
20. Emden, p. 161.
21. N. K. Hill, *Imperial Continental Gas Association from 1824-1900*.
22. Wolf, *Montefiore*, p. 23.
23. Hill, *op. cit.*
24. C. R. Fay, *Huskisson and his Age* (Longmans, 1951), pp. 146-8.
25. W. Schooling, *Alliance Insurance 1824-1924*.
26. *ibid.*
27. *ibid.*
28. *ibid.*
29. *Diaries*, Vol. 1, p. 25.
30. *ibid.*, pp. 88-91.
31. Psalm xcv.

Chapter 6

1. *Diaries*, Vol. 1, p. 208.
2. L. Wolf, *Moses Montefiore*, pp. 78-80.
3. *Diaries*, Vol. 1, p. 210.
4. *ibid.*
5. *ibid.*
6. Quoted by Wolf, *op. cit.*, p. 88.
7. A. Hyamson, *The Sephardim of England*, p. 251.
8. G. Kirk, *A Short History of the Middle East* (Methuen, 1955), p. 78.
9. W. Baring Pemberton, *Palmerston*

(Batchworth Press, 1954), p. 105.
10. *Diaries*, p. 243.
11. *ibid.*, p. 244.
12. S. Lipman, *Judith Montefiore*, p. 299.
13. *Diaries*, p. 247.
14. *ibid.*, p. 252.
15. *ibid.*, p. 261.
16. *ibid.*, p. 279.
17. *ibid.*, p. 290.
18. Quoted by Wolf, *op. cit.*, p. 100.
19. *The Times*, 6/7/1859.

Chapter 7

1. W. Moneypenny and Buckle, *Life of Disraeli* (Murray, 1912), Vol. II, p. 30.
2. 21/7/1838.
3. C. Roth, *History of the Jews in England* (O.U.P., 1964), p. 249.

4. *ibid.*, p. 250.
5. Emden, *The Jews of England*, pp. 107-8.
6. N. K. Hill, *Imperial Continental Gas Association*.
7. Emden, *op. cit.*, p. 110.

8. Emden, *op. cit.*, p. 115.
9. *John Bull*, 7/5/1827.
10. A. Hyamson, *The Sephardim of England*, p. 297.
11. *Diaries*, Vol. 1, p. 61.
12. *Edinburgh Review*, January 1831.
13. Roth, *op. cit.*, p. 253.
14. *Diaries*, p. 66.
15. *ibid.*, p. 78.
16. *ibid.*, p. 79.
17. *The City or the Physiology of London Business with Sketches on Change and at the Coffee Houses* (Baily Bros, 1845).
18. Hannah Cohen, *Changing Faces* (Martin Hopkinson, 1937), pp. 5-6.
19. *The City or Physiology of London Business*.
20. Briggs and Jordan, *Economic History of England* (University Tutorial Press, 1962), p. 425.
21. T. E. Gregory, *The Westminster Bank* (Oxford, 1936), Vol. II, p. 201.
22. 23/7/1873.
23. Gregory, *op. cit.*, p. 202.
24. Hannah Cohen, *op. cit.*, p. 60.
25. A. Hyamson, *David Salomons* (Methuen, 1939).
26. *Diaries*, Vol. 1, p. 108.
27. *ibid.*, p. 117.
28. *ibid.*, p. 122.
29. 10/11/55.
30. Wolf, *Essays in Jewish History*, p. 329.

Chapter 8

1. *Diaries*, Vol. 1, p. 110.
2. *Sir Francis Henry Goldsmid, a Memoir* (Kegan Paul, 1882), p. 34.
3. *The Diary of Samuel Pepys* (Bell, 1952), ed. H. B. Wheatley, Vol. 3, p. 284.
4. Hyamson, *The Sephardim of England*, p. 274.
5. Roth, *History of the Great Synagogue*, p. 254.
6. L. Wolf, *Essays in Jewish History*, p. 324.
7. Hyamson, *op. cit.*, p. 287.
8. Roth, *op. cit.*, p. 253.
9. *Sir Francis Henry Goldsmid*, p. 141.
10. *ibid.*, p. 157.
11. *ibid.*, p. 149.

Chapter 9

1. Private papers in possession of Sir Henry d'Avigdor-Goldsmid.
2. *Diaries*, Vol. 1, p. 151.
3. Goldsmid papers.
4. *ibid.*
5. *ibid.*
6. *ibid.*
7. *ibid.*
8. *ibid.*
9. *ibid.*
10. *ibid.*
11. *The Wanderer*, unpublished paper by Sir Henry d' Avigdor-Goldsmid.

12. Hyamson, *The Sephardim*, p. 391.
13. Private communication fromMrs E. Noble,a great-grand-daughter of Countess d'Avigdor.
14. Private communication from Sir Henry.

15. *The Wanderer.*
16. *ibid.*
17. *ibid.*
18. Goldsmid papers.

Chapter 10

1. L. Abrahams, in *Transactions of the Jewish Historical Society*, Vol. 4, p. 121.
2. Reeves, *The Rothschilds*, p. 206.
3. Corti, *Reign of the House of Rothschild*, Vol. II, p. 114.
4. T. Johnston, *The Financiers and the Nation*, p. 9 (Methuen, 1934).
5. Moneypenny and Buckle, *Life of Disraeli*, Vol. 3, p. 31.
6. Spencer Walpole, *Life of Lord John Russell* (Longmans, 1889), Vol. 2, p. 93.
7. P. Magnus, *Gladstone* (John Murray, 1954), p. 91.
8. Moneypenny, p. 67.
9. *ibid.*, pp. 68-9.

10. Wolf, *Essays in Jewish History*, p. 333.
11. A. Hyamson, *Sir David Salomons*, (Methuen, 1939), pp. 79-80.
12. Morton, *The Rothschilds*, p. 150.
13. V. D. Lipman, *Three Centuries of Anglo-Jewish History*, (Jewish Historical Society, 1961), p. 96.
14. A. Hyamson in *Transactions of Jewish Historical Society*, Vol. 17, p. 98.
15. *ibid.* p. 99.
16. *ibid.*, p. 99.
17. *ibid.*, p. 100.
18. Emden, *The Jews of England*, p. 285.

Chapter 11

1. *Diaries*, Vol. 1, pp. 316-17.
2. *ibid.*, p. 334.
3. *ibid.*, p. 334.
4. *ibid.*, p. 336.
5. *ibid.*, p. 348.
6. Vol. 11, p. 7.
7. Magnus, *Gladstone* (Murray, 1954), p. 236.
8. Corti, *Reign of the House of Rothschild*, p. 297.
9. *The Times*, 19/11/1858.
10. L. Wolf, *Sir Moses Montefiore*, p. 155 (Harper Bros. N.Y., 1885).
11. *The Times*, 9/11/1859.
12. Quoted by Wolf, *op. cit.*, p. 157.

13. *Diaries*, Vol. 11, p. 89.
14. Wolf, *op. cit.*, p. 163.
15. *Diaries*, Vol. 1, p. 37.
16. Wolf, *op. cit.*, p. 172.
17. *Diaries*, Vol. II, p. 128.
18. Quoted by Wolf, *op. cit.*, p. 171.
19. J. Montefiore, *Notes on a Private Journey* (Lea & Co, London, 1885), p. 74.
20. S. Lipman, *Judith Montefiore*, pp. 300-1.
21. Wolf, *op. cit.*, p. 173.
22. J. Montefiore, *Notes on a Private Journey*, p. 115.
23. *ibid.*, p. 209.

24. J. Montefiore, *Notes on a Private Journey*, p. 126.
25. Wolf, *op. cit.*, p. 186.
26. *Diaries*, Vol. II, p. 157.
27. T. Hodgkin, *A Journey to Morocco* (Gautley Newby, London, 1866), p. 12.
28. *ibid.*, p. 29.
29. *Diaries*, Vol. II, p. 157.
30. Wolf, *op. cit.*, p. 213.

31. *Diaries*, Vol. II, p. 200.
32. *ibid.*, p. 205.
33. *ibid.*, p. 206.
34. *ibid.*, p. 216.
35. *ibid.*, p. 300.
36. *ibid.*, p. 301.
37. *ibid.*, p. 337.
38. *Kent Coast Times*, 27/11/1873.
39. *Diaries*, Vol. II, p. 260.
40. *ibid.*, p. 338.

Chapter 12

1. *Economist*, 16/7/1870.
2. Moneypenny and Buckle, Vol. III, p. 19.
3. F. M. L. Thompson, *The English Landed Gentry in the 19th Century* (Routledge, 1963), p. 36.
4. Gibbs, *A History of Aylesbury* (Bucks Advertiser, 1885), p. 300.
5. N. Pevsner, *Buckinghamshire* (Penguin Books, 1960), p. 206.
6. R. R. James, *Rosebery* (Weidenfeld and Nicolson, 1963), p. 80.
7. Asquith, *Memories and Reflections* (Cassell, 1928), Vol. II, p. 187.
8. Quoted by Roth, *The Magnificent Rothschilds* (Hale, 1939), p. 218.
9. L. Cohen, *Lady Rothschild and Her Daughters* (Murray, 1935), p. 126.

10. Svent Eriksen, *Waddesdon Manor* (National Trust, 1968), p. 68.
11. Roth, *The Magnificent Rothschilds*, pp. 149-50.
12. V. Cowles, *Edward VII and His Circle* (Hamish Hamilton, 1956), p. 138.
13. Asquith, *op. cit.*, p. 200.
14. B. Dugdale, *Arthur James Balfour* (Hutchinson 1936), Vol. I, p. 258.
15. H. V. Eckardstein, *10 Years at the Court of St James's* (Butterworth, 1921), p. 221.
16. Lady Battersea, *Reminiscences* (Macmillan, 1922), p. 45.
17. S. Jackson, *The Sassoons* (Heinemann, 1968), p. 70.
18. Roth, *op. cit.*, pp. 180-3.

Chapter 13

1. J. Wechsberg, *The Merchant Bankers* (Weidenfeld & Nicolson, 1967), p. 343.
2. *The Times*, 5/6/1879.
3. Moneypenny and Buckle, Vol. V, p. 413.
4. *ibid.*, p. 440.
5. *ibid.*, p. 443.
6. *ibid.*, p. 447.

7. *ibid.*, p. 449.
8. Wolf, *Essays in Jewish History*, p. 307.
9. M. Lane, *Jerusalem Post*, 2/11/1967.
10. C. Roth, p. 134.
11. M. Rothschild, *Karl Jordan, a Biography, Transactions of the Royal Entomological Society of London*.

12. M. Lane, *op. cit.*
13. *ibid.*
14. V. Weizmann, *The Impossible Takes a Little Longer* (Hamish Hamilton, 1967), p. 78.
15. M. Lane, *op. cit.*
16. F. Owen, *Tempestuous Journey* (Hutchinson, 1954), p. 184.
17. *ibid.*
18. J. Clapham, *The Bank of England* (Cambridge University Press, 1944), Vol. II, p. 328.
19. *ibid.*, p. 329.
20. *ibid.*, p. 331.
21. *The Times*, 15/11/1890.
22. Roth, *op. cit.*, p. 106.
23. Roth, p. 112.
24. R. Palin, *Rothschild Relish* (Cassell, 1970), p. 43.

Chapter 14

1. L. Cohen, *Lady Rothschild and her Daughters* (Murray, 1935), p. 9.
2. *Lady de Rothschild* (Humphreys, 1912), p. 3.
3. *ibid.*, p. 5.
4. Cohen, p. 18.
5. *ibid.*, p. 15.
6. *ibid.*, p. 30.
7. *ibid.*, pp. 31-2.
8. *ibid.*, p. 33.
9. Lady Battersea, *Reminiscences*, p. 62.
10. Cohen, p. 99.
11. N. Pevsner, *Buckinghamshire*, p. 53.
12. *Lady de Rothschild*, pp. 106-11.
13. *ibid.*, p. 103.
14. *Cohen*, pp. 46-7.
15. Moneypenny and Buckle, Vol. V, p. 430.
16. Lady Battersea, pp. 234-5.
17. L. Cohen, p. 68.
18. *ibid.*, p. 66.
19. *ibid.*, pp. 11-12.
20. *ibid.*, p. 120.
21. *Hughenden Papers*.
22. Brit. Mus. Additional MSS. 47948.
23. Cohen, p. 156.
24. Lady Battersea, p. 167.
25. *Battersea Papers*, B.M. Add. MSS. 47995.
26. Lady Battersea, p. 172.
27. *ibid.*, p. 174.
28. *ibid.*, p. 173.
29. B.M. Add. MSS. 47911.
30. Lady Battersea, p. 195.
31. B.M. Add. MSS. 47910.
32. B.M. Add. MSS. 47948.
33. B.M. Add. MSS. 47948.
34. Lady Battersea, p. 417.
35. Cohen, p. 280.

Chapter 15

1. Crewe, *Lord Rosebery* (Murray, 1931), Vol. I, p. 44.
2. R. R. James, *Lord Rosebery* (Weidenfeld & Nicolson, 1969).
3. *ibid.*, p. 57
4. *ibid.*, p. 52
5. *ibid.*, p. 52
6. Crewe, p. 114.
7. *ibid.*, p. 115.
8. *Jewish Chronicle*, 7/10/1877
9. James, p. 85
10. Brit Mus. Add. MSS. 44288.
11. *Vanity Fair*, 23/3/1878.
12. *Jewish Chronicle*, 25/5/1878.

13. Roy Jenkins, *Sir Charles Dilke* (Collins, 1968), p. 112.
14. James, p. 158
15. *ibid.*, p. 112.
16. *ibid.*, p. 179.
17. *ibid.*, p. 189.
18. Jenkins, p. 353.
19. B.M. Add. MSS. 44288.
20. Crewe, p. 119.

21. B.M. Add. MSS. 47948.
22. *Hamilton Papers*, Brit. Mus. Add. MSS. 48610.
23. Crewe, pp. 367-70.
24. E. C. Collier, *A Victorian Diarist*, p. 205 (Murray, 1944).
25. W. Churchill, *Great Contemporaries* (Odhams, 1947), p. 11.

Chapter 16

1. L. Wolf, *Essays in Jewish History*, p. 217.
2. A. Hyamson, *The Sephardim of England*, p. 200.
3. See Chapter 8, p. 74.
4. Sir A. Mocatta, *Frederic David Mocatta*, Address to the Jewish Historical Society of England, 12/11/1969.
5. *ibid.*
6. Ada Mocatta, *F. D. Mocatta* (Baines & Scarsbrook, 1911), p. 91.
7. V. D. Lipman, *A Century of Social Service* (Routledge, 1959), p. 138.
8. *Jewish Chronicle*, 17/6/1892.
9. Lipman, p. 93.

10. L. P. Gartner, *The Jewish Immigrant in England* (Allen and Unwin, 1959), p. 5.
11. *Gaster Papers*, Mocatta Library.
12. Sir A. Mocatta.
13. Lipman, p. 110.
14. Ada Mocatta, p. 43.
15. *ibid.*, p. 35.
16. *ibid.*, p. 45.
17. *ibid.*, p. 86.
18. *Gaster Papers*.
19. Ada Mocatta, pp. 9-10.
20. *ibid.*, p. 40.
21. *ibid.*, p. 87.
22. *ibid.*, p. 39.
23. *Jewish Chronicle*, 20/1/1905.
24. Sir A. Mocatta.
25. *Jewish Chronicle*, 13/11/1891.

Chapter 17

1. R. Henriques, *Sir Robert Waley Cohen*, p. 22.
2. L. Wolf, *Essays in Jewish History*, p. 186.
3. H. Cohen, *Changing Faces*, p. 36.
4. *ibid.*, p. 27.
5. *ibid.*, p. 40.
6. R. Truptil, *British Banks* (Jonathan Cape, 1936), p. 62.
7. W. King, *History of the London*

Discount Market (Routledge, 1936), p. 267.
8. J. Mills, *The British Jews*, 1853. Quoted by V. D. Lipman.
9. V. D. Lipman, *A History of Social Service*, p. 4.
10. *ibid.*, p. 26.
11. *ibid.*, p. 2.
12. *ibid.*, p. 79-80.
13. *ibid.*, pp. 90-1.

14. L. P. Gartner, *The Jewish Immigrant in England* (Allen & Unwin, 1959), p. 24.
15. Board of Guardians, *Annual Report* (1900), p. 16.
16. Lipman, p. 94.
17. *ibid.*, p. 92.
18. *Contemporary Essays on Clifton College*, p. 52.
19. H. Cohen, p. 86.
20. *ibid.*, p. 145.
21. *ibid.*, p. 25.
22. See p. 70.
23. H. Cohen, p. 49.
24. *ibid.*, p. 60.
25. *ibid.*, p. 55.
26. *ibid.*, p. 87.
27. *ibid.*, p. 173.
28. *ibid.*, p. 267.
29. *ibid.*, p. 263.
30. H. Cohen, *Let Stephen Speak*, p. 25 (published privately).
31. *ibid.*, p. 26.
32. *ibid.*, p. 52.
33. *ibid.*, p. 102.
34. *ibid.*, p. 141.
35. *ibid.*, p. 149.
36. *ibid.*, p. 54.
37. Mr Polack in conversation with author.
38. In conversation with author.
39. C. P. Snow, *The Conscience of the Rich* (Macmillan, 1958), p. 100.
40. *ibid.*, p. 47.
41. House of Commons, 2/12/53.
42. L. Cohen, *Claude Montefiore* (Faber, 1940), p. 231.
43. In interview with author.

Chapter 18

1. *Daily News*, 13/1/1911
2. Lilian Montagu, *Baron Swaythling* p. 12 (printed privately 1913).
3. C. B. Fry, *Life Worth Living* (Eyre & Spottiswoode, 1939), p. 185.
4. Montagu, p. 69.
5. *ibid.*, p. 79.
6. *Jewish Chronicle*, 23/1/1880.
7. *ibid.*, 5/12/1884.
8. V. D. Lipman, *A Social History of the Jews in England*, p. 128.
9. Montagu, p. 54.
10. *ibid.*, p. 14.
11. *ibid.*, p. 16.
12. *ibid.*, p. 12.
13. E. Conrad, *In Memory of Lily Montagu* (Polak & Van Genapp), p. 45.
14. *ibid.*, p. 18.
15. *ibid.*, p. 55.
16. *ibid.*, p. 7.
17. Quoted by E. Conrad, *Lily H. Montagu* (National Federation of Temple Sisterhoods, New York, 1953), p. 18.
18. *ibid.*, p. 19.
19. Conrad, *In Memory*, p. 36.
20. *ibid.*, p. 19.
21. *ibid.*, p. 79.

Chapter 19

1. *Fifty Cartoons by Max Beerbohm* (Heinemann, 1913).
2. W. Paget, *In My Tower* (Hutchinson, 1924), Vol. II, p. 474.

3. S. Lee, *Edward VII* (Macmillan, 1925), Vol. I, p. 474.
4. *ibid.*, Vol. II, p. 60.
5. H. V. Eckardstein, *Ten Years at the Court of St. James's* (Butterworth, 1921), p. 53.
6. Margot Asquith, *Autobiography* (Eyre & Spottiswoode, 1920), Vol. I, p. 67.
7. K. Grunwald, *Turkenhirsch* (Oldbourne Press, 1966), p. 107.
8. *ibid.*, p. 10.
9. *ibid.*, p. 95.
10. Lee, Vol. II, p. 594.
11. S. Jackson, *The Sassoons* (Heinemann, 1968), p. 30.
12. *ibid.*, p. 119.
13. *ibid.*, p. 31.
14. *ibid.*, p. 31.
15. *ibid.*, p. 35.
16. *ibid.*, p. 44.
17. *ibid.*, p. 86.
18. Lady Battersea, *Reminiscences*, p. 48.
19. Jackson, p. 82.
20. P. Magnus, *King Edward VII* (Penguin Books, 1967), p. 277.
21. *ibid.*, p. 251.
22. Jackson, p. 72.
23. *ibid.*, p. 86.
24. Hyamson, *The Sephardim of England*, p. 398.
25. Jackson, p. 208.
26. *ibid.*, p. 84.
27. *ibid.*, p. 117.
28. *ibid.*, p. 146.
29. H. Nicolson, *Diaries and Letters 1930-39* (Collins, 1966), p. 76.
30. R. Blake, *The Unknown Prime Minister* (Eyre & Spottiswoode, 1955), p. 101.
31. Jackson, p. 183.
32. Lord Beaverbrook, *Men and Power* (Hutchinson, 1956), p. 176.
33. T. Jones, *A Diary with Letters* (Oxford University Press, 1954), p. 204.
34. R. R. James, ed., *The Diaries of Sir Henry Channon* (Penguin Books 1970), p. 250.
35. *ibid.*, p. 34.
36. *ibid.*, p. 15.
37. *ibid.*, p. 40.
38. *ibid.*, p. 94.
39. *ibid.*, p. 250.
40. Jackson, p. 138.
41. *ibid.*, p. 206.
42. *ibid.*, p. 156.
43. *ibid.*, p. 136.
44. *ibid.*, p. 203.
45. *ibid.*, p. 210.
46. *ibid.*, p. 283.
47. *ibid.*, p. 79.
48. *ibid.*, p. 95.
49. *ibid.*, p. 133.
50. S. Sassoon, *Memoirs of a Fox-hunting Man* (Faber, 1960), p. 172.

Chapter 20

1. *The Diaries of Theodore Herzl* ed. M. Lowenthal (Gollancz, 1958), p. 39.
2. *ibid.*, p. 13.
3. *ibid.*, p. 19.
4. *ibid.*, p. 188.
5. *ibid.*, p. 193.
6. *ibid.*, p. 83.
7. *ibid.*, p. 83.
8. *ibid.*, p. 83.

9. *ibid.*, p. 206.
10. N. Bentwich, *My 77 Years* (Routledge, 1962), p. 12.
11. *Herzl Diaries*, p. 350.
12. *ibid.*, pp. 364-76.
13. *ibid.*, p. 367.
14. *ibid.*, p. 477.
15. Chaim Weizmann, *Trial and Error* (Hamish Hamilton, 1949), p. 144.
16. S. Jackson, *The Sassoons*, p. 177.

17. L. Stein, *The Balfour Declaration* (Vallentine Mitchell, 1961), p. 10.
18. I. Cohen, *A Short History of Zionism* (Muller, 1951), p. 17.
19. N. Bentwich, *Remember the Days*, pp. 230-1
20. *The Times*, 1/6/1896.
21. *Herzl Diaries*, p. 193.
22. In an address to the Anglo-Jewish Association 30/8/1897.
23. *Herzl Diaries*, p. 88.

Chapter 21

1. C. Weizmann, *Trial and Error*, p. 144.
2. *Cambridge Independent Press*, 21/11/23.
3. S. D. Waley, *Edwin Montagu* (Asia Publishing House, 1964), p. 11.
4. *ibid.*, p. 13-14.
5. *ibid.*, p. 31.
6. Alfred Duff Cooper, *Old Men Forget* (Hart-Davis, 1953), p. 52.
7. *Daily Mail*, 7/7/1910.
8. Waley, p. 47.
9. *Nation*, 11/3/1911.
10. *Nation*, 18/3/1911.
11. Waley, p. 58.
12. *ibid.*, p. 59.
13. R. Jenkins, *Asquith* (Collins, Fontana, 1967), p. 408.
14. *ibid.*, p. 410.
15. Waley, p. 63.
16. Beaverbrook, *Politicians and the War* (Oldbourne, 1960), Vol. I, p. 60.
17. Waley, pp. 66-7.
18. *ibid.*, p. 58.
19. *ibid.*, p. 67.

20. Jenkins, p. 408.
21. Waley, p. 93.
22. *ibid.*, p. 105.
23. James Pope-Hennessy, *Lord Crewe* (Constable, 1955), p. 188.
24. Waley, p. 113.
25. Lloyd George, *War Memoirs* (Nicolson & Watson, 1934), p. 1067.
26. F. Owen, *Tempestuous Journey* (Hutchinson, 1954), p. 416.
27. *ibid.*, p. 417.
28. *ibid.*, p. 417.
29. Randolph Churchill, *Lord Derby* (Heinemann, 1959), pp. 281-2.
30. C. Sykes, *Two Studies in Virtue* (Collins, 1953), p. 213.
31. F. Owen, p. 427.
32. *Cabinet Papers*, 23/4/32, p. 10.
33. *The Times*, 24/5/17.
34. L. Stein, *The Balfour Declaration* (Vallentine Mitchell, 1961), p. 459.
35. Stein, p. 497.
36. *ibid.*, p. 502.
37. *ibid.*, p. 504.
38. *Cabinet Papers* 21/58 p. 1.
39. *ibid.*, pp. 1-9.

40. Blanche Dugdale, *Arthur Balfour* (Hutchinson, 1936), Vol. 2, p. 226.
41. *An Indian Diary* ed. V. Montagu (Heinemann, 1930), p. 18.
42. Viscount Samuel, *Memoirs* (Cresset, 1945), p. 170.
43. C. Bermant, *Troubled Eden* (Vallentine Mitchell, 1969), pp. 159-60.
44. Beaverbrook, *Men and Power* (Hutchinson, 1956), p. 292.
45. Waley, p. 83.
46. *ibid.*, p. 83.
47. *ibid.*, p. 84.
48. Robert Blake, *The Unknown Prime Minister*, p. 421.
49. *Morning Post*, 10/7/1917.
50. Hansard XCVII 1695-6.
51. *Commd. Paper*, 9109.
52. Waley, pp. 206-7.
53. Croft, *My Life of Strife* (Hutchinson, 1948), p. 149.
54. Winterton, *Orders of the Day* (Cassell, 1953), p. 112.
55. *ibid.*, p. 112.
56. Quoted by Sykes in *Two Studies in Virtue*, p. 213.
57. *ibid.*, p. 285.
58. Duff Cooper, p. 52.

Chapter 22

1. A. J. Franklin, *Records of the Franklin Family* (Routledge, 1915)
2. R. J. D. Hart, *The Samuel Family of Liverpool and London* (Routledge, 1958).
3. Hart, p. 74.
4. *ibid.*, p. 2.
5. *ibid.*, p. 117.
6. *The Times*, 14/11/1967.
7. D. Hopkinson, *Family Inheritance* (Staples, 1954), p. 30.
8. *ibid.*, p. 31.
9. *ibid.*, p. 35.
10. *ibid.*, p. 60-1.
11. M. Stocks, *Eleanor Rathbone* (Gollancz, 1950), p. 109.
12. N. Bentwich, *My 77 Years*, p. 41.
13. R. Storrs, *Orientations* (Nicholson & Watson, 1937), p. 434.
14. Bentwich, p. 99.
15. *ibid.*, p. 98.
16. Bentwich and Kisch, *Kisch* (Vallentine Mitchell, 1966), p. 59.
17. *ibid.*, p. 192.
18. *ibid.*, p. 193.
19. *The Times*, 10/5/1965.
20. L. Wolf, *Essays in Jewish History*, p. 352.
21. I. Morris, *Madly Singing in the Mountains* (Allen & Unwin, 1970), p. 86.
22. *ibid.*, p. 90.
23. *ibid.*, p. 87.
24. *ibid.*, p. 67.
25. Cabinet Papers, 23/4, p. 9.
26. L. Stein, *The Balfour Declaration*, p. 565.
27. *The Jewish Chronicle 1841-1941* (Jewish Chronicle, 1949), p. 41.
28. V. D. Lipman, *A Century of Social Service*, p. 22.
29. M. Gibbon, *Netta* (Routledge, 1960), p. 12.
30. *ibid.*, p. 118.
31. *ibid.*, p. 158.
32. *ibid.*, p. 50.
33. *ibid.*, p. 151.

34. F. Mumby, *Publishing and Bookselling* (Jonathan Cape, 1956), p. 312.

35. J. D. Watson, *The Double Helix*

(Weidenfeld & Nicolson, 1968), p. 225

36. *ibid.*, p. 226.

Chapter 23

1. Quoted in R. Henriques, *Marcus Samuel* (Barrie & Rockliff, 1960), p. 550.

2. V. D. Lipman, *A Century of Social Service*, p. 23.

3. R. Henriques, p. 40.

4. *ibid.*, p. 39.

5. *ibid.*, p. 53.

6. *ibid.*, p. 50.

7. *ibid.*, p. 618.

8. Quoted by Lord Birkenhead, *Contemporary Personalities* (Cassell, 1924), p. 305.

9. D. Keir, *The Bowring Story* (Bodley Head, 1962), p. 219.

10. R. Henriques, p. 85.

11. *ibid.*, p. 93.

12. *ibid.*, p. 143.

13. *ibid.*, p. 198.

14. *ibid.*, p. 159.

15. *ibid.*, p. 124.

16. *ibid.*, p. 53.

17. The third Lord Bearsted in conversation with the author.

18. R. Henriques, p. 135.

19. *ibid.*, p. 227.

20. *ibid.*, p. 220.

21. *ibid.*, p. 238.

22. *Petroleum Times*, 21/1/1927.

23. R. Henriques, p. 379.

24. Lord Birkenhead, p. 300.

25. In conversation with author.

26. Henriques, p. 402.

27. *ibid.*, p. 263.

28. *ibid.*, p. 160.

29. Lord Bearsted.

30. *The Times*, 18/1/1927.

31. Henriques, p. 229.

32. *ibid.*, p. 423.

33. *ibid.*, p. 429.

34. *ibid.*, pp. 439-40.

35. *ibid.*, p. 464.

36. *ibid.*, p. 473.

37. *ibid.*, p. 493.

38. In conversation with author.

39. Henriques, p. 567.

40. *ibid.*, p. 40.

41. *ibid.*, p. 530.

42. *ibid.*, p. 527.

43. *ibid.*, p. 651.

44. A. J. Mander, *From the Dreadnaughts to Scapa Flow* (Oxford University Press, 1961), Vol. 1, p. 270.

45. Henriques, p. 400.

46. L. P. Elwell-Sutton, *Persian Oil* (Lawrence & Wishart, 1955), p. 23.

47. Henriques, p. 581.

48. *ibid.*, p. 586.

49. R. Henriques, *Sir Robert Waley Cohen* (Secker & Warburg, 1966), p. 93.

50. Birkenhead, p. 318.

51. Henriques, p. 639.

52. *ibid.*, p. 642.

53. *The Times*, 18/1/1927.

Chapter 24

1. L. Cohen, *Lady Louisa de Rothschild* (John Murray, 1935), p. 23.
2. L. Cohen, *Some Recollections of C. G. Montefiore* (Faber, 1940), p. 27.
3. *ibid.*, p. 59.
4. 'The Jewish Religious Union', p. 2, *M. Montefiore Papers*, Vol. 411, London Library.
5. *ibid.*, p. 10-11.
6. *ibid.*, p. 11.
7. R. Apple, *The Hampstead Synagogue* (Vallentine Mitchell, 1967), p. 38.
8. C. G. Montefiore, *The Dangers of Zionism* (Jewish Religious Union, 1918), p. 3.
9. *ibid.*, pp. 6-7.
10. L. Cohen, *C. G. Montefiore*, p. 253.
11. *ibid.*, p. 323.
12. *ibid.*, p. 205.
13. Lady Battersea, *Reminiscences*, p. 419.
14. 'Report of the International Conference on the Suppression of Traffic in Girls and Women', 1927, p. 41, *Montefiore Papers*, Vol. 534.
15. *C. G. Montefiore*, p. 128.
16. C. Temple Paterson, *The University of Southampton* (University of Southampton, 1962), p. 124.
17. *C. G. Montefiore*, p. 31.
18. *ibid.*, p. 36.
19. *ibid.*, p. 72.
20. *ibid.*, p. 71.
21. *Leonard G. Montefiore* ed. L. Stein and C. C. Aronsfeld (Vallentine Mitchell, 1964), p. 17.
22. *ibid.*, p. 13.
23. *ibid.*, p. 15.
24. In conversation with author.
25. *C. G. Montefiore*, p. 228.
26. *ibid.*, p. 252.
27. W. R. Matthews, *Memoirs and Meanings* (Hodder & Stoughton, 1969), p. 134.
28. Quoted by C. Temple Paterson, p. 124.
29. Matthews, p. 133.

Chapter 25

1. J. Bowle, *Viscount Samuel* (Gollancz, 1957), p. 22.
2. *ibid.*, p. 43. Unpublished notes for *A Lifetime in Jerusalem*.
3. E. Samuel, *A Lifetime in Jerusalem* (Vallentine Mitchell, 1970), p.14.
4. Samuel, *Memoirs* (Cresset Press, 1945), p. 251.
5. Bowle, p. 352.
6. Samuel, p. 8.
7. *ibid.*, p. 251.
8. Samuel, *Liberalism, Its Principles and Proposals* (Grant Richards, 1902), p. 4.
9. *ibid.*, p. 29.
10. *ibid.*, p. 387.
11. Bowle, p. 32.
12. *New Witness*, 8/8/1912.
13. Samuel, *Memoirs*, p. 77.
14. Bowle, p. 92.
15. *ibid.*, p. 101.
16. H. G. Wells, *The New Machiavelli* (Bodley Head, 1911), p. 295.
17. E. Samuel, p. 8.
18. Wells, p. 316.
19. Charles Landstone in *Jewish Chronicle*, 28/8/1969.
20. Bowle, p. 110.

21. R. Jenkins, *Asquith* (Collins, Fontana ed., 1967), p. 381.
22. Samuel, *Memoirs*, p. 109.
23. Bowle, p. 125.
24. *ibid.*, p. 128.
25. F. Owen, *Tempestuous Journey* (Hutchinson, 1954), p. 320.
26. Samuel, *Memoirs*, pp. 119-20.
27. *ibid.*, pp. 122-3.
28. *ibid.*, p. 125.
29. Lloyd George, *War Memoirs*, Vol. III, p. 1075.
30. Samuel, *Memoirs*, p. 125.
31. Bowle, p. 191.
32. Asquith, *Memories and Reflections* (Cassell, 1928), Vol. II, pp. 59-60.
33. C. Weizmann, *Trial and Error*, p. 191.
34. Samuel, *Memoirs*, p. 140.
35. Bowle, pp. 172-7.
36. Asquith, Vol. II, p. 65.
37. R. Storrs, *Orientations* (Nicholson & Watson, 1937), p. 459.
38. *Isaiah*, p. 40.
39. Samuel, *Memoirs*, p. 150.
40. Weizmann, p. 342.
41. I. Cohen, *A Short History of Zionism*, p. 106.

42. R. St John, *Ben Gurion* (Jarrolds, 1959), p. 57.
43. I. Cohen, p. 106.
44. Samuel, *Memoirs*, p. 179.
45. Storrs, pp. 457-9.
46. Samuel, *Memoirs*, p. 181.
47. H. Nicholson, *King George V* (Constable, 1952), p. 461.
48. L. Amery, *My Political Life* (Hutchinson, 1955), Vol. III, p. 68.
49. Owen, p. 720.
50. K. Feiling, *Neville Chamberlain* (Macmillan, 1946), p. 195.
51. Samuel, *Memoirs*, p. 210.
52. Davidson, *Memoirs of a Conservative* (Weidenfeld & Nicolson, 1969), p. 373.
53. Bowle, p. 287.
54. Amery, Vol. III, p. 16.
55. A. Toynbee, *Acquaintances* (Oxford University Press, 1967), p. 303.
56. Samuel, *Memoirs*, p. 267.
57. Bowle, pp. 320-1.
58. E. Samuel, p. 21.
59. C. Hill, *Both Sides of the Hill* (Heinemann, 1964), p. 166.
60. E. Samuel, p. 14.
61. Toynbee, p. 314.

Chapter 26

1. R. Henriques, *Sir Robert Waley Cohen* (Secker & Warburg, 1966), p. 228.
2. R. Henriques, unpublished manuscript.
3. *ibid.*
4. N. G. L. Hammond, *Centenary Essays on Clifton College* (Arrowsmith, 1962), p. 175.
5. Unpublished manuscript.
6. *ibid.*

7. Henriques, p. 54
8. R. Henriques, *Marcus Samuel* (Barrie & Rockliff, 1960), p. 348.
9. R. Henriques, *From a Biography* (Secker & Warburg, 1969), p. 19.
10. Henriques, *From a Biography*, p. 107.
11. *ibid.*, p. 103.
12. *ibid.*, p. 104.
13. *ibid.*, p. 107.
14. *ibid.*, p. 199.

15. Henriques, *From a Biography*, p. 290.
16. *ibid.*, p. 321.
17. *ibid.*, p. 313.
18. *ibid.*, p. 350.
19. In conversation with author.
20. Henriques, p. 179.
21. George Webber, *Sir Robert Waley*

Cohen (Jewish Memorial Council, 1953), p. 7.
22. Webber, p. 8.
23. C. Weizmann, *Trial and Error*, p. 227.
24. Henriques, p. 375.
25. *ibid.*, p. 338.
26. *ibid.*, p. 338.

Chapter 27

1. *Fiftieth Anniversary Review* (Bernhard Baron Settlement), p. 4.
2. Sir Israel Brodie, K.B.E., in conversation with the author.
3. *Anniversary Review*, p. 5.
4. R. Henriques, *Sir Basil Henriques*, Social Pioneers, No 42 (Council for Social Welfare).
5. *Anniversary Review*, p. 11.
6. *ibid.*, p. 13.
7. *ibid.*, p. 17.
8. S. Brodstsky, *Memoirs* (Weidenfeld & Nicolson, 1960), p. 243.
9. R. Henriques, *Sir Basil Henriques*.
10. *Anniversary Review*, p. 49.
11. *Sir Basil Henriques*.
12. In conversation with author.
13. Dr A. Ungar in communication to author.
14. *ibid.*

15. *ibid.*
16. *Anniversary Review*, p. 18.
17. *ibid.*, p. 17.
18. L. Cohen, *Claude Montefiore* (Faber & Faber, 1940), p. 246.
19. Dr Ungar.
20. *Sunday Times*, 20/1/57.
21. Robert Henriques, *From a Biography of Myself* (Secker & Warburg, 1969).
22. *ibid.*, p. 20.
23. *ibid.*, p. 21.
24. *ibid.*, p. 21.
25. Veronica Henriques in Foreword to the above, p. xvii.
26. *ibid.*, p. xvi.
27. *ibid.*, p. xix.
28. *ibid.*, p. xx.
29. *From a Biography of Myself*, pp. 171-2.

Chapter 28

1. Nicolas Tomalin, *Sunday Times*, 1/11/70.
2. *New Statesman*, 6/11/70.
3. M. Rothschild, *Catalogue of Rothschild Collection of Fleas*, Vol. I, (London, 1953).
4. *ibid.*

5. Communication from Dr Miriam Rothschild.
6. *Observer*, 1/11/70.
7. R. Palin, *Rothschild Relish*, p. 187.
8. E. de Rothschild in *Atlantic Advocate*, July, 1967.

9. *The Times*, 23/9/70.
10. *ibid.*, 23/9/70.
11. *ibid.*, 23/9/70.
12. E. de Rothschild, *Window on the World* (Peter Davies, 1949), pp. 172-3.
13. *ibid.*, p. 207.
14. C. Bermant, *Troubled Eden* (Vallentine Mitchell, 1969), p. 140.
15. *Daily Express*, 21/9/64.
16. *The Times*, 25/4/37.
17. In conversation with author.
18. *ibid.*
19. A. Temple Paterson, *The University of Southampton* (Southampton University Press, 1962), p. 148.
20. Quoted by S. Aris, *The Jewish Entrepreneur* (Cape, 1970), p. 51.

21. In conversation with author.
22. L. Fraser, *All to the Good* (Heinemann, 1963), p. 226.
23. T. Green, *Gold* (Michael Joseph, 1968), p. 101.
24. I. Montagu, *The Youngest Son* (Lawrence & Wishart, 1970), p. 21.
25. In conversation with author.
26. In private communication to author.
27. Sir Henry in letter to author.
28. In conversation with author.
29. *Evening Standard*, 4/6/59.
30. *City Press*, 16/1/53.
31. *ibid.*, 23/1/53.
32. *Horse & Hounds*, 19/1/63.
33. In conversation with author.
34. In conversation with author.

Chapter 29

1. P. Mathias, *The First Industrial Revolution* (Methuen, 1969), p. 160.
2. Mitchell and Deane, *Abstract of British Historical Statistics* (Cambridge University Press, 1962), pp. 303-6.
3. Mathias, p. 161.
4. *ibid.*, p. 164.

Index

Index